Financial Accounting Theory

CANADIAN EDITION

WILLIAM R. SCOTT
UNIVERSITY OF WATERLOO

PRENTICE HALL CANADA INC.
SCARBOROUGH, ONTARIO

To Mary Ann, Julie, Martha,
Kathy, Paul and Cary

Canadian Cataloguing in Publication Data

Scott, William R. (William Robert), 1931–
    Financial accounting theory

Canadian ed.
ISBN 0-13-565896-9

1. Accounting. I. Title.

HF5635.S36   657'.044   C96-931067.6

© 1997 Prentice-Hall Canada Inc.,
Scarborough, Ontario
A Viacom Company

Acquisitions Editor: Patrick Ferrier
Developmental Editor: Lesley Mann
Copy Editor: Rodney Rawlings
Production Editor: Mary Ann McCutcheon
Production Coordinator: Jane Schell
Art Direction: Kyle Gell
Interior and Cover Design: Carole Giguère
Page Layout: Niche Electronic Publishing

1 2 3 4 5   RRD   01 00 99 98 97

Printed and bound in the United States

Every reasonable effort has been made to obtain per-
missions for all articles and data used in this edition.
If errors or omissions have occurred, they will be corrected in future editions provided written notification
has been received by the publisher.

We welcome readers' comments, which can be sent by
e-mail to
    collegeinfo_pubcanada@prenhall.com

The articles "GE Posts 6.2% Rise in 4th-Quarter Net, Record 1992 Profit,""Now It's SEC vs. the Lawyers," "The Pros Get Trounced in Stock Contest," "U.S. Deloitte Said to Be Close to Thrift Pact," "SEC Rules Forces More Disclosure," "Exxon Is Told to Pay $5 Billion for Valdez Spill," "Natural-Gas Producers Bristle at 'Snapshot' Accounting," "Presidential Life Is Accused by SEC of Overstatement," "Wrongheaded Hit at Retiree Benefits," "Treasury Aide Charges SEC Proposals on Accounting Could Hamper Lending," "Accountants Worry Clinton Tax Plans Will Skew Results, Thwart Comparisons," "Accounting Rule-Making Board's Proposal Draws Fire," "FASB Approves Plan Requiring Banks to Value Most Debt at Market Prices," "Big Advertisers Could Face Reduced Profits If Proposed Accounting Rule Wins Approval," "Big Firms Get Around Big One-Time Earnings Hits to Save Executive Bonuses," "IBM Will Try Big Bonus Plan to Spur Effort," "Study of CEOs' Compensation Finds Surprises," "Former Critic of Big Stock Plans for CEOs Now Supports Them," "SEC to Push for Data on Pay of Executives," "Taking Stock: Big Firms Rely More on Options but Fail to End Pay Criticism," "FASB Moves to Make Firms Deduct Options," "Bausch & Lomb Posts 4th-Quarter Loss, Says SEC Has Begun Accounting Probe," "RJR Nabisco's Use of Accounting Technique Dealing with Goodwill Is Getting a Hard Look," "Few Support Any New Rules on Derivatives," "Bank Regulators Expected to Drop Plan Pegged to Market Value of Securities," "Big Board, SEC Fight over Foreign Stocks, "SEC Investigating Harley Stock Plunge: Angry Investors See a Leak of Results," and "Rash of Trading Ahead of Big Deals Raised Eyebrows" paraphased by permission of *Wall Street Journal*, © Dow Jones & Company, Inc. All rights reserved.

Prentice Hall Canada acknowledges that certain materials in the Work are reproduced from or adaptations of *Financial Accounting 5*, copyright CGA-Canada, 1995.

CONTENTS

PREFACE

This book began as a series of lesson notes for a financial accounting theory course of the Certified General Accountants' Association of Canada. The lesson notes grew out of a conviction that we have learned a great deal about the role of financial accounting and reporting in our society from securities markets and information economics-based research conducted over many years, and that financial accounting theory comes into its own when we formally recognize the information asymmetries that pervade business relationships.

The challenge was to organize this large body of research into a unifying framework and to explain it in a manner such that professionally oriented students would both understand and accept it as relevant to the financial accounting environment and ultimately to their own professional careers.

The lesson-notes material, of which this book represents an extension and updating, seems to have achieved its goals. In addition to being part of the CGA program of professional studies for a number of years it has been extensively class-tested in financial accounting theory courses at the University of Waterloo and several other universities, both at the senior undergraduate and professional Master's levels. I am encouraged by the fact that, by and large, the students comprehend the material and, indeed, will object if the instructor follows it too closely in class. This frees up class time to expand coverage of areas of interest to individual instructors and/or to motivate particular topics by means of articles from the financial press.

Despite its theoretical orientation, the book does not ignore the institutional structure of financial accounting and standard setting. It features considerable coverage of financial accounting standards. Many important standards, such as reserve recognition accounting, management discussion and analysis, foreign exchange translation, postretirement benefits, financial instruments, marking-to-market and ceiling tests, are described and critically evaluated. The structure of standard-setting bodies is also described, and the role of structure in helping to engineer the consent necessary for a successful standard is evaluated. While the text discussion concentrates on relating standards to the theoretical framework of the book, this does not provide students with the occasion to learn the contents of the standards themselves.

I have also used this material in Ph.D seminars. Here, I concentrate on the research articles which underlie the text discussion. Nevertheless, the students appreciate the framework of the book as a way of putting specific research papers into perspective. Indeed, the book proceeds in large part by selecting important research papers for description and commentary, and provides extensive references to other research papers underlying the text discussion. Assignment of the research papers themselves could be especially useful for instructors who wish to dig into methodological issues which, with some exceptions, are downplayed in the book itself.

Supplements

The Instructor's Manual includes solutions to the end-of-chapter Questions and Problems. It also discusses the Learning Objectives for each chapter and suggests teaching approaches that could be used. In addition, it comments on other issues for consideration and suggests supplementary references.

 For students who wish to explore the Internet as a dynamic source for up-to-the-minute information, the Bibliography concludes with a list of some of the most useful and interesting Web sites that relate to finance and accounting.

Acknowledgements

I have received a lot of assistance in writing this book. First, I thank CGA Canada for their encouragement and support over a number of years. Much of the material in the questions and problems has been reprinted or adapted from the *Financial Accounting 5* course and examinations of the Certified General Accountants' Association of Canada. These are acknowledged where used.

I also thank Prentice Hall, in particular Bill Webber and P.J. Boardman. In addition to their own support, their review process has provided extremely helpful commentary which has enabled me to greatly improve the manuscript. At Prentice Hall Canada I would like to thank Patrick Ferrier, Mary Ann McCutcheon, Lisa Penttilä and Rodney Rawlings. I extend my thanks and appreciation to the following reviewers as well: Lisa Feil, CGA Canada; Rick Burke, University of Saskatchewan; Nabil Elias, University of Manitoba; Claude Lanfranconi, University of Western Ontario; John Macintosh, York University; Pamela Ritchie, University of New Brunswick; and Lynda Carson, CGA Canada. I acknowledge the financial assistance of the Ontario Chartered Accountants' Chair in Accounting at the University of Waterloo, which has enabled teaching relief and other support in the preparation of the manuscript.

I also thank numerous colleagues and students for advice and feedback. These include Phelim Boyle, Dennis Chung, Len Eckel, Haim Falk, Jennifer Kao, David Manry, Bill Richardson, Gordon Richardson, Dean Smith and, especially, Sati Bandyopadhyay.

I thank the large number of researchers whose work underlies this book. As previously mentioned, numerous research papers are described and referenced. However, there are many other worthy papers which I have not referenced. This implies no disrespect or lack of appreciation for the contributions of these authors to financial accounting theory. Rather, it has been simply impossible to include them all, both for reasons of space, and the boundaries of my own knowledge.

I am grateful to Carolyn Holden for skilful, timely and cheerful typing of the manuscript in the face of numerous revisions, and to Jill Nucci for research assistance.

Finally, I thank my wife and family who, in many ways, have been involved in the learning process leading to this book.

Introduction

1.1   *The Objective of This Book*

This book is about accounting, not how to account. It argues that accounting students, having been exposed to the methodology and practice of accounting, need at least one course which critically examines the broader implications of financial accounting for the fair and efficient operation of our economy. Its objective is to give the reader an understanding of the current financial accounting and reporting environment.

1.2   *The Complexity of Information in Financial Accounting and Reporting*

This environment is both very complex and very challenging. It is complex because the product of accounting is **information**—a powerful and important commodity. One reason for the complexity of information is that individuals are not unanimous in their reaction to it. For example, a sophisticated investor may react positively to the valuation of certain firm assets at market value on the grounds that this will help to predict future firm performance. Other investors may be less positive, perhaps because they feel that market value information is unreliable, or simply because they are used to historical cost information. Furthermore, managers, who will have to report the market values, might react quite negatively. Market values are typically beyond management control, yet managers' performance is measured, at least in part, by reported net income, which can be affected by changes in market values under this basis of reporting.

Another reason for the complexity of information is that it does more than affect individual decisions. In affecting decisions it also affects the operation of markets, such as securities markets and managerial labour markets. The proper operation of such markets is important to the efficiency and fairness of the economy itself.

The challenge for financial accountants, then, is to survive and prosper in a complex environment characterized by conflicting pressures from different groups with an interest in financial reporting. This book argues that the prospects for survival and prosperity will be enhanced if accountants have a critical awareness of the impact of financial reporting on investors, managers, and the economy. The alternative to awareness is simply to accept the reporting environment as given. However, this is a very short-term strategy, since environments are constantly changing and evolving.

1.3   *The Role of Accounting Research*

A book about accounting theory must inevitably draw on accounting research, much of which is contained in academic journals. There are two complementary ways that we can view the role of research. The first is to consider its effects on accounting practice. For example, a decision usefulness approach underlies Section 1000 of the *CICA Handbook*, and the Conceptual Framework of the Financial Accounting Standards Board (FASB) in the United States. The essence of this approach is that investors should be supplied with information to help them make good investment decisions. One has only to compare the current annual report of a public company with those issued in the 1960s and prior to see the tremendous increase in disclosure over the 25 years or so since decision usefulness formally became an important concept in accounting theory.

Yet, this increase in disclosure did not "just happen." It is based on fundamental research into the theory of investor decision-making and the theory of capital markets, which have guided the accountant in what information to supply. Furthermore, the theory has been subjected to extensive empirical testing, which has established that, on average, investors use financial accounting information much as the theory predicts.

Independently of whether it affects current practice, however, there is a second important view of the role of research. This is to improve our *understanding* of the accounting environment, which we argued above should not be taken for granted. For example, fundamental research into models of conflict resolution, in particular agency theory models, has improved our understanding of managers' interests in financial reporting, of the role of executive compensation plans in motivating and controlling management's operation of the firm, and of the ways in which such plans use accounting information. This in turn leads to an improved understanding of managers' interests in accounting policy choice and why they may want to bias or otherwise manipulate reported net income, or, at least, to have some ability to manage the "bottom line." Research such as this enables us to understand the boundaries of management's legitimate role in financial reporting, and why the accountant is frequently caught between the interests of investors and managers. In this book, we use both of the above views. Our approach to research is to selectively choose important research papers, describe them intuitively, and explain how they fit into our overall framework of financial accounting theory and practice.

1.4 The Importance of Information Asymmetry

This book is based on information economics. This is a unifying theme which formally recognizes that some parties to business transactions may have an information advantage over others. When this happens, the economy is said to be characterized by **information asymmetry**. We shall consider two major types of information asymmetry.

The first is **adverse selection**. For our purposes, adverse selection occurs because some persons, such as firm managers and other insiders, will know more about the current condition and future prospects of the firm than outside investors. There are various ways that managers and other insiders can exploit their information advantage at the expense of outsiders, for example, by biasing or otherwise managing the information released to investors. This may affect the ability of investors to make good investment decisions. In addition, if rational investors are concerned about the possibility of biased information release, they will be wary of buying firms' securities, with the result that capital and managerial labour markets will not function as well as they should. We can then think of financial accounting and reporting as a mechanism to control the adverse selection problem by credibly converting inside information into outside information.

> *Adverse selection is a type of information asymmetry whereby one or more parties to a business transaction, or potential transaction, have an information advantage over other parties.*

The second type of information asymmetry is **moral hazard**. In our context, this problem occurs because of the separation of ownership and control that characterizes most large business entities. It is effectively impossible for shareholders and creditors to observe the extent and quality of top manager effort on their behalf. The manager may be tempted to shirk on effort, blaming any deterioration of firm performance on factors beyond his or her control. Obviously, if this happens, there are serious implications both for investors and for the efficient operation of the economy.

We can then view accounting net income as a measure of managerial performance. This helps to control the moral hazard problem in two complementary ways. First, net income can serve as an input into executive compensation contracts to motivate manager performance. Second, net income can inform the securities and managerial labour markets, so that a manager who shirks will suffer a decline in income, reputation, and market value over time.

Moral hazard is a type of information asymmetry whereby one or more parties to a business transaction, or potential transaction, can observe their actions in fulfillment of the transaction but other parties cannot.

1.5   The Fundamental Problem of Financial Accounting Theory

It turns out that the "best" measure of net income to inform investors, that is, to control adverse selection, need not be the same as the best measure to motivate manager performance, that is, to control moral hazard. Investors' interests are best served by information that provides a useful tradeoff between relevance and reliability, where relevant information is that which enables investors to assess the firm's future economic prospects, and reliable information is that which is precise and free of bias or other management manipulation.

Managers' interests are best served by information that is highly correlated with their effort in running the firm. But information that is relevant for investors, such as market values of assets and liabilities, may be very volatile in its impact on reported net income. Also, to the extent that reliable market values are not available, value-oriented information may be more subject to bias and manipulation than historical-cost-based information. Both of these effects reduce correlation with effort. Given that there is only one bottom line, the fundamental problem of financial accounting theory is how to reconcile these different roles for accounting information.

1.6   Regulation as a Reaction to the Fundamental Problem

There are two basic reactions to the fundamental problem. One is, in effect, to ask "What problem?" That is, why not let market forces determine how much and what kinds of information firms should produce? We can think of investors and other financial statement users as demanders of information and of managers as suppliers. Then, just as in markets for apples and automobiles, the forces of demand and supply can determine the quantity produced.

This view argues, in effect, that market forces can sufficiently control the adverse selection and moral hazard problems so that investors are protected, and managerial labour markets and securities markets will work reasonably well. Indeed, as we shall see, there are a surprising number of ways whereby managers can credibly supply information, including accounting information. Furthermore, investors as a group are surprisingly sophisticated in ferreting out the implications of information for future firm performance.

The second reaction is to turn to **regulation** to protect investors, on the grounds that information is such a complex and important commodity that market forces alone fail to adequately control the problems of moral hazard and adverse selection. This leads directly to the role of standard setting, which is viewed in this book as a form of regulation which lays down generally accepted accounting principles (GAAP).

The rigorous determination of the "right" amount of regulation is an extremely complex issue of social choice. At the present time we simply do not know which of the above two reactions to the fundamental problem is on the right track. Certainly, we witness lots of regulation in accounting, and there appears to be no slowing down in the rate at which new standards are coming on line. Consequently, it may seem that society has resolved the question of extent of regulation for us.

Yet, we live in a time of deregulation. Recent years have witnessed substantial deregulation of major industries such as transportation, telecommunications, and financial services, where deregulation was once thought unthinkable. The reason why it is important to ask whether similar deregulation should take place in the information "industry" is because regulation has a cost—a fact often ignored by standard setters. Again, however, the answer to the question of whether the benefits of regulation outweigh the costs is not known.

1.7   *Some Historical Perspective*

One way to address the question of regulation is to examine the workings of securities markets prior to substantial regulation. In the United States, the securities acts of 1933 and 1934 created the Securities and Exchange Commission (SEC) and the present disclosure-based regulatory structure of securities markets in that country. Prior to 1933, these markets were relatively unregulated. Was the establishment of the SEC a "knee-jerk" overreaction to the 1929 stock market crash and ensuing Great Depression, or were there substantial failures in these markets which inevitably led to social catastrophe?

Merino and Neimark (1982) (MN) examined the conditions leading up to the securities acts of 1933 and 1934. In the process, they reported on some of the security market practices of the 1920s and prior. Apparently, voluntary disclosure was widespread, as also noted by Benston (1973). However, MN claim that such disclosure was more to support "potential competition," that is, the encouragement of competition by enabling potential entrants to identify high-profit industries, than to inform investors. Investors were "protected" by a "2-tiered" market structure whereby prices were set by knowledgeable insiders, subject to a self-imposed "moral regulation" to control the problems of adverse selection and moral hazard. Unfortunately, moral regulation was not always effective, and MN refer to numerous instances of manipulative financial reporting and other abuses, which were widely believed to be the immediate causes of the 1929 crash.

The 1933–34 securities legislation can then be regarded as a movement away from a potential competition rationale for disclosure towards the supplying of better-quality information to investors as a way to control manipulative financial practices. Thus, if the question is one of regulation versus deregulation,[1] MN's depiction of events seems to support regulation.

If so, we may expect that regulation will be with us for the foreseeable future. However, given the complexity of information, the extent of regulation (that is, the number and content of accounting standards) must be determined by a political process rather than by rigorous economic calculation. In effect, the measure of the success of a new standard is not whether it is correct in some abstract, theoretical sense but whether different interest groups are willing to support it. As we shall see, the structure of standard setting bodies such as the Accounting Standards Board (ASB) of the Canadian Institute of Chartered Accountants and the FASB in the United States is designed to facilitate the attainment of the consensus which is necessary for such support.

1.8   *The Organization of This Book*

Figure 1.1 summarizes how this book operationalizes the framework for the study of financial accounting theory outlined above. There are four main components of the figure, and we will discuss each in turn.

1.8.1   *IDEAL CONDITIONS*

Before considering the problems introduced into accounting by information asymmetry, it is worthwhile to consider what accounting would be like under ideal conditions. This is the subject matter of Chapter 2, and is depicted by the leftmost oval of Figure 1.1. By ideal conditions we mean an economy characterized by perfect and complete markets or, equivalently, by a lack of information asymmetry and other barriers to fair and efficient market operation. Such conditions are also called "first best." Then, asset and liability valuation is on the basis of expected present values of future cash flows. Arbitrage ensures that present values and market values are equal. Financial statements are both completely relevant and completely reliable, and investors and managers would have no scope for disagreement over accounting policy choice and no incentives to call for regulation. We will often refer to present value- and market value-based accounting as **current value** accounting.

Unfortunately, or perhaps fortunately, ideal conditions do not prevail in practice. Nevertheless, they provide a useful benchmark against which more realistic

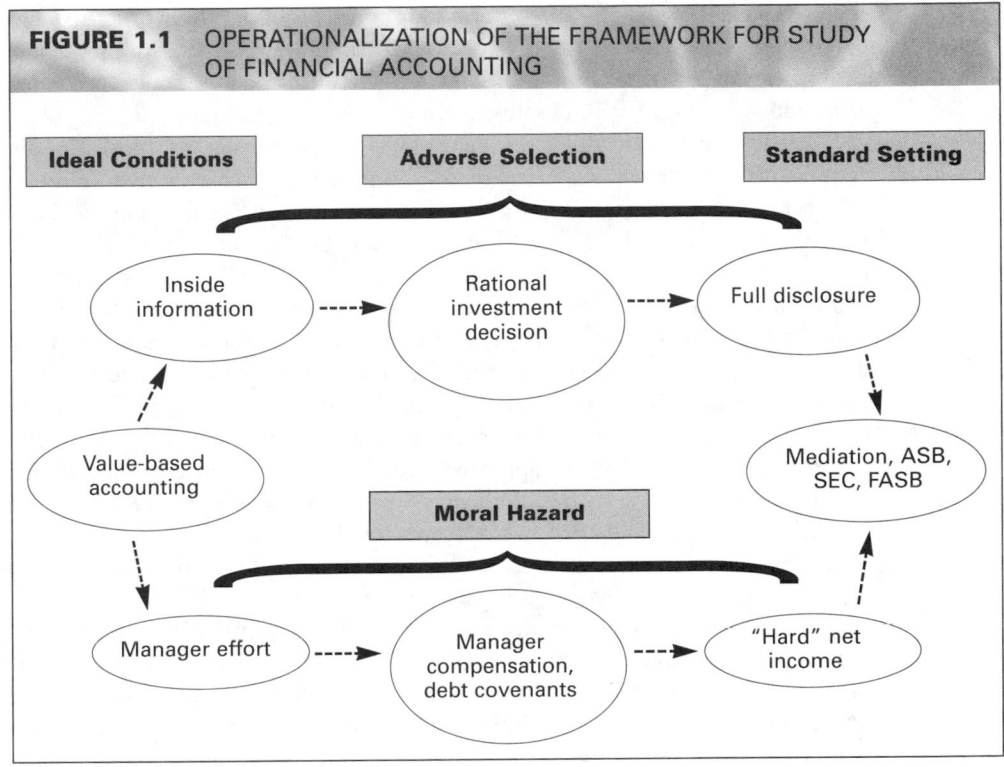

FIGURE 1.1 OPERATIONALIZATION OF THE FRAMEWORK FOR STUDY OF FINANCIAL ACCOUNTING

"second best" accounting conditions can be compared. For example, we will see that there are numerous instances of the actual use of current value accounting techniques in financial reporting. Reserve recognition accounting for oil and gas companies is an example. Furthermore, the use of such techniques is increasing, as in recent standards requiring mark-to-market accounting for financial instruments. A study of accounting under ideal conditions is useful, because it helps us to see what the real problems and challenges of current value accounting are when the ideal conditions that they require do not hold.

1.8.2 ADVERSE SELECTION

The top three ovals of Figure 1.1 represent the second component of the framework. This is the adverse selection problem, that is, the problem of communication from the firm to outside investors. Here, the accounting role is to provide a "level playing field" through full disclosure of relevant, reliable, timely, and cost-effective information to investors and other financial statement users.

To understand how financial accounting can help to control the adverse selection problem, it is desirable to have an appreciation of how investors make decisions. This is because knowledge of investor decision processes is essential if the accountant is to know what information they need. The study of investment decision-making is a large topic, since investors undoubtedly make decisions in a variety of ways, ranging from intuition to "hot tips" to random occurrences such as a sudden need for cash to sophisticated computer-based models.

The approach we shall take in this book is to assume that most investors are **rational**, that is, they make decisions so as to maximize their expected utility, or satisfaction, from wealth. This theory of rational investment decision has been widely studied. In making the rationality assumption we do not imply that all investors make decisions this way, but only that the theory captures the average behaviour of those investors who want to make informed investment decisions.

The reporting of information that is useful to rational investors is called the **decision usefulness** approach. For example, the theory implies that investors may want information about the riskiness of their investments, in addition to expected returns. Chapter 3 develops the decision usefulness approach to financial reporting, and shows that this approach underlies the pronouncements of major standard setting bodies, such as the Conceptual Framework of the FASB.

When a large number of rational investors interact in a properly working securities market, the market becomes **efficient**. Chapter 4 develops the theory of efficient security markets, and its implications for financial reporting. The accounting reaction to security market efficiency has been **full disclosure**, that is, the supplying of large amounts of information to help investors make their own predictions of future firm performance. This is called the **information perspective** on decision usefulness. An implication is that the form of disclosure does not matter—it can be in footnotes, or in supplementary disclosures such as reserve recognition accounting and management discussion and analysis, in addition to the financial statements proper. The market is regarded as sufficiently sophisticated that it can digest the implications of public information from any source.

Any theory needs to be tested. If accountants are to take the theory and implications of rational investment decision and security market efficiency seriously, they need some evidence that investors react to full disclosure as the theory predicts. Chapter 5 examines some of the empirical evidence in this regard. This evidence provides encouragement that investors do in fact find financial statement information useful.

Earlier, we suggested that ideal conditions are needed before current value accounting comes into its own. The reason is that only under ideal conditions can accounting information be both completely relevant and completely reliable. When conditions are not ideal, current-value-based information loses reliability, thereby opening itself up to possible bias and manipulation. Traditionally, accountants have felt that, lacking ideal conditions, historical cost accounting provides a useful tradeoff between relevance and reliability.

Interestingly, recent years have seen a considerable increase in the use of current valuations in financial statements, including for leases, pensions, other postretirement benefits and financial instruments. This is called the **measurement**

perspective on decision usefulness. It seems that accountants are expanding their approach to decision usefulness by taking more responsibility for incorporating measurements of current values into the accounts. Chapter 6 explores possible reasons for this and evaluates some recent measurement-based standards.

1.8.3 MORAL HAZARD

The bottom three ovals of Figure 1.1 represent the third component of the book. Here, the information asymmetry problem is moral hazard, arising from the unobservability of the manager's effort in running the firm. The accounting role is to provide a performance measure to report on the results of manager effort.

Moral hazard has important implications for financial accounting. Note first that the information and securities markets-oriented role of accounting just described suggests that firms' accounting policy choices should not affect their share prices. Given full disclosure of these policies, the market will look through them and establish an efficient valuation of the firm that is independent of, for example, depreciation policy, capitalization policy, and timing of revenue recognition.

This implies that firm managers need not be concerned about accounting policy choice, since the value of the firm should be unaffected. Yet, anyone with any exposure to accounting practice will know that managers are quite concerned about accounting policies and, indeed, a careful examination of accounting policies actually chosen provides a rich web of information about the state of the firm. The source of management's concern lies in the moral hazard problem.

Chapter 7 begins our study of how moral hazard leads to managers' interest in accounting policy, by documenting the existence of economic consequences. Essentially **economic consequences** means that accounting policies matter. By analyzing reactions to certain accounting standards, the chapter shows that accounting policies can matter not only to managers but also to investors and government.

The question then is: *Why* do accounting policies matter? This leads directly to **positive accounting theory**, described in Chapter 8. This is a theory which attempts to understand why accounting policies matter and to predict which particular accounting policies firms will choose. The theory is based on a view of the firm as a "nexus of contracts." That is, a business entity can be described by the various contracts it enters into, and if we want to understand why managers prefer certain accounting policies and oppose others, we should look at the firm's contracts.

Two common types of contracts have been particularly studied in positive accounting theory. These are manager compensation contracts and debt contracts. Here, we think of the contracting parties as the users of financial statement information. Thus, compensation contracts involve the manager and the board of directors, and debt contracts involve lenders and the manager. The user decision problem is how best to use financial statement information in the contract. For example, compensation contracts often base manager remuneration on reported net income, and debt contracts usually contain covenants, which constrain the manager's dividend and financing policies if certain financial ratios, such as debt-to-equity, exceed specified levels, or if certain levels of working capital and shareholders' equity are not maintained. Given that important contracts such as these depend on financial statement information, we can begin to see why accounting policies matter—accounting policies can affect compensation through the amount of reported net income and can affect the values of debt covenant ratios.

Once we recognize the role of accounting information in contracting, other questions arise. Specifically, what are the best accounting policies to use in these contracts? We begin to answer this question in Chapter 9, which gives an introductory outline of game theory and, in particular, of agency theory. Agency theory provides a rationale for compensation contracts which base manager remuneration on some measure of firm performance. It also explains the inclusion of debt covenants in lending agreements. Contract provisions such as these enable the moral hazard problems of shirking and creditor exploitation to be controlled.

Unfortunately, while moral hazard problems may be controlled, they cannot be eliminated. This is because such contract provisions are costly. Specifically, they impose **risk** on managers. For example, managers cannot completely control firm performance due to events such as strikes, changes in interest rates, and so on. Then, if manager compensation depends on firm performance, it is risky. Risk is costly, and not only because managers have to be compensated for bearing risk; costs also result because managers react to risk in various ways. For example, they may engage in earnings management, they may react negatively to accounting policies that increase the volatility of reported net income, and they may even change firm operating and financing policies. The best accounting policies for controlling moral hazard, then, are those which maximize performance incentives for managers while minimizing the risks imposed.

Chapter 10 looks more closely at executive compensation contracts. Executive compensation attracts a lot of attention, one reason being that the amounts involved are quite large. We will use the agency theory outlined in Chapter 9 to focus our understanding of executive compensation and will see that net income, in conjunction with other performance measures such as share price, has an important role to play not only in motivating manager effort but in controlling both risk and the length of the manager's decision horizon.

We mentioned above that managers may react to risk by engaging in earnings management. At first glance, earnings management may seem undesirable, since it implies a biasing or other manipulation of reported net income by the manager. Certainly, earnings management is bad if carried to an extreme, since investors and other users would quickly lose confidence in financial reporting. However, there is a good side to earnings management as well. For example, it gives management some flexibility to reduce the impact of unforeseen events on net income, thereby reducing the costly consequences of violation of covenants in debt contracts. Also, earnings management can be a vehicle for the release of inside information to investors. These and other aspects of earnings management are pursued in Chapter 11.

The accounting reaction to the use of financial accounting information for contracting purposes is to produce a "hard" performance measure, that is, a reported net income that is highly correlated with the manager's effort in running the firm.[2] Hardness will be enhanced if net income is reasonably free of management manipulation or bias and is not excessively volatile from factors beyond the manager's control.

We can now see the source of the fundamental problem of financial accounting theory more clearly. An income measure that is reasonably correlated with manager effort may be a different measure than the one which best informs investors. To the extent that market forces cannot resolve which method should predominate, standard setting becomes quite complex.

1.8.4   STANDARD SETTING

This leads to the fourth component of the framework, namely standard setting, shown on the right side of Figure 1.1. As discussed earlier, standard setting can be viewed as a regulatory response to failures in the supply of information to capital markets. However, the standard setter quickly gets caught up in mediation between the conflicting interests of investors and managers. The conflict arises because of the differing information needs that arise from the two major types of information asymmetry. Conflict also means that the regulatory process is quite costly. Some of the cost-benefit tradeoffs of regulation in accounting are considered in Chapter 12.

The final chapter of the book proposes two theories of regulation, describes the current structure of standard setting, and considers with which theory the current structure is most consistent. It also examines some of the economic and political factors that the standard setter should consider as it tries to mediate standards which both investors and management are willing to accept. The chapter also includes a very brief outline of the structure of international standard setting, to show that financial accounting and reporting is a part of the globalization of financial markets that has taken place in recent years.

1.9   Relevance of Financial Accounting Theory to Accounting Practice

The framework just described provides a way of organizing our study of financial accounting theory. However, this book also recognizes an obligation to convince you that the theory is relevant to accounting practice. This is accomplished in two main ways. First, the various theories and research underlying financial accounting are described and explained in plain language, and their relevance is demonstrated by means of numerous references to accounting practice. For example, Chapter 3 describes how investors may make rational investment decisions, and then goes on to demonstrate that this decision theory underlies the conceptual framework of the FASB. Also, the book contains numerous instances where accounting standards are described and critically evaluated. In addition to enabling you to learn the contents of these standards, you can better understand and apply them when you have a grounding in the underlying reasoning on which they are based. The second approach to demonstrating relevance is through review and assignment problems. A real attempt has been made to select relevant problem material to illustrate and motivate the concepts.

Recent years have been challenging, even exciting, times for financial accounting theory. We have learned a tremendous amount about the important role of financial accounting in our economy from the information economics research outlined above. If this book enables you to better understand and appreciate this role, it will have attained its objective.

Notes

1. Actually, MN pose a much deeper question. Widespread share ownership had long been seen as a way of reconciling increasingly large and powerful corporations with the popular belief in individualism, property rights, and democracy, whereby the "little guy" could take part in the corporate governance process. With the 1929 crash and subsequent revelation of manipulative abuses, a new approach was required which would both restore public confidence in securities markets and be acceptable to powerful corporate interest groups. MN suggest that the creation of the SEC was an embodiment of such a new approach.

2. The term "hardness" was introduced by Ijiri (1975), who defined it as difficulty of manipulation of financial reports by persons with a vested interest in those reports.

Accounting Under Ideal Conditions

2.1   Overview

We will begin our study of financial accounting theory by considering the present value model. This model provides the utmost in relevant information to financial statement users. In this context we define relevant information as information about the firm's future economic prospects, that is, its dividends, cash flows, and profitability.

Our concern is with the conditions under which relevant financial statements will also be reliable, where we define reliable information as information which is precise and free from bias. We will also explore the conditions under which market values of assets and liabilities can serve as indirect measures of value. This will be the case under ideal conditions (to be defined later). If conditions are not ideal (which is usually the case), fundamental problems are created for asset valuation and income measurement.

2.2   The Present Value Model Under Certainty

The present value model is widely used in economics and finance and has had considerable impact on accounting over the years. We first consider a simple version of the model under conditions of certainty. By "certainty" we mean that the future cash flows of the firm and the interest rate in the economy are publicly known with certainty. We denote these as **ideal conditions**.

EXAMPLE 2.1 THEORETICAL ILLUSTRATION OF THE PRESENT VALUE MODEL UNDER CERTAINTY

Consider P.V. Ltd., a one-asset firm with no liabilities. Assume that the asset will generate end-of-year cash flows of $100 each year for two years and then will have zero value. Assume also that the risk-free interest rate in the economy is 10%. Then, at time 0 (the beginning of the first year of the asset's life), the present value of the firm's future cash flows, denoted by PA_0, is:

$$
\begin{aligned}
PA_0 &= \$100 \div 1.10 + \$100 \div (1.10)^2 \\
&= \$90.91 + \$82.64 \\
&= \$173.55
\end{aligned}
$$

We can then prepare a present value opening balance sheet as follows:

P.V. LTD.
BALANCE SHEET
As at Time 0

Capital asset, at present value $173.55   Shareholders' equity $173.55

Now, move on to time 1, one year later. At that time, the present value of the remaining cash flows from the firm's asset is:

$$
\begin{aligned}
PA_1 &= \$100 \div 1.10 \\
&= \$90.91
\end{aligned}
$$

The firm's income statement for year 1 would be:

P.V. LTD.
INCOME STATEMENT
For Year 1

Sales (cash received)	$100.00
Depreciation expense	82.64
Net income	$ 17.36

Depreciation expense is calculated as $173.55 − $90.91 = $82.64—that is, the decline in the present value of the future receipts from the asset over the year. This way of calculating depreciation differs from the way that accountants usually calculate it. Nevertheless, it is the appropriate approach under the ideal conditions of this example, namely, future cash flows known with certainty and a fixed risk-free interest rate.

Then, the end-of-year-1 balance sheet is:

P.V. LTD. BALANCE SHEET As at End of Year				
Financial Asset			**Shareholders' Equity**	
Cash		$100.00	Opening value	$173.55
Capital Asset			Net income	17.36
Opening value	$173.55			
Accumulated				
depreciation	82.64	90.91		
		$190.91		$190.91

This assumes that the firm pays no dividend. A dividend can be easily incorporated by reducing cash and shareholders' equity by the amount of the dividend.

Note the following points about Example 2.1:

1. The net book value of the capital asset at any year-end is equal to the present value of the future cash flows from that asset, discounted at 10%. Depreciation expense is the change in present value over the year.

2. Net income for the year is equal to the year's cash flow of $100 less the $82.64 decline in the present value of the asset. Note that it is also equal to $PA_0 \times 10\% = \$173.55 \times 10\% = \$17.36$. This amount is sometimes called **accretion of discount,** that is, the opening present value multiplied by the interest rate. The term arises because the stream of cash receipts is one year closer at the end of the year than it was at the beginning. The $17.36 is also referred to as *ex ante* or **expected** net income since, at time 0, the firm expects to earn $17.36. Of course, because all conditions are known with certainty, the expected net income will equal the *ex post* or **realized** net income.

3. Define **relevant** financial statements as those which give information to investors about the firm's future economic prospects. Example 2.1 is entirely relevant. To see this, note first that, fundamentally, economic prospects are defined by the firm's stream of future dividends—it is dividends which provide a payoff to investors, the present value of which serves to establish firm value.

Then, it might seem that the firm's dividend policy will affect its value, since the timing of dividends will affect their present value. However, under ideal conditions, this is not the case, a condition called **dividend irrelevancy**.

To see why dividend policy does not matter under ideal conditions, note that as long as investors can invest any dividends they receive at the *same rate* of return as the firm earns on cash flows *not* paid in dividends, the present value of an investor's overall interest in the firm is independent of the timing of dividends. This holds in our example since there is only one interest rate in the economy. In effect, the firm's cash flows establish the size of the "pot" that is ultimately available to investors and it does not matter if this pot is distributed sooner or later. If it is distributed during the current year, investors can earn 10% on the distributions. If it is distributed in a subsequent year, the firm earns 10% on amounts not distributed, but this accrues to investors through an increase in the value of their investment. The present value to the investor is the same either way.

Under dividend irrelevancy, cash flows are just as relevant as dividends, because cash flows establish the firm's dividend-paying ability. As a result, the financial statements under Example 2.1 are entirely relevant.

4. As an accountant, you might be wondering why the firm's **net income** seems to play no role in firm valuation. This is quite true—it doesn't, under ideal conditions of certainty. The reason is that future cash flows are known and hence can be discounted to provide balance sheet valuations. Net income is then quite trivial, being simply accretion of discount as pointed out above. In effect, under ideal conditions, the balance sheet contains all the relevant information and the income statement contains none.[1] Even though net income is "true and correct," it conveys no information because investors can always figure it out by multiplying the opening balance sheet value by the interest rate. To put this another way, there is no information in the current net income that helps investors predict future economic prospects of the firm. These are already known to investors by assumption. This is an important point and we shall return to it later. For now, suffice it to say that when ideal conditions do not hold the income statement assumes a much more significant role.

5. If we define **reliable** financial statements as being precise and free from bias, Example 2.1 is entirely reliable, since we have assumed that future cash flows and the interest rate are known with certainty. Lack of reliability harms rational investors in two related ways. First, information that is imprecise will need revision later. This can upset investors' decision calculations. Second, for reasons outlined in Chapter 1, managers may bias or otherwise manipulate financial statement information, which can also upset investor decisions. When information is perfectly

reliable, neither of these problems can arise. For example, any attempt by management to bias the financial statements would be immediately detected since future cash flows and the interest rate are publicly known.

6. Under the ideal conditions of future cash flows known with certainty and the economy's risk-free interest rate given, the market value of the asset will be equal to its present value. To see this, consider the following argument: Given an interest rate of 10%, no one would be willing to pay more than $173.55 for the asset at time 0—if they did, they would be earning less than 10%. Also, the owners of the asset would not sell it for less than $173.55—if offered less than $173.55, they would be better off to retain it and earn 10%. If they needed the money they could borrow at 10% against the asset as security. Thus, the only possible equilibrium market price is $173.55. This argument is a simple example of the principle of **arbitrage**. If market prices for goods and services are such that it is possible to make a profit by simply buying in one market and selling in another, these are called arbitrage profits. However, it seems reasonable to expect that, if future cash flows and the risk-free rate are publicly known, the scramble of self-interested individuals to make these quick profits would eliminate any price discrepancies.

7. Arbitrage means that there are two ways to determine asset value. We can calculate the discounted present value of future cash flows, as in Example 2.1. We will call this the **direct** approach. Alternatively, we can use market value. We will call this the **indirect** approach. Under ideal conditions, the two approaches yield identical results.

    As P.V. Ltd. owns only one asset and has no liabilities, the firm's market value would also be $173.55 at time 0, being the sum of the financial assets and the present value of future cash receipts from the capital asset. Thus, the total market value of P.V.'s shares outstanding would be $173.55. In more general terms, if a firm owns more than one asset, the market value of the firm would be the sum of the value of its financial assets plus the value of the joint future receipts from its capital assets, less the present value of any liabilities. At points in time after time 0, the firm's market value continues to equal the sum of its financial assets plus capital assets, net of liabilities. Note, however, that dividend policy affects the amount of financial assets. To the extent that the firm does not pay out all of its profits in dividends, it will invest this cash to earn a return. Question 2, at the end of this chapter, illustrates this point. See also the discussion of dividend irrelevancy above.

The purpose of Example 2.1 is to demonstrate that under the ideal conditions of future cash flows known with certainty and a fixed risk-free interest rate in the economy, it is possible to prepare relevant financial statements that are also reliable. The process of arbitrage ensures that the market value of an asset equals the present value of its future cash flows. The market value of the firm is then the value of its financial assets plus the value of its capital assets (less liabilities).

Net income for the period equals cash flow less the change in the value of its financial and capital assets during the period or, equivalently, the firm's opening value multiplied by the interest rate. However, even though net income can be perfectly calculated, it has no information content, because investors can easily calculate it for themselves. All of the "action" is on the balance sheet, which shows the value of the firm.

Because of dividend irrelevancy, all of these conclusions are independent of the firm's dividend policy.

2.3   *The Present Value Model Under Uncertainty*

It is instructive to extend the present value model to the presence of uncertainty. With one major exception, most of the concepts carry over from Example 2.1. Again, we will proceed by means of an example.

EXAMPLE 2.2 THEORETICAL ILLUSTRATION OF THE PRESENT VALUE MODEL UNDER UNCERTAINTY

Let us continue Example 2.1 taking into account that the economy can be in a "bad" state or a "good" state during each year. If it is in the bad state, cash flows will be $100 for the year. If it is in the good state, however, cash flows will be $200 for the year. Assume that during each year the bad state and the good state occur with probability 0.5. This assumption implies that the state realizations are independent over the two years of the example. That is, the state realization in year 1 does not affect the probabilities[2] of state realization in year 2.

Uncertain future events such as the state of the economy are called **states of nature**, or **states** for short. Thus the states in this example are, for each year:

> **State 1:** Economy is bad.
> **State 2:** Economy is good.

Note that no one can control which state is realized—this is why they are called states of *nature*. Other examples of states that affect cash flows are weather, government policies, strikes by suppliers, equipment breakdowns, etc. In any realistic situation there will be a large number of possible states. However, our two-state example is sufficient to convey the idea—states of nature are a conceptual device to model those uncertain, uncontrollable future events whose realization affects the cash flows of the firm.

While at time 0 no one knows which state will occur, we assume that the *set* of possible states is publicly known and complete. That is, every possible future event that can affect cash flows is known to everyone. Thus, while no one knows for sure which state will occur, it is known that whatever state does happen must be an element of the set. Furthermore, we assume that the state realization is publicly observable—everyone will know which state actually happens. Finally, we assume that the state probabilities are **objective**, and publicly known. By objective we mean that if we imagine a long-run sequence of repetitions of our economy, the bad state will occur with relative frequency 0.5 (or whatever other state probability we were to assume). Think by analogy with rolling a pair of fair dice. We know that the probability of a seven, say, is 1/6, and that if we were to roll the dice a large number of times a seven will appear with relative frequency 1/6. Note that an implication of objective probabilities here is that the outcome of any particular roll tells us nothing about the true state of the dice—we know that they are fair. Thus, the probability of a seven on the next roll remains at 1/6, and similarly for the probability of any other outcome.

These assumptions extend the concept of ideal conditions, also called "first-best" conditions, to take uncertainty into account. To summarize:[3]

> *Ideal conditions* under uncertainty are characterized by: (1) a given, fixed interest rate at which the firm's future cash flows are discounted, (2) a complete and publicly known set of states of nature, (3) state realization publicly observable, and (4) state probabilities objective and publicly known.

Another way to think about ideal conditions here is that they are similar to conditions of certainty except that future cash flows are known *conditionally* on the states of nature. We will assume that P.V. Ltd.'s future cash flows are discounted at 10%.

Given these ideal conditions, we can now calculate the **expected present value** of P.V.'s future cash flows at time 0:

$$PA_0 = 0.5 \left(\frac{\$100}{1.10} + \frac{\$200}{1.10} \right) + 0.5 \left(\frac{\$100}{1.10^2} + \frac{\$200}{1.10^2} \right)$$
$$= 0.5 \times \$272.73 + 0.5 \times \$247.93$$
$$= \$136.36 + \$123.93$$
$$= \$260.33$$

We can then prepare P.V.'s opening balance sheet as:

P.V. LTD.
BALANCE SHEET
As at Time 0

Capital asset, at expected present value	$260.33	Shareholders' equity	$260.33

It is worthwhile to ask whether the time 0 market value of the asset, and hence of the firm, would be $260.33, as per the balance sheet. It is tempting

to answer yes, since this is the firm's expected value given dividend irrele-
vance. However, the introduction of uncertainty introduces an additional
consideration not present in the certainty model of Section 2.2. This is that
investors may be averse to risk. While the *expected* value of the firm is
$260.33 at time 0, it is shown below that the expected value of the firm at
the *end* of year 1 will be $236.36 or $336.36 depending on whether the bad
state or the good state happens in that year. Ask yourself whether you
would be indifferent between $260.33 for sure now or a 50/50 gamble of
$236.36 or $336.36 a year from now. The present value of the 50/50 gamble
is:

$$PA_0 = 0.5 \times \frac{\$236.36}{1.10} + 0.5 \times \frac{\$336.36}{1.10}$$
$$= 0.5 \times \$214.87 + 0.5 \times \$305.78$$
$$= \$107.44 + \$152.89$$
$$= \$260.33$$

the same as the sure thing. But, most people would prefer the sure thing,
since it is less risky. Then, the market value of the firm will be less than
$260.33, since to the extent that investors are collectively risk-averse they
will value the risky firm at less than its present value.

In this chapter, we will ignore this complication, by assuming that
investors are risk-neutral. Then, the firm's market value will be $260.33 at
time 0. This assumption of risk-neutral investors will be relaxed later, since
accountants have a role to play in informing investors about the firm's
riskiness as well as its expected value. The concept of a risk-averse
investor is introduced in Section 3.4 and the impact of risk on firm valuation is shown in Section 4.3. For now, suffice it to say that the expected
value of future cash flows is relevant for investors irrespective of their attitudes to risk.

Given risk-neutral valuation, the arbitrage principle will ensure that the
market value of the firm's asset, and of the firm itself, is $260.33. The arbi-
trage principle would still hold if investors were averse to risk but the market value would be driven to an amount less than $260.33.

To return to the example, you should verify that *expected* net income for
year 1—also called accretion of discount—is $0.10 \times \$260.33 = \$26.03$, analogous to the certainty case (see question 3).

Now, at the end of year 1 the present value of the remaining cash flows
from the asset is:

$$PA_1 = 0.5 \left(\frac{\$100}{1.10} + \frac{\$200}{1.10} \right) = \$136.36$$

Assuming that the year 1 state realization is bad economy, P.V.'s year 1
realized income statement is:

P.V. LTD.
INCOME STATEMENT
(bad economy)
For Year 1

Sales (cash received)	$100.00
Depreciation expense ($260.33 − $136.36)	123.97
Net loss	$ 23.97

The year-end balance sheet is:

P.V. LTD.
BALANCE SHEET
(bad economy)
As at End of Year 1

Financial Asset			**Shareholders' Equity**	
Cash		$100.00	Opening value	$260.33
Capital Asset			Net loss	23.97
Opening value	$260.33			
Accumulated depreciation	123.97	136.36		
		$236.36		$236.36

Again, arbitrage ensures that the market value of the asset is $136.36 and of the firm is $236.36 at time 1. We continue the assumption that the firm pays no dividend. Ideal conditions ensure that it makes no difference whether the firm pays a dividend or not, as in the certainty case. In other words, dividend irrelevancy continues to hold. Question 4 pursues this point.

The major difference between the uncertainty and certainty cases is that *expected net income and realized net income need not be the same.* To analyze this further, consider the following alternative calculation of net income given state 1:

P.V. LTD.
ALTERNATIVE INCOME STATEMENT
(bad economy)
For Year 1

Accretion of discount (0.10 × $260.33)		$26.03
Less: Abnormal earnings, as a result of bad-state realization:		
Expected cash flows (0.5 × $100 + 0.5 × $200)	$150	
Actual	100	50.00
Net loss		$23.97

Note that the negative $50 of unexpected cash flows results in a $50 "shock" to earnings for the year. The negative $50 earnings shock is called **abnormal earnings**, since it reduces expected earnings of $26.03 to a loss of $23.97. Under this calculation, net income consists of *expected* net income less the abnormal earnings for year 1 resulting from the bad-state realization of $50.

It should be noted that in our example abnormal earnings do not **persist**. That is, their effect dissipates completely in the year in which they occur. In general, this need not be the case. For example, if the bad-state realization was due to, say, a tax increase which affected economic activity, the abnormal effect on earnings may persist for several periods. We ignore this possibility here, to keep the example simple. However, we will return to the concept of persistence in Chapter 6.

Yet another way to calculate income, familiar from introductory accounting, is to calculate the change in balance sheet net assets for the year, adjusted for capital transactions. In this example, we have:

Net income = $236.36 − $260.33 − $0 = −$23.97

where capital transactions are zero. Thus, knowing the present values of all assets and liabilities enables one to calculate present-value-based net income.

Now, let's consider the accounting if the state realization is a good economy. At the end of year 1, the present value of the remaining cash flows is still $136.36, and the year 1 income statement is:

P.V. LTD.
INCOME STATEMENT
(good economy)
For Year 1

Sales (cash received)	$200.00
Depreciation expense ($260.33 − $136.36)	123.97
Net income	$ 76.03

Under the alternative calculation of net income, we have:

P.V. LTD.
ALTERNATIVE INCOME STATEMENT
(good economy)
For Year 1

Accretion of discount	$26.03
Add: Abnormal earnings, as a result of good-state realization ($200 − $150)	50.00
Net income	$76.03

The abnormal earnings of $50 is the difference between actual and expected cash flows for year 1, and these abnormal earnings increase expected earnings up to a profit of $76.03.

The year-end balance sheet is:

P.V. LTD.
BALANCE SHEET
(good economy)
As at End of Year 1

Financial Asset			**Shareholders' Equity**	
Cash		$200.00	Opening value	$260.33
Capital Asset			Net income	76.03
Opening value	$260.33			
Accumulated				
depreciation	123.97			136.36
		$336.36		$336.36

Again, arbitrage ensures that the firm's market value at time 1 will be $336.36, given risk-neutral investors.

Note the following points about Example 2.2:

1. It continues to be the case that financial statements are both completely relevant and completely reliable. They are relevant because balance sheet values are based on expected future cash flows, and dividend irrelevancy holds. They are reliable because ideal conditions ensure that present value calculations are precise and free of bias—a complete set of states of nature plus objective state probabilities, together with a given, fixed interest rate, enable a present value calculation that is incapable of error, or of being manipulated by management. All relevant future states are anticipated and objectively included in the expected present values. Of course, reliability here is in an *ex ante* sense. Expected time 1 value at time 0 will generally not equal actual value at time 1. Nevertheless, for investor decision-making purposes, beginning-of-period present value is what is needed, and this is completely reliable in our example.

2. Like the certainty case, there are still two ways of calculating relevant and reliable balance sheet values: we can calculate expected present values directly or we can use market values. Under ideal conditions, arbitrage forces the two ways to yield identical results.

3. Despite the fact that expected and realized net income need not be equal, the income statement still does not have any information content when abnormal earnings do not persist. Investors have sufficient information to calculate for themselves what realized net income will be, once they know the current year's state realization. This calculation is programmable and no accounting policy decisions are needed.

4.   At the risk of getting ahead of ourselves, let us see how the income statement *can* be informative. For this, we need only relax the assumption that state probabilities are objective. This puts us into the realm of **subjective** probabilities, which are formally introduced in Chapter 3. Then, investors no longer have "ready-made" state probabilities available to them for purposes of calculating expected future cash flows and income. Rather, they must assess these probabilities themselves, using whatever information is available. There is no longer any guarantee that in a long-run sequence of repetitions of the economy, the bad and good states will occur with the same relative frequencies as the probabilities assigned by the investor. The reason, of course, is that individuals are limited in their knowledge and forecasting ability. Note that if state probabilities are subjective, so are the resulting expected values. That is, the value of the firm is also subjective.

Subjective probabilities are a more reasonable assumption than objective probabilities, because the future performance of a business entity is much more complex and difficult to predict than a simple roll of fair dice. Since investors know that their predictions are subject to error, they will be alert for information sources that enable them to revise their probability assessments. The income statement is one such source. When state probabilities are subjective, the income statement can provide information about what these probabilities are. For example, observing a net income of $76.03 this year in Example 2.2 may cause you to increase your probability of the high state in future years. This would improve your ability to predict firm cash flows and profitability in *future* years.

If this argument is unclear to you, return to the analogy of rolling dice, but now assume that you do not know whether the dice are fair. What is your probability of rolling a seven? Obviously, this probability is no longer objective, and you must assess it on the basis of whatever information and prior experience you have. However, rolling the dice (cf. observing the income statement) provides information, and after a few rolls you should have a better idea of what their true state is. Just as improved knowledge of the true state of the dice will help you to predict future rolls, improved knowledge of the true state of the firm will help you to predict future profitability and investment returns. In Chapter 3 we will show how investors can use financial statement information to revise their subjective probabilities of future firm performance.

SUMMARY

The purpose of Example 2.2 was to extend the present value model to formally incorporate uncertainty, using the concept of states of nature. The definition of ideal conditions must be extended to include a complete and publicly known set of states of nature, with future cash flows known *conditionally* on state realization—that is, *if* the state of nature is …, *then* cash flows will be …. Also, ideal conditions now specify objective state probabilities and that the state realization be publicly observable. The logic of the present value model under certainty then carries over, except that market values are based on *expected* cash flows, assuming investors are risk-neutral.

The major difference between the certainty and uncertainty cases is that *expected* and *realized* net income need no longer be the same under uncertainty, and the difference is called abnormal earnings. Nevertheless, financial statements based on expected present values continue to be both relevant and reliable. They are relevant because they are based on expected future cash flows. They are reliable because financial statement values objectively reflect these expected future cash flows and, as in the certainty case, management manipulation is not possible.

All of these conclusions are independent of the firm's dividend policy, since dividend irrelevancy continues to hold.

2.4   *Reserve Recognition Accounting (RRA)*

2.4.1   *AN EXAMPLE OF RRA*

By now, you probably want to point out that the real world is *not* characterized by ideal conditions. This is quite true. Indeed, the present value model encounters serious problems when we try to apply it under less-than-ideal conditions. To illustrate these problems, we now consider reserve recognition accounting for oil and gas companies.[4]

In 1982, the FASB issued SFAS 69, which requires supplemental disclosure of certain information about the operations of publicly traded oil and gas companies. An interesting aspect of SFAS 69 is that disclosure of the estimated present value of future receipts from a company's proved oil and gas reserves is required. The estimate is known as the "standardized measure." The intent, presumably, is to provide investors with more relevant information about future cash flows than that contained in the conventional, historical-cost-based financial statements. Oil and gas companies, it can be argued, particularly need to give this type of supplementary disclosure, because the historical cost of oil and gas properties may bear little relationship to their value.

It can hardly be said that oil and gas companies operate under conditions of certainty. Consequently, we shall consider SFAS 69 in relation to our present value model under uncertainty in Example 2.2. Present value accounting applied to oil and gas reserves is known as **reserve recognition accounting (RRA)**.

Consider first Table 2.1, adapted from the 1993 annual report of Exxon Corporation. Note that the undiscounted future net cash flows are shown, and also the present value of these cash flows, discounted at 10%. No information is given about the riskiness of the estimates. This disclosure seems to conform fairly well to our theoretical Example 2.2. The $16,735 is the amount that would appear on Exxon's December 31, 1993 balance sheet for the asset "proved oil and gas reserves" (except that the information is supplementary here). It corresponds to the $136.36 valuation of the capital asset at time 1 in Example 2.2. It should

TABLE 2.1 EXXON CORPORATION AND CONSOLIDATED SUBSIDIARIES
STANDARDIZED MEASURE OF DISCOUNTED FUTURE CASH FLOWS
AS AT DECEMBER 31, 1993 (millions of dollars)

	United States	Canada	Europe	Australia and Far East	Other	Total
			Consolidated Subsidiaries			
As of December 31, 1991:						
Future cash inflows from sales of oil and gas	$44,929	$15,782	$44,202	$22,836	$2,141	$129,890
Future production and development costs	27,046	9,414	24,373	12,277	982	74,092
Future income tax expenses	4,967	2,595	8,528	3,999	543	20,632
Future net cash flows	12,916	3,773	11,301	6,560	616	35,166
Effect of discounting net cash flows at 10%	7,348	2,036	4,788	2,876	163	17,211
Discounted future net cash flows	$ 5,568	$ 1,737	$ 6,513	$ 3,684	$ 453	$ 17,955
As of December 31, 1992:						
Future cash inflows from sales of oil and gas	$48,897	$15,496	$41,248	$19,680	$1,814	$127,135
Future production and development costs	24,681	7,704	19,965	10,941	781	64,072
Future income tax expenses	7,334	3,183	7,987	3,464	476	22,444
Future net cash flows	16,882	4,609	13,296	5,275	557	40,619
Effect of discounting net cash flows at 10%	8,175	2,351	5,767	2,157	157	18,607
Discounted future net cash flows	$ 8,707	$ 2,258	$ 7,529	$ 3,118	$ 400	$ 22,012
As of December 31, 1993:						
Future cash flows from sales of oil and gas	$38,261	$11,816	$33,639	$18,190	$1,234	$103,140
Future production and development costs	19,980	6,677	18,295	11,287	593	56,832
Future income tax expenses	4,566	2,016	5,467	2,515	345	14,909
Future net cash flows	13,715	3,123	9,877	4,388	296	31,399
Effect of discounting net cash flows at 10%	6,695	1,552	4,387	1,951	79	14,664
Discounted future net cash flows	$ 7,020	$ 1,571	$ 5,490	$ 2,437	$ 217	$ 16,735

SOURCE: 1993 annual report of Exxon Corporation. Reprinted by permission.

be noted, however, that the 10% discount rate used by Exxon is not the single known rate in the economy. Rather, this rate is mandated by SFAS 69, presumably for comparability across firms. Also, as mentioned, the figures apply only to proved reserves and not all Exxon's assets.

Table 2.2 gives changes in the standardized measure.

TABLE 2.2 EXXON CORPORATION AND CONSOLIDATED SUBSIDIARIES CHANGES IN STANDARDIZED MEASURE OF DISCOUNTED FUTURE NET CASH FLOWS RELATING TO PROVED OIL AND GAS RESERVES FOR THE YEAR ENDED DECEMBER 31 (millions of dollars)

Consolidated Subsidiaries	1993	1992	1991
Value of reserves added during the year due to extensions, discoveries, improved recovery, and net purchases less related costs	$ 527	$1,452	$ 586
Changes in value of previous-year reserves due to:			
Sales and transfers of oil and gas produced during the year, net of production (lifting) costs	(6,975)	(7,765)	(7,696)
Development costs incurred during the year	2,947	3,305	3,306
Net change in prices and lifting and development costs	(10,229)	5,185	(29,877)
Revisions of previous reserves estimates	1,137	580	2,516
Accretion of discount	2,817	2,588	4,417
Net change in income taxes	4,499	(1,288)	13,041
Total change in the standardized measure during the year	$(5,277)	$4,057	$(13,707)

SOURCE: 1993 annual report of Exxon Corporation. Reprinted by permission.

To understand this statement, rework Example 2.2 (see Table 2.3) to show the changes in the book value of the capital asset during the year, assuming state 2 (good economy) is realized (a similar analysis applies to state 1).

TABLE 2.3 EXAMPLE 2.2: CHANGE IN BOOK VALUE OF CAPITAL ASSET DURING THE YEAR (state 2 realized)

Present value of capital asset, beginning of year (time 0)		$260.33
Less: Sales in year 1		200.00
		60.33
Add:		
Accretion of discount	$26.03	
Unexpected cash flows	50.00	76.03
BV of capital asset, end of year (time 1)		$136.36

Now, we rework Exxon's Changes in Standardized Measure (Table 2.2) statement into a format consistent with Table 2.3, as shown in Table 2.4.

TABLE 2.4 EXXON CORPORATION AND CONSOLIDATED SUBSIDIARIES REWORKED STANDARDIZED MEASURE FOR THE YEAR ENDED DECEMBER 31, 1993 (millions of dollars)

Present value of standardized measure at beginning of year		$22,012
Less: Sales in year		6,975
		15,037
Add:		
Accretion of discount	$ 2,817	
Present value of additional reserves added during year	527	
Development costs incurred during year	2,947	
Unexpected items—changes in value of previous-year reserves ($-10,229 + 1,137 + 4,499$)	(4,593)	1,698
Present value of standardized measure at end of year		$16,735

Check each of these numbers from the original Exxon statement in Tables 2.1 and 2.2. The $527 of additional present value proved during the year represents the ongoing nature of oil and gas exploration and could easily be added to Example 2.2. The $2,947 of development costs incurred during the year represents the increase in present value resulting from the expenditure of some of the development costs allowed for in the beginning-of-year present value.

The changes in estimates of −$4,593 should be considered carefully. Note, in particular, that there are a number of changes, including revisions of quantities, prices, and costs as well as income taxes. Note also that the amounts are fairly material. For example, the net change in prices and costs of −$10,229 is over 46% of present value at the beginning of 1993. The number and magnitude of these changes are the main differences between our Example 2.2, which assumed ideal conditions, and the "real world" environment in which Exxon operates. We shall return to this point shortly.

Note that the accretion of discount is not 10% of beginning-of-year present value as it was in Example 2.2. Unfortunately, the calculation of the $2,817 accretion is not given. Its failure to agree with its theoretical counterpart (beginning present value of $22,012 × 10% interest rate) presumably results from the added complexity derived from additional reserves proved during the year and from the changes in estimates. These changes are with respect to prices, costs, and their timing. Thus, the present value calculations are considerably more complex than in Example 2.2.

Finally, what would Exxon's 1993 present-value-based net income from proved oil and gas reserves be? This can be quite simply calculated as in Table 2.5. Again, the material impact on net income of changes in estimates is apparent. These amount to −163% of expected net income.

TABLE 2.5 EXXON CORPORATION AND CONSOLIDATED
SUBSIDIARIES INCOME STATEMENT FOR 1993 FROM PROVED OIL AND
GAS RESERVES (millions of dollars)

Sales in year	$ 6,975
Development costs incurred in year	(2,947)
Amortization expense (that is, decline in present value of reserves during the year [from Table 2.2])	(5,277)
Net loss from proved oil and gas reserves	$(1,249)

Or, in the alternative format:

Expected net income—accretion of discount	$ 2,817
Additional reserves proved during the year	527
Unexpected items—changes in value of previous-year reserves	(4,593)
	$(1,249)

Summary

The procedures used by Exxon to account for the results of its oil and gas operations under RRA seem to conform to the theoretical present value model under uncertainty, except that it is necessary to make material changes to the estimates.

2.4.2 CRITIQUE OF RRA

Management's Reaction

This necessity to make changes in estimates seems to be the Achilles' heel of RRA. Oil company managers, in particular, tend to regard RRA with reservation and suspicion. As an example, the following statement appears in Exxon's 1993 annual report (page F26):

> As required by the Financial Accounting Standards Board, the standardized measure of discounted future net cash flows is computed by applying year-end prices and costs, and a discount factor of 10 percent, to net proved reserves. The corporation believes that the standardized measure is not meaningful and may be misleading.

Usefulness to Investors

While it is clear that management opposes RRA, this does not necessarily mean that it does not provide useful information to investors. Certainly, RRA is more relevant than historical cost information, so it has the potential to be useful. To see the potential for relevance, compare the present-value-based 1993 net income from Table 2.5 with Exxon's historical-cost-based earnings from oil and gas,[5] given in Table 2.6.

TABLE 2.6 EXXON CORPORATION AND CONSOLIDATED SUBSIDIARIES EARNINGS FROM OIL AND GAS PRODUCING ACTIVITIES FOR THE YEAR ENDED DECEMBER 31, 1993 (millions of dollars)

			Consolidated Subsidiaries			
Results of Operations	**United States**	**Canada**	**Europe**	**Australia and Far East**	**Other**	**Total**
1993—Revenue						
Sales to third parties	$1,275	$ 346	$2,336	$1,655	$106	$5,718
Transfers	2,829	712	1,063	876	166	5,646
	4,104	1,058	3,399	2,531	272	11,364
Production costs excluding taxes	1,204	430	1,114	412	64	3,224
Exploration expenses	132	41	250	81	144	648
Depreciation and depletion	1,196	480	700	404	136	2,916
Taxes other than income	479	21	60	532	2	1,094
Related income tax	459	19	435	378	38	1,329
Results of producing activities	634	67	840	724	(112)	2,153
Other earnings	296	(35)	194	26	45	526
Total earnings	$ 930	$ 32	$1,034	$ 750	$ (67)	$2,679

SOURCE: 1993 annual report of Exxon Corporation. Reprinted by permission.

Comparison of net income under the two bases is complicated by the fact that the present value calculations relate only to proved reserves. However, let us take the $2,153 million total consolidated results of producing activities for 1993 in Table 2.6 as the historical cost analogue of the $1,249 million present-value-based loss in Table 2.5. We see immediately that the present-value-based earnings are considerably lower than their historical-cost-based counterpart. This seems reasonable, since Table 2.2 tells us that the present value of proved reserves declined by $5,277 million during the year. Under historical cost accounting, as you know, this decline in reserves would not show up in the income statement until sales started to fall off from the reduced reserves. In effect, the present-value-based income statement recognizes the decline "sooner." Thus, present value information has the potential for usefulness.

If RRA is in fact useful, we should observe some reaction in the price of Exxon's shares to the release of RRA information. Empirical evidence on the usefulness of RRA is reviewed in Chapter 5. For now, suffice it to say that it has been difficult to find evidence of usefulness.

Discussion

The above considerations, in particular management's opposition, suggest that RRA may have failed as a viable reporting product. What has gone wrong? The main point to realize is that Exxon does not operate under the ideal conditions of Examples 2.1 and 2.2. Consider the difficulties that Exxon's accountants would face in applying ideal conditions. First, interest rates in the economy are not fixed, although SFAS 69 deals with this by requiring a fixed, given rate of 10% for the discounting. Second, the set of states of nature affecting the amounts, prices, and timing of future production is much larger than the simple two-state set in Example 2.2, due to the complex environment in which oil and gas companies operate. However, in principle, it should be possible to come up with a reasonable list of future possibilities. Third, it is unlikely that the state realization would be publicly observable. Events like equipment breakdowns, production problems, and minor oil spills would most likely be inside information of Exxon. As a result, outsiders have no way of knowing whether the changes in estimates are accurate and unbiased, particularly since RRA is unaudited.

While these difficulties could probably be dealt with, a fourth problem is more fundamental. Objective state probabilities are not available. Consequently, subjective state probabilities need to be assessed by Exxon's engineers and accountants, with the result that the standardized measure is itself a subjective estimate.

Because of these difficulties in applying ideal conditions, the reliability of RRA information is severely compromised. This shows up in the number and materiality of revisions to estimates that need to be made, as shown in Table 2.4. It is not that estimates of expected future cash flows cannot be made. After all, RRA is "on line." Rather, lacking objective probabilities, these estimates become subject to revisions which threaten reliability to the point where the benefit of increased relevance is compromised. In effect, without ideal conditions, complete relevance and reliability are no longer jointly attainable. One must be traded off against the other.

2.4.3 SUMMARY

RRA represents a valiant attempt to convey relevant information to investors. On the surface, the present value information conforms quite closely to the theoretical present value model under uncertainty. If one digs deeper, however, serious problems of estimation are revealed. This is because oil and gas companies do not operate under the ideal conditions assumed by the theoretical model. As a result, reserve information loses reliability, as evidenced by the need for substantial annual revisions, as it gains relevance. It seems necessary to trade off these two desirable information qualities.

2.5   *Historical Cost Accounting Revisited*

As our discussion of RRA in Section 2.4 points out, it seems impossible to prepare financial statements that are both completely relevant and completely reliable. Consequently, relevance and reliability must be traded off. The historical cost basis of accounting can be thought of as one such tradeoff. Recall that under historical cost accounting the primary basis of valuation for several major asset categories, such as inventories, long-term portfolio investments, and capital assets including intangibles, is *cost*, or cost less amounts written off as amortization. On the liability side, long-term debt is also valued at cost, in the sense that the carrying value of such debt is based on interest rates in effect when the debt was issued—carrying value is not adjusted for subsequent interest rate changes.

Historical cost accounting is relatively reliable because the cost of an asset or liability to a firm is usually an objective number which is less subject to errors of estimation and bias than are present value calculations. Unfortunately, however, historical costs may lack relevance. While historical cost, market value, and present value may be similar as at the date of acquisition, market values and present values will change over time as market conditions change. Nevertheless, accountants continue to use the historical cost basis of accounting for major asset types because they are willing to trade off a considerable amount of relevance to obtain reasonable reliability. Consequently, historical cost accounting represents a particular tradeoff between the two.

2.5.1   THE CHALLENGE OF HISTORICAL COST ACCOUNTING

Historical cost accounting has a major challenge, however. Under historical cost accounting, it is necessary to match expenses with revenues, to determine earnings. The challenge is to do this in a manner which provides information to investors about the firm's *future* economic prospects.

Historical-cost-based earnings do have the potential to do this. One reason is their relative reliability, as mentioned above. More fundamentally, however, historical-cost-based earnings are a way to "smooth out" cash flows for the current period into a measure of the longer-run or persistent earning power that is implied by these cash flows.

To do this, the accountant has to calculate **accruals**, that is, to match costs with revenues. However, under non-ideal conditions, there is usually no unique way to do this, which complicates the ability of historical-cost-based earnings to reveal persistent earning power. To illustrate, we now consider three examples.

Depreciation

A major problem with matching is the amortization of capital assets. The matching principle deems it necessary to deduct amortization of capital assets from revenue for the period to arrive at net income. Yet, it does not state *how much* amortization should be accrued except for a vague indication that it should be systematic and rational. For example, paragraph 3060.31 of the *CICA Handbook* states that:

> Amortization should be recognized in a rational and systematic manner appropriate to the nature of a capital asset with a limited life and its use by the enterprise.

As a result of this vagueness, a variety of amortization methods are acceptable for use in practice, such as straight-line, declining-balance, and so on.

If it were possible to value capital assets on a present value basis for the financial statements, we would need only *one* amortization method—the change in the present value of the future receipts from the assets during the period, as illustrated in Examples 2.1 and 2.2. As it is not usually possible to value capital assets this way, the door is opened to a variety of amortization methods. This complicates the comparison of profitability across firms, because we must ascertain the amortization methods firms are using before making comparisons. It also means that firm managers have some room to manage their reported profitability through choice of amortization method or through changes to the method used. Thus, while one can argue, as we have above, that historical cost financial statements may be more reliable than those prepared on a present value or market value basis, this reliability will be eroded to the extent that managers can choose between alternative historical-cost-based accounting policies to manage reported net income for their own purposes. In other words, while historical cost accounting may be more reliable than value-based methods, it is by no means completely reliable.

Deferred Income Taxes

A major accounting controversy in Canada arose in 1953 when the *Income Tax Act* was amended to allow firms to choose the method of depreciation they wanted for their reported financial statements, while claiming maximum capital cost allowance on their tax returns. Prior to this, firms could not claim more capital cost allowance than the depreciation they recorded in their financial statements. Most firms responded to the 1953 amendment by using straight-line depreciation for financial reporting while claiming maximum capital cost allowance for tax purposes. This created a deferred tax problem, since taxes saved by claiming maximum capital cost allowance did not represent a permanent saving but merely a deferral of tax to later years, when maximum capital cost allowance was less than straight-line depreciation for capital assets.

The controversy was whether to record the deferred taxes (and resulting higher income tax expense) on the firm's financial statements. Some argued that they should be recorded, because the matching principle of historical cost accounting required that income tax expense should be matched with the amount of depreciation actually recorded on the financial statements. Others, however, felt that deferral was not required by the matching principle, because, in most cases (for example, if a firm was growing), the possibility that the deferred taxes would have to be repaid in some future year was remote. It does not make sense, they argued, to match costs that are unlikely to be paid with revenue. The controversy continued until 1963, when the *CICA Handbook* required that the deferral method be used henceforth. Paragraph 3470.13 states, "When timing differences occur between accounting income and taxable income, income taxes should be accounted for on the tax allocation basis...."

Note that the essential source of the deferred tax question is the multiplicity of acceptable depreciation methods under historical cost accounting. The problem arises because the method firms use on their financial statements can differ (and usually does differ) from the method allowed for tax purposes. If there was only one depreciation method, as under present value accounting, firms' book and tax figures would be the same and the deferred tax problem for depreciation would not arise.

Full-Cost Versus Successful-Efforts Approach in Oil and Gas Accounting

Under historical cost accounting, we need to know the *cost* of assets, so that they can be written off (matched) against revenues over their useful lives. We suggested earlier in this section that the cost of assets is usually reliably determinable. However, in some cases, even the cost of assets is not clear. Oil and gas accounting provides an interesting and important example.

There are two basic methods of determining the cost of oil and gas reserves. The **full-cost** approach capitalizes all costs of discovering reserves (subject to certain exceptions), including the costs of unsuccessful drilling. The argument is that the cost of successful wells includes the costs of dry holes drilled in the search for the successful ones. The **successful-efforts** approach capitalizes only the costs of successful wells and expenses dry holes, the rationale being that it is difficult to regard a dry hole in the ground as an asset.

Clearly, these two approaches can produce materially different recorded costs for oil and gas reserves, with the result that depreciation expense can also be materially different. In turn, this complicates the comparison of the reported net incomes of oil and gas firms, because different firms may use different methods for determining the cost of their reserves. For our purposes, however, simply note that the historical cost basis of accounting cannot settle the question of which method is preferable. The historical cost basis requires only that a cost of oil and gas reserves be established. It does not require a particular method for establishing what the cost should be. In fact, the *CICA Handbook* (paragraph 3060.25) allows both methods to be used in Canada (subject to certain exceptions).

Notice that use of RRA in the firm's accounts would eliminate the full-cost versus successful-efforts controversy. RRA values oil and gas reserves at their present values. It is *not* a cost-based approach, so the question of how to determine cost does not arise. Under RRA, depreciation expense is the change in the present value of oil and gas reserves resulting from extraction during the period.

2.5.2   *ACCOUNTANTS' REACTION TO THE CHALLENGE*

Since it seems impossible to prepare a complete set of present-value-based financial statements with sufficient reliability, the historical cost accounting framework will likely be with us for a long time to come. Consequently, the major accounting bodies have reacted to the challenge of historical-cost-based accounting by retaining its framework, but turning their attention to making financial statements more *useful*, within that framework. This is not to say that certain assets and liabilities cannot be reported on a present value or market value basis. Indeed, use of current values in the financial statements is increasing, as will be discussed in Chapter 6. Nevertheless, since major asset and liability categories, such as capital assets, continue to be accounted for on the historical cost basis, we can still say that this is the basic framework of accounting.

To increase the usefulness of historical cost accounting, accountants have tended to adopt a strategy of *full disclosure*. Thus, disclosure of accounting policies used enables investors to at least be aware of the particular policies the firm has chosen out of the multiplicity of policies that are available for most assets and liabilities. Also, **supplementary information** is given to help investors project current performance into the future. The RRA disclosure discussed in Section 2.4 is an example of such supplementary information.

2.5.3   *SUMMARY*

The continued use of historical cost accounting in financial reporting can be thought of as a consequence of the impossibility of preparing theoretically correct financial statements on a present value basis. Historical cost accounting represents a particular tradeoff between relevance and reliability of financial statements. Complete relevance is not attained, because historical-cost-based asset values need bear little resemblance to discounted present values. However, complete reliability is not attained either, since the possibility of management manipulation remains. The measurement of net income becomes a process of matching, rather than a simple calculation of accretion of discount, and the matching principle usually allows different ways of accounting for the same item. Frequently, accounting standard setting bodies step in to impose uniform accounting policies to reduce the multiplicity of policy choices.

Since it appears that historical cost accounting will be around for some time to come, accountants, over the last number of years, have reacted by trying to make the historical cost framework more useful. One way of increasing usefulness is to retain the historical cost framework but expand disclosure in the annual report, so as to help investors to make their own estimates of future economic prospects.

2.6   *Conclusions*

To prepare a complete set of financial statements on a present value basis, recall that it is necessary to value *all* of the firm's assets and liabilities this way, with net income being the change in the firm's present value during the period (adjusted for capital transactions such as dividends). Yet, we saw with RRA that severe problems arise when we try to apply the present value approach to even a single type of asset. These problems would be compounded if the approach was extended to all other assets and liabilities.

This leads to an important and interesting conclusion, namely that under the real-world conditions in which accounting operates, *net income does not exist as a well-defined economic construct.* As evidence, simply consider Exxon's 1993 RRA net loss of $1,249 in Table 2.5. How can we take this as well-defined, or "true," income when we know that next year there will be a flock of unanticipated changes to the estimates that underlie the 1993 income calculation?

A fundamental problem is the lack of objective state probabilities. With objective probabilities, present values of assets and liabilities correctly reflect the uncertainty facing the firm, since present values then take into account all possible future events and their probabilities. In this case, accounting information is completely relevant as well as completely reliable.

Furthermore, an indirect approach of basing the income calculation on changes in market values rather than present values runs into the problem that market values need not exist for all firm assets and liabilities, a condition known as **incomplete markets**. For example, while there may be a market price for a barrel of crude oil, what is the market value of Exxon's reserves? In the face of uncertainties over quantities, prices, and lifting costs, an attempt to establish their market value runs into the same estimation problems as RRA. As a result, a ready market value does not exist. If market values are not available for all firm assets and liabilities, an income measure based on market values is not possible. Beaver and Demski (1979) give formal arguments to show that income is not well defined when markets are incomplete.[6]

Lacking objective probabilities, the door is opened for subjective estimates of future firm performance. These estimates can be subject to wide error, however. As a result, accounting estimates based on present value lose reliability as they strive to maintain relevance.

Thus, a second conclusion is that accountants feel that historical-cost-based accounting represents a better way to account, since we observe historical cost accounting strongly rooted in practice. Some relevance is lost, but hopefully this is more than made up for by increased reliability.

You may be bothered by the claim that true net income does not exist. Should we devote our careers to measuring something that doesn't exist? However, we should be glad of the impossibility of ideal conditions. If they existed, no one would need accountants! As discussed in Examples 2.1 and 2.2, net income has no information content when conditions are ideal. The present value calculations and related income measurement could then be programmed in advance. All that is needed is the set of states, their probabilities, and knowledge of which state is realized, and accountants would not be needed for this. Thus, we can say of income measurement, "If we can solve it, we don't need it."

This lack of a theoretically correct concept of income is what makes accounting both frustrating and fascinating at the same time. It is frustrating because of the difficulty of agreeing on accounting policies. Different users will typically want different tradeoffs between relevance and reliability. As a result, there are often several ways of accounting for the same thing. It is fascinating because the lack of a well-defined concept of net income means that a great deal of *judgement* must go into the process of asset valuation and income measurement. It is judgement that makes accounting valuable and, indeed, provides the very basis of a profession.

Instead of dwelling on questions of existence, accountants have turned their efforts to making historical-cost-based financial statements more useful. We will now proceed to study decision usefulness.

Notes

1. This argument can be turned around. We could argue that if the firm's future income statements were known with certainty, in conjunction with the interest rate, then they would contain all relevant information and the balance sheet could be easily deduced. In effect, each statement contains all the information needed for the other. We view the balance sheet as more fundamental under ideal conditions of certainty, however.

2. The independence assumption is not crucial to the example. With slight added complexity we could allow for conditional probabilities, where the probability of state realization in year 2 depends on the state realization in year 1. For example, if the high state happened in year 1, this might increase the probability that the high state would also happen in year 2.

3. Somewhat weaker conditions than these would be sufficient to give a first-best economy. Our purpose here, however, is only to give a set of conditions sufficient to ensure that net income is well defined and without information content.

4. Reserve recognition accounting is not required, even as supplementary information, in Canada. Consequently, our consideration is with respect to practice in the United States.

5. SFAS 69 also requires the reporting of historical-cost-based results of operations for oil and gas producing activities.

6. For a counterargument, see Ohlson (1987).

Questions and Problems

1. Prepare the income statement for year 2 and the balance sheet at the end of year 2 for P.V. Ltd. in Example 2.1 under the assumption that P.V. Ltd. pays no dividends.   (CGA-Canada)

2. Show that an owner of P.V. Ltd. in Example 2.1 would not care whether P.V. Ltd. paid any dividend at the end of year 1. State precisely why this is the case.

    (CGA-Canada)

3. Calculate the expected net income for P.V. Ltd. for years 1 and 2 in Example 2.2. Explain why expected net income is also called "accretion of discount."

    (CGA-Canada)

4. Show that an owner of P.V. Ltd. in Example 2.2 would not care whether P.V. Ltd. paid any dividend at the end of year 1. Assume that the good-economy state was realized in year 1.   (CGA-Canada)

5. In Example 2.2, assume that P.V. Ltd. pays no dividends over its life, until a liquidating dividend is paid at the end of year 2 consisting of its cash on hand at that time.

    Required

    Verify that the market value of P.V. Ltd. at time 0 based on the present value of dividends equals $260.33, equal to P.V.'s market value based on expected future cash flows.

6. A simple example of the difference between ideal and non-ideal conditions is the rolling of a die.

    Required

    a. Calculate the expected value of a single roll of a fair die.

b. Now suppose that you are unsure whether the die is fair. How would you then calculate the expected value of a single roll?

c. Now roll the die four times. You obtain 6, 4, 1, 3. Does this information affect your belief that the die is fair? Explain.

7. Explain why, under ideal conditions, there is no need to make estimates when calculating expected present value.

8. Explain why estimates are required to calculate expected present value when conditions are *not* ideal.   (CGA-Canada)

9. Do you think that the market value of an oil and gas firm will be affected when RRA information is presented in addition to historical-cost-based earnings from oil and gas producing activities? Explain why or why not.

10. Explain why, under non-ideal conditions, it is necessary to trade off relevance and reliability. Define these two terms as part of your answer.   (CGA-Canada)

11. Why do you think Exxon's management is opposed to RRA?

12. Inventory is another asset for which there is a variety of ways to account under historical cost accounting, including first-in, first-out; last-in, first-out; average cost; etc.

a. How would inventory be accounted for under ideal conditions?

b. Give reasons why inventory is usually accounted for on a historical cost basis. Is accounting on this basis completely reliable? Why?

13. P Ltd. operates under ideal conditions. It has just bought a fixed asset for $3,100, which will generate $1,210 cash flow at the end of one year and $2,000 at the end of the second year. At that time, the asset will be useless in operations and P Ltd. plans to go out of business. The asset will have a known salvage value of $420 at the end of the second year. The interest rate in the economy is constant at 10% per annum.

P Ltd. finances the asset by issuing $605 par value of 12% coupon bonds to yield 10%. Interest is payable at the end of the first and second year, at which time the bonds mature. The balance of the cost of the asset is financed by the issuance of common shares.

Required

a. Prepare the present-value-based balance sheet as at the end of the first year. P Ltd. plans to pay no dividends in this year.

b. Give two reasons why ideal conditions are unlikely to hold.

c. If ideal conditions do not hold, but present-value-based financial statements are prepared anyway, is net income likely to be the same as you calculated in part **a**? Explain why or why not.   (CGA-Canada)

14. IC Ltd. operates under ideal conditions. The cash (net of cash expenses) revenue from its single asset is known to be receivable as follows: end of year 1, $100; end of year 2, $200; end of year 3, $100. At the end of year 3 the asset is worthless. Interest rates in the economy in which IC Ltd. operates are known to be 10% per annum over the next three years. The company pays no dividends. All cash on hand at year-end is invested at 10%.

    Required

    a. Prepare present-value-based balance sheets and income statements as follows:

        i. Balance sheet as at time 0 (beginning of operations)
        ii. Income statement for year 1
        iii. Balance sheet as at time 1 (end of first year of operations)
        iv. Income statement for year 2
        v. Balance sheet as at time 2 (end of second year of operations)

    b. Given the ideal conditions assumed, the market value of the asset must equal the present value of future receipts from the asset at all times. Explain why.

    c. Suppose that we relax the assumption of ideal conditions. Give two reasons why the present value approach to financial statement preparation becomes less reliable. (CGA-Canada)

15. XYZ Ltd. purchased an asset on January 1, 1995 with a useful life of two years at the end of which it has no residual value. The cash flows from the asset are uncertain. If the economy turns out to be "normal," the asset will generate $4,000 in cash flow each year; if the economy is "bad," it will generate $3,000 in cash flow per year; and if the economy is "good," the cash flow generated will be $5,000 per year. The chances of a "normal" economy being realized are 30%, the chances of a "bad" economy are 50%, and the chances of a "good" economy are 20%. State realization becomes publicly known at the end of 1995.

    Assumptions

    • Ideal conditions hold under uncertainty.
    • The economy-wide interest rate is 10%.
    • XYZ Ltd. finances the asset purchase partly by a bond issue and partly by a common share issue. The bond has a $3,000 face value and a 10% coupon rate and matures on December 31, 1996.
    • XYZ Ltd. has adopted the policy of paying out 50% of its net income as dividends to its shareholders.
    • The economy turns out to be "good."

Required

a. Calculate the present values of the asset at January 1, 1995 and December 31, 1995.

b. Prepare the present-value-based income statement of XYZ Ltd. for the year ended December 31, 1995.

c. Prepare the present-value-based balance sheet of XYZ Ltd. as at December 31, 1995.

d. Explain why, even under uncertainty, present-value-based financial statements are relevant and reliable provided ideal conditions hold.

e. Explain why shareholders of XYZ Ltd. are indifferent to whether they receive any dividend from the company　　　　　　　　　(CGA-Canada)

16. An area where discounting could possibly be applied is deferred income taxes. Consider a firm that purchases an asset costing $100,000 on January 1 of year 1. It is depreciated on a straight-line basis at 20% per year on the firm's books. Tax depreciation is 40% on a declining-balance basis. The income tax rate is 45%.

    The following schedule shows a simplified calculation of the deferred income tax balance for this asset over its life, assuming zero salvage value. This is the firm's only capital asset.

Year	Opening Tax B.V.	Additions	Tax Depreciation	Straight-Line Depreciation	Difference
1	—	100,000	40,000	20,000	20,000
2	60,000		24,000	20,000	4,000
3	36,000		14,400	20,000	(5,600)
4	21,600		8,640	20,000	(11,360)
5	12,960		12,960*	20,000	(7,040)

Year	Tax on Difference	Deferred Income Tax
1	9,000	9,000
2	1,800	10,800
3	(2,520)	8,280
4	(5,112)	3,168
5	(3,168)	0

*It is assumed that all of the remaining tax book value is claimed in year 5.

Required

a. Calculate the discounted present value of the deferred income tax liability at the end of each of years 1 to 5. Use a discount rate of 12%.

b. Why are the balances calculated in part **a** different from the undiscounted deferred income tax liabilities?

c. What problems would there be if the discounting approach was applied to the deferred tax liability of a large, complex firm with many capital assets etc.?

17. On January 1, 1995, ABC Ltd. started its business by purchasing a productive oil well. The proved oil reserves from the well are expected to generate $7,000 cash flow at the end of 1995, $6,000 at the end of 1996, and $5,000 at the end of 1997. Net sales is gross revenues less production costs. Net sales equals cash flows. On January 1, 1998, the oil well is expected to be dry. The management of ABC Ltd. wishes to prepare financial statements based on RRA in accordance with SFAS 69. The following information is known about the well at the end of 1995.

    • Actual cash flows in 1995 amounted to $6,500.

    • Changes in estimates: Due to improved recovery (of oil from the well), cash flows in 1996 and 1997 are estimated to be $6,500 and $6,000 respectively.

    Required

    a. Prepare the income statement of ABC Ltd. for 1995 from its proved oil reserves.

    b. Management of some firms have expressed serious concerns about the reliability of the RRA information. Outline two of these concerns.   (CGA-Canada)

18. On January 1, 1995, GAZ Ltd. purchased a producing oil well, with an estimated life of 15 years, and started operating it immediately. The management of GAZ Ltd. calculated the present value of future net cash flows from the well as $1,500,000. The discount rate used was 10%, which is the company's expected return on investment. During 1995, GAZ Ltd. recorded cash sales (net of production costs) of $600,000. GAZ Ltd. also paid $50,000 cash dividends during 1995.

    Required

    a. Prepare the income statement of GAZ Ltd. for the year ended December 31, 1995, using RRA.

    b. Prepare the balance sheet of GAZ Ltd. as at December 31, 1995, using RRA accounting.

    c. Summarize the perceived weaknesses of RRA accounting.

d. Why does SFAS 69 require that a 10% discount rate should be used by all oil and gas firms rather than allowing each firm to select its own discount rate?

(CGA-Canada)

19. The following RRA information is taken from the December 31, 1992 annual report of Chevron Corp.

CHEVRON CORP.
CHANGES IN THE STANDARDIZED MEASURE OF DISCOUNTED
FUTURE NET CASH FLOWS FROM PROVED RESERVES WORLDWIDE
For the Year Ended December 31, 1992
($ millions)

Present value at January 1, 1992	$11,410
Sales and transfer of oil and gas produced, net of production costs	(4,923)
Development costs incurred	1,525
Purchases of reserves	89
Sales of reserves	(1,723)
Extensions, discoveries, and improved recovery, less related costs	1,722
Revisions of previous quantity estimates	400
Net changes in prices, development, and production costs	2,232
Accretion of discount	1,880
Net change in income tax	1,138
Net change for the year	2,340
Present value at December 31, 1992	$13,750

SOURCE: December 31, 1992 annual report of Chevron Corp. Reprinted by permission.

Required

a. Prepare an income statement for 1992 on an RRA basis, similar to Table 2.5. That is, calculate net income in both the "sales less amortization" format and the "alternative" format.

b. Comment on why amortization expense is negative. Would you expect Chevron Corp.'s 1992 RRA net income as calculated in part a to be greater or less than Chevron Corp.'s 1992 net income from proved oil and gas reserves calculated on a historical cost basis? Explain.

c. Explain why the standardized measure is applied only to proved reserves.

d. SFAS 69 mandates a discount rate of 10% to be used in the present value calculations, rather than allowing each firm to choose its own rate. Why? Can you see any disadvantages to mandating a common discount rate?

3

The Decision Usefulness Approach to Financial Reporting

3.1   Overview

In Chapter 2 we concluded that the present value model faces some severe problems in practice. It is doubtful that a complete set of financial statements on this basis is feasible. This inability to value the whole firm on a present value basis means that a theoretically well-defined concept of net income does not exist in the complex, real world in which accountants operate.

In this chapter we will begin our study of how to tackle this problem. In Chapter 2 we saw that historical cost accounting makes more sense perhaps than many give it credit for, particularly when we recognize that it produces reliable information, even though historical cost information is not as relevant as market or present-value-based approaches to valuation.

Given that historical cost accounting for major classes of assets and liabilities is firmly fixed in practice, the next question is: How can financial statements based on historical costs be made more *useful?* This leads to an important concept in accounting—the concept of **decision usefulness**. To properly understand this concept, we need to consider other theories (that is, other than the present value model) from economics and finance. We, as accountants, cannot proceed to make financial statements more useful until we know just what usefulness means. We also need a precise definition of information. As it turns out, decision theories and capital market theories assist in conceptualizing the meaning of useful financial statement information.

The main purpose of this chapter is to introduce you to some of these theories and to discuss their relevance to accounting. As we shall see, major accounting standard setting bodies have picked up on these theories, to such an extent that they underlie many of the accounting standards and pronouncements issued by these bodies.

3.2   The Decision Usefulness Approach

As we can infer from Section 2.5, the decision usefulness approach to accounting theory takes the view that "if we can't prepare theoretically correct financial statements, at least we can try to make historical-cost-based statements more useful." This simple observation has had major implications for accounting theory and practice. In particular, we must now pay much closer attention than we did in Chapter 2 to financial statement users and their decision needs, since under non-ideal conditions it is no longer possible to read the value of the firm directly from the financial statements.

In adopting the decision usefulness approach, two major questions must be addressed. First, who are the users of financial statements? Clearly, there are many users. It is helpful to categorize them into broad groups, such as investors, lenders, managers, unions, standard setters, and governments. These groups are called **constituencies** of accounting.

Second, what are the decision problems of financial statement users? By understanding these decision problems, accountants will be better prepared to meet the information needs of the various constituencies. Financial statements can then be prepared with these information needs in mind. In other words, tailoring financial statement information to the specific needs of the users of those statements will lead to improved decision-making. In this way, the financial statements are made more *useful*.

Of course, determining the specific decision needs of users is by no means an obvious process. For example, what information does a holder of the firm's long-term debt need to make a rational decision about whether to sell certain holdings? Would this decision be helped or hindered by including deferred income taxes on the balance sheet?

In the face of difficult questions like these, accountants have turned to various theories in economics and finance for assistance. In this chapter we consider the single-person **theory of decision**. This theory is a good place to begin to understand how individuals may make rational decisions under uncertainty. The theory enables us to appreciate the concept of information, which enables decision-makers to sharpen up their subjective beliefs about future payoffs from their decisions.

We also consider the **theory of investment,** a specialization of decision theory to model the decision processes of a rational investor. In particular, the theory of investment helps us to understand the nature of *risk* in a portfolio investment context.

These theories are important to accountants because they have been adopted by major professional accounting standard setting bodies. An examination of some of the pronouncements of the Conceptual Framework project of the FASB (Section 3.8) shows that the above theories lurk just under the surface. Consequently, an understanding of the theories enables a deeper understanding of the pronouncements themselves.

SUMMARY

Accountants have adopted a decision usefulness approach to financial reporting as a reaction to the impossibility of preparing theoretically correct financial statements. However, the decision usefulness approach leads to the problems of identifying the users of financial statements and selecting the information they need to make good decisions. Accountants have decided that investors are a major constituency of users and have turned to various theories in economics and finance—in particular, to theories of decision and investment—to understand the type of financial statement information investors need.

3.3   *Single-Person Decision Theory*

Single-person decision theory takes the viewpoint of an individual who must make a decision under conditions of uncertainty.[1] It recognizes that state probabilities are no longer objective, as they are under ideal conditions, and sets out a formal procedure whereby the individual can make the best decision, by selecting from a set of alternatives. This procedure allows additional information to be obtained to revise the decision-maker's subjective assessment of the probabilities of what might happen after the decision is made. Decision theory is relevant to accounting because financial statements provide additional information which is useful for many decisions. Example 3.1 illustrates decision theory applied to a typical investment decision.

3.3.1   *DECISION THEORY APPLIED*

Bill Cautious has $10,000 to invest for one period. He has narrowed down his

---

EXAMPLE 3.1 A TYPICAL INVESTMENT DECISION

---

choice to two investments: shares of X Ltd. or risk-free government bonds yielding 2 1/4%. We will denote the act of buying the shares by a_1, and the bonds by a_2.

If he buys the shares, Bill faces risk. That is, the next-period return on the share investment is not known when Bill makes his decision. Bill feels that this return depends primarily on the long-run, or persistent, earning power of X Ltd. Consequently, he defines two states of nature:

State 1: High earning power

State 2: Low earning power

If X Ltd. is in state 1, the next-period net return will be $1,600, where net return is calculated as:

Net return = End-of-period market value + Dividends in period − Original investment

If X Ltd. is in state 2, next-period net return will be zero. The reason that net return varies with earning power, of course, is that market value will respond positively to earning power. Also, the higher is earning power the higher will be dividends, other things equal.

Note that if Bill buys the bonds, he receives interest of $225 next period, regardless of the state of nature. That is, the bond investment is treated as riskless.

The amounts to be received from a decision are called **payoffs**, which we can summarize by a **payoff table** as shown in Table 3.1. Note that in this decision problem the payoffs are in the form of net returns from an investment. We will use payoffs and (net) investment returns interchangeably throughout our discussion.

TABLE 3.1 PAYOFF TABLE FOR DECISION THEORY EXAMPLE 3.1

Act	State	
	HIGH	**LOW**
a_1 (buy shares)	$1,600	0
a_2 (buy bonds)	$225	$225

Now consider the state probabilities. Bill subjectively assesses the probability of state 1 (the high earning power state) as $P(H) = 0.30$. The probability of state 2 is then $P(L) = 0.70$. These probabilities incorporate all that Bill knows about X Ltd. to this point in time. These are called **prior probabilities**. He could base these probabilities, for example, on an analysis of X Ltd.'s past financial statements. Instead, or in addition, he could study the current market price of X Ltd. shares. If share price is low, it would indicate an unfavourable market evaluation of X's prospects, and Bill might also take this into account when assessing his state probabilities.

Bill is risk-averse. Let us assume that the amount of utility, or satisfaction, he derives from a payoff is equal to the square root of the amount of the payoff. Thus, if he receives $1,600, his utility is 40. This assumption of risk aversion is not necessary to our example. We could just as easily assume Bill was risk-neutral and evaluate the expected *dollar* amounts of the various payoffs. However, investors are generally risk-averse, so we will work in utilities rather than dollars. Section 3.4 considers risk aversion in greater detail.

Figure 3.1 gives a decision tree diagram for this decision problem. The leftmost numbers in parentheses are the probabilities of the states, the second column from the right shows the dollar amounts of the payoffs, and the rightmost column gives Bill's utility for each amount.

The decision theory tells us that, if he must decide now, Bill should choose the act with the highest **expected utility.** We will denote the expected utility of act a_1 by $EU(a_1)$, and so on.

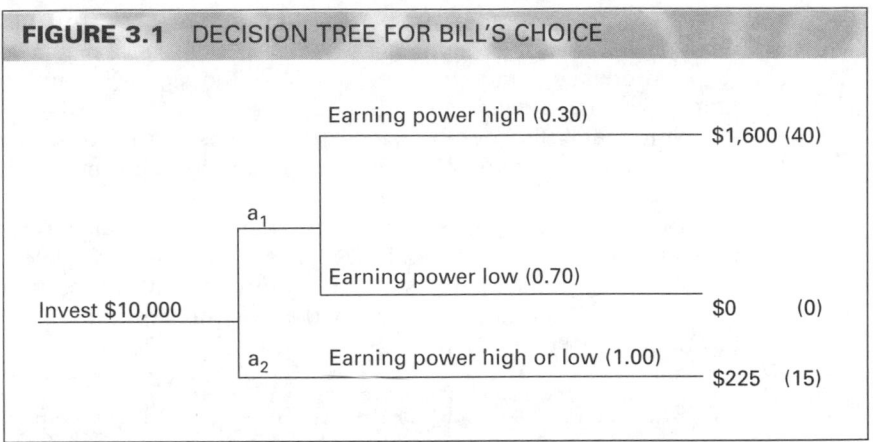

FIGURE 3.1   DECISION TREE FOR BILL'S CHOICE

$EU(a_1) = 0.30 \times 40 + 0.70 \times 0 = 12$

$EU(a_2) = 1.00 \times 15 = 15$

Therefore, it appears that Bill should choose a_2 and buy the bonds. (A possible alternative would be to diversify, that is, buy some of each type of security. We will rule this out for now by assuming that the brokerage fees for buying small amounts are prohibitive.)

However, Bill has another alternative: to obtain *more information* before deciding. Accordingly, let's assume that he decides to become more informed. The current year's annual report of X Ltd. is to be released within the next few days and Bill decides to wait for it, since it provides readily available and cost-effective evidence about the state of the firm. When the annual report comes, Bill notes that net income is quite high. In effect, the current financial statements show "good news" (GN).

On the basis of extensive experience in financial statement preparation and analysis, Bill knows that if X Ltd. really is a high-earning-power firm, there is an 80% probability that the current year's financial statements will show GN and 20% probability that they will show bad news (BN). Denote these conditional probabilities by $P(GN/H) = 0.80$ and $P(BN/H) = 0.20$ respectively.

Bill also knows that if X Ltd. is a low-earning-power firm, it is still possible that the financial statements show GN, since historical-cost-based net income is not completely relevant and reliable. Assume the probability that the current year's financial statements will show GN is 10%, giving a 90% probability that they will show BN. Denote these probabilities by $P(GN/L) = 0.10$ and $P(BN/L) = 0.90$ respectively.

Now, armed with the GN evidence from the current financial statements and the above conditional probabilities, Bill can use Bayes' theorem to calculate his **posterior** state probabilities (that is, posterior to the financial statement evidence). The posterior probability of the high-earning-power state is:

$$P(H/GN) = \frac{P(H)\ P(GN/H)}{P(H)\ P(GN/H) + P(L)\ P(GN/L)}$$

$$= \frac{0.30 \times 0.80}{(0.30 \times 0.80) + (0.70 \times 0.10)}$$

$$= 0.77$$

where:

P(H/GN) is the (posterior) probability of the high state given the good-news financial statement
P(H) is the prior probability of the high state
P(GN/H) is the probability that the financial statements show good news given that the firm is in the high state
P(GN/L) is the probability that the financial statements show good news given that the firm is in the low state

Then, the posterior probability P(L/GN) of X Ltd. being in a low-earning-power state is 1.00 − 0.77 = 0.23. If earning power is high, the pay-off from Bill's investment will be high ($1,600), and if it is low, the payoff will be low ($0).

Bill can now calculate the expected utility of each act on the basis of his posterior probabilities:

$EU(a_1/GN) = 0.77 \times 40 + 0.23 \times 0 = 30.8$
$EU(a_2/GN) = 1.00 \times 15 = 15$

Thus the GN current financial statement information has caused Bill's optimal decision to change to a_1—he should buy the shares of X Ltd.

3.3.2 THE INFORMATION SYSTEM

It is important to understand why financial statement information is useful here. To be useful, it must help predict future investment returns. Under historical cost accounting, the financial statements do not show expected future values directly (as they did under the ideal conditions of Examples 2.1 and 2.2). Nevertheless, financial statements will still be useful to investors to the extent that they enable a prediction that the good or bad news they contain will persist into the future. Think of a progression, from current good or bad news to future earning power to future expected investment returns.

Notice that we develop the decision process in terms of the investor using *current* financial statement information (here, the good or bad news in net income) to predict future earning power. Then, the prediction of earning power is used to predict future investment return, which is the investor's ultimate interest.

An alternative way of thinking about the decision process is that the investor uses current financial statement information to predict future **cash flows** of the firm, rather than earning power. Then, future cash flows can be used to predict future investment returns. This approach is consistent with ideal conditions. We saw in Examples 2.1 and 2.2 that it is future cash flows that determine the market value of the firm—net income as such had no information content. However, under non-ideal conditions it is less clear that predicting future cash flows is a better approach to predicting investment returns than predicting earning power. In the long run, the two approaches are essentially similar since, over time, cash flows and earnings will average out to be the same. That is, accruals, the difference between cash flows and net income, will net out to zero over time.

In the short run, however, one can argue that earning power has certain advantages in predicting future investment return. Because of accruals, earnings are less "lumpy" than cash flows, which are affected, for example, by capital asset acquisitions and disposals. Consequently, it can be difficult and time-consuming to back projections of operating cash flows out of accrual-based financial statements. Projecting future earnings is conceptually equivalent, and often much easier.[2] In addition, as we will see in Section 11.3, the amounts and timing of accruals can themselves have information content.

In this book, we will usually think of the investor as using the first approach, that is, using current financial statement information to predict future earning power. However, it will occasionally be convenient to predict future cash flows, one reason being that it is quite common.

To return to our example, the good news was that current earnings were high. This information enabled Bill to predict high future earning power with probability 0.77, and this is also the probability of the high future investment return. Of course, such information is a double-edged sword. Had the financial statements contained bad news, Bill's probability of high future earning power would have been lowered just as surely as it was raised by good news.

We may conclude that financial statements can still be useful to investors even though they do not report directly on future cash flows by means of present-value-based calculations. Here, it is the lack of ideal conditions that gives the income statement its information content—recall that there was really no information in net income in Examples 2.1 and 2.2.

The heart of the linkage between current and future financial statement information is the conditional probabilities P(GN/H) and P(BN/L). These probabilities are called an **information system**, which can be summarized by a table such as Table 3.2. Recall that, in our example, the probability that the current financial statements of X Ltd. show good news, conditional on the firm being in the high-earning-power state, is 0.80 etc. The 0.80 and 0.90 probabilities are called **main diagonal**; the others are called **off-main diagonal**.

*An **information system** is a table giving, conditional on each state of nature, the objective probability of each possible financial statement evidence item.*

TABLE 3.2 INFORMATION SYSTEM FOR DECISION THEORY EXAMPLE 3.1		
	Current Financial Statement Evidence	
	GN	**BN**
High	0.80	0.20
State		
Low	0.10	0.90

Note that financial statements are not perfect—this would be true only under ideal conditions. Thus, there is a 20% probability that even if the firm is in the high state the financial statements would show BN. This weakening of the contemporaneous relationship between current financial statement information and future firm performance is sometimes described as **noise** or as low earnings **quality** in the financial statements. Nevertheless, the information system is **informative**, since it enables Bill to sharpen up or, more precisely, to update his prior probabilities. For cases of fully informative and non-informative information systems, see question 2 at the end of this chapter.

Note also that the extent of informativeness depends, at least to some degree, on the relevance and reliability of the financial statements. For example, suppose X Ltd. was to switch to current value from historical cost for its capital assets. The resulting increase in relevance would tend to increase the main diagonal probabilities of the information system and lower the off-main diagonal ones. This is because current market values of assets are a better predictor of their future values (and hence of firm earning power) than are historical costs of capital assets. However, the use of current values would also decrease reliability, because current values are volatile and more subject to possible managerial bias, and this would have the opposite effect on the probabilities. Thus, it is difficult to say whether such an accounting policy change would increase or decrease the informativeness of the information system.

However, if it were possible to increase relevance without sacrificing reliability or vice versa, the result would be to increase financial statement usefulness. One way to accomplish this would be to present **supplementary** present value information, as in RRA. This would increase relevance for those who wanted to use supplemental information. However, the historical-cost-based primary statements are still available for those who are concerned about the reliability of RRA.

The concept of informativeness of an information system is useful in understanding the role of information in decision-making. The higher the main diagonal probabilities relative to the off-main diagonal ones, the more informative the system—or, equivalently, the less noise it contains. Consequently, the more informative an information system, the more decision useful it is. It enables better predictions of relevant states of nature and payoffs. In an investment context, these payoffs are returns on investments.

Decision theory and the concept of informativeness give us a precise way to define information:

> *Information* is evidence which has the potential to affect an individual's decision.

Notice that this is an *ex ante* definition. We would hardly expect an individual to gather evidence if he or she didn't expect to learn enough so as to possibly affect a decision. Bayes' theorem is then simply a device to process what has been learned. The crucial requirement for evidence to constitute information is that for at least some evidence that might be received, beliefs will be sufficiently affected that the optimal decision will change.

Also, the definition is individual-specific. As pointed out in Chapter 1, individuals may differ in their reaction to the same information source. For example, their prior probabilities may differ, so that posterior probabilities, and hence their decisions, may differ even when confronted with the same evidence.

The definition should really be interpreted net of cost. An information source may have the potential to affect an individual's decision but, if it is too costly, it is not information because it will not be used. It can be argued, however, that financial statements are a cost-effective information source because of the large number of potential users.

Finally, it should be emphasized that an individual's receipt of information and subsequent belief revision is really a continuous process. We can think of the individual as using Bayes' theorem every time a new information item comes along. Example 3.1 concentrated on belief revision following receipt of the annual report, but obviously there are many other information sources, such as newspapers, speeches and announcements, statistical reports, etc. that can also affect decisions. Hopefully, by supplying relevant and reliable information, financial statements will continue their role as an important source of information.

3.3.3   CONCLUSION

We conclude that decision theory is important because it helps us to understand why information is such a powerful commodity—it can affect the actions taken by investors. Accountants, who prepare much of the information required by investors, should be aware of this powerful role.

3.4   *The Rational, Risk–Averse Investor*

In decision theory, the concept of a rational individual simply means that in making decisions, the chosen act is the one that yields the highest expected utility. Note that this implies that the individual may search for additional information relevant to the decision, using it to revise state probabilities by means of Bayes' theorem.

Of course, whether individuals actually make decisions this way is difficult to say. Nevertheless, in thinking about questions of decision usefulness, it is helpful to assume that they do. As pointed out in Chapter 1, we do not mean to imply that all individuals make decisions as the theory suggests, but only that the theory captures the average behaviour of investors who want to make good investment decisions. Alternatively, we can argue that if investors want to make good decisions this is how they *should* proceed. If individuals do not make decisions in some rational, predictable manner it is difficult for accountants, or anyone else, to know what information they find useful. At any rate, implications of the theory have been subjected to much empirical testing, as we shall see in Chapter 5. To the extent that predictions of the theory are confirmed empirically, our confidence that the decision theory model is a reasonable one is strengthened.

It is also usually assumed that rational investors are risk-averse.[3] To see the intuition underlying this concept, consider yourself as an investor who is asked to flip a fair coin with your university instructor—suppose the coin is a penny. You would probably be willing to flip for pennies, if for no other reason than to humour the instructor. If the ante were raised, you would probably be willing to flip for dimes, quarters, even dollars. However, there would come a point where you would refuse—say flipping for $100,000 (if you didn't refuse, the instructor would).

Remind yourself that the expected payoff of flipping a fair coin is zero, regardless of the amount at stake. Thus, your increasing nervousness as the stakes are raised means that another effect, beyond the expected value of the gamble, is operating. This is risk aversion.

Note also that risk-averse individuals trade off expected return and risk. For example, if the coin was biased in your favour—say you have a 75% chance of winning—you would probably be willing to flip for higher stakes than if the coin was fair. In effect, you are now willing to bear more risk in exchange for a higher expected value—the expected value of your gamble is now $0.50 per dollar rather than 0.

To model risk aversion, decision theorists use the device of a **utility function**, which relates payoff amounts to the decision-maker's utility for those amounts. To portray a utility function, consider Figure 3.2. The solid line shows the utility function of Bill Cautious in Example 3.1. Bill's utility function is:

$$U(x) = \sqrt{x}, \ x \geq 0$$

where x is the amount of the payoff.

Based on his prior probabilities, Bill's expected payoff is (0.3 × $1,600 + 0.7 × 0) = $480. The expected *utility* of the payoff is at point C on the dotted line

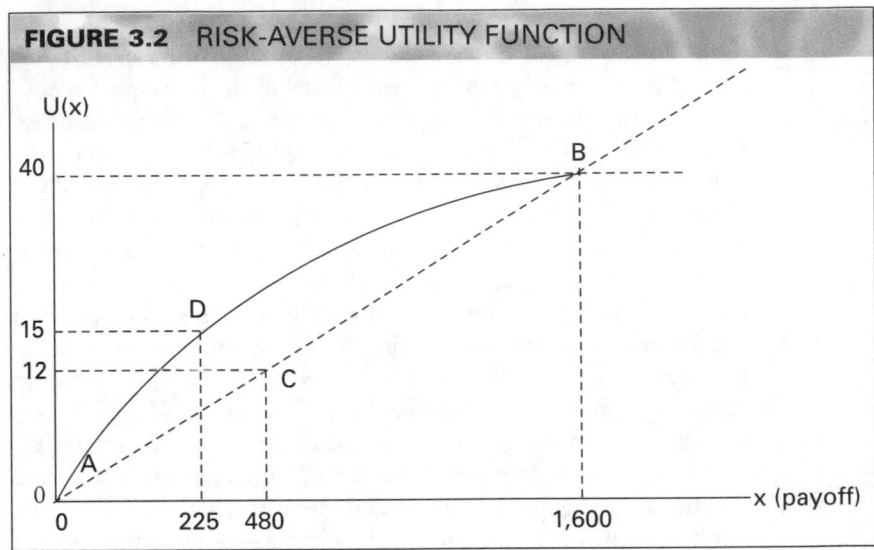

FIGURE 3.2 RISK-AVERSE UTILITY FUNCTION

joining A and B. This expected utility of $(0.3 \times 40 + 0.7 \times 0) = 12$ is less than the utility of 15 for the risk-free investment at point D on Figure 3.2. Consequently, Bill's rational decision is to choose the risk-free investment, if he were to act on the basis of his prior probabilities. This is the case even though the expected payoff of the risky investment ($480) is greater than the risk-free payoff ($225). This demonstrates that Bill is averse to risk.

To see how Bill's decision may change if the risky investment were less risky, assume that the possible payoffs are now $200 (with probability 0.7) and $1,133.33 (with probability 0.3) instead of the earlier $0 and $1,600. You should verify that the expected payoff is still $480 but the expected utility rises to 20.[4] Then, Bill's rational decision, a priori, is to buy the risky investment. The reduction in risk raises expected utility, holding expected payoff constant.

Despite the intuitive appeal of risk aversion, it is sometimes assumed that decision-makers are **risk-neutral**. This means that they evaluate risky investments strictly in terms of expected payoff—risk itself does not matter per se. We made this assumption in Example 2.2. Figure 3.3 shows the utility function of a risk-neutral decision-maker. A typical risk-neutral utility function is $U(x) = bx$, where b is the slope of the line. Here, utility is simply a linear function of the payoff.

Risk neutrality may be a reasonable assumption when the payoffs are small. However, risk aversion is the more realistic assumption in most cases. The concept of risk aversion is important to accountants, because it means that investors need information concerning the risk, as well as the expected value, of future returns.

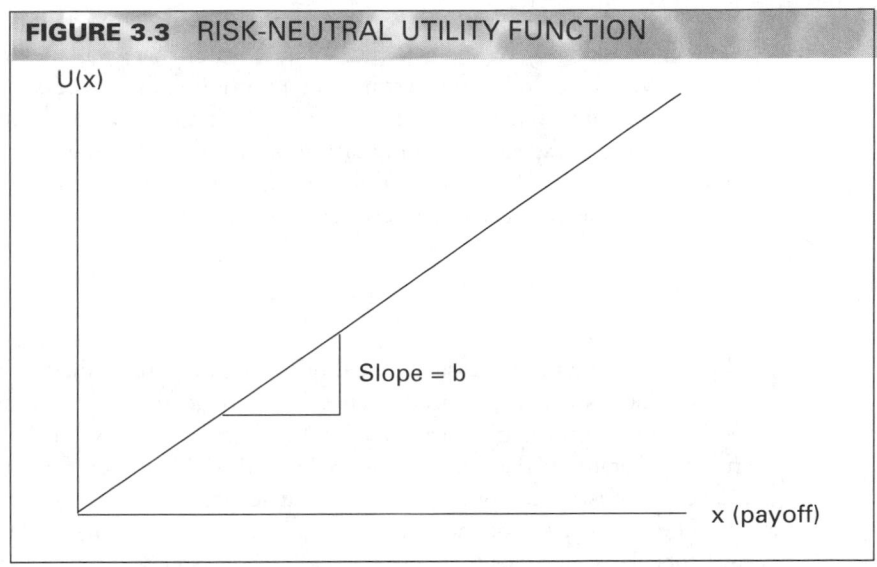

FIGURE 3.3 RISK-NEUTRAL UTILITY FUNCTION

3.5 *The Principle of Portfolio Diversification*

In Section 3.4, we stated that individual investors were typically assumed to be risk-averse. Consequently, for a given expected payoff from investments the rational investor wants the lowest possible risk or, equivalently, for a given risk, will want the highest possible expected payoff. In effect, the investor adopts a trade-off between risk and return; greater risk will be borne only if expected return is higher and vice versa.

One way investors can lower risk for a given expected return is to adopt a strategy of diversification, that is, to invest in a portfolio of securities. The principle of portfolio diversification shows us that some, but not all, risk can be eliminated by appropriate investment strategy. This principle has important implications for the nature of the risk information that investors need.

Before illustrating the diversification principle, we return briefly to our risk-averse investor. Note that before we can calculate an individual's expected utility for different investment acts, we need to know what that individual's utility function looks like. For example, Bill Cautious' utility function in Example 3.1 was $U(x) = \sqrt{x}$, $x \geq 0$. With this utility function and payoff probabilities, Bill's expected utilities for different acts were calculated and compared.

One might reasonably ask, "How do we know what an individual's utility function is?" To avoid this question, we shall now assume **mean-variance utility:**

$$U_i(a) = f_i(\bar{x}_a, \sigma_a^2)$$

where symbol a represents an investment act. For example, a could be an investment in a riskless government bond, or in a firm's shares, as in Example 3.1. Alternatively, it could be an investment in a portfolio of securities.

The equation states that the utility of an investment act a to investor i is a function f_i of the expected rate of return from that act $\bar{x}_a$ and the risk as measured by its variance σ_a^2. We assume that f_i is increasing in $\bar{x}_a$ and decreasing in σ_a^2. A specific example of a mean variance utility function is:

$$U_i(a) = 2\bar{x}_a - \sigma_a^2$$

which can be seen to increase in $\bar{x}_a$ and decrease in σ_a^2. Individuals will have different tradeoffs between expected rate of return and risk—for example, a more risk-averse investor might have $-2\sigma_a^2$ rather than $-\sigma_a^2$ as shown above. It is not true in general that the utility of an act depends only on its mean and variance. However, investigation of this is beyond our scope.

The significance of mean-variance utility to accountants is that it makes investors' decision needs more explicit—all investors need information about the expected values and riskiness of returns from investments, regardless of the specific forms of their utility functions. Without such an assumption, specific knowledge of investors' utility functions would be needed to fully deduce their information requirements.

With this background in mind, we now illustrate the principle of portfolio diversification by means of two examples.

EXAMPLE 3.2 THE PRINCIPLE OF PORTFOLIO DIVERSIFICATION (PART 1)

Suppose that a risk-averse investor (Toni Difelice) has $200 to invest and is considering investing all of it in the shares of firm A, currently trading for $20. Assume that Toni assesses a 0.74 probability[5] that the shares will increase in market value to $22 over the coming period and a 0.26 probability that they will decrease to $17. Assume also that A will pay a dividend of $1 per share at the end of the period (we could also make the dividend uncertain, but this would just add complexity without affecting the point to be made).

As in our decision theory Example 3.1, Toni's subjective probabilities could be posterior to her analysis of firm A's financial statements and the resulting application of Bayes' theorem. Alternatively, they could be her prior probabilities based on whatever other information is at her disposal. For present purposes, the extent to which Toni may have become informed does not matter. The important point is that she has assessed probabilities.

The payoffs from Toni's proposed investment are as follows:

If shares increase: $22 ×10 shares + $10 dividend = $230

If shares decrease: $17 ×10 shares + $10 dividend = $180

TABLE 3.3 CALCULATING EXPECTED RATE OF RETURN AND VARIANCE

Payoff	Rate of Return		Probability	Expected Rate of Return	Variance
$230	$\dfrac{230-200}{200} =$	0.15	0.74	0.1110	$(0.15 - 0.0850)^2 \times 0.74 = 0.0031$
$180	$\dfrac{180-200}{200} =$	−0.10	0.26	−0.0260	$(-0.10 - 0.0850)^2 \times 0.26 = \underline{0.0089}$
				$\overline{x}_a = \underline{\underline{0.0850}}$	$\sigma_a^2 = \underline{\underline{0.0120}}$

Table 3.3 shows the calculation of expected return and variance of this investment. Henceforth, we will work with the *rate* of return. As can be seen from Table 3.3, this just involves dividing net returns by the amount of investment ($200). Note that the rate of return for a period depends on the closing share price and any dividends paid during the period. The division by opening price is a standardization device—rates of return can be directly compared across securities while returns cannot. Also, rate of return fits in nicely with the assumption of mean-variance utility, which is in terms of the expected value and variance of rate of return.

The variance of return is 0.0120. The variance of an investment return serves as a measure of its riskiness. Since Toni is risk-averse, increasing riskiness will lower her utility, other things equal.

Assume that Toni's utility function is:

$$U_i(a) = 2\overline{x}_a - \sigma_a^2$$

as given above. Then, her utility for this investment is:

$$2 \times 0.0850 - 0.0120 = 0.1580$$

Toni now has to decide whether to take this investment act. If she feels that this utility is not sufficiently high for the risk involved, further search would be necessary to find a more attractive investment, or some other use for the $200 of capital.

EXAMPLE 3.3 THE PRINCIPLE OF PORTFOLIO DIVERSIFICATION (PART 2)

It turns out that Toni would not be rational to accept the above investment—a more attractive investment can be found. It is possible to find another investment decision which has the same expected return but lower risk. This is because of the **principle of portfolio diversification.**

To illustrate, assume that shares of firm B are also traded on the market, with a current market value of $10. These shares also pay a dividend of $1. Assume there is a 0.6750 probability that firm B's shares will increase in market value to $10.50 at the end of the period, and a 0.3250 probability that they will decrease to $8.50.

Now suppose that Toni decides to invest $200 in six shares of firm A at $20 and eight shares of firm B at $10. We must calculate Toni's expected utility for the portfolio consisting of six shares of firm A and eight shares of firm B. Notice that the same amount ($200) is invested, but that it is now spread over two different securities.

Four possible payoffs now exist from the portfolio: both shares increase in market value, one share increases and the other decreases, or both shares decrease. The amounts of the payoffs and their assumed probabilities are as follows:

TABLE 3.4   PAYOFFS AND THEIR PROBABILITIES

A		B		Dividends		Total Payoff	Probability
132	+	84	+	14	=	$230	0.5742
132	+	68	+	14	=	$214	0.1658
102	+	84	+	14	=	$200	0.1008
102	+	68	+	14	=	$184	0.1592
							1.0000

Recall that six shares of firm A and eight shares of firm B are held, and that the high payoff is $22 per share for firm A and $10.50 for firm B, plus a $1 dividend from each share. This gives the $230 payoff on the first line of the table. The other payoffs are similarly calculated.

Now let us consider more closely the probabilities we have assumed for the four possible payoffs. The returns from shares of firm A and firm B are correlated in our example. To see this, consider the first row in Table 3.4 with a total payoff of $230. This payoff will be realized if both shares A and B realize their high-payoff values. On the basis of our assumption about the probabilities of the individual payoffs of shares A and B, the probabilities of these two payoffs, when each share is considered separately, are 0.74 for A and 0.6750 for B. If the payoffs of shares A and B were independent, the probability of both shares realizing their high payoffs would be $0.74 \times 0.6750 = 0.4995$.

However, in any economy, there are states of nature, also called factors, which affect the returns of *all* shares, such as levels of interest rates, foreign exchange rates, the level of economic activity, and so on. These are called **market-wide** or **economy-wide** factors. Their presence means that if the return on one share is high, it is more likely that the returns on most other shares in the economy will also be high—more likely, that is, than would be the case if the returns on shares were independent. Thus, we have assumed that the probability that both shares A and B realize their high payoffs is 0.5742, greater than the 0.4995 that we would obtain under independence, to reflect these underlying common factors.

Similar reasoning applies to the last row of Table 3.4 with a payoff of $184. Here we have assumed that the joint probability of both firm A and firm B realizing their low payoffs is 0.1592, greater than the ($0.26 \times 0.3250 = 0.0845$) probability under independence. If market-wide state realizations are such that they work against high returns (that is, if the economy is performing poorly), then the probability that both shares realize low payoffs is greater than what would be expected under independence.

Of course, while share returns may be correlated because of common factors, they will not be perfectly correlated. It is still possible that one firm realizes a high return and another a low return—witness the two middle rows of Table 3.4. This is because, in addition to economy-wide factors, there are also **firm-specific** factors which affect the return of one firm only. Examples include the quality of a firm's management, new patents, strikes, machine breakdowns, and so on. Thus, the second row of the table represents a situation where firm A realizes a high return (say because of a new invention it has just patented) and firm B realizes a low return (say because of a critical machine failure in its assembly line). However, because of the presence of economy-wide factors, the probabilities for these high/low payoff realizations will also be different than under independence. This is true of Example 3.3.

It should be pointed out that the preceding argument assumes that the *only* source of correlation between returns on firms' shares is market-wide factors. In effect, we have partitioned states of nature that can affect share returns into two components—economy-wide and firm-specific. This is a simplification, since, for example, industry-wide factors could introduce additional returns correlation. However, the simplification is a widely used one and is sufficient for our purposes. It leads to an important measure of share riskiness (beta) which we will discuss shortly. For now, you should realize that the assumption implies that if *all* factors were economy-wide, returns on firms' shares would be perfectly correlated. If *all* factors were firm-specific, returns would be independent. As is usually the case, the truth lies somewhere in between. Consequently, the probabilities given in Table 3.4 assume that both types of factors are present.

The expected rate of return and variance of Toni's portfolio of A and B shares are calculated in Table 3.5 using the correlated probabilities. Thus, the expected rate of return of the portfolio is 0.0850, as before (we have forced this result by appropriate choice of the probabilities, to facilitate comparison), but the variance has decreased to 0.0074, from 0.0120. Since Toni is risk-averse, she would be better off to buy the portfolio of A and B shares rather than just A, because the expected return is the same, but the risk is lower.

TABLE 3.5 CALCULATING EXPECTED RATE OF RETURN AND VARIANCE

Payoff	Rate of Return		Probability	Expected Rate of Return	Variance
$230	$\dfrac{230-200}{200}=$	0.15	0.5742	0.0861	$(0.15-0.0850)^2 \times 0.5742 = 0.0024$
$214	$\dfrac{214-200}{200}=$	0.07	0.1658	0.0116	$(0.07-0.0850)^2 \times 0.1658 = 0.0000$
$200	$\dfrac{200-200}{200}=$	0.00	0.1008	0.0000	$(0.00-0.0850)^2 \times 0.1008 = 0.0007$
$184	$\dfrac{184-200}{200}=$	−0.08	0.1592	− 0.0127	$(-0.08-0.0850)^2 \times 0.1592 = 0.0043$
				$\overline{x}_a = 0.0850$	$\sigma_a{}^2 = 0.0074$

In fact, her utility now is:

$$U_i(a) = 2 \times 0.0850 - 0.0074$$
$$= 0.1626$$

up from 0.1580 for the single-share investment.

SUMMARY

Risk-averse investors can take advantage of the principle of portfolio diversification to reduce their risk, by investing in a portfolio of securities. This is because realization of firm-specific states of nature tend to cancel out across securities, leaving economy-wide factors as the main contributors to portfolio risk.

While individual attitudes to risk may differ, we can see investors' decision needs with particular clarity if we assume mean-variance utility. Then, regardless of the degree of risk aversion, we know that utility increases in expected return and decreases in variance of the portfolio.

3.6   *The Optimal Investment Decision*

If a portfolio of two shares is better than one, then a three-share portfolio should be better than two, and so on. Indeed, this is the case and, assuming no transaction costs such as brokerage fees, Toni should continue buying until the portfolio includes some of every security traded on the market. This is called "holding the market portfolio." Note again that the total amount invested remains at $200, but is spread over a greater number of securities.

Be sure you understand *why* the same amount invested in a portfolio can yield lower risk than if it were invested in a single firm for the same expected rate of return. The reason is simply that when more than one risky investment is held, *the firm-specific risks tend to cancel out*. If one share realizes a low return, there is always the chance that another share will realize a high return. The larger the number of different firms' shares in the portfolio, the more this effect can operate. As a result, the riskiness of returns is reduced, which we have illustrated above by means of our variance calculations. Of course, in the presence of economy-wide risk, there is not a complete cancelling-out. At a minimum, that is, when the market portfolio is held, the economy-wide factors will remain to contribute to portfolio risk, and this risk cannot be diversified away. Such non-diversifiable risk is called **systematic risk.**

Conceptually, the market portfolio includes all assets available for investment in the economy. As a practical matter, the market portfolio is usually taken as all the securities traded on a major stock exchange. The return on the market portfolio can then be proxied by the return on a market index for that exchange, such as the Dow Jones Index of the New York Stock Exchange, the Toronto Stock Exchange 300 Index, etc.

Now return to our investor Toni Difelice. Toni decides to buy the market portfolio after hearing about the benefits of diversification. Her first task is to assess the expected return and variance of the market portfolio. She subjectively assesses a 0.8 probability that the Toronto Stock Exchange 300 Index will increase by 10% and a 0.2 probability that it will increase by 2 1/2%. Then, denoting the expected return and variance of the market portfolio by $\bar{x}_M$ and σ_M^2 respectively:

$$\bar{x}_M = 0.10 \times 0.8 + 0.0250 \times 0.2 = 0.0850$$
$$\sigma_M^2 = (0.10 - 0.0850)^2 \times 0.8 + (0.0250 - 0.0850)^2 \times 0.2$$
$$= 0.0002 + 0.0007$$
$$= 0.0009$$

This gives Toni a utility of:

$$2\bar{x}_m - \sigma_M^2 = 0.1700 - 0.0009$$
$$= 0.1691$$

which is greater than the 0.1626 utility of the two-share portfolio in Example 3.3.

The question now is: Is this Toni's optimal investment decision? The answer is probably not. If Toni were quite risk-averse, she might prefer a portfolio with lower risk than 0.0009, and would be willing to have a lower expected return as a result.

One strategy she might follow would be to sell some of the high-risk stocks in her portfolio. But, if she does this, she is no longer holding the market portfolio, so some of the benefits of diversification are lost. How can Toni adjust portfolio risk to her desired level without losing the benefits of diversification?

The answer lies in the **risk-free asset.** If a risk-free asset, such as treasury bills yielding, say, 4%, is available, an investor could sell some of the market portfolio (that is, sell some of all securities, so that the market portfolio is still held but total investment in it is lower) and use the proceeds to buy the risk-free asset. This strategy is depicted in Figure 3.4 as a move from X, where only the market portfolio is held, to Y. Risk is lower at Y, but so is expected return, compared to X. However, if the investor is quite risk-averse this could raise utility.

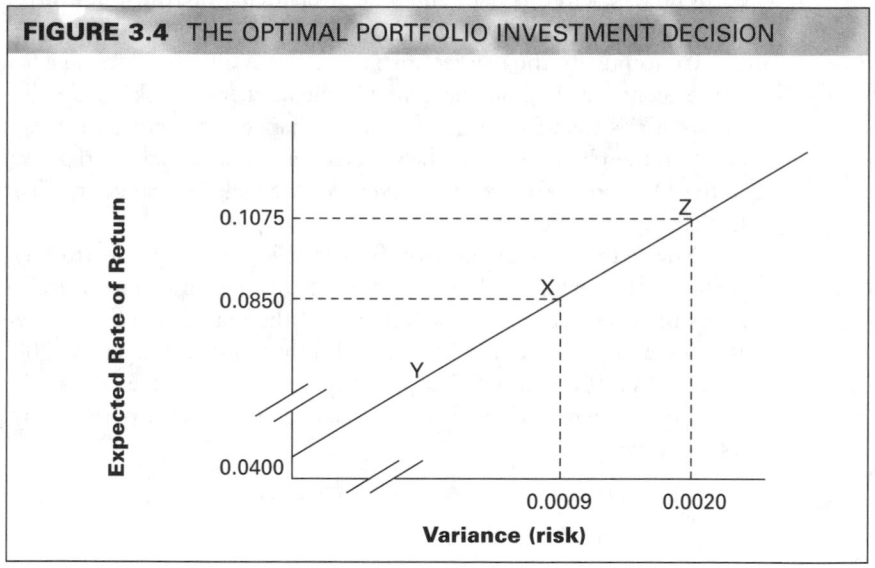

FIGURE 3.4 THE OPTIMAL PORTFOLIO INVESTMENT DECISION

Conversely, if Toni were less risk-averse, she may prefer to borrow at the risk-free rate and buy more of the market portfolio, thereby moving to Z, with higher expected return and risk.

In this way, each investor can secure a desired risk-return tradeoff while continuing to enjoy the maximum risk-reduction effects of diversification.

To illustrate, suppose that Toni borrows $100 at a rate of 0.04 and buys an additional $100 of the market portfolio. Then:

$$\overline{x}_a = \left(\frac{300}{200} \times 0.0850 - \frac{100}{200} \times 0.0400 \right)$$

$$= (0.1275 - 0.0200)$$

$$= 0.1075$$

$$\sigma_a^{\;2} = \left(\frac{300}{200} \right)^2 \times 0.0009$$

$$= 0.0020$$

yielding utility of $2 \times 0.1075 - 0.0020 = 0.2130$. This yields Toni a higher util-ity than simply holding the market portfolio (0.1691). Toni will continue to bor-row until the amount borrowed and reinvested yields an $\overline{x}_a$ and $\sigma_a^{\;2}$ that maximizes her utility. In fact, if she can borrow all she wants at 4%, she would borrow $9,800, which would yield her utility of 2.33.

SUMMARY

When transaction costs are ignored, a risk-averse investor's optimal invest-ment decision is to buy that combination of market portfolio and risk-free asset that yields the best tradeoff between expected return and risk. This trade-off is individual-specific—it depends on the investor's utility function. Some investors may wish to reduce their investment in the market portfolio and buy the risk-free asset with the proceeds. Others may wish to borrow at the risk-free rate and increase their investment. Either way, all investors can enjoy the full benefits of diversification while at the same time attaining their optimal risk-return tradeoff.

3.7   Portfolio Risk

3.7.1   CALCULATING AND INTERPRETING BETA

The principle of diversification leads to an important risk measure of a secu-rity in the theory of investment. This is **beta**, which measures the co-move-ment between changes in the price of a security and changes in the market value of the market portfolio. To illustrate, we will calculate the betas of shares of firms A and B in Example 3.3, in relation to the market portfolio M given in Section 3.6.

EXAMPLE 3.4 CALCULATING BETA

The beta of A shares, denoted by β_A, is given by:

$$\beta_A = \frac{Cov(A,M)}{Var(M)}$$

where Cov(A,M) is the covariance of the returns on A with the returns on the market portfolio M. In effect, β_A measures how strongly the return on A varies as the market varies. For example, a high-beta security would undergo wide swings in returns as market conditions change. Shares of airlines and aircraft manufacturers are examples, since these industries are sensitive to economic conditions. Shares of electric utilities and fast food firms would be low-beta, since the returns of such firms are less subject to the state of the economy.

Division by Var(M) is simply a standardization device, to express Cov(A,M) in units of market variance. For example, if the returns on the Toronto and New York Stock Exchanges have different variances, standardization by the variance of returns on the respective exchanges enables betas of Canadian and U.S. firms to be compared.

To calculate the beta of security A, assume that the conditional payoff probabilities of A are as follows:

• When return on M is high:

Probability return on A is high = 0.90
Probability return on A is low = 0.10

• When return on M is low:

Probability return on A is high = 0.10
Probability return on A is low = 0.90

These probabilities could be estimated by examining past data on the returns on A shares in relation to the returns on M. Cov(A,M) is calculated in Table 3.6.

TABLE 3.6 CALCULATION OF COVARIANCE

A	M	Payoff Probabilities		
High	High	$(0.15 - 0.0850)(0.10 - 0.0850) \times 0.72$	=	0.0007
High	Low	$(0.15 - 0.0850)(0.0250 - 0.0850) \times 0.02$	=	−0.0001
Low	High	$(-0.10 - 0.0850)(0.10 - 0.0850) \times 0.08$	=	−0.0002
Low	Low	$(-0.10 - 0.0850)(0.0250 - 0.0850) \times 0.18$	=	0.0020
		Cov(A,M)	=	0.0024

The values 0.15 and 0.0850 are the high return and the expected return respectively of A (see Table 3.3). Similarly 0.10 and 0.0850 are the high return and the expected return of M (see Section 3.6). The probability that both A and M pay off high is:

$$\text{Prob(A high and M high)} = \text{Prob(M high) Prob(A high/M high)}$$
$$= 0.8 \times 0.9$$
$$= 0.72$$

You should verify the remaining lines in the table.

Then, recalling from Section 3.6 that $\sigma_M^2 = \text{Var(M)} = 0.0009$, we obtain:

$$\beta_A = \frac{0.0024}{0.0009} = 2.6667$$

For security B in Example 3.3, assume that the conditional payoff probabilities are:

- When return on M is high:

    Probability return on B is high = 0.7917
    Probability return on B is low = 0.2083

- When return on M is low:

    Probability return on B is high = 0.2083
    Probability return on B is low = 0.7917

Then:

$$\beta_B = \frac{0.0014}{0.0009} = 1.5556$$

You should verify this calculation.[6]

Note that β_B is lower than β_A. Thus, an investor who buys B shares is more insulated from the ups and downs of the stock market. This is the sense in which a low-beta security has low risk.[7]

3.7.2 *PORTFOLIO EXPECTED VALUE AND VARIANCE*

Since risk-averse investors with mean-variance utility functions need to know the expected value and variance of their investment portfolios, we here give formulae for their calculation. In the process, we shall see that beta measures the amount of systematic risk contributed by a security to a portfolio.

For the expected value of return on a portfolio P, we have:

$$\bar{x}_P = k_1 \bar{x}_1 + k_2 \bar{x}_2 + ... + k_n \bar{x}_n$$

where $\bar{x}_P$ is the expected return on P, $\bar{x}_1$ is the expected return on security 1, etc., k_1 is the proportion of total portfolio investment in security 1, etc., and there are n securities in the portfolio.

In Example 3.3, n = 2, k_1 = \$120/\$200 = 0.6, k_2 = $(1 - k_1)$ = 0.4, and the expected returns on the two securities in Toni's portfolio were both 0.0850. Then, the formula gives:

$$\bar{x}_P = 0.6 \times 0.0850 + 0.4 \times 0.0850 = 0.0850$$

which, of course, agrees with the direct calculation in Table 3.5.

For the variance of portfolio return, we have the following formula:

$$Var(P) = \sigma_P^2 = k_1^2 \sigma_1^2 + k_2^2 \sigma_2^2 + ... + k_n^2 \sigma_n^2 + 2k_1 k_2 \, Cov(x_1,x_2) + 2k_1 k_3 \, Cov(x_1,x_3)$$
$$+ ... + 2k_{n-1} k_n \, Cov(x_{n-1},x_n)$$

That is, the variance of P is the weighted sum of the variances of the individual securities in P plus the weighted sum of covariances of all the pairs of securities in P.

In Example 3.3, the formula reduces to:

$$Var(A + B) = k_1^2 \, Var(A) + (1 - k_1)^2 \, Var(B) + 2k_1(1 - k_1) \, Cov(A,B)$$

The main point here is that portfolio variance depends not only on the variances of the component securities, but also, if the security returns are correlated, on the covariance between them (if the returns on A and B are uncorrelated, $Cov(A,B) = 0$).

In an investment context, the returns on A and B are most definitely correlated because of economy-wide factors. In fact, we have assumed that economy-wide factors are the *only* source of correlation between security returns. Then, we can write the covariance between A and B in terms of their covariances with the market portfolio M:

$$Cov(A,B) = \frac{Cov(A,M) \, Cov(B,M)}{Var(M)}$$
$$= Var(M)\beta_A \beta_B$$

The portfolio variance becomes:[8]

$$Var(A + B) = 0.6^2\,Var(A) + 0.4^2\,Var(B) + 2 \times 0.6 \times 0.4\,Var(M)\beta_A\beta_B$$
$$= 0.36 \times 0.0120 + 0.16 \times 0.0088 + 0.48 \times 0.0009 \times 2.6667 \times 1.5556$$
$$= 0.0043 + 0.0014 + 0.0017$$
$$= 0.0074$$

which agrees with the direct calculation in Table 3.5. Thus, we see that securities A and B contribute systematic risk of 0.0017 to the portfolio variance of 0.0074, or about 23%.

3.7.3 PORTFOLIO RISK AS THE NUMBER OF SECURITIES INCREASES

A contribution of 23% may not seem like much. However, consider what happens as the number of securities in the portfolio increases. Let there now be n securities in portfolio P. To simplify a bit, we will assume that an equal amount is invested in each security, so that the proportion of each security in P is 1/n of the total amount invested. Then:

$$Var(P) = \frac{1}{n^2}\sigma_1^2 + \frac{1}{n^2}\sigma_2^2 + ... + \frac{1}{n^2}\sigma_n^2 + \frac{2}{n^2}\,Cov(x_1,x_2) + \frac{2}{n^2}\,Cov(x_1,x_3) + ... + \frac{2}{n^2}Cov(x_{n-1},x_n)$$

$$= \frac{1}{n^2}\left[\sigma_1^2 + \sigma_2^2 + ... + \sigma_n^2\right] + \frac{2}{n^2}\,Var(M)\left[\beta_1\beta_2 + \beta_1\beta_3 + ... + \beta_{n-1}\beta_n\right]$$

There are n variance terms in the formula. However, the number of covariance terms goes up quite quickly relative to n. In fact, there are $n(n-1) \div 2$ covariance terms. For example, if n = 10, there are 10 variance terms but 45 covariance terms.

This means that, even for portfolios that contain a small number of securities, *most of the risk is systematic risk*. For example, for n = 10, the coefficient of the variance terms is only 1/100, so that the variances of the 10 securities contribute only 10% of their average variance to the portfolio variance. However, while the coefficient of the systematic risk terms is only 2/100, there are 45 terms, so the covariances contribute fully 90% of their average covariance to the portfolio variance. In other words, *most of the benefits of diversification can be attained with only a few securities in the portfolio*. This is fortunate, since brokerage and other transactions costs would prevent most investors from buying the market portfolio. From an accounting standpoint, this means that for most investors, useful information is that which helps them assess securities' expected returns and betas.

3.7.4 SUMMARY

When transactions costs are not ignored, a risk-averse investor's optimal investment decision is to buy relatively few securities, rather than the market portfolio. In this way, most of the benefits of diversification can be attained, at reasonable cost.

Information about securities' expected returns and betas is useful to such investors. This enables them to estimate the expected return and riskiness of various portfolios that they may be considering. They can then choose the portfolio that gives them their most preferred risk-return tradeoff, subject to the level of transactions costs that they are willing to bear.

3.8   *The Reaction of Professional Accounting Bodies to the Decision Usefulness Approach*

It is interesting to note that major professional accounting bodies have adopted the decision usefulness approach. For example, Section 1000 of the *CICA Handbook* states (paragraph 1000.15):

> The objective of financial statements is to communicate information that is useful to investors, members, contributors, creditors and other users ... in making their respective resource allocation decisions and/or assessing management stewardship.

However, the earliest and most complete statement of this adoption comes from the FASB in its Conceptual Framework project. The Conceptual Framework specifically mentions investors' needs for information about the uncertainty of future investment returns as well as their expected values. While Section 1508 of the *CICA Handbook* lays down conditions for disclosure of measurement uncertainty, Section 1000 per se does not mention risk. In view of our demonstration above that rational investors need information about risk as well as expected value of returns, we shall concentrate here on the Conceptual Framework.

According to *Statement of Financial Accounting Concepts* (1978) (SFAC 1), the purpose of the project is "to set forth fundamentals on which financial accounting and reporting standards will be based." SFAC 1 gives a series of objectives of financial reporting. Its first objective of financial reporting is to:

> provide information that is useful to present and potential investors and creditors and other users in making rational investment, credit, and similar decisions.

Note particularly the use of the word "rational" in this objective. This is the tie-in to the economic decision theory. As pointed out in Section 3.4, decision-makers who proceed in accordance with the theory, that is, those who make decisions so as to maximize their expected utility, are referred to as rational.

Note also that a variety of constituencies are included in this most general objective (present and potential investors and creditors and other users) and also that a wide variety of decisions are contemplated (investment, credit, and similar decisions). This immediately raises the question of what particular decision-makers and decisions are involved. Thus, SFAC 1 states that the second objective of financial reporting is to:

> provide information to help present and potential investors and creditors and other users in assessing the amounts, timing and uncertainty of prospective cash receipts from dividends or interest.

Thus, we can see that the primary decision addressed in SFAC 1 is the investment decision in firms' shares or debt. Specifically, cash receipts from dividends or interest are *payoffs*, similar to those in the payoff table (Table 3.1) of Example 3.1. Note that these investment decisions apply to potential investors as well as present ones. This means that financial statements must communicate useful information to the market, not just to existing investors in the firm.

Note also that the second objective is future-oriented—it calls for information about "prospective" cash receipts from dividends or interest. There is a clear recognition that investors need information to help them estimate *future* payoffs from their investments. In particular, the second objective states that investors need to assess "the amounts, timing and uncertainty" of prospective returns. While the terms used are somewhat different, these will be recognized as relating to the expected value and risk of future returns. Thus, the second objective also contains a clear recognition that (risk-averse) investors will want information about risk of returns as well as their expected amounts, just as the theory of investment predicts.

The question now arises: How can historical-cost-based financial statements be useful in predicting future returns? This is probably the major difficulty that the FASB's Conceptual Framework has faced. Given that historical cost accounting is firmly fixed in practice, it is necessary to establish some linkage between past firm performance and future prospects. Without such linkage, the decision-oriented objectives of SFAC 1 would not be attainable.

We can see the linkage clearly, however, by drawing on the decision theory model. In particular, refer to the information system (Table 3.2) for Example 3.1. The table provides a probabilistic relationship between current financial statement information (GN or BN) and the future-oriented states of nature (high or low earning power) which will determine future investment payoffs. In effect, current financial statement information and future returns are linked via the conditional probabilities of the information system.

Consistent with the information system linkage, SFAC 1 states:

> Although investment and credit decisions reflect investors' and creditors' expectations about future enterprise performance, those expectations are commonly based at least partly on evaluations of past enterprise performance.

This is the crucial argument that enables the Conceptual Framework to maintain that past-oriented, historical-cost-based financial statement information can be useful to forward-looking investors. It is consistent with the decision usefulness approach which purports that information is useful if it helps investors make their own estimates of future returns.

In SFAC 2, the FASB goes on to consider the characteristics that are necessary if financial statement information is to be useful for investor decision-making. This is another crucial and delicate aspect of the whole conceptual framework—how can financial statement information be presented so as to be of maximum use to investors in predicting future returns? Once again, the answer lies in the concepts of **relevance** and **reliability**.

In Chapter 2, we defined relevant financial statements as ones which showed the discounted present values of the cash flows from the firm's assets and liabilities. The SFAC 2 definition is somewhat broader:

> Relevant accounting information is capable of making a difference in a decision by helping users to form predictions about the outcomes of past, present, and future events or to confirm or correct prior expectations. Information can make a difference to decisions by improving decision makers' capacities to predict or by providing feedback on earlier expectations. Usually, information does both at once, because knowledge about the outcomes of actions already taken will generally improve decision makers' abilities to predict the results of similar future actions. Without a knowledge of the past, the basis for a prediction will usually be lacking. Without an interest in the future, knowledge of the past is sterile.

The essence of the SFAC 2 definition is that information is relevant if it helps financial statement users to form their own predictions of events (such as future profitability). Again, this is consistent with the decision usefulness approach. Thus, we can say that under the ideal conditions of Chapter 2, relevant financial statement information consists of (the discounted present values of) future payoffs, or expected future payoffs. Under less-than-ideal conditions, relevant financial statement information consists of information which helps investors form *their own* expectations of future payoffs. By extending the definition of relevance to include information which can help investors form their own payoff estimates, the scope for information to be relevant is greatly enlarged.

It is also worth noting that the FASB notion of relevance is consistent with the definition of information in decision theory. Recall that information is that which has the potential to change individual decisions, that is, it can "make a difference." In effect, evidence is not really information unless it is capable of affecting user decisions. This role of information comes across with particular clarity in Bayes' theorem. Recall that Bayes' theorem provides a vehicle for investors to update their prior beliefs about relevant states of nature on the basis of new information, as illustrated in Example 3.1.

Another desirable information characteristic in SFAC 2 is reliability. In Chapter 2 we defined reliable information as information that is *precise and free from bias*. According to SFAC 2:

> To be reliable, information must have representational faithfulness and it must be verifiable and neutral.

This characteristic can be reconciled with our definition. We can equate representational faithfulness and neutrality with freedom from bias. For example, if financial statement information is biased due to managerial misrepresentation towards a predetermined result, that information would be neither representationally faithful nor neutral.

Also, the precision of financial statement information can be equated with representational faithfulness and verifiability. We saw in Section 2.4 that a major problem with RRA was the imprecision of the discounted reserves valuation, with the consequence that major adjustments of prior years' valuations were frequently required. In effect, the estimates were not sufficiently precise for purposes of estimating an oil company's future cash flows; hence they were not representationally faithful to the resources or events those numbers purport to represent. In addition, they would lack verifiability in the sense that independent measurers would be likely to achieve different RRA estimates under similar circumstances.

SFAC 2 goes on to explore other desirable characteristics of useful financial statement information, which we will not review here. As previously mentioned, the main point to realize is that, to be useful for investment decision purposes, financial statement information need not necessarily involve a direct prediction of future firm payoffs. Rather, if the information has certain desirable characteristics, such as relevance and reliability, it can be an informative input to help investors form their own predictions of these payoffs.

SUMMARY

The FASB's SFAC 1 represents an important adaptation of decision theory to financial accounting and reporting. Furthermore, this theory is oriented in SFAC 1 to the theory of decision-making for investors, which has been much studied in economics and finance.

SFAC 2 operationalizes the decision usefulness approach by developing the characteristics that accounting information should have in order to be useful. In essence, accounting information should provide an informative information system that links current financial statements with future state realizations and payoffs. Two major informative characteristics are *relevance* and *reliability*. Relevant information is information that has the capacity to affect investors' beliefs about future returns. Reliable information faithfully represents what it purports to measure. It should be precise and free from bias.

3.9   *Conclusions on Decision Usefulness*

The decision usefulness approach to financial reporting implies that accountants need to understand the decision problems of financial statement users. Single-person decision theory and its specialization to the portfolio investment decision provides an understanding of the needs of rational, risk-averse investors. This theory tells us that such investors need information to help them assess securities' expected returns and the riskiness of these returns. In the theory of investment, beta is an important risk measure, being the standardized covariance of a security's return with the return on the market portfolio. This covariance risk is the main component of the riskiness of a diversified portfolio, even if the portfolio contains only a relatively few securities.

Historical-cost-based financial statements are an important and cost-effective source of information for investors, even though they do not report directly on future investment payoffs. They provide an information system which can help investors to predict future firm profitability or cash flows which, in turn, predict future returns. This predictive role is enhanced to the extent that financial statements are relevant and reliable.

Major accounting standard setting bodies such as the CICA and the FASB have adopted the decision usefulness approach. This is evidenced by their conceptual frameworks, which show a clear recognition of the role of financial reporting in providing relevant and reliable information for investors.

Notes

1.   For a formal development of the concepts of decision theory, including utility theory, the information system, and the value of information, see Laffont (1989), especially Chapters 1, 2, and 4. See also Demski (1972), especially Chapters 1 to 3. For an excellent intuitive development of the theory, see Raiffa (1968).

2.   I am indebted to Professor Charles Lee for this point.

3.   For a formal development and analysis of risk aversion, see Pratt (1964), or Laffont (1989), Chapter 2.

4.   The expected payoff is:

$0.7 \times \$200 + 0.3 \times \$1,133.33 = \$480$

Expected utility is:

$$0.7 \times \sqrt{200} + 0.3 \times \sqrt{1{,}133.33} \quad \begin{aligned} &= 0.7 \times 14.14 + 0.3 \times 33.66 \\ &= 9.90 + 10.10 \\ &= 20 \end{aligned}$$

5. Note that we have suppressed the set of states of nature in this example. That is, Toni assesses payoff probabilities directly, rather than routing them through states. Thus, instead of saying "The probability that firm A is in high earning power state is 0.74 and if A really is in this state the payoff will be \$220," we simply say "The probability of the \$220 payoff is 0.74." This simplification has certain analytical advantages and is frequently used.

6. The expected return of B is:
$$0.6750 \times \frac{92 - 80}{80} + 0.3250 \times \frac{76 - 80}{80}$$

$$= 0.6750 \times 0.15 + 0.3250 \times -0.05 = 0.0850$$

(See Example 3.3.)

Cov(B,M) is calculated as:

		Payoff
B	**M**	
High	High	$(0.15 - 0.085)(0.10 \quad - 0.085) \times 0.6333 \quad = \quad 0.0006$
High	Low	$(0.15 - 0.085)(0.025 - 0.085) \times 0.0417 = -0.0002$
Low	High	$(-0.05 - 0.085)(0.10 \quad\; 0.085) \times 0.1667 \; = -0.0003$
Low	Low	$(-0.05 - 0.085)(0.025 - 0.085) \times 0.1583 \; = \quad 0.0013$
		Cov(B,M) $= \quad 0.0014$

The probability of B high and M high is given by $0.8 \times 0.7917 = 0.6333$. You should now verify the remaining lines.

7. This raises the question: Who would buy A shares if B shares were available? Both securities have an expected rate of return of 0.0850, but the risk of A, as measured by its beta, is 2.6667, which is higher than B's of 1.5556. However, we do not claim that portfolio A + B is an optimal investment decision. These securities are used only to illustrate portfolio diversification.

What would probably happen, should this situation actually occur, is that the market price of A would fall until its expected return rose sufficiently to overcome its greater riskiness.

8. $\text{Var(B)} = \sigma_B{}^2 = 0.6750 \times (0.15 - 0.0850)^2 + 0.3250 \times (-0.05 - 0.0850)^2$
$= 0.0029 + 0.0059$
$= 0.0088$

Questions and Problems

1. Suppose you are a member of the CICA staff and are charged with preparing guidelines for financial reporting to other constituencies of financial statement users (that is, other than investors). What financial information would the following constituencies find useful? How could this information be used?

    a. Managers
    b. Labour unions
    c. Government   (CGA-Canada)

2. Refer to Table 3.2, the information system table for Example 3.1. Prepare a similar table for a **perfect**, or **fully informative**, information system, that is, an information system that perfectly reveals the true state of nature. Do the same for a **non-informative** information system, that is, one that reveals nothing about the true state.

    Use the probabilities from the two tables you have prepared to revise state probabilities by means of Bayes' theorem, using the prior probabilities and GN message given in Example 3.1. Comment on the results.   (CGA-Canada)

3. What would the utility function of a **risk-taking** investor look like? What sort of portfolio would such an individual be likely to invest in? What information would the investor need?   (CGA-Canada)

4. An investor's utility function is:

    $$U_i(a) = 3\bar{x} - \frac{1}{2}\sigma_x{}^2$$

    Act a_1 has $\bar{x} = 0.88$, $\sigma_x{}^2 = 0.512$, yielding $U_i(a_1) = 2.384$. Act a_2 has $\bar{x} = 0.80$.

    What $\sigma_x{}^2$ would this act require to yield the same utility as a_1? Comment on the result with regard to risk and expected return.   (CGA-Canada)

5. Refer to Figure 3.4. Suppose Toni's utility function is:

    $$U_i(a) = \frac{1}{2}\bar{x} - 16\sigma_x{}^2$$

    Calculate Toni's utility at point Z on Figure 3.4 and compare it with her utility at point X. Which act does Toni prefer? Explain.   (CGA-Canada)

6. What is the beta of:

    a. The market portfolio

b. The risk-free asset

c. Portfolio A + B in Example 3.3 and Section 3.7 (CGA-Canada)

7. Explain why most of the benefits of diversification can be attained with only a relatively few securities in the portfolio. Assume that an equal amount is invested in each security. Does the riskiness of the return on a diversified portfolio approach zero as the number of securities in the portfolio gets larger? Explain.

(CGA-Canada)

8. The FASB states in SFAC 1:

> Information about enterprise earnings based on accrual accounting generally provides a better indicator of an enterprise's present and continuing ability to generate favourable cash flows than information limited to the financial effects of cash receipts and payments.

In other words, the FASB is arguing that net income is a better predictor of future cash flows than cash flows themselves. This may seem surprising.

Why do you think the FASB makes this argument? (CGA-Canada)

9. Verify the statement made at the end of Section 3.6 that if Toni Difelice can borrow all she wants at 4% she would borrow $9,800, yielding utility of 2.33.

10. Give some reasons why the off-main diagonal probabilities of an information system such as that depicted in Table 3.2 are non-zero. Use the concepts of relevance and reliability in your answer. Explain why an information system is more useful the lower the off-main diagonal probabilities are.

11. a. State the decision usefulness approach to accounting theory.

b. What two questions arise once the decision usefulness approach is adopted?

c. What primary constituency of financial statement users has been adopted by the major professional accounting bodies as a guide to the reporting of decision-useful financial information?

d. According to the FASB Conceptual Framework's second objective of financial reporting, what information is needed by the constituency of users that you have identified in part c?

e. Explain why information about the riskiness of securities is useful to investors. (CGA-Canada)

12. Mr. Smart is an investor with $15,000 to invest. He has narrowed his choice down to two possible investments:

• Mutual fund

• Common shares in Buyme Corporation

Mr. Smart is risk-averse. The amount of utility he derives from a payoff is:

Utility = 2ln(payoff)

where ln denotes natural logarithm. The decision tree for Mr. Smart's problem appears as in Figure 3.5.

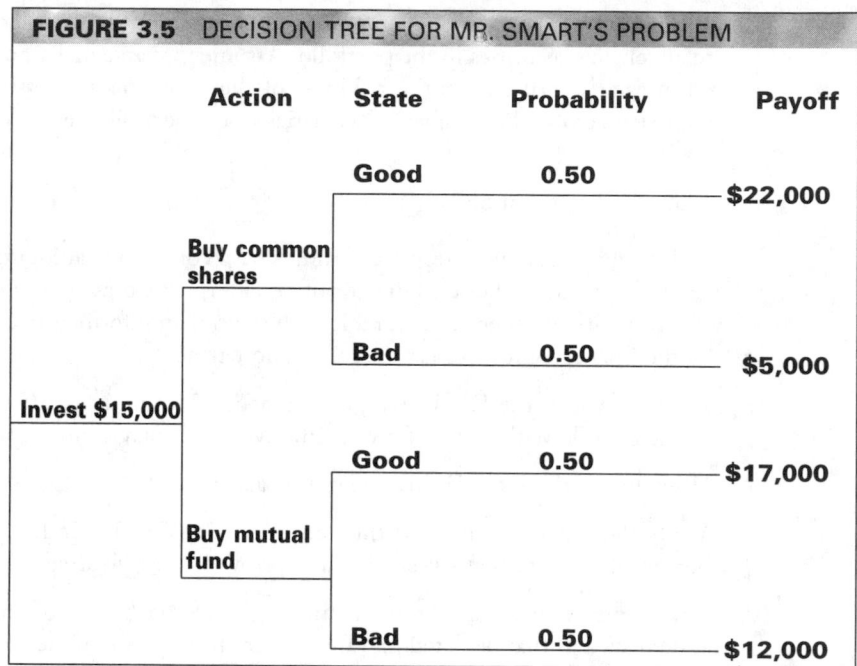

FIGURE 3.5   DECISION TREE FOR MR. SMART'S PROBLEM

	Action	State	Probability	Payoff
	Buy common shares	Good	0.50	$22,000
		Bad	0.50	$5,000
Invest $15,000	Buy mutual fund	Good	0.50	$17,000
		Bad	0.50	$12,000

Because of a planned major purchase, Mr. Smart intends to sell his investment one year later. The payoffs represent the proceeds from the sale of the investment and receipt of any dividends. The probabilities represent Mr. Smart's prior probabilities about the state of the economy (good or bad) over the coming year.

Required

a. Calculate Mr. Smart's expected utility for each action and indicate which action he would choose if he acted on the basis of his prior information.

b. Now, suppose Mr. Smart decides that he would like to obtain more information about the state of the economy rather than simply accepting that it is just as likely to be good as bad. He decides to take a sample of current annual reports of major corporations. Every annual report shows that its firm is doing well, with increased profits over the previous year. The probability that there would be such healthy profits if the state of the economy actually was good is 0.75. The probability of such healthy profits is only 0.10 if the state of the economy actually was bad.

Use Bayes' theorem to calculate Mr. Smart's posterior probabilities of the high and low states of the economy. Will he change his decision?

Note: Round your calculations to two decimal places.   (CGA-Canada)

13. John Save plans to invest $5,000 in one of the following instruments:

    - Bonds of J Ltd., yielding 12%
    - Canada Savings Bonds, yielding 8%

    On the basis of his knowledge of current economic conditions and the outlook for the industry of J Ltd., John assesses the prior probability that J Ltd. will go bankrupt as 0.05. If this happens, John will lose both principal and interest and receive no money at the end of the year. If J Ltd. does not go bankrupt, John plans to sell the bonds, plus interest, at the end of one year.

    Of course, the probability that the Canada Savings Bonds will fail to pay off is zero. John also plans to sell these, plus interest, one year later.

    John is risk-averse, and decides to choose that investment which yields the highest expected utility. Assume that John's utility for an amount of $x is given by $\sqrt{x}$, that is, his utility is the square root of the money received.

    Required

    a. On the basis of his prior probabilities, which investment should John choose?

    b. Rather than choosing on the basis of his prior probabilities, assume that John decides to analyze the current financial statements of J Ltd. These financial statements can look "good" (G) or "bad" (B). After his analysis, John realizes that the statements look good. On the basis of his extensive understanding of financial statement analysis, he knows that the probability that the financial statements would look good given that the firm was actually heading for bankruptcy is 0.10, that is:

    $$P(G/S_1) = 0.10$$

    where S_1 denotes the state of heading for bankruptcy.

    Similarly, John knows that:

    $$P(G/S_2) = 0.80$$

    where S_2 denotes the state of not heading for bankruptcy.

    Advise John as to which investment he should now take. Use Bayes' theorem.

    c. Suppose that a new accounting standard makes biasing and manipulation of earnings much more difficult. Would $P(G/S_1)$ rise or fall? Explain why.

    Note: Round your calculations to four decimal places.   (CGA-Canada)

14. "A theoretically correct measure of income does not exist in the real world in which accountants must operate."

Required

a. What is meant by the phrase "a theoretically correct measure of income"?

b. Why does a theoretically correct measure of income not exist in the real world? Discuss.

c. Discuss how the historical cost basis of accounting trades off relevance against reliability.

d. Give two examples of problems or weaknesses associated with historical cost accounting. (CGA-Canada)

15. Consider the common stock of A Ltd. and the common stock of B Ltd. These two common stocks have the same expected return and the same variance of return.

You are a risk-averse investor and have a fixed sum of money to invest. You are considering the following two choices:

a. Investing the entire sum of money in common stock of A Ltd.

b. Investing in a portfolio with the investment equally distributed between common stock of A Ltd. and common stock of B Ltd.

Required

Discuss whether you would choose alternative **a** or **b** or whether you are indifferent between them. Explain your choice. (CGA-Canada)

16. "It is possible to reduce risk in a portfolio by diversification."

Required

a. Do you agree with this statement? If so, why? Discuss.

b. Can the risk of a portfolio be reduced to zero by diversification? Discuss.

c. Why is beta the most relevant measure of risk in a diversified portfolio? (CGA-Canada)

17. a. Consider the common stock of A Ltd., which is currently trading at $40 per share. In the future, there is a 40% chance that the price of A Ltd. will rise to $80 per share and a 60% chance that it will fall to $35.

The stock of B Ltd. is currently trading at $20 per share. In the future, there is a 60% chance the stock price of B Ltd. will rise to $30 and a 40% chance it will rise to $21.25.

Assume that the returns of A Ltd. and B Ltd. are independent. As an investor with $800 to invest, would you prefer a portfolio of 20 shares of A Ltd., or a second portfolio consisting of 10 shares of A Ltd. and 20 shares of B Ltd.? Give reasons for your choice, and show any calculations used to support your answer. Carry any calculations to four decimal places.

b. Consider the common stock of D Ltd., which is currently trading at $92 per share. In the future, there is a 50% chance the value of D Ltd. will rise to $100 per share and a 50% chance it will fall to $90 per share.

The stock of M Ltd. is currently trading at $23 per share. In the future, there is a 50% chance the value of M Ltd. will rise to $25 per share and a 50% chance it will fall to $22.50 per share.

M Ltd. and D Ltd. are both in the same industry and are located side by side: as a result, their stocks rise and fall in price together. In other words, the returns on D and M are perfectly correlated. You are an investor with $1,840 to invest. Would you prefer a portfolio of 10 shares of D Ltd. and 40 shares of M Ltd. or one of 20 shares of D Ltd.? Give reasons for your choice. (*Hint:* You should be able to answer without calculations.)

c. Consider the common stock of X Printers, a textbook manufacturing firm, which is currently trading at $100 per share. Financial analysts estimate that there is a 50% chance the stock price of X Printers will rise to $150 per share in the next period and a 50% chance that it will fall to $80.

Another textbook manufacturing stock currently trading is that of Y Printing, which also trades at $100 per share. Analysts estimate that there is a 50% chance that Y's stock price will rise to $130 per share in the next period and a 50% chance that it will fall to $90.

Now consider a portfolio of 10 shares of X Printers and 10 shares of Y Printing. Because both firms are in the same industry, they are both strongly affected by certain market-wide factors. Accordingly, there is a 40% chance that the two stock prices will rise simultaneously, a 40% chance that both will fall, a 10% chance that X's price will rise while Y's price falls, and a 10% chance of the opposite occurring.

As an investor with $2,000 to invest, would you prefer the above portfolio (portfolio X + Y) or one with 20 shares of X Printers (portfolio X)? Give reasons for your choice. Show calculations where required and carry to four decimal places.

d. How would financial statement information be useful to analysts and investors in assessing the various probabilities that share prices would rise or fall? Explain. (CGA-Canada)

Efficient Securities Markets

4.1   Overview

In this chapter, we consider the interaction of investors in a securities market. The theory of efficient securities markets predicts that the security prices that result from this interaction have some appealing properties. In essence, these prices "properly reflect" the collective knowledge and information-processing ability of investors. The process by which prices do this is quite complex and not yet fully understood. Nevertheless, the general outlines of the process are easy to see, and we shall concentrate on these.

Security market efficiency has important implications for financial accounting. One implication is that it leads directly to the concept of *full disclosure*. Efficiency implies that it is the information content of disclosure, not the form of disclosure itself, that is valued by the market. Thus, information can be released as easily in footnotes and supplementary disclosures as in the financial statements themselves.

Indeed, accounting is viewed as being in competition with other information sources such as news media, financial analysts, and even market price itself, in efficient market theory. Accounting will survive only if it is a relevant, reliable, timely, and cost-effective vehicle for communicating information to investors.

Efficient security market theory also alerts us to what is the primary theoretical reason for the existence of accounting, namely information asymmetry. When some market participants know more than others, pressure arises to find mechanisms whereby the better informed, who wish to do so, can credibly communicate their information to others, and whereby those with information disadvantage can protect themselves from possible exploitation by the better informed. Insider trading is an example of such exploitation.

We can then think of accounting as a mechanism to enable communication of relevant information from inside the firm to outside. In addition to enabling better investor decisions, this has social benefits through improving the operation of securities markets.

By and large, financial accounting standard setting bodies have accepted the full disclosure approach. To illustrate this, we will examine two relatively recent standards from an informational perspective.

4.2   *Efficient Securities Markets*

4.2.1   *THE MEANING OF EFFICIENCY*

In Chapter 3 we studied the optimal investment decisions of rational investors. Now consider what happens when a large number of rational individuals interact in a securities market. Our interest is in the characteristics of the market prices of securities traded in the market, and how these prices are affected by new information.

If information was free, it is apparent that investors would want to take advantage of it. For instance, under the ideal conditions of Example 2.2, investors would want to know which state of nature was realized, since this affects the future cash flows and dividends of the firm. By assumption, information is free under ideal conditions since state realization is publicly observable. Thus, all investors would use this information, and the process of arbitrage ensures that the market value of the firm then adjusts to reflect the revised cash flow expectations that result, as illustrated in Example 2.2.

Unfortunately, information is not free under non-ideal conditions. Investors have to form their own subjective estimates of firms' future profitability, cash flows, or dividends. Furthermore, these estimates will need revision as new information comes along. Each investor then faces a cost-benefit tradeoff with respect to how much information to acquire. There are a variety of relevant information sources—the financial press, tips from friends and associates, changes in economic conditions, advice from analysts and brokers, etc. We can think of investors as continuously revising their subjective state probabilities as such information is received. From our standpoint, of course, a major source of cost-effective information is firms' annual reports. Probability revision arising from financial statement information was illustrated in Example 3.1.

At least some investors spend considerable time and money to use these information sources to guide their investment decisions. Such investors are called **informed**. Bill Cautious, in Example 3.1, is an example of such an investor.

It should be apparent that informed investors will want to move *quickly* upon receipt of new information. If they do not, other investors will get there first and the market value of the security in question will adjust so as to reduce or eliminate the benefit of the new information.

When a sufficient number of investors behave this way, the market becomes *efficient*. There are several definitions of an efficient securities market. The definition that we shall use here is called the **semi-strong form**.

> *An efficient securities market is one where the prices of securities traded on that market at all times "properly reflect" all information that is publicly known about those securities.*

Three points are particularly noteworthy. First, market prices are efficient with respect to *publicly known* information. Thus, the definition does not rule out the possibility of inside information. Persons who possess inside information, in effect, know more than the market. If they wish to take advantage of their inside information, insiders may be able to earn excess profits on their investments. This is because the market prices of these investments, reflecting only outside or publicly available information, do not incorporate the knowledge that insiders possess.

Second, market efficiency is a *relative* concept. The market is efficient relative to a stock of publicly available information. There is nothing in the definition to suggest that the market is omniscient and that market prices always reflect real underlying firm value. Market prices can certainly be wrong in the presence of inside information, for example.

The definition does imply, however, that once new or corrected information becomes publicly available, the market price will quickly adjust to this new information. This adjustment occurs because rational investors will scramble to revise their beliefs about future returns as soon as new information, from whatever source, becomes known. As a result, the expected returns and risk of their existing portfolios will change and they will enter the market to restore their optimal risk/return tradeoffs. The resulting buy-and-sell decisions will quickly change security prices to reflect the new information.

Third, investing is **fair game** if the market is efficient. This means that over time, the price of a security is just as likely to go down as up; that is, it should fluctuate randomly.[1] The reason is that anything about a firm that can be *expected*, such as the seasonal nature of its business or the retirement of its chief executive, will be properly reflected in its security price by the efficient market as soon as the expectation is formed. That is, the market's expectation of the effect of such events on the value of the firm is on average *unbiased*. The only reason that prices will change is if some relevant, but *unexpected*, information comes along. By definition, unexpected events occur randomly. Thus, if we examine the time series formed by the sequence of prices for a particular security, this series should fluctuate randomly over time. A time series that exhibits such behaviour is sometimes called a **random walk**.

4.2.2   HOW DO MARKET PRICES PROPERLY REFLECT ALL AVAILABLE INFORMATION?

We now consider *how* market prices properly reflect all available information. This process is by no means obvious or transparent. As described previously, rational, informed investors will demand information about securities. However, there is no guarantee that a particular individual will properly interpret that information. That is, the decision theory model provides a way to process information but nothing guarantees that the processing is correct. For example, the investor may misspecify one or more of the various probabilities required by Bayes' theorem or may err in the calculation of the conditional returns. In a sense, the decision theory model is like an automobile. It provides a vehicle to process information, but nothing guarantees that the vehicle will be properly driven.

As a result, it is quite likely that different investors will interpret the same information differently, even though they all proceed rationally. They may have different prior beliefs, or they may differ in one or more inputs into the decision theory model. Yet, investors interact in a market, each making buy/sell decisions about various securities. Since the market price of a security is the result of the demand for and supply of the security by investors, how can the market price properly reflect all available information when the individuals making the demand and supply decisions are fallible or, at least, different?

An interesting insight into this question can be gained from an example in Beaver (1989, p. 150, Table 6-1). The example relates to forecasting the results of football games. The *Chicago Daily News*, during 1966–68, printed weekly the predictions of each of its sports staff as to who would win that weekend's college football games. Table 4.1, taken from Beaver, summarizes the outcomes of these predictions.

TABLE 4.1 FORECASTING OUTCOMES OF FOOTBALL GAMES

	1966	**1967**	**1968**
Total forecasters (including consensus)	15	15	16
Total forecasts made per forecaster	180	220	219
Rank of consensus*	1 (tie)	2	2
Median rank of forecasters	8	8	8.5
Rank of best forecasters:			
J. Carmichael (1966)	1 (tie)	8	16
D. Nightingale (1966)	1 (tie)	11	5
A. Biondo (1967)	7	1	6
H. Duck (1968)	8	10	1

*When all three years are combined, the consensus outperforms every one of the forecasters (that is, ranks first).

SOURCE: William H. Beaver, *Financial Reporting: An Accounting Revolution* ® 1981, p. 162, Table 6-1. Reprinted by permission of Prentice-Hall Inc., Upper Saddle River, New Jersey. Data are from "Here's How Our Staff Picks 'Em," *Chicago Daily News*, November 25, 1966 (p. 43), November 24, 1967 (p. 38), and November 29, 1968 (p. 43). Reprinted by permission of *Chicago Sun-Times* © 1995.

Note the following points from Table 4.1. First, there were a number of different forecasters (15–16) and a large number of forecasts were made (619 over the three years). Second, no one individual forecaster dominated in terms of forecasting ability. The best forecasters in 1966 were well down the list in subsequent years, and vice versa. Third, note the consistent performance of the consensus forecast. The consensus forecast was also published weekly by the *Chicago Daily News* and, for each game, consisted of the team favoured to win by the majority of those forecasting. It is clear that the consensus forecast has a quality which transcends the forecasting ability of the individual forecasters from which the consensus is derived.

To translate the example into a securities market context, we can think of the forecasters as investors in a security and the forecasts as their various buy/sell decisions. The consensus forecast is analogous to the market price, since it is a type of average of the various individual forecasting decisions.

The rationale behind the example is not hard to see. It appears that the various errors made by individual forecasters tend to cancel out when the consensus is formed, leaving a "market price" that outperforms the ability of any of the market participants.

Of course, just because a consensus forecast outperforms individual forecasters of football games does not by itself mean that the same phenomenon carries over to security prices. Essentially, what is required is that investors' estimates of security values must on average be unbiased. This is an example of **rational expectations**; that is, the market does not systematically misinterpret the valuation implications of a stock of information, but rather puts a valuation on securities that is *on average* correct or unbiased. As mentioned, this does not mean that any individual investor will necessarily be correct, but it does mean that *on average* the market uses all available information.

There are other possible explanations for market efficiency than the rational expectations argument. For example, financial analysts may be sufficiently adept at evaluating security value that, when investors follow their recommendations, the resulting prices properly reflect available information about these securities.

4.2.3   SUMMARY

In an efficient securities market, prices properly reflect all available information, and the market price of securities on such a market will fluctuate randomly over time. Efficiency is defined relative to a stock of information. If this stock of information is incomplete, say because of inside information, or wrong, security prices will be wrong. Thus, market efficiency does not guarantee that security prices are accurate. It does suggest, however, that prices are unbiased and will react quickly to new or revised information.

The quantity and quality of publicly available information will be enhanced by prompt and full reporting. However, individual investors may have different prior beliefs and/or may interpret the same information differently. Nevertheless, roughly speaking, we can think of these differences as "averaging out," so that the market price has superior quality to the quality of the information processing of the individuals trading on the market.

4.3   *A Capital Asset Pricing Model*

We are now in a position to formalize the relationship between the efficient market price of a security, its risk, and the expected rate of return on a security. We shall do so by means of the well-known Sharpe-Lintner capital asset pricing model (CAPM) (Sharpe, 1964; Lintner, 1965).

First, we need some preliminaries. Define R_{jt}, the net rate of return on the shares of firm j for time period t, as:

$$R_{jt} = \frac{P_{jt} + D_{jt} - P_{j,t-1}}{P_{j,t-1}} = \frac{P_{jt} + D_{jt}}{P_{j,t-1}} - 1$$

where:

P_{jt} is the market price of firm j's shares at the end of period t

D_{jt} is dividends paid by firm j during period t

$P_{j,t-1}$ is the market price of firm j's shares at the beginning of period t

This is the return concept used in Examples 3.2 and 3.3. It is a *net* rate of return given that the opening market price is subtracted in the numerator. We can also define a *gross rate of return* as $1 + R_{jt}$, where:

$$1 + R_{jt} = \frac{P_{jt} + D_{jt}}{P_{j,t-1}}$$

Since the only difference between the two rate of return concepts is the 1, we can use them interchangeably. In fact, to conform to common practice, we will usually refer to both net and gross rates of return as simply **returns**.

We can think of returns as either *ex post* or *ex ante*. Ex post, we are at the end of period t and looking back to calculate the return actually realized during the period. Alternatively, we can stand at the beginning of period t and think of an *ex ante* or expected return as:

$$E(R_{jt}) = \frac{E(P_{jt} + D_{jt})}{P_{j,t-1}} - 1 \tag{4.1}$$

That is, expected return for period t is based on the expected price at the end of the period plus any dividends expected during the period, divided by the beginning-of-period price.

Now, consider an economy with a large number of investors like Toni Difelice (Examples 3.2 and 3.3). Recall that Toni is risk-averse and has a mean-variance utility function. As shown in Tables 3.5 and 3.6, Toni can calculate the expected rates of return, the variances of return, and the covariances of return for each security in the market. Assume that there is a risk-free asset in the economy, with return R_f. Assume also that security markets are efficient and transaction costs are zero. Then, the Sharpe-Lintner CAPM shows that:

$$E(R_{jt}) = R_f(1 - \beta_j) + \beta_j E(R_{Mt}) \tag{4.2}$$

where β_j is the beta of share j and R_{Mt} is the return on the market portfolio for period t.

Note that the model is in terms of the market's *expected* returns. Equation 4.2 states that at the beginning of period t the expected return for the period equals a constant $R_f(1 - \beta_j)$ plus another constant β_j times the expected return on the market portfolio. Strictly speaking, markets do not have expectations—individuals do. One way to think of the market's expectations is that the price of a share behaves *as if* the market held a certain expectation about its future performance. More fundamentally, the market price of a share includes a sort of average of the expectations of all informed investors, much like the consensus forecast in the Beaver football example (Section 4.2.2) includes an average expectation of the forecasters.

Note also the role of the current market price $P_{j,t-1}$ in the model. Given expected end-of-period price P_{jt} and dividends D_{jt}, we see that $P_{j,t-1}$ will adjust so that Equation 4.1 holds. That is, a share's current price will adjust so that its expected return equals the return demanded by the market in that share which, from Equation 4.2, is a function only of R_f, R_{Mt}, and β_j.

It is not difficult to see the intuition of the model. Since rational investors like Toni Difelice will fully diversify when transactions costs are zero, the only risk measure in the formula is β_j. Firm-specific risk does not affect share price because it disappears in fully diversified portfolios. Also, note that the higher is β_j the higher is expected return, other things equal. This is consistent with risk aversion, since risk-averse investors will require a higher expected return to compensate for higher risk. Thus, the current price $P_{j,t-1}$ will be lower the higher is beta, other things equal.

Note also how information affects current market price. Suppose that at the beginning of period t some new information comes along that raises investors' expectations of P_{jt} (and possibly also of D_{jt}). This will throw Equation 4.1 out of balance, so that $P_{j,t-1}$, the current price, must rise to restore equality. This, of course, is consistent with market efficiency, which states that the market price of a security will react immediately to new information.

For our purposes, there are three main uses for the CAPM formula. First, it brings out clearly how share prices depend on investors' expectations of rate of return. If these expectations change (the numerator of Equation 4.1), current price $P_{j,t-1}$ (the denominator) will immediately change to reflect these new expectations. For a given change in expectations, and given R_f and $E(R_{Mt})$, the amount of the change in current price depends only on the share's beta. To put this another way, the larger the change in expectations, the larger the change in price, other things equal.

Second, by reverting to an *ex post* view of returns, the CAPM provides us with a way of separating the realized return on a share into expected and unexpected components. To see this, consider the following version of the model, where we are now at the end of period t and looking back:

$$R_{jt} = \alpha_j + \beta_j R_{Mt} + \epsilon_{jt}$$

This version of CAPM is called the **market model**. It states that the realized return R_{jt} for the period is the sum of the beginning-of-period *expected* return ($\alpha_j + \beta_j R_{Mt}$) and the *unexpected* or **abnormal**[2] return ϵ_{jt}. The expected return comes from the CAPM, with $\alpha_j = R_f(1 - \beta_j)$. The ϵ_{jt} captures the impact on R_{jt} of all those events during period t that were not expected at the beginning of the period. By definition in an efficient market, $E(\epsilon_{jt}) = 0$, since new information comes along randomly. But, in any period t the *realized* value of ϵ_{jt} will not be zero. Thus, the market model enables an *ex post* separation of the realized return R_{jt} into expected ($\alpha_j + \beta_j R_{Mt}$) and unexpected or abnormal (ϵ_{jt}) components.

Third, the market model provides a convenient way to estimate a stock's beta, which, as we saw in Section 3.7, is an important risk measure for investors. Notice that the market model is presented in the form of a regression equation. By obtaining past data on R_{jt} and R_{Mt}, the coefficients of the regression model can be estimated by least-squares regression. If we assume that the market is able to form accurate expectations of R_{Mt} (so that R_{Mt} is a good proxy for $E(R_{Mt})$ which is unobservable) and if we assume that β_j is stable over time, then the coefficient of R_{Mt} from least-squares regression is a good estimate[3] of β_j. Furthermore, the reasonableness of the estimation can be checked by comparing the estimated coefficient α_j with $(1 - \beta_j)R_f$—the two should be the same.

Also, as we will see in Chapter 5, much empirical research in accounting has required an accurate estimate of beta, and we will return to its estimation in Section 5.7. For now, it is important to realize that the CAPM provides an important and useful way to model the market's expectation of returns, and that the model depends crucially on security market efficiency.

4.4   *Implications of Efficient Securities Markets for Financial Reporting*

4.4.1   IMPLICATIONS

Security market efficiency has several important implications for financial accounting and reporting. A readable and persuasive examination of these implications appears in an article by W. H. Beaver, "What Should Be the FASB's Objectives?" (1973). Here, we will briefly consider the most important implications of Beaver's argument.

According to Beaver, the first major implication is that accounting policies adopted by firms do not affect their security prices, as long as these policies have no differential cash flow effects, the particular policies used are disclosed, and sufficient information is given so that the reader can convert across different policies. Thus, Beaver would regard accounting disputes such as a firm's choice of amortization method, the deferral versus flow-through of deferred income taxes, and the full-cost versus successful-efforts approach for oil and gas firms as essentially "tempests in a teapot." Notice that a firm's choice between different accounting policies in each of these disputes involves only "paper" effects. The policy chosen will affect reported net income, but will not directly affect future cash flows and dividends. For example, an oil and gas firm's proceeds from sale of crude and refined products will not depend directly on whether it uses full-cost or successful-efforts accounting. In particular, the amount of income tax the firm must pay will not be affected by its accounting policy choice in any of these three disputed areas since the tax department has its own way of calculating expenses and income in each area, independent of how the firm accounts for them on its books. If investors are interested in future cash flows and dividends and their impact on security values, and if choosing between accounting policies does not directly influence these variables, the firm's choice between accounting policies should not matter.

Thus, the efficient market argument is that as long as firms disclose their selected policy, and any additional information needed to convert from one method to another, investors are able to make the necessary calculations to see through to the resulting differences in reported net income. That is, the market can see through to the ultimate cash flow and dividend implications regardless of which accounting policy is actually used for reporting. Thus, the efficient market is not "fooled" by differing accounting policies when comparing different firms' securities. This suggests that management should not care about which particular accounting policies they use as long as those policies have no direct cash flow effects.

We thus see that full disclosure extends to disclosure of the firm's accounting policies. This is recognized by standard setters. For example, the *CICA Handbook*, paragraph 1505.04, states:

> A clear and concise description of the significant accounting policies of an enterprise should be included as an integral part of the financial statements.

A second implication follows—namely, efficient securities markets go hand in hand with full disclosure. If a firm's management possesses relevant information about the firm and if this can be disclosed at little or no cost, management should then disclose this information on a timely basis unless it is certain that the information is already known to investors from other sources. More generally, management should develop and report information about the firm as long as the benefits to investors exceed the costs. The reasons are twofold. First, market efficiency implies that investors will use all available, relevant information as they strive to improve their predictions of future returns, so that additional information will not be "wasted." Second, the more information a firm publishes about itself, the more information is publicly available about that firm. Consequently, investors' confidence in the securities market is enhanced.

Third, market efficiency implies that firms should not be overly concerned about the naive investor—that is, financial statement information need not be presented in a manner so simple that everyone can understand it. The reasoning here is actually quite subtle: if *enough* investors understand the disclosed information, this is sufficient to ensure that the market price of a firm's shares is the same as it would be if all investors understood it. This is because the investors who do understand the financial information will engage in buy/sell decisions on the basis of the disclosed information, which will move the market price towards its efficient level. Also, naive investors can hire other persons (such as financial analysts or investment fund managers) to interpret the information for them, or can mimic the buy/sell decisions of more knowledgeable investors. As a result, any information advantage that the knowledgable investors may have is quickly dissipated. In other words, the naive investors can *trust* the efficient market to price securities so that they always reflect all that is publicly known about the firms that have issued them, even though these investors may not have complete knowledge and understanding themselves. This is sometimes referred to as investors being **price-protected** by the efficient market.

Since Beaver's paper, accountants have recognized that there are a variety of reasons for trading securities. For example, some investors may make a rational decision to rely on market price as a good indicator of future payoffs, rather than incur the costs of becoming informed. Others may trade for a variety of non-portfolio reasons—perhaps an unexpected need for cash has arisen. Consequently, "naive" may not be the best word to describe uninformed investors. This is considered further in Section 4.5.

A final implication is that accountants are in competition with other providers of information, such as financial analysts, media, disclosures by company officials, and so on. That is, belief revision is a continuous process, as pointed out in Section 3.3.2. Thus, if accountants do not provide useful, cost-effective information, we would expect that the usefulness of the accounting function would decline over time as other information sources take over—accountants have no *inherent* right to survive in the competitive marketplace for information. However, we observe little tendency for this to happen, suggesting that, by and large, accounting information is generally useful to investors. Empirical evidence about security market response to financial accounting information is reviewed in Chapter 5.

Beaver's paper was published in 1973. Consequently, it predates SFAC 1 (issued in 1978) and SFAC 2 (1980) by several years. However, it provides a good example of the early enthusiasm of accounting theorists for efficient security markets. It also highlights the type of disclosure-oriented thinking that led to the formal statement of the usefulness criterion by the FASB in SFAC 1.

4.4.2　SUMMARY

Beaver argues that security market efficiency has several implications for financial reporting. First, managers and accountants should not be concerned about which accounting policies firms use unless different accounting policies have direct cash flow effects. Many accounting policy alternatives, that accountants have argued long and hard about, do not have such cash flow effects. Second, firms should disclose as much information about themselves as is feasible—the fact of disclosure and not the form it takes is what is important. The efficient market will prefer the least costly form of disclosure, other things equal. One can argue, however, that financial statements are a cost-effective disclosure medium. Third, firms need not be concerned about the naive investor when choosing disclosure policies and formats. Such persons are price-protected, because efficient security prices properly reflect all that is publicly known about those securities. Furthermore, there are a variety of mediums, such as financial analysts and investment funds, whereby investors can take advantage of sophisticated information without needing to fully understand it themselves. Finally, the efficient market is interested in relevant information from any source, not just accounting reports.

4.5　*The Informativeness of Price*

4.5.1　A LOGICAL INCONSISTENCY

The careful reader may have noticed an inconsistency in our discussion of efficient securities markets to this point. Recall that efficiency implies that the market price of a security at all times properly reflects all that is publicly known about that security. What is it that drives market price to have this "properly reflects" characteristic? It is the actions of informed investors who are always striving to obtain and process information so as to make good buy/sell decisions. By analogy with the football example in Section 4.2.2, price aggregates information since informed investors' buy/sell decisions will affect the market price of a security and these decisions are based on information.

However, by the definition of market efficiency, all available information is already reflected in market price. That is, the price is **fully informative**. Since information acquisition is costly, and investors could not expect to beat the market when the market price already reflects all publicly known information, investors would simply stop gathering information and rely on market price as the best indicator of future security returns. For example, a simple decision rule would be to buy when price is rising and sell when price starts to fall.

The logical inconsistency, then, is that if prices fully reflect available information, there is no motivation for investors to acquire information; hence, prices will not fully reflect available information. In terms of football forecasting, the forecasters would stop putting effort into their forecasts because they can't beat the consensus forecast, but then the consensus forecast would lose its superior forecasting ability. Technically speaking, the problem here is that stable equilibrium prices do not exist, as shown by Grossman (1976).

This has potentially serious implications for accounting theory, since a lack of equilibrium makes it problematic whether financial statement information is useful to investors. Also, it is contrary to what we observe. SFAC 1 (Section 3.8) certainly implies that investors find financial reporting useful, for example.

However, there is an easy way out of the inconsistency. This is to recognize that there are other sources of demand and supply for securities than the buy/sell decisions of rational informed investors. For example, people may buy or sell securities for a variety of unpredictable reasons—they may decide to retire early, they may need money to pay gambling debts, they may have received a "hot tip," etc. Such persons are called **liquidity traders** or **noise traders**. Their buy/sell decisions will affect a security's market price, but the decisions come at random—they are not based on a rational evaluation of relevant information. As a result, market price is no longer fully informative. For example, a decline in a security's market price might be due either to lower expected future returns or to a major sale by a cash-strapped owner, and an investor would not know the real reason. Thus, shares may be mispriced, even on an efficient market.

Of course, security market prices will still be **partially informative** under the above scenario. After all, at least some buy/sell decisions are made on the basis of rational evaluation of relevant information, and these will drive prices in the direction of fully reflecting available information. When price is partially informative, rational investors can derive *some* information about future returns from price. The important point, however, is that they have the opportunity, at a cost, to further sharpen up their beliefs by their own private information-gathering activities. Presumably, some of this additional information will come from their analysis of financial statements.

The extent to which investors do this will depend on a number of factors, such as how informative price is, the quality of financial statement information, and the costs of analysis and interpretation. These factors lead to empirical predictions about how security market prices respond to financial statement information.

For example, we might expect that price will be more informative for large firms, since they are more "in the news" than small firms, and hence, their market price will incorporate considerable information. This reduces the ability of financial statements to add to what is already known about such firms. Thus, we would predict that security prices will respond less to financial statement information for large firms than for small firms.

Furthermore, note that firm management may have an incentive to cater to this desire of investors to ferret out information. For example, management of a firm that is undervalued may engage in **voluntary disclosure**, that is, disclosure of information beyond the minimum requirement of GAAP and other reporting standards. Such disclosure can have credibility, even if unaudited, since legal liability imposes discipline on managers' reporting decisions. Unfortunately, there are limitations on voluntary disclosure, not only because the legal system may be unable to completely enforce credibility, but because management will not want to reveal information that would give away competitive advantage.

However, voluntary disclosure is much more complex and subtle than simply disclosing information. Management can signal inside information by its choice of accounting policies and, indeed, by the nature and extent of voluntary disclosure itself. This means that there are potential rewards to investors, and analysts, for careful and complete analyses of firms' annual reports. Such analyses may identify mispricing and can quickly be turned into profitable investment decisions.

Also, an increase in the quality of financial statement information, other things equal, should lead investors to increase their utilization of financial statement information relative to price. For example, the requirement by the Ontario Securities Commission (OSC) that firms include management discussion and analysis (MD&A) in their annual reports and the 1989 Section 4250 of the *CICA Handbook* relating to **future-oriented financial information (FOFI)** may increase market price reactions to annual reports. Annual reports should have higher information content with MD&A and/or FOFI relative to the preexisting information content of market price. Empirical evidence on the decision usefulness of financial statement information will be considered in Chapter 5. MD&A and FOFI are discussed in Section 4.8.

We conclude that the term "properly reflects" in the efficient securities market definition has to be interpreted with care. It does not mean that security prices are fully informative with respect to available information at all points in time. Indeed, if it did, this would have adverse implications for the usefulness of financial statements. Rather, the term should be interpreted as reflecting a tension between the level of informativeness allowed by noise and liquidity traders, and the ability of investors and analysts to identify mispriced securities through analysis of accounting policy choice, of the nature and extent of voluntary disclosure, and, indeed, of all other available information. With this interpretation in mind, it is important to point out that the implications of security market efficiency as outlined by Beaver in Section 4.4 continue to apply. In particular, the importance of full disclosure remains.

4.5.2   SUMMARY

While the ability of a market price to *average out* the errors of individual, fallible investors, as we saw in the football forecasting example, is on the right track, the process of price formation in securities markets is much more complex than this. Through consideration of ways that rational investors can become more informed by careful analysis of managers' disclosure decisions, and through other sources of demand and supply for securities than those from rational, informed investors, accountants are beginning to understand the role of information in price. This does not mean that efficient securities market concepts are invalid, but rather that these concepts must be interpreted with care.

Improved understanding of the process of price formation leads to empirical predictions of how security prices respond to accounting information and, ultimately, to more useful financial statements.

4.6   Information Asymmetry

4.6.1   THE CONCEPT OF INFORMATION ASYMMETRY

In this section, we continue our close look at the notion of "publicly available" information in the efficient securities market definition. This leads directly to what is undoubtedly the most important concept of financial accounting theory—*information asymmetry*. Frequently, one type of participant in the market (sellers, for example) will know something about the asset being traded that another type of participant (buyers) does not know. When this situation exists, the market is said to be characterized by information asymmetry. As mentioned in Chapter 1, there are two major types of information asymmetry—adverse selection and moral hazard. We now consider these in greater detail.

One effect of information asymmetry is to hamper the proper operation of markets. In Examples 2.1 and 2.2, there was no information asymmetry, by the definition of ideal conditions. Then we saw that market values and present values were equal. This is not necessarily true when information asymmetry is present.

These effects were studied by Akerlof (1970). An example of a market characterized by information asymmetry is the used car market. The owner of a car will know more about its true condition, and hence its future stream of benefits, than would a potential buyer. The owner may try to take advantage of this by bringing a "lemon" to market, hoping to get more than it is worth from an unsuspecting buyer. However, the buyers will be aware of this temptation and, since they don't have the information to distinguish between lemons and good cars, will lower the price they are willing to pay for any used car. As a result, many cars—the good ones—will have a market value that is less than the real value of their future stream of benefits. The arbitrage effect, whereby cars of similar service potential must sell for similar prices, operates less effectively when it is difficult to know exactly what the service potential of a used car is. Thus, owners of good cars are less likely to bring them to market. In other words, the market for used cars does not work as well as it might.

In extreme cases, a market may collapse completely as a result of information asymmetry. To illustrate, consider the market for insurance policies. You may wish to buy insurance against the possibility of failing to attain your university or college degree. You would be better off with such a policy, at least if the cost was fair. Illness, for example, may prevent your completion of the course of studies, and you could eliminate this risk of illness if you had a policy that reimbursed you for your loss of the present value of the increased future income that would follow the attainment of your degree. However, if you owned such a policy, you would probably **shirk** your studies, even if you were perfectly healthy. Why put in all the time and effort to complete your course of studies when, by merely failing, you could receive equivalent compensation from your insurance policy?

As a result, no insurance company would sell you a policy that would reimburse you for your full income loss if you failed to attain your degree. Essentially, the problem is one of information asymmetry. You have a major information advantage over the company, because the company can only observe whether you fail, not whether your sickness caused you to fail. This is called a *moral hazard* problem, for you are tempted to cheat the company by shirking your studies. Note that requiring a medical certificate would not be of much use here, because of the difficulty in establishing that it was the illness that led to the failure.

Another difficulty the insurance company would face is that people who were sick would flock to enroll in university programs (called an adverse selection problem, because people whose health is adverse to the insurance company's best interests self-select themselves to buy insurance). Then, when their illness led to their failure, they could collect on their policies and still enjoy the monetary fruits of a degree.

Faced with information disadvantages of this magnitude, the company responds by not writing insurance policies of the type described. Hence, no market develops. Obviously, if there is no market for an asset, such as a university degree, it is impossible to value this asset using market value.

It is interesting to note the variety of devices that markets use to reduce the effects of information asymmetry. Thus, used car markets are characterized by guarantees, safety certificates, test drives, dealers who attempt to establish a good reputation, and so on. Insurance markets are characterized by medical examinations for life insurance, co-insurance and deductible clauses for fire insurance, premium reductions for good driving records, and so on. However, because they are costly, these devices do not completely eliminate the problem. Nevertheless, they may be sufficiently effective to at least allow the market to operate, albeit not as properly as it would in the absence of information asymmetry.

The presence of risks, such as the impact of illness on earning power, that individuals would like to protect themselves against but cannot because a market does not develop, is a consequence of incomplete markets. Recall from Section 2.6 that incompleteness results when estimation problems, such as in oil company reserves, prevent market prices from developing. Here, we see that information asymmetry is another source of incompleteness.

Incompleteness of markets also results when markets exist but do not work properly. For example, despite the devices mentioned above that enable the used car market to operate, a used car buyer still bears a risk of buying a vehicle of different quality from what he or she wants and is paying for. That is, if price does not perfectly reflect the quality of a commodity, individuals are unable to buy the exact quality they want, so they bear more risk than they would like. As a result, they would like to see market incompleteness reduced. But because of adverse selection and the cost of devices to overcome it, it may not be cost-effective to eliminate it completely. Nevertheless, we will now argue that financial accounting has a role to play in improving the operation of markets, thereby at least reducing the problem of incompleteness.

One of the reasons why information asymmetry is of such importance to accounting theory is that *securities markets* are subject to information asymmetry problems. This is because of the presence of inside information and insider trading. Even if security market prices fully reflect all publicly available information, including that which can be inferred from firms' accounting policy and disclosure decisions, it is still likely that insiders know more than outsiders about the true quality of the firm. If so, they may take advantage of their information to earn excess profits. This is another example of the adverse selection problem, since insiders will be attracted by this opportunity which is *adverse* to the interests of investors. Of course, investors will be aware of this possibility and will lower the amounts that they would otherwise be willing to pay for shares, to reflect their expected losses at the hands of insiders. Just like the used car market, the efficient securities market does not work as well as it might.

> We can think of *financial reporting* as a device to reduce the adverse selection problem, thereby improving the operation of securities markets and reducing incompleteness.

To reduce adverse selection, accountants have adopted policies of **full disclosure**, to expand the set of information that is publicly available. Also, **timeless** of reporting will reduce the ability of insiders to profit from their information advantage.

Of course, since financial reporting is costly, it is unlikely that the problem of inside information can be eliminated. Nevertheless, full and timely disclosure will increase the usefulness of financial reporting to investors by expanding the set of publicly available information. This should help with Beaver's concern that accounting is in competition with other information sources, including price itself.

4.6.2   *SUMMARY*

Under ideal conditions, the firm's market value fully reflects *all* information. When conditions are not ideal, market value fully reflects all *publicly available* information, if security markets are efficient.

The difference between these two information sets includes **inside information**. The ability of insiders to profit from their information advantage is an example of the adverse selection problem. Full and timely disclosure will reduce this problem, thereby making financial reporting more useful to investors and improving the working of securities markets. Since reporting is costly, however, the inside information problem will still be present.

4.7   *The Social Significance of Properly Working Securities Markets*

In a capitalist economy, securities markets are the primary vehicle whereby capital is raised and allocated to competing investment needs. Consequently, it is socially desirable that these markets work properly in the sense that security prices should provide correct values to guide the flow of investment funds. For example, a firm that has high-expected-value capital projects will be encouraged to invest in them if it receives a high price for its securities. Conversely, investment should be discouraged in firms that do not have high-expected-value capital projects. This will happen if security prices properly reflect underlying value. Of course, this is exactly what society wants, since investment capital is in scarce supply. Social welfare will be enhanced if scarce capital goes to the most productive alternatives.

In this chapter, we have formally faced up to the existence of information asymmetry and, in particular, the problem of inside information, whereby managers and other insiders have an information advantage over outside investors. It is not hard to see that this adverse selection problem operates against proper securities market operation, since insiders may withhold, delay, or bias the release of relevant information for their own advantage.

It is also important to note that investors will be aware of this possibility. Then, a "lemons" phenomenon, as described in Section 4.6 for the used car market, would also come into play here. Investors would recognize that the market is not a "level playing field" and would either withdraw from the market or lower the amount they are willing to pay for *any* security. Then, firms with high-quality investment projects will not receive a high price for their securities, and the market is not working as well as it should. If too many investors withdraw, the market becomes **thin** or, equivalently, it loses **breadth**. A problem with thin markets is that investors may not be able to buy or sell all they want of a security at the market price.

Of course, developed capitalist economies have a variety of mechanisms for promoting the proper operation of securities markets. One such approach is to impose **penalties** on the market. Thus, we witness government securities commissions such as the SEC in the United States and the OSC in Ontario. These agencies create and enforce regulations to, for example, control insider trading and promote prompt disclosure of significant events, with penalties for violation.

However, the natural operation of a market can provide **incentives** for the release of inside information even in the absence of penalties for abuse. For example, a variety of mechanisms are available whereby firms with high-quality investment projects can credibly communicate this to the market, thereby enhancing the price they obtain for their securities. **Signalling** is one such mechanism—for example, insiders may retain a substantial equity position in new projects, thereby signalling to the market their beliefs in their high-quality project. The higher the project quality, the greater the incentive to signal. Signals will be considered in greater detail in Chapter 12.

For present purposes, a related incentive mechanism is full disclosure. Firms with high- (or low-) quality projects have an incentive to engage in full disclosure in their financial reports.[4] If such disclosures are credible, investors will remove them from the "lemons" category and will, as a result, be willing to pay prices for their securities that properly reflect underlying values.

Obviously, penalty-based and incentive-based mechanisms are not mutually exclusive—we witness both in our economy. The penalty approach is like a "stick" and requires regulation to enforce it. The need for regulation will be reduced, however, to the extent that "carrots" are available to enable firms that wish to do so to credibly reveal their information, thereby enabling them to receive a fair price for their securities.

We may conclude that the social benefits of properly working securities markets will be attained if the following two conditions are met:

- All relevant information is in the public domain, at least up to the ability of penalties and incentives to cost-effectively motivate the release of inside information.

- Security market prices are efficient relative to this information.

4.8   *Examples of Full Disclosure*

4.8.1   *INTRODUCTION*

In this section, we shall consider two examples of accounting standards of which firms may avail themselves to increase the quality of their financial disclosure.

The first is **management discussion and analysis** pursuant to OSC Policy Statement 5.10, issued in 1989. The second is FOFI pursuant to Section 4250 of the *CICA Handbook*, also issued in 1989.

Besides being of interest in their own right, these two standards provide important illustrations of how the amount of relevant information in the public domain can be increased. The MD&A standard is in between the carrot and stick approaches to information release. It is required of firms to which Statement 5.10 applies. However, it is written in fairly general terms so that firms have latitude in the extent to which they release MD&A information. Also, it need only include information available without undue effort or expense and which is not already clear from the financial statements. The second standard (FOFI) is voluntary; hence, it is a carrot approach. Section 4250 applies only if firms decide to release a forecast. The signalling implications of forecasting will be discussed in Chapter 12. Here, our interest is in its full-disclosure aspects.

4.8.2   *MANAGEMENT DISCUSSION AND ANALYSIS*

Objectives of MD&A

Statement 5.10 requires certain firms in the OSC's jurisdiction to prepare an "Annual Information Form (AIF) and Management's Discussion and Analysis of Financial Condition and Results of Operations (MD&A)." Our coverage will concentrate on MD&A.

The MD&A requirements apply only to relatively large firms, that is, firms with shareholders' equity greater than $10 million and with revenues greater than $10 million. The requirements came into effect for fiscal years ending on or after December 31, 1989 although in certain cases these deadlines were extended.

According to the Introduction to Statement 5.10, the primary objective is to:

enhance investor understanding of the issuer's business by providing supplemental analysis and background material to allow a fuller understanding of the nature of an issuer, its operations and known prospects for the future.

Thus, we see that the objective of MD&A is derived from the decision usefulness approach introduced in Section 3.2. In particular, the emphasis is on assisting the user to assess the future prospects of the firm. Note that this is not accomplished in Statement 5.10 through the financial statements, nor even by direct forecasts of future profits. Rather, the argument is:

There are practical constraints on the amount of information that can be effectively conveyed in financial statements, which are subject to generally accepted accounting and auditing standards. Important transactions,

events and conditions are not always fully reflected in the financial statements and some are not easily expressed in dollar amounts. Additional
disclosure and analysis beyond the financial statements is necessary to
provide an adequate basis for assessment of an issuer's recent history and
outlook for the future. This Policy Statement requires such expanded
disclosure.

The "additional disclosure and analysis" referred to is oriented to management
discussion of its current financial statements and future prospects.

Disclosure Requirements

Generally, the MD&A disclosure requirement is to discuss those aspects of the
financial statements and other statistical data that enhance the reader's understanding of financial condition, changes in financial condition, and results of
operations. More specifically, discussion is required under the following aspects:

- Discussion of current operations and financial condition is required.

- Specific requirements are set out to disclose information on risks and
  uncertainties. This is consistent with our discussion of the FASB
  Conceptual Framework in Section 3.8, in particular with SFAC1's second
  objective of financial reporting, which includes assessment of the uncertainty of prospective cash flows and dividends.

- Information about the nature and magnitude of "financial instruments" is
  required. In addition to bonds and shares, this term includes mortgage-
  backed securities and hedging instruments. Thus, the Policy Statement
  requires disclosure of financial instruments that typically do not appear
  on financial statements, such as futures contracts, options, and swaps.
  This represents at least a start at bringing "off-balance-sheet financing"
  into the open.

- Many of the requirements are designed to help users interpret the financial statements. For example, "known trends" that will have a favourable
  or unfavourable effect on liquidity, capital resources, and continuing
  operations are to be described. Again, this assists the user to assess the
  future liquidity and profitability of the firm.

- The Policy Statement contains a number of provisions to assist firms in
  complying. Thus, firms whose securities are also traded in the United
  States (and hence must comply with the MD&A requirements of the
  SEC) can submit their SEC reports to the OSC in satisfaction of the
  OSC's MD&A requirements. That is, they do not have to prepare the
  same information twice. Small firms do not have to comply. Firms whose
  MD&A disclosures could put them at a competitive disadvantage can

apply for exemption from reporting of "sensitive information." Also, firms need only include in MD&A information that is available "without undue effort or expense and which does not clearly appear in the issuer's financial statements." Finally, specific auditor involvement in the MD&A disclosures is not required. Presumably, these conditions have been included in response to management concerns about the costs and sensitive nature of compliance. Thus, Statement 5.10 includes a combination of carrot and stick mechanisms to promote information release, as discussed in Section 4.7.

Discussion of MD&A Disclosure

Strictly speaking, MD&A is not part of the financial statements (presumably, this explains why MD&A is an OSC standard rather than a *CICA Handbook* standard). Nevertheless, it is not hard to see that it is consistent with the spirit of the Conceptual Framework, where the emphasis is on supplying information to enable investors to assess the future prospects of the enterprise. This forward-looking approach is evident in MD&A, for example in the requirements to describe known trends and uncertainties.

More generally, MD&A is consistent with the decision usefulness approach. The information that it provides should be helpful in better enabling users to assess the probabilities of future profitability, cash flows, or dividends from their investments. Thus, the thrust of MD&A is to assist users in making their own assessments, rather than providing these assessments directly.

In addition, MD&A can improve the proper working of securities markets to the extent that it expands the set of relevant information available to investors. In effect, it has the potential to reduce inside information.

An Example of MD&A Disclosure

Exhibit 4.1 reproduces the MD&A in the 1993 annual report of Mark's Work Wearhouse. The firm's shares are traded on the Toronto Stock Exchange; consequently, it is subject to OSC requirements.

EXHIBIT 4.1   MD&A from 1993 Annual Report of Mark's Work Wearhouse

Fiscal 1993 was a year of transition: the Company concluded both the downsizing started in late fiscal 1991 and the refinancing put in motion in the second half of fiscal 1992.

OPERATIONS

Corporate store sales were unimpressive early in the year. Same-store sales were down 2% to the end of the first quarter, but recovered to a flat position by the end of the second quarter and remained there through the third quarter. Sales strengthened significantly in the fourth quarter, as the Company's improved purchasing and event marketing programs began to take hold. The result was an overall corporate same-store sales increase of 3% for the year. This improved sales trend has continued into the first quarter of fiscal 1994. There were 77 comparable stores in fiscal 1993 of the 91 corporate stores open at January 30, 1993 and the 86 open at January 25, 1992. Of these 77 stores, 51 (or 66%) had sales increases over last year. Sales by category increased or decreased as follows:

CORPORATE STORE SALES BY CATEGORY

	Increase	Decrease
Workwear apparel	—	8.9%
Men's casual wear	16.1%	—
Western wear	53.2%	—
Brand name bottoms	—	12.0%
Industrial footwear	0.6%	—
Accessories	—	0.9%
Casual outerwear	20.0%	—
Industrial outerwear	—	9.9%
Private label bottoms	17.0%	—
Casual footwear	—	10.9%
Children's wear	—	66.4%
Ladies' wear	—	2.0%

The significant sales increases in casual wear and decreases in the workwear categories had two main causes: high unemployment in workwear-related vocations, and short-term supply programs caused by the demise of certain Canadian workwear manufacturers. Sales of private label bottoms increased as the Company began to implement its strategy of increasing its private label business. Children's wear is not a significant business for the Company, and the western wear growth relates to a very low sales base. Going forward, the Company will aim to recoup the sales lost during the recession in workwear and brand name bottoms, while continuing to focus on increasing its casual wear and private label bottoms businesses.

There were 40 comparable franchise stores of the 45 open at January 30, 1993 and the 57 open at January 25, 1992. Of these 40 stores, 32 (or 80%) increased sales over the previous year. The overall same-store franchise sales increase for the year was 11%. If we exclude the nine franchise stores that performed exceptionally well, the comparable store sales increase drops to 5.3%.

Along with this modest sales growth, the Company improved margins from 35.2% for the year ending January 25, 1992 to 36.3% for the year ending January 30, 1993. In the area of purchase markup, there was an improvement of $2,600,000 over the previous year on similar total sales, for a full two points of markup. This was achieved not by retail price increases, but through a blend of business changes and better buying. Markdowns in dollars were virtually identical to a year ago. But because shrinkage and freight charges increased and fewer volume rebates were earned, gross margin dollars improved by only $1,607,000. The markup on our opening inventories continued to improve, to 41.2% at January 30, 1993 from 40.2% at January 25, 1992 and 39.1% at January 26, 1991.

Front line expenses increased by $724,000, as follows:

Front Line Expenses

	Fiscal 1992	Fiscal 1993	Variance (000s)
Staff	$ 9,538	$11,115	$ 1,577
Advertising	$ 8,032	$ 7,018	$ (1,014)
Other	$ 3,467	$ 3,906	$ 439
Occupancy	$14,556	$14,886	$ 330
Depreciation	$ 2,238	$ 1,736	$ (502)
Interest— short term	$ 1,258	$ 1,152	$ (106)

The six new corporate stores and five repossessed franchise stores, less the six corporate stores closures that operated for part of the year, accounted for most of the front line expense increases.

The franchise contribution decreased by $525,000. As the Company repossessed five franchise stores and closed seven other franchise locations, it took $1,098,000 of writeoffs—$468,000 more than in fiscal 1992. The Company believes that most of its franchise problems are now behind it.

During fiscal 1993 back line costs were reduced by $3,652,000, as follows:

Back Line Expenses

	Fiscal 1992	Fiscal 1993	Variance (000s)
Staff	$8,743	$6,631	$(2,112)
Other	$2,441	$2,665	$ 224
Occupancy	$ 985	$ 888	$ (97)
Depreciation	$1,566	$1,294	$ (272)

Software developmemt costs	$ 660	$1,342	$ 682
Interest— long term	$1,096	$ 978	$ (118)
Senior executive settlements	$1,959	$ —	$(1,959)

The combination of the $1,607,000 increase in gross margin dollars, the $724,000 increase in front line expenses, the $525,000 decrease in franchise contribution and the $3,652,000 decrease in back line costs produced a $4,010,000 improvement from operations, or $3,567,000 after taxes.

BALANCE SHEET

During the course of fiscal 1993 the Company concluded the following refinancings:

REFINANCING IN FISCAL 1993
(thousands)

Subordinated debentures Series A (excludes accrued interest)	$3,850
Subordinated debentures Series B (excludes some repayments)	$ 800
8,000,000 common shares issued to institutional investors (net of issues costs)	$7,204
450,821 common shares issued to employees	$ 456

These refinancings, coupled with improved operations showing cash flow in the black, resulted in $14,870,000 of working capital at January 30, 1993. This was $10,474,000 ahead of the prior year's $4,396,000. The Company's much improved working capital position was highlighted by reduced inventories, franchise receivables, supplier payables and bank indebtedness. The current ratio at January 30, 1993 was 1.64/1 compared to 1.11/1 at January 25, 1992 and 1.15/1 at January 26, 1991.

The Company has also improved its debt-to-equity ratio, to 2.04/1 at January 30, 1993 from 4.07/1 at January 25, 1992 and 2.71/1 at January 26, 1991.

The Company has managed current and debt-to-equity ratios to the target levels set in the financial objectives section of this report. More than $3,000,000 of capital expenditures are planned for fiscal 1994 (exclusive of computer lease activities) and the repayment of the Series A Subordinated Debentures is required on February 1, 1994. The Company therefore concluded a rights offering on March 18, 1993 yielding $3,600,000 of net equity. This additional equity, combined with expected operating results, will keep the Company's current and debt-to-equity ratios as at January 29, 1994 within the guidelines set out in our financial objectives.

SOURCE: 1993 annual report of Mark's Work Wearhouse, #30, 1035–64 Avenue S.E., Calgary, Alberta T2H 2J7. Reprinted by permission.

With respect to the discussion of financial results, the company goes well beyond a simple rehashing of information already available from the comparative financial statements. Note the detailed information about sales categories and trends. Note also the distinction between "front line" expenses (expenses of people who come face to face with customers) and "back line" expenses (providing support to the front line). Front-line expenses have increased for the year, in keeping with the company's drive to return to profitability, while back-line expenses have decreased, reflecting efforts to control costs. The discussion of refinancing in relation to planned capital expenditures and target ratios should help convince the reader that the company knows clearly where it wants to go. The discussion of risks and uncertainties also goes well beyond minimum MD&A requirements. Planned levels of certain risk measures and of some major sources of uncertainty are candidly discussed.

Summary

MD&A represents a major step taken by a government regulatory body to set standards that go beyond the requirements of GAAP. The reason for this, presumably, is that the accounting recommendations of the *CICA Handbook* relate primarily to financial statements and their footnotes, whereas the concern of the SEC here is with regulating the discussion by management contained in the annual reports.

The specific requirements of MD&A are of interest in their own right, because they lay out major reporting standards and responsibilities for management. These apply to all firms that are required to register with the SEC.

MD&A is also of interest because it further illustrates how the decision usefulness approach to financial reporting has influenced, and been accepted by, a major standard setting body. It has the potential to expand the set of information available to the market.

4.8.3 FUTURE-ORIENTED FINANCIAL INFORMATION

Financial Forecasting Standards

We now consider another standard that has the potential for a further expansion of the information available to investors. In September 1989, the CICA adopted Section 4250, dealing with future-oriented financial information (FOFI). According to this section, the "objective of presenting future-oriented financial information is to provide external users with information that assists them in evaluating any entity's financial prospects" (paragraph 4250.02).

Section 4250 does not *require* that FOFI be presented. Rather, it provides standards for measurement, presentation, and disclosure for those firms that do decide to disclose FOFI to external users. FOFI is thus an incentive mechanism available to those who wish to develop a reputation for full, timely disclosure.

Despite, or perhaps because of, its voluntary nature, Section 4250 represents a major extension of the full-disclosure principle. It applies both to *forecasts* (prepared using assumptions that reflect the entity's planned courses of action for the period covered) and to *projections* (prepared using assumptions that reflect the entity's planned courses of action for the period covered, together with one or more assumptions that are not necessarily the most probable in management's judgement). Thus, projections are prepared to answer "what if" questions, whereas forecasts are estimates of the most probable outcomes of planned activities. Here, we will consider only forecasts.

Section 4250 recognizes that a forecast is only as good as its underlying assumptions. For example, these should be reasonable and supportable and reflect the *most probable* economic conditions and planned courses of action. Statistically speaking, the most probable value of a random variable is its **mode**, which may differ from the arithmetic mean. Nevertheless, we may take this most probable requirement as being reasonably consistent with an expected value approach to decision-making under uncertainty.

It is interesting that Section 4250 avoids many of the estimation problems of RRA. Thus, "The period covered by future-oriented financial information should not extend beyond the point in time for which such information can be reasonably estimated" (paragraph 4250.15). The section goes on to suggest that this period would normally be one year. Thus, the problems arising from frequent and material revisions to the estimates, which we saw in Chapter 2 as a major problem with the practical application of RRA, should be minimized. Also, because of the short time horizon of the forecast, discounting, and resulting difficult choice of a discount rate, would not normally be needed.

Another interesting point is how Section 4250 takes steps to maximize the usefulness of the FOFI to the user. In addition to requiring disclosure of significant assumptions, it requires that FOFI "should be prepared in accordance with the accounting policies expected to be used in presenting historical financial statements for the future period" (paragraph 4250.18), and "should be presented in the format of historical financial statements and include at least an income statement" (paragraph 4250.20). Clearly, the intent here is to present the FOFI in common and well-understood format so as to enhance the user's ability to compare it with subsequent actual results.

Thus, we see that Section 4250 provides a major opportunity for improved disclosure. It goes well beyond the simple statement of SFAC1 that users' expectations about the future enterprise performance are at least partly based on "evaluations of past enterprise performance." While the responsibility for estimation of future profitability still remains with the user, particularly for projections beyond one year, FOFI disclosures certainly provide an important and potentially useful linkage between past and future. Furthermore, they do this in a manner which does not compromise the integrity of the generally accepted historical cost financial statements.

An Example of a Financial Forecast

Exhibit 4.2 gives extracts from the 1994 financial forecast of Mark's Work Wearhouse, from its 1993 annual report.

EXHIBIT 4.2   Financial Forecast from 1993 Annual Report of Mark's Work Wearhouse

Earnings per Common Share for the 52 weeks ending January 29, 1994 are forecast to be in the range of two cents to seven cents per share.

This forecast represents, in management's judgement, the most likely set of conditions and the Company's most likely course of action. The reader is cautioned that some assumptions used preparing our forecast, although considered reasonable at the time of preparation, may prove to be incorrect. The actual results achieved during the forecast period will inevitably vary from the forecast results, and variations may be material.

The Company completed these forecasts on March 24, 1993. The financial reports issued by the Company to its shareholders during the forecast year will contain either a statement that there are no significant changes to be made to the forecast or an updated earnings per share forecast accompanied by explanations of significant changes.

KEY ASSUMPTIONS

	Actual 53 Weeks Ended January 30, 1993	Forecast (unaudited) 52 Weeks Ended January 29, 1994	
		Conservative	Operating Budget
Same corporate store sales increase	3.0%	3.0%	5.8%
Same franchise store sales increase	11.0%	7.0%	7.0%
Extra week of sales in fiscal 1993	$1,700,000	$(1,700,000)	$(1,700,000)
Gross margin	36.2%	38.6%	38.6%
Inventory turnover	2.3 times	2.4 times	2.6 times
Number of corporate store openings	6 stores	8 stores	8 stores
Sales increases from part-year fiscal 1993 corporate stores becoming full-year stores in fiscal 1994	$ —	$14,521,000	$15,755,000
Number of franchise stores	45 stores	44 stores	44 stores
Operating line—interest rates	8.6%	8.0%	8.0%
Capital expenditures			
Real estate and other	$1,578,000	$ 3,000,000	$ 3,000,000
Systems	$1,582,000	$ 966,000	$ 966,000
New equity financing (net)	$7,660,000	$ 3,600,000	$ 3,600,000
Long-term debt financing			
Subordinate debt	$4,650,000	$ —	$ —
Capital leases	$2,106,000	$ 1,532,000	$ 1,532,000
Long-term debt repayments			
Subordinate debt	$ —	$ 4,925,000	$ 4,925,000
Capital leases	$ 942,000	$ 1,609,000	$ 1,609,000

SOURCE: 1993 annual report of Mark's Work Wearhouse, #30, 1035—64 Avenue S.E., Calgary, Alberta T2H 2J7. Reprinted by permission.

The following points should be noted about the Mark's Work Wearhouse forecast. First, the period covered is one year, and no discounting is applied. Also, the forecast information is presented in the same format as the summarized actual 1993 historical-cost-based results. Mark's Work Wearhouse has opted for a range forecast, also allowed by Section 4250. Second, notice that key assumptions are given, again in comparison with realized values for the current year. Mark's Work Wearhouse's forecast represents an interesting example of what can be done to convey relevant information to financial statement users beyond the minimum requirements of GAAP and MD&A.

Summary

It is interesting to contemplate why Mark's Work Wearhouse goes well beyond minimal disclosure requirements. One reason may be a relatively less litigious environment than other jurisdictions, such as the United States. The company may feel that it is unlikely to be sued if its financial forecast and other forward-looking information are not satisfied.

However, another reason may be that Mark's Work Wearhouse, particularly since it was in a loss position in 1993, may want to communicate inside information about its expectations of future profitability. This information is revealed not only by the amounts of forecasted profits but by the firm's willingness to put itself "under the gun" of a general-use forecast. Yet another reason may be that Mark's Work Wearhouse, being a relatively small public corporation, may feel a greater need to reveal information about itself than very large corporations, about which more is known from media and other sources.

4.9   Summary and Conclusions

Efficient securities market theory has major implications for financial accounting. One of these is that efficiency is defined relative to a stock of publicly known information. Financial reporting has a role to play in improving the amount, timing, and accuracy of this stock.

Examples of full disclosure standards include MD&A and financial forecasts. Both of these standards have the potential to convey information beyond that contained in the conventional historical-cost-based financial statements. This potential is not only in the information contained in the disclosure per se. The very act of disclosing or not disclosing a forecast, or the extent to which the firm goes beyond the general MD&A requirements, also tells the market something about the firm.

Full disclosure has two main benefits, which can be attained simultaneously. One is to enable investors to make better decisions. The other is to improve the ability of securities markets to direct investment to its most productive uses. The reason why these benefits are attained simultaneously, of course, is that better information enables more-informed buy/sell decisions, and it is demand and supply that determines market price.

Another implication of efficient securities market theory appears in Beaver's 1973 analysis. This is that the specific accounting policies adopted by firms do not matter as long as they have no differential cash flow effects across those policies, full disclosure is made of the particular policies used, and investors have sufficient information to convert from one policy to another. The reason, according to efficient market theory, is that investors as a whole will *look through* reported net income to its underlying implications for future cash flows. In so doing, they will take into account the specific accounting policies used in calculating net income. Thus, firms' choices of amortization policy, of successful-efforts or full-cost accounting for oil and gas exploration, of deferral or flow-through for deferred income taxes, and so on, will not affect the efficient market prices of their securities, providing the specific accounting policies they are using are fully disclosed. Thus, we see that the full-disclosure principle extends to disclosure of accounting policies.

Accountants are improving their understanding of the role of information in determining price. In essence, market price aggregates the collective information processing and decision-making abilities of investors. Thus, market price itself has considerable information content, which individuals may use as an input into their decisions.

This process contains a logical contradiction, however, since if price is fully informative, no one would bother to collect additional, costly, information. In effect, market price contains within it the seeds of its own destruction. However, we can identify two factors to prevent this from happening:

- Noise and liquidity traders introduce a random component to market price, which prevents market price from being fully informative about future value.

- Information asymmetry, in particular the presence of inside information, means that not all relevant information is in the public domain. Then, investors have the potential to earn extra profits if they can ferret out some of this inside information. Improved disclosure, as in MD&A and forecasting, may provide investors with some help in this regard.

As Beaver (1973) put it, accountants are in competition with other information sources. We now know that market price is one of these other sources. Think of market price as aggregating all relevant "other" information up to the time of release of the financial statements. The question then is: Is it cost-effective for rational investors to inform themselves by utilizing the financial statements? Again, the accountants' answer is the concept of full disclosure. By increasing the information content of financial reporting, not only do accountants help preserve their competitive advantage, they also improve social welfare by reducing the adverse impact of inside information.

We thus see that if historical-cost-based accounting can meet the competitive challenge, it will be useful to investors by cost-effectively supplying relevant and reliable information. Furthermore, relevance can be enhanced by full disclosure, as in footnotes, MD&A, and forecasts. If investors do in fact find accounting information useful, this should show up as a response of security prices to this information. In the next chapter, we will examine empirical evidence in this regard.

Notes

1. More generally, the random fluctuation could be about a trend line. For example, the price of a security may have an upward trend over time.

2. This abnormal return should not be confused with abnormal earnings of P.V. Ltd. in Example 2.2. While the idea is the same, abnormal return here refers to a *market* return, whereas abnormal earnings refer to *accounting* net income.

3. Estimating beta by least-squares regression is not inconsistent with the calculation of beta described in Section 3.7.1. The regression approach merely provides a convenient framework to carry out the estimation. To see this, note the definition of the coefficient of an independent variable in a regression model—it is the amount of change in the dependent variable (R_{jt}) for a unit change in the independent variable (R_{Mt}). This is exactly the definition of beta. As explained in Section 3.7.1, beta measures the strength of the variation in a security's return as the market return varies.

4. This argument assumes that the disclosure is truthful. Truthful disclosure can be encouraged by, for example, an audit.

Questions and Problems

1. Two firms, of the same size and risk, release their annual reports on the same day. It turns out that they each report the same amount of net income. Following the release, the share price of one firm rose strongly while the other rose hardly at all.

   Explain how it is possible for the market to react positively to one firm's annual report and hardly at all to the other when the firms are similar in size, risk, and profitability. (CGA-Canada)

2. Shares of firm A and firm B are traded on an efficient market. The two firms are of the same size and risk. They both report the same net income. However, you see in the footnotes that firm A uses the LIFO inventory method and declining-balance amortization for capital assets, while firm B uses the FIFO inventory method and straight-line amortization. (CGA-Canada)

   Which firm's shares should sell at the higher price-to-earnings ratio, all other things being equal? Assume a period of rising prices.

3. Some firms, such as Mark's Work Wearhouse (see Section 4.8.3) report financial forecasts. Yet few firms report the present value of their future cash receipts. Why do you think firms seem to be more willing to report FOFI than present values? Which do you think is more useful to users of financial statements? (CGA-Canada)

4. Using the concept of information asymmetry, answer the following questions:

    a. You observe that used cars sold by new car dealers sell for a higher price, for models of same make, year, and condition, than used cars sold by used car dealers. Why?

    b. Why would a fire insurance policy contain a $150 deductible provision?

    c. Why would a life insurance company require a medical examination before approving applications for new policies?

    d. A firm plans to raise additional capital by means of a new issue of common shares. Before doing so, it hires a well-known investment house to help design and market the issue, and also switches auditors from a small, local firm to a "Big Six" firm. Why?   (CGA-Canada)

5. To what extent might the financial press provide a relevant source of information for investors? Would this information source conflict with or complement financial statement information? Explain.   (CGA-Canada)

6. Normally, we think of the audit as a mechanism to add credibility to financial statement information. Explain, in decision theory terms, how increased credibility is useful to investors.

    Could the audit have information content beyond the credibility it adds to the financial statements? Explain.   (CGA-Canada)

7. On January 21, 1993 the *Wall Street Journal* reported that General Electric Co.'s fourth-quarter 1992 earnings rose 6.2% to $1.34 billion or $1.57 a share, setting a new record and bringing the earnings for 1992 to $4.73 billion or $5.51 a share. After adjusting for extraordinary items, 1992 earnings from continuing operations were up about 10% from the previous year.

    The *Journal* also reported that forecasts made by analysts averaged $1.61 per share for the fourth quarter of 1992, and from $5.50 to $5.60 per share for the whole year. One analyst was quoted as saying that 1992 "wasn't a bad year for GE" despite the downturn in the stock market on the day of the earnings announcement.

    Yet, on the same day the fourth-quarter earnings were announced, General Electric Co.'s stock price fell $1.50 to $82.625 on the New York Stock Exchange.

    Required

    a. Give two reasons to explain why this could happen.

    b. Use the Sharpe-Lintner CAPM (Equations 4.1 and 4.2) to explain how the new information caused the current price slip. Calculations are not required.

    c. Give another reason, that is, other than GE's earnings announcement, that could have caused the share price decline.

8. Atlas Ltd. is a listed public company. It is in a volatile industry. The market price of its shares is highly sensitive to its earnings. The company's annual meeting is to be held soon, and the president is concerned, expecting to be attacked strongly by a dissident group of shareholders.

One issue the dissidents are expected to focus on is the company's depreciation policy. They will claim that the annual declining-balance depreciation charges are excessive—that the company's "conservative" depreciation policy seriously understates annual earnings per share, causing the shares' market price to be artificially low. Threats have even been made of suing management and the board of directors to "recover the resulting loss in market value, relative to shareholders in companies with less conservative depreciation policies, suffered by Atlas shareholders."

The president has asked you to help prepare a defence against the expected attack on the company's depreciation policy.

Required

Write a memo summarizing how you would recommend the president respond to this attack. (CGA-Canada)

9. The article "GM to Take Charge of $20.8-Billion" here reproduced from the *Globe and Mail* (February 2, 1993) describes the potential impact of SFAS 106, "Accounting for Postretirement Benefits Other Than Pensions," on General Motors and Ford. For example, it appears that General Motors will be required to record a liability of $20.8 billion, reducing its shareholders' equity from $27.8 billion to $7 billion, about a 75% reduction.

Required

Describe and explain how you would expect the securities markets to react to this information.

10. The article by Baruch Lev here reproduced appeared in the *Wall Street Journal* (November 30, 1992).

GM TO TAKE CHARGE
OF $20.8-BILLION

ATLANTA—General Motors Corp. will take a $20.8-billion (U.S.) charge against 1992 earnings to account for a new way of estimating retiree health care costs, the auto maker's directors decided yesterday.

The charge, which will not affect the struggling auto maker's cash flow, will leave GM with the largest annual loss of any U.S. corporation, eclipsing the company's 1991 loss of $4.45-billion, which was a record at that time.

Including accounting changes, other charges and losses on its North American operations, GM's 1992 loss could approach $23-billion.

The $20.8-billion is a non-cash charge. It reduces GM's net worth to about $7-billion, still sufficient to pay stock dividends under the laws of Delaware, where GM is incorporated.

Separately, GM said it would take a $744-million fourth-quarter restructuring charge for its National Car Rental Systems business. In a recent U.S. Securities and Exchange Commission filing, GM estimated that charge at about $300-million.

The accounting change, required by the Financial Accounting Standards Board of all publicly traded U.S. companies, has had a major effect on each of the Big Three U.S. auto makers.

Ford Motor Co. said it would take a $7.5-billion charge against 1992 earnings to account for the change. Chrysler Corp. said it has not decided whether to take its $4.7-billion charge as a lump sum in the first quarter or spread it over 20 years, as the standard allows.

GM had estimated its charge for adopting the new accounting standard at $16-billion to $24-billion. The $20.8-billion actual charge includes its workers, GM Hughes Electronics Corp. and its financial subsidiary, General Motors Acceptance Corp.

The company's EDS Corp. subsidiary does not pay health benefits, so it was exempt.

SOURCE: *Globe and Mail*, February 2, 1993. Reprinted by permission of The Associated Press.

THE CURSE OF GREAT EXPECTATIONS

Hewlett-Packard's shareholders lost $3 billion on Friday, Aug. 7, when its stock price plunged nearly 18%. Did the giant electronics manufacturer suffer a sales or earnings setback? Did a new product line flop? Or perhaps severe financial difficulties surfaced? Far from it.

In recessed world markets, H-P's sales and earnings had continually increased for the preceding 10 quarters, with 40% boosts in the previous two; no major products failed; H-P's competitive position did not erode precipitously; and its financial leverage—a measure of risk—is among the lowest of any major U.S. company. The reason for the Friday price dive was H-P's announcement that, while sales were up 15% in the July quarter, earnings were flat, falling short of analysts' expectations.

H-P's case is not unique. Harley-Davidson lost 31% of its market value on Oct. 23 and 24, 1991, when it announced quarterly earnings of 49 cents per share (a hefty increase of 36%). The reason? Analysts' expectations had ranged between 60 and 80 cents.

Even meeting analysts' expectations is no longer a recipe for price stability. The Gap's announcement (March 5) of a nearly 30% increase in quarterly sales and a 50% increase in earnings was deemed disappointing (its price dropped 5%) since, in the words of one analyst, "Investors had become conditioned to believe that earnings would exceed expectations."

The large price drops caused by unmet, or even just-met, analysts' expectations are detrimental to corporations, their managers and shareholders. The earnings disappointment often causes an overreaction (Harley-Davidson's stock regained 25% of the initial drop within three trading days of the earnings announcement). This results in undue losses to investors who sold in the panic. Furthermore, repeated earnings surprises shake investors' confidence in the stock's stability, thereby raising the company's cost of capital, which in turn impedes its growth.

But perhaps the most costly consequence of unmet expectations is litigation against managers and auditors. Of course, the fact that an earnings announcement is surprisingly low does not necessarily imply that managers had prior information and had failed to warn investors. Managers are often as surprised as outsiders when they first learn the new earnings figure. Nevertheless, in a Pavlovian reaction, some lawyers file class action suits whenever a share price drops below a certain range, alleging managers' failure to warn investors ahead of time. The fact that over 90% of these suits settle out of court practically ensures plaintiff lawyers a handsome return on such activity.

Ironically, the record of those analysts whose forecasts are highly regarded is, on average, far from impeccable. While analysts' annual earnings estimates appear more accurate than "naive" extrapolations mechanically derived from past earnings, the accuracy of short horizon analysts' forecasts (made up to 60 days before the earnings announcements) is not significantly better than estimates based on only an average of past earnings. Research also indicates that analysts are often oblivious to certain simple and repeated patterns in quarterly earnings of corporations. And analysts, in revising their forecasts, appear to overreact to corporate announcements of large earnings changes. Most intriguing is the consistent finding that analysts tend to generate optimistic forecasts.

What's wrong with a bit of optimism in this time of widespread economic gloom? Nothing much, except that optimistic forecasts inevitably lead to disappointments when earnings are released. When these releases result in sharp price declines, costly lawsuits ensue and executives are diverted from managing their businesses. The threat of litigation even drives some managers to meet analysts' expectations at all costs, including manipulating financial reports. This is detrimental to investors and to the competitiveness of the business sector.

Much of the overreaction to earnings announcements that increase stock price volatility can be prevented by the continuous communication of relevant, forward-looking information to the investment community. Such communication, however, is now severely curtailed by managers' concern about being sued for supposedly misleading investors. In a study of 300 companies with the largest deviations (surprises) of earnings from analysts' consensus forecasts, I find that only one firm in 15 preceded the earnings announcement with a quantitative, prospective disclosure concerning earnings or sales (e.g., earnings will range between $2.50 and $3 per share). With such a low level of communication, large surprises are inevitable.

Effective communication calls for a disclosure strategy whereby major plans (e.g., new investments, business alliances, product development) and their expected effects on short-and long-term earnings are routinely announced. This would provide investors with valuable prospective information, decreasing their reliance on analysts. Such communication would also lead to a convergence between managers' and analysts' perceptions. When the opinions and forecasts of analysts are way out of line with those of management, it might be advisable to guide (not manipulate) analysts. For example, in November of last year,

Kimberly-Clark's CEO publicly cautioned analysts that they were overly optimistic about the firm's 1992 performance.

Sometimes the effectiveness of managers' disclosures has to be enhanced by a real action—such as a dividend boost, a stock repurchase, or an increase in the stock ownership of managers and board members. In September 1991, General Dynamics released an upbeat earnings forecast. Apparently aware of investors' skepticism about the prospects of defense contractors, the company announced a plan for a dividend increase and a stock repurchase.

To maintain managers' credibility, it is important to communicate promptly both good and bad news. It is also important to refrain from masking the latter by accounting gimmickry, and to outline what is being done to cope with adversity.

A consistent, proactive disclosure strategy would go a long way toward minimizing stock price volatility, ensuring that shareholder values properly reflect a company's real worth, and—contrary to widespread managerial belief—mitigating the threat of litigation.

Required

a. The article points out major price declines for shares of firms when earnings do not meet analysts' expectations. Are such declines consistent with security market efficiency? Explain.

b. Explain why "the continuous communication of relevant, forward-looking information to the investment community" would be good for investors and for the competitiveness of the business sector.

c. Why would "a consistent, proactive disclosure strategy" go a long way towards mitigating the threat of litigation, rather than increasing it?

11. As discussed in Section 4.8.3, firms may present financial forecasts as part of their annual report. However, it seems that such forecasts are rare, particularly in the United States. An article entitled "Now It's SEC vs. the Lawyers" that appeared in the *Wall Street Journal* (October 28, 1994) suggests a reason: firms may be liable for lawsuits when forecast information is not borne out by subsequent actual results.

According to the article, in 1989 there was an estimated $529 million paid out for security class-action suits. These settlement payments rose to $1.4 billion in 1993. As a result, most companies are unwilling to provide forward-looking estimates, thereby restricting the release of relevant investor information. The SEC, whose job is to protect investors, would like to see this restriction lessened.

The article suggests that the SEC adopt a "business judgement rule." Under this rule the SEC would protect officers and directors that make "good-faith mistakes" against class-action lawsuits that arise from unmet "forward-looking information." However, this rule in no way implies that managers have "an invitation to commit fraud." The SEC will take action against companies whose forecast information demonstrates "a conflict, a lack of good faith, or a failure of honest and reasonable belief."

Required

a. To the extent that firms are discouraged from providing financial forecasts by the prospect of litigation, how could this lead to a negative impact on the proper operation of security markets? Can you give an argument that a litigious environment might actually help proper operation of security markets?

b. The article argues that it would be a "big win for investors" if the SEC was able to encourage more financial forecasting by adopting the business judgement rule. Explain how such a rule may be good for investors.

12. An article entitled "The Pros Get Trounced in Stock Contest" appeared in the *Wall Street Journal* on March 4, 1993. It describes the outcome of the most recent contest, sponsored by the *Journal*, between four investment analysts and a group using a dart-throwing investment strategy.

The "Investment Dartboard Stock-Picking" series of contests began in 1988. Each contest runs for a six-month period. The article states that the contest is between four professional investors who choose a portfolio according to their expertise, and reporters who throw darts randomly at the stock listings to choose a "Dartboard Portfolio."

According to the article, "for the six-month period ended Feb. 28," the team of four experts did their worst picking since the games began in 1988. "The pros trailed the darts by an astonishing margin of 42.3 percentage points." There was a 2.5% rise in the Dow Jones Industrial Average, while the average loss for the pros was 26.7% and the dart-throwers had a gain of 15.6%. However, the cumulative score over all contests now has the analysts leading 18 to 15.

Required

a. Use efficient security markets theory to explain how "dart-throwing" may be a desirable investment strategy.

b. To what extent does the cumulative score of 18 to 15 provide evidence in favour of security market efficiency? Explain.

c. It appears that the contests do not control for possible risk differences between the analysts' and the dart-throwing portfolios. How would you determine whether risk differences were affecting the results? Suppose that on average the analysts chose riskier strategies than the dart-throwers. Would this affect your answer in part **b**? Explain.

The Information Perspective on Decision Usefulness

5.1 Overview

There is a saying that "the proof of the pudding is in the eating." If the efficient markets theory and the decision theories underlying it are reasonable descriptions of reality on average, we should observe the market values of securities responding in predictable ways to new information.

This leads to an examination of empirical research in accounting. Despite the difficulties of designing experiments to test the implications of decision usefulness, accounting research has established that security market prices do in fact respond to at least the net income component of accounting information. The first solid evidence of this was provided by Ball and Brown in 1968. Since then, a large number of empirical studies have documented additional aspects of security market response.

On the basis of these studies, it does seem that accounting information is useful to investors in helping them estimate the expected values and risks of security returns. One has only to contemplate the use of Bayes' theorem in Example 3.1 to see that if accounting information did not have information content there would be no revision of beliefs upon receipt, hence no triggering of buy/sell decisions. Without buy/sell decisions, there would be no price changes. In essence, information is useful if it leads investors to change their beliefs and actions. Furthermore, the degree of usefulness can be measured by the extent of price change following release of the information.

This equating of usefulness to information content is called the **information perspective** on financial reporting, an approach which has dominated financial accounting theory and research since 1968. As we have seen in Sections 3.8 and 4.8, it has also been adopted by major accounting standard setting bodies. The information approach takes the view that investors want to make *their own* predictions of future security returns (instead of having accountants do it for them, as under ideal conditions) and will "gobble up" all useful information in this regard. As mentioned, empirical research has shown that at least some accounting information is perceived as useful. Furthermore, the information approach implies that empirical research can help accountants to further increase usefulness by letting market response guide them as to what information is and is not valued by investors.

> The **information perspective** *on financial reporting is an approach which recognizes individual responsibility for predicting future firm performance and which concentrates on providing useful information for this purpose. The approach recognizes that the market will react to useful information from any source, including financial statements.*

One must be careful, however, when equating usefulness with the extent of security price change. It does *not* follow that *society* will necessarily be better off if accountants base their decisions of what financial statement information to present on the basis of market response to that information. Information is a very complex commodity and its private and social values are not the same. One reason is *cost*. Financial statement users do not generally pay directly for this information. As a result, they may find information useful even though it costs society more (in the form of higher product prices to help firms pay for generating and reporting the information) than the increased usefulness is worth. Furthermore, information affects people differently, requiring complex cost-benefit tradeoffs to balance the competing interests of different constituencies.

These social considerations do not invalidate the information perspective. Accountants can still strive to improve their competitive position in the information marketplace by providing useful information. And, it is still true that securities markets will be more efficient to the extent that security prices provide good indicators of investment opportunities. However, what accountants cannot do is claim that the "best" accounting policy is the one that produces the greatest market response.

5.2 Outline of the Research Problem

5.2.1 REASONS FOR MARKET RESPONSE

We begin by reviewing the reasons why we would predict that the market price of a firm's shares will respond to its financial statement information. For most of this chapter we will confine financial statement information to reported net income. The information content of net income is a topic that has received extensive empirical investigation. Information content of other financial statement components will be discussed in Section 5.8 and in Chapter 6.

Consider the following predictions about investor behaviour, in response to financial statement information:

1. Investors have prior beliefs about the expected return and risk of a firm's shares. These prior beliefs will be based on all publicly available information, including market price, up to just prior to the release of the firm's current net income. Even though they are based on publicly available information, these prior beliefs need not all be the same, because investors will differ in the amount of information they obtain and in their abilities to interpret it. These prior beliefs may also include expectations about the firm's current and future earning power, since future security returns will depend at least in part on profitability.

2. Upon release of current year's net income, certain investors will decide to become more informed, by analyzing the income number. For example, if net income is high, or higher than expected, this is good news. Some investors, by means of Bayes' theorem, would revise upward their beliefs about future earning power and returns. Other investors, who perhaps had high expectations for what current net income should be, might interpret the same net income number as bad news.

3. Investors who have revised their beliefs about future profitability and returns upward will be inclined to buy the firm's shares at their current market price, and vice versa for those who have revised their beliefs downward (their evaluations of the riskiness of these shares may also be revised).

4. We would expect to observe the volume of shares traded to increase shortly after the firm reports its net income. Furthermore, this volume should be greater the greater are the differences in investors' prior beliefs and in their interpretations of the current financial information. If the investors who interpret reported net income as good news (and hence have increased their expectations of future profitability and returns) outweigh those who interpret it as bad news, we would expect to observe an increase in the market price of the firm's shares, and vice versa.

Beaver (1968), in a classic study, examined trading volume reaction. He found a dramatic increase in volume during the week of release of earnings announcements. Further details of Beaver's findings are included in question 8 at the end of this chapter. In the balance of this chapter we will concentrate on market price reaction. Market price reaction provides a stronger test of decision usefulness than volume reaction, because we have better models to predict price reaction, such as the CAPM, discussed in section 4.3. It is less clear how to make precise directional predictions for volume.

You will recognize that the preceding predictions follow the decision theory and efficient markets theory of Chapters 3 and 4 quite closely. If these theories are to have relevance to accountants, their predictions should be borne out empirically. An empirical researcher could test these predictions by obtaining a sample of firms that issue annual reports and investigating whether the volume and price reactions to good or bad news in earnings occur as the theories lead us to believe. This is not as easy as it might seem, however, for a number of reasons, as we shall discuss next.

5.2.2   *FINDING THE MARKET RESPONSE*

1.   Efficient market theory implies that the market will react quickly to new information. As a result, it is important to know *when* current year's reported net income first became publicly known. If the researcher looked for volume and price effects even a few days too late, no effects may be observed even though they had existed.

     Researchers have solved this problem by using the date the firm's net income was reported in the financial media such as the *Wall Street Journal*. If the efficient market is going to react, it should do so in a **narrow window** of a few days surrounding this date.

2.   The good or bad news in reported net income is usually evaluated relative to what investors *expected*. If a firm reported net income of, say, $2 million, and this was what investors had expected (from, say, quarterly reports, speeches by company officials, analysts' predictions, and, perhaps, forward-looking information in MD&A and forecasts), there would hardly be much information content in reported net income. Investors would have already revised their beliefs on the basis of the earlier information. Things would be different, however, if investors had expected $2 million and reported net income was $3 million. This good news would trigger rapid belief revision about the future prospects of the firm.

     This means that researchers must obtain a proxy for what investors expected net income to be. This can be accomplished by using analysts' forecasts of earnings for the quarter or year in question. Alternatively, expected net income can be estimated by projecting the time series of the firm's past reported net incomes. A simple projection model would be to expect that current year's net income will be the same as last year's. Then, the change in net income is a proxy for its unexpected component. Evidence by Brown, Griffin, Hagerman, and Zmijewski (1987), who studied the quarterly forecasting performance of one forecasting organization (Value Line), suggests that analysts outperform time series models in terms of accuracy. Yet another alternative, used in some earlier studies, is to calculate an accounting beta, that is, to estimate the past linear relationship between a firm's reported net income and the average net income of all firms. Given average net income for all firms for the current year, the firm's expected net income can be estimated on the basis of this relationship. For example, if over the last five years a firm's net income has averaged 1.2 times that of all firms and if average net income for all firms this year is $100, then expected net income for the firm in question is taken as $120.

3. There are always many events taking place which affect a firm's share volume and price. This means that a market response to reported net income can be hard to find. For example, suppose a firm released its current year's net income, containing good news, on the same day the federal government first announced a substantial increase in the deficit. Such an announcement would probably affect prices of all or most securities on the market, which in turn might swamp the price impact of the firm's earnings release. Thus, it is desirable to separate the impact of these factors on share returns.

5.2.3   SEPARATING MARKET-WIDE AND FIRM-SPECIFIC FACTORS

As described in Section 4.3, the market model is widely used to *ex post* separate market-wide and firm-specific factors that affect security returns. Figure 5.1 gives a graphical illustration of the market model for firm j for period t, where we take the length of the period as one day. Longer time periods, such as a week, month, or year, and even shorter periods, are also used by researchers.

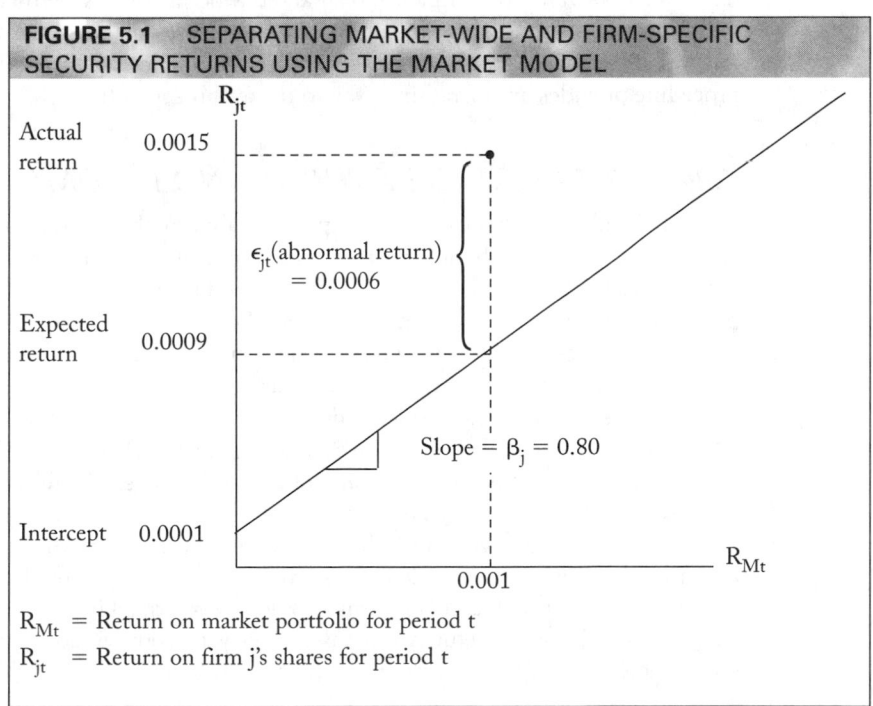

FIGURE 5.1   SEPARATING MARKET-WIDE AND FIRM-SPECIFIC SECURITY RETURNS USING THE MARKET MODEL

R_{jt}

Actual return   0.0015

ϵ_{jt}(abnormal return) = 0.0006

Expected return   0.0009

Slope = β_j = 0.80

Intercept   0.0001

0.001

R_{Mt}

R_{Mt} = Return on market portfolio for period t
R_{jt} = Return on firm j's shares for period t

The figure shows the relationship between the return on firm j's shares and the return on the market portfolio (proxied, for example, by the Dow Jones Index).

Consider the equation of the market model, repeated here from Section 4.3:

$$R_{jt} = \alpha_j + \beta_j R_{Mt} + \epsilon_{jt}$$

As described in Section 4.3, the researcher will obtain past data on R_{jt} and R_{Mt} and use regression analysis to estimate the coefficients of the model. Suppose that this yields $\alpha_j = 0.0001$ and $\beta_j = 0.80$, as shown in the figure.[1]

Now, armed with this estimate of the market model for firm j, the researcher can consult the *Wall Street Journal* to find the day of the firm's current earnings announcement. Call this day "day 0." Suppose that for day 0 the return on the Dow Jones Index was 0.001.[2] Then, the estimated market model for firm j is used to predict the return on firm j's shares for this day. As shown in Figure 5.1, this expected return[3] is 0.0009. Now assume that the *actual* return on firm j's shares for day 0 is 0.0015. Then, the difference between actual and expected returns is 0.0006 (that is, $\epsilon_{jt} = 0.0006$ for this day). This 0.0006 is an estimate of the *abnormal* (also called unexpected or firm-specific) return on firm j's shares for that day.[4] This abnormal return is also interpreted as the rate of return on firm j's shares for day 0 *after removing* the influence of market-wide factors. Note that this interpretation is consistent with Example 3.3, where we separated the factors that affect share returns into market-wide and firm-specific categories. The present procedure provides an operational way to make this separation.

5.2.4 COMPARING RETURNS AND INCOME

The empirical researcher can now compare the abnormal share return on day 0 as calculated above with the unexpected component of the firm's current reported net income. If this unexpected net income is "good news" (that is, a positive unexpected net income) then, given security market efficiency, a positive abnormal return constitutes evidence that investors on average are reacting favourably to the unexpected good news in earnings. A similar line of reasoning applies if the current earnings announcement is bad news.

To increase the power of the investigation, the researcher may wish to similarly compare a few days on either side of day 0. It is possible, for example, that the efficient market might learn of the good or bad earnings news a day or two early. Conversely, positive or negative abnormal returns may continue for a day or two after day 0 while the market digests the information, although market efficiency implies that any excess returns should die out quickly. Consequently, the summing of abnormal returns for a 3-to-5-day narrow window around day 0 seems more reasonable than examining day 0 only. It also helps protect against the possibility that the date of publication of current earnings in the financial media may not be a completely accurate estimate of the date of their public availability.

If positive and negative abnormal returns surrounding good or bad earnings news are found to hold across a sample of firms, the researcher may conclude that predictions based on the decision theory and efficient security markets theory are supported. This would in turn support the decision usefulness approach to financial accounting and reporting, because, if investors did not find the reported net income information useful, a market response would hardly be observed.

Of course, this methodology is not foolproof—a number of assumptions and estimations have to be made along the way. One complication is that other firm-specific information frequently comes along around the time of a firm's earnings announcement. For example, if firm j announced a stock split or a change in its dividend on the same day that it released its current earnings, it would be hard to know if a market response was due to one or the other. However, researchers can cope with this by simply removing such firms from the sample.

Another complication is the estimation of a firm's beta, needed to separate market-wide and firm-specific returns as in Figure 5.1. As mentioned, this estimation is usually based on a regression analysis of past data using the market model. Then, the estimated beta is the slope of the regression line. However, a firm's beta may change over time, as its operations and/or its capital structure change, for example. If the estimated beta is different from the true beta, this affects the calculation of abnormal return, possibly biasing the results of the investigation.

There are a variety of ways to cope with this complication. For example, it may be possible to get a "second opinion" on beta by estimating it from financial statement information rather than from market data. (This is considered in Section 5.7.) Alternatively, beta may be estimated from a period after the earnings announcement and compared with the estimate from a period before the announcement.

Also there are ways to separate market-wide and firm-specific returns that ignore beta. For example, we can estimate firm-specific returns by the difference between firm j's stock return during period 0 and the average return on its shares over some prior period. Or, we can take the difference between firm j's return during period 0 and the return on the market portfolio for the same period.

The rationale for these simpler procedures is that the market model is just that—a model. There is no guarantee that it adequately captures the real process generating share returns. Also, there are a variety of market portfolio return indices available, of which the Dow Jones Index is only one. Which one should be used? Thus, because of modelling and measurement problems, estimation of beta may introduce more error into the abnormal returns calculation than it removes by controlling for risk.[5]

These issues were examined by Brown and Warner (1980) in a simulation study. Despite modelling and measurement problems such as those mentioned above, Brown and Warner concluded that, for monthly return windows, the market model-based procedure outlined in Section 5.2.3 performed reasonably well relative to alternatives, including the two mentioned above. Consequently, this is the procedure we shall concentrate on.

Using the market model procedure, it does appear that the market reacts to earnings information much as the theories predict. We will now review the first solid evidence of this reaction, the famous 1968 Ball and Brown study.

5.3 The Ball and Brown Study

5.3.1 METHODOLOGY AND FINDINGS

In 1968, Ball and Brown (BB) began a tradition of empirical capital markets research in accounting which continues to this day. They were the first to provide convincing scientific evidence that firms' security market prices responded to the information content of financial statements. A review of their paper is worthwhile because their basic methodology, and adaptations and extensions of it, continues to be used. Their paper continues to provide guidance, as well as encouragement, to those who wish to better understand the decision usefulness of financial reporting.

BB examined a sample of 261 New York Stock Exchange (NYSE) firms over nine years from 1957 to 1965. They concentrated on the information content of earnings, to the exclusion of other potentially informative financial statement components such as liquidity and capital structure. One reason for this, as mentioned earlier, was that earnings for NYSE firms were typically announced in the media prior to actual release of the annual report so that it was relatively easy to determine when the information first became publicly available.

BB's first task was to measure the information content of earnings. The measure they used was quite coarse, being simply whether reported earnings were greater than what the market had expected (GN), or less than expected (BN). Of course, this requires a proxy for the market's expectation. BB used two. The first proxy was based on the **accounting beta** discussed in Section 5.2.2. As they put it:

> If, in prior years, the income of a firm has been related to the incomes of other firms in a particular way, then knowledge of that past relation, together with a knowledge of the incomes of those other firms for the present year, yields a conditional expectation for the present income of the firm. Thus, apart from confirmation effects, the amount of new information conveyed by the present income number can be approximated by the difference between the actual change in income and its conditional expectation. (BB, page 161)

The second proxy was to assume that the market's expectation of current earnings was equal to last year's actual earnings, from which it follows that unexpected earnings is simply the change in earnings. This simple time series approach yielded results similar to those of using accounting beta. We will confine our attention to the accounting beta proxy.

To obtain "knowledge of that past relation," BB examined pre-1957 data for each firm in their sample. For example, suppose that in the years leading up to 1957 firm j's earning changes[6] averaged 75% of the earnings changes of the firms in the sample. Also suppose that the average earnings change for all the sample firms in 1957 was[7] +$100. Then, the proxy for the 1957 expected earnings change of firm j was +$75. In effect, this procedure assumes that the market knew of this past relationship and, in addition, that the market had a good idea in early 1958 how firms in general were doing 1957-earnings-wise and set its expectations for firm j accordingly. Now, suppose that firm j announced its 1957 earnings change in February 1958 as +$90. This exceeds the expectation, so BB would classify firm j as GN for 1957. This procedure was repeated for all the years 1957–65 and for all sample firms. Thus, every earnings release in the sample was classified as GN or BN, relative to expectations.

The next task was to evaluate the market return on the shares of the sample firms near the time of each earnings announcement. This was done, for the most part, according to the abnormal returns procedure illustrated in Figure 5.1. The only difference was that BB used monthly returns (daily returns were not available on computer tape in 1968).

Analogously to Figure 5.1, suppose that the return on the NYSE market portfolio in February 1958 was 0.001, yielding an expected return for February of 0.0009. BB would then calculate the actual return on firm j shares for February 1958. Suppose this was 0.0015, yielding an abnormal return for February of 0.0006. Since firm j's 1957 earnings were reported in February 1958 and since its shares earned 0.0006 over and above the market in this month, one might suspect that the reason for the positive abnormal return was that investors were reacting favourably to the GN information in earnings.

The question then was: Was this pattern repeated across the sample? The answer was yes. If we take all the GN earnings announcements in the sample (there were 1,231), the *average* abnormal security market return in the month of earnings release was strongly positive. Conversely, the average abnormal return for the 1,109 bad news earnings announcements in the sample was strongly negative. This provides substantial evidence that the market did respond to the good or bad news in earnings during a narrow window consisting of the month of earnings announcement release.

An interesting and important aspect of the BB study was that they repeated their abnormal security market returns calculation for a **wide window** consisting of each of the 11 months prior to and the 6 months following the month of earnings release (month 0). BB calculated average abnormal returns for each month of this 18-month-wide window. The results are shown in Figure 5.2, taken from BB:

FIGURE 5.2 ABNORMAL RETURNS FOR GN AND BN FIRMS

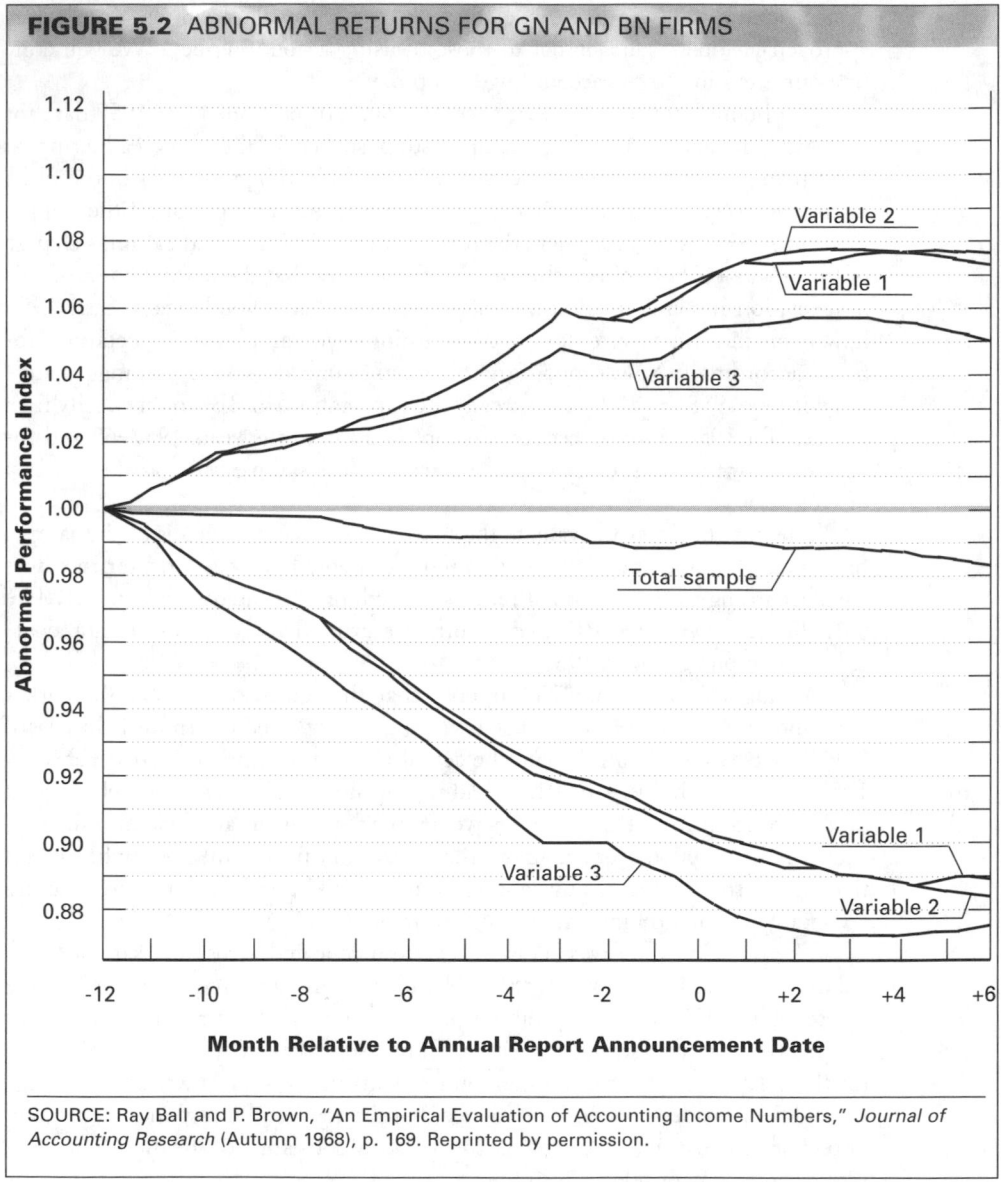

SOURCE: Ray Ball and P. Brown, "An Empirical Evaluation of Accounting Income Numbers," *Journal of Accounting Research* (Autumn 1968), p. 169. Reprinted by permission.

Variable 1 in Figure 5.2 uses reported net income as an earnings measure. Variable 2 takes earnings per share as the earnings measure. Variable 3 uses the time series approach to calculating expected earnings per share (variables 1 and 2 used the accounting beta approach). As can be seen, all variables give the same general results. The upper part of Figure 5.2 shows cumulative average abnormal returns for the GN earnings announcement firms in the sample; the bottom part shows the same for the BN announcement firms.

5.3.2 CAUSATION VERSUS ASSOCIATION

Note that the returns are *cumulative* in the diagram. Furthermore, while there was a substantial increase (for GN) and decrease (for BN) in average abnormal returns in the narrow window consisting of month 0, as described above, the market began to *anticipate* the GN or BN as much as a year early. As can be seen, if an investor had bought the shares of all GN firms one year before the good news was released and held them until the end of the month of release, there would have been an extra return of more than 7% over and above the market-wide return. Similarly, an abnormal loss of almost 9% would have been incurred on a portfolio of BN firms bought one year before the bad news was released.[8]

These longer-run returns suggest an important distinction between wide- and narrow-window studies of information content. If a security market reaction to accounting information is observed during a narrow window of a few days (or, in the case of BB, a month) surrounding an earnings announcement, it can be argued that the accounting information is the *cause* of the market reaction. The reason is that during a narrow window there are relatively few other firm-specific factors than net income to affect share returns. Also, if other factors do occur, such as stock splits or dividend announcements, the affected firms can be removed from the sample, as mentioned. Thus, a narrow-window association between security returns and accounting information suggests that accounting disclosures are the *source* of new information to investors.

Evaluation of returns over a wide window, however, opens returns up to a host of other factors. For example, a firm may have discovered new oil and gas reserves, be engaged in promising R&D projects, and have rising sales and market share. As the market learns this information from media and other sources, share price would begin to rise, because of the partly informative nature of security prices. That is, in an efficient market, security prices reflect all available information, not just accounting information. Thus, firms that in a real sense are doing well would have their share prices, and hence the abnormal return on their shares, bid up by the efficient market.

While historical-cost-based net income tends to lag behind the market in reflecting events like these, as the window is widened the relative effect of the lag decreases. That is, over a long period of time the sum of net incomes reported over that period captures more of the effects of economic factors such as those described above, even though there may be a lag in their initial recognition. This effect was studied by Easton, Harris, and Ohlson (1992), who found that the association between security returns and historical-cost-based earnings improved as the window was widened, up to 10 years. A similar effect was observed by Warfield and Wild (1992), who found that the association between security returns and earnings for annual reporting periods averaged over 10 times the association for quarterly periods.

While the relationship between security returns and reported net income may improve for wider windows, it is important to point out that it can no longer be argued that reported net income *causes* abnormal returns. The most that can be argued is that net income and returns are *associated*. That is, both are positively correlated with the real, underlying, economic performance of the firm.

Both causation and association results are consistent with accounting evidence having information content. In the long run, the total income earned by the firm is the same, regardless of the basis of accounting and in the limit will approach income under ideal conditions (on this point, see question 18). But a short window association provides stronger support for decision usefulness, since it suggests that it is the accounting information that actually drives investor belief revision and hence security returns.

5.3.3   EARNINGS LEVELS VERSUS EARNINGS CHANGES

Recall that BB defined the information content of earnings by the difference between actual and expected, where expected earnings was estimated either by an accounting beta relationship with market-wide earnings or by last year's actual earnings. Reasons for working with unexpected earnings were given in Section 5.2.2.

However, in Example 3.1, Bill Cautious used the *level* of earnings. Specifically, the GN in earnings was that they were "high." Thus, we have two competing constructs for the GN in earnings:

High, as in Example 3.1

Higher than expected, as in BB

and conversely for BN. Both constructs will lead to investors' belief revisions, but which one provides a tighter linkage between current and future firm performance, that is, which one has the higher main diagonal probabilities in the information system?

Under ideal conditions of certainty, the answer is clear (since there are no unexpected earnings under certainty). Recall P.V. Ltd. in Example 2.1. P.V.'s net income for period t = 1 was $17.36. Ohlson (1991) shows that the market value of the firm at time t can be expressed as:

$$P_t = \frac{1 + R_f}{R_f} NI_t - D_t \qquad (5.1)$$

$$= \frac{1.10}{0.10} \times 17.36 - 0$$

$$= \$190.96$$

for t = 1, where $R_f = 0.10$ is the rate of interest and dividends D_t are zero. Except for a slight rounding error, this agrees with the market value of P.V. Ltd. at the end of period 1 of $190.91 in Example 2.1.

We can also express this relationship in terms of the market return, by dividing by opening firm value:

$$R_f = \frac{P_t - D_t}{P_{t-1}} - 1$$

$$= \frac{190.96}{173.55} - 1$$

$$= 0.10$$

The point is that since P_t can be expressed in terms of NI_t—see Equation 5.1—it is the *level* of net income that explains market returns.

Ohlson shows that this result carries over to the case of ideal conditions under uncertainty. Specifically:

$$P_t = \frac{1}{R_f}[(1 + R_f)(NI_t - D_t) - a_t] \qquad (5.2)$$

where a_t is abnormal earnings. For P.V. Ltd. in Example 2.2, we have, for the bad-state realization:

$$P_t = \frac{1}{0.10}[1.10\,(-23.97 - 0) + 50]$$

$$= \frac{1}{0.10}(-26.37 + 50)$$

$$= \frac{1}{0.10} \times 23.63$$

$$= 236.30$$

as per the balance sheet of P.V. at the end of year 1. The −$50 of abnormal earnings for year 1 are added back because they do not persist, and hence have no predictive ability for future earning power.

In terms of market return:

$$R_t = \frac{P_t - D_t}{P_{t-1}} - 1$$

$$= \frac{236.30}{260.33} - 1$$

$$= -0.09$$

and again, since P_t contains NI_t—see Equation 5.2—we see that it is the level of net income, not unexpected net income, that explains R_t, the realized return for period t = 1.

When we relax ideal conditions, however, matters become less clear. Then, it is an empirical issue whether earnings or unexpected earnings better explain security returns. This was examined by Easton and Harris (1991). They compared the ability of the level of reported net income and the change in reported net income (where the change in net income proxies for unexpected earnings) to explain one-year security returns of a large sample of firms over the period 1969–86. Using regression analysis, they documented an association between security returns and the *change* in net income, consistent with BB. Interestingly, however, there was an even stronger association between returns and the *level* of net income. Furthermore, both variables combined did a significantly better job of explaining returns than either variable separately. These results suggest that the theoretical implications of earnings as a fundamental component of firm value and security returns carry over reasonably to non-ideal conditions, at least when returns are measured over a wide window of one year.

5.3.4   OUTCOMES OF THE BB STUDY

Despite questions such as those raised by Ohlson, one of the most important outcomes of BB was that it opened up a large number of additional usefulness issues. A logical next step is to ask whether the *magnitude* of unexpected earnings is related to the *magnitude* of the security market response—recall that BB's analysis was based only on the *sign* of unexpected earnings. That is, the information content of earnings in BB's study was classified only into GN or BN. As previously mentioned, this is a fairly coarse measure.

The question of magnitude of response was investigated, for example, by Beaver, Clarke, and Wright (BCW) in 1979. They examined a sample of 276 NYSE firms with December 31 year-ends, over the 10-year period from 1965 to 1974. For each sample firm, for each year of the sample period, they used an accounting beta approach to estimate expected annual earnings changes. The amounts of the unexpected earnings changes were then taken as the difference between expected and actual earnings change. They used the market model procedure described in Sections 4.3 and 5.2.3 to estimate the abnormal security returns associated with these unexpected earnings changes.

Upon comparison of unexpected earnings changes with abnormal security returns, BCW found that the greater the change in unexpected earnings, the greater the security market response. This result is consistent with the CAPM (Section 4.3) and with the decision usefulness approach, since the larger are unexpected earnings changes the more investors will revise upwards their estimates of future firm earning power and resulting returns from their investments, other things equal.

Also, since 1968, accounting researchers have studied security market response to net income on other stock exchanges, in other countries, and for quarterly earnings reports, with similar results. The approach has been applied to study market response to the information contained in new accounting standards, auditor changes, etc.

The information content of the accruals component of net income, in relation to the cash flow component, has also been studied. If we think of net income as consisting of operating cash flows ±33 net accruals, one might expect a stronger market response to the cash flow income component, since "A bird in the hand is worth two in the bush." While Wilson (1987) obtained some evidence during 1981–82 that the market favoured cash flows over accruals, Bernard and Stober (1989) were unable to replicate or otherwise explain this evidence in a study conducted over a longer time period.

Perhaps this ambiguity is to be expected, since accruals contain a discretionary component. For example, management has some discretion over the allowance for doubtful accounts, inventory valuation and depreciation policy, which could affect the information content of accruals. On the one hand, if management uses accruals to bias or otherwise manipulate reported net income, this would reduce their informativeness. On the other hand, as we will discuss in Section 11.3, management may use accruals policy to signal its inside information, which would increase informativeness. Since these effects work in opposite directions, it may indeed be difficult to find a distinction empirically between cash flows and accruals with respect to market reaction.

We will return to the question of earnings management in Chapter 11. Here, we will concentrate on what is probably the most important extension of BB, earnings response coefficients. This line of research asks a different question than BCW, namely, for a *given* amount of unexpected earnings, is the security market response greater for some firms than for others?

5.4   *Earnings Response Coefficients*

Recall that the abnormal security market returns identified by BB were *averages*, that is, they showed that on average their GN firms enjoyed positive abnormal returns, and negative for their BN firms. Of course, an average can conceal wide variation about the average. Thus, it is likely that some firms' abnormal returns were well above average and others' were well below.

This raises the question of *why* the market might respond more strongly to the good or bad news in earnings for some firms than for others. If answers to this question can be found, accountants can improve their understanding of how accounting information is useful to investors. This, in turn, could lead to the preparation of more useful financial statements.

Consequently, one of the most important directions that empirical financial accounting research has taken since the BB study is the identification and explanation of differential market response to earnings information. This is called **earnings response coefficient (ERC)** research.[9]

> *An **earnings response** coefficient measures the extent of a security's abnormal market return in response to the unexpected component of reported earnings of the firm issuing that security.*

5.4.1   *REASONS FOR DIFFERENTIAL MARKET RESPONSE*

A number of reasons can be suggested for differential market response to historical-cost-based earnings. We will review these in turn.

Beta

The riskier is the sequence of a firm's future expected returns, the lower will be its value to a risk-averse investor, other things equal. For a diversified investor, the relevant risk measure of a security is its beta, explained in Section 3.7. Since investors look to current earnings as an indicator of earning power and future returns, the riskier are these future returns the lower will be investors' reactions to a given amount of unexpected earnings.

To illustrate this, think of Toni Difelice in Example 3.2. Toni's utility increases in the expected value and decreases in the risk of the return on her portfolio. Suppose that Toni is an informed investor and thus quickly evaluates financial statement information. She notices that one of her securities has just released GN earnings information. As a result, Toni revises upwards her expected rate of return on this security and decides to buy more of it. However, if this security has high beta, this will increase her portfolio risk.[10] Consequently, she would not buy as much more as she would if the security was low beta. In effect, the high beta acts as a brake on Toni's demand for the GN security. Since all risk-averse informed investors will think this way, the demand for the firm's shares, as it releases its GN, will be lower the higher is its beta, other things equal. Of course, lower demand implies a lower increase in market price and return in response to the GN, hence, a lower ERC.

Empirical evidence of a lower ERC for higher-beta securities has been found by Collins and Kothari (1989) and by Easton and Zmijewski (1989).

Capital Structure

For highly levered firms, an increase, say, in earnings (before interest) adds strength and safety to bonds and other outstanding debt, so that much of the good news in earnings goes to the debtholders rather than the shareholders. Thus, the ERC for a highly levered firm should be lower than that of a firm with little or no debt, other things equal. Empirical evidence of a lower ERC for more highly levered firms has been reported by Dhaliwal, Lee, and Fargher (1991).

Persistence

We would expect that the ERC will be higher the more the good or bad news in current earnings is expected to **persist** into the future. Thus, if current GN is due to the successful introduction of a new product or vigorous cost-cutting by management, the market response should be higher than if the GN was due to, say, a gain on disposal of plant and equipment. In the latter case, if the market had not anticipated the gain, the ERC would be 1, since the net assets of the firm increase by the amount of the gain but there is no reason to expect the unusual gain to recur. Indeed, if the market had completely anticipated the increase in value of the asset that was sold, the ERC would be 0. In the new product and cost-cutting cases, the ERC should be greater than 1, since the revenue increases or cost savings will continue to benefit future income statements. Evidence that ERCs are higher the higher the persistence of unexpected current earnings changes is presented by Kormendi and Lipe (1987).

Persistence is a challenging and useful concept. One reason, advanced by Ramakrishnan and Thomas (1991) (R&T) is that different components of net income may have different persistence. For example, suppose that in the same year a firm successfully introduces a new product it also reports a gain on disposal of plant and equipment. Then, the persistence of earnings is an average of the differing persistence of the components of earnings. R&T distinguish three types of earnings events:

- Permanent, expected to persist indefinitely
- Transitory, affecting earnings in the current year but not future years
- Price-irrelevant, persistence of zero

The ERCs for these are $(1 + R_f)/R_f$ (where R_f is the risk-free rate of interest under ideal conditions), 1, and 0 respectively.

In effect, there are three ERCs, all of which may be present in the same income statement. R&T suggest that instead of trying to estimate an average ERC, investors should attempt to identify the three types separately and assign different ERCs to each. In so doing, they can identify the firm's permanent, or persistent, earning power. This implies that accountants should provide lots of classification and detail on the income statement.

To understand the ERC for permanent earnings, note that it can be written as $1 + 1/R_f$. Thus, under ideal conditions, the market response to $1 of permanent earnings consists of the current year's "instalment" of 1 plus the present value of the perpetuity of future instalments of $1/R_f$. (This ignores riskiness of the future instalments, which is appropriate if investors are risk-neutral or the permanent earnings are firm-specific.)

Another aspect of ERCs is that their persistence can depend on the firm's accounting policies. For example, suppose that a firm uses market value accounting for its assets and liabilities. Assume that there is a $100 unexpected increase in the market value of an asset this period, resulting from a permanent increase in the price of its product. Then, net income will include GN of $100, since, under market value accounting all changes in market values are included in income as they occur (if this is not clear to you, review Examples 2.1 and 2.2). Then, since unexpected changes in market value come along randomly, by definition, the efficient market will not expect the effect of the $100 GN on earnings to persist.

Now suppose instead that the firm uses historical cost accounting and that the annual increase in contribution margin is $9.09. Then, under historical cost accounting there will be only $9.09 of GN in earnings this year. The reason, of course, is that under historical cost accounting, a portion of the increase in market value is brought into income each period as it is realized, and not all at once as under market value accounting. However, the efficient market will recognize that the current $9.09 GN is only the "first instalment" of a longer series of earnings increases.[11] In other words, the GN in current earnings is expected to persist.

In the market value accounting case, the ERC will be 1, since the GN in earnings is $100 and this is also the increase in the market value of the firm. Under historical cost accounting the ERC will be $(1.10/0.10) = 11$, assuming $R_f = 0.10$. The GN in earnings is $9.09, but the efficient market value increase is still $100, since the market capitalizes this future earnings stream.

Also, zero-persistence income statement components can result from choice of accounting policy. Suppose, for example, that a firm capitalizes a large amount of organization costs. This could result in GN on the current income statement, which is freed of the costs because of their capitalization. However, assuming the organization costs have no salvage value, the market would not react to the "GN," that is, its persistence is zero. As another example, suppose that a firm writes off research costs currently in accordance with section 3450 of the *CICA Handbook*. This could produce BN in current earnings. However, to the extent the market perceives that the research costs as having future value, it would not react to this BN so that, again, persistence is zero. The possibility of zero persistence suggests once more the need for detailed income statement disclosure, including a statement of accounting policies.

Earnings Quality

Intuitively, we would expect a higher ERC for higher-quality earnings. Formal consideration of the concept of earnings quality requires that quality be defined, however. This can be done by means of the information system, such as the one depicted in Table 3.2. Recall that the information system associated with an income statement captures the linkage between current reported earnings and future firm performance—the higher the main diagonal probabilities the tighter the linkage. Thus we can define the quality of earnings by the magnitude of the main diagonal probabilities of the associated information system. The higher the quality, the higher we would expect the ERC to be, since investors are better able to infer future firm performance from current performance.

As a practical matter, measurement of earnings quality is less clear, since information system probabilities are not directly observable. One promising approach to measurement is used by Lev and Thiagarajan (1993) (L&T). They identify 12 "fundamentals" used by financial analysts in evaluating earnings quality. For example, one fundamental is the change in accounts receivable, relative to sales. If accounts receivable increase, this may suggest a decline in earnings quality—the firm may have attracted higher earnings by a more generous credit policy, or the firm may simply be managing its receivables less effectively. Other fundamentals were change in inventory, order backlog, etc.

For each firm in their sample, L&T calculated a measure of earnings quality by assigning a score of 1 or 0 to each of that firm's 12 fundamentals, then adding the scores. For example, for accounts receivable, a 1 is assigned if that firm's receivables, relative to sales, are down for the year, suggesting higher earnings quality, and a 0 score is assigned if receivables are up. L&T then partitioned their sample firms each year into five groups of decreasing earnings quality according to their measure. Next, using regression analysis, they estimated average ERCs for each group. They found that the higher-quality-earnings groups had higher ERCs, consistent with the theoretical expectation.

It can also be argued that earnings persistence and earnings quality are positively related. Suppose that a firm reports increased earnings this year and, in addition, accounts receivable are down suggesting an increase in earnings quality. Then, to the extent that credit policy is not changed very often, the market would expect the GN in earnings to persist. L&T examined the relationship between earnings quality and persistence for their sample firms and found that firms with both high persistence and high earnings quality had higher ERCs, on average, than firms with high persistence and low earnings quality, and similarly for low-persistence firms. These results support a positive relationship between persistence and quality of earnings.

Growth Opportunities

For reasons related to the above persistence and earnings quality arguments, the GN or BN in current earnings may suggest future growth prospects for the firm, and hence a higher ERC. One might think that historical-cost-based net income really cannot say anything about the future growth of the firm. However, this is not necessarily the case. Suppose that current net income reveals unexpectedly high profitability for some of the firm's recent investment projects. This may indicate to the market that the firm will enjoy strong growth in the future. One reason, of course, is that to the extent the high profitability persists, the future profits will increase the firm's assets. In addition, success with current projects may suggest to the market that this firm is also capable of identifying and implementing additional successful projects in future, so that it becomes labelled as a growth firm. Such firms can easily attract capital and this is an additional source of growth. Thus, to the extent that current good news in earnings suggests growth opportunities, the ERC will be high.

To illustrate, extend the persistence example above by assuming that the $9.09 of current permanent earnings increase is expected to grow by 5% per year. The present value at 10% of a perpetuity which increases by 5% per year is $1/(0.10 - 0.05) = 20$, greater than $1/0.10 = 10$ under no-growth. Thus, the ERC is 21 rather than 11 as before.

Evidence that the ERC is higher for firms that the market regards as possessing growth opportunities is shown by Collins and Kothari (1989). They use the ratio of market value of equity to book value of equity as a measure of growth opportunities and find a positive relationship between this measure and the ERCs of their sample firms, not inconsistent with the above argument.

The Informativeness of Price

We have suggested on several previous occasions that market price itself is partially informative about the future value of the firm. Recall that the reason is that market price aggregates all publicly known information about the firm, not just accounting information. Consequently, the more informative is price, the less will be the information content of current accounting earnings, other things equal.

A proxy for the informativeness of price is *firm size*, since larger firms are more in the news. However, Easton and Zmijewski (1989) found that firm size was not a significant explanatory variable for the ERC. The reason is probably that firm size proxies for other firm characteristics, such as risk and growth, as much as it proxies for the informativeness of share price. Once these factors are controlled for, any significant effect of size on the ERC seems to go away. Collins and Kothari (1989) dealt with size by moving the wide window over which security returns were measured earlier in time for large firms. This substantially improved the relationship between changes in earnings and security returns, the argument being that the market anticipates changes in earning power sooner for large firms. Once this was done, size appeared to have no explanatory power for the ERC.

5.4.2   IMPLICATIONS OF ERC RESEARCH

Be sure that you see the reason *why* accountants should be interested in the market's response to financial accounting information. Essentially, the reason is that improved understanding of market response suggests ways that they can further improve the decision usefulness of financial statements. For example, lower informativeness of price for smaller firms implies that expanded disclosure for these firms would be useful for investors, contrary to a common argument that larger firms should have greater reporting responsibilities.

Also, the finding that ERCs are lower for highly levered firms supports arguments to expand disclosure of the nature and magnitude of financial instruments, including those that are "off-balance-sheet." If the relative size of a firm's liabilities affects the market's response to net income, then it is desirable that all liabilities be disclosed.

The importance of growth opportunities to investors suggests, for example, the desirability of disclosure of segment information, since profitability information by segments would better enable investors to isolate the profitable, and unprofitable, operations of the firm.

Finally, the importance of persistence and quality of earnings to the ERC means that disclosure of the *components* of net income is useful for investors. This implication is discussed further in Section 5.5.

5.4.3   SUMMARY

The information content of reported net income can be measured by the extent of security price change or, equivalently, by the size of the abnormal market return, around the time the market learns the current net income. This is because informed investors may revise their beliefs about future earnings and returns on the basis of current earnings information. Revised beliefs trigger buy/sell decisions, as investors move to restore the risk/return tradeoffs in their portfolios to desired levels. If there was no information content in net income there would be no belief revision, no resulting buy/sell decisions, and hence no associated price changes.

For a given amount of unexpected net income, the extent of security price change or abnormal returns depends on factors such as firm size, capital structure, risk, growth prospects, persistence, and earnings quality.

Following the pioneering study of Ball and Brown, empirical research has demonstrated a differential market response depending on these factors. These empirical results are really quite remarkable. First, they have overcome substantial statistical and experimental design problems. Second, they show that the market is, on average, very sophisticated in its ability to evaluate accounting information. This supports the theory of security market efficiency and the decision theories that underlie it. Finally, they support the decision usefulness approach to financial reporting.

Indeed, the extent to which historical-cost-based net income can provide "clues" about future firm performance may seem surprising. The key, of course, is the information system probabilities, as shown in Table 3.2. In effect, the higher the main diagonal probabilities, the greater we would expect the ERC to be. This supports the FASB's contention in its Conceptual Framework that investors' expectations are based "at least partly on evaluations of past enterprise performance" (Section 3.8). As accountants gain a better understanding of investor response to financial statement information, their ability to provide useful information to investors will further increase.

5.5 Extraordinary Items

In the previous section, we mentioned Ramakrishnan and Thomas' suggestion (1991) that investors separately estimate permanent, transitory, and price-irrelevant types of earnings. An interesting example of the importance of earnings persistence can be found in the reporting of events which are unusual and/or infrequent. Since these items may not recur regularly, their persistence will be low. This means that they must be fully disclosed; otherwise, the market may get an exaggerated impression of their persistence.

The reporting of **extraordinary items** is specified by Section 3480 of the *CICA Handbook*. In 1989, Section 3480 was revised to introduce greater consistency in the reporting of extraordinary items on the income statement. According to paragraph 3480.02:

Extraordinary items are items which result from transactions or events that have all of the following characteristics:

(a) they are not expected to occur frequently over several years;

(b) they do not typify the normal business activities of the entity; and

(c) they do not depend primarily on decisions or determinations by management or owners.

The last characteristic in the definition was added in the 1989 revision. Prior to that time, only the first two characteristics applied. The result was to eliminate a large number of former extraordinary items such as, for example, gains or losses on disposals of land held for future expansion. After 1989 such gains or losses would be included *before* income from continuing operations, because management controls the timing of such transactions.

This revision seems to resolve the issue of **classificatory smoothing**, whereby management could smooth (or otherwise manage) operating earnings by choosing to classify unusual items above or below the operating earnings line. Evidence that managers in the United States behaved as if they smoothed income before extraordinary items by means of classificatory smoothing was reported by Barnea, Ronen, and Sadan (1976). By requiring those unusual items whose amounts and/or timing could be controlled by management to be consistently reported as part of operating income, the ability to engage in classificatory smoothing was effectively eliminated. It therefore appeared that the new Section 3480 represented an improvement in financial reporting.

However, the nature of the improvement can be questioned, based on the ERC research outlined in our Section 5.4. Specifically, unusual items have low persistence. For example, a gain on sale of land would have persistence of 1. Other unusual items could have persistence as low as zero, to the extent that they are not value-relevant at all.

The impact of the 1989 revisions to Section 3480 caused a number of low-persistence unusual items to move from extraordinary items up to the operating section of the income statement. This places a heavy burden on the firm to fully disclose these items. Otherwise, these items could become buried in operations, and the market may overestimate their persistence or, at least, spend considerable time and effort trying to disentangle them.

This issue was investigated by Betts and Richardson (1992). They examined a sample of 102 TSE firms over the period from 1980 to 1989 inclusive (before the revisions to Section 3480). They found evidence of classificatory smoothing during this period, supporting the reason for the 1989 revisions. However, they also found that, prior to 1989, extraordinary items had lower ERCs than operating earnings. This supports the concerns that, when most of these extraordinary items were moved into operating income effective 1989, the potential existed for the market to misinterpret their persistence. Indeed, Betts and Richardson quote a prominent financial analyst organization that stated in 1992:

> Our quantitative team spends a great deal of time and effort each month separating earnings of Canadian companies into their recurring and non-recurring components. ... This process is very difficult due to the weak disclosure policies of a number of our companies.

Thus, the question appears to be open whether Section 3480 actually succeeded in improving financial reporting. From our standpoint, however, Section 3480 represents an interesting example of how theory can be brought to bear to re-examine an issue that was thought resolved.

5.6   A Caveat About the "Best" Accounting Policy

To this point, we have argued that accountants can be guided by security market reaction in determining usefulness of financial accounting information. From this, it is tempting to conclude that the "best" accounting policy is the one that produces the greatest market price response. For example, if net income reported by oil and gas firms under successful-efforts accounting produces a greater market reaction than net income reported under full-cost accounting, successful-efforts should be used, because investors find it more useful.

However, we must be extremely careful about this conclusion. Accountants may be better off to the extent that they provide useful information to investors, but it does not follow that *society* will necessarily be better off.

The reason is that information has characteristics of a **public good**. A public good is a good such that consumption by one person does not destroy it for use by another. Consumption of a **private good**—such as an apple—eliminates its usefulness for other consumers. However, an investor can use the information in an annual report without eliminating its usefulness to other investors.

Consequently, suppliers of public goods may have trouble charging for these products, so that we often witness them being supplied by governmental or quasi-governmental agencies—roads and national defence, for example. If a firm was to try to charge investors for its annual report, it would probably not attract many customers, because a single annual report, once sold, could be circulated to many users. Instead, we observe governments through securities legislation and corporations acts, *requiring* firms to issue annual reports.

Of course, firms' annual reports are not "free." Investors will eventually pay for them through higher product prices. Nevertheless, investors perceive them as free, since the extent to which they use the annual report information will not affect the product prices they pay. Also, investors may incur costs to inform themselves, either directly, or indirectly through paying for analyst or other information services. Nevertheless, the basic "raw material" is perceived as free and investors will do what any other rational consumer will do when prices are low—consume more of it. As a result, *investors may perceive accounting information as useful even though from society's standpoint the costs of this information (through higher product prices) outweigh the benefits to investors and capital markets.*

Also, as mentioned in Chapter 1, information affects different people differently. Thus, information may be useful to investors but managers may object to supplying it. As a result, the social value of such information depends on both the benefits to investors and the costs to managers. Such fundamental cost-benefit tradeoffs are extremely difficult to make.

Think of information as a commodity, demanded by investors and supplied by firms through accountants. Because of the public-good aspect of information, we cannot rely on the forces of demand and supply to produce the socially "right" or first-best amount of production, as we can for private goods produced under competition. The essential reason is that the price system does not, and probably cannot, operate to charge investors the full costs of the information they use. Consequently, from a social perspective we cannot rely on the extent of security market response to tell us which accounting policies should be used (or, equivalently, "how much" information to produce). Formal arguments to support this conclusion were given by Gonedes and Dopuch (1974).

We will return to the question of regulation of information production in Chapters 12 and 13. For now, the point to realize is that it is still true that accountants can be guided by market response to maintain and improve their competitive position as suppliers to the competitive marketplace for information. It is also true that securities markets will work better to the extent security prices provide good indications of underlying real investment opportunities. However, these social considerations do suggest that, as a general rule, accounting standard setting bodies should be wary of using security market response to guide their decisions.

Interestingly, an exception to this rule seems to have occurred with respect to standard setters' decisions to eliminate current cost accounting. SFAS 33, which required U.S. firms to report supplemental current cost information for certain assets, was discontinued in 1986. Discontinuance was based in part on the influential study by Beaver and Landsman (1983), who failed to find any incremental security market reaction to current cost information over and above the information content of historical-cost-based net income.[12] In Canada, Hanna, Kennedy, and Richardson (1990) recommended the discontinuance of Section 4510 of the *CICA Handbook*, which laid down procedures for supplemental current cost disclosures. They were unable to find evidence of usefulness of this information and the section was withdrawn in 1992. It is difficult to disagree with decisions to cease production of information which no one finds useful. Nevertheless, from a social perspective, no one knows whether this decision was correct, due to the difficulties of measuring social costs and benefits.

5.7 Estimating Beta

To this point, we have looked at the usefulness of earnings information in evaluating the expected return on a security. In Section 3.7 we saw that the expected return on a portfolio is just a weighted average of the expected returns of the securities in the portfolio, where the weights are the proportions of each security in total portfolio investment. However, investor utility also depends on portfolio risk. In this section we will consider the usefulness of financial statement information in evaluating portfolio risk.

Recall from Section 3.7 that, for all but the least diversified investors, portfolio risk depends mainly on the betas of the securities in the portfolio. Consequently, to be useful in evaluating portfolio risk, financial statement information must be useful in estimating beta. Securities' betas are also used by empirical researchers to separate market-wide and firm-specific security returns—see Figure 5.1.

As discussed in Sections 4.3 and 5.2.3, the primary way to estimate beta is to obtain past data on the relationship between a security's return and the return on the market portfolio. Recall that this involves estimation of the market model, that is, the following regression equation:

$$R_{jt} = \alpha_j + \beta_j R_{Mt} + \epsilon_{jt}$$

where R_{jt} is the return on security j for period t and R_{Mt} represents the return on the market portfolio for period t (see note 2). The ϵ_{jt} term is a random error, assumed to have a mean of zero, and uncorrelated with R_{Mt}. Past data is then obtained for R_{jt} and R_{Mt} and the coefficients α_j and β_j are estimated by least-squares regression.

It is important to point out that the estimate of beta obtained from a regression equation is just that, an *estimate*. In regression analysis, or any other statistical estimation technique for that matter, the true value of beta will never be known. The accuracy of the estimate depends on factors such as sample size, whether β_{jt} and R_{Mt} can be observed without error, whether ϵ_{jt} is uncorrelated with R_{Mt}, and on whether the true beta, whatever it is, is stable over time. These factors are beyond our concern here.

However, the fact that beta is an estimate does raise the question of whether financial-statement-based risk measures can improve the estimate or, at least, serve as a check on the regression estimate. If so, this would be particularly useful if a firm's beta were to *change*. Beta may change if a firm's operating or financing characteristics change—for example if it enters a new line of business or engages in significant debt financing. If security betas should change, this could upset the investor's optimal risk/return tradeoff described in Section 3.6, and investors would want to know about it so as to rebalance their portfolios.

Notice, though, that it may take some time to reestimate β_j by running another regression analysis, since it is necessary to wait until enough post-change observations of R_{jt} and R_{Mt} are obtained to provide an accurate reestimate. However, if beta is related to financial-statement-based risk measures, these latter measures will be useful because they are available sooner.

It turns out that the relationships between beta and certain accounting risk measures are surprisingly high. To show these, we shall briefly consider one of the original studies in this area, by Beaver, Kettler, and Scholes (BKS) in 1970.

BKS studied a sample of 307 NYSE firms traded on the New York Stock Exchange for two periods: 1947–56 (period 1) and 1957–65 (period 2). They used regression analysis as described above to estimate each stock's beta for period 1 and for period 2. Then, they calculated various risk measures from the financial statements for each firm for each year. The four risk measures that we shall consider are:

- **Dividend payout**, defined as the ratio of common stock cash dividends to net income
- **Leverage**, defined as the ratio of senior securities to total assets
- **Earnings variability**, defined as the standard deviation of the price-to-earnings ratio over the period
- **Accounting beta** (Section 5.2)

For each risk measure, BKS then formed 61 portfolios of five securities each from their sample firms and arranged the portfolios in decreasing order of the magnitude of that risk measure. For example, for dividend payout, the first portfolio consisted of the five firms in their sample with the highest payout ratios during the period, the second portfolio of those with the next five highest payout ratios, etc. This procedure was repeated for the other risk measures, giving for each measure 61 portfolios ranked by their riskiness according to that measure.

To see the intuition for this, consider an investor who adopts a strategy of buying a five-security portfolio on the basis of dividend payout (or other accounting risk measure). If the investor wants highest risk, portfolio 1 would be purchased; if lowest risk is wanted, portfolio 61 would be purchased; etc. To what extent would the risk of the portfolio chosen this way correspond to its risk as measured by beta?

To answer this question BKS calculated the correlation coefficients between the accounting-based measures of portfolio risk and the betas of those portfolios (the beta of a portfolio was taken as the average of the betas of its five securities). The results were as follows:

TABLE 5.1 CORRELATION COEFFICIENTS BETWEEN ACCOUNTING RISK MEASURES AND BETA, FOR FIVE-SECURITY PORTFOLIOS		
	PERIOD 1 1947–56	PERIOD 2 1957–65
Dividend payout	–0.79	–0.50
Leverage	0.41	0.48
Earnings variability	0.90	0.82
Accounting beta	0.68	0.46

SOURCE: BKS, Table 5. Reprinted by permission.

Notice that the signs are what we would expect (for example, the higher the dividend payout, the lower the risk) and that at least two of the correlations are quite high. Furthermore, there is reasonable consistency between periods 1 and 2. The results support an argument that financial-statement-based risk measures can be useful in predicting beta.

The reasons for these results, however, are not obvious. The most likely reason is that both accounting-based risk measures and security betas are correlated with the underlying operating and financial riskiness of the firm. In fact, it can be shown theoretically that beta is related to both these aspects of firm risk. Then, in a study such as BKS, this will show up as beta and accounting risk measures associated with each other.

Since 1970, other researchers have found similar results. Indeed, several commercial services have sprung up to sell beta estimates to investors and at least some of these base their estimates in part on accounting risk measures. To the extent that these services earn a profit this speaks well for the ability of financial statements to provide useful risk information.

5.8   *The Information Content of RRA*

In this section we depart again from our concentration on the information content of historical-cost-based net income in order to consider the informativeness of other financial statement information. Specifically, we will consider whether RRA information has additional information content over historical cost net income and book value. Recall from Section 2.4 that SFAS 69 requires oil and gas firms to report supplementary present value information about proved reserves.

A priori, we would expect that if supplemental current value-oriented information was going to be useful for investors, it would be in the oil and gas industry. One could argue, for example, that historical cost and market values are especially likely to diverge in this industry—a lucky firm might, at low cost, find a bonanza. More importantly, we pointed out the implications of inside information in Section 4.6. Since so much of the value of an exploring/producing oil company depends on its reserves, shares of such a firm seem especially susceptible to the problems of information asymmetry. Consequently, the market should be particularly interested in reserves information. We shall see, however, that empirical results are not nearly as clear-cut as these arguments suggest.

The theoretical and empirical ability of RRA to explain the market's evaluation of oil and gas reserves was extensively investigated by Magliolo (1986), in tests conducted on a sample of firms over 1979–83, inclusive. In one set of tests, Magliolo compared the undiscounted value of net reserves reported in RRA to an estimate of the market's valuation of those reserves. This RRA information did not perform according to theory in its ability to explain market value. Indeed, RRA was outperformed by reserve information provided by an investment service. This service makes a number of adjustments to the current operating data of oil and gas firms to arrive at an economic estimate of revenues and costs. The implication is that RRA, at least, contains considerable error in its measure of reserve value.

Magliolo also examined the ability of the elements of an RRA-based income statement (see Table 2.5 for such a statement) to explain *changes* in the market's valuation of reserves. He found that additional reserves proved during the year had significant explanatory power, although some of it appeared to be anticipated by the market, which suggests that other, more timely information sources are available to investors. Other components of the RRA income statement had little explanatory ability. Magliolo concluded that, overall, RRA does not measure the market values of oil and gas reserves as theory would predict.

Other researchers have also investigated the information content of RRA. Doran, Collins, and Dhaliwal (1988) (DCD) studied a sample of 173 producing oil and gas firms over the six-year period 1979–84. They studied the sub-periods 1979–81 and 1982–84 separately.[13]

For each sample observation, DCD calculated monthly abnormal returns as in Figure 5.1 for a 12-month period ending on the firm's year-end (December

31), and summed them for each observation to give a 12-month abnormal return. The question then was, to what extent did RRA information have incremental ability, in addition to the change in historical cost net income, to explain the abnormal return? You will recognize that this approach is similar to that discussed in Sections 5.2 and 5.3, except that now two variables are being used to explain abnormal security returns, rather than one. To the extent that the two-variable model does a better job of explaining abnormal returns than a model using only historical-cost-based net income, it can be argued that the supplemental RRA information is useful for investors, in the sense that it has information content about future returns and dividends over and above the information content of historical cost net income.

Using regression analysis, DCD showed that during 1979–81 *both* historical cost and RRA information had significant explanatory power, supporting the incremental usefulness of RRA. However, during 1982–84, *neither* variable had significant explanatory power. Thus, their results were mixed. DCD attributed this to the fact that oil and gas market prices were much more volatile during the earlier period. Consequently, investors would be particularly interested in information about reserves and expected market prices during 1979–81.

Nevertheless, the fact that they also found historical-cost-based net income not to have significant explanatory power for abnormal returns during 1982–84 is puzzling, since this conflicts with the wealth of evidence about the usefulness of income discussed in Sections 5.3 and 5.4. DCD attribute this result to the fact that the market was expecting an oil glut during 1982–84 and that the effects of this expectation on oil company share prices swamped the impact of reported net income.[14]

Despite these explanations, DCD's results have to be interpreted as providing, at best, fairly weak evidence in favour of RRA. This lack of strong results also shows up in other studies. For example, Harris and Ohlson (1987) (HO) examined the ability of RRA information to explain the market value of the oil and gas assets[15] of producing firms, rather than abnormal returns as in DCD. Using a sample of 273 observations over the five-year period from 1979 to 1983, they found that the book value of oil and gas assets[16] had significant explanatory power for the market value of these assets. RRA information also had some explanatory power, but less than historical cost.

HO also examined the usefulness of reserve quantity information. SFAS 69 (paragraphs 10, 11) requires that quantities of proved oil and gas reserves, and changes in the quantities during the year, be disclosed. HO found that quantity information had no incremental explanatory power beyond RRA. In other words, when both quantity information and RRA information are available it seems that investors go for RRA.

It should be pointed out that the DCD study was "wide window," that is, security returns were measured over a 12-month period. Thus, even if a significant association between security returns and RRA was found, this does not mean that the RRA information *causes* abnormal security returns. The most that can be said is that security market price and RRA both reflect the underlying value of future returns from oil and gas properties. This does not necessarily mean that RRA information is not useful, since, knowing that RRA reflects underlying value, investors may use this information in their investment decisions. It does mean, however, that RRA competes with information from other sources. For example, Ghicas and Pastena (1989) also examined the incremental information content of RRA. However, they introduced financial analyst forecasts of oil company values as a *third* explanatory variable. They found that when recent analyst information was available any ability that RRA had to explain oil company value disappeared. Thus, a further constraint on the decision usefulness of RRA is that it may be superseded by other, more timely sources of information, consistent with Magliolo's finding.

Even if we ignore the question of timeliness, however, the difficulty that empirical research has had to demonstrate decision usefulness of RRA is surprising. Given the apparent sophistication of security market reaction to reported net income, one would expect a similar reaction to relevant balance sheet and supplementary information.

Several reasons can be suggested for the weak results for RRA. One is reliability. Perhaps RRA is too imprecise to be useful, again consistent with the results of Magliolo. Also, we saw in Section 2.4 that management is lukewarm about the usefulness of RRA, claiming low reliability. Second, the research faces more severe methodological difficulties than it does in finding a market reaction to net income. One problem is in finding the point in time that the market first becomes aware of the RRA information. For net income, media publication of the earnings announcement provides a reasonable event date. However, given the inside nature of oil and gas reserves information and its importance to firm value, analysts and others may work particularly hard to ferret it out in advance of the annual report. If a reasonable event date for the release of reserve information cannot be found, return studies must use wide windows, which are open to a large number of influences on price in addition to accounting information.

A third reason may be that historical-cost-based information about oil and gas reserves may be more value-relevant than implied by our discussion above. HO suggest that oil companies will not throw money away on exploration and development but, rather, will only spend it if the expected benefits at least equal the costs. This means that the higher is the book value of an oil company's oil and gas properties, the more the company thinks they are worth (allowing for risk), and vice versa. If this argument that book value makes economic sense is combined with the greater reliability of historical cost information than RRA, it is not surprising that the market may find historical cost book value more useful.

In a followup study, HO (1990) investigated the information content of historical cost reserves information more closely. They continued to find that historical cost dominated RRA. Furthermore, their results suggest that the market, if anything, underuses the information content of historical cost reserves information. This finding is of interest because it raises the possibility that the market may not be as sophisticated in its evaluation of information as efficient market theory assumes.

However, one must be cautious in accusing the market of a lack of sophistication. Instead of searching for a direct link between other financial statement information and abnormal security returns, as the above studies have done, there is an indirect approach which links other information to the quality of earnings. To illustrate, suppose that an oil company reports high earnings this year, but supplemental oil and gas information shows that its reserves have declined substantially over the year. An interpretation of this information is that the firm has used up its reserves to increase sales in the short run. If so, the quality of current earnings is reduced, since they contain a transitory component that will dissipate if new reserves are not found. Then, the market's reaction to the supplemental reserve information may be more easily found in a low ERC than in a direct reaction to the reserve information itself.

While their study was not specifically oriented to oil and gas firms, this approach was used by Lev and Thiagarajan (1991) (L&T). Parts of their research were reviewed in Section 5.4.1. Recall that they identified 12 fundamental variables that affect earnings quality. Several of these were based on balance sheet information, such as the change in accounts receivable. When L&T added these fundamentals as additional explanatory variables in an ERC regression analysis, there was a substantial increase in ability to explain abnormal security returns beyond the explanatory power of unexpected earnings alone. This suggests that the market, aided perhaps by analysts, is quite sophisticated in its evaluation of earnings, using balance sheet information to augment the information content of the earnings announcement itself.

5.9 Summary and Conclusions

The empirical literature in financial accounting is vast, and we have looked only at certain parts of it. Nevertheless, we have seen that, for the most part, the security market response to reported net income is impressive in terms of its sophistication. Results of empirical research in this area support the efficient markets theory and related decision theories.

In addition to providing information to enable investors to revise expected security returns, financial accounting information can assist when estimating firm riskiness. This is all the more surprising because beta, the primary risk measure for a diversified investor, is not directly related to financial statement variables.

What is puzzling, however, is that the market does not seem to respond to non-earnings information as strongly as it does to earnings information. RRA was examined as an example of non-earnings information where, a priori, a strong market response would be expected. The extent to which the lack of strong market response to non-earnings information such as RRA is due to methodological difficulties, to its low reliability, to availability of alternative information sources, or to failure of efficient market theory itself is not fully understood at the present time, although it may be that investors route their reaction to such information through their perceptions of earnings quality.

As stated earlier, the approach to financial accounting theory which equates the extent of security price change with information content and hence with decision usefulness is known as the information perspective. The essence of this approach is that investors are viewed as attempting to predict future returns from their investments. They seek all relevant information in this regard, not necessarily just accounting information. To maximize their competitive position as suppliers of information, accountants may then seek to use the extent of security market response to various types of accounting information as a guide to its usefulness to investors. This motivates their interest in empirical research on decision usefulness. Furthermore, the more information accountants can move from inside to outside the firm, the better can capital markets guide the flow of scarce investment funds.

Despite these considerations, accountants must be careful of concluding that the accounting policies and disclosures which produce the greatest market response are the best for society. This is not necessarily true, due to the public-good nature of accounting information. Investors who do not bear the full costs of the information they use will not necessarily demand the "right" amount of it, since they do not bear the full costs. These concerns limit the ability of decision usefulness research to guide accounting standard setters.

Despite these social considerations, the information perspective has dominated financial accounting theory and research since the Ball and Brown paper of 1968. It has led to a tremendous amount of empirical investigation which has enriched our understanding of the decision usefulness of accounting information for investors.

Notes

1. From Section 4.3, this estimate of α_j should equal $(1 - \beta_j)R_f$, where R_f is the risk-free rate of interest. Here, $\alpha_j = 0.0001$ implies $R_f = 0.0005$ per day.

2. The market return for day 0 is calculated as follows:

$$R_{M0} = \frac{\text{Level of DJ Index, end of day 0} + \text{Dividends on DJ Index on day 0}}{\text{Level of DJ Index, beginning of day 0}} - 1$$

Sometimes, because of data problems, the dividends are omitted.

3. Calculated as: $E(R_{j0}) = \alpha_j + \beta_j R_{M0}$
   $$= 0.0001 + 0.80 \times 0.001$$
   $$= 0.0009$$

4. Again, this abnormal return should not be confused with abnormal earnings of P.V. Ltd. in Example 2.2. While the idea is the same, abnormal return here refers to a *market* return, whereas abnormal earnings refer to *accounting* net income.

5. Yet another way is to work with total share returns rather than abnormal returns, that is, to not factor out expected return at all. See, for example, Easton and Harris (1991).

6. Note that BB worked with earnings *changes*, rather than earnings themselves. This is further discussed in Section 5.3.3.

7. Since BB conducted their study in 1968, they could look back and calculate the average 1957 earnings change for their sample firms.

8. Note that the loss on bad news firms can be converted into a gain by selling short the shares of the bad news firms.

9. For reasons explained in Section 5.3.2, the interpretation of a narrow-window ERC is different from a wide-window ERC. Here we will refer, somewhat loosely, to both types as simply ERCs.

10. Recall from Section 3.7 that in reasonably diversified portfolios, most of the portfolio risk stems from the betas of the securities in the portfolio. Thus, if Toni were to buy more shares of a security whose beta is greater than the average beta of the securities presently in the portfolio, this will raise the average, hence increasing portfolio risk.

11. This assumes that the market knows that the increase in market value is $100. Possibly, this would be known from sources other than the financial statements. If not, considerable onus is put on the firm for full disclosure. Perhaps MD&A provides a vehicle for management to reveal this information.

12. A number of reasons other than lack of usefulness can be suggested for these results. First, the market may value the information but is able to estimate it from other sources. Second, the information may be relevant but unreliable, since a large number of assumptions and estimates go into its preparation. Third, the market may have reacted to the information but the research

methodology was not sufficiently powerful to find it. For example, the Beaver and Landsman (1983) study was criticized by Bernard (1987) on methodological grounds. Indeed, some evidence of security market reaction has been found in studies subsequent to Beaver and Landsman. Thus, Bernard and Ruland (1987) found some information content for current cost information, at least in certain industries.

13. SFAS 69 came into effect in 1982. However, the SEC required disclosure of information similar to RRA information from 1979 to 1981.

14. Note that the procedure to separate economy-wide returns and abnormal returns illustrated in Figure 5.1 does *not* remove industry-wide returns. These will be buried in abnormal returns under the Figure 5.1 procedure, because all firms in DCD's sample were in the oil and gas industry. This illustrates one of the difficulties of working with data from a single industry in empirical studies.

15. HO estimated the market value of oil and gas assets by subtracting the book value of net non-oil and gas assets from the market value of the firm's capital stock and marketable debt.

16. HO's significant result held for both book value on a successful-efforts basis and on a full-cost basis.

Questions and Problems

1. Explain the information perspective on financial reporting. Does it rely on the historical cost basis of accounting? (CGA-Canada)

2. Refer to the separation of market-wide and firm-specific security returns as shown in Figure 5.1. What factors could reduce the accuracy of the estimate of abnormal returns? (CGA-Canada)

3. Explain why the market might begin to anticipate the GN or BN in earnings as much as a year in advance, as Ball and Brown found in Figure 5.2. (CGA-Canada)

4. Give examples of components of net income with:

   a. High persistence

   b. Persistence of 1

   c. Persistence of 0 (CGA-Canada)

5. Explain why it is necessary to find the exact time that the market first became aware of an item of accounting information if any security price reaction to this information is to be detected. Can such a time always be found? Explain why or why not. What can researchers do when the exact time cannot be isolated? (CGA-Canada)

6. A researcher finds evidence of a security price reaction to an item of accounting information during a narrow window of three days surrounding the date of release of this information and claims that it was the accounting information that caused the security price reaction. Another researcher finds evidence of security price reaction to a different item of accounting information during a wide window beginning 12 months prior to the release of the financial statements containing that item. This researcher does not claim that the accounting information caused the security price reaction but only that the information and the market price reaction were associated.

   Explain why one can claim causation for a narrow window but not for a wide window. Which price reaction constitutes the stronger evidence for usefulness of accounting information? Explain.

7. XYZ Ltd. is a large retail bookstore chain listed on a major stock exchange, and its reported net income for the year ended December 31, 1995 is $5 million. The earnings were announced to the public on December 31, 1995.

   Financial analysts had predicted the company's net income for 1995 to be $7 million. The financial analysts' prediction of $7 million net income was in effect up until the release of the 1995 earnings on December 31, 1995.

   Assumptions

   • No other news about XYZ Ltd. was released to the public on December 31, 1995.

   • No macroeconomic information was released to the public on December 31, 1995.

   • Financial analysts' forecasts about XYZ Ltd.'s net income represented the market's expectations about XYZ Ltd.'s income.

   Required

   a. Would you expect a change in price of XYZ Ltd.'s common stock on December 31, 1995? If so, why? Discuss.

   b. Consider the two situations below:

      i. The deviation of forecasted earnings from actual earnings of $2 million ($7 million − $5 million) is completely accounted for by the closing down of a number of its retail outlets.

      ii. The deviation of the forecasted earnings from actual earnings of $2 million is completely accounted for by a fire in the XYZ Ltd.'s largest retail outlet which had caused the outlet to be closed temporarily for six months.

      In which of these two scenarios would you expect the price change of XYZ Ltd.'s common stock to be greater? Discuss.   (CGA-Canada)

8. In a classic study, Beaver (1968) examined the trading volume of firms' securities around the time of their earnings announcements. Specifically, he examined 506 annual earnings announcements of 143 NYSE firms over the years 1961–65 inclusive (261 weeks).

For each earnings announcement, Beaver calculated the average daily trading volume (of the shares of the firm making that announcement) for each week of a 17-week window surrounding week 0 (the week in which the earnings announcement was made). For each firm in the sample, he also calculated the average daily trading volume outside its 17-week window. This was taken as the normal trading volume for that firm's shares.

For each week in the 17-week window, Beaver averaged the trading volumes over the 506 earnings announcements in the sample. The results are shown in Figure 5.3 below. The dotted line in the figure shows the average normal trading volume outside the 17-week window.

As can be seen from the figure, there was a dramatic increase in trading volume, relative to normal, in week 0. Also, volume is below normal during most of the weeks leading up to week 0.

FIGURE 5.3   VOLUME ANALYSIS

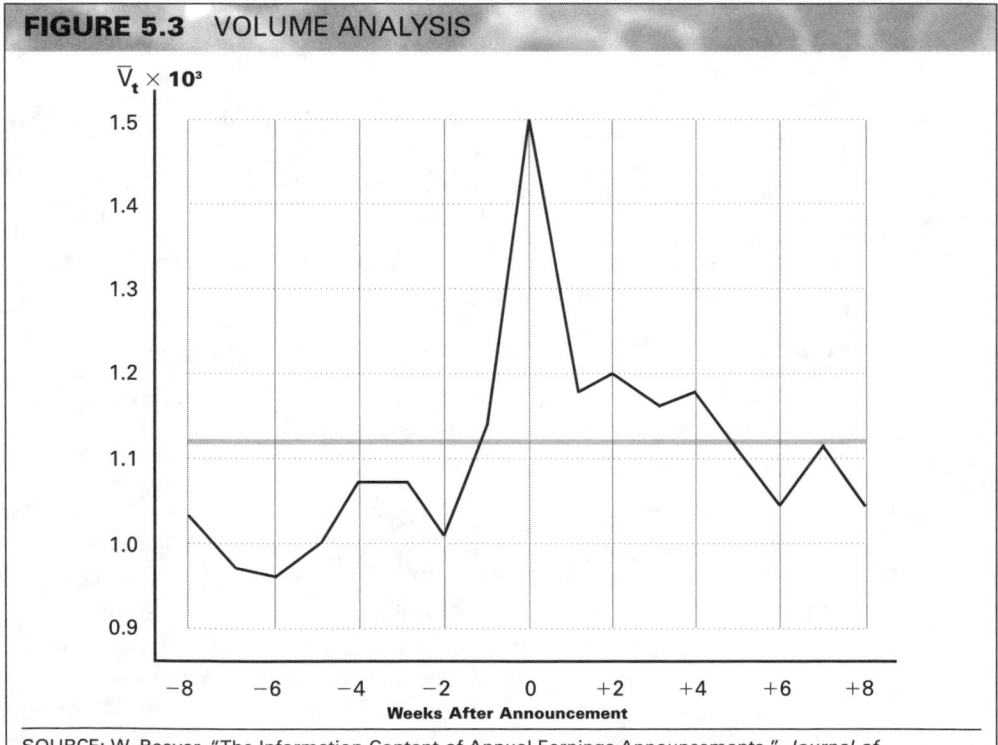

SOURCE: W. Beaver, "The Information Content of Annual Earnings Announcements," *Journal of Accounting Research*, Supplement, 1968: 67–92. Reprinted by permission.

Required

a. Why do you think trading volume increased in week 0?

b. Why do you think trading volume was below normal in the weeks leading up to week 0?

c. Do Beaver's volume results support the decision usefulness of earnings information? Explain.

d. Which is the better indicator of decision usefulness, the abnormal return measure (Figure 5.1) or the volume measure? Explain.   (CGA-Canada)

9. Explain the impact of firm size on the ERC.   (CGA-Canada)

10. X Ltd. is a rapidly growing firm that uses conservative, high-quality accounting policies. Y Ltd. is growing more slowly and is a rarity in that it uses market value accounting for its capital assets and related amortization.

   Otherwise, X Ltd. and Y Ltd. are quite similar. They are the same size, and have similar capital structures and similar betas.

   Required

   a. Both X and Y Ltd. report the same GN in earnings this year. Which firm would you expect to have the greater security market response (ERC) to this good earnings news? Explain.

   b. Suppose that X Ltd. had a much higher debt-to-equity ratio and beta than Y Ltd. Would your answer to part **a** change? Explain.   (CGA-Canada)

11. On the basis of the empirical evidence presented in this chapter, do you feel the FASB is correct in its claim in SFAC 1 (see Section 3.8) that investors' expectations about future enterprise performance "are commonly based at least partly on evaluations of past enterprise performance"?   (CGA-Canada)

12. By defining extraordinary items to be infrequent, not typical of normal business activities, and not depending on management decision, Section 3480 of the *CICA Handbook* greatly increases the need for adequate disclosure of the components of reported net income. Explain why.

13. a. Describe the usual approach to estimating beta risk of a security from stock market data.

   b. Discuss two sources of problems of estimating beta accurately using this approach.

   c. Name three financial-statement-based risk measures which have been found to be correlated with security beta. What is a likely reason why accounting-based risk measures and security betas are correlated?

      (CGA-Canada)

14. Shown below are the income statement and comparative balance sheets of N Ltd., from its 1995 annual report. The 1995 statement of changes in financial position of N Ltd. (not attached) shows operating cash flow as $2,386.

Required

a. What is the amount of net accruals included in N Ltd.'s 1995 net income?

b. Use the information in the income statement and balance sheets of N Ltd. to calculate the various individual accruals and reconcile to the net total in part **a**.

c. We know from the empirical research described in this chapter that share price responds to net income. We also know that net income can be disaggregated into operating cash flow and net income components. Which component—cash flow or accruals—do you think would produce the strongest share price response? Explain.   (CGA-Canada)

N LTD.
INCOME STATEMENT
Year Ended December 31, 1995

Contract income	$11,684
Cost of contracts	9,073
Gross profit	2,611
General and administrative expenses	1,346
Depreciation	176
Interest	16
	1,538
Operating profit	1,073
Equity income from affiliates	165
Other income	52
	217
Income before income taxes and extraordinary items	1,290
Income taxes:	
Current	584
Deferred	59
	643
Income before extraordinary items	647
Extraordinary items	—
Net income for year	$ 647

N LTD.
BALANCE SHEETS
As at December 31

	1995	1994
Assets		
Current assets:		
Cash	$ 693	$ —
Trade accounts receivable	2,107	3,464
Income taxes recoverable	—	506
Inventories	810	410
Prepaid expenses	61	99
	3,671	4,479
Investments in affiliated companies	405	203
Machinery and equipment	1,532	1,632
	$5,608	$6,314
Liabilities		
Current liabilities:		
Bank indebtedness	$ —	$1,291
Accounts payable and accrued liabilities	398	497
Income taxes payable	282	34
Deferred income taxes	83	64
	763	1,886
Deferred income taxes	62	22
	825	1,908
Shareholders' Equity		
Share capital	2,268	2,268
Capital contributed on issue of warrants	80	80
Retained earnings	3,895	3,275
Excess of appraised value of fixed		
assets over depreciated cost	1,175	1,307
	7,418	6,930
Less: Cost of shares purchased	2,635	2,524
	4,783	4,406
	$5,608	$6,314

15. Why does financial statement information have characteristics of a public good? What does this imply about using the *extent* of security market reaction to accounting information to guide accountants? Standard setters? (CGA-Canada)

16. You estimate empirically the ERC of firm J as 0.38. Firm K is identical to firm J in terms of size, earning power, persistence of earnings, and risk. Unlike firm J, however, firm K supplements its income statement with a financial forecast. You estimate firm K's ERC as 0.57. Which firm's net income report appears to be more useful to investors? Explain. Does this mean that all firms should be required to prepare financial forecasts? Explain.

17. In 1991, the AICPA established a Special Committee on Financial Reporting. This committee, made up of several leaders in public accounting, industry, and academia, was charged with reviewing the current financial reporting model and making recommendations on what information management should make available to investors and creditors.

     In 1994, the Committee made several recommendations in a report entitled "Report of AICPA Special Committee on Financial Reporting" that it argued should help investors and other users to improve their assessment of a firm's prospects, thereby increasing the decision usefulness of annual reports. Here are two of their recommendations:

     • The Committee recommended that companies differentiate between core activities and non-core activities in their income statement, balance sheet, and cash flow statement. "A company's core activities—usual and recurring events—provide the best historical data from which users discern trends and relationships and make their predictions about the future." Non-core activities are defined as "unusual and nonrecurring activities or events (non-core effects) as well as interest charges. Without adjustment, non-core effects can distort or mask an important trend or relationship in the company's ongoing business."

     • Many companies are faced with litigations from investors who feel that they did not live up to their forecasted forward-looking information. "Because of this, managements see disclosure of forward-looking information, even though helpful to users, as providing ammunition for future groundless lawsuits." This means that a lot of managers are reluctant to disclose forward-looking information. In the light of this situation, the Committee recommended that there be "safe harbours" in order to eliminate "unwarranted litigation" when disclosing forward-looking information. The Committee further suggested that standard setters include rules that are "specific enough to enable companies to demonstrate compliance with requirements."

SOURCE: Excerpts reprinted with permission from report of the AICPA Special Committee on Financial Reporting. © 1994 by American Institute of Certified Public Accountants, Inc.

Required

a. To what extent will the proposed additional disclosures suggested above replace MD&A?

b. Use the concept of earnings persistence to explain why the Committee recommends separate reporting of the results of "core" activities on the income statement.

c. What benefits for investors may result, if, as proposed, court protection is provided for companies that disclose and make forecasts about their forward-looking information?

18. It is important to realize that different bases of accounting, such as present value accounting and historical-cost-based accounting, do not affect total earnings over the life of the firm, but only the timing of the recognition of those earnings. In effect, over the life of the firm, the firm "earns what it earns," and different bases of accounting will all produce earnings that add up to this total.

If this is so, then we would expect that the greater the number of time periods over which we aggregate a firm's historical cost earnings, the closer the resulting total will be to economic earnings, that is, the earnings total that would be produced over the same periods under ideal conditions.

This was studied by Easton, Harris, and Ohlson (1992) (EHO) and by Warfield and Wild (1992) (WW). EHO proxied economic income by the return on the firm's shares on the securities market. When this return was aggregated over varying periods of time (up to 10 years) and compared with historical-cost-based earnings returns for similar periods, the comparison improved as the time period lengthened. WW studied a similar phenomenon for shorter periods. They found, for example, that the association between economic and accounting income for quarterly time periods was on average about 1/10 of their association for an annual period, consistent with historical-cost-based net income lagging behind economic income in its recognition of relevant economic events.

Required

a. In Example 2.1, calculate net income for years 1 and 2 assuming that P.V. Ltd. used straight-line depreciation for its capital asset, while retaining all other assumptions. Verify that total net income over the two-year life of P.V. Ltd. equals the total net income that P.V. Ltd. would report using present value depreciation.

b. Do the same in Example 2.2, assuming that the state realization is bad and good in years 1 and 2 respectively.

The Measurement Perspective on Decision Usefulness

6.1 Overview

Our major purpose in this chapter is to enquire whether a further increase in decision usefulness can be attained by moving to a more measurement-oriented approach to financial reporting. By a measurement approach or perspective we mean a recognition by accountants of an increased responsibility to incorporate current values, also called fair values, into the financial statements proper. This approach is to be distinguished from the information perspective which has dominated Chapters 3, 4, and 5, where accountants rely on efficient security market theory to justify historical-cost-based financial statements supplemented by lots of additional disclosure. Of course, if a measurement perspective is to be useful, it must not be at the cost of a substantial reduction in reliability.

Recent years have witnessed an increasing presence of a measurement approach to financial reporting. That is, there is an increasing number of situations where accountants are overriding historical costs.

> The **measurement perspective** on financial reporting is an approach under which accountants undertake a responsibility to incorporate current values into the financial statements proper, providing that this can be done with reasonable reliability, thereby recognizing an increased obligation to assist investors to predict future firm performance.

While it is unlikely that a measurement perspective will *replace* the historical cost basis of accounting, it does seem to be the case that the relative balance of cost-based versus current-value-based information in the financial statements is moving in the current value direction. This may seem strange, given the problems that techniques such as RRA and current cost accounting have experienced. In this chapter we will suggest reasons why the measurement perspective is gaining increased recognition.

There always has been a considerable measurement component in the financial statements—cash, accounts receivable, current liabilities, and so forth. However, recent years have seen several new accounting standards which involve increased attention to measurement, relating to leases, pensions, capital assets, and acquisitions. Furthermore, new standards which involve an even greater use of current values, such as marking-to-market, are being developed and implemented. We will review some of these standards and, in the process, we will see the variety of ways that are being used to operationalize the measurement perspective.

Firms are increasingly making use of complex financial instruments to manage the risks to which they are exposed. In this chapter, we will review existing standards relating to hedge accounting and derivatives.

6.2 Reasons for Valuations

6.2.1 INTRODUCTION

A number of considerations come together to suggest that the decision usefulness of financial reporting may be enhanced by increased attention to measurement. From an empirical direction, it seems that reported net income explains only a small part of the variation of security prices around the date of earnings announcements. This raises questions about the relevance of historical-cost-based reporting. Also from an empirical direction, there is increasing evidence that security markets may not be as efficient as previously believed. This suggests that investors may need more help in assessing probabilities of future returns than they obtain from historical cost statements.

From a theoretical direction, the clean surplus theory of Ohlson shows that the market value of the firm can be expressed in terms of income statement and balance sheet variables. While the clean surplus theory applies to any basis of accounting, its demonstration that firm value depends on fundamental accounting variables is consistent with a measurement perspective.

Finally, increased attention to measurement is supported from a practical direction. In recent years, auditors have been subjected to major lawsuits, particularly following failures of financial institutions. In retrospect, it appears that asset values of failed institutions may have been seriously overstated. Accounting standards which require marking-to-market, ceiling tests, and other current-value-based techniques may help to reduce auditor liability in this regard.

We now review each of these considerations in more detail.

6.2.2 THE EXPLANATORY POWER OF NET INCOME

In Chapter 5 we saw that empirical accounting research has established that security prices do respond to the information content of net income. The ERC research, in particular, suggests that the market is quite sophisticated in its ability to extract value implications from financial statements prepared on the historical cost basis.

However, Lev (1989) has pointed out that the market's response to the good or bad news in earnings is really quite small, even *after* the impact of economy-wide events has been allowed for as explained in Figure 5.1. In fact, only 2 to 5% of the abnormal variability of narrow-window security returns around the date of release of earnings information can be attributed to earnings itself.[1] The proportion of variability explained goes up somewhat for wider windows—see our discussion in Section 5.3.2. Nevertheless, most of the variability of security returns seems due to factors other than the change of earnings.

An understanding of Lev's point requires an appreciation of the difference between **statistical significance** and **practical significance**. A statistic such as the ERC can be significantly different from zero, but yet can be quite small. Thus, we can be quite sure that there *is* a security market response to earnings (as opposed to *no* response) but at the same time we can be disappointed that the response is not larger than it is. To put it another way, suppose that, on average, security prices change by $1 during a short window of three or four days around the date of earnings announcements. Then, Lev's point is that only about 2 to 5¢ of this change is due to the earnings announcement itself, even after allowing for market-wide price changes during this period.

Of course, we would never expect net income to explain *all* of a security's abnormal return, except under ideal conditions. The information perspective recognizes that there is always a large number of other relevant information sources and, indeed, that accountants are in competition with these other sources. Even if accountants were the *only* source of information to the market, our discussion of the informativeness of price in Section 4.5, and the resulting need to recognize the presence of noise and liquidity traders, tells us that accounting information cannot explain all of abnormal return variability.

Nevertheless, a "market share" for net income of only 2 to 5% seems low, even after the above counterarguments are taken into account. Lev attributes this low share to poor earnings quality, a charge that has led to empirical research into the sources of low quality. For example, Collins, Kothari, Shanken, and Sloan (1994) present evidence that it is due to a lack of timeliness of historical-cost-based earnings. This leads to the suggestion that perhaps earnings quality could be improved by introducing a measurement perspective into the financial statements, providing that the increased timeliness of current-value-based earnings is not outweighed by a decrease in reliability. At the very least, Lev's concerns suggest that there is still lots of room for accountants to improve the usefulness of earnings information.

6.2.3   EFFICIENT SECURITY MARKET ANOMALIES

The research described in Chapter 5 assumes security market efficiency. Thus, a finding that firms' security prices respond to the good or bad news in earnings on or before the date of the earnings announcement supports not only the hypothesis that accounting information is useful, but also the hypothesis of efficient security markets on which the research is based. Interestingly, there is increasing evidence that security markets may not be as efficient as previously believed. Recall from our discussion of Beaver's 1973 paper in Section 4.4 that, as long as there was full disclosure of relevant information, the *form* of disclosure did not matter—it could be buried in footnotes or even provided by other, more timely or cost-effective sources. The underlying assumption was that there were enough informed, sophisticated investors that all information would be quickly incorporated into security price in an unbiased manner. However, recent evidence raises questions that, at the least, suggest investors may need more help in assessing the implications of financial statements for future returns than the information approach has assumed. We now consider some of these **efficient security market anomalies**.

Post-announcement Drift

As just mentioned, once a firm's current earnings announcement becomes known, the information content should be quickly digested by the market and incorporated into security price. There should be no further market reaction to the good or bad news in earnings. However, it has long been known that this is not exactly what happens. For firms that report good news in earnings, their abnormal returns tend to drift upward for at least 60 days following the earnings announcement. Similarly, firms that report bad earnings news have their abnormal returns drift downward for a similar period. Indeed, one can see some evidence of this **post-announcement drift** in the 1968 Ball and Brown study—see Figure 5.2.[2]

Reasons for post-announcement drift have been extensively studied. For example, Foster, Olsen, and Shevlin (1984) examined several possible explanations for its existence following quarterly earnings announcements. Their results suggested that apparent post-announcement drift may be an artifact of the earnings expectation model used by the researcher. Most studies of market response to earnings announcements measure their information content by some proxy for *unexpected* earnings. When Foster, Olsen, and Shevlin proxied unexpected earnings by the change in earnings from the same quarter last year, they found strong evidence of the existence of post-announcement drift. However, with other proxies for unexpected earnings there appeared to be no such drift. Since we do not know which earnings expectation model is the correct one (or even whether unexpected earnings are the appropriate construct—see our discussion in Section 5.3.3), the Foster, Olsen, and Shevlin results tended to leave the existence of post-announcement drift up in the air, so to speak.

Be sure you see the significance of post-announcement drift. If it exists, investors could earn arbitrage profits, before transactions costs, by buying shares of good news firms on the day of their earnings announcements and selling short shares of bad news firms. But, if investors scrambled to do this, the prices of good news firms' shares would rise right away, and those of bad news firms' shares would fall, thereby eliminating the post-announcement drift. Consequently, post-announcement drift poses a real puzzle for efficient market theory.

Subsequently, Bernard and Thomas (1989) (BT) examined this issue. In a large sample of firms over the period from 1974–86, they documented the presence of post-announcement drift. Indeed, an investor following the strategy of buying GN firms and selling short BN, on day 0, and holding for 60 days would have earned an average annual return of 18%, over and above the market-wide return, before transactions costs, in their sample.

BT then set out to try to explain *why* post-announcement drift persists. One possible explanation would be changes in firms' riskiness (as measured by beta) after they announce GN or BN.[3] However, BT present convincing arguments and evidence against a risk-based explanation.

Another possible explanation is based on transactions costs. It is possible that the profits from the investment strategy merely represent the level of transactions costs required to earn the profits.[4] BT present some evidence that transactions costs limit the amount of the post-announcement drift. Nevertheless, the 18% return that they report seems high to be completely explained by transactions costs.

However, the most interesting possible explanation is that *investors appear to underestimate the implications of current earnings for future earnings.* As BT point out, it is a known fact that quarterly earnings changes are positively correlated. That is, if a firm reports, say, GN this quarter, in the sense that this quarter's earnings are greater than the same quarter last year, there is a greater-than-50% chance that its next-quarter earnings will also be greater than last year's. Rational investors should anticipate this and, as they bid up the price of the firm's shares in response to the *current* GN, they should also bid them up some more due to the increased probability of GN in *future* periods. However, BT present evidence that this does not happen, suggesting that post-announcement drift results from the market taking considerable time to figure this out. In terms of the information system given in Table 3.2, BT's results suggest that Bill Cautious understates the main diagonal probabilities.

While risk-based and transactions-cost-based explanations for post-announcement drift, were they correct, are consistent with security market efficiency, the serial correlation explanation is not. Consequently, BT's findings represent a serious and important challenge to security market efficiency.

Market Efficiency with Respect to Non-earnings Information

There is more information in the financial statements than just net income. Given that the market responds to net income information, it seems reasonable to expect that it would also respond to relevant balance sheet and supplementary information. However, evidence of such response has been difficult to find. We have already seen, in Section 5.8, that evidence about the decision usefulness of RRA information is fairly weak.

One possible reason is that the market may not fully use the non-earnings information. More specifically, it may not appreciate the extent to which current balance sheet information, such as financial ratios or unusual accruals, may predict future earnings. While Lev and Thiagarajan (1991) (see Section 5.4.1) find evidence that the market does respond to certain balance sheet information, results of other studies suggest that it may wait until the balance sheet information shows up in future earnings or cash flows before reacting. If so, this would raise further questions about market efficiency, and it should be possible to use the non-earnings information to devise an investment strategy to "beat the market." Evidence that the market does wait, and details of a strategy that does appear to beat the market, appear in a paper by Ou and Penman (1989) (OP), which we now describe.

OP began their study by deriving a list of 68 financial ratios. They obtained a large sample of firms and, for each firm, calculated each ratio for each of the years 1965 to 1972 inclusive. Then, for each ratio, they investigated how well that ratio predicted whether net income would rise or fall in the next year. Some ratios predicted better than others. For example, the return on total assets proved to be highly associated with the change in next year's net income—the higher the ratio in one year the greater the probability that net income would increase the next. However, the ratio of sales to accounts receivable, also called accounts receivable turnover, did not predict the change in next year's net income very well.

OP then took the 16 ratios that predicted *best* in the above investigation and used them as independent variables to estimate a *multivariate* regression model to predict changes in next year's net incomes. This model then represents their sample's best predictor of next year's earning changes, since it takes the 68 ratios they began with, distills them to the 16 best on an individual-ratio basis, and uses these 16 in a multivariate prediction model.

Armed with this model, OP then applied it to predicting the earnings changes of their sample firms during 1973 to 1983. That is, the prediction model was estimated over the period from 1968 to 1972 and then used to make predictions from 1973 to 1983. For each firm and for each of the years 1973 to 1983, the prediction from the multivariate model is in the form of a *probability* that net income will rise in the following year.

OP then used these predictions as the basis for the following investment strategy. For each firm and for each year, *buy* that firm's shares at the market price *three months* after the firm's year end *if* the multivariate regression model predicts that the probability of that firm's net income rising next year is 0.6 or more (the three months is to allow sufficient time for the firm's financial statements to be released and for the market to digest their contents). Conversely, if the model's prediction is that the probability of net income rising is 0.4 or less, *sell short* that firm's shares three months after its year-end.

Notice that this investment strategy is implementable—it is based on information that is actually available to investors at the time. Also, in theory, the strategy need not require any capital investment by the investor, because the proceeds from the short sales can be used to pay for the shares that are bought. (In practice, some capital would be required due to restrictions on short sales and, of course, brokerage fees and other transactions costs.)

Once bought, shares were held for 24 months and then sold at the market price at that time. Shares sold short were purchased at the market price 24 months later to satisfy the short-sale obligation.

The reasoning behind this investment strategy is quite straightforward. We know from Ball and Brown that firms that report GN earnings enjoy an increase in share price, and suffer a decrease for BN. If we can predict in advance, using ratio information from previous years, which firms will report GN and which BN, then we may be able to capture these gains by the above investment strategy.

The question then is, does this investment strategy beat the market? To answer this question, OP calculated the profit or loss on each transaction, which was then converted into a rate of return. These returns were then aggregated to give the total return over all transactions. Next, it was necessary to adjust for the market-wide rate of return on stocks, so as to express returns net of the performance of the market as a whole. For example, if OP's investment strategy produced a return of 8%, but the whole market rose by 10%, one could hardly say that the strategy beat the market. However, when market-wide returns were removed, OP found that their strategy earned a return of 14.53% over two years, *in excess of market-wide return*, before transactions costs. As the chances of this happening by chance are almost zero, their investment strategy appears to have been successful in beating the market. Again, it is possible that transactions costs could explain this return, but 14.53% does seem high to be fully explained on these grounds.

OP then went on to check that this result was not because of risk differences between the firms in their sample and market-wide risk. Similar to Bernard and Thomas, it is possible that OP's prediction model identifies high-risk firms, and the 14.53% return they report merely represents the fact that risk-averse investors demand higher returns for higher risk. OP conducted tests to check on this and concluded that risk was not driving their results.

Assuming that transactions costs and risk do not fully explain the excess returns on their investment strategy, OP's results are surprising, because under efficient market theory those results should not have occurred. The investment strategy was based solely on information that was available to all investors—financial ratios from firms' financial statements. Efficient market theory suggests that this ratio information will quickly and efficiently be incorporated into market prices. The share prices of the firms that OP bought or sold short should have already adjusted to reflect the probable increases or decreases in next year's net incomes by the time they bought them, in which case their investment strategy would not have earned excess returns. The fact that OP did earn excess returns suggests that the market did not fully digest all the information contained in financial ratios. Rather, the market price only adjusted as the next two years' earnings increases or decreases were actually announced. But by then, OP had already bought or sold short. Consequently, the OP results serve as another anomaly for efficient security market theory.

The OP results have generated considerable additional investigation. In a related study, Holthausen and Larcker (1992) (H&L) also documented excess returns to a financial statement ratio-based investment strategy. They used ratios to predict the sign of excess returns directly, rather than routing the prediction through the change in earnings. In addition, H&L repeated the OP investment strategy over a later time period (1978-88) but found that excess returns were not earned. This latter result suggests the possibility that OP's results were specific to the time period they examined.

Greig (1992) reexamined the OP results and concluded that their excess returns were due more likely to the effects of firm size on expected returns than to a failure of the market to fully evaluate accounting information. There is evidence that firm size explains share returns in addition to beta (Banz, 1981). On the basis of more elaborate controls for firm size than in OP, Greig's results suggest that OP's excess returns go away when size is fully taken into account. Greig also presented evidence that the H&L results may also be explained by firm size.

Stober (1992) documented excess returns to the OP investment strategy. He showed, however, that the excess returns continue for up to six years following the release of the financial statements. If the OP excess returns are due to a deviation of share price from fundamental value, one would hardly expect that it would take six years before the market caught on. In other words, while the market may wait until the information in ratios shows up in earnings, it is unlikely that it would wait this long, suggesting that the OP results reflect some permanent difference in expected returns such as firm size or risk rather than a deviation from fundamental values.

It should be noted, however, that even if the OP results are due to size effects, this does not necessarily rule out support for market inefficiency. Given the theory underlying the CAPM, the only firm-specific factor affecting a share's expected return is its beta—see Section 4.3. Thus, if the market also looks to firm size in setting expected returns this, in itself, may suggest inefficiency.

A counterargument, though, is given by Ball (1992) and Tinic (1990). This is that the securities market may be efficient but the CAPM is misspecified. Thus, beta may not be the only firm-specific variable that, in theory, determines expected return. Until fundamental theoretical issues such as this are resolved, we may conclude that the OP results remain as a challenge to the efficient market hypothesis.

The Pricing of Closed-end Fund IPOs

Hanley, Lee, and Seguin (1996) (HLS) analyzed the market price and trading volume behaviour of a sample of 65 initial public offerings (IPOs) of closed-end funds[5] between January 1, 1988 and May 31, 1989. Their sample included essentially all of the new closed-end funds on the NYSE and the American Stock Exchange (AMEX) during this period.

It seems to be a fact of life in the marketplace that the shares of newly issued closed-end funds tend to drop in price during the first few months after the initial offering. The HLS sample was no exception—the average cumulative return by 100 days after issue was −6.8%. However, by looking more closely at how this significant negative return came about, HLS came up with some interesting findings. First, the price declines did not begin immediately, but began 30 days or more after issue, usually with a sharp drop.

Second, the market appeared to be characterized by the presence of "flippers." These are large investors who buy a large number of shares of the IPO and then sell them immediately once trading begins. HLS found that, in the first few days of trading, volume was extremely high and the great majority of the trades that took place were seller-initiated. This is consistent with the presence of flippers.

The question then is: If there is a large immediate imbalance of sellers over buyers, why do the funds' share prices not start to decline for 30 or more days? The answer seems to be price management by the issues' underwriters. By over-allotting the IPO to small investors in an amount equal to the expected volume of flipping, the underwriter can use the flipped shares to fill the over-allotted orders. Since supply and demand then remain in balance, the market price does not begin to decline until the stabilization policy is discontinued, some 30 days later. However, by that point, the "big guys" are out of the market and, it seems, the initial offering price has been maintained long enough that the subsequent price decline does not unduly tarnish the underwriters' reputations in the eyes of the small investors, who will now see the value of their holdings decrease by an average of 6.8%.

The HLS paper illustrates a tendency in recent security market research to model the **micro-structure** of the market. The paper gives formal attention to underwriters—the supply side of the IPO market, and to two classes of investors—large and small. In our consideration of the market to this point we have simply thought of it as being composed of a large number of investors who make buy/sell decisions, with market price as the result. While this is satisfactory for many purposes, the HLS paper does point out that the structure of the market is not this simple—there are different classes of buyers and sellers with different degrees of market power. Market price can be affected by the strategic actions of these groups, in addition to the forces of demand and supply. At the very least, the HLS paper serves as another illustration of our conclusion in Section 4.5.1 that the theory that market price fully reflects all available information must be interpreted with care.

For present purposes, however, the unanswered question is why one group of investors—the small purchasers of IPOs of closed-end funds—allowed itself to be systematically manipulated by large investors. Granted, they may not know what is going on, but certainly the poor performance of such funds in the few months following issue would be a matter of public record. The rational thing to do would be to wait 100 days and then buy. The fact that this does not seem to happen is yet another apparent anomaly for efficient securities markets.

Conclusions About Security Market Efficiency

Despite the apparent anomalies discussed above, it is very difficult to "prove" either market efficiency or inefficiency. Some of these difficulties were examined by Foster (1979). While there are literally thousands of studies, such as Ball and Brown in Section 5.3 and the ERC studies of Section 5.4, whose results are consistent with efficient security market predictions, Foster points out that we do not know whether the *magnitude* of price response in these studies is what it should be under efficiency. For example, Ball and Brown reported an average excess return of 7% for their GN firms, but perhaps this should have been 10%, or 3%, given an efficient market. It should be noted, though, that the direction and speed of response, and the anticipation of the GN or BN in earnings that Ball and Brown reported, are as predicted by efficient market theory.

Another problem, which could be responsible for the anomalies, is that inside information and publicly available information are not completely separate categories, but shade into one another. Thus one must be careful to look at the information available to the market before drawing conclusions about anomalies. Furthermore, as Foster points out, the extent of publicly available information depends on the transactions costs that investors are willing to bear (see note 4). The investment strategies required to earn arbitrage profits may be quite costly in terms of investor time and effort, requiring substantial monitoring of earnings announcements, annual reports, and market prices, including development of the required expertise. Thus, profits even as high as the 18% per annum reported by Bernard and Thomas and the 14.53% over two years in Ou and Penman may appear to be anomalies only because the costs of the investment strategies required to actually earn them are at least this high. Even the losses of small investors in closed-end fund IPOs can be explained in this manner. Small investors may feel that the losses they suffer from using the advice of underwriters, brokers, fund managers, and other investment experts are less than the costs they would incur to develop the necessary information and expertise themselves.

If we accept this argument, security market efficiency can then be reconciled with the anomalies, at least up to the level of transactions costs. To put it another way, we would hardly expect the market to be efficient with respect to more information than it is cost-effective for investors to acquire.

The problem with a transactions-cost-based defence of efficiency, however, is that *any* apparent anomaly can be dismissed on cost grounds. If cost is used to explain everything, then it explains nothing. That is, unless we know what the costs of an investment strategy *should* be, we do not know whether the profits earned by investment strategies such as those of Bernard and Thomas and Ou and Penman, or the losses of investors in closed-end fund IPOs, are anomalous.

A second way to possibly explain anomalies is by *risk differences*, as previously discussed. However, at least for the BT and HLS results, this explanation does not seem convincing or relevant.

The third way to view these anomalies is to accept them, but recognize that security market efficiency is a matter of *degree*. Instead of asking if the market is efficient, which may be the wrong question, we can think of the market as being *reasonably* efficient—close enough that the theory is not invalidated, but recognizing that certain anomalies may occur. Perhaps the real test of security market efficiency is whether the arbitrage opportunities from post-announcement drift, financial ratio analysis, and other anomalies not reported here[6] will disappear once they are pointed out to the market.

Despite our continuing faith in security market efficiency, it is important to note that the presence of anomalies such as the three outlined above lend support to the measurement perspective. To the extent that investors are unable, or find it too costly, to fully develop the information content of historical-cost-based financial statements, perhaps accountants should undertake to do more of it for them, by incorporating more current values into the statements on their behalf. If this can be done without substantial loss of reliability, the ability of net income to predict future performance will increase and investors will have more scope to gather information from the balance sheet than under historical cost accounting.

6.2.4 OHLSON'S CLEAN SURPLUS THEORY

Three Formulae for Firm Value

The Ohlson clean surplus theory provides a framework consistent with the measurement perspective, by showing how the market value of the firm, hence security returns, can be expressed in terms of fundamental balance sheet and income statement components. The theory assumes ideal conditions, including dividend irrelevancy. Nevertheless, it has had some success in explaining and predicting actual firm value. Our outline of the theory is based on a simplified version of Feltham and Ohlson (1995) (F&O).

Much of the theory has already been included in earlier discussions, particularly Example 2.2 of P.V. Ltd. operating under ideal conditions of uncertainty. You may wish to review Example 2.2 at this time. In this section we will pull together these earlier discussions, and extend the P.V. Ltd. example to allow for earnings persistence.

F&O begin by pointing out that the fundamental determinant of a firm's value is its dividend stream. Assume, for P.V. Ltd. in Example 2.2, that the bad-economy state was realized in year 1 and recall that P.V. pays no dividends, until a liquidating dividend at time 2. Then, the present value of dividends at time 1 is just the expected present value of the cash on hand at time 2:

$$PA_1 = \frac{0.5}{1.10}(\$110 + \$100) + \frac{0.5}{1.10}(\$110 + \$200)$$

$$= \$95.45 + \$140.91$$

$$= \$236.36$$

Recall that cash flows per period are $100 if the bad state happens and $200 for the good state. The first term inside the brackets represents the cash on hand at time 1 invested at a return of $R_f = 0.10$ in period 2.

Given dividend irrelevancy, P.V.'s market value can also be expressed in terms of its future cash flows. Continuing our assumption that the bad state happened in period 1:

$$PA_1 = \$100 + 0.5 \times \frac{\$100}{1.10} + 0.5 \times \frac{\$200}{1.10}$$

$$= \$100 + \$136.36$$

$$= \$236.36$$

where the first term is cash on hand at time 1, that is, the present value of $100 cash is just $100.

The market value of the firm can also be expressed in terms of financial statement variables.

F&O show that:

$$PA_t = bv_t + g_t$$

at any time t, where bv_t is the net book value of the firm's assets per the balance sheet and g_t is the expected present value of future abnormal earnings. For this relationship to hold it is necessary that all items of gain or loss go through the income statement, which is the source of the term "clean surplus" in the theory. For P.V. Ltd., assuming the bad state in period 1:

$$PA_1 = \$236.36 + \$0$$

$$= \$236.36$$

where $bv_1 = \$236.36$ is read directly from the balance sheet—see Example 2.2.

Note that the expected value of abnormal earnings is zero. This illustrates a special case of the F&O model called **unbiased accounting**. When accounting is unbiased, and abnormal earnings do not persist, all of firm value appears on the balance sheet. In effect, the income statement has no information content, as we noted in Example 2.2.

The above formula for PA_t holds for any basis of accounting, not just unbiased accounting under ideal conditions. For example, if P.V. Ltd. used historical cost accounting, bv_t may be biased downwards relative to its market value. As a result, the firm has *unrecorded* goodwill $g_t > 0$.

Then, the clean surplus theory leads directly to the measurement perspective, since it suggests that the accountant should measure bv_t as completely and accurately as possible, so as to reduce the need for the market to estimate g_t from other sources. For example, valuing at least some assets and liabilities at market value and recording intangible assets such as advertising and R&D on the books may benefit investors, if it can be done with reasonable reliability, in the sense that more firm value is included in bv_t and less in g_t. This argument is supported by the evidence of efficient security market anomalies in Section 6.2.3, where we suggested that investors may not be as adept at figuring out g_t from other sources as the information perspective has assumed.

Earnings Persistence

F&O then introduce the important concept of *earnings persistence* into the theory. Specifically, they assume that:

$$ox_t{}^a = \omega ox_{t-1}{}^a + \widetilde{\epsilon}_t$$

where $ox_t{}^a$ is abnormal earnings for year t. The $\widetilde{\epsilon}_t$ are the effects of state realization in period t on earnings, where the "~" indicates that these effects are random, as at the beginning of the period. As in Example 2.2, the expected value of state realization is zero and realizations are independent from one period to the next.

The ω is a persistence parameter, where $0 \leq \omega < 1$. For $\omega = 0$, we have the case of Example 2.2. However, $\omega > 0$ is not unreasonable. Often, the effects of state realization in one year will persist into future years. For example, the bad-state realization in year 1 of Example 2.2 may be because of a rise in interest rates, the economic effects of which will likely persist beyond the current year. Then, ω captures the proportion of the $-\$50$ abnormal earnings in year 1 that would continue into the following year.

However, note that $\omega < 1$, that is, abnormal earnings of any particular year will die out over time. For example, the effects of a rise in interest rates will eventually dissipate. More generally, forces of competition will eventually eliminate positive, or negative, abnormal earnings.

Note also that persistence is related to its empirical counterpart in the ERC research. Recall from Section 5.4.1 that ERCs are higher the greater the persistence in earnings. As we will see below, this is exactly what clean surplus theory predicts—the higher ω is, the greater the impact of the income statement on firm value.

Finally, note that the theory assumes that the set of possible values of $\tilde{\epsilon}_t$ and their probabilities are known to investors, consistent with ideal conditions. It is also assumed that investors know ω. If these assumptions are relaxed, rational investors will want information about $\tilde{\epsilon}_t$ and ω and can use Bayes' theorem to update their subjective state probabilities. Thus, nothing in the theory conflicts with the role of decision theory that was explained in Chapter 3.

EXAMPLE 6.1 PRESENT VALUE MODEL UNDER UNCERTAINTY AND PERSISTENCE

We now extend Example 2.2 to allow for persistence. Continue all the assumptions of that example and add the further assumption ω = 0.40. Thus, if the bad-economy state happens in year 1, not only will there be −$50 of abnormal earnings in that year, but 40% of this amount will persist to reduce operating earnings in year 2, and conversely for the good state.

We begin with the depreciation schedule for P.V.'s capital asset, based on the expected decline in the asset's present value as at time 0. This depreciation schedule is the same as in Example 2.2, that is:

Depreciation, year 1 = $260.33 − $136.36 = $123.97
Depreciation, year 2 = $136.36 − 0   = $136.36
                                           $260.33

Now, assume that the bad state happens in year 1. (A similar analysis applies if the good state happens.) First, we calculate P.V.'s market value at time 1 based on expected future dividends:

$$PA_1 = \frac{0.5}{1.10}(\$110 - 0.40 \times \$50 + \$100) + \frac{0.5}{1.10}(\$110 - 0.40 \times \$50 + \$200)$$

$$= \frac{0.5}{1.10} \times \$190 + \frac{0.5}{1.10} \times \$290$$

$$= \$86.36 + \$131.82$$

$$= \$218.18$$

Note the effect of persistence—40% of year 1 abnormal earnings will persist to reduce year 2 cash flows. Otherwise, the calculation is identical with Example 2.2. We see that the effect of persistence of the bad state is to reduce the time 1 firm value by 236.36 − 218.18 = $18.18, the present value of the −$20 of reduced future cash flows.

F&O also show that the firm's market value can be expressed in terms of financial statement variables:

$$PA_t = bv_t + \alpha \text{ (abnormal earnings in year t)}$$

where $\alpha = \omega/(1 + R_f)$ is a capitalization factor.[7] Then, in our example, for t = 1:

Cash on hand	= $100.00
Book value of asset, based on depreciation schedule, $260.33 − $123.97	= $136.36
bv_t	= $236.36

This gives:

$$PA_1 = \$236.36 + \frac{0.40}{1.10} \times -\$50$$

$$= \$236.36 - \$18.18$$

$$= \$218.18$$

The implications of this formula are twofold. First, even under ideal conditions, *all the action is no longer on the balance sheet*. The income statement is important too, because it reveals the current year's abnormal earnings, 40% of which will persist into future periods. Thus, we can regard abnormal earnings as 40% persistent in this example.

Second, the formula implies that investors will want information to help them assess persistent earnings, since these are important to the future performance of the firm. Our discussion of extraordinary items in Section 5.5 showed how accountants can help in this regard, by appropriate classification of items with low persistence. Also, the formula is consistent with the empirical impact of persistence on the ERC as outlined in Section 5.4.1, where we saw that greater persistence is associated with stronger investor reaction to current earnings.

Finally, the clean surplus theory's assumption of ideal conditions should be emphasized again. In particular, the theory ignores information asymmetry. The extent to which it carries over to more realistic conditions is thus an empirical matter. However, we have just mentioned that empirical ERC results seem consistent with the model. Also, in Section 5.3.3 we reported on the results of Easton and Harris (1991), who found that levels of earnings better explained security returns than earnings changes. Note that the F&O model is in terms of levels of earnings. In addition, empirical results consistent with the model are reported by Fairfield (1994).

6.2.5 *AUDITORS' LEGAL LIABILITY*

Perhaps the main source of pressure in favour of the measurement perspective comes as a reaction to spectacular failures of large firms, particularly financial institutions. Many such failures have taken place in the United States. For example, an article in the *Wall Street Journal* (March 11, 1994, p. A2) reports that Resolution Trust Corp. has lawsuits against Deloitte and Touche totalling $1.4 billion, and the Federal Deposit Insurance Corp. has lawsuits of another $450 million. The charges arise from alleged clean audit opinions issued to savings and loan associations that, in retrospect, were insolvent. The article describes a proposed settlement of these lawsuits in excess of $300 million. While considerably less than the amounts at suit, this would still be the second-largest liability settlement surrounding the savings and loan debacle. (The largest was a $400 million settlement by Ernst and Young for similar charges.)

Under historical cost accounting it can happen that firms that are here today, in the sense that their balance sheets and income statements show them to be going concerns, are gone tomorrow. While accountants and auditors may claim that information about impending failure was implicit in the notes or other sources, or was not their responsibility, there is a certain logic to questions raised by those who ask why the primary financial statements did not more clearly foresee the disaster. Auditors often have considerable difficulty in defending themselves from the lawsuits that usually accompany business failure.

Furthermore, these legal liability pressures are likely to continue to increase. For example, Jensen (1993) points out that as technology advances, more and more firms are finding themselves with substantial excess capacity. The resulting need to downsize leads to mergers and acquisitions, reorganizations, layoffs, or bankruptcy. All of these events put severe pressure on the adequacy of historical-cost-based net income and asset valuation.

In addition, firms are facing increasing pressures to behave in socially and environmentally responsible ways. Many firms face substantial future liabilities in this regard, for example in site restoration costs, which severely strain the concept of matching costs and revenues.

One way that accountants and auditors can protect themselves against these pressures is to adopt a measurement perspective, that is, introduce more current valuation into the accounts. Then, they can point out that the financial statements *anticipated* the value changes leading to bankruptcy, merger, downsizing, environmental liabilities, etc. Of course, this requires greater use of estimates and judgement but, because of legal liability, accountants may be more willing to adopt at least those current valuations that can be attained without substantial loss of reliability.

6.2.6 *SUMMARY*

Recall that the information perspective on financial reporting is content to accept the historical cost basis of accounting, and rely on full disclosure to enhance usefulness to investors. The form of disclosure does not matter, since it is assumed that there are enough rational, informed investors to quickly and correctly incorporate any reasonable form into the efficient market price. Empirical research has confirmed that the market finds net income information, at least, to be useful. In effect, empirical research under the information perspective tends to accept the efficient market price and to evaluate the usefulness of accounting information in terms of its association with this market price.

However, there are a number of questions about the information perspective. First, a "market share" of 2 to 5% for net income seems low and, despite theoretical support, it has been difficult to find much market reaction at all to non-earnings accounting information. Second, securities markets themselves may not be as fully efficient as had previously been believed, suggesting that investors might need some help in figuring out the full implications of accounting information for future returns. Finally, legal liability may force accountants to increase valuation-based numbers in the financial statements. These questions are reinforced by the development of a theory, the Ohlson clean surplus theory, that emphasizes the fundamental role of financial accounting information in determining firm value. This theory implies a more basic role for financial statements in reporting on firm value than the information perspective, which views accounting information as one of many information sources competing for the attention of the efficient market. Thus, the clean surplus theory leads naturally to the measurement perspective.

Of course, for reasons given in Sections 2.4 and 2.5, the measurement perspective would never extend to a complete set of financial statements on a current value basis. Historical cost is unlikely to be displaced as the primary accounting basis for capital assets, for example. Rather, the question is one of degree—to what degree will current values supplant costs in useful financial reporting? Consequently, our next task is to review GAAP from a valuation perspective. There always has been a substantial present value and market value component to the financial statements. But, as we shall see, recent years have witnessed a number of new current value standards.

6.3   *Longstanding Valuation Examples*

Even though financial statements are conventionally referred to as based on historical cost, they contain a substantial current value component. As a preliminary to a discussion of recent measurement-oriented standards, we will review some common longstanding instances of market- and present-value-based valuations.

6.3.1 POST-REVENUE REALIZATION ASSETS AND LIABILITIES

For most firms,[8] post-revenue realization assets and liabilities include cash, accounts receivable, and accounts payable. Cash, by definition, is valued at market. Accounts receivable, net of allowance for doubtful accounts, can be regarded as valued at present value. Current liabilities such as accounts payable can also be regarded as valued at present value. In the case of both accounts receivable and payable, we can argue that the length of time to collection/payment is sufficiently short that discounting is not needed, so that, effectively, they are valued on a present value basis. Valuation of post-revenue realization assets and liabilities is useful to investors who may wish to evaluate a firm's short-run solvency.

6.3.2 CASH FLOWS FIXED BY CONTRACT

Another common situation where measurement is at least partly on a present value basis occurs when cash flows surrounding assets and liabilities are fixed by contract, as in debt, leases, and pensions. We will briefly examine each of these.

Discount Amortization on Long-Term Bonds

Two methods are available for the amortization of discount or premium on bonds—the straight-line method and the effective-interest method. Under this latter method, the discount or premium is amortized so as to produce an interest expense or income each period at the effective rate established at issuance or acquisition. This constitutes an application of the present value model under certainty. We now illustrate the interest method applied to an investment in bonds intended to be held to maturity.

EXAMPLE 6.2 INTEREST METHOD OF DISCOUNT AMORTIZATION

A firm buys $10,000 par value of bonds on December 31, 1994, paying $8,869.92, to yield an **effective rate** of return of 12% per annum. The discount on the bonds is thus $1,130.08. The bonds pay interest annually on December 31, at a coupon rate of 10% and are due in 10 years, that is, on December 31, 2004.

First, we show that the price of the bonds on December 31, 1994 is equal to the present value of the future receipts from the bonds, discounted at the effective rate of 12%:

$$\text{PV of future receipts} = \text{PV of principal} + \text{PV of interest}$$

$$= \frac{\$10,000}{(1.12)^{10}} + 5.65022 \times \$1,000$$

$$= \$3,219.70 + \$5,650.22$$

$$= \$8,869.92$$

The first term is the present value of the bond principal, due in 10 years, at 12%. The second term is the present value at 12% of the annuity formed by the future $1,000 interest payments. The annuity factor of 5.65022 can be verified from an interest table.

Given that the current interest rate in the economy for an investment of this quality is 12%, the market price of the bonds must equal the present value of $8,869.92. This argument follows from the same arbitrage principle stated in Section 2.2. If the market price of the bonds were higher than this amount, investors would not buy them, because the yield would be less than 12% and they could earn 12% elsewhere on an investment of similar quality. Thus, the price would fall. If the market price were lower than $8,869.92, investors would clamour to buy them, because they would then be earning more than the market rate of interest. Thus, the price would rise. The only possible equilibrium price is $8,869.92. Consequently, on December 31, 1994, the investment's book value, market value, and present value are all equal.

Next, we show that one year later, on December 31, 1995, the book value also equals present value providing that the interest method of discount amortization is used and the effective rate of 12%, established at date of purchase, is held constant.

On December 31, 1995, nine years remain in the life of the bonds. Consequently, the present value of the future receipts from the bonds is now:

$$\text{PV of future receipts} = \frac{\$10,000}{(1.12)^9} + 5.32821 \times \$1,000$$

$$= \$8,934.31$$

Thus, the new present value of the bonds is $8,934.31. Under the interest method of discount amortization, the following journal entry is made:

Dec. 31, 1995

Investment in bonds 64.39
    Interest income...64.39
To amortize discount: $8,934.31 − $8,869.92.

The new book value of the bonds is $8,934.31, equal to the present value of future receipts. This equality with present value will continue to hold in future years as long as the interest method of discount amortization is used.

Finally, we show that the investment income from the bonds for the year is equal to 12% multiplied by the opening book value of the bonds:

Cash received from interest in the year	$1,000.00
Discount amortization	64.39
Income from the bonds	$1,064.39

This is equal to 12% × the opening book value: 12% × 8,869.92 = $1,064.39.

Example 6.2 corresponds directly with our previous theoretical illustration in Example 2.1—at each financial statement date, book value equals the discounted present value of future receipts from the asset, and the annual income from the asset equals the opening book value multiplied by the interest rate.

Note that, by the contractual nature of bonds, the future receipts are known with reasonable certainty. Of course, bonds held as an investment are subject to **credit risk**—the risk that the issuer may not perform according to the terms of the contract. According to the *CICA Handbook*, paragraph 3050.20, if the value of the bonds becomes impaired, and the impairment is other than temporary, the carrying value of the bonds would have to be written down.

It should also be emphasized that we are holding the interest rate constant in Example 6.2, at the 12% rate established on the date of purchase. Consequently, the accounting for bonds here is only a *partial* application of the measurement approach, since no recognition is given to interest rate changes after acquisition. This limits the decision usefulness of the present value information. However, it should be noted that paragraph 3050.33 of the *CICA Handbook* requires supplemental disclosure of the quoted market value of marketable securities held as portfolio investments. Thus, supplementary information may be available to investors who want to know the impact of interest rate and other changes affecting market value.

Leases

Another important example of the contractual application of the present value model is found in **leases** (*CICA Handbook*, Section 3065), where capital leases and related obligations are valued at the present value of the minimum lease payments, using the interest rate implicit in the lease.

Pension Obligations

Yet another example is **pension obligations** (*CICA Handbook*, Section 3460) where, for defined benefit plans, the actuarial present value of accrued pension benefits must be disclosed. Also, pension fund assets should be valued at "market-related values."

Because of the complexity of many lease and pension contracts, the question of whether the certainty or uncertainty present value models apply is moot. For leases, Section 3065 requires that the present value of the minimum lease payments equal "usually 90% or more" of the fair value of the leased property at inception before the lease can be regarded as a capital lease by the lessee. This implies a high degree of certainty of future cash flows before capitalization is appropriate.

For pensions, however, accounting practice seems closer to the uncertainty model of Example 2.2. For example, paragraph 3460.17 requires that "best estimates" should be used in actuarial valuations. Section 3460 also contains extensive discussions about accounting for changes in estimates arising from past service (paragraph 3460.43), changes in assumptions (paragraph 3460.46), experience gains and losses (paragraph 3460.52), and plan settlements and curtailments (paragraph 3460.54).

6.3.3   THE LOWER-OF-COST-OR-MARKET RULE

What if future cash flows are not established by contract? Can the measurement perspective still be applied? Here we consider the well-known lower-of-cost-or-market rule as a partial application of a valuation approach. As we know, lower of cost or market applies primarily to inventories and marketable securities, both areas where current market values are reasonably reliable. Here, we will consider the rule as applied to marketable securities.

The *CICA Handbook*, paragraph 3010.06, specifies that "When the market value of temporary investments has declined below the carrying value, they should be carried at market value." Also, as mentioned, paragraph 3050.20 states that for long-term investments, "When there has been a loss in value of an investment that is other than a temporary decline, the investment should be written down to recognize the loss."

It is interesting that the lower-of-cost-or-market rule is only a partial application of the present value model. That is, asset values are written down when the market is below cost, but are not written up above cost. Indeed, once the asset is written down, the written-down value becomes the new "cost" and may not be written up again. The lower-of-cost-or-market rule is usually justified in terms of conservatism. It is more difficult to justify in terms of decision usefulness, however, since one would think that if market value information is useful, it would be useful when value is greater than cost as well as when it is less than cost. Presumably, accountants must feel that their exposure to legal liability is greater for an asset overstatement than for an equivalent amount of understatement. Nevertheless, the rule remains an interesting and important partial application of the measurement approach to financial reporting.

6.3.4   CEILING TESTS FOR CAPITAL ASSETS

We next consider **ceiling tests for capital assets**. In Canada, the ceiling test is imposed by Section 3060, *CICA Handbook*, issued in October 1990. While the primary basis of recording capital assets continues to be historical cost, Section 3060 requires write-downs when the net carrying amount of the capital asset exceeds the net recoverable amount.

The calculation of the net recoverable amount requires the estimation of future net cash flows from use of a capital asset. The net cash flows are essentially operating cash inflows or revenues, less operating cash outflows or expenses, plus residual or salvage value. Also, when directly attributable to the capital asset, the following are to be deducted from the estimated future net cash flows:

- **General and Administrative Costs** The relevant cash outflows are defined to include directly attributable general and administrative costs. While deducting such costs may convert a recoverability test into a going-concern test, it can be argued that capital assets must recover all such costs.

- **Future Removal and Site Restoration Expenses** The costs for dismantling a property should be accrued as a liability. Also, consistent with the growing demand for environmental accountability, site restoration costs should be accrued when they are likely to be incurred as a result of environmental law or contract, or because the enterprise has a restoration policy. However, sometimes it will be difficult to restore a site to its original condition (for example, strip mining); therefore, accruals for complete restorations are not always required.

- **Income Taxes** The after-tax basis is applied to the recoverability test so that results for similar assets are more comparable.

Furthermore, the determination of the net recoverable amount is to be based on the "most probable set of economic conditions." Thus, it constitutes an application of the present value model under uncertainty, as in Example 2.2. However, there is a major difference. Paragraph 3060.53 states that the estimated future cash flows are "not discounted in computing net recoverable amount since the purpose of the calculation is to determine recovery, not valuation." This orientation to cost recovery rather than valuation seems hard to justify. For example, timing of cash flows will differ across assets. Yet the standard would value two assets with the same total cash flows identically, even though the cash flows of one asset will be realized later than the other. Furthermore, the rate of return reported on subsequent use of the asset will be downwardly biased. A cynical explanation for the lack of discounting is that because a low discount rate means high present value (ceteris paribus), the standard setters wish to minimize the number of times a write-down will need to be recorded. At the very least, this could seriously delay the recognition of losses.

Another difference from Example 2.2, of course, is the partial nature of ceiling tests, that is, capital assets may be written down, but not written up, to net recoverable value. In this regard, the standard is similar to the lower-of-cost-or-market rule.

We should also point out that the ceiling test applies to oil and gas resources. Unlike RRA, however, future net revenues from proved resources are not discounted in the calculation of the ceiling. Any excess of book values over the ceiling should be written off, but (also unlike RRA) no write-up is applied if the ceiling is greater than book value.

However, despite the partial nature of its application, and despite its denial of discounting, the ceiling test represents an important extension of the measurement perspective to a major class of assets.

6.3.5   PUSH-DOWN ACCOUNTING

When one firm acquires control of another in an arm's-length transaction, Section 1625 of the *CICA Handbook*, issued December 1992, allows (but does not require) the assets and liabilities of the acquired firm be comprehensively revalued, with the resulting values recorded on the books of the acquired firm. This is called **push-down accounting**. The result is that the assets and liabilities are recorded on the books of the *acquired* firm at their market values as established in the acquisition transactions. In addition, paragraph 1625.05 requires comprehensive revaluation following a financial reorganization, provided the reorganization is significant enough to result in a substantial realignment of interests. Thus, Section 1625 constitutes another major example of the introduction of a measurement perspective into financial statements.

6.3.6   CONCLUSIONS

The above is only a partial listing of longstanding present-value- and market-based valuations in generally accepted financial accounting. For a more complete discussion, see Weil (1990). For our purposes, the main point to realize is that a considerable amount of measurement perspective is already inherent in financial statements, even though those statements are regarded as primarily historical-cost-based.

The foregoing examples, however, understate the extent of measurement perspective in current GAAP. We now turn to a consideration of more recent current-value-oriented accounting standards.

6.4   More Recent Current-Value-Oriented Standards

6.4.1   POSTRETIREMENT BENEFITS

While Canadian standard setters do not yet require accrual accounting for postretirement benefits other than pensions, an important standard is in place in the United States, namely SFAS 106, issued in 1990. This standard requires accrual accounting for postretirement benefits (PRBs), consisting of health care, insurance, and related benefits provided to retired employees. Prior to SFAS 106, these were usually accounted for on a cash basis. However, the standard takes the view that PRBs are a form of deferred compensation, which should be recognized as employee services are rendered. In particular, the accumulated PRB obligation is the actuarial present value of the benefits expected to be paid to or on behalf of current and retired employees. Also, the periodic cost of PRBs includes service cost and accretion of discount, less the return on any plan assets. Furthermore, if the firm's PRB plan bases benefits on future compensation levels, increases in compensation must be estimated for purposes of the present value calculations.

Upon adoption of SFAS 106, the firm may record the entire accumulated PRB obligation as an expense of the current period. This amount can be surprisingly large. For example, the *Globe and Mail* (February 2, 1993) reported a $20.8 billion one-time charge by General Motors Corp. to record its PRB obligation, a reduction in its shareholders' equity of about 75% (see Chapter 4, question 9). Alternatively, the accumulated obligation may be recognized annually as part of PRB cost over a period in most cases of up to 20 years.

For our purposes, the important aspect of SFAS 106 is its use of discounted present value to calculate the PRB cost and obligation. As such, it represents a major example of the measurement approach in financial reporting.

6.4.2   IMPAIRED LOANS

Section 3025 of the *CICA Handbook*, released in 1994, relates to impaired loans. This standard requires that loans be written down by the lender to their **estimated realizable amount** when they become impaired or restructured. This amount is based on the expected future cash flows to be derived from the loans, discounted at the rate of interest implicit in the loan transaction. Any loss resulting from such a write-down is to be recorded in current income. Furthermore, under certain conditions the net carrying value of impaired loans *is to be adjusted for subsequent changes in the estimated realizable amount*, with the resulting charge or credit reflected in the income statement.

It is this latter provision that is of particular interest, suggesting a movement away from the lower-of-cost-or-market rule. Thus, the impaired loans standard indicates a clear extension of the valuation approach by standard setters. This is confirmed in paragraph 3025.55, which states that "disclosure of the net charge or credit to income in respect of loan impairment allows users of financial statements to assess the effect on net income of changes in expectations with respect to the amounts and timing of future cash flows from loans."

6.5   *Financial Instruments*

6.5.1   INTRODUCTION

In Canada, accounting for **financial instruments**[9] is laid down by Section 3860 of the *CICA Handbook*, issued in 1995. Section 3860 deals primarily with the definition and disclosure of financial instruments. It does not specify how they should be valued on firm's books. Consequently, this standard is more in keeping with the information perspective than with the measurement perspective, the topic of this chapter. Standard setters in the United States have gone further in the direction of the measurement perspective with respect to financial instruments than is currently the case in Canada. Consequently, we shall supplement our discussion by reference to U.S. standards where appropriate.

Firms issue or acquire financial instruments for a variety of reasons. For example, they may manage their capital structure by means of convertible debt or securitizations. They may manage their cash flows, for example by issuing zero-coupon debt. Securitization may also enable lower financing costs. Another major reason is to *manage risk*. It is this role of financial instruments that we shall concentrate on here. We begin by considering **hedge accounting**.

6.5.2   *HEDGE ACCOUNTING*

In recent years, a variety of complex financial instruments has developed to enable firms to better manage the risks and uncertainties to which they are exposed. Many of these risks and uncertainties arise from **market risk**—changes in interest rates, commodity prices, and foreign exchange rates. The accounting for these complex financial instruments, when used to hedge risks and uncertainties, involves difficult issues of valuation and revenue recognition, which standard setting bodies are only beginning to address.

Firms have long used hedges to offset some of the risks they face. The essence of a hedge is that if a firm owns, say, a risky asset it can hedge this risk by acquiring a **hedging instrument**—some other asset or liability whose value moves in the direction opposite from that of the value of the item to be hedged. Thus, a gain or loss on the risky asset is offset by a loss or gain on the hedging instrument.

In the United States hedge accounting is specified by SFAS 80, *Accounting for Futures Contracts*, issued in 1984. While not a new standard, it is included here pending issuance of a new standard, because it continues to provide guidance both in Canada and in the United States.

A futures contract, according to SFAS 80, is a particular type of financial instrument that obligates the purchaser or seller to accept or make delivery of a standardized quantity of a commodity or financial instrument in the future, or else make settlement in cash. Such contracts are traded on security exchanges. Obviously, their market value depends on the market price of the underlying commodity or security to which they relate and their market value will fluctuate as the underlying market prices fluctuate. Thus, they have potential to hedge against market risk.

Under SFAS 80, the change in the market value of a futures contract shall be recognized as a gain or loss of the period during which the change takes place, *unless* it is a hedge of an exposure to price or interest rate risk.[10] To be a hedge, two criteria must be met. First, the *item to be hedged* must expose the *enterprise* to price or interest rate risk. This is not always as easy to establish as one might think. Suppose, for example, that a firm is owed US$100 and owes US$80 to another party. Then the firm enters into a $100 foreign exchange futures contract to fully hedge the US$100 owing to it. The question is, does the $100 owing to the firm (the item to be hedged) expose the enterprise to foreign exchange risk? The answer appears to be substantially no, since the US$80 owing already hedges all but $20 of the risk of the $100 asset. Consequently, it is doubtful whether the $100 foreign exchange contract in this case constitutes a hedge. In effect, while hedges occur at the transactions level, their impact on risk is evaluated at the enterprise level under SFAS 80. In this case, the enterprise has a greater exposure to foreign exchange risk after the foreign exchange contract ($80) than it did before ($20).

This example illustrates the important point that a firm's own assets and liabilities can hedge each other. For example, if a firm owns risky securities and at the same time has interest-bearing debt outstanding, the market value of the assets will tend to move in the opposite direction to changes in the market value of the liabilities. This will particularly be the case if the firm tailors the amount, duration, and other characteristics of the debt so as to match the risk characteristics of the securities. As we shall see, if current-value-based accounting is then imposed on the assets but not on the liabilities, this will increase the volatility of reported net income, if gains or losses from asset revaluations are included in income.

The second criterion for a hedge is that the futures contract reduces exposure by being highly negatively correlated with the hedged item. That is, if there is a change in the value of the hedged item, there should be a corresponding opposite change in the market value of the futures contract. Note that the correlation need not be perfect, only "high." Under non-ideal conditions, there may not exist a perfect hedge. For example, a bank may have trouble finding a perfect hedge for interest rate changes on its deposit liabilities. The risk from lack of perfect correlation is called **basis risk**.

One way of estimating the correlation between the hedged item and the hedging instrument is the *cumulative dollar offset* method. For example, suppose that 18 months ago a firm hedged the risk of an existing variable interest rate liability by purchasing a treasury bill futures contract. Suppose also that due to rising interest rates, the fair value of its liability has decreased by $1,500 to date, but the market value of its treasury bill futures contract has fallen by $1,300. Then the ratio of loss to gain is $-1,500 \div 1,300 = -1.15$. Since this is reasonably close to a perfect ratio of -1, this supports the continuing acceptance of the futures contract as a hedge.

If the two criteria are met, then under **deferred hedge accounting**, the gain of $1,500 and the loss of $1,300 are both deferred until the futures contract is closed out.[11] Be sure you see the significance of the futures contract being regarded as a hedge. Suppose it were *not* regarded as a hedge, say because the -1.15 above was considered to be too far from -1. Then, under SFAS 80 it would be necessary to record the $1,300 loss on the futures contract currently. This could have a material effect on the firm's reported net income.

Whether a futures contract is regarded as a hedge or not can have extreme consequences. A case in point is Franklin Savings Association of Ottawa, Kansas.[12] Franklin, during the 1980s, engaged in an aggressive strategy of using funds from deposits to buy mortgage-backed securities and other risky derivative financial instruments. It hedged the interest rate risk of these instruments by the use of sophisticated and complex hedging instruments. At the end of its June 30, 1989 fiscal year, Franklin had accumulated losses on these hedging instruments of $365 million, which it deferred under SFAS 80.

The Office of Thrift Supervision became increasingly concerned about the firm's investment and hedging strategies and questioned the deferral of the $365 million of losses. The issue boiled down to one of correlation between losses and gains resulting from interest rate changes under Franklin's hedging strategy. By some methods of measuring this correlation, Franklin "passed." By other methods, including a version of the cumulative dollar offset measure described above, it "failed."

In the face of this conflicting evidence, the Office of Thrift Supervision decided that the deferred losses be written off. Since Franklin's statutory capital was only $380 million, this put it into technical insolvency, takeover by the regulatory authorities, and possible ultimate liquidation.

Other aspects of SFAS 80 are also worthy of mention. In our earlier example, suppose that interest rates had fallen rather than risen, and that to date there was a $1,500 increase in the fair value of the liability and a $1,300 increase in the market value of the hedge. Suppose also that the firm expects the $200 net loss to continue until the futures contract matures. Then, it would be necessary to provide for the $200 anticipated loss currently. This will be recognized as a sort of "net" version of the lower of cost or market rule.

Also, hedges can be classified as hedges for an *existing* asset or liability or for an *anticipated* transaction. If the hedge is of an existing asset or liability, a change in market value of the hedging instrument is deferred by adjusting the carrying value of the hedged item. If the hedge is of an anticipated transaction, then any change in the market value of the hedging instrument is deferred and included as an adjustment of the revenue from/cost of the transaction when it occurs. SFAS80 gives conditions that must be met for a future transaction to be regarded as anticipated. For example, it must be probable that the anticipated transaction will take place.

While Section 3860 of the *CICA Handbook* does not specify the accounting for hedging of anticipated future transactions, it does require (paragraph 3860.92) disclosure, including a description of the anticipated transactions and related hedging instruments, the amount of any deferred gains or losses, and the expected timing of recognition of such gains and losses.

6.5.3   *FAIR VALUE OF FINANCIAL INSTRUMENTS*

SFAS 107 (1992) introduces the term **fair value** of financial instruments. Generally, fair value means current market value, but, if this is not available, fair value can be determined by management estimate, market value of a similar instrument, or discounted present value. Fair value can also be determined by means of a valuation model (to be discussed below). Consistent with SFAS 107, Section 3860 defines fair value as "the amount of the consideration that would be agreed upon in an arm's length transaction between knowledgeable, willing parties who are under no obligation to act."

Of course, fair value disclosure has long been required for many assets, such as marketable securities held as temporary and long-term investments. However, SFAS 107 and Section 3860 require supplemental disclosure of fair value for almost all financial instruments for which it is practicable to make reliable estimates, including liabilities as well as assets. A major exclusion is **core deposit intangibles** of a financial institution. These are values arising from the long-term relationship between a financial institution and its depositors. Long-term depositors are unlikely to all demand their money back at one time. Furthermore, they may be paid a relatively low rate of interest. SFAS 107 regards core deposit intangibles as intangible assets rather than financial instruments.

6.5.4   VALUATION OF DEBT AND EQUITY SECURITIES

Like Section 3860, SFAS 107 requires disclosure of *supplemental* fair value information. As a result, these standards do not affect the valuation of financial instruments on the balance sheet itself, and do not impact reported net income. SFAS 115, effective in 1994, however, has the potential to impact both balance sheet and earnings, thereby moving towards a measurement perspective. Since a comparable Canadian standard is not yet in place, we now describe SFAS 115.

SFAS 115 applies to investments in debt securities and to investments in equity securities with readily determinable fair values. It requires that these assets be classified at acquisition into one of 3 categories:

- **Held-to-Maturity** Debt securities for which the entity has a "positive intent and ability" to hold to maturity
- **Trading** Securities held for a short time for the purpose of selling them
- **Available-for-Sale** All other securities to which SFAS 115 applies

While held-to-maturity securities are valued at amortized cost, both trading and available-for-sale securities are valued at fair value. Unrealized gains and losses from such valuations are included in income, for trading securities. For available-for-sale securities, unrealized gains and losses are included in a separate component of shareholders' equity.

To understand this seemingly inconsistent juxtaposition of accounting policies, two major problems need to be pointed out. This first problem is **gains trading**, also called "cherry picking." This is a practice that financial institutions, in particular, have been suspected of using as a way to manage their reported earnings. Gains trading can be employed when investment portfolios are valued at cost or amortized cost, and when at least some securities have risen in value. Then, the institution can realize a gain by selling securities that have risen in value, while continuing to hold securities that may have fallen in value. No loss is recognized on these latter securities, because they continue to be carried at cost.

Note that gains trading is not possible if securities are valued at fair value, with unrealized gains and losses included in income. However, it is interesting to note that SFAS 115 has the potential to make the problem of gains trading worse rather than better. When securities are transferred from held-to-maturity to trading, SFAS 115 requires that the transfer be accounted for at fair value, with any gain or loss included in income. Thus, to gains trade, the firm need only reclassify held-to-maturity securities as trading—no sale of securities is needed.

However, SFAS 115 protects against this possibility by placing stringent conditions on transfers into and out of held-to-maturity. For example, if a firm intends to hold a debt security for an indefinite period, this does not qualify as held-to-maturity. Also, transfers out of held-to-maturity require events that are "isolated, nonrecurring, and unusual for the reporting enterprise that could not have been reasonably anticipated. ..."

The second problem is one of volatility of reported net income. SFAS 115 applies only to financial assets. However, as discussed in Section 6.5.2 above, financial institutions may coordinate the duration and other characteristics of their financial assets and liabilities in order to create a natural hedge of changes in values. It then seems reasonable that if financial assets are carried at fair values so should financial liabilities. Otherwise, the volatility of net income that results from recognizing unrealized gains and losses from only financial assets is greater than the real volatility the firm has chosen through its natural hedging activities. It is for this reason, presumably, that SFAS 115 stipulates that certain securities (held-to-maturity) need not be carried at fair value and that gains and losses on others (available-for-sale) are excluded from earnings.

One might ask why, if gains trading is to be eliminated, SFAS 115 does not simply require that financial liabilities also be carried at fair value, rather than going through the contortions just described. After all, SFAS 107 already requires disclosure of fair values of financial liabilities as supplemental information.

The difficulty is that financial institutions are a major industry affected by SFAS 115 and that, to date, a practicable method of valuing the demand deposit liabilities of financial institutions does not exist. It may seem reasonable to value demand deposits at their face value, since this is the amount that depositors can demand; however, this ignores the value of core deposit intangibles, which are excluded from SFAS 107. The face amount of deposit liabilities should be reduced by this intangible asset for a fair valuation. Yet this introduces problems of estimating the timing of withdrawals and discounting, which are currently unresolved. In the face of these difficulties, SFAS 115 opts for retention of historical cost accounting for held-to-maturity securities and exclusion of unrealized gains and losses on available-for-sale securities from income, rather than requiring fair values for financial liabilities. While this does not eliminate the possibility of gains trading, the FASB must feel that the stringent controls over transfers between categories will keep the problem within bounds.

Despite these compromises, SFAS 115 represents a clear extension of the measurement perspective beyond the realm of supplemental disclosure and into the financial statements proper. Major classes of financial assets are to be fair-valued and, for one of these classes at least, unrealized gains and losses are included in income.

6.5.5 *DERIVATIVE FINANCIAL INSTRUMENTS*

Derivative financial instruments are financial instruments whose value *derives* from some underlying asset. A common example is an **option**. For example, consider a call option which gives a right to buy a share for $20 over some future time period. The higher the market value of the share, the more valuable the option, other things equal. Thus, the value of the option derives from the value of the underlying share. Other examples of derivatives include futures, forward and swap contracts, interest rate caps and floors, and fixed-rate loan commitments. These instruments convey a benefit to the holder if there is a favourable movement in the underlying value. If the underlying value moves unfavourably, there may or may not be a loss to the holder.

SFAS 105 and 107 already require disclosure of certain information about derivatives held or issued by a firm. For example, SFAS 105 requires disclosure of information about off-balance-sheet risk. To illustrate, suppose that a firm enters into a forward contract whereby it will pay $10,000 for a block of shares in six months' time. If the share price falls below $10,000 (that is, the underlying price moves unfavourably), the forward contract will become a liability (that is, the holder suffers a loss). Consequently, the forward contract has off-balance-sheet risk, in which case its face value and other terms including credit risk must be disclosed under SFAS 105. Somewhat similar requirements are included in Section 3860.

Also, both Section 3860 and SFAS 107 require disclosure of the fair value of financial instruments, including derivatives. Thus, actively traded options would be disclosed at their current market value. If the options are not traded, both standards allow the use of models of derivative value. The famous Black-Scholes (1973) option pricing model is an example. Suppose that you own a non-traded call option giving you the right to buy a share of X Ltd. stock for $10 at any time over the next year. The current market value of the underlying X Ltd. stock is $9. Thus, you would not want to exercise the option right now. However, the option still has value since the share price might rise above $10 over the year. What is the current fair value of the option?

The Black-Scholes model values this option as a function of the following five variables:

- Current market price of X Ltd. stock—$9
- Variability of return of X Ltd. stock
- Exercise price of the option—$10
- Time to expiration—one year
- Risk-free interest rate in the economy

The first two of these inputs to the model are observable characteristics of the underlying asset. Thus, given values for the last three variables, we see how the value of the option *derives* from the underlying asset. Specifically, it depends on the current market price and return variability of the X shares. Since Black-Scholes, models to value other, more complex derivative financial instruments have been developed. Thus, under appropriate conditions,[13] models provide a way to implement the fair value calculations required by SFAS 107, even if current market values are not available.

6.6   *Summary and Conclusions*

There are numerous instances of the use of current values in financial reporting, and the list is growing. Many longstanding uses involve only partial application of a measurement perspective, as in lower-of-cost-or-market, long-term debt, ceiling tests, and push-down accounting. Thus, under lower-of-cost-or-market and ceiling tests, written-down assets are not written up again if value increases. Also, the present value of long-term debt is not adjusted for changes in interest rates, and once subsidiary asset values are pushed down they are not revalued subsequently. Nevertheless, partial applications of current value have the potential to be decision useful to the extent they reveal a material change in the firm's financial position and prospects.

However, recent standards suggest the clear extension of a measurement perspective so as to periodically measure both value increases and decreases. Thus, under Section 3025 of the *CICA Handbook*, impaired loans may be written up if impairment is reduced. Under SFAS 115, in the United States, trading and available-for-sale securities are marked-to-market each period. Furthermore, PRBs are reported at present value each period under SFAS 106. While the information is supplemental, Section 3860, as well as several FASB standards in the United States, require periodic disclosure of fair value and risk information for a variety of financial instruments. Certainly, it appears that decision usefulness is moving more and more into the arena of measurement.

Why do we observe an increasing use of current valuations for financial instruments, as described above, while other measurement perspective approaches such as RRA and current cost information for property, plant, and equipment seem to have failed? The answer may lie in the degree of proper operation of markets. If markets work properly, market values of assets and liabilities provide a reliable measure of fair value. Hopefully, markets for financial instruments work reasonably well. However, markets for oil and gas reserves and for property, plant, and equipment do not work well when they are plagued by thinness and by a lack of objective probabilities for measuring the expected values of future cash flows. Presumably, the increase in relevance from reporting the fair values of financial instruments outweighs any reduction in reliability, while the opposite is the case for oil and gas reserves and current values of property, plant, and equipment.

Indeed, research by Barth (1994) supports the decision usefulness of fair value accounting for investments. In a study of U.S. banks using 1990 data,[14] Barth found that the fair values of banks' investment securities had significant explanatory power for the market value of banks' shares, and that this explanatory power was considerably greater than that of historical-cost-based carrying values for these investments. These results strongly support the decision usefulness of fair value investment information for investors.

Barth found only marginal explanatory power of unrealized gains and losses on investments in explaining returns on bank shares, however. After further investigation she concluded that there was considerable measurement error in unrealized gains and losses, which reduces their reliability and hence their decision usefulness.

It is important to note that the use of fair value in no way undermines the desirability of full disclosure that was discussed in Chapter 4. If financial reporting and other mechanisms fail to overcome problems of information asymmetry, market values will not reflect all relevant information and hence will not properly measure fair value. This concern applies just as much to markets for financial instruments as to markets for shares. Thus, the market prices of financial instruments will not reflect their fair value unless the firms that issue them fully disclose their results of operations, financial position, and risks.

There is, however, an important difference between the information perspective on decision usefulness described in Chapter 5 and the measurement perspective described in this chapter. Recall that the information perspective takes the view that accountants can retain historical cost as the primary basis of valuation, on the grounds that it is an appropriate tradeoff between relevance and reliability, and expand on historical cost with lots of additional information in footnotes and in supplementary information such as RRA, MD&A, financial forecasts, and fair values. Given security market efficiency, all of this information will be quickly incorporated into share price in an unbiased manner. This information perspective reflects the early enthusiasm of accountants for efficient security market theory, and it is supported by substantial empirical evidence that the market responds to financial accounting information as the theory predicts.

A measurement perspective, however, implies a slight "backing off" by accountants from this early enthusiasm, and an assumption of greater responsibility for incorporating fair values into the financial statements proper. In effect, accountants are doing some of investors' work for them through increased use of valuations. If the securities market was fully efficient, this would not be necessary to the extent that value information was available in supplementary form or elsewhere.

A number of factors come together to support this measurement perspective. Empirically, historical-cost-based net income explains only about 2 to 5% of the variability of abnormal security returns around the release date of current earnings. Also, the evidence of efficient securities market anomalies supports a concern that markets may not be as efficient as previously believed. Both of these observations suggest that there is considerable scope to further increase decision usefulness of financial statements by proactive design of measurement techniques that increase value relevance without substantial loss of reliability.

A lack of value relevance becomes particularly apparent when firms fail, with little or no warning. This characterizes the failure of numerous financial institutions, such as savings and loans in the United States. These failures have been accompanied by evidence of abuse of historical-cost-based valuations, such as gains trading and deficiencies in reporting on risk. When failure happens, the legal system responds, and, in turn, standard setters respond by mandating more value and risk disclosures. Presumably, they feel that more fair value information will reduce the potential for successful lawsuits as well as improve public confidence in financial reporting.

Finally, Ohlson's clean surplus theory provides a framework supportive of a measurement perspective, by demonstrating that the market value of the firm can be expressed in terms of fundamental income statement and balance sheet values. Then, it seems natural to give more attention to fair reporting of these values.

Whether the recent valuation-oriented standards described in this chapter will increase the market share of financial accounting information in explaining share returns, and will reduce auditor liability, remains to be seen.

Despite some of the anomalies outlined in this chapter, this book continues to assume security market efficiency, on the grounds that efficiency is a matter of degree. While anomalies may suggest somewhat less efficiency than was thought originally, there is a large body of evidence consistent with the theory, which demonstrates a remarkable degree of sophistication by the market. The ERC literature is an example.

One final point: An implication of security market efficiency is that firms' accounting policy choices and their impact on reported net income will not affect their share prices, as long as policy choices, and changes in policies, are disclosed and cash flows are not directly affected. Thus, if two firms are identical except that one reports lower earnings because of, say, a more conservative depreciation policy, their market values should be similar. This suggests that managers should not be concerned about accounting policy choice, because these choices will not affect their cost of capital.

However, managers *are* concerned about accounting policy choice. Indeed, increased adoption of measurement-oriented accounting standards is increasing their concerns, as we shall see. This poses another anomaly for efficient securities market theory. Either managers do not accept the theory or other factors are at work—or both. We now turn to a consideration of other factors which, as we shall see, can reconcile market efficiency and legitimate manager concern over accounting policy choice.

Notes

1. The proportion of variability is measured by the R^2 statistic from the regression of abnormal security returns on unexpected earnings.

2. Note that in Figure 5.2 the cumulative abnormal returns for the GN firms—the upper portion of the figure—continue upward for two or three months following month 0. The continuing downward drift after month 0 for the BN firms is even more pronounced.

3. For example, firms' betas may shift when they announce good or bad earnings news. If the beta shift were positive for GN firms and negative for BN firms, this could explain post-announcement drift as simply an artifact of the higher (for GN firms) and lower (for BN firms) returns that investors would demand to compensate for the changes in risk. Recall from our discussion in Sections 3.4, 3.5, and 3.6 that risk-averse investors trade off risk and return. Consequently, if a firm's risk (beta) increases, investors will require a higher return on that firm's shares, which will manifest itself as increased abnormal returns in the days following the earnings announcement, and the converse for firms whose risk decreases. While BT present evidence that betas do shift in the manner described above following earnings announcements, the magnitude of the shifts is much smaller than what would be required to explain the magnitude of the post-announcement drift. A variety of other tests also fail to support a risk-based explanation for the drift.

4. Suppose that transactions costs were 5% of the amount invested. Then, if it was possible to gross 5% by a strategy of buying GN firms and selling short BN firms, transactions costs would consume the 5% profit, so investors would not bother. Thus, what might appear to be a profitable investment strategy might merely reflect the level of transactions costs required to earn those profits.

5. Closed-end funds are investment companies whose only income-generating assets are portfolios of publicly traded shares.

6. Several other anomalies have been reported in the finance literature. For example, consider the so-called January effect. There is evidence that share returns, especially the shares of smaller firms, are higher in January than in other months.

7. Our expression for α differs slightly from that of F&O. They assume that the firm has an infinite life, whereas our assumption is that P.V. Ltd. has a two-year life.

8. Some firms, gold mines for example, recognize revenue upon completion of production or, equivalently, value their inventory at market value. For such firms, post-revenue realization assets would also include inventories. Other firms, for example those selling on a long-term instalment receivable basis, sometimes defer revenue recognition until cash is collected or, equivalently, value their accounts receivable at cost. Post-revenue realization assets for these firms would exclude accounts receivable.

9. The CICA Handbook, paragraph 3860.05, defines a financial instrument as follows:

> A **financial instrument** is any contract that gives rise to both a financial asset of one party and a financial liability or equity instrument of another party.
>
> A **financial asset** is any asset that is:
> (i) cash;
> (ii) a contractual right to receive cash or another financial asset from another party;
> (iii) a contractual right to exchange financial instruments with another party under conditions that are potentially favourable; or
> (iv) an equity instrument of another entity.
>
> A **financial liability** is any liability that is a contractual obligation:
> (i) to deliver cash or another financial asset to another party; or
> (ii) to exchange financial instruments with another party under conditions that are potentially unfavourable.

Note that this is quite a broad definition, which affects most firms. It includes post-revenue realization assets and liabilities, fixed-term securities, and capitalized leases, for example.

10. SFAS 80 applies to price or interest rate risk, but not to foreign exchange rate risk, which is included in SFAS 52. Practically speaking, however, the rules SFAS 80 lays down also apply to foreign exchange rate risk. In Canada, hedge

accounting for foreign exchange risk is laid down by paragraphs 1650.47–55 of the *CICA Handbook*.

11. An alternative is mark-to-market hedge accounting, in which both the hedged item and the related hedging instrument are marked-to-market, with the net gain or loss reported in current net income.

12. I am indebted to Mark Finn, University of Chicago, for material on Franklin Savings Association. For further information on Franklin, see Milligan (1991).

13. It should be pointed out that these valuation models assume that the markets on which the underlying securities are traded work well. If, because of adverse selection or other problems, they do not work well, then just as the market price of the underlying security may not reflect true value, the derived value of the derivative security may not reflect its true value. Thus, the availability of valuation models in no way reduces the need for financial reporting to be an effective vehicle for fully disclosing information to the market, as discussed in Section 4.7.

14. While the date of Barth's data precedes the effective dates of SFAS 107 (1992) and SFAS 115 (1994), banks had been disclosing the fair value of their investments as supplementary information for some time.

Questions and Problems

1. Why does a measurement perspective on financial reporting suggest more value-relevant information in the financial statements proper, when efficient security markets theory implies that footnote or other disclosure would be just as good? (CGA-Canada)

2. What will be the impact on reliability of financial statement information as accountants adopt the measurement perspective? (CGA-Canada)

3. Lev, in his article "On the Usefulness of Earnings" (1989), points out the low ability of reported net income to explain variations in security prices around the date of release of earnings information. Lev attributes this low explanatory power to low earnings quality.

   Required
   a. Define earnings quality. Relate your answer to the concept of an information system in single-person decision theory.
   b. What other reasons might there be for the low explanatory power of earnings?
   c. How might an increased use of valuations in financial statements raise earnings quality, and hence the impact of earnings on security prices?

4. For what reasons might transactions costs, including investors' time to figure out and operate strategies that appear to beat the market, not be a completely adequate explanation for the apparent efficient security market anomalies?

5. Under generally accepted accounting principles, certain current assets such as cash, accounts receivable, and marketable securities (when current value is below cost) are carried at present value and/or market value. Does this violate the historical cost basis of accounting? Explain.

   Note: A good answer will draw on the realization principle.   (CGA-Canada)

6. Under generally accepted accounting principles, certain liabilities are carried on a present value basis. Long-term bonds and lease liabilities are examples. Does this constitute a violation of the historical cost basis of accounting? Explain.

   Note: In your answer, state whether the interest rate used in the discounting calculations should be held constant or changed as interest rates in the economy change.

7. Explain why a firm may not necessarily reduce its price risks to zero by means of hedging transactions.   (CGA-Canada)

8. Explain what "post-announcement drift" is. Why is this an anomaly for security market efficiency?

9. The article here reproduced, "Beating The Market: Yes, It Can Be Done," appeared in *The Economist* (December 5, 1992). The article critically evaluates evidence of efficient security market anomalies.

BEATING THE MARKET

Yes, It Can Be Done

The death, when it was announced this year, sent shock waves along Wall Street. Life would never be the same again, wailed the obituaries. Had some star analyst passed away, or the head of a top investment bank? Or maybe another crooked company boss had slipped from his yacht? In fact, the deceased was not a he or a she, but an it. "Beta," screamed the papers, was dead.

Beta? Why would the average Wall-Streeter mourn the second letter of the Greek alphabet? Beta is one of the best-known measures of risk used by investors. It plays a key role in lots of tricky financial activities, from portfolio management to pricing derivatives, working out the cost of capital and deciding if a firm should go ahead with its investment plans, calculating or even setting top executives' pay. Without beta, these tasks are hard indeed.

It now seems that the reports of beta's death were much exaggerated. The press based its sensational headlines on a study of share-price changes by two well-known financial economists, Eugene Fama and Kenneth French, of Chicago University. But, says the academic grapevine, several other economists are soon to publish work contradicting Messrs. Fama and French. Beta lives on. Yet it is wounded: Wall Street's faith in it has been shaken.

Investors may soon be grappling with even bigger doubts. Beta is the most familiar product of what economists call the "theory of efficient markets." Disputes about beta are just part of growing debate about that whole theory. Many economists now question whether financial markets can any longer be called efficient.

Welcome to the real world, many people will conclude. To them, inefficient markets are a plain fact. What, after all, could be less efficient than the crashing stockmarkets and lurching exchange rates that are now all too familiar? This misses the point, however. When economists talk about efficiency, they use the word in a precise sense quite different from what most people mean by it. And until recently the economists' definition explained real-world events pretty well. It also underpinned much of what investors do.

WALKING AT RANDOM

Efficient-market theory was born in 1953. Maurice Kendall, a British statistician, found that, instead of behaving in predictable ways, shares and commodity prices followed a "random walk." At any moment it was impossible to tell what prices would be a moment later. This, said theorists, is because prices are "efficient"—they reflect all available facts. Future prices differ from current prices only if buyers or sellers get new information. This, by definition, is unpredictable (or "random").

But why should prices be efficient? Put simply, if they are not, it means the market is ignoring price-sensitive information. But this gives whoever has that information a chance to make big profits by trading on it. As soon as he does so, the overlooked information is incorporated in the price. This will make it "efficient."

This led to the theory's main claim. If prices are unpredictable, investors should not be able consistently to beat the market. Share-picking and foreign-exchange speculation should not pay. Put more precisely, one investor should be able to earn higher returns than another only by taking bigger risks—markets reward risk-taking—or if he is lucky (and luck rarely lasts). After allowing for differences in asset-riskiness, no investor should regularly earn higher ("excess") returns than the herd.

By the end of the 1960s, the theory had been refined. In principle, all markets could be efficient, whatever the product traded. In practice some markets are more efficient than others. Liquidity—how easy it is to buy and sell—boosts efficiency. So do visible, up-to-date prices, which help people to spot wrong prices fast. So does the availability of many similar products, so that relative prices can be compared. Financial markets enjoy all these advantages, and so are more likely to be efficient than are most.

Economists also graded and defined the efficiency of markets according to the information that prices reflected. "Strong" efficiency means that all relevant information—whether published or not—is reflected in prices. With "semi-strong" efficiency, prices reflect all information that is publicly available. With "weak" efficiency, the current price reflects, at least, all information contained in earlier prices of that asset. This last kind means that looking at past and current prices should tell you nothing about what will happen to prices in future. If price changes follow predictable trends, the market is not even weakly efficient.

Economists soon learned that strong efficiency was to be found rarely, if at all. But numerous studies backed up Mr. Kendall's results, finding that financial markets displayed both weak and semi-strong efficiency. Efficient-market theory was built into a host of practical theories and investment strategies. The best-known are the capital-asset-pricing model (which created beta), the arbitrage-pricing theory and the Black-Scholes option-pricing model. The effect of such theories was huge. By the mid-1980s they had transformed the way people (or, at least, professional investors and financiers) understood and used financial markets. It was they that drove the rapid growth in futures and options markets and swaps, for instance.

CALENDAR EFFECTS AND OTHER FLAWS

While the influence of efficient-market theories soared on Wall Street, however, academics started to have doubts. Faster, cheaper computers and bigger databases made possible more and better research. This had a simple aim: to unearth trading strategies that would, in the past, have produced what economists call "excess returns"—returns that are above average even after allowing for the investment being riskier (or less risky) than average.

A first wave of evidence, in the mid-1980s, cast doubt on semi-strong efficiency, finding cases where information was publicly available yet returns were predictably high (or low). "Calendar effects"

were the most striking: at certain times of the year, and on certain days of the week, prices predictably rise (or fall) by more (or less) than on the average day, and the related returns vary correspondingly.

One example is the "January effect": shares of small companies beat the market in January. There is a "turn-of-the-month effect": all prices tend to rise by more than average on the last trading day of the month and on the first three of the new month. They do the same on Friday, but fall on Monday—the "weekend effect." There is a "holiday effect": prices rise more than average on the day before a public holiday.

Robert Schiller, of Yale University, looked at one sort of information that affects share prices—changes in dividends. He found that the market overreacted to these. It was far more volatile than efficient-market theory would predict. Others have looked for simple trading rules that make extra profits. In stockmarkets, for instance, it has long paid to buy shares with a below-average ratio of market price to book value. This "value investing" was practised by skilled investors like Warren Buffett well before economists rumbled it.

In a new study based on many years' data, Ken Froot, of Harvard University, shows that short-term interest rates forecast returns in foreign-exchange stock, bond and commodity markets at the same time. His simple rule? A fall of one percentage point in (annualised) short rates is usually associated with an extra three percentage points in (annualised) excess returns to investors trading in accordance with that interest-rate change.

Others have found profitable trading rules that are based solely on tracking changes in the price of an asset over time. These suggest that markets are not even weakly efficient. Stephen Taylor, of Lancaster University, found that several rules based solely on trends in past exchange rates produced above-average returns in foreign-exchange markets over the ten years to December 1991. Take, for instance, the "double moving average" rule. The trader uses a short and a long moving average. He sells when the shorter average falls below the long-term average, and buys when the short-term average exceeds the longer one. This rule produced average annual returns of 14.2%, compared with an 8% average return on American Treasury bills.

Most of the work on weak efficiency has been far from simple. The current fad among finance economists is to use complicated computer models that churn long series of prices until they find predictable patterns. Trading on the basis of these patterns, only possible with a big, fast computer, would have brought investors excess returns.

Academics have also found that market volatility varies predictably. If prices are jumpy one day, they will probably be jumpy the next day too; if they are flat one day, they will probably be flat the next.

Reassuringly, some of the more blatant effects weakened after academics drew attention to them. But enough evidence remains to make a strong case against the efficient-market theory. Armed with the right rules or computer software, investors can, it seems, earn juicy excess returns—as can (and do) many of the academics who discover them, whether by trading directly or taking jobs as investment advisors.

RETHINKING RISK

Yet few economists are prepared to abandon the efficient market. As Charles Goodhart, of the London School of Economics, points out, no one has thought up a better theory. Instead, academics have tried to reinterpret the awkward evidence in less-threatening ways. They have shown that, at times, trading costs would have wiped out apparent excess returns. And, more basically, they have rethought risk.

The simple efficient-market rule, remember, is that investors should not be able to earn excess profits after account is taken of the riskiness of their investment relative to the average. Most studies assume that the "price of risk"—how much extra profit an investor needs to expect before he will take extra risk—never changes: offer an investor an identically risky investment at two different times and he will want the same amount of extra profit each time.

But what if the price of risk varies over time? For instance, as people get richer they may become more willing to take risks; in a recession, less so. If the price of risk varies, what studies show as "inefficient" excess returns might, if they were earned, say, during a recession, turn out really to have been "efficient" average returns; the returns would indeed be higher, but only because the risk component in them was larger.

Academic journals have been filled to bursting over recent years with papers explaining away excess returns by varying the price of risk and with papers arguing the opposite. Alas, no clear conclusion has emerged. That may be inevitable. Measuring changes in the price of risk is mostly guesswork. Yet these guesses largely determine a study's results.

This may, then, be a blind alley. Indeed, so may much of the empirical research on both sides of the efficient-market debate. In a recent paper, Fischer Black, co-author of option-pricing theory and now with Goldman Sachs, launched a fierce attack on "data-mining": people digging into data until they find what looks like a trend. For instance, some academics have claimed that shares of small firms consistently outperform those of big firms, an apparent inefficiency. To Mr. Black, this "sounds like people searched over thousands of rules till they found one that worked in the past. Then they reported it, as if past performance were indicative of future performance. As we might expect, in real life the rule did not work any more." Needless to say, Mr. Black prefers theory.

THE HUNT FOR LOSERS

Can efficient-market theory and evidence of inefficiency be reconciled? Many economists now think so. If some people gain from market inefficiency, they point out, others must lose from it. And though it is obvious why winners stay in the market, it is not clear why the losers do so. So theorists should find out who the losers are, and try to understand why it is that they are willing to lose. In short, allow that the way markets work is efficient, but that some of the people investing in markets are not.

This may make efficient-market theory a more useful tool than it was when used simply as a rod to beat inefficiency-finding heretics. For instance, show persistent losers that—and why—they are losers, and there is a chance they may do something about it.

This approach means changes to the theory, though. Economists (like bookmakers long before them) now distinguish two types of punter: "smart," informed traders and "noise" traders. Smart traders consistently earn excess profits, because noise traders consistently lose. In early versions of efficient-market theory, arbitrage—trading by smart investors—would have driven noise traders out of the market and kept prices efficient. Now economists think complete arbitrage unlikely, not least because the smart money available is not unlimited.

This has a curious knock-on effect. Without complete arbitrage, there is no reason to expect smart traders to keep prices rational. If they know that noise traders are unduly bullish, it may pay them to jump on the bandwagon rather than bid prices down. This produces an added complication: an efficient price after smart trading may now look to economists like an inefficient one.

The search for persistent losers has only just begun. Though some likely candidates have been lined up—central banks, individual investors, company pension funds—most studies are hotly disputed. The problem is to find plausible explanations why particular groups should lose.

One tack is to identify institutional factors that may lead investors to take bad decisions. For example, most central banks are affected by political pressures. They are probably the main long-term losers in the foreign-exchange markets, reckons Lancaster University's Mr. Taylor. Huge losses by the Bank of England on this September's "Black Wednesday"—when sterling had to drop out of the European exchange-rate mechanism—seem to confirm this, though the evidence is blurred by central banks' reluctance to reveal their blunders.

Another sort of pressure may distort investment by company pension funds. The sponsor of the fund hires professional managers to do this investing, and reviews their performance each year. But even good managers are likely to do badly in one year or another. So—argues Bill Sharpe, the Nobel-prize-winning author of the capital-asset-pricing model—the managers may over-invest in those shares that they can most easily justify to the sponsors. These shares may be overpriced, so making underperformance more likely; but if the fund does underperform, it is a lot less embarrassing to meet sponsors with a fistful of Microsoft shares than with shares in unknown firms.

Psychology may explain some losers. Consider closed-end mutual funds (known in Britain as investment trusts). These invest in shares, and the price of their own shares should—you might think—almost exactly reflect the market value of those underlying assets. In fact, though, they usually trade at a discount. How can one account for this blatant market inefficiency? Richard Thaler, of Cornell University, has an answer. Investors in closed-end funds are almost all individuals; the discount is a good indicator of their collective optimism (or pessimism), reckons Mr. Thaler. Shifts in the discounts of closed-end funds are paralleled by changes in the price of other assets in which individuals invest heavily. In other words, investment by individuals may be mood-driven, rather than having much to do with the merits of what they invest in.

ONWARD TO GREATER EFFICIENCY

The world, then, is not as simple as economists once thought. The possibility of making long-term profits by playing the foreign-exchange markets or by picking stocks can no longer be ruled out on grounds of principle. It may even be that the trendy, high-tech trading software, based on "neural networks" and "artificial intelligence," that is now selling well on Wall Street, is not as gimmicky as it seems. But that does not mean that anything goes. Far from it. Rather than dismissing markets as inefficient, studies are likely to pay growing attention to losers, with the possibility that these losers will learn and adapt.

Nor does proof of inefficiency in markets mean, as some people believe, that governments should intervene, especially at times of market turbulence. Government action will probably just create more noise. Black Wednesday shows how efficiently markets can mug inefficient governments and their lackeys.

One last point. Though evidence of market inefficiency has soared in recent years, that does not mean markets have become less efficient. More likely, it means academics have got better computers and bigger databases, and that there are more of them data-crunching. If fact, most economists believe financial markets are more efficient now than ever before, thanks not least to shrinking official intervention. Theorists may argue about betas or market efficiency, but investors should not imagine that making money will get any easier.

Required

a. Explain how variations over time in the risk/return tradeoff demanded by market investors may explain apparent efficient market anomalies.

b. The article suggests that the real test of market efficiency is whether "losers," such as noise traders and large institutional investors, will change their behaviour once their "irrationality" is pointed out to them. Would you expect that apparent anomalies such as post-announcement drift and excess returns from financial ratio analysis would persist following publication of articles such as Bernard and Thomas and Ou and Penman? Explain why or why not.

10. An article entitled "U.S., Deloitte Said to Be Close to Thrift Pact" appeared in the *Wall Street Journal* on March 11, 1994. It reported on the liabilities faced by certain large accounting firms as a result of the failure of numerous savings and loan associations in the 1980s. For example, Deloitte & Touche faces 15 lawsuits totalling $1.4 billion.

The *Journal* suggests that Deloitte & Touche is close to reaching an agreement whereby they would pay more than $300 million to settle these litigations, most of which stem from alleged "counts of malpractice, including allegations that Deloitte … issued clean audit opinions to deeply insolvent institutions." If this agreement is finalized it would "be the second-largest settlement the government has secured in its efforts to punish professionals who provided services to savings and loans that later collapsed." The largest was a $400 million settlement with Ernst & Young in 1992.

Another example includes the biggest U.S. accounting firm, Arthur Andersen & Co., who "in August paid $65 million to settle government charges of professional negligence in its audits of failed financial institutions."

Required

a. Suppose that savings and loan associations had used mark-to-market accounting for their various financial instruments. To what extent do you think this would have reduced the number of savings and loan failures?

b. For those savings and loans that would have failed regardless of their accounting policy for financial instruments, to what extent do you think auditor liability would have been reduced if GAAP had required mark-to-market accounting for financial instruments?

11. The article here reproduced, "Market Value: The Debate Rages," appeared in *Financial Executive* (January/February 1993). It reports on a debate over the prospect of mark-to-market accounting for marketable debt and equity securities. It is interesting to observe the SEC representative (Mr. Schuetze) defend himself against the concerns of two senior financial institution accountants. The financial institution industry would be greatly affected by market value accounting. The FASB, represented by Mr. Leisenring, seems to be caught in the middle.

MARKET VALUE:
THE DEBATE RAGES

*S*ecurities and Exchange Commission Chairman Richard Breeden lit a new fire under the decades-old debate over market-value accounting when he announced several years ago that the historical cost model is no longer relevant in our volatile world.

The Financial Accounting Standards Board initiated its financial instruments project in 1986. Since that time, the FASB has issued a number of exposure drafts and several statements of accounting standards. The FASB's most recent exposure draft, *"Accounting for Certain Investments in Debt and Equity Securities,"* was issued in September 1992.

The provisions of the new ED have inspired heated discussion. One such debate occurred at Financial Executive Institute's recent conference on financial reporting issues. The participants in that debate were four well-known and outspoken experts on the issue: Thomas E. Jones, executive vice president, Citibank; Patrick W. Kenny, group executive—finance and administration, Aetna; James J. Leisenring, vice chairman, Financial Accounting Standards Board; and Walter Schuetze, chief accountant, Securities and Exchange Commission. Donald J. Kirk, professor of accounting, Columbia University and former FASB chairman, moderated the panel. Reproduced here is the substance of their debate.

DONALD KIRK: Fair-value accounting and the alleged shortcomings of the historical cost accounting model have been on the agenda of practically every professional or regulatory entity in recent years.

Let's start our discussion with the SEC's chief accountant, Walter Schuetze.

WALTER SCHUETZE: The SEC has been urging the Financial Accounting Standards Board to require that marketable debt and equity securities be accounted for at fair value or market value in the face of the financial statements. There are those who argue that footnote disclosure of fair value is enough. They point out that the AICPA's Statement of Position 90-11 and FASB Statements 12 and 60 already require disclosure of the fair value of marketable debt and equity securities. Statement 107 ["Disclosures About Fair Value of Financial Instruments"], which went into effect in December, requires the disclosure of market value for additional items.

Financial analysts are not clamoring for formal accounting for marketable debt and equity securities at market prices, and some are even opposed to formal mark-to-market accounting. They would, however, oppose eliminating the disclosures of market value.

So why am I pushing so hard for formal mark-to-market for marketable securities? Because historical cost is not useful or relevant for decision-making, especially by retail investors and policymakers. Retail investors use the information published by investor services, which does not include the footnote disclosures. And policymakers look at industry-wide statistics when they set policy; again they don't read the footnote disclosures. Both groups assume that capital based on generally accepted accounting principles is the real amount of capital. But we know that isn't a correct assumption.

During the last year, as more and more financial institutions have reexamined their accounting for securities held for investment, the center of this debate has shifted from *whether* to mark-to-market to *how* to mark-to-market. How to identify those liabilities that need to be marked to market if it is decided that liabilities need to be marked to market. How to get a good number for assets that are not traded every day, for example, for foreclosed assets that must be marked to market under current accounting standards at the time of foreclosure, for loans that are going over to a collecting bank to be sold, for disclosures under Statement 107.

The SEC addressed the "how" question for foreclosed assets and for in-substance foreclosed assets in its Financial Reporting Release 28, issued in December 1986. The release specifies that current market prices should be used to value foreclosed assets at the time of foreclosure even if those market prices come from an auction market where the buyers hope to profit by holding the assets for future price increases.

Fair-value accounting will soon be applied to loan impairment. The FASB has proposed that formally restructured loans be remeasured at their fair values. [The FASB exposure draft, "Accounting by Creditors for Impairment of a Loan," was issued in June 1992.] Some commentators on the exposure draft have suggested that all impaired loans should be measured at fair values. Others, of course,

believe that no change in practice is necessary.

Fair-value accounting has another application in writing down the carrying amounts of impaired non-monetary assets. When an asset is acquired, the acquisition price is its fair value. That fair value is, at least in theory, the present value of a series of future cash flows. When identifying and measuring impairment, we need to look at the fair value of that asset at subsequent balance-sheet dates. And if fair value is not readily available, we need to estimate that amount by projecting the cash flows from the asset and discount that amount using a risk rate appropriate to those cash flows.

So fair value is the relevant attribute in identifying and measuring impaired assets when historical cost is no longer relevant or useful for decision-making.

JAMES LEISENRING: This debate is not about market-value accounting per se. Most people concede that market value or discounted present value are essentially the same in initial measurement. Rather, the debate is about subsequent measurement.

Many of our constituents say that the FASB is moving toward across-the-board market-value accounting. Our project on impairment, for example, has attracted a great many comment letters suggesting that any notion of marking down to a recoverable amount that is something less than historical cost is in essence market-value accounting. We have another neutral discussion memorandum, "New-Basis Accounting," which is often referred to as the push-down issue. The DM discusses a variety of circumstances where new bases might be recognized. A good many comment letters on this DM suggest that it too is part of the grand move to market-value accounting.

In truth, the FASB never realized that this was the issue. We were looking at what happened when actual cost of a given transaction was pushed down into financial statements. We did not see it as a movement toward subsequent measurement at market value.

The majority of members of the Board that voted for the loan impairment exposure draft would emphatically deny that it represents market-value accounting. The ED would not adopt market value as an ongoing measurement for troubled debt restructurings. It's a judgment that a new measurement should take place because the loan has been restructured. When there is an impairment but not a restructured loan, the impaired loan is not measured at a market rate of interest but at the same discount rate used at the inception of the loan. Neither of these two approaches is market-value accounting.

Many have argued market-value accounting is imprecise and doesn't provide comparable information. I agree that we do have to go through a learning process to estimate market values of some instruments. But historical costs are surely not comparable. They will always show that $1,000 spent for a 4-percent bond in 1992 is exactly the same as $1,000 spent for a 13-percent bond in 1983, both of which will still be on the balance sheet at $1,000. To imply that the two $1,000 expenditures are comparable is misleading.

Relevance is the current arena for our debate. Market-value accounting advocates say that the most relevant information about an entity's financial instruments at each reporting date is their market values and the gains and losses from economic events that occurred within the reporting period. Historical-cost advocates say that market values are the least relevant because they represent a liquidation value—a liquidation amount that in all likelihood will not be realized.

This last point leads me to the argument that we hear most frequently, and that concerns volatility. Gains and losses on investment securities for financial institutions have been very volatile for years. As the ED on accounting for debt and equity securities points out, market-value accounting actually is less volatile in the period in which the gains and losses are realized than it is to recognize all realized gain or loss in one period. This suggests to me that volatility is not the real argument; rather it is control over the recognition of the volatility.

PATRICK KENNY: Insurance entities operate an asset/liability matched business. The relationship between the two sides of the balance sheet is maintained by carefully matching the duration of the assets to that of the liabilities and by constantly monitoring that relationship to respond to business conditions. From a financial reporting perspective, if we change the way we value the asset side of this relationship, it only stands to reason that similar changes must be made to the liability side.

The application of market-value accounting to one side of the balance sheet does not adequately portray the economics of an asset/liability matched business. I don't want to downplay the complexities of determining fair-value liabilities, but it is better to take on that challenge than to adopt the one-sided approach suggested in the FASB's exposure draft on debt and equity securities.

The FASB generally took a balanced approach to disclosure of market-value information in Statement 107. It think Statement 107 will present useful information, and I strongly recommend that we allow financial statement users some time to use that information and to understand the relevance of that information before we proceed down the road to market-value accounting.

While the FASB is debating the merits of market-value accounting, the SEC has taken a more aggressive approach. The SEC now requires financial reporting that, for insurance companies at least, is more restrictive than today's generally accepted accounting principles and differs from FASB's exposure draft. This inconsistency is confusing and possibly misleading to financial statement users and preparers. And it places an unnecessary burden on companies to restate financial statements to conform to the SEC's aggressive interpretation of accounting standards that may well change.

It is important to keep in mind that this issue affects not only the financial services industry, but manufacturing and other industries as well.

THOMAS JONES: I am not against mark-to-market accounting in its proper place. Citicorp has tens of billions of dollars of assets marked to market every day. I'm also not against mark-to-market accounting because of the results. For example, substantial loan-loss reserves are already on the books, and because pressure for this kind of change always happens at the end of a downturn, the economic cycle is likely to help rather than hinder the numbers.

But I am against the way mark-to-market is being handled. Every time you look around there's another camel's nose under the tent. Loan impairment is one. Securities is another—although I will admit that some of us should be embarrassed about the number of times securities portfolios that were supposed to be held to maturity were turned over. But the market-value accounting discussion is a subtle undercurrent. It's being done piecemeal, and it's not out in the open being debated on the merits.

Let's take financial instruments. Because it's being done in bits and pieces, we need to do the work two or three times. Statement 107 is mark-to-market disclosure, and if mark-to-market accounting on loans and securities follows, we will take on an entire new workload. All of this makes us uncompetitive with companies outside the U.S. that don't have this problem. This piecemeal treatment establishes a bad precedent.

I also argue that market-value accounting is bad accounting. The stampede to mark-to-market was caused by generally accepted accounting principles (GAAP). Accounting for S&Ls wasn't under GAAP anyway. We're mixing up regulation with accounting. If we force mark-to-market on an industry such as real estate, which is going through a severe downturn, we'll get liquidation accounting, not going-concern accounting. And that's not GAAP.

Business—the preparers—are supportive of things that need to be done. Take OPEB [Statement 106, "Employers' Accounting for Postretirement Benefits Other Than Pensions"], for example. Most businesses recognized the necessity for change, even though it has been very damaging to their reported earnings.

But most business people don't see anyone getting such tremendous value from broad application of mark-to-market. I'm not against mark-to-market where it makes sense, but I am very much against mark-to-market across the balance sheet.

So mark-to-market is a victory of liquidation accounting over going-concern accounting and doesn't necessarily reflect the underlying purpose of the assets.

That leads to bad policy, at least from a bank's point of view. The purpose of a commercial bank is to make loans to customers and then, within the limits of possibility, provide liquidity for them through bad times. Marking loan portfolios to market will force banks to take a short-term view that is inconsistent with their fundamental business proposition.

So I make the case that mark-to-market accounting is bad accounting, bad policy and bad precedent.

KIRK: Tom Jones finds evidence that the more the FASB denies it's marching towards current-value accounting, the more people are convinced it is. The question is, Walter, can the man on the street, that retail investor, decipher the meaning of an income statement if all these unrealized gains and losses are in that income?

SCHUETZE: The exclusion of these amounts from the face of the financial statements omits important information for the individual investor, for the sophisticated investor, and for the policymakers. It's more than just the retail investor.

But the SEC is not targeting market-value accounting. To be sure, we want market value for marketable debt and equity securities, but we are not talking about market value for loans, for plants, for patents, for copyrights, or the like.

LEISENRING: The FASB has purposely kept unrealized gains and losses on

marketable debt and securities out of the income statement for two reasons: first, because liabilities are not included and, second, because they are unrealized.

KIRK: But by running unrealized gains and losses through equity, you haven't solved what the SEC has said is a bad practice—gains trading, or cherry picking. Why didn't the FASB solve that particular issue in the way the SEC thinks it should be solved?

LEISENRING: The only way it can be solved is to put all gains and losses through earnings. It's very difficult to demonstrate that investment securities haven't been abused. But we haven't solved the cherry-picking issue, and we have to accept that.

SCHUETZE: I think the financial analysts would be better served if realized gains and losses are shown below the line. The primary reason the analysts do not want recognition of realized gains and losses is that it messes up their predictions. But if they would agree to formal recognition of market values in the face of the financial statements with realized and unrealized gains and losses below the line in the income statement, that would be worthwhile.

JONES: We're underestimating the users of financial statements. When a company has a quarter in which it has a lot of income from a one-time gain or sale of investment securities, there isn't a user who doesn't exclude that immediately. I don't think it's as big an issue as we're making it.

KIRK: I want to switch to the appropriateness of valuing the asset side and not the liabilities side. Do you think that marking a financial institution's bond portfolios to market would be misleading if its liabilities were not also marked to market?

KENNY: Yes.

JONES: I agree.

LEISENRING: As the ED suggests, we would have liked to have reached some conclusions about liabilities but could not. Some Board members took the view that for deposits, for example, and for some values in life insurance contracts, the only notion of market value that has any relevance is the settlement amount. If someone can walk in the bank and demand a million dollars, it is not necessarily going to enhance financial reporting to record the liability at, say, $950,000 because of changes in interest rates. A study that KPMG did recently for the Association of Reserve City Bankers ["Estimating Fair Value for Financial Instruments"] acknowledges this. In fact it says that those deposits are already at market on balance sheets. The study goes on to advocate the recognition of the so-called core-deposit intangible. But that was a much broader question than we could come to grips with in the context of equity and debt securities.

KIRK: What will this move towards market-value accounting do to the behavior of companies? If we look at it in terms of the financial institutions, the representations are that people will change their investment horizons, and that if we move it towards loans, it may also change banks' lending practices. What's the reaction of the SEC to such representations as that?

SCHUETZE: I say again we're not talking about mark-to-market on the loan and real estate portfolios.

KIRK: What about banks changing the duration or maturities of government securities they own as a reaction to the proposals?

SCHUETZE: I don't know if banks will do that. Accounting standards ought to produce information that is neutral, that does not influence behavior in one way or another. Bank holdings of marketable securities on the historical cost standard exceed their commercial and industrial loan portfolios, perhaps because the Basel Accords require no capital whatsoever with respect to interest-rate risk. We should not use accounting standards to regulate action. Rather, accounting standards should produce information that is neutral and that investors can use in capital-raising and capital-allocation decisions.

JONES: I'm delighted to hear that the SEC is not interested in mark-to-market accounting more broadly, but I have a hard time believing it. Statement 107 is already a good step on the way. And the loan impairment project is basically mark-to-market. This is a financial institution issue right now, but, believe me, it's coming down the pike for everyone sooner or later. And I don't know if everyone realizes what is being asked for.

With the FASB's proposal on loan impairment, we are being asked to forecast the timing and the amounts of all future cash flows on every loan that gets into difficulty. We've talked about the difficulty of measuring liabilities, but in this case you're talking about measuring assets. It is almost impossible. And because it happens at the beginning of an economic downturn, it front-ends the future interest cost as well. Front-ending the entire principal loss and future interest loss for all the financial institutions at the start of a recession is not much help. I hope it occurs after I've retired.

KENNY: I also think that it will cause financial institutions to invest shorter rather than longer. So this accounting information is hardly neutral.

LEISENRING: But loan impairment accounting as it has been proposed by the FASB is *not* mark-to-market accounting. When you measure something at initial recognition that purports to be a present-value measurement, what should you do about changes in the factors that determined the initial measurement? Should you incorporate, in a subsequent measurement, your new estimate of the inbound cash flow stream, or should you not?

And should you incorporate in your measurement the observation that interest rates have or have not changed? The Board decided that reflecting the change in interest rates would be remeasuring at market and should not be done. But it did say you should consistently measure the item at its present value of the assumed inbound cash flow stream at the interest rate inherent at the inception of the loan. this decision does impose the burden of determining the timing of cash, but it should not impose a new burden to think about the amount. Presumably, you cannot meet existing standards without thinking about the amount of a loan that you're going to collect.

KIRK: What would be an acceptable standard that would respond to the concerns raised?

JONES: There's no objection to the concept of mark-to-market when there is a deep, liquid market that the company intends to access. In the days when the banks were being chastised for the LDC debt, the mark-to-market cry was very loud, and there was absolutely no market at all. These days there is a fair amount of market and, lo and behold, most banks have either written down to or reserved up

to the market value, and it isn't an issue.

It's absurd to think about a deep liquid market for commercial real estate loans today, but over time that will change. In the absence of a market, the loan-loss reserve is designed to help customers through bad times. The loan-loss reserves bring the value on the balance sheet down to a recoverable value. That is the substitute right now for mark-to-market.

SCHUETZE: But we have a ton, a long ton, of anecdotal evidence that the reserve for bad debts in many financial institutions did not measure up. Under the loan impairment standard we're going to get a much better measure of the actual impairment when companies have to foreclose and sell the foreclosed asset.

JONES: But that's a totally different issue. Obviously foreclosed assets have been written down to market value. What I'm talking about are the loans that are already in difficulty and for which we're going to have to predict the future principal and interest cash flows.

SCHUETZE: If you're talking about collateralized loans, maybe it's easier to just get the fair value of the collateral and use that number to measure the impairment. But we have lots of signature loans where we're going to have to try to measure impairment. You're not suggesting that we not make a reasonably good stab at that, are you, Tom?

JONES: Hey, listen, for a guy who is not pushing market-value accounting, you're doing a good job right now.

KIRK: What is the attitude of the SEC and the FASB with regard to the possibility of valuing intangibles and attempting to value operating assets of other sorts?

SCHUETZE: The SEC has not addressed operating assets. We do have a rule that requires oil and gas companies using full-cost accounting to write down the cost of their assets when it is in excess of certain ceilings. But, other than that, we have not looked at this issue.

I note that the Association of Investment Management and Research, in a statement of position that it issued in the fall, recommended that all unidentifiable intangibles be written off to equity. They apparently do not find those representations useful. They also recommend that all executory obligations be recognized on the face of the balance sheet.

LEISENRING: Of course we're interested in certain intangible accounting questions, but again that's not necessarily mark-to-market accounting.

The AICPA has the advertising cost capitalization issue, an issue of soft-cost recognition. Last spring we approved for exposure their statement of position ["Reporting on Advertising Costs"], although some of us certainly had some qualms about it. It, again, is not mark-to-market accounting, but it is recognition of

an asset that has previously been considered too soft for recognition. I would predict we will have more of these questions. We're much more of a service economy than we once were, but our model is oriented to bricks and mortar. So it's inevitable that we will continue to have questions about recognition of intangible assets.

KIRK: Won't the subjective nature of many fair-value estimates for the purpose of measuring impairment shoot holes in what should be bullet-proof balance sheets?

SCHUETZE: To be sure, in the absence of a liquid market, getting estimates of fair value is difficult. However, once historical cost is impaired, it has lost its relevance. When we look for a substitute number, we need to look for the one that is the most relevant. If we have a number that is verifiable but not relevant, the most relevant number should always win out. It is going to be a difficult learning process to go through these measurements, but what we're after is numbers that have relevance for investors.

SOURCE: Excerpted with permission from *Financial Executive*, January/February 1993, © 1993 by Financial Executives Institute, 10 Madison Avenue, P.O. Box 1938, Morristown, New Jersey 07962-1938; (201) 898-4600.

Required

a. According to Messrs. Schuetze and Leisenring, what are the advantages of mark-to-market accounting for marketable securities?

b. What concerns about marking-to-market are expressed by Messrs. Kenny and Jones?

c. Explain Mr. Leisenring's statement that "the only way it [that is, gains trading] can be solved is to put all gains and losses through earnings."

d. Do you agree with Mr. Leisenring's denial that the proposed loan impairment standard (now SFAS 114) "represents market-value accounting"? Explain.

12. Refer to the article "Market Value: The Debate Rages" (see question 11). There, Mr. Kenny, the insurance industry representative, points out that "insurance

entities operate an asset/liability matched business." That is, the maturities of assets and liabilities are matched. This provides a sort of natural hedging against interest rate risk. Mr. Kenny argues that if the FASB forces insurance companies to mark financial assets to market, they should also require that financial liabilities be marked to market.

a. Assuming that unrealized gains/losses on marking financial assets to market are included in income, but not for liabilities, what effect would this have on reported net income?

b. Mr. Kenny refers to SFAS 107. This standard already requires that market value information about financial assets and liabilities be given, but does not require the information to be actually recorded on the books, as marking-to-market does. Why does Mr. Kenny seem to prefer SFAS 107 over marking-to-market?

c. Would the market value of a firm be affected differently according to whether market value information is shown in a footnote, as in SFAS 107, or included in the financial statements proper, as in marking-to-market?

d. Assuming that marking-to-market for financial assets is adopted, how might concerns about the resulting volatility of reported net income be reduced? (CGA-Canada)

13. Potential environmental liabilities faced by firms provide a major challenge for the matching concept and for full disclosure. According to SFAS 5, loss contingencies are not accrued on the firm's books unless it is probable that a liability exists *and* the amount can be reasonably estimated. Frequently, environmental liabilities do not meet these tests. However, potential environmental liabilities may be disclosed as supplemental information in the footnotes.

An article entitled "SEC Rule Forces More Disclosure" appeared in the *Wall Street Journal* on December 13, 1993. It outlines SEC concerns that disclosure of environmental liabilities by many firms is insufficient.

According to the article, in June 1993 the SEC issued a staff accounting bulletin which suggested that firms need to disclose a lot more information about their present and future environmental liabilities. The article states that as of now (1993), "companies aren't required to disclose liabilities of less than 5% of either their profits or assets." However, "under the new SEC rule companies will have to disclose some environmental liabilities even if they fall below the 5% threshold."

In addition, the bulletin prevents firms from using expected insurance recoveries to offset expected liabilities. The article quotes *Best's Review*, an insurance-company rating publication, as stating that the industry "is clearly underreserved if called upon to fund current [environmental] cleanup estimates." The bulletin also prevents discounting of future liabilities "to a smaller amount." There will be considerable fines and penalties given by the SEC for lack of disclosure. For example, the SEC can "fine the company up to $500,000 for each violation."

These potential penalties and fines put pressure on companies. For example, Lawrence Komatz, vice president and controller of Rockwell International Corp., states that the SEC "put us through the wringer about our lack of disclosure." Also, John Wulff of Union Carbide called the SEC bulletin "a pain in the neck," indicating the company would add some additional disclosure in its next annual report.

Required

a. Explain, in decision theory terms, why investors may find information about potential environmental liabilities to be useful. Consider the tradeoff between relevance and reliability in your answer.

b. Do you agree with the SEC that expected insurance recoveries may not be used to offset environmental liabilities and that future liabilities are not to be discounted? Explain.

14. An article entitled "Exxon Is Told to Pay $5 Billion for Valdez Spill" appeared in the *Wall Street Journal* on September 19, 1994. The article states that Exxon Corp. has "to pay $5 billion to fishermen and other Alaskans as punishment for the 1989 Valdez oil spill, the largest punitive award ever against a corporation."

According to the *Journal*, most oil industry analysts say that the penalty will not greatly affect Exxon's "operations, strategies or even dividend policy because the company is so large and profitable," although Lee Raymond, Exxon's chairman, said the verdict "is totally unwarranted" and "excessive by any legal or practical measure."

The plaintiffs were asking for $20 billion but were awarded only $5 billion. On the New York Stock Exchange, "Exxon traded at $58.75, before the jury's decision, but afterward surged $1.50 to $60.25 a share in after-hours trading."

The following is an extract from Note 14 in Exxon's December 31, 1993 annual report, relating to contingent liabilities following from the oil spill.

Litigation and Other Contingencies

A number of lawsuits, including class actions, have been brought in various courts against Exxon Corporation and certain of its subsidiaries relating to the release of crude oil from the tanker *Exxon Valdez* in 1989. Most of these lawsuits seek unspecified compensatory and punitive damages; several lawsuits seek damages in varying specified amounts. Certain of the lawsuits seek injunctive relief. The claims of many individuals have been dismissed or settled. Most of the remaining actions are scheduled for trial in federal court commencing May 2, 1994. Other actions will likely be tried in state court later in 1994. The cost to the corporation from these lawsuits is not possible to predict; however, it is believed that the final outcome will not have a materially adverse effect upon the corporation's operations or financial condition.

SOURCE: 1993 annual report of Exxon Corporation. Reprinted by permission.

Required

a. As an informed investor attempting to value the common stock of Exxon prior to September 19, 1994, do you feel that the contingency disclosure in the 1993 annual report is adequate under the circumstances? Explain why or why not.

b. Explain why the security price of Exxon rose on September 18, 1994 despite record punitive damages.

15. While ceiling tests for all capital assets were not yet in place in the United States in 1992, the SEC did enforce a ceiling test on the oil and gas reserves of producers. Essentially, a write-down was required if the book value of reserves exceeded their present value. In this regard, the SEC ceiling test was similar to that of Section 3060 of the *CICA Handbook*.

An article entitled "Natural-Gas Producers Bristle at 'Snapshot' Accounting" appeared in the *Wall Street Journal* on April 17, 1992. It described the annoyance of affected firms, some of whom were forced to make substantial write-downs as a result of the ceiling test.

The SEC's ceiling test requires corporations to value their energy reserves at a price that "is whatever the company is able to sell its gas or oil for on the last day of the accounting period." According to the article, the SEC states that this test is necessary in order "'to insure that investors receive disclosures based on accounting that reflects recoverable value of assets.'" However, Bob Alexander, president of Alexander Energy Co., feels that this is not a good rule because "'the ceiling calculation takes a snapshot of a price on one day.'" Mr. Alexander along with others feels that this rule should be replaced by "a 12-month weighted average price to eliminate seasonal fluctuations."

Not all companies are required to use the ceiling test on their oil and gas reserves; the test is only for those companies that use full-cost accounting, which excludes successful-effort users.

According to the article, if the book value of oil and gas reserves is higher than the ceiling calculation, the company must write down the reserves to the ceiling. The article, for example, states that Enserch Exploration had to take a $50 million write-down of its reserves in 1991. These large write-downs often lead to a decrease in stock price even though it is a non-cash adjustment. Analyst Catherine Montgomery "believes the market sometimes reads too much into the write-downs," adding "I think that serious investors, institutions and analysts understand these write-downs. ... But the average investor out there has a knee-jerk response and stock prices may be affected."

Required

a. Explain why firms using the full-cost method of accounting for reserves are more likely than successful-effort firms to be affected by the ceiling test. The article stated that full-cost firms "have to apply the ceiling test to their oil and gas reserves every quarter; successful efforts users never do." Do you agree that successful-effort firms *never* have to apply a ceiling test? Explain.

b. Use efficient security market theory to critically evaluate a claim made in the article that ceiling test write-downs can adversely affect stock price. Do you agree with this claim? Explain.

c. The article pointed out that once ceiling test write-downs are made, assets cannot be written up again if prices recover. Presumably, this accounts for the concern expressed by oil company managers about "snapshot" accounting. Why does the ceiling test impose write-downs but not allow subsequent write-ups? As an informed investor in the oil and gas industry, would you support regular adjustment of book values of oil and gas reserves to market value? Explain.

16. The article by Sutton and Johnson reproduced here, "Current Values: Finding a Way Forward," appeared in *Financial Executive* (January/February 1993). The authors make proposals for increased use of valuations in financial reporting.

CURRENT VALUES: FINDING A WAY FORWARD

New initiatives in accounting are always controversial. The current debate over using current values to measure and report marketable securities in financial statements certainly is no exception.

Market-value proponents have no doubt that current value is the best way to determine comprehensive income and measure an investment's contribution to the owner's net worth. Opponents to market value are equally certain historical cost is best. This morning's investment value will inevitably change, they say, probably by this afternoon, and those changes in value, which are not realized, are irrelevant in measuring company performance.

We suggest a way forward. Our framework would retain the essential structure of the current accounting model, but would provide for greater recognition of market values in the financial statements. Financial assets that have ready markets would be carried at market value on the balance sheet. Unrealized changes in the values of these assets would be excluded from the traditional measurement of earnings. Rather, these changes in values, which are provisional until the asset is sold, would be captured and reported in a new, fourth financial statement that we call a "Statement of Changes in Provisional Values."

WHY THE DEBATE?

Today's complex economic and regulatory environments have tested the limits of the current accounting model. In addition to competition and escalating costs, companies cope with a broad array of financial market risks. For example, a sudden increase in interest rates can adversely affect a financial institution that has not matched the duration of its assets and liabilities. A stronger dollar can erode the profits of a multinational consumer products company when it has an important market share in another country. Exacerbating the risks of the financial markets is their volatility.

GAINS TRADING

Many regulators, including the SEC, are critical of certain practices that are rooted in the historical-cost accounting model. One particularly troublesome practice is known as gains trading, in which the investor hopes to profit from changes in the direction of future interest rates. In its simplest form, the investor, believing that interest rates will decline, accumulates a portfolio of fixed-rate debt instruments. If interest rates decline as anticipated, the investor sells the securities. Under the historical-cost model, the resulting gains are realized and included in profits.

But if interest rates rise and the value of the investments declines, the investor most likely will elect to hold the securities as long-term investments. Traditionally, the ability and intent to hold debt securities to maturity have permitted the investor to carry those instruments at historical cost. Under the historical-cost accounting model, the investor has not realized a loss, even though the economic value of the investments has declined.

These outcomes are a consequence of the transaction-oriented, historical-cost accounting framework, under which gains and losses on investments are often reported only at the time they are sold. Critics point to the apparent contradiction of reporting profits in the income statement while the balance sheet may actually be weakened by unrecognized declines in the value of securities held.

A company can also use its investment portfolio to manage its interest-rate risk. Assume, for example, that a bank has a negative gap—its interest-rate-sensitive liabilities exceed its interest-rate-sensitive assets. If interest rates climb, the bank is exposed. By selling fixed-maturity debt securities and reinvesting the proceeds in variable-rate or short-term instruments, the bank can narrow or close the negative gap. At large financial institutions, portfolio adjustments to help balance asset and liability exposures occur frequently.

Although the motivations are vastly different, gains trading and portfolio management both result in a sale of debt instruments in advance of maturity. Current-value advocates question how the maturity value of a debt instrument has relevance if the investor will sell the debt instrument before its maturity and at an amount that reflects market conditions at the time of sale.

Today's accounting model is perceived to be relatively simple. But historical cost is a misnomer for what is a relatively complex accounting framework. It would more aptly be described as a mixed-attribute model. Original cost, fair value, or an amount in between can each be the right answer under the current framework, depending on the circumstances. For example, a financial institution might own two identical debt securities, but account for one at market if it is held for trading, and account for the other at amortized cost if it is held for long-term investment.

Given that the right choice often depends on the quality of the asset and the intent of management, it is no wonder that management, auditors, and financial statement readers have difficulty communicating.

WHEN DOES CURRENT VALUE MAKE SENSE?

In a typical operating cycle, assets move through the balance sheet—from manufacturing plants to short-term marketable securities—on their way to cash. At some point during the trip, the current value of the asset becomes more relevant than its historical cost. Operating on the premise that investors and creditors ultimately focus on the cash flow, we suggest that financial reporting should depart from historical-cost measurements in favor of current values when current values most closely approximate the asset's ability to realize cash.

The concept is best demonstrated at the extremes. Assume, for example, that a manufacturer enjoys eight consecutive record quarters. Surplus cash is invested in short-term U.S. Treasury bills, while management evaluates whether to increase the dividend, expand overseas, or some combination of the two. Few would argue that the historical cost of the Treasury bills is a better measure of their ability to generate cash than their market value. But if the manufacturer declares the dividend and sells the investments, current value is the best measure of the available cash.

Let's also assume that the manufacturer owns a state-of-the-art research facility, which is the spawning ground for the ideas that give the manufacturer its competitive edge. The current market value of the facility is a fraction of its cost. Many of the improvements that have been made to the facility have no other use, and real estate and credit conditions have depressed land prices. But the company's engineers keep turning out ideas; the innovations translate into products that are manufactured and sold; and the receivables from the sales are ultimately collected to produce cash. The research facility's worth is as a spawning ground of ideas, not as a store of monetary value.

Sometimes determining when the next step in the operating cycle is cash is complicated by factors beyond management's control. A conglomerate might instruct its investment bankers to identify suitable buyers for a profitable electronic component subsidiary. Should an electronics component company sell at a multiple of 15 times earnings, or is 12 more realistic? And who are the prospective buyers? A commercial bank might hold a bridge loan that it made to a highly leveraged, troubled company. Can the bank sell the note? If not, how and when will it be settled? In circumstances such as these, the ability to convert an asset to cash or to estimate the proceeds that could be received are not so clear. The practical solution for the present: Use current values when the next step is cash and the asset is readily marketable.

HOW SHOULD CHANGES BE IMPLEMENTED?

Some historical-cost advocates claim that even limited changes to the mixed-attribute model are seriously flawed. Long-term investments can go up or down in value many times during an extended holding period; as a result, interim changes in value have little significance. A second defect, charge the critics, is that current-value proponents focus principally on assets. When the value of a company's investment falls because interest rates increase, an offsetting economic gain is often embedded in the investor's liability structure. Both criticisms have merit.

The longer the term of a fixed-rate debt instrument, the more impact changes in interest rates will have on the investment's value. Critics of current-value measurement point out that investors will favor shorter-term investments to avoid the roller coaster effect on reported income.

One solution would be to uncouple the income statement and the balance sheet. Under current accounting standards, most gains and losses are reported in the income statement. We propose that standard-setters give serious consideration to introducing a fourth financial statement, the "Statement of Changes in Provisional Values" (in addition to the balance sheet, income statement, and statement of cash flows) to deal with conflicts in the objectives of reporting financial position as of a point in time and reporting earnings for a period of time.

Under the approach, assets could be adjusted to current values on the balance sheet. Earnings could continue to be measured and displayed in the income statement as it is now. Changes in provisional values, including unrealized gains and losses not recognized in earnings, would be reported in the "Statement of Changes in Provisional Values" and as an increase or decrease in stockholders' equity.

FAIR-VALUE LIABILITIES

A company can benefit from changes in market conditions if it has the right capital structure. A company's fixed-rate debt, for example, might immunize it from the economic loss of holding low coupon interest bearing investments in a rising interest rate environment. Critics of current-value accounting believe that these facts are too often ignored. One solution, favored by some, is to use historical-cost measurements on the theory that the unrecognized changes in asset values are offset by corresponding effects on liabilities.

A more realistic solution would be to measure both investments and related liabilities at current values. Although a company's capital structure can help to avoid the effect of unexpected changes in market conditions, ignoring the current value of both assets and liabilities implies that the change in the value of each, if measured, would perfectly offset. The difficulty, however, is that accountants have little understanding of what the fair value of a liability represents and little experience in trying to communicate the sources and effects of changes in value.

These issues need to be carefully studied. To date, one of the major unresolved issues in expanding the use of current values has been a lack of consensus on how to deal with liabilities.

WHAT NEXT?

The current accounting model is better suited to a more stable, less global commercial environment. Most businesses have recognized the need to address changing and sometimes hostile market forces, and manage their operating and financial activities to avoid the risks and capitalize on the opportunities. Changes are needed to recognize the primary interest of users of financial reporting in information that will best enable them to assess an entity's prospects for future cash flows.

Tailoring the model to fit the circumstances of the economic environment of today will require care. A company's capital structure as well as its investment portfolio needs to be considered. And the alterations should accommodate reporting provisional value changes without distorting the concept of earnings that management and financial statement users have come to understand.

SOURCE: Excerpted with permission from *Financial Executive,* January/February 1993, © 1993 by Financial Executives Institute, 10 Madison Avenue, P.O. Box 1938, Morristown, New Jersey 07962-1938; (201) 898-4600.

Required

a. The authors describe gains trading practices. Evaluate the extent to which SFAS 115 will prevent this practice.

b. The authors do not advocate current value accounting for all assets and liabilities. Rather, they suggest that "financial reporting should depart from historical cost measurements in favor of current values when current values most closely approximate the assets' ability to realize cash." Evaluate this proposal in terms of relevance and reliability. Also, relate your answer to the "clean surplus" theory of Ohlson.

c. The authors suggest a new "Statement of Changes in Provisional Values," as a way to avoid the volatility that results when gains and losses are included in net income. As an informed investor, would this suggestion help you assess the future profitability and cash flows of the firm? Why do you think the authors make this suggestion?

d. The authors point out that a firm's capital structure can help protect it against unexpected changes in value, that is, gains and losses on changes in asset values can be offset by losses and gains on liabilities. To what extent does this self-hedging phenomenon reduce the need for valuations in the accounts? Explain.

17. One of the problems of valuing assets and liabilities on a present value basis under non-ideal conditions is the choice of a discount rate. SFAS 69 "solved" this problem for RRA by mandating a 10% rate. However, SFAS 87, dealing with accounting for pensions, allows firms to choose the rate at which they discount future pension liabilities. Thus, SFAS 87 (paragraph 44) states that "assumed discount rates shall reflect the rates at which the pension benefits

could be effectively settled" and(paragraph 201) "material changes in long-term rates should [not] be ignored solely to avoid adjusting assumed discount rates."

This raises questions about what discount rate should be used for pension assets and liabilities, and whether the rate should be adjusted as interest rates in the economy change. For example, a decline in interest rates could result in a major increase in the estimated pension liability.

Required

a. As an informed investor in a large firm with a defined benefit pension plan, explain how present value information on pension plan net liabilities would be useful to you in evaluating the future profitability and cash flows of the firm.

b. An alternative to revising the discount rate as interest rates in the economy change is simply to disclose the rate actually used (SFAS 87 requires this disclosure—paragraph 54d.). As an informed investor, would you feel that supplementary disclosure of the discount rate actually used is satisfactory or do you think that the recorded book value of the pension liability should be adjusted as interest rates change? Explain.

c. Can you think of a reason why it may be desirable to allow firms to choose their own discount rates, as in SFAS 87, rather than requiring all firms to use the same rate, as in SFAS 69?

18. An article entitled "Presidential Life Is Accused by SEC of Overstatement" appeared in the *Wall Street Journal* on September 23, 1992. It describes a "cease and desist" order issued by the SEC following a claimed overstatement by Presidential Life Corporation of the fair value of certain of its security investments.

According to the article, the SEC believed that Presidential Life did not use generally accepted accounting principles to account for its junk bonds, and did not disclose the risks of the portfolio. Many of these bonds "had declined sharply in market price in 1989 and … most of the issuers of its junk bonds were either in bankruptcy or near default."

According to the SEC, this led to a $20.7 million overstatement of Presidential's 1989 pre-tax profit. "The SEC also alleged that Presidential misled investors when the company told investors in 1989 that 'the company believes its investments in high yield/high risk obligations will have no material adverse effects.'"

Required

a. To what extent would SFAS 115, had it been in effect at the time, have prevented the claimed misstatements? Explain.

b. The corporation plans to contest the SEC's charge. Suppose that you were in charge of preparing counterarguments to the SEC. What would these arguments be?

Economic Consequences

7.1   *Overview*

You may have noticed that there has been little discussion of management's interests in financial reporting to this point. Since management is a major constituency of accounting, our theory will be incomplete unless this omission is remedied.

This will involve us in a new line of thought which, at first glance, differs sharply from the investor-decision-based and efficient-market-oriented theories discussed earlier. Our first task is to understand the concept of **economic consequences**. In the process, we will also learn about some of the accounting problems in three major areas of accounting policy choice—foreign exchange conversion, government assistance, and costs of oil and gas exploration.

> *Economic consequences is a concept which asserts that, despite the implications of efficient security market theory, accounting policy choice can affect firm value.*

Essentially, the notion of economic consequences is that firms' accounting policies, and changes in policies, *matter*. Primarily, they matter to management. But, if they matter to management, accounting policies matter to the investors who own the firms, because managers may well change the actual operation of their firms due to changes in accounting policies. An example would be changes in accounting policies relating to oil and gas company reserves. Changes in such accounting policies, according to economic consequences arguments, may alter managers' exploration and development activities, which in turn may affect firm value. Furthermore, if these changes are negative and if many investors are affected, investors may bring pressure to bear on their elected representatives. Consequently, politicians will also be interested in firms' accounting policies and in the standard setting bodies that determine them.

It is important to point out that the term "accounting policy" refers to *any* accounting policy, not just one which affects a firm's cash flows. Suppose that a firm changes from declining-balance to straight-line depreciation. This will not in itself affect the firm's cash flows. Nor will there be any effect on income taxes paid, since tax authorities have their own capital cost allowance regulations. However, the new depreciation policy will certainly affect reported net income. Thus, according to economic consequences doctrine, the accounting policy change will matter, despite the lack of cash flow effects. Under efficient market theory the change will not matter (except for possible signalling effects) because future cash flows, and hence the market value of the firm, are not directly affected.

An understanding of the concept of economic consequences of accounting policy choice is important for several reasons. First, the concept is interesting in its own right. Many of the most interesting events in accounting practice derive from economic consequences. Second, a suggestion that accounting policies do not matter is at odds with accountants' experience. Much of financial accounting is devoted to discussion and argument about which accounting policies should be used in various circumstances, and many debates and conflicts over financial statement presentation involve accounting policy choice. Economic consequences is consistent with real-world experience.

Third, the presence of economic consequences raises the question of why they exist. Reasons were suggested in Section 1.8.3. Briefly, these arise from contracts that firms enter into, in particular executive compensation contracts and debt contracts. Given that accounting policies matter, the particular policies that firms use, and the timing and nature of changes to these policies, can be an important source of information to investors despite the implications of efficient security market theory. Indeed, managers who wish to do so can exploit this information source by using accounting policy choice as a credible signal of inside information.

This chapter is devoted to documenting the existence of economic consequences. Development of the reasons for their existence will require four additional chapters. The positive theory view of the firm as a nexus of contracts is developed in Chapter 8. The conflicts that arise from the moral hazard problem, which lead to a need for compensation and debt contracts in the first place, are described in Chapter 9. Chapter 10 considers executive compensation contracts in greater detail and Chapter 11 examines managers' use of accounting policy choice to manage reported earnings.

7.2   The Rise of Economic Consequences

One of the most persuasive accounts of the existence of economic consequences appears in an early article by Stephen Zeff (1978) entitled "The Rise of 'Economic Consequences.'" The basic questions that it raises are still relevant today.

Zeff defines economic consequences as "the impact of accounting reports on the decision-making behavior of business, government and creditors." The essence of the definition is that accounting reports can *affect* the real decisions made by managers and others, rather than simply *reflecting* the results of these decisions.

Zeff documents several instances in the United States where business, industry associations, and governments attempted to influence, or did influence, accounting standards set by the Accounting Principles Board (predecessor to the FASB) and its predecessor, the Committee on Accounting Procedure (CAP).

This "third party intervention," as Zeff calls it, greatly complicated the setting of accounting standards. If accounting policies did not matter, choice of such policies would be strictly between the standard setting bodies and the accountants and auditors whose task was to implement the standards. Presumably, these are the primary parties involved in accounting policy choice. If only these parties were involved, the traditional accounting model, based on well-known concepts such as matching of costs and revenues, realization, and conservatism, could be applied and no one other than the parties involved would care what specific policies were used. In other words, accounting policy choice would be *neutral* in its effects.

As an example of an economic consequences argument, Zeff discusses the attempts by several U.S. corporations to implement replacement cost accounting during 1947 to 1948, a period of high inflation. Here, the third-party constituency that intervened was management, who argued in favour of replacement cost depreciation to bolster arguments for lower taxes and lower wage increases, and to counter a public perception of excess profitability. The efficient market argument would be that such intervention was unnecessary because the market would see through the high reported net incomes produced by historical cost depreciation during inflation. If so, it should not be necessary to "remind" users by formal adoption of replacement cost depreciation. It is interesting to note that the CAP held its ground in 1948 and reaffirmed historical cost accounting.

Zeff goes on to outline the response of standard setting bodies to these various interventions. One response was to broaden the representation on the standard setting bodies themselves—for example, the Financial Executives Institute, representing management, is represented on the Financial Accounting Foundation (the body that oversees the FASB). Also, the use of exposure drafts of proposed new standards became common as a device to allow a variety of constituencies to comment on proposed accounting policy changes.

As Zeff puts it, standard setting bodies face a dilemma. To retain credibility with accountants, they need to set accounting policies in accordance with the financial accounting model and its traditional concepts of matching and realization. Yet, we have seen in Section 2.5 that such historical-cost-based concepts seldom lead to a unique accounting policy choice. That is, since net income does not exist as a well-defined economic construct under non-ideal conditions, there is no theory that clearly prescribes what accounting policies should be used, other than a vague requirement that some tradeoff between relevance and reliability is necessary. This opens the door for various other constituencies to get into the act and argue for their preferred accounting policies. In short, standard setting bodies must operate not only in the accounting theory domain, but also in the political domain. Zeff refers to this as a "delicate balancing" act. That is, without a theory to guide accounting policy choice, we must find some way of reaching a consensus on accounting policies. In a democratic setting, this implies involvement in the political domain. While a need for delicate balancing complicates the task of standard setters, it makes the study of the standard setting process, and of accounting theory in general, much more challenging and interesting.

SUMMARY

Despite the implications of efficient market theory, it appears that accounting policy choices have economic consequences for the various constituencies of financial statement users, even if these policies do not directly affect firm cash flows. Furthermore, different constituencies may prefer different accounting policies. This complicates the setting of accounting standards, which require a delicate balancing of accounting and political considerations. Standard setting bodies have responded by bringing different constituencies onto their boards and by issuing exposure drafts to give all interested parties an opportunity to comment on proposed standards.

7.3   *Foreign Exchange Translation: Practice and Theory*

7.3.1   *INTRODUCTION*

We now examine three areas where economic consequences have been particularly apparent. The first of these is accounting for foreign exchange translation.

Firms often enter into a variety of dealings involving foreign currencies. Frequently, these dealings result in gains and losses due to changes in exchange rates. We can distinguish two main sources of gains and losses. First, we have *transaction* gains and losses. For example, firms may buy or sell products in foreign markets, or borrow money abroad. If exchange rates change before these transactions are completed, the firm may experience a gain or loss. To illustrate, suppose a firm sells 100 units of product to a U.K. customer and agrees to accept payment of £6 per unit in pounds. If the exchange rate is £1 = 2.40, it would record the sale as 100 × 6 × \$2.40 = \$1,440. However, if the exchange rate falls to £1 = \$2.30 before payment is received, the firm would receive 100 × 6 × \$2.30 = \$1,380, incurring a foreign exchange loss of $60. Note that once the foreign transaction is closed out, the gain or loss is **realized**. Of course, the firm may enter into a hedging-type contract to protect itself against such a loss. Nevertheless, there may still be foreign exchange gains or losses, because it may be difficult to hedge certain contracts, and/or the firm may choose to bear all or part of the foreign exchange risk itself.

A second source of foreign exchange gains and losses derives from the ownership of foreign subsidiary companies. Then, for consolidation purposes (or for purposes of applying the equity method if the foreign subsidiary is not consolidated) it is necessary to translate the foreign subsidiary's financial statements into the currency of the parent company. This process frequently gives rise to **translation gains and losses**, also called **translation adjustments** or **differentials**. These gains and losses tend to be **unrealized**.

The accounting for and reporting of translation adjustments has created great difficulties for standard setting bodies and multinational firms. Consequently, these will be the main focus of our discussion. An early U. S. standard in this area was SFAS 8, which generated much opposition from management and was replaced six years later by SFAS 52. The process leading from SFAS 8 to SFAS 52 provides an interesting and important glimpse of economic consequences in action, whereby the interests of the various constituencies involved were rebalanced.

We will concentrate on balance sheet translation procedures (as opposed to the income and funds statements), because they lead to translation adjustments. We will also focus mainly on the U.S. experience, since developments in that country have tended to lead those in Canada in this area, and have also generated the greatest controversy.

7.3.2 REVIEW OF SFAS 8

In 1975, the FASB issued SFAS 8. This standard required use of the so-called **temporal method** of translation. To understand this method we first need to review the distinction between nonmonetary and monetary balance sheet items.

- **Nonmonetary items** consist mainly of inventories and capital assets. The key point to notice is that the amount of cash flows received from these may fluctuate because of changing market conditions or price levels. Thus, the market value of inventories may fall, adversely affecting the sales price. Also, the firm may adjust its prices in response to inflation, in which case the future cash flows from use of the firm's capital assets would be affected.

- **Monetary items** consist of items such as cash and accounts receivable and, on the liability side, accounts payable and bonds payable. Note that the amounts received or paid out from them is fixed with respect to amounts. Thus, changing economic conditions do not affect the fact that a firm is owed $100 on account or owes $1,000 of long-term debt. Monetary items are distinctly different from nonmonetary items, because the amount of money to be received or paid for the former is fixed by contract, whereas for the latter, the amount to be received may vary with changing prices and other economic conditions.

Under the temporal method of translation, nonmonetary items on the balance sheet of a foreign subsidiary are translated into the currency of the parent company at the exchange rate in effect when those assets were acquired. We will call this rate the **historical rate**. Monetary items, however, are translated at the exchange rate in effect as of the date of the financial statements, that is, the **current rate**. If the current rate changes during the year, then the translated amount of the monetary asset or liability would also change from its opening balance, *even if the balance had not changed in the foreign currency*. This creates a translation adjustment.

EXAMPLE 7.1 FOREIGN EXCHANGE TRANSLATION USING THE TEMPORAL METHOD

For this example and also for the rest of our discussion of foreign exchange conversion, we will assume that a U.S. parent has a 100%-owned U.K. subsidiary (UKS Ltd.), with the following balance sheet as at the beginning of the year:

UKS LTD. OPENING BALANCE SHEET			
Cash	£ 100	Accounts payable	£ 200
Accounts receivable	200	Bonds payable	2,000
Inventory	500	Shareholders' equity	600
Capital assets (net)	2,000		
	£2,800		£2,800

Thus, the subsidiary had net monetary liabilities of £1,900. The inventory and capital assets are nonmonetary.

Assume that the exchange rate at the beginning of the year was £1 = US$2.40 and that this rate was in effect when the inventory and capital assets were acquired.

Then the condensed opening balance sheet, translated into U.S. dollars, using the temporal method, would have been:

UKS LTD.
OPENING BALANCE SHEET

Nonmonetary assets (£2,500 @ $2.40)	$6,000	Net monetary liabilities (£1,900 @ $2.40)		$4,560
		Shareholders' equity (£600 @ $2.40)		1,440
	$6,000			$6,000

The nonmonetary assets and shareholders' equity are translated at the historical rate ($2.40). The net monetary liabilities are translated at the current rate (also $2.40 at first of year). This balance sheet is now ready for consolidation with that of the parent as at the beginning of the year.

Now, assume that at year-end the pound has fallen to £1 = US$2.30. Assume also that UKS's year-end condensed balance sheet looks exactly the same (in £) as it did at the first of the year. (This will simplify the example by eliminating the need to translate the income statement and will not affect the point to be made.) Then, the year-end balance sheet, translated into dollars, is:

UKS LTD.
YEAR-END BALANCE SHEET

Nonmonetary assets (£2,500 @ $2.40)	$6,000	Net monetary liabilities (£1,900 @ $2.30)		$4,370
		Shareholders' equity (£600 @ $2.40)	1,440	
		Add: Translation gain	190	1,630
	$6,000			$6,000

Nonmonetary assets and shareholders' equity are translated at historical rates. Net monetary liabilities are translated at the current rate. This throws the translated balance sheet out of balance by a credit of $190. This amount is the translation gain, arising from the fact that the parent company could pay off the net monetary liabilities with US$190 less at the end of the year than it could at the first of the year. Note that this gain is unrealized. Under SFAS 8, the $190 translation gain would appear on the consolidated income statement for the year.

The years following the issuance of SFAS 8 were marked by volatile exchange rates. Consequently, translation adjustments such as the one illustrated above tended to materially impact reported net income. Management had no control over this impact—it could not control exchange rate movements, and the method of accounting for translation adjustments was mandated. Prior to SFAS 8, the impact of translation adjustments on net income was less severe (and more controllable by management), because translation gains and losses could be deferred and amortized (this is still the case in Canada).

Impact of SFAS 8 on Massey-Ferguson Limited

The following table documents the impact of SFAS 8 on the reported earnings of Massey-Ferguson Limited (now Varity Corp.). These figures were taken from the annual reports of Massey-Ferguson for the years indicated.

TABLE 7.1 MASSEY-FERGUSON LIMITED—IMPACT OF SFAS 8 ON REPORTED INCOME, 1976 TO 1981 INCLUSIVE (US$000s)

Year	Income (Loss) Before Translation Adjustments (after tax)	Translation Adjustments		Reported Net Income (Loss)
1976	$ 125,731	dr	$ 7,817	$ 117,914
1977	55,019	dr	22,299	32,720
1978	(165,796)	dr	90,913	(256,709)
1979	12,100	cr	24,900	37,000
1980	(175,300)	dr	49,900	(225,200)
1981	(384,800)	cr	190,000	(194,800)

Note that translation adjustments varied from a debit of $90.913 million to a credit of $190 million over this period. In 1979, two-thirds of reported net income of $37 million arose from translation adjustments. In 1981, the favourable translation adjustment cut the net loss almost in half.

The material impact on reported net income, and the volatile nature of this impact, are obvious. The impacts in 1978 and 1980 must have been particularly frustrating to Massey-Ferguson, since it was struggling to recover from a loss position during this period. The following comment, taken from Massey-Ferguson's 1978 annual report, illustrates its frustration and is typical of management reaction generally:

> Massey-Ferguson's management remains skeptical of the FASB 8 theory of translation as a practical tool for the management of a multinational corporation.

As pointed out earlier, a major part of management's concern about "FASB 8" (we use "SFAS 8" to refer to the same pronouncement) arose from the non-controllability of the translation adjustment. The response of Massey-Ferguson's management to this controllability problem is worth noting. Their 1980 annual report stated:

> we established a concept of operating income as a measure of management's performance. We defined operating income as total revenue less those recurring expenses which are within the control of management. It excludes extraordinary items, net exchange adjustments and reorganization expense.

From this, it is clear that management did not want translation adjustments included in the measurement of their performance. Nevertheless, the bottom line would still be net income, after translation adjustments. It would be interesting to know how many financial statement users accepted management's concept and looked above the bottom line in their evaluations of Massey-Ferguson.

7.3.3   REVIEW OF SFAS 52

As a result of widespread concerns similar to those raised by Massey-Ferguson's management, the FASB decided in 1979 to reexamine accounting for foreign currency translation. The result was SFAS 52, issued in December, 1981. Some of the major features of SFAS 52 are as follows:

Functional Currency

Before translation into U.S. dollars, the financial statements of the foreign subsidiary under SFAS 52 are expressed in that subsidiary's functional currency, which is defined as the currency of the primary economic environment in which the subsidiary operates. For example, if a U.S. parent has a **self-sustaining** (that is, financially and operationally independent) subsidiary in the United Kingdom that operates primarily in the U.K. market, the functional currency would be the pound. However, complex situations can arise where the functional currency is a question of judgement. For example, if the U.K. subsidiary operated primarily in Africa, would the functional currency be the pound, or the currency of the particular African nation in which it operated? As another example, suppose a U.S. parent has a U.K. subsidiary that ships all of its product back to the United States. In this case, the subsidiary would be deemed to be an **integrated foreign operation** rather than self-sustaining, and its functional currency is deemed by SFAS 52 to be the currency of the parent, that is, the U.S. dollar.

Current Rate Translation Method

Once the foreign subsidiary's financial statements are expressed in its functional currency, they are to be translated into U.S. dollars (unless the functional currency is already U.S. dollars) using the **current rate method**. This is done by simply multiplying each asset and liability item on the subsidiary's balance sheet by the current exchange rate (share capital continues to use the historical rate). The result is the "same" set of subsidiary financial statements (except for shareholders' equity), but each item is expressed in U.S. dollars rather than in the functional currency.

Recall that under the temporal method used in SFAS 8, only monetary assets and liabilities were translated at the current rate. Nonmonetary assets, such as inventories and capital assets, were translated at historical rates. Understanding the difference between the current rate and temporal methods requires a consideration of the concept of **exposure**.

Essentially, exposure measures the amount of assets or liabilities subject to risk of foreign exchange rate fluctuations. Under SFAS 8, as we have just mentioned, inventories and capital assets are translated at historical exchange rates; hence, they are not exposed. The exposure is with respect to monetary items. Under SFAS 52, all assets and liabilities are translated at the current rate and hence their net amount is exposed. Thus, we can say that exposure under SFAS 8 was equal to the subsidiary's *net monetary liabilities*, while under SFAS 52 it is equal to the *shareholders' equity* of the subsidiary. Observe that when assets and liabilities are both exposed, they hedge each other with respect to foreign exchange gains and losses. Consequently, under SFAS 52, exchange gains and losses on inventories and capital assets hedge losses and gains on monetary liabilities. Under SFAS 8, no such hedging took place because inventories and capital assets were translated at historical rates. Under SFAS 8, hedging only took place between *monetary* assets and liabilities.

EXAMPLE 7.2 FOREIGN EXCHANGE TRANSLATION USING THE CURRENT RATE METHOD

We now extend Example 7.1 to the SFAS 52 current rate translation method, assuming that the U.K. subsidiary is self-sustaining.

The opening translated balance sheet is identical to that in Example 7.1 because the historical and current rates were equal at that time.

Recall that the year-end exchange rate was £1 = $2.30. Therefore, the year-end translated balance sheet is:

UKS LTD.
YEAR-END BALANCE SHEET

Nonmonetary assets (£2,500 @ $2.30)	$5,750	Net monetary liabilities (£1,900 @ $2.30)		$4,370
		Shareholders' equity (£600 @ $2.40)	$1,440	
		Less: Cumulative translation loss	60	1,380
	$5,750			$5,750

The cumulative translation loss is calculated as the net exposure of £2,500 − £1,900 = dr £600 multiplied by the decline of $0.10 in the exchange rate during the year. For a self-sustaining foreign subsidiary, the amounts of such gains and losses are accumulated in a separate shareholders' equity account and not written off to current net income as in SFAS 8.

Note that the translation gain for the year of $190 under SFAS 8 has turned into a loss of $60 under SFAS 52. However, there is no particular significance to this. Whether translation adjustments under SFAS 52 are more or less than under SFAS 8 would depend on the subsidiary's capital structure. For example, if the subsidiary has a large amount of debt outstanding, as in this example, we would expect lower gains when the value of the foreign currency falls, because the nonmonetary assets hedge the net monetary liabilities under SFAS 52. However, if the subsidiary has little or no debt, opposite results could easily occur.

These differences in exposure lead to a major distinction between SFAS 8 and SFAS 52. The temporal method used in SFAS 8 was essentially a line-by-line approach where the emphasis was on the correct translation of individual assets and liabilities from the standpoint of the consolidated entity. For example, with respect to capital assets, the view was that the foreign subsidiary's capital assets essentially belong to the consolidated entity. Since GAAP normally require that capital assets be carried at cost, this can be accomplished by translating the subsidiary's capital assets at the historical rate, that is, the rate in effect when the assets were acquired. In this way, the capital assets are included on the consolidated balance sheet at the same gross values each year and represent the actual cost, in U.S. dollars, of the subsidiary's assets to the consolidated entity. Similar reasoning applies to inventories—from the consolidated entity's standpoint the cost of inventories is established by translating them at the historical rate.

However, the historical cost principle does not apply to monetary items under GAAP. Generally, monetary items are valued at the amounts expected to be received or paid. By translating the foreign subsidiary's accounts receivable, for example, at the current rate, SFAS 8 included these receivables on the consolidated balance sheet at the amount they would realize if they were collected and remitted back to head office. Similar reasoning applies to accounts payable, bonds payable, and other monetary liabilities of the subsidiary. By translating these at the current rate, the consolidated balance sheet includes them at the amount of U.S. dollars that would be required to pay them off at the balance sheet date.

The current rate method of SFAS 52 takes a different approach than SFAS 8. It takes the view that the (self-sustaining) foreign subsidiary is a separate operation, with the parent company's exposure being its net investment in the subsidiary. Be sure you realize that if all assets and liabilities of the subsidiary are translated at the current rate, this is equivalent to the parent company's exposure being equal to the shareholders' equity of the subsidiary. Then, the translation adjustment for the year will be equal to the change in the exchange rate during the year multiplied by the subsidiary's shareholder's equity, as shown in Example 7.2. (Recall that this example made the simplifying assumption that the opening and closing balance sheets were identical. If this were not the case, the change in shareholders' equity during the year would have to be considered.) This result is consistent with the view that the foreign subsidiary is a separate operation and that the exposure of the consolidated entity is limited to its net investment in that operation.

It is also worth noting that, under the current rate method, the various ratios and other relationships on the subsidiary's functional currency balance sheet are preserved when the balance sheet is translated. This was not the case under the SFAS 8 temporal method given that different items were translated at different rates.

While the approaches of SFAS 8 and SFAS 52 are quite different, we have not expressed an opinion as to which one might be better. We will return to this point shortly, when we consider some of the economics of exchange rate determination.

Integrated Foreign Operations

An exception to using the current rate translation method in SFAS 52 arises with integrated foreign operations. Then, as we mentioned, the functional currency of the integrated foreign subsidiary is deemed to be the U.S. dollar. This means that the financial statements of the subsidiary must be translated from its domestic currency to U.S. dollars. SFAS 52 stipulates that this translation be done using the temporal method. In effect, when the foreign subsidiary is integrated with the parent company's operations, SFAS 52 requires that the SFAS 8 method be used for translation.

The FASB's reason for this is not hard to see. We saw in our coverage of the current rate translation method that it applied to the general case of a self-sustaining foreign subsidiary. In that case, SFAS 52 took the view that the foreign subsidiary was a separate operation and the parent's exposure was limited to its net investment in the subsidiary. This view makes far less sense when the subsidiary is essentially an extension of the operations of the parent. Then, it seems reasonable to translate the subsidiary's balance sheet so that the translated amounts appear as they would if the parent company had acquired the assets and liabilities of the subsidiary and recorded them on its own books. In other words, the line-by-line approach of SFAS 8 seems more reasonable when the foreign subsidiary is integrated. This is accomplished under SFAS 52 by defining the functional currency of an integrated subsidiary as the U.S. dollar and then mandating the temporal method of translation from the local currency of the subsidiary to its functional currency. (If this seems confusing, you may wish to look ahead to the summary of translation methods at the end of this section.)

Highly Inflationary Economies

Another exception to the rule arises when the subsidiary is not highly integrated but operates in an economic environment which is highly inflationary (relative to the U.S. economy). Once again, SFAS 52 requires that the functional currency of the subsidiary be the U.S. dollar, that is, that the SFAS 8 temporal method be used for translation from the local currency of the subsidiary into the functional currency. This avoids the **disappearing asset** phenomenon. The value of the currency of a highly inflationary economy will fall over time relative to the U.S. dollar, because, by the definition of inflation, the purchasing power of a currency becomes less and less as inflation progresses. If the current rate translation method were used under such conditions for long-lived assets, the translated value of the assets would also become less and less over time. The temporal method avoids this by translating long-lived assets, such as plant and equipment, at the historical rate.

Treatment of Translation Adjustments

Perhaps the most significant element of SFAS 52 is its treatment of the gains or losses arising from translation adjustments. The immediate write-off of such gains or losses was the aspect of SFAS 8 that drew the most management ire, as Massey-Ferguson demonstrated, because this tended to create large, uncontrollable impacts on net income. SFAS 52 avoids this problem by creating a new section in shareholders' equity called **cumulative translation gain (or loss)**. Here, the accumulated translation adjustments are deferred on the balance sheet into an unrealized gain or loss account, separate from retained earnings. Since this removes translation gains or losses from net income, it effectively gives management what it seems to want—a more controllable measure of net income.

Note, however, that translation adjustments that arise in the two exception cases—integrated foreign operations and highly inflationary economies—must be included in current net income under SFAS 52, just as under SFAS 8.

Summary of Translation Methods Under SFAS 52

Figure 7.1 summarizes the various translation methods required under SFAS 52. Think of a three-stage process. Stage 1 is the foreign subsidiary's financial statements in its local currency. In stage 2, these financial statements are translated into the subsidiary's functional currency using the temporal method (unless the local currency *is* the functional currency). In stage 3, the functional currency statements are translated (unless the functional currency is the U.S. dollar) into U.S. dollars using the current rate method.

FIGURE 7.1 SUMMARY OF TRANSLATION METHODS UNDER SFAS 52

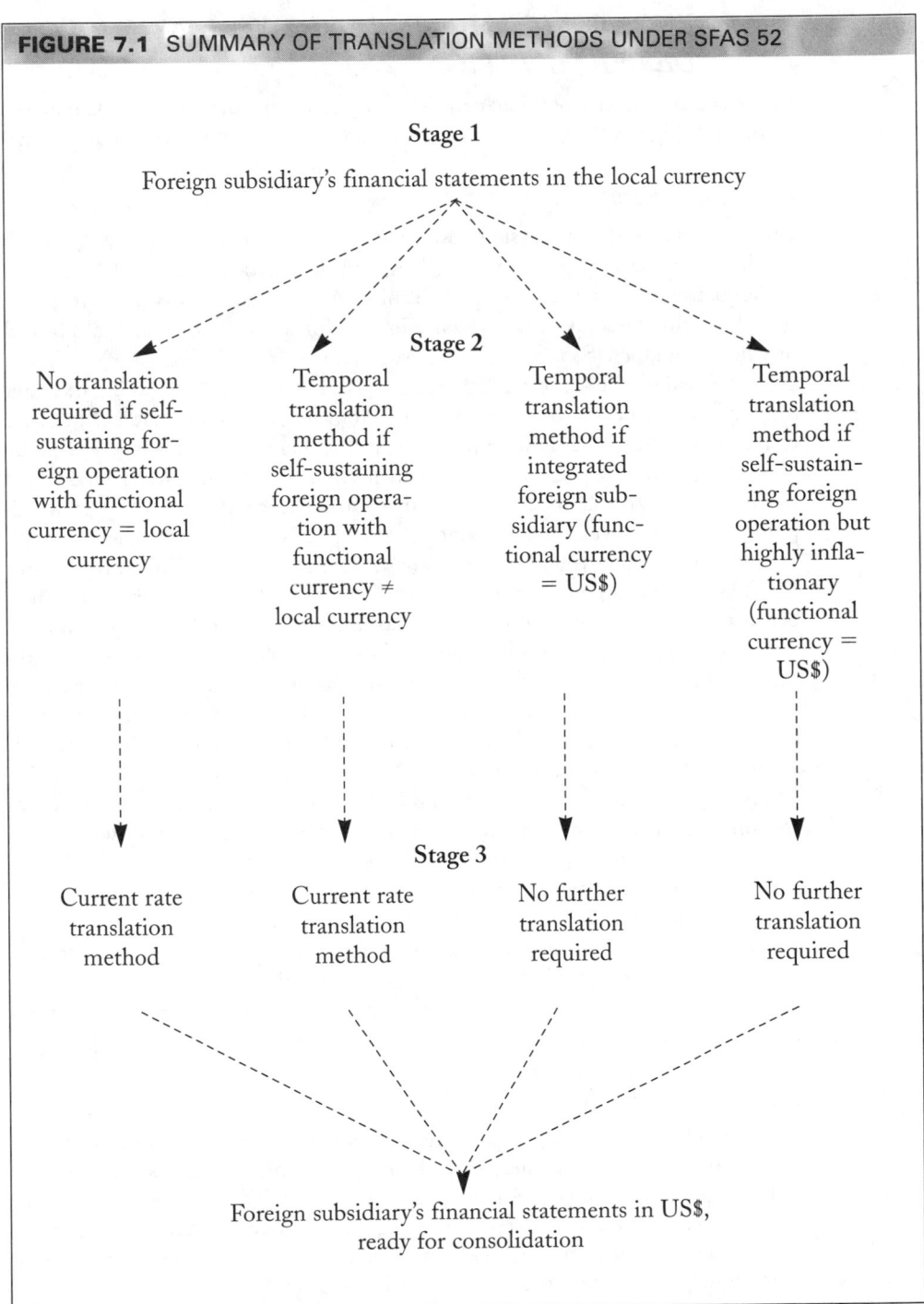

7.3.4   ECONOMIC THEORIES OF EXCHANGE RATE DETERMINATION

In this section we briefly outline two alternative economic theories to explain movements in foreign exchange rates: purchasing power parity and interest rate parity.

Purchasing Power Parity

The basic idea of the purchasing power parity theory is that a currency represents purchasing power over goods and services, and that market forces will operate on the exchange rates so as to keep purchasing power constant across different countries. For example, suppose that you live in the United States and can buy a bushel of wheat there for US$5. Suppose that you can also buy a bushel of wheat in the United Kingdom for £2. If the exchange rate is £1 = US$2.40 you would be better off to buy your wheat in the U.K. (we ignore transportation costs here). Other U.S. residents would feel the same way. Consequently, there would be a big demand by U.S. residents to buy pounds to pay for their U.K. wheat purchases. This demand would tend to raise the price of the pound until it reached £1 = $2.50, at which point it would cost you the same amount of U.S. dollars to buy a bushel of wheat, regardless of whether you bought it in the United States or the United Kingdom.

The purchasing power parity theory also applies to inflationary economies, because inflation is one reason why purchasing power may differ across countries. A country that is experiencing high inflation relative to other countries can expect, other things equal, to see a continuing decline in the value of its currency on foreign exchange markets and a deficit in its balance of payments. One reason for wheat being as high as $5 per bushel in the United States may be because of domestic inflation. Then, as the example suggests, the value of the U.S. dollar falls relative to the foreign currency and the U.S. balance of payments is in deficit as consumers rush to buy the foreign currency to pay for their foreign wheat purchases. In effect, rising prices in one country tend to encourage imports and discourage exports. The value of that country's currency on foreign exchange markets will then fall in an attempt to restore equilibrium.

Empirical tests of the purchasing power parity theory have shown that the theory holds up reasonably well over long periods of time, but that a variety of other factors can cause exchange rates to behave differently in the short run from what the theory would predict.

Interest Rate Parity

Another theory of exchange rate determination is based on interest rates. The basic idea of the interest rate parity theory is that higher interest rates in one country will encourage capital flows into that country. This creates a demand for that country's currency on foreign exchange markets and, other things equal, a higher value for that currency. In effect, foreign exchange rates will adjust so that the (risk-adjusted) rates of return are equal across countries.

Of course, the two theories are not mutually exclusive. For example, a country with a high balance of payments deficit for goods and services may not experience a decline in the value of its currency, as purchasing power parity would predict, to the extent that the country provides an attractive environment to foreign investors. There are many examples of countries financing an excess of imports over exports, that is, a current account deficit, by capital inflows. However, the two theories differ primarily in their assumptions about the primary engine that drives exchange rate movements. The interest rate parity theory works by means of capital flows between countries while purchasing power parity theory works by means of flows of goods and services.

For our purposes, the key point is that the purchasing power parity theory implies an inverse relationship between price levels for goods and services in a country and the value of that country's currency on the foreign exchange market. Thus, high domestic prices imply a balance of payments deficit leading to a reduced currency value, and vice versa. The interest rate parity theory makes no such connection, because it concentrates on capital flows rather than prices for goods and services.

We can now consider the influence of the above theories on accounting for exchange conversion and resulting translation adjustments.

7.3.5   CRITIQUE OF SFAS 8 AND SFAS 52

According to SFAS 52, the basic objective of foreign currency translation is to provide information that is generally compatible with the expected economic effects of a rate change on an enterprise's cash flows and equity. This goal seems reasonable, and consistent with SFAC 1 of the FASB Conceptual Framework. Consequently, we will adopt it as the basis for our critique.

SFAS 52 also refers to a pervasive criticism that translation results under SFAS 8 do not reflect the underlying reality of foreign operations. Certainly, Massey-Ferguson's management would agree with this criticism. However, we will argue that SFAS 8 was consistent with the purchasing power parity theory and, to a lesser extent, with the interest rate parity theory of exchange rate movements. However, it is difficult to see SFAS 52 as consistent with either of these theories.

Suppose that a U.S. parent company has a self-sustaining foreign subsidiary and that the foreign currency weakens in relation to the U.S. dollar. Consider first the inventory, capital assets, and other nonmonetary assets of the subsidiary. A weakening of the foreign currency would cause a nominal loss with respect to these nonmonetary items from the parent's standpoint—they are now worth less in terms of the U.S. dollar.

However, the subsidiary will also expect an offsetting gain. Recall that under the purchasing power parity theory, a weakening of the foreign currency would follow from rising prices in the foreign economy relative to those in the United States. This means that the nominal foreign currency cash flows from the nonmonetary assets would be expected to increase, as the self-sustaining subsidiary raises its selling prices commensurately with the inflation in the foreign economy. Such an increase in expected cash flows represents a nominal gain, and under purchasing power parity theory such a gain would offset the loss on translation—this is the inverse relationship we referred to in the previous section.

Now notice that this was the effect achieved under SFAS 8. No losses or gains on nonmonetary assets were recorded under SFAS 8 when foreign exchange rates changed, because such assets were translated at historical rates. Thus, SFAS 8 seemed consistent with purchasing power parity theory, at least with respect to nonmonetary assets.

Now consider a subsidiary with net monetary liabilities (a similar argument applies if the subsidiary has net monetary assets). By definition, the future cash flows associated with monetary items are fixed; the future payments with respect to a bond issue would be fixed by contract, for example. Thus, the firm has no ability to "change its prices" with respect to monetary assets or liabilities. Hence, the gain that the firm enjoys with respect to net monetary liabilities when the foreign currency falls in value—it takes fewer U.S. dollars to pay these liabilities off—is not offset by a change in related cash flows. Consequently, SFAS 8 was also consistent with purchasing power parity theory through its requirement that translation gains or losses on net monetary liabilities be included in income.

It also seems that SFAS 8 was consistent with interest rate parity theory, at least as far as net monetary liabilities were concerned. Under interest rate parity, a foreign currency will weaken on exchange markets if interest rates in the foreign economy fall relative to those in other countries. Lower interest rates in the foreign economy mean that the consolidated entity could repay its net monetary liabilities and reborrow at the lower rate, that is, it *gains* (assuming no penalty for refinancing). Therefore, inclusion of translation gains and losses on net monetary liabilities under SFAS 8 also seems consistent with interest rate parity theory.

Since interest rate parity theory makes no direct connection between price levels in the foreign economy and the exchange rate, it seems difficult to judge whether it is consistent with SFAS 8's translation of nonmonetary assets at historical rates.

Summary

We can therefore conclude that SFAS 8 was consistent with purchasing power parity theory and, for monetary items, with interest rate parity theory as well. Thus, it was consistent with our criterion of compatibility with the expected economic effects of rate changes on cash flows and equity.

Yet SFAS 8 came under severe attack from managers and was replaced in 1981 by SFAS 52. Why might this be?

SFAS 8's treatment of nonmonetary assets seems an unlikely reason, as no translation gains or losses were recognized with respect to these assets. This was in line with the conventional accounting treatment of inventories and capital assets on the books of the U.S. parent, where historical cost was the generally accepted basis of accounting.

Most likely, the problem stemmed from the gains or losses on net monetary liabilities. If the foreign subsidiary had borrowed heavily, the exposure could be quite high. Certainly, economic theory held that gains or losses on monetary items took place when exchange rates changed. The problem was that these translation adjustments were *unrealized*. Thus, by requiring them to be included in current income, SFAS 8 forced an accounting which was not only volatile but inconsistent with generally accepted historical cost accounting at the time, where, following the lower-of-cost-or-market rule, unrealized losses were sometimes recognized but recognition of unrealized gains in income was unusual. The foreign exchange gains or losses on monetary items would only be realized as these were collected or paid off, and this could take years.

It should be emphasized, however, that volatility per se is not sufficient reason to discard an accounting standard. Any business operates in a volatile price risk environment, particularly multinational firms. Ideally, the volatility of reported net income should reflect the volatility of the firm's real operations and capital structure (net of any hedging activities). Thus, one can argue that if firms choose to operate in volatile foreign environments, reported net income, to be relevant, should reflect that chosen volatility. As discussed above, reasonable arguments can be given that SFAS 8 did just this.

However, the Achilles' heel of SFAS 8, like RRA, was probably that by including unrealized translation gains and losses in income, it ignored the question of reliability. The inclusion of unrealized gains or losses in income introduced a volatile and uncontrollable element. In SFAS 8, it came from fluctuations in foreign exchange rates. In RRA, it came from fluctuations in amounts and prices of petroleum reserves. The effect on net income was much the same. However, it was much more serious as far as SFAS 8 was concerned, because the fluctuations affected *reported* net income—RRA is supplementary information only. In both cases, the theory did not seem to be sufficiently powerful to offset the practical measurement problems.

SFAS 52 seems to be a retreat to more conventional accounting, at least for self-sustaining foreign subsidiaries. Management's acceptance of SFAS 52 is no doubt due to the exclusion of translation adjustments from income, and their relegation to a separate component of shareholders' equity.

It is difficult to see much connection between economic theory and SFAS 52. In fairness, however, recall that SFAS 52 retains the SFAS 8 approach for subsidiaries that are in a highly inflationary environment. Here, the purchasing power parity theory seems particularly relevant.

7.3.6 *THE ECONOMIC CONSEQUENCES OF SFAS 8*

It is clear that the management of multinational corporations intervened in the standard setting process with respect to foreign exchange translation. The reaction of Massey-Ferguson management was typical, and consistent with the economic consequences effects described by Zeff. It appears that the intervention of the management constituency was sufficiently powerful that the FASB retreated from SFAS 8 to a more politically acceptable or, in Zeff's terms, a more "delicately balanced," alternative, despite considerable support for SFAS 8 in economic theory.

Yet SFAS 8 had no direct cash flow effects. The exchange gains and losses were paper items only. Thus, under efficient market theory, prices of the shares of affected multinational corporations would not be affected by the exchange gains or losses; that is, the market values of these shares should not be affected by the particular methods used for foreign exchange conversion. In other words, there should be no economic consequences. What, then, was the basis of management's concern? The material and uncontrollable volatility introduced by the inclusion of unrealized foreign exchange gains and losses in current net income must have been a major contributing factor.

In this regard, it is interesting to note the relationship between the failure of SFAS 8 and of RRA. RRA failed (at least, in the opinion of management) because of severe measurement problems which necessitated frequent and material adjustments to previously reported amounts. It seems that any accounting practice that departs extensively from the characteristic of reliability becomes problematic. Presumably, with respect to SFAS 8, management had no confidence in the reported foreign exchange gains and losses as a reliable measure of their performance. The economic theory of exchange rate determination that we have described seems to ignore questions of reliability, being based on market prices, which undergo constant change. (An exchange rate is a market price, since it gives the market price of one currency in terms of another.)

Nevertheless, it is interesting to note a slight difference in management's arguments against SFAS 8, in relation to those against RRA. Opposition to RRA focussed on its lack of usefulness to financial statement users. For SFAS 8, the arguments were more direct—management didn't like it. Foreign exchange adjustments affected the bottom line, whereas for RRA, the information was supplemental only. As a result, management must have taken it much more seriously and attacked it directly rather than indirectly through a claimed lack of relevance to users.

Summary

You should concentrate on two aspects of foreign exchange translation. First, there are the theoretical and technical aspects of foreign exchange accounting. Our discussion here has looked almost exclusively at those aspects surrounding translation of foreign subsidiary balance sheets in preparation for consolidation with the parent, and with the effects of such translation on the reported net income of the consolidated entity.

The second aspect of foreign exchange accounting is its fascinating and important illustration of economic consequences. Here, the interplay between

SFAS 8 and SFAS 52 is relevant. Clearly, managements of multinational corporations were disturbed about the impact of SFAS 8 on the bottom line. The adoption of SFAS 52 can then be interpreted as a revision of foreign currency translation standards to more delicately balance the competing economic and political considerations surrounding accounting policy choice.

7.4   *The ERCs of Multinational Firms*

As argued above, the volatility introduced into reported net income by SFAS 8 will increase decision usefulness if it properly reflects the underlying volatility of the foreign firm's operations. However, decision usefulness will decrease to the extent that the volatility simply creates "noise" in net income. You will recognize this as another instance of the tradeoff between relevance and reliability. In terms of the information system diagram of Table 3.2, greater relevance will increase the main diagonal probabilities, leading to greater belief revision following an earnings announcement. However, noise will lower these probabilities, leading to less belief revision. Which effect dominates is an empirical question.

The question can be addressed by examining the ERCs of affected firms. This was done by Collins and Salatka (1993) (C&S), who examined the quarterly earnings response coefficients of a sample of 27 U.S. multinational companies during the SFAS 8 (1976–80 inclusive) and SFAS 52 (1983–87) periods. C&S argued that the noise effect should dominate. Thus, they predicted that the ERCs of multinational firms during the SFAS 8 period should be *lower* than[1] the ERCs of the same firms during SFAS 52. Also, they argued that the ERCs of a control sample of 27 non-multinational firms[2] should not change between the two periods, because the non-multinationals would be unaffected by the transition from one standard to the other. The control sample was chosen to be similar to the multinational sample in terms of size and industries.

Using similar reasoning, C&S also argued that, during the SFAS 8 period, the ERCs of the multinational firms should be lower than those of the control firms and, during the SFAS 52 period, the multinational firms' ERCs should be the same as those of the control firms. The four ERC relationships are shown in Table 7.2. The equality and inequality signs show the *predicted* relationships.

By and large, C&S found evidence consistent with their arguments that SFAS 8 earnings were noisier.[3] The average ERC of the multinational firms was significantly higher under SFAS 52 than under SFAS 8 (top row of the table). Also, during the SFAS 8 period the average ERC of the multinational firms was less than that of the control firms (left column), and equality between ERCs was evidenced during the SFAS 52 period (right column). However, they found that the ERCs of the control firms *increased* from SFAS 8 to SFAS 52, contrary to their expectation of equality (bottom row).

TABLE 7.2 COLLINS AND SALATKA ERC STUDY—SIMPLIFIED RESEARCH DESIGN

	SFAS 8 Period		SFAS 52 Period
Multinational Firms	Average ERC of sample of 27 multinational firms	<	Average ERC of same sample of 27 multinational firms
	∧		‖
Control Firms	Average ERC of 27 similar non multinational firms	=	Average ERC of same sample of 27 non-multinational firms

Thus, the evidence was consistent with three of their four predictions. As C&S admit, these results provide fairly weak evidence in favour of their hypothesis of lower earnings quality under SFAS 8. The increased ERCs of the control firms between periods is problematic because it opens up the possibility that some other effects were operating to increase the ERCs of *all* firms over time, including the multinationals. Consequently, it is not completely clear whether the observed increase in the ERCs of the multinationals was due to the switch to SFAS 52.

Perhaps the weakness of evidence here is not surprising. Given the variety of factors that affect the ERC, as discussed in Section 5.4, it is hard to isolate the effect of any one factor, such as the volatility introduced by SFAS 8. In effect, it is difficult to find a control sample that is identical to the multinational sample in all respects except the applicability of SFAS 8.

Second, in view of our previous study of economic theories of exchange rate determination, perhaps the quality of SFAS 8 earnings was not as bad as C&S suggest. While SFAS 8 earnings may have been volatile, this volatility would have real information content (rather than just "noise") to the extent that SFAS 8 captured the economic reality of foreign operations.

Despite these problems, C&S concluded that their evidence was consistent with an increase in the earnings quality of multinational firms upon adoption of SFAS 52, thereby supporting the decision usefulness of SFAS 52 over SFAS 8. For our purposes, whether we agree with this conclusion or not, their study provides an informative example of how empirical ERC methodology can be brought to bear on an important and controversial accounting policy issue.

7.5   *Accounting for Government Assistance*

Governments frequently provide benefits to firms in order to influence those firms' decisions in a manner desired by government policy. For example, governments may provide incentives for firms to locate in designated areas, ranging from grants, conditional on the firm meeting certain commitments, to municipal tax relief. Other programs may be designed to encourage firms to become more capital-intensive, to assist the capital goods sector of the economy and/or to enhance international competitiveness. Assistance to stimulate research and development is another common government policy.

Government assistance plans that do not involve capital items are relatively straightforward in terms of accounting. Thus, if a firm receives a payment representing a reduction of municipal taxes in a particular year, this should go to reduce the municipal tax cost of that year. These suggestions are consistent with the *CICA Handbook*, which requires that "Government assistance towards current expenses or revenues should be included in the determination of net income for the period" (paragraph 3800.20).

Accounting for government assistance with respect to capital items can be considerably more complex. For example, assume that a firm receives a substantial grant for locating its new plant in a designated area. We can immediately see several possible alternatives to account for the grant:

1. The amount of the grant could be brought into income in the year in which it is received (more precisely, in the year in which the firm becomes entitled to receive it). Because the firm has done what is required to earn the grant, it should be recognized as income of that period.

2. The grant could be credited to the cost of the new plant. Because the grant was given to encourage the firm to locate its plant in the designated area, the cost of the plant should be reduced accordingly.

3. The grant could be regarded as deferred revenue and brought into revenue over the life of the plant. Clearly, this alternative would tend to have the same effect on net income as the second alternative, although the balance sheet would be different—it would show a deferred credit for the unrecognized portion of the grant, whereas the second alternative would show a lower valuation for capital assets and related amortization.

It is important to note that the choice of alternative can have a material effect on reported net income. While, as mentioned, alternatives 2 and 3 would tend to produce a similar net income, alternative 1 would result in a substantially higher net income in the first year of the grant, with lower incomes in subsequent years.

Conventional accounting theory seems incapable of resolving the question of which method is best. The matching of cost and revenue principle produces ambiguous results; it could be used to justify alternative 1 by arguing that the effort required to earn the grant was carried out when the plant was built in the designated area. Consequently the grant should be matched with this effort by bringing it into revenue as soon as the firm qualifies for it. This argument would be particularly valid if the costs of constructing and operating the plant were not materially higher in the designated area. However, the same matching principle can be used to justify alternatives 2 and 3, by arguing that since the grant was received specifically for the new plant, it belongs to the whole useful life of the plant. Consequently, it should be used to reduce amortization expense (alternative 2) or recognized as revenue over this period (alternative 3). Only then would the revenues generated from the new plant be properly matched with the costs of earning them.

The lack of resolution of arguments such as these has made it necessary for a standard setting body to step in. Indeed, since 1975 the *CICA Handbook* (paragraph 3800.26) has required that:

> Government assistance towards the acquisition of fixed assets should be either:
> (a) deducted from the related fixed assets with any depreciation calculated on the net amount, or
> (b) deferred and amortized to income on the same basis as the related depreciable fixed assets are depreciated. The amount of the deferral and the basis of amortization should be disclosed.

Thus, in terms of our example, the *CICA Handbook* allows alternatives 2 and 3 and does not allow alternative 1.

7.5.1   PIP GRANT ACCOUNTING CONTROVERSY

A particularly interesting example of economic consequences took place in Canada with respect to the accounting for government grants to encourage exploration for oil and gas. This occurred during the early 1980s when the Liberal government introduced the National Energy Policy (NEP), whose goal was the energy self-sufficiency of Canada. One aspect of the NEP was a new 8% tax on revenue from producing oil and gas wells. The Petroleum and Gas Revenue Tax (PGRT) was to be paid by all oil companies in Canada.

A second aspect of the NEP was the Petroleum Incentive Program (PIP), a system of government grants based on exploration expenditures. To qualify for the maximum grant (80% of exploration expenditures) a firm had to be largely Canadian-owned and explore in remote areas, such as the Beaufort Sea or off Canada's east coast.

Clearly, the NEP and, in particular, the PIP grants program were fraught with political implications. It could be interpreted as discriminating against Alberta, because oil and gas exploration in that province was not in a remote area, and as discriminating against foreign-owned oil companies. For an interesting account of the PIP grant controversy, see Crandall (1983).

Some of the accounting implications of the NEP program were noncontroversial. The new PGRT was straightforward. It would reduce the reported net incomes and cash flows of all oil companies operating in Canada by 8% of oil and gas revenues.

The PIP grants were more complex. Since oil and gas wells are long-term assets, they would fall under paragraph 3800.26 of the *CICA Handbook*, that is, the PIP grants had to be brought in as revenue over the useful life of the related exploration expenditures. In Canada, the full-cost method of accounting for oil and gas exploration expenditures was widespread around the time of the NEP. Consequently, the useful life of exploration expenditures would be quite long, regardless of whether those expenditures resulted in successful wells. In other words, the PIP grants would be reflected in net income only over an extended period, despite the fact that the cash flow from grants would be received right away.

Clearly, combining the accounting impacts of the PGRT and PIP would result in a drop in reported net income, even for firms that qualified for the maximum PIP. The 8% PGRT would reduce net income currently, but the offsetting PIP grants were to be taken into income only over a period of years. Executives of affected oil companies became extremely concerned about this implication.

This raises the question of why the executives were so concerned. As Crandall points out, "the cash flow prospects were favourable or neutral." Thus, on balance, there seemed to be no reduction in prospects of future cash flows for firms that qualified for maximum PIP. Hence, according to efficient market theory, the securities market valuation for such firms should either rise or be unaffected. Yet, according to Crandall:

> Most of them knew they would have to go to the financial markets to raise the funds needed for the exploration contemplated by the NEP. They believed that the underwriters would want to price their securities at a less favourable rate if they reported a lower net income because of the CICA stand. The validity of this view is controversial, but there is no question that it was widely believed.

Certainly, something was bothering the oil company executives, to the point where they brought pressure to bear on the federal government to remedy the situation. It seems that efficient market theory is not able to explain these reactions.

The federal government shared the oil companies' concerns, fearing that lower oil company reported profits would hamper attainment of the goals of the NEP. It brought pressure to bear on the CICA to amend or waive the requirements of Section 3800, even to the point of threatening legislation if the CICA failed to act. Apparently, the federal government did not subscribe to efficient security market theory either.

In the face of these pressures, the CICA held its ground. Ultimately, the government decided not to legislate. The CICA had the support of other powerful constituencies, such as the Ontario Securities Commission. Also, it may have felt that direct intervention would compromise the integrity of the standard setting process in Canada.

In this particular instance the CICA won. Regardless of the outcome, however, the PIP grant controversy has enlightened us about economic consequences.

It certainly demonstrates that accounting standards cannot be set in a vacuum and that their economic consequences can extend well into the political system.

SUMMARY

Two aspects of the accounting for government assistance are worthy of note. First, we have another example of our by-now-familiar argument that the matching of costs and revenues concept usually allows different ways to account for the same thing. Uniform policies to account for government assistance are in place only because they are mandated by the *CICA Handbook.* The second aspect is that the PIP grants controversy, a specific instance of disagreement over the accounting for government grants, represents an important and close-to-home example of economic consequences in action. We see many of the same reactions of management to a mandated accounting policy that we saw with SFAS 52, although for PIP grants the concern and influence of the government were particularly apparent.

7.6   *Stock Market Reaction to Successful-Efforts Accounting in the Oil and Gas Industry*

Our third illustration of economic consequences also pertains to oil and gas, although its focus is somewhat different. The previous two examples have been concerned with management and government reaction to accounting policies. Here we will look at investor reaction. Recall again that under the efficient market theory developed in Chapter 4, there should be no effect on the market price of firms' shares arising from a change in accounting policy if that policy change does not influence cash flows. Consequently, if a share price reaction is observed following a change in accounting policy that has no cash flow effects, such an observation would either raise further questions about efficient market theory or reinforce economic consequences arguments. It should by no means be taken for granted that such a share price reaction would be observed, however. Empirical research is needed to investigate this issue.

Our coverage here is based on an article by Lev, "The Impact of Accounting Regulation on the Stock Market: The Case of Oil and Gas Companies" (1979). Lev's study concerns SFAS 19, issued in 1977. That statement required that all U.S. oil and gas firms account for their exploration costs using the successful-efforts (SE) method. Recall that we discussed SE in relation to the alternative full-cost (FC) method in Section 2.5; you may wish to review the discussion at this time. While use of successful efforts is no longer required under GAAP, Lev's article is still relevant today, because it remains one of the few studies to document a market response to an accounting policy change that had no cash flow effects.

Since the choice of accounting policy for oil and gas exploration costs represents another instance of policy choice with no direct cash flow effects, efficient market theory predicts that there should be no managerial or governmental objections to the use of SE. Yet, economic consequence arguments were very much in evidence with respect to SFAS 19. In particular, there were concerns about possible adverse impacts on competition in the oil and gas industry and on oil and gas exploration. The source of these concerns was that most small oil and gas firms used FC. Since SE tended to produce lower reported net income than FC, especially for actively exploring firms,[4] it was feared that the lower reported net incomes would make it more difficult for small firms to raise capital, thus reducing competition and extent of exploration.

Consequently, Lev set out to determine whether the security prices of oil and gas firms were affected by the imposition of SE. If the concerns about SE, expressed by the government and the smaller oil and gas firms, were well founded, the answer should be yes, strengthening the economic consequences argument.

Lev's study is called an **events study**. While the reasoning and methodology are much the same as the empirical research reviewed in Sections 5.3 and 5.4, the focus is on finding a security market reaction to a *non-earnings* event, in this case the prospect of the FASB imposing successful efforts.

While the publication of an earnings announcement in the financial press works well as an estimate of the date on which the market becomes aware of current earnings, it can be much more difficult to establish the comparable date for an events study. Lev took the event date as July 18, 1977, the date that the FASB issued the exposure draft for SFAS 19. It was always possible that some other event occurring around this date could trigger oil stock price changes, rather than the event of interest. However, Lev carefully examined news reports surrounding July 18 that might have related to oil and gas and concluded that this was not the case.

Lev secured a sample of 49 FC firms (firms that had been using FC and hence would be required to switch to SE under SFAS 19) and a control sample of 34 SE firms. The daily stock returns for these firms were examined for a seven-day period surrounding July 18, using the same abnormal returns procedure that was described in Section 5.2 and used by Ball and Brown and in ERC studies.

He found a significant average negative, abnormal return for the shares of 49 sample FC firms affected by SE on the day following the release of the exposure draft. For the 34 sample firms that were already using SE, and were relatively unaffected by the exposure draft, there was little average negative return.

Lev reran his analysis using the "raw" returns, that is, the total daily share returns without separation into economy-wide and firm-specific components. He found roughly similar results, consistent with no major economy-wide events taking place on or about July 18, 1977.

Other researchers have also investigated security price reaction to changes in accounting standards. With respect to oil and gas, Dyckman and Smith (1979) and Kross (1982) found no significant reaction, while Lys (1984) did. It is instructive to contemplate possible reasons for market reaction. As discussed by Lev, one possibility is security market inefficiency—perhaps this is another anomaly. However, in view of the large number of empirical studies whose results are consistent with security market efficiency, this explanation seems unlikely. Other reasons can be suggested. One is that managers of FC firms may run into difficulties raising capital and/or may reduce their exploration activities once they were forced to use SE. Another reason is that the reduction in reported net income and shareholders' equity following a switch to SE might affect management bonuses and debt covenant ratios. The market could have been reacting to possible dysfunctional manager response to problems such as these. In the final analysis, however, we simply do not know why the market reacted as it did in Lev's study.

Nevertheless, while we may not know the reason, Lev's result does suggest that the market *did* react to an accounting event with no cash flow implications. Consequently, it is evidence that mandated accounting policy changes *can* have security price effects, thereby strengthening the economic consequences argument.

7.7　The Relationship Between Efficient Market Theory and Economic Consequences

At this point, we may have another anomaly. Efficient market theory predicts no security price reaction to accounting policy changes that do not impact underlying profitability and cash flows. If there is no security price reaction (implying no change in firms' costs of capital), it is unclear why management and governments should be particularly concerned about the accounting policies that firms use. In other words, efficient market theory implies the importance of full disclosure, including disclosure of accounting policies. However, once full disclosure of accounting policies is made, the market will interpret the value of the firm's securities in the light of the policies used and will not be fooled by variations in reported net income that arise solely from differences in accounting policies.

Yet, in three important areas of accounting policy choice, we have seen that three major constituencies of financial statement users—management, government, and investors—have indeed reacted to paper changes in accounting policy. The strength of management reaction seems particularly surprising, even involving appeals to government authority to intervene on its behalf. These various reactions are summarized in the concept of economic consequences, that is, accounting policy choice can matter even in the absence of cash flow effects.

Thus, accounting policies have the potential to affect real management decisions, including decisions to intervene either for or against proposed accounting standards. This "tail wagging the dog" aspect of economic consequences is all the more surprising because much evidence suggests that major security exchanges are reasonably described by the efficient market model.

Thus, our next task is to do what any discipline does when confronted with observations that are inconsistent with existing theory. We search for a more general theory that includes the existing theory but which also has the potential to explain the inconsistent observations. We begin this task in the next chapter.

Notes

1. Essentially, their argument is one of persistence. If net income contains noise, the noise will not persist, by definition. From Section 5.4.1 we saw that the ERC decreased with lower persistence.

2. Multinational firms were defined as firms with 12% or more of their sales consisting of foreign sales. Non-multinational firms had less than 12% foreign sales. The average proportions of foreign sales for the 27 multinationals in the sample was 0.32, and 0.07 for non-multinationals. Thus, the non-multinationals would have some influence from SFAS 8, although much less than for the multinationals. Note that this works against C&S finding the effects they seek.

3. Recall the caveat in Section 5.6. What is being investigated by C&S is whether the market may have reacted differently to different accounting standards. If it does, this may imply different degrees of decision usefulness for investors. However, there is no implication that the standard that produces the greatest market reaction is the best from a social standpoint.

4. Lev refers to a FASB staff study of the impact of SFAS 19, which found 64% of firms using FC would have their reported earnings decreased by 5% or more under SFAS 19. Also, 74% of FC firms would have their shareholders' equity reduced by 5% or more.

Questions and Problems

1. ABC Inc., a U.S. company, has a 100%-owned self-sustaining U.K. subsidiary, XYZ Ltd. The balance sheet of XYZ Ltd. as on December 31, 199X is shown below.

XYZ LTD.
BALANCE SHEET
As at December 31, 199X

Cash	£ 675	Bonds payable	£4,950
Capital asset (net)	5,625	Shareholders' equity	1,350
	£6,300		£6,300

When the capital asset was acquired, the exchange rate was £1 = US$2.50. On December 31, 199X, the exchange rate was £1 = US$2.20. XYZ Ltd. incorporated on January 1, 199X and the capital asset was acquired on that day.

Required

a. Calculate the translation gain or loss which would arise if XYZ Ltd.'s balance sheet is translated to U.S. dollars using:

   i. Translation rules as laid down in SFAS 8
   ii. Translation rules as laid down in SFAS 52

b. What is the amount of the impact of the translation gains or losses as calculated in part **a** on the income statement of the U.S. parent, ABC Inc. under:

   i. SFAS 8 rules?
   ii. SFAS 52 rules?

c. Why did managers oppose continuance of SFAS 8? Discuss.

d. How did SFAS 52 attempt to address managers' criticisms of SFAS 8?

(CGA-Canada)

2. Table 7.4 shows the March 31, 1991 comparative balance sheet of Caleb Wines Ltd. Caleb Wines Ltd. is the Canadian subsidiary of Supreme Wines Corporation of California.

Required

a. Calculate the parent company's exposure to foreign exchange fluctuations as at March 31, 1991 with respect to Caleb Wines Ltd., assuming SFAS 8 was in place.

b. Assume that Caleb Wines Ltd. is not an integrated foreign operation and that the Canadian economy is not highly inflationary. Calculate the parent company's exposure to foreign exchange fluctuations with respect to Caleb Wines Ltd., assuming SFAS 52 was in place.

c. Suppose that the Canadian dollar declines by 3% relative to the U.S. dollar. How much foreign exchange gain or loss would the parent company record in the 1991 consolidated income statement under part **a** and

CALEB WINES LTD.
CONSOLIDATED BALANCE SHEETS
As at March 31, 1991 and March 31, 1990

	1991	1990
	$	$
ASSETS		
CURRENT ASSETS		
Cash and short-term investments	19,437,331	17,201,126
Accounts receivable	7,304,883	4,622,061
Inventories of wine and supplies	15,899,825	17,031,305
Prepaid expenses	485,021	890,601
	43,127,060	39,745,093
FIXED ASSETS (Note 2)	10,942,219	11,472,294
Deferred Charges (net of amortization)	179,400	246,942
	54,248,679	51,464,329
LIABILITIES		
CURRENT LIABILITIES		
Accounts payable and accrued liabilities	2,642,149	2,062,655
Dividends payable	656,959	656,959
Income and other taxes payable	2,233,872	1,528,245
Current portion of long-term debt (Note 3)	175,000	175,000
	5,707,980	4,422,859
LONG-TERM DEBT (Note 3)	1,498,000	1,738,000
DEFERRED INCOME TAXES	1,887,000	2,022,000
MINORITY INTEREST IN NET ASSETS		
of Subsidiary Companies	252,563	237,501
	9,345,543	8,420,360
SHAREHOLDERS' EQUITY		
CAPITAL STOCK (Notes 4 and 5)	2,069,867	2,069,867
Retained Earnings	42,833,269	40,974,102
	44,903,136	43,043,969
	54,248,679	51,464,329

Signed on Behalf of the Board

_____
                    Director

_____
                    Director

under part **b**? Base your calculations on March 31, 1991 balance sheet values.

d. If Caleb Wines Ltd. was an integrated foreign operation of its parent company, how much gain or loss would the parent record in the 1991 consolidated income statement?

3. a. The SFAS 8 method of foreign exchange translation required that capital assets on the balance sheet of a foreign subsidiary be translated into the currency of the parent company at the historical exchange rate. Is this consistent with GAAP for capital assets in general? Discuss.

b. According to SFAS 52, if the foreign subsidiary operates in a highly inflationary economy, the functional currency of the subsidiary will be the U.S. dollar, even if the subsidiary is not an integrated operation. That is, in these circumstances the SFAS 8 temporal method is required to be used. Explain the rationale behind this requirement from the perspective of the "disappearing asset" phenomenon.   (CGA-Canada)

4. In his article "The Impact of Accounting Regulation on the Stock Market: The Case of Oil and Gas Companies" (Section 7.6), Lev examined the daily returns on a portfolio of oil and gas company's common shares affected by SFAS 19. At the time, this standard would have required firms to use the successful-efforts method of accounting for the costs of oil and gas exploration.

Lev found that there was an average decline of 4.5% in the share prices of firms that would be affected by the new standard during a three-day period following the release of the exposure draft (July 18, 1977), which announced the FASB's intention to impose successful-efforts accounting. This illustrates the economic consequences of an accounting policy change that would have no direct impact on affected firms' cash flows.

Required

a. Why did Lev examine share returns around the date of the exposure draft (July 18, 1977) rather than the date SFAS 19 was issued (December 5, 1977)?

b. Why did Lev examine daily stock returns instead of returns over a longer period, such as a week?

c. Lev chronicled other events that may have affected oil company share prices around July 18, 1977, such as political developments, developments in the oil and gas market, etc. Why did he do this?   (CGA-Canada)

5. In his article "The Impact of Accounting Regulation on the Stock Market: The Case of Oil and Gas Companies," Lev refers to the negative reaction to the oil and gas exposure draft by small oil and gas producers that were currently using the full-cost method. These small producers argued that successful-efforts accounting would reduce their ability to raise capital, with consequent effects on oil and gas exploration and on the level of competition in the industry.

Required

Evaluate these arguments from the standpoint of efficient security markets theory.

6. Before 1993, postretirement benefits were accounted for on a cash basis, allowing companies to account for these benefits as they were paid to employees. However, after December 15, 1992, FASB implemented SFAS 106, a standard that requires companies to account for postretirement benefits on an accrual basis.

   According to SFAS 106 (paragraph 124), "accrual accounting will more appropriately reflect the financial effects of an employer's existing promise to provide those benefits and the events that affect that promise in financial statements, as those events occur." Furthermore, SFAS 106 (paragraph 20) states that "the expected postretirement benefit obligation for an employee is the actuarial present value as of a particular date of the postretirement benefits expected to be paid by the employer's plan to or for the employee."

   This new rule has had economic consequences, whereby firms moved to reduce their postretirement benefits. For example, as reported in the *Wall Street Journal* (November 4, 1992), McDonnell Douglas Corp. cut benefits to retired employees upon realizing that it faced a $1.2 billion charge against earnings from SFAS 106.

   Required

   a. What is the after-tax impact on a firm's cash flows following adoption of SFAS 106, assuming benefits are not cut?

   b. Why would some firms move to reduce retiree benefits following adoption of SFAS 106?

   c. Give an argument how a firm's share price might rise following the reporting of a major charge for adoption of SFAS 106.

7. An article entitled "Wrongheaded Hit at Retiree Benefits," by Robert G. Ripston, appeared in the *Wall Street Journal* on December 28, 1992. The article discusses some potential economic consequences of SFAS 106. FASB Statement 106 requires companies to "accrue on a current basis for the future costs of medical expenses and other benefits promised [to] retirees."

   According to the article, this has led companies to take drastic steps. For example, Primerica "ask[ed] its 7,800 retirees to agree to pay the cost of continuing health benefits or do without coverage."

   The article suggests that there are many problems facing companies that adopt this new rule. For instance, there are a lot of assumptions made when calculating future "medical costs 10 to 20 years from now." There are considerable costs associated with legal fees in order for companies to find ways to lessen the effect of accruing postretirement benefits. Furthermore, there have been litigations brought on by workers who are upset because their company has reduced or eliminated their postretirement benefits.

Required

a. Mr. Ripston states that "some firms have already taken the expense on their balance sheets, resulting in a significant increase in their liability." Give a journal entry to record, say, a $170 million after-tax provision for retiree benefits upon adoption of SFAS 106.

b. Mr. Ripston suggests "a less burdensome middle ground might have involved some greater level of disclosure of these liabilities and their nature short of requiring full accrual." In view of some of the efficient security market anomalies described in Section 6.2.3, do you feel that this suggestion has merit? Explain why or why not.

c. Among the claimed economic consequences of SFAS 106 is that "the future competitiveness of American business—and the future health and well-being of millions of retirees—should not be determined on the basis of a mere bookkeeping rule." Explain why you agree or disagree with Mr. Ripston here.

8. An article entitled "Treasury Aide Charges SEC Proposals on Accounting Could Hamper Lending" appeared in the *Wall Street Journal* on May 19, 1992. It describes the concerns of Deputy Treasury Secretary John Robson about the economic consequences of proposed new accounting standards for banks by the SEC. Secretary Robson argues that these standards "could discourage banks from lending." According to the article, there are three issues that concern Secretary Robson:

- The SEC has a proposal on how to account for "insubstance foreclosures." An "insubstance foreclosure" occurs when a lender defaults on his or her obligation and the bank assumes control of the building and/or other property put up for collateral by the lender, without formally seizing the property. "At issue is what value the bank gives the property and how quickly it has to write it off, thus reducing earnings and lending capacity. 'Federal bank and thrift regulators have developed some reasonable, real world examples to guide examiners on what is ... an insubstance foreclosure. ... [However,] the SEC staff seems to want even more rigid definitions of insubstance foreclosure [and] that [will] seriously thwart'" the flexibility of those examining whether or not they are dealing with an insubstance foreclosure. Mr. Robson believes that this new proposal "would discourage banks from helping troubled borrowers work through their problems."

- The SEC wants to propose "mark-to-market" accounting for government securities held by banks. This means that banks would account for their government securities at market as opposed to historical cost. However, according to the article many are concerned that "mark-to-market" accounting "could produce volatile swings in bank earnings."

- The SEC wants to propose "that banks be forced to hold more capital against government securities." Mr. Robson feels "that this could discourage banks from lending."

Required

a. Explain how the first issue that concerns Secretary Robson could operate to reduce banks' lending.

b. Do the same for the second issue, namely mark-to-market accounting for government securities in the banks' investment portfolios. Include in your answer consideration of how volatile swings in bank earnings could affect banks' willingness to make long-term loans.

c. To what extent do you agree with the concern expressed by Secretary Robson about the ability of the proposed accounting policies to affect banks' lending decisions? Explain your answer.

9. An article entitled "Accountants Worry Clinton Tax Plans Will Skew Results, Thwart Comparisons" appeared in the *Wall Street Journal* on March 29, 1993. The article describes two of the financial reporting implications of U.S. President Clinton's tax proposal for 1993.

The first implication arises from the proposed reintroduction of the investment tax credit which was eliminated in 1986, a key part of the president's "economic stimulus package." According to the article, in 1971 Congress passed a bill to allow two methods to account for investment tax credits: defer the credit over the useful life of the asset or credit it to earnings right away. "It was the only time that Congress overruled accountants and regulators who wanted all companies to spread the credit's benefits providing for uniform disclosure to investors and financial analysts."

According to the article, Stephen A. Zeff, an accounting professor at Rice University, feels that the FASB should not allow companies to account for the investment tax credit in two different ways. Timothy Lucas, FASB's research director, believes that Professor Zeff is right because two methods of accounting for the same thing can become confusing to the reader of financial statements.

The second implication arises from the requirements of SFAS 109, *Accounting for Income Taxes* (1992). Unlike Section 3470.20 of the *CICA Handbook*, which requires the deferral method of income tax allocation, SFAS 109 requires the accrual method, that is, when income tax rates change, the balances of deferred income tax asset and liability accounts are adjusted to reflect the new rates, with the resulting charge or credit included in income from continuing operations. The amount of this charge or credit can have a material effect on the bottom line.

The article states that President Clinton would like to increase the tax rate from 34% to 36%, and suggests that "the president's proposed boost in corporate tax rates could affect corporate profits significantly by forcing some companies to reserve more and others less for future tax liabilities, depending on their tax-credit history." In addition, "under the new accounting rule, when tax rates are boosted, profits of companies with future tax deductions and net loss carryforwards generally rise while profits of companies that defer some tax payments to the future, [such as the excess of tax over book depreciation], generally decline." For example, the article points out that Northrop Corp., under a 34% tax rate, had $200.8 million in profit for 1991. However, if the new proposal of a 36% tax rate were implemented, Northrop Corp.'s profit would have decreased $33.4 million to $167.4 million.

Required

a. With respect to the proposed investment tax credit, describe an accounting policy that reports the highest net income in the year the credit is granted. Describe an accounting policy that reports the lowest net income in that year.

b. What is the purpose of an investment tax credit? Why do you think the U.S. Congress overruled the accountants and regulators who, in 1971, wanted to spread the credit over the life of the asset?

c. With respect to the material impact of the tax rate increase on reported profits under SFAS 109, what economic consequences could there be?

d. Given the efficient security market anomalies discussed in Section 6.2.3, to what extent would you, as an investor in firms whose reported profits are affected by SFAS 109, agree with Professor Zeff's concern about lack of comparability if firms can spread the proposed investment tax credit over the life of the asset or use it immediately?

e. Use the concept of earnings persistence to explain the desirability of full disclosure of the effects of a tax rate increase on profit from continuing operations, under the accrual method of SFAS 109.

10. An article entitled "Accounting Rule-Making Board's Proposal Draws Fire," by Lee Berton, appeared in the *Wall Street Journal* on January 5, 1994. It describes the concerns of small businesses about a FASB proposal to charge the value of employee stock options to expense. Under current GAAP, there is usually no expense recorded for such options.

According to the article, small businesses feel that this new proposal will hurt them the most, because they use stock option plans instead of high salaries to lure top executives. This enables smaller businesses to compete with larger businesses "for executive talent."

The article refers to a recent Coopers & Lybrand survey, which found that the FASB proposal would reduce reported profits of start-up or high-tech firms by 27%, compared with 3.4% for mature, larger firms.

Craig M. Swanson, vice president of finance for Protocol Systems Inc., a medical equipment maker, is quoted in the article as saying that 200 of their 250 employees receive stock options. However, if the FASB proposal were implemented, he would only give stock options to the top executives. Mr. Swanson states that "without options, talented people won't want to take the risk of growing with us."

In addition, the article gives an example of a restaurant chain, Outback Steakhouse Inc., where Robert Merritt, senior vice president and chief financial officer, states that they use stock options in order to keep their employees "interested in the overall performance of the company." He insists that dropping stock options "could make it harder to convince employees that their hard work enhances their own wealth."

In defence of the proposal, the article quotes FASB chairman Dennis Beresford as saying "We are aware of the concerns of small businesses. ... But we feel that issuing stock options without any cost gives the issuing company an unfair advantage and is an accounting loophole that needs to be addressed."

Required

a. What economic consequences might there be if the FASB proposal goes through?

b. Do you agree with Mr. Beresford's reply, despite possible economic consequences? Explain why or why not.

11. The AICPA Special Committee on Financial Reporting (see Chapter 5, Question 17) made several additional recommendations:

- The Committee recommended that there be an improvement in the disclosure of segmented information. "Segment reporting should be improved by better aligning the information in business reporting with the segment information that companies report internally to senior management or to the board."

- The Committee recommended that there be an improvement in the disclosure of financial instruments such as swaps, caps, and floors, to name a few. Users want answers to questions such as: What is the risk associated with the instruments? How are the instruments accounted for in the financial statements? and many other questions.

- The Committee recommended that there be an improvement in the disclosure of the risk associated with off-balance-sheet financing for such items as long-term leases, joint ventures, long-term purchase agreements, and many others.

- The Committee recommended that risk and uncertainties associated with a company's assets and liabilities should be disclosed in the notes to the financial statements.

- The Committee recommended that there be an increase in auditor involvement. For example, "allow for flexible auditor association with business reporting, whereby the elements of information on which auditors report and the level of auditor involvement with those elements are decided by agreement between a company and the users of its business reporting."

SOURCE: Excerpts reprinted with permission from report of the AICPA Special Committee on Financial Reporting. © 1994 by American Institute of Certified Public Accountants, Inc.

Required

a. Evaluate the relevance and reliability of the proposed additional information for investors.

b. The FEI, as reported in the *Wall Street Journal*, August 16, 1994, claims adverse economic consequences if the Committee's proposals are put into effect. These include increased share price volatility leading to higher cost of capital. Outline the FEI's likely reasoning in arriving at this claim.

c. Do you agree with the FEI's claims in part **b**? Explain why or why not.

12. In the article here reproduced, "Commentary," from *Accounting Horizons* (March 1990), Arthur Wyatt (a former member of the FASB) gives a vigorous defence of the proposals leading up to SFAS 106. Mr. Wyatt argues that the economic consequences of improved accounting for postretirement benefits will be good, not bad.

COMMENTARY

OPEB Costs: The FASB Establishes Accountability

One of the most popular games in town these days is carping at (or about) the FASB. Virtually no one is happy about what the FASB is doing. It is both too conceptual and too practical, issues too many standards or not enough guidance, moves too quickly or at a snail's pace.

In the midst of all this carping the Board is about to issue a standard providing guidance on accounting for the costs of other postretirement benefits (OPEB). Based on reactions in comment letters to the exposure draft of the Board's proposals and comments at public hearings, almost no one is satisfied with what the Board is proposing.

Maybe it is appropriate, however, to step back from the technical recommendations in the Board's proposals to put this project in perspective. The technical issues have been evaluated, criticized, and berated in many settings, mostly without shedding any new light on the underlying phenomena or the most appropriate accountability for those phenomena. What few seem to recognize, however, is that this FASB project has focused attention on a significant social problem in the U.S. Amidst all the criticisms corporate America is reassessing its commitments under postretirement health care programs. After more than a decade plan structures are being modified, influenced by useful information on costs and benefits. Criticisms persist while the critics benefit from FASB initiatives.

The Board, in fact, deserves the highest praise for tackling the accounting aspects of a substantial social phenomenon and for focusing attention on the existing accountability shortcomings. The importance of the Board's OPEB project lies not in the details of its technical provisions but in its willingness (some would say eagerness) to confront accountability issues that no other group in our society (government or private) was willing to confront.

That the Board's technical conclusions fall short of a forthright resolution of the accountability issues is distressing to some, but the shortcomings are far overshadowed by the focus on a significant business and social issue that the Board's initiatives have produced. That the business community is heaping scorn, rather than praise, on the Board for its proposals is distressing, even deplorable. What the FASB project has really done is to shed light on a serious business problem facing many companies, possibly even saving some managements from the effects of their own often uninformed and uneconomic decisions.

Throughout the Board's exposure process it was often told that company records were not adequate to develop the data needed to establish the level of accountability proposed by the Board. In other cases, as those data reached upper management levels, revisions to existing plans were proposed. Often those revisions reduced previous benefits, and in some cases led to defined contribution plans and even substitute employee stock ownership plans. Other companies are currently in the midst of a reassessment of their commitments and how best to gain control of costs.

How is it that the technical accounting wizards of Norwalk could create such an impact? The answer to this question lies in some fundamental notions of accountability. Financial reporting rests importantly on the notion of management accountability for transactions consummated, contracts entered into, and other events having measurable economic consequences. Clearly, the granting of postretirement benefits by management to employees as a part of a compensation package for services rendered is the type of action for which managements should expect to be held accountable. The issue the Board is dealing with is whether accountability should commence with the granting of the benefits or later with the expenditure of cash to settle claims made.

How accounting practice for postretirement benefits evolved to embrace accountability only at expenditure date would be interesting to pursue, but of greater importance is the current effort by the Board to bring accountability in this area into line with accountability for other aspects of an employee compensation package. The fact that the discrepancy in accountability between the two approaches is of such great financial significance simply heightens the profile of the issue. Thus, strong arguments can be made that the business community, rather than being so critical of the Board, should be:

1. Praising the Board for drawing attention to an important social issue—the financing responsibility for retiree health care, or at least that portion that has been agreed to be borne by the private sector.
2. Encouraging the Board to pursue the issues to the fullest so that all necessary information becomes publicly available to indicate the magnitude of the problem.
3. Working overtime to develop data necessary to measure the magnitude of the problem—rather than arguing that the data are impossible to develop. One really has to question how responsible a management has been to grant specified significant benefits to employees the magnitude of which are unmeasurable because of the absence of reliable data.

In many other transaction areas over the years accountants, including standard setters, have found that accrual accounting achieves better the reporting of accountability, or stewardship, than does cash basis accounting. Thus, the FASB inclination toward accrual accounting notions to establish standards for reporting on postretirement benefits is neither innovative nor surprising. Rather, the accounting for postretirement benefits simply provides new—and dramatic— evidence of the superiority of accrual accounting over cash basis accounting in dealing both with notions of accountability and income determination. Many critics of the Board's proposal seem less interested in establishing a valid standard of accountability than in protecting past misguided practices that improved the appearance—but not the reality—of balance sheets and income statements.

While many forces influence the ultimate decision by the FASB to undertake a project, with the OPEB project it is clear that at least one force was concerned about the accountability achieved under existing practice. Thus, it would appear that criticisms of the Board's specific proposals would focus importantly on whether appropriate accountability levels have been achieved. Stated differently, the real question is, will the proposal in the exposure draft provide information that will permit a reasonable evaluation of the depth of the problem a management faces in connection with an existing arrangement with its employees. Those who favor, for example, precluding immediate recognition of the existing obligation should be expected to justify that phasing the existing liability in over future periods does not mask, or cover up, the magnitude of today's obligations.

Different societies have dealt with the problem of health care costs for retired workers in different ways. A few have ignored the problem. Most have had the obligations undertaken by the government. In the United States we have a mixed pattern—some governmental assumption through Medicare and Medicaid, some private sector assumption through benefits earned during working years, and some assumed by individual citizens through personal insurance programs and cost-sharing arrangements. To the extent a business entity has agreed to provide these benefits to its workers after their retirement, it is essential that the costs and related obligations be reported fully and forthrightly on a timely basis. The FASB project is aimed at this objective.

Postretirement health care benefits impose an obligation on a company just as do wages currently paid and other employee benefit costs. All of these costs require consideration in product pricing strategies. If it is factually accurate that managements are unable to determine the magnitude of postretirement health care benefits, a significant cost component may have been overlooked, at least in part, as pricing strategies evolved. The focus the FASB project places on this cost component will benefit industry over time.

Accounting for any given phenomenon—such as postretirement health care costs—serves well its purpose when it leads to the reporting of the economic effects of the contractual agreements that exist. Accounting is not expected to change the economics, but to reveal data to enable an assessment of the economics. Accounting can, on the other hand, preclude understanding of the economics by fostering incomplete or misleading information. Such information can then lead to bad economic decisions by those who use the information. In assuming the burden of addressing the accounting issues in the postretirement benefit area, the Board has assumed the responsibility to refine the presentation of information about this phenomenon that will minimize the likelihood of bad economic decisions. Some critics argue that the result of the proposed FASB standard will be a reduction, even a substantial reduction, in corporate postretirement benefits for their employees. This, the argument runs, is socially undesirable, an adverse economic consequence of an FASB action. Such an argument, if valid, suggests that the major foundation of existing postretirement programs is the absence of a need for accountability of their consequences. If, in fact, existing postretirement health care programs cannot withstand the scrutiny provided by full accountability for those plans, changes in health care coverages may well be desirable.

The Board deserves praise for dealing forthrightly with such a sensitive and emotional issue. Those who are critical of the Board's efforts in this area need to consider whether their alternatives would add to the problem or enhance the solution. Too many fail to appreciate the benefits that will flow from having more complete and forthright data on health care obligations. Amidst all the carping and criticism, the FASB project on other postretirement benefits may contribute in some small way to a better understanding of the social issue of retiree health care burdens.

SOURCE: *Accounting Horizons*, March 1990. Reprinted by permission.

Required

a. Explain why Mr. Wyatt argues that "past misguided practices that improved the appearance—but not the reality—of balance sheets and income statements" should be changed. In your answer, consider whether accrual accounting is more useful to investors than cash basis accounting for postretirement benefits.

b. According to Mr. Wyatt, what social benefits will result if improved accounting for postretirement benefits is adopted?

c. Do you agree that "Accounting is not expected to change the economics, but to reveal data to enable an assessment of the economics." Explain.

13. Reproduced here is an excerpt from the MD&A of Gulf Canada Resources Limited, in its December 31, 1992 annual report. Of interest is the table of sensitivities, which shows the impact on earnings and cash flows of changes in certain production and price variables for the coming year.

RISKS AND UNCERTAINTIES

The results of operations are subject to uncontrollable elements such as changes in oil and gas prices and fluctuations in exchange and interest rates. Gulf utilizes a variety of risk management techniques to mitigate the effect of these elements.

1. Over 80 per cent of Gulf's gross revenues are attributable to liquids, and Gulf employs an active price management strategy to provide downside protection against a drop in the world oil price. For 1993, Gulf has established a minimum hedge price of US$20.39 per barrel for over half of its Western Canada conventional production. This was achieved through a combination of collars in the range of US$20.00 to US$23.00, forward sales and options.

2. Gulf's liquids sales revenues are sensitive to the U.S.-dollar expenditures relating to debt, capital spending and miscellaneous expenses. In order to reduce its exposure to exchange rate fluctuations in 1993, Gulf has entered into foreign exchange contracts fixing a total of approximately US$120 million receipts at an average exchange rate of approximately Cdn$1.25 to US$1.

3. Interest rate swaps and forward rate agreements effectively convert the rate on approximately 35 per cent of the variable-rate long-term debt obligations into an average fixed rate of 7.3 per cent. In addition, Gulf has entered into swap agreements to fix approximately 70 per cent of its dividend obligations on the series 1 senior preference shares at a rate of approximately 8.9 per cent.

OUTLOOK

Gulf's stategic direction, capital spending plans, and production volume and price expectations for 1993 are incorporated in the Outlook section on Page 5 and in the Outlook sections on Pages 10 and 15 of the Operating Review.

Sensitivities

Based on current estimates of production and prices, the estimated effect on the Company's financial results for 1993 of a change in the following factors is set out below (in millions of dollars):

	Earnings	Cash Generation
Prices:		
US$1.00/bbl change in WTI oil	17	30
Western Canada production:		
1 mbbl/d change in conventional crude	3	5
10 mmcf/d change in natural gas	2	3
Interest rate:		
One per cent change in interest rates	4	7
Exchange rate:		
One per cent U.S. change in the value of the Canadian dollar	—	5

SOURCE: December 31, 1992 annual report of Gulf Canada Resources Limited. Reprinted by permission of Gulf Canada Resources Limited.

Required

Taking into account the fact that Gulf uses a variety of risk-management techniques, evaluate the relevance and reliability of this "sensitivities" method of disclosing the impact of risk on the firm's operations.

The Positive Theory of Accounting

8.1 Outline of Positive Accounting Theory

Given that economic consequences exist, we must ask *why*. To explain this phenomenon we now introduce a theory that is consistent with the existence of economic consequences—**positive accounting theory (PAT)**. For our purposes, the term "positive" refers to a theory that attempts to make good predictions of real-world events. Thus:

> *Positive accounting theory (PAT) is concerned with predicting such actions as the choices of accounting policies by firms and how firms will respond to proposed new accounting standards.*

For example, can we predict which oil and gas firms will use successful-efforts accounting for their exploration costs and which will use full-cost? Can we predict which firms will react favourably to new mark-to-market accounting standards for financial instruments, and which will be opposed?

PAT takes the view that firms organize themselves in the most efficient manner, so as to maximize their prospects for survival[1]—some firms are more decentralized than others, some firms conduct activities inside while other firms contract out the same activities, some firms finance more with debt than others, etc. The most efficient form of organization for a particular firm depends on factors such as its legal and institutional environment, its technology, the degree of competition in its industry, etc. Taken together, these factors determine the set of investment opportunities available to the firm, and hence its prospects.

A firm[2] can be viewed as a nexus of **contracts**, that is, its organization can be largely described by the set of contracts it enters into. For example, contracts with employees (including managers), with suppliers, and with capital providers are central to the firm's operations. The firm will want to minimize the various **contracting costs** associated with these contracts, such as costs of negotiation, monitoring of contract performance, possible renegotiation, and expected costs of bankruptcy or other failures.

Many of these contracts involve accounting variables. Thus, employee promotion and remuneration may be based on accounting-based performance measures such as net income. Contracts with suppliers may depend on liquidity and financing variables. Lenders may demand protection in the form of maintenance of certain financial ratios such as debt-to-equity or times interest earned, or minimum levels of working capital or equity.

PAT argues that firms' accounting policies will be chosen as part of the broader problem of minimizing contracting costs, so as to attain efficient corporate governance. For example, Mian and Smith (1990) study the accounting policy choice of whether to consolidate a subsidiary company. They argue that the greater the interdependence between parent and subsidiary the more efficient it is (that is, the lower the contracting costs) to prepare consolidated financial statements. The reason is that the greater the interdependence the more desirable it is to evaluate the *joint* results of parent and subsidiary operations. Consolidated financial statements provide a basis for joint evaluation. It is more efficient to monitor manager performance by use of consolidated financial-statement-based performance measures than by performance measures based on separate parent and subsidiary financial statements when interdependence is high. Thus Mian and Smith predict that the greater the integration between parent and subsidiary the more likely the parent will prepare consolidated statements. This argument can be extended to predict that if consolidated financial statements are prepared for internal monitoring of manager performance it is less costly to also prepare consolidated statements for external reporting. Mian and Smith present empirical evidence consistent with these predictions.

It should be noted that PAT does not go so far as to suggest that firms (and standard setters) should completely specify the accounting policies they will use. This would be too costly. It is desirable to give managers some flexibility to choose accounting policies so that they can adapt to new or unforseen circumstances. For example, a new accounting standard may reduce firms' debt-to-equity ratios (SFAS 106 dealing with postretirement benefits is such a standard—see Section 6.4.1) to the point where violation of debt covenants is of concern. It would probably be costly for management to, say, switch from the LIFO to the FIFO inventory method as a way to increase equity even after allowing for income tax effects, rather than to renegotiate the debt contract or suffer the expected costs of technical violation.

Though usually the set of available accounting policies can be taken as those allowed under GAAP, there is no reason, other than cost, why the set cannot be further restricted by contract. However, giving management flexibility to choose from a set of accounting policies opens up the possibility of **opportunistic behaviour**. That is, PAT assumes that managers are rational (like investors) and will choose accounting policies in their own best interests if able to do so. Thus, managers of actively exploring oil companies whose remuneration contracts are based on reported net income may choose full-cost accounting over successful-efforts so as to smooth out income and increase the present value of their bonus streams, even though higher reported income under successful-efforts may increase probabilities of higher taxes and entry of additional firms into the industry. Of course, such opportunistic behaviour will be anticipated when the manager's remuneration contract is being negotiated and the firm will price-protect itself by lowering the manager's formal remuneration by the expected amount of opportunism. That is, given competition in the labour market for managers, managers will be willing to work for a lower compensation from the company if they can augment their utility by means of opportunistic behaviour. As a result, given the remuneration contract, managers have an incentive to behave opportunistically to the extent they have the ability to choose from a set of accounting policies.

The optimal set of accounting policies for the firm then represents the best tradeoff between tightly prescribing accounting policies so as to minimize contracting costs under current circumstances, and giving managers flexibility to change accounting policies in the face of changing circumstances, including resulting costs of opportunistic behaviour. PAT emphasizes the need for empirical investigation to determine just what these accounting policies are and how they vary from firm to firm depending on its organizational structure. Ultimately the objective of the theory is to understand and predict accounting policy choice across different firms.

Thus, PAT does not attempt to tell individuals or constituencies what they *should* do. Theories that do this are called **normative**. This book draws on both positive and normative theories. The single-person decision theory and the theory of investment described in Chapters 3 and 4 are examples of normative theories—if individuals wish to make a decision in the face of uncertainty so as to maximize expected utility, they should proceed as the theories recommend.

Whether normative theories have good predictive abilities depends on the extent to which individuals actually make decisions as those theories prescribe. Certainly, some normative theories have predictive ability—we do observe individuals diversifying their portfolio investments, for example. However, we can still have a good normative theory even though it may not make good predictions. One reason is that it may take time for people to figure out the theory. Individuals may not follow a normative theory because they do not understand it, because they prefer some other theory, or simply because of inertia. For example, investors may not follow a diversified investment strategy because they believe in technical analysis,[3] and may concentrate their investments in firms that technical analysts recommend. But, if a normative theory is a good one, we should see it being increasingly adopted over time as people learn about it. However, unlike a positive theory, predictive ability is not the main criterion by which a normative theory should be judged. Rather, it is judged by its logical consistency with underlying assumptions of how rational individuals should behave.

Some people become engaged in the question of which theoretical approach is the correct one. See, for example, Boland and Gordon (1992) and Demski (1988). For our purposes, however, it is sufficient to recognize that both normative and positive approaches to theory development and testing are valuable. To the extent that decision-makers proceed normatively, positive and normative theories will make similar predictions. By insisting on empirical testing of these predictions, positive theory helps to keep the normative predictions on track. In effect, the two approaches complement each other.

8.2   *The Three Hypotheses of Positive Accounting Theory*

The predictions made by PAT are largely organized around three hypotheses, formulated by Watts and Zimmerman (1986). We will give these hypotheses in their "opportunistic" form, since according to Watts and Zimmerman (1990), this is how they have most frequently been interpreted.

1.   **The bonus plan hypothesis**   All other things being equal, managers of firms with bonus plans are more likely to choose accounting procedures that shift reported earnings from future periods to the current period.

     This hypothesis seems reasonable. Firm managers, like everyone else, would like high remuneration. If their remuneration depends, at least in part, on a bonus related to reported net income, then they may be able to increase their current bonus by reporting as high a net income as possible. One way to do this is to choose accounting policies that increase current reported earnings. Of course, because of the nature of the accrual process, this will tend to lower future reported earnings and bonuses, other things equal. However, the present value of the manager's utility from his or her future bonus stream will be increased by shifting it towards the present.

2.   **The debt covenant hypothesis**   All other things being equal, the closer a firm is to violation of accounting-based debt covenants, the more likely the firm manager is to select accounting procedures that shift reported earnings from future periods to the current period.

     The reasoning is that increasing reported net income will reduce the probability of technical default. Most debt agreements contain covenants that the borrower must meet during the term of the agreement. For example, a borrowing firm may covenant to maintain specified levels of debt-to-equity, interest coverage, working capital, and/or shareholders' equity. If such covenants are violated, the debt agreement may impose penalties, such as constraints on dividends or additional borrowing.

Clearly, the prospect of covenant violation constrains management's actions in running the firm. To prevent, or at least postpone, such violation, management may adopt accounting policies to raise current earnings. According to the debt covenant hypothesis, as the firm approaches default, or if it actually is in default, it is more likely to do this.

3. **The political cost hypothesis**   All other things being equal, the greater the political costs faced by a firm, the more likely the manager is to choose accounting procedures that defer reported earnings from current to future periods.

    The political cost hypothesis introduces a political dimension into accounting policy choice. For example, political costs can be imposed by high profitability, which may attract media and consumer attention. Such attention can quickly translate into political "heat" on the firm and politicians may respond with new taxes or other regulations. This has happened to oil companies, for example, during periods of restricted crude oil supply and rising gasoline prices. Resulting public anger has led, in the United States, to special taxes on oil companies to take back the excess profits. As a result, oil company managers may feel that, for example, switching to LIFO would reduce the likelihood of this happening again.

    Often, sheer size can lead to political costs. Very large firms may be held to higher performance standards, for example with respect to environmental responsibility, simply because they are felt to be large and powerful. If the large firms are also highly profitable, such political costs will be magnified.

    Also, firms may face political costs at particular points in time. Foreign competition may lead to reduced profitability unless affected firms can influence the political process to grant import protection. One way to do this would be to adopt income-decreasing accounting policies in an attempt to convince the government that profits are suffering.

These three hypotheses form an important component of PAT. Note that they all lead to empirically testable predictions. For example, managers of firms with bonus plans are predicted to choose less conservative accounting policies than managers of firms without such plans. Also, we would expect that managers of firms with bonus plans would oppose proposed accounting standards that may lower reported net income and/or increase its volatility, since such standards would make it more difficult to maximize current reported earnings by choice of accounting policy. Similarly, the debt covenant hypothesis predicts that managers of firms with high debt-to-equity ratios will choose less conservative accounting policies than managers of firms with low ratios, and will be more likely to oppose new standards that limit their ability to do this. Also, the political cost hypothesis predicts that managers of very large firms will choose more conservative accounting policies than managers of smaller firms, and will be less likely to oppose new standards that may lower reported net income.

8.3   Empirical PAT Research

Positive accounting theory has generated a large amount of empirical research. For example, the Lev (1979) paper discussed in Section 7.6 is a PAT study. Lev makes no recommendations on how firms and investors *should* react to the SFAS 19 exposure draft. Rather, the emphasis is on how investors *did* react to the prospect of full-cost oil and gas firms being required to switch to successful efforts. Thus Lev's study helps us to understand *why* different firms may choose different accounting policies, why some managers may object to changes in these policies, and why investors may react to the potential impact of an accounting policy change on net income. Indeed, Lev includes both the bonus plan and debt covenant hypotheses as possible reasons for the market's unfavourable reaction to the prospect of full-cost firms being forced to switch to successful-efforts. To the extent that managers would behave opportunistically to preserve their bonuses and avoid debt covenant violation, the efficient market would be expected to react negatively.

Much PAT research has been devoted to testing the implications of the three hypotheses described above. For example, the bonus plan hypothesis was investigated by Healy (1985), who found evidence that managers of firms with bonus plans based on reported net income systematically adopted accrual policies so as to maximize their expected bonuses. Healy's paper and some of the research that followed from it are discussed in Section 11.2.

Sweeney (1994) reports on tests of the debt covenant hypothesis. She studied a sample of 130 U.S. manufacturing firms that were first-time debt covenant violators during the period 1980–89, plus a control sample of 130 firms of similar size and industry that did not violate debt covenants.

Sweeney obtained information about the existence and nature of debt covenant violations from firms' annual reports, including MD&A. She found that the most frequently violated covenants were with respect to maintenance of working capital and shareholders' equity. Debt-to-equity and interest coverage ratios were violated relatively infrequently. Many of the sample firms disclosed the nature of the costs they incurred because of covenant violation. These included increased security, restrictions on further borrowing, and higher interest rates.

Sweeney found that in an eight-year period beginning five years prior to the year of default, the defaulting firms made, on average, significantly more voluntary income-increasing accounting policy changes than the control sample firms, and that the average cumulative impact on reported net income of these changes was significantly greater for the defaulting firms. Examples of income-increasing accounting changes include changes in pension plan assumptions, pension terminations, adoption of FIFO inventory, and liquidation of LIFO inventory layers.

In addition to voluntary changes in accounting policies such as those just mentioned, firms may be able to manipulate reported net income by the timing of adoption of new accounting standards. For example, SFAS 52 relating to foreign currency translation was issued in December, 1981. However, its effective date was for fiscal years beginning on or after December 15, 1982, with early adoption encouraged. This meant that a firm with a December 31 year-end could wait until its December 31, 1983 annual report before adopting SFAS 52, or could adopt as early as its December 31, 1981 annual report. A firm whose reported net income would increase under SFAS 52 relative to its income under SFAS 8 would adopt early if it was close to or in violation of debt covenants, according to the debt covenant hypothesis. Sweeney found that her sample of defaulting firms did tend to adopt mandatory income-increasing standards early, and to delay adoption of income-decreasing standards. The control sample firms did not exhibit this behaviour. Sweeney's voluntary and mandatory accounting policy results are consistent with opportunistic accounting policy choice by managers, at the expense of creditors, as predicted by the debt covenant hypothesis.

Sweeney also reports that of her 130 sample defaulting firms, only 53 firms actually made accounting policy changes during the eight-year period surrounding violation. That is, the results given above are despite the fact that 77 firms made no income-increasing changes at all. This raises a question as to the generality of the opportunistic form of the debt covenant hypothesis.

To investigate why some defaulting firms adopted accounting policies to increase reported net income and why some did not, Sweeney identified those defaulting firms that had both "accounting flexibility" and low default costs. If firms had little flexibility to make income-increasing accounting changes (for example, they may already be using FIFO inventory accounting and straight-line depreciation) and if they bore no costs of covenant violation (firms that did not report costs of violation in their annual reports were taken as not bearing such costs), they would hardly be expected to make income-increasing accounting changes. She found that firms in her defaulting sample that had both little flexibility and low default costs made significantly fewer income-increasing changes than firms that did not have these characteristics, suggesting that managers are quite rational in their responses to covenant violation. They appear to trade off the costs of accounting policy change against the benefits.

This result is of interest, because it implies that the opportunistic version of the debt covenant hypothesis does not tell the whole story, and that the efficient contracting version of PAT is also operative. We will return to efficient contracting below.

With respect to the political cost hypothesis, much empirical investigation has been based on firm size. However, this measure of political cost is complicated by the correlation of size with other firm characteristics, such as profitability and risk. Also, the bonus plan and debt covenant hypotheses work in the opposite direction to size in their accounting policy predictions, so that it is necessary to control for their effects.

These considerations suggest that empirical investigation of the political cost hypothesis should look at situations where political costs are particularly salient. One such situation occurs when firms are under pressure from foreign imports.

Jones (1991) studied the actions of firms to lower reported net income during import relief investigations. The granting of relief to firms that are unfairly affected by foreign competition is, in part, a political decision. Trade legislation allows for the granting of assistance such as tariff protection to firms in industries that are unfairly affected by foreign competition. In the United States, the International Trade Commission (ITC) is responsible for investigating whether there is injury. This investigation will consider economic factors such as sales and profits of affected firms. However, there is also a considerable political dimension to the granting of relief, since consumers will end up paying higher prices, and there may be retaliation by foreign countries. A determination of injury by the ITC goes initially to the president, who has 60 days to decide whether to grant relief. If relief is not granted, Congress may step in and override the president.

Thus, it is by no means clear that a deterioration of profitability is sufficient for relief to be granted. As a result, affected firms have an incentive to choose accounting policies to lower their reported net income even more, so as to bolster their case. Of course, this incentive will be known to the ITC, politicians, and the public. However, as Jones points out, these constituencies may not have the motivation to adjust for any opportunistic downward manipulation of earnings. For example, the effect of higher prices which would follow the granting of relief to an industry may not be sufficiently great for it to be cost-effective for consumers to lobby against it. Even the ITC may not be fully motivated to adjust for manipulation of earnings if it was a priori sympathetic to the petitioning firms. These disincentives to unwind any earnings manipulation are strengthened if it is difficult to detect.

An effective way to reduce reported earnings in a hard-to-detect manner is to manipulate accounting policies relating to accruals. For example, a firm may increase depreciation and amortization charges, it may record excessive liabilities for product guarantees, contingencies, and rebates, and it may record generous provisions for doubtful accounts and obsolescence of inventories. These are called **discretionary accruals**.

Jones examined whether firms used discretionary accruals to lower reported earnings. She collected a sample of 23 firms from five industries involved in six import relief investigations by the ITC over the period 1980–85 inclusive.

It is easy to determine a firm's **total accruals** for the year. One approach is to take the difference between operating cash flows and net income. Accruals are interpreted quite broadly here, being the net effect of all recorded operating events during the year other than cash flows. Thus changes in accounts receivable and payable are accruals, as are changes in inventories. Depreciation expense is a negative accrual, being that portion of the cost of property, plant, and equipment that is written off in the year. Jones used an equivalent approach, by taking the change in non-cash working capital for the year from the comparative balance sheets, plus depreciation expense, as her measure of total accruals.

However, separating total accruals into discretionary and non-discretionary components presents a major challenge. This is because non-discretionary accruals are correlated with the level of business activity. For example, if a firm is suffering from foreign competition it may have lower receivables, it may have to delay payment of current liabilities, and it may have to write off large amounts of slow-moving inventory. These are negative accruals, but they can hardly be regarded as discretionary. How can the researcher, who does not have access to the firm's records and so must work from the financial statements, separate them out of total accruals so as to get at the discretionary component?

Jones' approach to this problem was to estimate the following regression equation for each firm j in her sample, over a period prior to the year of the ITC investigation:[4]

$$TA_{jt} = \alpha_j + \beta_{1j}\Delta REV_{jt} + \beta_{2j}PPE_{jt} + \epsilon_{jt}$$

where:

TA_{jt} = total accruals for firm j in year t

ΔREV_{jt} = revenues for firm j in year t less revenues for year $t - 1$

PPE_{jt} = gross property, plant, and equipment in year t for firm j

ϵ_{jt} = a residual term that captures all impacts on TA_{jt} other than those from ΔREV_{jt} and PPE_{jt}

The purpose of ΔREV_{jt} is to control for non-discretionary accruals of current assets and liabilities, on the grounds that these depend on changes in business activity as measured by revenues. Also, PPE_{jt} controls for the non-discretionary component of depreciation expense, on the grounds that this depends on the firm's investment in capital assets.

With this regression model estimated for each sample firm, Jones used it to predict non-discretionary accruals during the ITC investigation years. That is:

$$U_{jp} = TA_{jp} - (\alpha_j + \beta_{1j}\Delta REV_{jp} + \beta_{2j}PPE_{jp})$$

where p is the year of investigation, TA_{jp} is firm j's total accruals for this year, and the quantity in brackets is the predicted non-discretionary accruals for the year, from the regression model. The term U_{jp} is thus an estimate of discretionary accruals for year p for firm j. The political cost hypothesis predicts that the U_{jp} will be negative, that is, that firms use discretionary accruals to force down reported net income.

Jones found evidence of the predicted behaviour. For almost all firms in the sample, discretionary accruals as measured above were significantly negative in the ITC investigation years. Significant negative accruals were not found in the years immediately preceding and following the investigations. These results, while perhaps not as strong as might be expected, suggest that affected firms were systematically choosing accrual policies so as to improve their case for import protection, consistent with the political cost hypothesis.

The above are just a few of numerous studies to test the predictions of PAT. More extensive discussions are contained in Watts and Zimmerman (1986, 1990). It does appear that these three hypotheses have empirical validity in explaining differential manager reaction to accounting policy choices. Estimation of discretionary accruals is an important component of much PAT research. We will return to it in our review of earnings management in Chapter 11.

While these hypotheses may explain manager reaction, the evidence is less strong that they can explain *investor* reaction to accounting policy change. In fact, the Lev study reviewed in Section 7.6 is one of the few to find a clear security market reaction to a paper policy change. However, even Lev does not clarify whether his results were due to positive theory variables or to security market inefficiency. More generally, Bernard (1989) states that evidence that the market responds to the economic consequences of other standards than oil and gas has been hard to come by. Whether market value effects are present, but existing empirical methodology cannot uncover them, or whether the three hypotheses are not good predictors of security market reaction to economic consequences appears to be an open question.

8.4 Distinguishing the Opportunistic and Efficient Contracting Versions of PAT

As mentioned, the three hypotheses of PAT have been stated above in opportunistic form, that is, they assume that managers choose accounting policies to maximize their own expected utility relative to their remuneration and debt contracts and political costs. These hypotheses can also be stated in "efficiency" form, on the assumption that internal control systems, including monitoring by the board of directors, limit opportunism, and motivate managers to choose accounting policies that minimize contracting costs.

Frequently, these two forms of PAT make similar predictions. For example, from the bonus plan hypothesis a manager may choose straight-line depreciation over, say, declining-balance so as to opportunistically increase remuneration.

However, this same policy could be chosen under the bonus hypothesis for efficiency reasons. Suppose that straight-line depreciation best measures the opportunity cost to the firm of using its fixed assets. Then, straight-line depreciation results in a reported income that better measures manager performance. As a result, this policy would more efficiently motivate the manager (which is the purpose of the bonus in the first place) relative to other possible depreciation policies. Also, as Sweeney (1994) points out, if a firm in danger of default on its debt covenants runs down its LIFO inventory, this could be regarded as an opportunistic increase in profits at the expense of creditors. Alternatively, if the threatened default arises from a fall in business activity, reducing inventories could be an efficient business strategy to increase cash flows, particularly if the firm is in a tax loss position.

Consequently, it can be difficult to tell whether firms' observed accounting policy choices are driven by opportunism or efficiency. Yet, without being able to distinguish these possibilities, it can hardly be said that we understand the process of accounting policy choice.

Current PAT research is addressing this problem. For example, Christie and Zimmerman (1994) investigated the extent of income-increasing accounting choices in a sample of firms that had become takeover targets. Their reasoning was that if opportunistic accounting policy choice was taking place, it would be most rampant in firms that subsequently were taken over, as existing management struggled to maintain their jobs and reputations by maximizing reported net income and financial position. Christie and Zimmerman found that, even in such a sample, the effects of income-increasing accounting choices were relatively small. From this, they reasoned that the extent of opportunism in the population of firms at large was even less.

Earlier, we mentioned that Sweeney (1994) found that managers were mindful of the costs versus benefits of accounting policy change, and appeared to change accounting policies in the face of debt covenant problems only when it was cost-effective to do so. If only the opportunistic version of the debt covenant hypothesis held, managers would be less concerned about costs in their attempts to manoeuvre out of their covenant problems.

Sweeney presents additional evidence in favour of the efficiency version of PAT, by identifying four firms in her sample that could have delayed default by switching from LIFO but chose not to do so. All of these firms would have incurred substantial tax costs if they had switched. She identified another three firms that apparently decided not to incur the costs of changing accounting policies because the income effects of doing so would not have been large enough to delay default.

Overall, Sweeney's results support both versions of PAT but suggest that a detailed, firm-specific analysis is needed to separate the two.

The research of Dechow (1994) also relates to the two versions of PAT. She argued that if accruals are largely the result of opportunistic manipulation of reported earnings, the efficient market will reject them in favour of cash flows, in which case cash flows should be more highly associated with share returns than net income. Alternatively, if accruals reflect efficient contracting, net income should be more highly associated with share returns than cash flows. Her empirical tests found net income to be more highly associated with returns than cash flows.

Dechow also argued that when accruals are relatively large (as, for example, in rapidly growing firms), net income should be even more highly associated with share returns, relative to cash flows, than when the firm is in steady state (in which case cash flows and net income will be equal). Her empirical tests found this to be the case, adding further support to efficient contracting.

8.5   Conclusions

PAT attempts to understand and predict firms' accounting policy choices. At its most general level it asserts that accounting policy choice is part of the firm's overall need to minimize its contracting costs. The accounting policies that do this are largely determined by the firm's organizational structure, which in turn is determined by its environment. Thus, accounting policy choice is part of the overall process of corporate governance.

PAT has led to a rich empirical literature. Three aspects of the firm's organizational structure and environment have been particularly singled out for study— its management compensation contracts, its capital structure, and its exposure to political costs.

PAT does not imply that a firm's accounting policy choice should be uniquely specified. Rather, it is usually more efficient to have a set of accounting policies, from which management may choose. This set can be taken as the set of policies allowed by GAAP or it can be further restricted by contract. Allowing management some flexibility in accounting policy choice enables a flexible response to changes in the firm's environment and to unforeseen contract outcomes. However, it also opens the door to opportunistic management behaviour in accounting policy choice.

From the perspective of PAT, it is not hard to see why accounting policies can have economic consequences. From an efficiency perspective, the set of available policies affects the firm's flexibility. From an opportunistic perspective, the ability of management to select accounting policies for its own advantage is affected. Either way, changes in the set of available policies will matter to management. New accounting standards may restrict the allowable accounting policies, as in SFAS 19 for oil and gas. Other standards may lower reported net income, as in SFAS 106, or increase its volatility, as in SFAS 8. Thus, we would expect management to react, and the more a new policy interferes with existing contracts and/or reduces accounting policy choice, the stronger this reaction should be. Note that nothing in this argument necessarily conflicts with security market efficiency.

However, the foregoing arguments are incomplete and raise additional questions. In particular, *why* do firms and managers enter into bonus agreements and *why* do firms accept covenants in lending agreements? Before we have a complete resolution of the efficient markets/economic consequences anomaly, these questions must be answered. As we shall see in Chapter 9, the answer lies in the concept of information asymmetry.

Notes

1. This is the "economic Darwinism" argument of Alchian (1950).

2. In the following discussion it will be helpful to distinguish between the firm and its manager. We can think of the firm as represented by the board of directors.

3. Technical analysis is an approach to investing which studies past market performance for systematic patterns and attempts to predict future market performance by projecting these patterns. It is inconsistent with security market efficiency, which predicts that share price fluctuations will be random.

4. To standardize for firm size, Jones divides both sides of this equation by total assets.

Questions and Problems

1. Explain the difference between a normative and a positive theory. Give an example of each.

2. Can a positive theory make good predictions even though it may not capture exactly the underlying decision processes by which individuals make decisions? Explain.

3. How is a firm's susceptibility to political costs often measured in positive accounting theory? Do you think this is a good measure? Explain.

4. Use the "efficiency" form of positive accounting theory to explain why managers would prefer a *set* of generally accepted accounting policies from which to choose, rather than have GAAP completely prescribe accounting policy choice.

Use the "opportunistic" form of positive accounting theory to explain the same thing.

5. A new accounting standard requires a firm to accrue major new liabilities for employee pensions and benefits. As a result, its debt-to-equity ratio rises to the point where technical violation of covenants in its borrowing agreements is threatened. Management knows that renegotiation of these covenants would be difficult and costly.

   Suggest some accounting policy choices which could reduce the likelihood of technical violation. Ideally, any changes in policies should not violate GAAP, not affect the firm's real operations, and not reduce cash flows. Justify your suggestions.

6. An article entitled "FASB Approves Plan Requiring Banks to Value Most Debt at Market Prices" appeared in the *Wall Street Journal* on February 4, 1993. The article describes "strong opposition" from the banking industry for the FASB's proposal to require mark-to-market accounting for debt securities, leading up to SFAS 115. "The new rule essentially would force banks to value their investment portfolios closer to their actual market value, rather than the initial cost." According to the article, the opposition stems from banks' concerns that such valuation "would cause sharp fluctuations in the value of their capital." Therefore, banks would be forced to carry less volatile, shorter-maturing bonds that have a smaller return.

   Also, the FASB has proposed a revision to allow at least some debt securities to continue to be valued at initial cost, but only if the banks are willing to retain the securities to maturity. According to the American Bankers Association, this "will help ease the volatility problem." However, it appears that the revision will not completely satisfy the banking industry, because "the FASB proposal's criteria are so strict that few debt securities would qualify for this treatment since the banks must guarantee that the debt will be held to maturity."

   Required
   Positive accounting theory predicts that managers will be concerned about new accounting standards that increase the volatility of reported earnings.

   a. Use the "opportunistic" form of the bonus plan and the debt covenant hypotheses to explain managements' concerns.

   b. Use the "efficiency" form of the same hypotheses to explain managements' concerns.

7. An article entitled "Big Advertisers Could Face Reduced Profits If Proposed Accounting Rule Wins Approval" appeared in the *Wall Street Journal* on January 8, 1992. It describes pressures for greater uniformity in accounting for costs of advertising. It seems that accounting policies differ across firms with respect to deferring versus expensing such costs. Both the AICPA and the SEC are advocating a tightening of the rules.

As of early 1992, accounting standards allowed companies to deduct the cost of advertising as it was incurred. "Or, if the company ... show[ed] a long-term benefit from advertising, it ... [could] defer such costs, 'capitalizing' them as an asset on the balance sheet, and delaying the impact on earnings."

According to the article, "the new rule would force companies to deduct ad costs ... [right away], or when the first in a series of ads is run."

The article states that those companies that capitalize their advertising costs will see lower profits if they are forced to expense them right away. For example, L.A. Gear in 1991 decided on their own to stop deferring more than $8.3 million in advertising and promotional costs. L.A. Gear resorted to expensing these costs right away. "A sharp sales drop, combined with the change in accounting policy, caused L.A. Gear to report a loss of almost $28 million for the nine months ended Aug. 31, 1991, compared with year-earlier profit of $38.4 million, or $1.91 a share." Other companies that would be affected by the proposal include Procter & Gamble, with 1990 advertising outlays of $2.3 billion, Sears Roebuck ($1.5 billion), and McDonald's ($760 million).

Required

a. Use efficient security market theory to explain why it may not matter how advertising costs are accounted for.

b. Use positive accounting theory to explain why it may be desirable to allow differences in accounting policies for advertising costs.

c. If theories predict that imposed uniformity of accounting policies may not be necessary, or even desirable, why would the AICPA and the SEC be pushing for greater uniformity?

d. The article describes different practices across firms with respect to accounting for advertising. For example, Procter & Gamble, Sears, and McDonald's capitalize at least some costs, while L.A. Gear does not. Use the bonus plan hypothesis of positive accounting theory to predict which firms would be most likely to defer all or part of their advertising costs. Do the same for the debt covenant hypothesis and the political cost hypothesis.

8. The article reproduced here from the *New York Times* (September 16, 1990), "Fearing Backlash, Big Oil Companies Will Trim Profits," describes strategies of oil industry executives to hold down their reported profits in the wake of increasing crude oil prices following the Iraqi invasion of Kuwait.

While the impact on profits of holding down the selling price of gasoline is obvious, the article describes another strategy, namely "to increase the amount of money they set aside, or hold in reserve, for future environmental expenses, for ... maintenance programs and for potential legal claims."

FEARING BACKLASH, BIG OIL COMPANIES WILL TRIM PROFITS

Fearful of public and Congressional outcry over the large profits that many oil companies are likely to report for the fiscal quarter that ends in two weeks, industry executives are trying to find ways to hold down those profits.

Their strategy takes two tacks. One is to hold down the increases in the retail price of gasoline. That may be news to motorists who have seen gas prices rise an average of 23 cents a gallon since the Iraqi invasion of Kuwait last month, but oil industry executives say a 36-cent-a-gallon increase would have been needed to offset the sharp increase in crude oil prices, which have nearly doubled this summer.

The oil companies' second strategy for reducing profits is to increase the amount of money they set aside, or hold in reserve, for future environmental expenses, for refinery and chemical-plant maintenance programs and for potential legal claims. Such a step is commonplace in the industry and conforms with accounting standards.

In trying to hold down profits, the oil industry is heeding the advice of the White House and senior Republicans in Congress.

Calls for Restraint

In a speech on Aug. 8, President Bush urged the oil companies to show restraint in raising gasoline prices. The next day, Senator Bob Dole of Kansas, the minority leader, sent a telegram to the chief executives of 11 major oil companies, warning that if gasoline price increases were not checked, the outcry would be overwhelming.

"I can assure you that it will be very difficult to stop legislation controlling the prices of petroleum products or taxing profits resulting from these increases should not action be taken by the oil industry," he said in the telegram.

The industry is anxious to avoid a replay of the 1970s, when angry consumers and legislators pilloried Big Oil as oil prices and company profits soared. A windfall profit tax took several billion dollars away from oil companies before crude oil prices plunged below $10 after 1985. Bryan Jacoboski, an analyst at Paine Webber, said oil executives suppose now that "the best way to avoid any windfall profit tax is not to report any windfall profits."

One warning of potential backlash came Thursday, when Senator Kent Conrad, a North Dakota Democrat, told Energy Secretary James D. Watkins, "There will be universal outrage" if reports of soaring oil profits appear.

Mr. Watkins replied that antitrust officials in the Justice Department were the Administration's first line of defense against profiteering. He also said oil companies that engaged in the practice would be "hammered" by the Administration.

Senator Conrad said in an interview Friday: "If there is a significant surge in profits, we all know there will be a public reaction. I'm not engaged in oil-industry bashing. I am trying to understand what the President means when he says we will not allow profiteering. Where is the plan?"

Nonetheless, profit increases of more than 40 percent from those reported in the comparable fiscal quarter last year seem certain for at least four major oil companies, and many others are expected to show profits of close to 20 percent, Wall Street securities analysts say. In gen-eral, oil companies that will profit the most are those that produce a great deal of crude oil and thus will benefit from the near-doubling of crude oil prices.

"It's a great time to be a producer of oil, but it's a bad time to be a retail seller of gasoline," Mr. Jacoboski said.

Holding down prices at the gas pump could also help the larger oil companies in the future because smaller competitors might be squeezed out of gasoline retailing.

Required

a. What pricing and accounting policy behaviour is predicted by the bonus plan and debt covenant hypotheses of positive accounting theory, in response to increasing crude oil prices? Explain.

b. The article implies that "Big Oil" companies are the ones concerned about a possible backlash. Use the political cost hypothesis of positive accounting theory to explain why only "Big Oil" companies would be so concerned.

c. What inventory accounting policy would "Big Oil" companies find most effective in holding down profits? Explain.

d. In view of efficient security market theory, do you think the strategy of holding down reported profits by means of accounting policy choice will be effective in avoiding a backlash? Explain why or why not.

An Analysis of Conflict

9.1 Overview

In this chapter, we look at economic consequences in more detail. To properly understand economic consequences, it is necessary to consider some models from **game theory**. Game theory attempts to model and predict the outcome of conflict between rational individuals. Certainly, economic consequences are characterized by **conflict**. We will also consider **agency theory**. This is a version of game theory that models the process of **contracting** between two or more persons. Since each party to a contract attempts to get the best deal for him/herself, agency theory also involves conflict.

As pointed out in Chapter 8, business firms enter into many contracts. Two particularly important contracts are **employment contracts** between the firm and its managers and **lending contracts** between the firm and its lenders. Both of these types of contracts often depend on the firm's reported net income. Employment contracts frequently base managerial bonuses on net income, and lending contracts usually incorporate protection for the lenders in the form of covenants which, for example, bind the firm not to exceed a certain debt-to-equity ratio, or not to pay dividends if the interest coverage ratio falls below a certain level.

Game theory can help us understand how managers, investors, and other affected parties can rationally deal with the economic consequences of financial reporting. Consequently, game theory and agency theory are relevant to accounting. Small wonder that accounting policies have economic consequences when important contracts are affected by those policies. Game theory helps us to see why contracts frequently depend on financial statements.

It can be argued that the historical cost basis of accounting has desirable properties which make it useful for contracting purposes. These properties are not necessarily the same as those which provide the most useful information to investors, leading to the fundamental problem of financial accounting theory outlined in Section 1.5.

Finally, the contract-based role for financial statements that emerges from game theory enables us to complete our reconciliation of the theory of efficient securities markets and economic consequences. We shall see that it is possible for securities markets to be efficient and for accounting policies to have economic consequences once the conflict implications for financial reporting are understood.

9.2   *Understanding Game Theory*

In this chapter, we will study the **economic theory of games**, or **game theory** for short. This is a large topic—we can only scratch the surface here. Nevertheless, we shall see that game theory underlies many of the current issues in financial accounting theory.

Essentially, game theory models the interaction of two or more *players*. Frequently, this interaction occurs in the presence of uncertainty and information asymmetry. Each player is assumed to maximize his or her expected utility, just as the investors did in our decision theory and investment decision examples in Chapter 3. The difference is that game theory, in addition to taking into account any uncertainty arising from random realization of states of nature, requires that the players formally take the actions of the other players into account. Actions of other players can be extremely difficult to predict, because the action chosen by one player will depend on what action that player thinks the other players will take, and vice versa. Consequently, game theory tends to be more complex than decision theory and the theory of investment. However, the formal recognition of conflict between rational parties greatly expands the range of situations addressed by the theory.

Another way to view game theory is that the actual number of players lies "in between" the number in single-person decision theory and in markets. On the one hand, in decision theory, there is a *single* player, playing a game against nature—nature's play may be thought of as the realization of one of the states of nature. At the other extreme, we can think of a market as a game with a *large* number of players. If the market is perfect in the economic sense, the number of players is so large that the actions of any one player cannot influence what happens on the market—this is the notion of a *price-taker* in economics, as in our investment decision Example 3.2, where Toni Difelice took the market prices of securities as given.

However, in game theory the number of players, while greater than one, is sufficiently small that the actions of one player *do* influence the other players—hence the conflict aspect of a game where the players take the actions of the other players into account. The decision problems facing firms in cartels or in oligopolistic industries (where each of a few producers affect, but do not control, the market) can be modelled as games, for example.

There are many different types of games. One basis for classifying games is as **cooperative** or **non-cooperative**. In a cooperative game, the parties can enter into a **binding agreement**. A cartel is an example of a cooperative game. Cartels work best where it is possible to enforce binding agreements on members not to bolt the cartel in favour of high short-term profits. If such agreements are not possible, the cartel would be more like a non-cooperative game. An oligopolistic industry is an example of a non-cooperative game, at least in jurisdictions where agreements in restraint of trade are illegal. We will illustrate both types of games in our development.

9.3 A Non-cooperative Game Model of Manager-Investor Conflict

In Section 3.2, we introduced the concept of **constituencies** of financial statement users. Conflict between constituencies can be modelled as a game, since the decision needs of different constituencies may not coincide. As we explored in Chapter 3, investors will desire relevant and reliable financial statement information to assist in assessing the expected values and risks of their investments. Managers, however, may not wish to reveal all the information that investors desire. They may prefer to omit certain liabilities from the balance sheet, on the grounds that this will make it easier to raise capital by facilitating contracts with lenders. Also, they may prefer not to reveal which accounting policies are being used so as to have room to "manage" reported profits by change of accounting policy if necessary. In addition, management may fear that releasing too much information will benefit their competition. These are just some of the actions that managers may take to present the firm in the best light by biasing, or otherwise manipulating, the financial statements for either efficient contracting or opportunistic purposes. The investor, of course, will be aware of this possibility and will take it into account in making an investment decision. Firm management, in turn, will be aware of possible investor reaction when preparing the financial statements. Game theory provides a formal framework for studying this conflict situation and for predicting the decisions the parties will make.

We will model this situation as a **non-cooperative game**, since it is difficult to envisage a binding agreement between manager and investor about what specific information is to be supplied. For one thing, such an agreement could be very costly, since similar agreements would have to be negotiated with all users. But different users may have varied decision problems and hence different information needs, so that many different sets of financial statements would be needed. Even if such binding agreements were made, they would be difficult and costly to enforce, because each user would need to conduct, or hire, an audit investigation of the firm to monitor management compliance with the agreement. In other contexts, binding agreements may be illegal, as when an oligopolistic industry enters into an agreement in restraint of trade.

To illustrate this game between the manager and the investor, consider Example 9.1.

EXAMPLE 9.1 MANAGER-INVESTOR RELATIONS AS A NON-COOPERATIVE GAME

We assume the manager has two strategies, one of which must be chosen. (See Table 9.1.) We will call the first of these "distort" (D), which we can think of as underinvesting in the internal control system and choosing accounting policies to maximize or otherwise bias reported net income. The second strategy is to choose "honest" (H), which we can think of as maintaining a strong internal control system and preparing relevant and reliable financial statements. The investor also has two strategies—to buy shares in the manager's firm or to refuse to buy, denoted by B and R respectively.

TABLE 9.1 UTILITY PAYOFFS IN A NON-COOPERATIVE GAME

		Manager	
		HONEST (H)	**DISTORT (D)**
	BUY (B)	60, 40	20, 80
Investor			
	REFUSE TO BUY (R)	35, 20	35, 30

The numbers in Table 9.1 represent the utility payoffs to the investor and manager respectively for each possible strategy combination. Thus, if the manager chooses H and the investor B, the investor receives a utility of 60 and the manager receives 40, and so on for the other three pairs of numbers in the table. You should analyze the relationship between the payoffs to make sure they appear reasonable. For example, if the investor chooses B, a higher utility is attained by the investor when the manager is honest (60) than when the manager distorts the information (20). Similarly, if the investor refuses to buy, the manager would prefer to choose D (if the manager distorts the information, less money and effort is put into the internal control system and into relevant and reliable reporting).

It is important to emphasize the assumption that each party has *complete information* about the other. Thus, the investor knows the strategies available to the manager and the manager's payoffs and vice versa. Game theory can be extended to relax these assumptions, but this is beyond our scope. This completeness of information does not extend to choice of strategy, however. Each player chooses his or her strategy without knowing the strategy choice of the other in this game.

What **strategy pair** will be chosen? The term means simply a statement of the strategy chosen by each player. Thus, BH is a strategy pair whereby the investor buys (B) and the manager is honest (H). Review Table 9.1 and make your own prediction before reading on.

We can rule out the RH and BD strategy pairs easily. If the manager chooses H, the investor will reason that it would be better to choose B, because it yields a utility of 60 as opposed to one of 35 from R. Thus, RH would be unlikely to happen. Similarly, if the manager chooses D, the investor would reason that it would be better to choose R, so BD would be unlikely.

Now consider the BH pair. If the investor chooses B, the manager would then prefer D. Thus, it seems BH must be ruled out also. The only strategy pair not subject to this problem is RD. If the manager chooses D, the investor would prefer R. Similarly, if the investor chooses R, the manager would prefer D. RD is the only strategy pair such that *given* the strategy choice of the other player, each player is content with his or her strategy. Such a strategy pair is called a **Nash equilibrium**. Thus, RD is the predicted outcome of the game.

However, RD is not a completely satisfactory outcome of the game in Example 9.1. Notice that *both parties would be better off* if BH were chosen rather than RD. But, as we have argued, if the investor chooses B rather than R, he or she knows that the rational manager would then switch to D and the investor would end up with 20 rather than the 35 from choosing R. Consequently, the investor would not choose B. The Nash equilibrium outcome RD in this game is unfortunate, because it means, at least for payoff values assumed, that the market for the firms' shares would not work very well—no one would buy them.

It is interesting to speculate what might happen next. Perhaps the parties would get together and enter into a binding agreement to choose BH, after all. However, the investor would have to be convinced the agreement was in fact binding on the manager and could be enforced. Another possibility would be to change the payoffs of the game, by introducing severe penalties for distortion. This may lower the manager's payoffs for BD and RD to, say, zero. Then it can be verified that BH would be a Nash equilibrium. This would require the intervention of some central authority, however.

Yet another approach would be to think of the game in a *long-run* perspective. If this game were repeated many times, and the manager always chose H, a reputation for honesty would be established and investors would start choosing B. This would give the manager a long-run average of 40, rather than the 30 that would be obtained on a one-shot basis. Extensions of game theory to incorporate these possibilities are beyond the scope of this example. Nevertheless, game theory provides a powerful and flexible methodology for studying problems of conflict.

Note the essential difference between single-person decision theory and game theory approaches. In our earlier decision theory Example 3.1, Bill Cautious assessed *probabilities* of what would happen—he ended up with a 0.77 probability of the high payoff, and so on. The assumption in decision theory is that the high or low payoffs are generated by some random mechanism called **nature**. Thus, a decision theory problem is sometimes called a game against nature, because some impartial force (nature) is assumed to generate the high or low payoffs with the probabilities as given. While we gave considerable attention to how investors may assess these probabilities, and revise them as new information was obtained, we made an implicit assumption throughout Example 3.1 that the particular decision chosen by the investor would not affect what these probabilities were. That is, nature does not "think."

This assumption is fine for many decision problems. Indeed, as we outlined in Chapters 3 and 4, much progress has been made in understanding the decision needs of users through study of the decision theory approach. However, the approach breaks down when the payoffs are generated by a *thinking opponent* (the manager) rather than by nature. In Example 9.1, once the manager realizes the investor's decision is to buy shares, he or she would choose the distort strategy D. Thus, it is not correct for the investor to assign probabilities to the manager's action choice when the manager's action is not chosen probabilistically. Similarly, it would not be correct for the manager to assign probabilities to the investor's action.[1] Such behaviour, by either or both decision-makers, would be unlikely to lead to good decisions in the conflict situation.

How can we use a game such as the one modelled in Example 9.1 in financial accounting theory? The essential point to realize here is that such models enable us to *better understand the process of accounting policy choice*. Recall that in Chapter 3 we developed a considerable body of theory to enable us to understand the information needs of investors. In that chapter we showed that major professional accounting standard setting bodies appear to have adopted the decision usefulness approach that follows from the theory. What we did *not* consider in those chapters, however, was whether firm management would be *willing* to adopt the full disclosure policies that accounting standard setters have proposed. Indeed, the important message in Chapter 7 was that managers appear unwilling to sit idly by, and adopt whatever accounting policies are suggested by the standard setters (representing the interests of investors). It is certainly clear that management has *its own* interests at stake in accounting policy choice and cannot be assumed to necessarily adopt full-disclosure or other accounting policies solely on the grounds that they will be useful to investors. This is shown in our Example 9.1 by the utility of the manager being lower under H than under D. In essence, the interests of the investor and manager constituencies may *conflict*.

By modelling this conflict situation as a game, we can understand the problems surrounding policy choice more clearly. In particular, we see that, depending on the payoffs of the game, it may indeed be in a manager's interests to distort the financial statements, at least in the short run. Thus, any accounting body concerned about implementing a new pronouncement must be concerned with the resulting payoffs to *both* investors and management. Only by ensuring that the payoffs to management are such that management will accept the new policy can a smooth implementation be assured.

Of course, any accountant with practical experience in choosing a firm's accounting policies will know about management's interest in and concern about these policies, without having to be convinced by a game theory example. Our point is that such interest and concern is exactly what is predicted by the game theory. Better understanding of this conflict situation by accounting standard setters will result in more realistic accounting policy choices, which should avoid the economic consequences disputes that were documented in Chapter 7.

There are other conflict situations in financial accounting that can be studied in a game context. For example, Darrough and Stoughton (1990) (D&S) analyze a game between a monopolistic firm (the incumbent) and a potential entrant to the industry (the entrant). The incumbent needs to raise equity capital for a new project. It has inside information about itself that can be either favourable or unfavourable about its future prospects. If the information is favourable, its disclosure will lower the incumbent's cost of capital for its new equity issue. However, the favourable news will also encourage the entrant to enter the industry. If the information is unfavourable, its disclosure[2] will deter the entrant but raise cost of capital. What should the incumbent do?

The answer depends on how profitable the incumbent is. If existing monopoly profits are high and the need for equity capital is moderate, the dominant consideration for the incumbent is to deter entry. Then, D&S show that if the entrant has high prior probability that the incumbent's inside information is favourable and/or the costs of entry to the industry are low, the incumbent firm will fully disclose its inside information, good or bad. If its inside information is unfavourable, its loss of profits if the entrant enters outweighs the higher cost of capital, so the incumbent will disclose. If its inside information is favourable, the incumbent will disclose even if this attracts entry since profits will still be satisfactory, particularly in view of the lower cost of capital following the favourable disclosure.

Other outcomes are possible, however. D&S show that if the entrant has low prior probability that the incumbent's inside information is favourable, the incumbent will not disclose favourable or unfavourable information. Even the incumbent with favourable news will be better off not disclosing if the higher profits from discouraging entry outweigh the increased cost of capital that results.

These conclusions are of interest, because they suggest that the question of full disclosure extends into industry structure. In the D&S model, the greater the competition in an industry (measured by the threat of entry), the better the disclosure. This reinforces our conclusion from positive accounting theory that full disclosure to investors is not the only consideration affecting managers' accounting policy choices.

Yet the implications of the D&S analysis have a deeper significance. By delineating conditions under which firms may or may not disclose voluntarily, conditions under which standard setting may or may not be needed are identified.

Since D&S, other papers have refined and extended the above considerations. See, for example, Darrough (1993), Newman and Sansing (1993), and Feltham and Xie (1994).

9.3.1   SUMMARY

Non-cooperative game theory enables us to model the conflict situation that often exists between different constituencies of financial statement users. Even a very simple game-theoretic model shows that an accounting standard setting body that fails to consider the interests of all constituencies affected by accounting policy choice is in danger of making policy recommendations that are difficult to implement. Furthermore, conflict analysis can be used to examine conditions under which standards may or may not be needed, since under some conditions firms may be motivated to release even unfavourable information voluntarily.

9.4   Some Models of Cooperative Game Theory

9.4.1   INTRODUCTION

While the non-cooperative game in Example 9.1 illustrates some of the implications of conflict between user constituencies, many other areas of accounting exhibit **cooperative** behaviour. Recall that the essence of cooperation here is that the players in a game situation can enter into agreements which they perceive as binding. Such agreements are often called **contracts**. There are many such contractual agreements that have accounting implications.

In this section we will be concerned with two important types of contracts that have implications for financial accounting theory. These are **employment contracts** between the firm and its top manager and **lending contracts** between the firm manager and the bondholder. In these contracts, we can think of one of the parties as the principal, and the other the agent. For example, in an employment contract, the firm owner is the principal and the top manager is the agent hired to run the firm on the owner's behalf. This type of game theory is called **agency theory**.

Agency theory is a branch of game theory which studies the design of contracts to motivate a rational agent to act on behalf of a principal when the agent's interests would otherwise conflict with those of the principal.

Actually, agency theory contracts have characteristics of both cooperative and non-cooperative games. They are non-cooperative in that both parties choose their actions non-cooperatively. The two parties do not specifically agree to take certain actions—rather, the actions are motivated by the contract itself. Nevertheless, each party must be able to commit to the contract, that is, to bind him/herself to "play by the rules." For example, it is assumed that the manager in an employment contract will not grab the total firm profits and head for a foreign jurisdiction. Such commitment may be enforced by the legal system, by use of bonding or escrow arrangements or, perhaps, by the reputations of the contracting parties. Consequently, for our discussion, we shall include them under cooperative games.

9.4.2 AGENCY THEORY: AN EMPLOYMENT CONTRACT BETWEEN FIRM OWNER AND MANAGER

Much of agency theory can be introduced by means of a simple owner-manager contract illustration.

It should be noted in the following example that the use of two persons is a modelling device to keep the example as simple as possible. The owner and the manager are proxies for a large number of similar investors and managers with conflicting interests. In effect, the firm exhibits a separation of ownership and control, captured by modelling the firm as two rational individuals with conflicting interests.

EXAMPLE 9.2 A FIRM OWNER-MANAGER AGENCY PROBLEM

Consider a simple firm consisting of a single owner (the principal) and a single manager (the agent). The firm operates for one period. It faces uncertainty which, as usual, we express in the form of random states of nature. Assume that there are two such states, denoted by θ_1 and θ_2. State θ_1 represents "good times" and θ_2 "bad times." If good times occur, the firm's end-of-period payoff will be $x_1 = \$100$. Given bad times, the end-of-period payoff will be $x_2 = \$50$.

We will think of the payoff here as the firm's net income. (Note, however, that in a one-period model, net income, cash flows, and dividends are identical.)

Each state realization leads to a specific payoff. If θ_1 occurs, net income $= x_1 = \$100$, and if θ_2 occurs, $x_2 = \$50$. Thus, we can work just as well with the probabilities of the payoffs as with the probabilities of the states of nature themselves. That is, the probability that θ_1 happens is the same as the probability that the payoff is x_1, and so on. If the probability of θ_1 is 0.6, we can say that the probability of x_1 is 0.6, rather than the more awkward "The probability of θ_1 is 0.6 and, if θ_1 occurs, $x_1 = \$100$." Consequently, we will suppress direct reference to states of nature for the remainder of the example.

Now, assume that the owner does not operate the firm, that this is the responsibility of the manager. Assume that, after being hired, the manager has two action choices—**work hard**, denoted by a_1, or **shirk**, denoted by a_2. The action choice of the manager will affect the probability distribution of the payoffs. Let these probability distributions be as follows:

- If the manager works hard:

$$P(x_1/a_1) = 0.6$$
$$P(x_2/a_1) = \underline{0.4}$$
$$\underline{1.0}$$

- If the manager shirks:

$$P(x_1/a_2) = 0.3$$
$$P(x_2/a_2) = \underline{0.7}$$
$$\underline{1.0}$$

Recall that x_1 represents the high payoff. If the manager works hard the probability of x_1 is greater (0.6) than it would be under shirking (0.3). In statistical terms, the payoff distribution conditional on a_1 stochastically dominates (in the first degree) the distribution conditional on a_2. This is a critical point to realize—the action of the agent affects the distribution of the payoffs. In particular, the greater the effort put into the operation of the firm by the manager, the higher the probability of the high payoff and the lower the probability of the low payoff.

Of course, this is just what we would expect. Harder work by the manager increases the probability that the firm will do well. It is still possible for low payoff to occur—it is unlikely that the manager's efforts could completely ensure the high payoff, because of factors beyond his or her control—but the probability of the low payoff decreases as effort increases. In other words, at least some of the factors affecting the payoff are under managerial control.

It should also be pointed out that effort should be interpreted quite broadly. Effort goes beyond such a literal interpretation as the number of hours worked, and includes such factors as the care the manager takes in running the firm, the diligence with which subordinates are motivated and supervised, the absence of perquisite-taking, and so on. In effect, effort is a modelling device that encompasses the whole range of activities undertaken by a manager.

We summarize the example up to this point in Table 9.2. The dollar amounts in the table represent reported net incomes under each of the four payoff/act combinations. The probabilities are conditional on the chosen act, that is, if a_1 is chosen by the manager the probability of x_1 is 0.6, whereas it is 0.3 if a_2 is chosen, and so on.

We assume that the payoff is *observable* to both parties. Note that this puts the onus on the firm's accounting system and financial statements to report information fully and accurately, so that both players in the game are willing to accept reported net income as a measure of the payoff. We will return to this point in Section 9.5.1.

TABLE 9.2 PAYOFFS FOR AGENCY EXAMPLE

	Manager's Effort			
	a_1 (work hard)		a_2 (shirk)	
	Payoff	**Probability**	**Payoff**	**Probability**
x_1 (high payoff)	$100	0.6	$100	0.3
x_2 (low payoff)	50	0.4	50	0.7

Now, consider this problem from the standpoint of the owner of the firm. The owner wishes to hire the manager to operate the firm, that is, the owner will have no direct control over the act taken. Clearly, the owner would like the manager to work hard, that is, to choose a_1, because the probability of the high payoff is higher conditional on a_1 than on a_2.

To illustrate this more formally, assume that the owner is risk-neutral, and that the utility from a given payoff is equal to the dollar amount of that payoff. Assume also that the manager receives a fixed salary of $25. Then, the owner's expected utility conditional on each act is:

$$
\begin{aligned}
EU_O(a_1) &= 0.6(100 - 25) + 0.4(50 - 25) \\
&= 0.6 \times 75 + 0.4 \times 25 \\
&= 45 + 10 \\
&= 55
\end{aligned}
$$

$$
\begin{aligned}
EU_O(a_2) &= 0.3(100 - 25) + 0.7(50 - 25) \\
&= 0.3 \times 75 + 0.7 \times 25 \\
&= 22.50 + 17.50 \\
&= 40
\end{aligned}
$$

where $EU_O(a_1)$ denotes the owner's expected utility given that the manager chooses a_1, and similarly for a_2. Just as in decision theory, we assume the players' wish to maximize their expected utilities. Consequently, the owner wants the manager to choose a_1, because its expected utility to the owner is greater. It should be clear that this result will hold for any probabilities such that the probability of x_1 given a_1 is greater than it is given a_2. Also, our assumption that the owner is risk-neutral could be relaxed and replaced by an assumption of risk aversion.

Now consider matters from the manager's standpoint. Let the manager be risk-averse. Specifically, assume that his or her utility from remuneration equals the square root of the remuneration.

Will the manager *want* to work for the owner? Most managers have alternative opportunities for the use of their time. We will assume that the manager's **reservation utility** is 3 (that is, the manager's expected utility from operating the firm must be at least 3 units or he or she would go elsewhere). Of course, the manager would prefer to receive a utility greater than 3, if possible. However, other managers would also like to work for this firm. If the manager asks for more than 3, the owner may well hire someone else. Consequently, given reasonable competition in the labour market for managers, we expect the manager to be willing to work for a utility of 3.

Now, given that the manager is hired, will a_1 in fact be chosen, as desired by the owner? First, it is important to remind ourselves that in game theory, and in agency theory in particular, one player will not choose an act desired by another player just because that player says so. Rather, each player chooses that act that maximizes his or her own expected utility. This observation is implicit in the three hypotheses of positive accounting theory discussed in Chapter 8.

Consequently, if the manager chooses a_1, it must be because the manager's expected utility is greater for a_1 than for a_2. Note that this assumption differs from much economic analysis, where it is assumed that firms act in a manner to maximize their profits. This expected utility-maximizing behaviour by all parties is one of the important and distinguishing characteristics of positive accounting theory and the economic theory of games.

Next, assume that the manager is **effort-averse**. This means that the manager dislikes effort and that the greater the level of effort the greater the dislike. In effect, the disutility of effort is subtracted from the utility of remuneration.

Consequently, we will assume:

Disutility of effort level $a_1 = 2$

Disutility of effort level $a_2 = 1.7$

We can now calculate the manager's expected utility, net of the disutility of effort, for each act. Recall that the manager is assumed to receive a salary of $25.

$$EU_m(a_1) = \sqrt{25} - 2 \quad = 3$$

$$EU_m(a_2) = \sqrt{25} - 1.7 \quad = 3.3$$

where $EU_m(a_1)$ denotes the expected utility of the manager, given that the manager chooses a_1, and similarly for a_2.

We see, then, that the manager will prefer to choose a_2, contrary to the wishes of the owner. This result is not very surprising. Most people, even managers, would prefer to take it easy, all other things being equal. Here, other things *are* equal, because the manager receives a salary of $25 regardless. This tendency of an agent to shirk is an exemple of moral hazard.

Designing a Contract to Control Moral Hazard

The question now is, what should the owner do in a situation such as that described in Example 9.2? One possibility is for the owner to refuse to hire the manager. But any other salaried manager would also choose a_2. Consequently, the owner could either go out of business or run the firm him/herself. These latter two possibilities are unlikely, however. The running of an organization is a complex and specialized task for which the owner may not have the required skills and, after all, we do witness a separation of ownership and management in all but the smallest organizations. In fact, our owner has a number of other options, which we will now consider.

HIRE THE MANAGER AND PUT UP WITH a_2 The owner could proceed anyway, letting the manager get away with a_2 and putting up with a utility of 40 rather than 55. This also seems unlikely, however, since we shall see that the owner can do better than this.

DIRECT MONITORING   If the owner could costlessly observe the manager's chosen act, this would solve the problem. Then, the contract could be amended to pay the manager a salary of $25 if a_1 was taken and, say, $12 otherwise. It is easy to verify that the manager would then choose a_1, because choosing a_2 would result in only $12 remuneration.

This type of contract is called **first-best**. It gives the owner the maximum attainable utility (55) and gives the agent the reservation utility (3). Under the assumptions of Example 9.2, no other contract can improve on this.

The first-best contract also has desirable **risk-sharing** properties. Note that under this contract the manager bears no risk, because a fixed salary is received regardless of the payoff. Since the manager is risk-averse, this is desirable. The owner bears all the risk of the random payoff. Since the owner is risk-neutral, he or she does not mind bearing risk. Indeed, we could argue that a function of business ownership is to bear risk. If the owner was risk-averse, rather than risk-neutral, the first-best contract would involve the owner and manager sharing the risk. However, demonstration of this is beyond our scope.

Unfortunately, the first-best contract is frequently unattainable. This would seem to be the case in an owner-manager contract, because it is unlikely that the owner could monitor the agent's effort in a managerial setting. The nature of managerial effort is so complex that it would be effectively impossible for a remote owner to establish whether the manager was in fact "working hard." We thus have a case of **information asymmetry**—the manager knows the effort level, but the owner does not. As mentioned previously, this particular form of information asymmetry is called moral hazard.

INDIRECT MONITORING   Given that managerial effort is not directly observable, it may be possible under some conditions to impute the effort. To illustrate, let us change our example slightly. See Table 9.3. The only difference

TABLE 9.3 PAYOFFS FOR AGENCY EXAMPLE

	Manager's Effort			
	a_1 (work hard)		a_2 (shirk)	
	Payoff	Probability	Payoff	Probability
x_1 (high payoff)	$100	0.6	$100	0.3
x_2 (low payoff)	50	0.4	40	0.7

between this table and Table 9.2 is that the payoff for (x_2, a_2) is now $40 rather than $50. In agency theory terms, this is a case of **moving support**, that is, the set of possible payoffs is different (it moves) depending on which act is taken. Table 9.2 is a case of **fixed support**—the set of possible payoffs is fixed at (100, 50), regardless of the action choice.

It is apparent from Table 9.3 that if the owner observes a payoff of $40 it will be known that the manager chose a_2 even though effort is not directly observable. Then the owner could amend the contract to offer the manager a salary of $25 unless the payoff was $40, in which case the salary would be $12. It is easy to check that the manager would then choose a_1:

$$EU_m(a_1) = \sqrt{25} - 2 \qquad\qquad = 3$$
$$EU_m(a_2) = 0.3\sqrt{25} + 0.7\sqrt{12} - 1.7 = 2.22$$

The penalty of $13 if the $40 payoff happens is sufficient cause for the agent to choose a_1.

Indirect monitoring will *not* work for the fixed-support case of Table 9.2, however. The reason is that if a payoff of $50 is observed, this is consistent with either a_1 or a_2, and similarly for the $100 payoff. Thus, the owner cannot impute the act from payoff observability.

It seems, then, that we cannot rely on indirect monitoring to ensure that the first-best contract will be attained. First, many contracting situations may be characterized by fixed support. For example, reported net income can be any positive or negative number. If a firm reports, say, a loss of $1 million the owner cannot be certain whether this loss resulted from low manager effort or an unfortunate realization of the state of nature.

Second, even if moving support holds, legal and institutional factors may prevent the owner from penalizing the manager sufficiently to force a_1. For example, minimum wage laws may prevent the owner from being able to impose a remuneration of $12.

OWNER RENTS FIRM TO THE MANAGER   At this point, the owner may well be tempted to say to the manager, "O.K., I give up—*you* take the firm and run it and pay me a rental of $47.38." Then, the owner no longer cares what action the manager takes, since a rental of $47.38 is received regardless. This is referred to as **internalizing** the manager's decision problem.

Such arrangements do exist, or they have existed in the past, in the form of tenant farming. Tenant farming is usually regarded as inefficient, however, and it is easy to see why. The manager's expected utility would be:

$$
\begin{aligned}
EU_m(a_1) &= 0.6\sqrt{100 - 47.38} + 0.4\sqrt{50 - 47.38} - 2 \\
&= 0.6 \times 7.25 + 0.4 \times 1.62 - 2 \\
&= 4.35 + 0.65 - 2 \\
&= 3.00
\end{aligned}
$$

$$
\begin{aligned}
EU_m(a_2) &= 0.3\sqrt{100 - 47.38} + 0.7\sqrt{50 - 47.38} - 1.7 \\
&= 0.3 \times 7.25 + 0.7 \times 1.62 - 1.7 \\
&= 2.18 + 1.13 - 1.7 \\
&= 1.61
\end{aligned}
$$

Thus, the manager will choose a_1 and receive reservation utility of 3.

Note, however, that the owner receives a utility of 47.38 in this contract, compared to 55 in the first-best contract. Consequently, the owner is worse off. The reason is that this contracting arrangement has inefficient risk-sharing characteristics. The owner is risk-neutral, and hence is willing to bear risk, but there is no risk for the owner because a fixed rental is received. The risk-averse manager, who dislikes risk, is forced to bear it all. The owner must lower the rental from $55 to $47.38 to enable the manager to receive reservation utility of 3, costing the owner $7.62 in lost utility. This $7.62 is called an **agency cost** (Jensen and Meckling, 1976), and is another component of contracting costs, which the owner will want to minimize.

GIVE THE MANAGER A SHARE OF THE PAYOFF   Finally, we come to what is often the most efficient alternative if the first-best contract is not attainable. This is to give the manager a share of the payoff. Suppose that the owner offers the manager 32% of the payoff. Then, the manager's expected utility from each act is as follows:

$$
\begin{aligned}
EU_m(a_1) &= 0.6\sqrt{0.32 \times 100} + 0.4\sqrt{0.32 \times 50} - 2 \\
&= 0.6 \times 5.66 + 0.4 \times 4.00 - 2 \\
&= 3.40 + 1.60 - 2 \\
&= 3.00
\end{aligned}
$$

$$
\begin{aligned}
EU_m(a_2) &= 0.3\sqrt{0.32 \times 100} + 0.7\sqrt{0.32 \times 50} - 1.7 \\
&= 0.3 \times 5.66 + 0.7 \times 4.00 - 1.7 \\
&= 1.70 + 2.80 - 1.7 \\
&= 2.80
\end{aligned}
$$

Thus, the manager will choose a_1 instead of a_2, as desired by the principal.

Note that it is the *contract* that provides the motivation here, as we mentioned earlier.[3] Given the terms of the contract, the manager *wants* to take a_1. This aspect of the contract is called **incentive-compatibility**, since the agent's incentive to take a_1 is compatible with the owner's best interests. (The first-best contract, if it is attainable, is also incentive-compatible, because the prospect of low remuneration following a_2 motivates the manager to take a_1.) We then say that the owner's and manager's interests are **aligned**, since they both want the firm to do well.

It is instructive to look more closely at the owner's expected utility in this payoff-sharing contract:

$$
\begin{aligned}
EU_O(a_1) &= 0.6(100 - 32) + 0.4(50 - 16) \\
&= 0.6 \times 68 + 0.4 \times 34 \\
&= 40.8 + 13.6 \\
&= 54.4
\end{aligned}
$$

This is less than the owner's utility of 55 in the first-best contract. The agency cost of this contract is thus 0.6, less than the 7.62 agency cost of the rental contract. The profit sharing contract is more efficient than the rental contract. The reason is not difficult to see. In the rental contract the risk-averse manager bears all the risk. Here, manager and owner share the risk. While both contracts motivate a_1, a lower **risk premium** (0.6 compared to 7.62) is needed to enable the manager's reservation utility to be attained. This lower risk premium translates into increased expected utility for the owner (54.4 compared to 47.38).

However, while the profit sharing contract may be more efficient, it is not first-best. The most efficient contract short of first-best is called **second-best**. The agency cost of the second-best contract is the irreducible minimum resulting from the unobservability of the agent's effort and resulting moral hazard problem. It is the cost to the principal of motivating the agent's effort by means of a profit sharing contract. To put this another way, the manager needs to bear *some* risk to convince the owner that the work-hard effort alternative will be chosen.

Agency costs are one of the costs of contracting that are part of positive accounting theory. As discussed in Section 8.1, a firm will want to arrange its contracts as efficiently as possible, and we pointed out there that the efficient contracts will depend on the firm's form of organization and its environment. We can now see more clearly the nature of this dependence. For example, consider a firm in a high-tech industry. Survival in such an environment requires a great deal of research and development, much of which must be written off currently under Section 3450 of the *CICA Handbook*. Consequently, reported net income of such firms is not a good measure of manager effort, to the extent that current research costs have benefits for the future. Thus, positive accounting theory predicts that high-tech firms will tend to base manager remuneration on some other payoff measure than net income, such as share price,[4] and that the remuneration contract would include stock options which may reduce the risk to the manager of share price volatility. Such a contract would have a strong incentive effect while minimizing agency costs resulting from the risk imposed on the manager.

As another example, consider a closely held firm. The organization structure of such a firm would exhibit high manager share ownership and manager representation on the board of directors. Then, the manager's incentive to exert effort is at least partly internalized, and the most efficient remuneration contract would need to impose only relatively low risk on the manager (since risk is already imposed by share ownership). Note also that membership on the board of directors gives the manager some control over risk through the ability to influence firm operating and financing policies. Then, positive accounting theory predicts that there will be a lower profit sharing component in the manager's remuneration contract, relative to those of firms that are widely held. Research by Lambert and Larcker (1987) that found evidence of efficiencies such as these is outlined in Section 10.4.

Summary

We can make the following observations:

1. Observability of an agent's effort seems unlikely in an owner-manager context, because of the separation of ownership and control that characterizes firms in a developed industrial society. This is an example of information asymmetry leading to moral hazard, in that, after the contract is signed, the rational manager will, if possible, take advantage of the lack of effort observability to shirk. Agency theory, a branch of game theory, studies the problem of designing a contract to control moral hazard. The optimal contract does so with the lowest possible agency cost.

2. The nature of the optimal contract depends crucially on what can be jointly observed. Contracts can only be written in terms of performance measures that are jointly observable by both principal and agent:

   - If the agent's effort can be jointly observed, directly or indirectly, a fixed salary (subject to a penalty if the contracted-for effort level is not taken) will be optimal when the principal is risk-neutral. Such a contract is called first-best. Here, *effort* is the performance measure.

   - If the agent's effort cannot be observed, but payoff can, the optimal contract will give the agent a share of the payoff. This will motivate the agent to work hard, but is second-best, because it imposes additional risk on the agent. Here, the *payoff* is the performance measure. Since the payoff is frequently expressed in terms of net income, this creates an opportunity for the accounting system to report a net income number that reflects as closely as possible the results of the manager's effort in running the firm. The higher the correlation of net income with effort, the closer the second-best contract to first-best, and hence the lower the agency costs borne by the owner. We denote such an income measure as "hard."

- If neither effort nor payoff can be observed, the optimal contract is a rental contract, whereby the principal rents the firm to the manager for a fixed rental fee, thus internalizing the agent's effort decision. Here, there is *no* performance measure. Such contracts tend to be unsatisfactory, because they impose all of the risk on the agent.

3. There are alternative measures of firm performance to net income, such as share price. The most efficient payoff measure, or combination of measures, depends on the firm's organizational structure and environment.

9.4.3 AGENCY THEORY: A BONDHOLDER-MANAGER LENDING CONTRACT

We now consider another moral hazard problem, namely a contract between a lender and a firm, such as a bondholder and the firm manager. We will regard the bondholder as the principal and the manager as the agent.

EXAMPLE 9.3 A LENDER-MANAGER AGENCY PROBLEM

A risk-neutral lender faces a choice of lending $100 to a firm or investing the $100 in government bonds yielding 10%. The firm offers 12% interest, contracting to repay the loan one year later, that is, to repay $112. However, unlike for government bonds, there is credit risk, that is, a possibility that the firm will go bankrupt, in which case the lender would lose both the principal and the interest.

The firm manager can choose one of two acts. The first act, denoted by a_1, is to pay no dividends while the loan is outstanding. The second act, a_2, is to pay high dividends. If the manager chooses a_1, assume that the lender assesses the probability of bankruptcy as 0.01, so that there is a 0.99 probability of receiving repayment, including $12 interest. However, if a_2 is chosen, the lender assesses the probability of bankruptcy as 0.1, because the high dividends will reduce the firm's solvency. Thus, under a_2, the probability of repayment will be only 0.9.

Assume that the manager is paid by means of an incentive contract consisting of a salary plus a bonus based on the firm's net income. Then, since dividends are not charged against income, the manager's remuneration is unaffected by the act chosen, that is, the manager is indifferent between the two acts. Thus, there is no compelling reason to assume that the manager will or will not take a_1, the lender's preferred act. After thinking about this, the lender assesses equal probabilities for each act of the manager, that is, the probability of a_1 is 0.5 and similarly for a_2. Table 9.4 summarizes this scenario.

TABLE 9.4 PAYOFFS FOR LENDER-MANAGER CONTRACT				
	Manager's Act			
	a_1 (no dividends)		a_2 (high dividends)	
	Payoff	Probability	Payoff	Probability
x_1 (interest paid)	$ 12	0.99	$ 12	0.9
x_2 (bankrupt)	−100	0.01	−100	0.1

The payoff amounts in the table exclude the $100 loaned. Thus, the lender either earns an interest income of $12 or loses the $100 investment. We could add $100 to each payoff, to express returns gross of the $100 loaned, without affecting the results.

The probabilities in the table are conditional on the manager's chosen act. Thus, if a_1 is taken, the probability of the lender receiving the interest is 0.99; hence, the probability of the lender receiving nothing is $1.00 - 0.99 = 0.01$, and so on. Recall that we have also assumed that the chances are 50/50 that a_1 will be chosen.

Will the lender be willing to lend $100 to the firm? The alternative is to buy government bonds, with a return of 10%, or $10 in total. The expected profit from investing in the firm is:

$$\text{ETR} = 0.5(12 \times 0.99 - 100 \times 0.01) + 0.5(12 \times 0.9 - 100 \times 0.1)$$
$$= 0.5 \times 10.88 \times 0.5 \times 0.80$$
$$= 5.44 + 0.40$$
$$= 97$$

where ETR denotes expected total return.

The first term in brackets represents the lender's expected return conditional on a_1. There is a 0.5 probability that a_1 will be chosen. Similarly, the second term in brackets is the expected return conditional on a_2, also multiplied by the 0.5 probability that a_2 will be chosen.

Thus, the ETR is only $5.84 or 5.84% on the amount loaned. The reason, or course, is the probability of bankruptcy, particularly if a_2 is taken, which forces the expected return down to well below the nominal rate of 12%. Our lender, who can earn 10% elsewhere, will not make the loan.

What nominal rate would the firm have to offer in order to attract the lender? This can be calculated as follows:

$$10.00 = 0.5(0.99R - 100 \times 0.01) + 0.5(0.9R - 100 \times 0.1)$$

where R is the required nominal rate. The left side is the lender's required total return. Upon solving for R, we obtain:

$$R = \frac{15.50}{0.945} = 16.40$$

Thus, the firm would have to offer a nominal rate of return of over 16% in order to attract the lender.

The 16% interest rate in Example 9.3 would probably seem too high to the manager, particularly since he or she shares in net income. Consequently, the manager may try to find some more efficient contractual arrangement that would lower the interest rate. One possibility would be to *commit* to take a_1. This could be done by writing a covenant into the lending agreement. An example of a covenant would be to pay no dividends if the interest coverage ratio (ratio of net income before interest and taxes to annual interest payments) is below a specified level. Another example would be to not undertake any additional borrowing (which would dilute the security of existing lenders) if the debt-to-equity ratio is above a specified level. Since covenants are legally binding, the lender will change the assessed probabilities of the acts. Assume the probability that the manager will take a_1 is now assessed by the lender as 1, and 0 for a_2. Thus, if the firm offers a nominal rate of 12%, the lender's ETR is:

$$1(12 \times 0.99 - 100 \times 0.01) + 0(12 \times 0.9 - 100 \times 0.1) = 10.88$$

Since this exceeds the required $10, the lender would now make the loan.

Note that since covenants depend on financial-statement-based ratios, the probability of technical violation will depend on the accounting policies used to calculate these ratios. One possibility would be to allow the manager to choose accounting policies from GAAP, giving some flexibility to reduce the risk of violation. However, if GAAP change, this flexibility could be impaired, thereby imposing costs on the firm. Consequently, an alternative would be to reduce the set of accounting policies by specifying in the contract the specific policies to be used for covenant ratio calculation.

Again, the most efficient contract depends on organizational and environmental variables. For example, if the firm already has a lot of debt outstanding it may wish to eliminate the risk of GAAP changing by specifying accounting policies in the contract, even though this would increase negotiation costs and reduce flexibility. Also, the choice would be affected by other factors such as the size of the debt issue (smaller size, less to worry about) and the profitability and financial position of the firm (better position, less likelihood of covenant violation in the first place). The most efficient contract is the one that best trades off the security offered to lenders with the expected contracting costs. For an example of a positive theory study which successfully predicts the choice of debt contract form on the basis of firm characteristics such as those mentioned above, see Thornton and Bryant (1986).

Summary

The main point to realize in Example 9.3 is the existence of a moral hazard problem between lenders and firm managers—managers may act contrary to the best interests of the lenders. Rational lenders will anticipate this behaviour, however, and thereby raise the interest rates they demand for their loans. As a result, the manager has an incentive to commit not to act in a manner that is against the lenders' interests. This can be done by inserting covenants into the lending agreement whereby the manager agrees to limit dividends or additional borrowing while the loan is outstanding. Consequently, the firm is able to borrow at lower rates.

The most efficient lending contract is the one that best trades off the interest cost demanded by lenders with the various costs of contracting, including the costs of debt covenants.

9.5   *Implications of Agency Theory for Accounting*

9.5.1   *HOLMSTRÖM'S AGENCY MODEL*

In a widely referenced paper, Holmström (1979) gives a rigorous development of the agency model. We now review aspects of his model from an accounting perspective.

Holmström assumes that the agent's effort is unobservable by the principal but that the payoff is jointly observable, consistent with Example 9.2. This reminds us that if a payoff is to serve as a basis for contracting, it must be observable to both parties. The question then is: Is net income sufficiently observable that principal and agent are willing to use it as a measure of payoff? If not, other payoff measures, such as share price, may take over.

The answer to this question is not obvious. Granted, both parties can observe a number called net income. But, since the manager controls the firm's accounting system and accounting policies, is net income sufficiently credible that the owner is willing to pay a bonus to the manager based on that reported number? If not, he or she would be unwilling to enter into a contract based on net income.

Thus, we see that contracting implies a role for GAAP and for an audit. GAAP are needed as a cost-effective way to put limits on the manager's ability to influence reported net income by selecting from alternative accounting policies.

Both parties should know the rules as to how net income is calculated. GAAP serve to provide this needed structure.

Auditing is needed to add credibility to the reported net income number. This credibility has several sources. First, the owner can be reasonably certain of the integrity of the audited internal control systems underlying the firm's accounting system so that the likelihood of fraud or error in net income is low. Second, the auditor will ensure that GAAP are adhered to, so that net income is determined in accordance with a set of publicly known rules. Third, the professional status of the auditor reassures the owner that the auditor is independent and unlikely to be unduly influenced by the manager. Certainly, agency theory implies that a strong and active auditing profession, which enforces competent and ethical behaviour by its members, is key to the financial reporting process.

The usefulness of net income for contracting also depends on the basis of accounting. It can be argued that historical-cost-based income has desirable properties in this regard. For example, it may be less susceptible to manager manipulation and bias than current-value-based net income, at least when markets do not work well. Also, current-value-based net income may be volatile, since market values fluctuate over time, and this volatility will be out of manager control. Thus, historical-cost-based income may be harder than income based on current values.

Given payoff observability, Holmström shows formally that a contract based on the payoff is less efficient than first-best, as illustrated by our Example 9.2. As in our example, the source of the efficiency loss is the necessity for the risk-averse agent to bear additional risk in order to overcome the tendency to shirk.

This raises the question of whether the second-best contract could be made more efficient by basing it on a second variable in addition to payoff. For example, as we have implied earlier, share price also conveys information about manager performance. Rather than using one measure or the other, would basing the contract on *both* net income and share price reduce the agency costs of the second-best contract?

Holmström shows that the answer to this question is yes, provided that the second variable is also jointly observable, and conveys some information about manager effort beyond that contained in the payoff measure itself.[5] This will typically be the case for share price. As discussed above, net income is not a perfectly hard measure of effort—despite GAAP and auditing, some manager ability to manipulate and bias net income remains. Also, the efficient security market price is based on more information than just accounting information, so that we would expect it to convey additional information about manager effort.

Of course, share price tends to be quite volatile, being affected by economy-wide events over which the manager has no control. Nevertheless, Holmström's analysis shows that no matter how noisy the second variable is, it can be used to increase the efficiency of the second-best contract if it contains at least some additional effort information.[6]

Thus, an interesting implication of the Holmström model is that, just as net income competes with other information sources for investors under efficient security market theory, it competes with other information sources for motivating managers under agency theory. As we will see in Chapter 10, this prediction is borne out in practice.

To meet this competition as a measure of manager performance, net income should be hard. As mentioned earlier, hardness will be affected by the relative proportions of historical-cost-based and current-value-based measurements in net income. This leads directly to the fundamental problem of financial accounting theory stated in Section 1.5. To the extent that historical-cost-based net income is highly correlated with manager effort, it will be useful for contracting. But current-value-based net income can be useful for investor decision-making. Then, the best measure of net income for informing investors need not be the same as the best measure for contracting, as recognized by Gjesdal (1981).

9.5.2 RIGIDITY OF CONTRACTS

Additional implications of agency theory for accounting follow from the fact that contracts tend to be *rigid* once signed. The reasons for this rigidity need some discussion. Otherwise, we might ask, if economic consequences have their roots in the contracts that managers enter into, why not just *renegotiate* the contracts following a change in GAAP or other circumstances?

Note first that it is generally impossible to anticipate all contingencies when entering into a contract. For example, unless the contract is of very short duration, it would be difficult to predict changes in GAAP which could affect the contract. Contracts that do not anticipate all possible state realizations are termed **incomplete.**

Given incomplete contracts, renegotiation might be possible to some extent, but it does not seem that renegotiation following a change in GAAP is sufficient to alleviate management's concerns about accounting policies (perhaps introducing provisions for renegotiation into a contract *before* it is signed would be useful, but this is beyond our scope). The reason is that contracts can be surprisingly difficult to renegotiate. For example, suppose that a new GAAP accounting policy lowers reported net income and increases its variability. The manager goes to the bondholder and explains that, through no one's fault, the accounting rules have changed and requests that the coverage ratio covenant be reduced from 2.5:1 to 2:1. This, the manager argues, would restore the bondholder's protection to what it was before the rule change. Why should the bondholder agree to such a request? In doing so, he or she is giving something away—namely the increased protection against excessive dividends that resulted from the new accounting policy. To be willing to do this, the bondholder may well require something in return, such as a higher interest rate. The problem for the manager is further complicated if, as is usually the case, there are many bondholders. Agreement would then be required from all of them, or, at least, a majority.

The manager's compensation contract with the firm owner would be similarly difficult to amend. If the manager requests, say, a higher bonus rate, to correct for an accounting policy change that lowers reported net income, the compensation committee of the board of directors may want something in return, or even reopen the entire contract for renegotiation.

In effect, a consequence of entering into contracts is just that—they are contracts, and hence tend towards rigidity. The manager who is unfavourably affected by a change of the accounting rules in midstream may well take out his or her displeasure on the accountants who introduced the rule change rather than on the other parties to the contract.

9.6   *Reconciliation of Efficient Securities Market Theory with Economic Consequences*

We are now in a position to complete our resolution of the anomaly stated in Section 7.7, namely, why *accounting policies appear to have economic consequences even though they have no direct effects on the cash flows of affected firms.*

Note first that the contracting-based argument we have just given for managers' concerns about changes in accounting policies does not depend on these changes having direct cash flow effects. The arguments would be the same regardless of whether such effects were present or not.

Rather, it is the rigidities produced by the signing of binding contracts that create managers' concerns, and which lead to their intervention in the standard setting process. These rigidities have nothing to do with whether accounting policy changes affect cash flows.

Given these rigidities, it should be clear from our agency theory examples (Examples 9.2 and 9.3) that net income and other financial statement numbers *matter* to managers. One reason, of course, is that the manager's remuneration is frequently based on net income. Another reason is that contracts between lenders and borrowers, especially long-term ones, usually contain covenants whereby the manager commits not to take certain actions that may be contrary to the lender's interests. Such covenants are typically based on the firm's financial statements. As a result of these considerations, we would expect managers to look very closely at any accounting policy changes that may affect reported net income and/or other financial statement values.

Thus, economic consequences and efficient securities markets are not inconsistent. Rather, they can be reconciled by positive accounting theory, with normative support from agency theory which suggests *why* firms enter into employment and debt contracts that depend on accounting information. Nothing in the above arguments leading to managerial concern about accounting policies conflicts with security market efficiency.

Similarly, nothing in the theory of efficient securities markets conflicts with managerial concern about accounting policies. Joint consideration of both theories, though, helps us to see that managers may well intervene in accounting policies, even though those policies would improve the decision usefulness of financial statements to investors. Thus, in the final analysis, the interaction between managers and investors is a game, as modelled in Sections 9.3 and 9.4.

Of course, agency theory is not the only explanation for economic consequences. Another possibility is simply that managers do not accept security market efficiency, believing that investor reaction and cost of capital are affected by accounting policy choice irrespective of any impact on cash flows. This may have been the case, for example, in the PIP grant controversy reviewed in Section 7.5. A related possibility is that managers do accept market efficiency but wish to use accounting policy choice as a vehicle for communicating inside information to the market. We will explore this argument in Chapter 11.

Other economic consequences explanations derive from the political cost hypothesis (Section 8.2) and from concern over competitive disadvantage following from certain disclosures, as modelled by Darrough and Stoughton (Section 9.3). However, given compensation contracts that align managers' interests with those of owners, we can argue that these explanations derive from game theory as well.

While game theory is consistent with managers' concerns about accounting policies, the theory also helps us to understand Lev's finding (Section 7.6), that investors were also concerned about such policies. One interpretation of Lev's finding is that the securities market is inefficient. Security prices fell in response to the prospect of an accounting policy change that would tend to lower reported net income of affected firms but would not affect their cash flows.

An alternative interpretation, however, is that Lev's finding is evidence of market efficiency, rather than inefficiency. To see this, consider once again the impact of successful-efforts on reported net income, namely, that it will tend to lower income and make it more variable. Both of these effects will increase the probability of violation of covenants in borrowing agreements. Since violation can have serious implications, the efficient market bids down the share prices accordingly. Alternatively, managers may change the way they operate the firm following an accounting policy change. For example, in response to the increased volatility of reported net income, managers of firms affected by the switch to successful-efforts may adopt safer exploration policies. Since these policies may offer significantly lower expected returns than the policies they replace, investors may bid down share prices in response. Thus, when contracting effects are recognized, security market reaction to a paper change in accounting policy may support the theory of market efficiency rather than inefficiency.

9.7   *Conclusions*

The various conflict-based theories described in this chapter have important implications for financial accounting theory. These can be summarized as follows:

1. An important implication is that these theories enable a reconciliation of efficient market theory and economic consequences. Early applications of efficient market theory to financial accounting (as, for example, in Beaver's early article, discussed in Section 4.4) suggested that accountants concentrate on full disclosure of information useful for investors' decision needs. The form of disclosure and the particular accounting policies used did not matter, as the market would see through these to their ultimate cash flow implications.

   Certainly, accountants have adopted the decision usefulness approach and its full-disclosure implications. Frequently, however, as noted in Chapter 7, management intervened in the standard setting process. This was not predicted by efficient securities market theory, since under that theory the market value of a firm's securities should be independent of its accounting policies, unless cash flows were affected. Why would management care about accounting policies if these do not affect its cost of capital? An answer is that changes in accounting policies can affect provisions in contracts that firm managers have entered into, thereby affecting their welfare and the welfare of the firm.

   The reason why accounting policies can affect manager and firm welfare should be carefully considered. The basic problem is one of information asymmetry. In an owner-manager context, the manager knows his or her own effort in running the firm on the owner's behalf, but typically the owner cannot observe this effort. Knowing this, the manager faces a temptation to shirk. Thus, there is a moral hazard problem between owner and manager. To control moral hazard, the owner can offer the manager a share of reported net income. This sharing in the results of personal effort motivates the manager to work harder. However, it also means that the manager has a personal interest in how net income is measured. The firm will want to induce the desired effort as efficiently as possible.

   When managers enter into borrowing contracts with lenders, similar implications for manager and firm welfare occur. Borrowing contracts typically contain covenants that restrict the payment of dividends depending on the values of certain financial-statement-based ratios, such as interest coverage. Since covenant violations can be costly to the firm, both the manager and the firm will have a personal interest in accounting policy changes that affect the probability of covenant violation, particularly if they share in firm profits.

Thus, economic consequences can be seen as a rational result of the rigidities introduced by entering into binding contracts. The conflict situation between managers, who may object to accounting policies that have adverse economic consequences for them and their firms, and investors, who desire full disclosure, can be modelled as a non-cooperative game.

2. Another implication of agency theory is that historical-cost-based net income has desirable properties for contracting purposes, including the fact that its rules are well known, so that contracting parties have a good "feel" for how it responds to differing economic circumstances. Also, historical-cost-based net income is reasonably reliable, relative to valuation-based alternatives, and it appears to be reasonably correlated with manager effort. These hardness properties of historical-cost-based net income lead, however, to the fundamental problem of financial accounting theory, namely the reconciliation of the information needs of investors with those of contracting.

3. Finally, agency theory implies that generally accepted accounting principles and auditing are important to giving net income the credibility it needs to serve as a basis for contracting.

For these reasons, game theory is an important component of financial accounting theory. In addition to enabling a better understanding of the conflicting interests of various constituencies affected by financial reporting, it has encouraged research into executive compensation and earnings management. Chapters 10 and 11 will review some of this research.

Notes

1. The discussion here assumes only pure strategies, that is, strategies where one act is chosen with probability 1. It is possible to have mixed-strategy solutions, where players randomize between acts over which they are indifferent. Then, this statement would need modification.

2. Darrough and Stoughton assume that if disclosure is made, it is honest. This assumption can be motivated by an audit and/or by severe penalties for fraudulent disclosure.

3. Note that the employment contract here is linear in the payoff, that is, 32% of net income. It is possible that a non-linear contract would be more efficient. This is beyond our scope here.

4. There is an implicit assumption of efficient security markets here.

5. More precisely, for the second variable to reduce agency costs it must be false that the payoff measure is a sufficient statistic for the pair of variables (payoff, second variable) with respect to effort.

6. Holmström points out that if the contract with the manager is confined to a limited class, such as the linear contract assumed in Example 9.2, this result may not hold.

Questions and Problems

1. The instability of economic cartels such as OPEC (Organization of Petroleum Exporting Countries) can be explained, at least in part, by game theory considerations. Typically such cartels attempt to agree to restrict oil production and keep prices to customers high. Frequently, however, some countries violate these agreements.

   Use the following depiction of a two-country non-cooperative game to explain why violation occurs. That is, explain in words which strategy pair is likely to be played in this game and why. Identify the Nash equilibrium of this game.

		Country 1	
		Keep	**Violate**
Country 2	**Keep**	100, 100	40, 200
	Violate	200, 40	50, 50

   In each box, the first number represents country 2's payoff and the second country 1's payoff.   (CGA-Canada)

2. U-Haul, a "do-it-yourself" moving company, is doing a booming business these days. The reason is that some companies relocating employees are changing the way they reimburse moving expenses. Before the change, moves were very expensive, because the companies paid for everything. Now, the companies pay a fixed amount to the employee, who can keep the savings, if there are any. Explain this change using agency theory concepts. Also, note that U-Haul offers to reimburse customers for the cost of oil used during the move, while customers have to pay for their own gasoline. Why?   (CGA-Canada)

3. A manufacturer of farm equipment is headed for financial distress. Bonuses of management are based on net income relative to budget. There has been a recent change in management, occurring in early 1995. To the surprise of the new manager, the outgoing manager had sharply increased 1994 production, resulting in excessive levels of inventory on hand at the end of 1994. The manufacturer uses absorption costing for its inventories.

    Required

    a. Explain why the old management increased production and inventories.

    b. How might the remuneration plan of management be changed to reduce the likelihood that this would happen in the future?   (CGA-Canada)

4. Suppose there is a company with a number of divisions which are profit centres, all sharing a production facility (for example, a computer). The user divisions are always submitting rush orders to the operator of the common production facility. The division involved (division A) claims the order is urgent and that delay will result in significant profit losses to the company, a claim which is very difficult for the operator of the common facility to verify or refute. What sometimes results is a job being given priority which causes a delay of some other division's job, where the cost of delay to the company (forgone profits due to, say, impatient customers going elsewhere) is well in excess of the cost of delay to division A. Assume that each division manager receives a bonus based solely on the profits of his or her division, in addition to fixed salary.

    Required

    a. Explain why the behaviour of division A's manager is predictable, in terms of agency theory.

    b. Can you think of a solution to this agency problem? Explain why your solution works.   (CGA-Canada)

5. The PIP grant accounting controversy discussed in Section 7.5 can be analyzed as a non-cooperative game. Let the two players be the government and the CICA. Each player faces two strategies: the "cooperate" strategy happens when one player goes along with the preferred accounting policy of the other; the "strong" strategy involves one player sticking to its own policy regardless of the wishes of the other.

    Hypothetical, but reasonable, payoffs for each player are summarized in the following table.

		CICA	
		Cooperate	**Strong**
	Cooperate	50, 50	8, 60
Government			
	Strong	20, 10	12, 15

In each box, the first number represents the government's payoff and the second number the CICA's payoff. To illustrate, consider the lower left box. Here, the government plays strong, that is, it demands that the CICA waive the requirements of Section 3800 and the CICA agrees. The government receives a payoff of 20 in this case, because it is seen as the dominant player. However, because this strategy erodes its relationship with the CICA and with other constituencies who feel that standard setting should be done in the private sector, its payoff is less than the 50 it would receive if both players had cooperated. The CICA receives a very low payoff of 10, because it is perceived as capitulating to the government's demands. Similar reasoning applies to the other three boxes of the table.

Required

a. On the basis of the discussion in Section 7.5, which strategy pair did the players choose?

b. Is this strategy pair a Nash equilibrium? Explain.

c. Both parties would have been better off if they had cooperated. Explain why this strategy pair was unlikely to have been chosen.

6. The shareholders of X Ltd. will vote at the forthcoming annual meeting on a proposal to establish a bonus plan, based on firm performance, for X Ltd. management. Proponents of the plan argue that management will work harder under a bonus plan and that expected earnings will thereby increase. However, a dissident shareholder group argues that there is little point in granting a bonus plan, because management will bias or otherwise manage earnings to increase their bonus, rather than working harder.

Upon investigation, you estimate that if the bonus plan is granted, expected earnings will be $150 if management does not manage earnings and $140 if it does, *before* management remuneration in each case. Management remuneration, including the bonus, would be $50 if it does not manage earnings and $60 if it does. Of course, earnings not paid as management remuneration will go to the shareholders.

If the bonus plan is not granted, expected earnings will be $140 before management remuneration if management does not manage earnings and $100 if it does. Management remuneration would be $30 in either case, with the balance of earnings going to the shareholders.

Required

a. Prepare a payoff table for the above game between shareholders and management.

b. Which strategy pair will be chosen? That is, identify a Nash equilibrium for the game. Assume both players are risk-neutral.

c. What is the main advantage of a game theory approach to modelling the management's decision whether to manage earnings, rather than modelling it as a single-person decision theory problem of the manager? (CGA-Canada)

7. Mr. Kao, the owner of Kao Industries, wants to hire a manager to operate the firm while he takes an extended trip abroad. He wants the manager to work hard (60 hours per week) rather than shirk (40 hours per week). The payoff table for Kao Industries under each alternative is as follows:

KAO INDUSTRIES PAYOFF TABLE FOR YEAR		
Net Income for Year (before manager remuneration)	Probability (a_1 = 60 hours)	Probability (a_2 = 40 hours)
$400	0.7	0.2
200	0.2	0.3
0	0.1	0.5

Kao is negotiating with a potential manager about the remuneration contract. The manager's disutility for effort for the year is:

$$\text{Disutility of effort} = \frac{h^2}{800}$$

where h is the number of hours worked per week.

Required

a. Show calculations to verify that for a fixed annual salary paid to the manager, Mr. Kao will prefer that the manager work hard. Mr. Kao is risk-neutral.

b. For any fixed annual salary, will the manager prefer to work hard or to shirk? Explain.

c. Suppose that Mr. Kao offers the manager a fixed annual salary of $10, plus 10% of net income. The manager's utility for money is equal to the square root of the money received. Assuming that the manager takes the job, which act would he or she take? Show your calculations.   (CGA-Canada)

8. The shareholders of UVW Ltd. are unhappy about the top manager's performance. While the manager's effort in running the firm cannot be observed, it is felt that he or she works about 40 hours a week. The manager's annual salary at present is $160,000.

A new incentive contract is being considered by the shareholders, whereby the manager would receive a salary of $100,000 per annum plus a bonus of 25% of reported net income before salary and bonus.

You are asked to analyze the expected impact of the new bonus plan on the manager. You estimate that if the manager works 60 hours per week (a_1), net income before manager remuneration will be $1,040,000 per annum with probability of 0.7, and $90,000 per year with probability of 0.3. Under the present salary-based remuneration, whereby the manager works 40 hours per week (a_2), analysis of past profitability shows that annual net income has been $1,040,000 only 0.1 of the time and $90,000 the other 0.9.

You also ascertain that the manager's utility for money is equal to the square root of the money received, and that disutility for effort is four times the number of hours worked per week.

Required

a. Show calculations to verify that under the present-salary-based remuneration plan the manager will prefer to work 40 hours per week over 60 hours.

b. Which act, a_1 or a_2, will the manager prefer under the new incentive contract? Show calculations.

c. A new accounting standard is proposed that, while it will not change future expected net income, will greatly increase the volatility of net income. Explain why the manager would object to the proposed new standard.

(CGA-Canada)

9.   Mr. K is contemplating a one-year 8% loan of $500 to firm J. Mr. K demands at least a 6% expected return per annum on loans like this.

K is concerned that the firm may not be able to pay the interest and/or principal at the end of the year. A further concern is that if he makes the loan, firm J may engage in additional borrowing. If so, K's security would be diluted and the firm would become more risky. Since firm J is growing rapidly, K is sure that the firm would engage in additional borrowing if he makes the loan.

K examines firm J's most recent annual report and calculates an interest coverage ratio (ratio of net income before interest and taxes to interest expense) of 4, including the contemplated $500 loan.

Upon considering all of these matters, K assesses the following probabilities:

Payoff	Probability
θ_1: Interest and principal repaid	0.80
θ_2: Reorganization, principal repaid but not interest	0.18
θ_3: Bankruptcy, nothing repaid	0.02
	1.00

Required

a. Should Mr. K make the loan? Show calculations.

b. Firm J offers to add a covenant to its lending agreement with Mr. K, undertaking not to engage in any additional borrowing if its interest coverage ratio falls below 4 before the next year-end. Mr. K estimates that there is a 60% probability that the interest coverage ratio will fall below 4. If it does, there would be no dilution of his equity by additional borrowing, and he feels the lower coverage ratio would still be adequate. He assesses that his payoff probabilities would then be:

Payoff	Probability
θ_1	0.95
θ_2	0.04
θ_3	0.01

If the coverage ratio does not fall below 4, the resulting additional borrowing and dilution of security would cause him to assess payoff probabilities as:

Payoff	Probability
θ_1	0.85
θ_2	0.14
θ_3	0.01

Should Mr. K now make the loan? Show calculations.   (CGA-Canada)

10. The article here reproduced from *CA Magazine* (December 1992), "US Survey Shows Opposition to Fair Market Value Accounting," describes a survey of users and preparers of financial statements in the banking industry. Apparently, both constituencies oppose accounting based on fair value. The views of preparers is especially noteworthy. For example, only 5% believe fair value reporting more accurately reflects an institution's financial position.

The survey results seem consistent with agency theory, which suggests that a managerial performance measure should be highly correlated with manager effort.

US SURVEY SHOWS OPPOSITION TO FAIR MARKET VALUE ACCOUNTING

Ninety percent of bankers, analysts and other users of financial statements in the US oppose the adoption of fair market value accounting, says a study conducted by KPMG Peat Marwick for the Association of Reserve City Bankers. As of this month, certain US financial institutions will be required to disclose the fair market value for financial instruments. The new reporting requirements arise out of the FDIC Improvement Act of 1991 and the Financial Accounting Standards Board's Standard 107.

The KPMG study, conducted over a six-month period earlier this year, revealed that most users of financial information regard the debate about replacing traditional historical cost accounting with fair market value as "the musings of theoreticians who are not directly involved in making investment decisions." The overwhelming choice (95%) for an alternative format was to use historical cost combined with supplemental fair value disclosure. The next most frequent choice was to continue the current historical cost model alone (76%), followed by the use of two versions of financial statements—one based on historical cost and one on fair value (58%). Only 5% of financial statement preparers believed fair value reporting more accurately reflected an institution's financial position.

The survey showed a marked difference between the perceptions of preparers and users of financial statements. At least 50% of financial statement users said they expect an error rate of less than 5% in fair value estimates, whereas few preparers say they expect to meet that goal; they felt the cost of obtaining the estimates would affect precision. And while a majority of users believed fair value disclosures would be useful for the instruments surveyed, 73% of financial statement preparers said they are not reliable or comparable.

Users and preparers agree that existing statement formats and disclosures are adequate for most types of information. A few areas emerged as having inadequate disclosure: off-balance-sheet instruments, problem loans, loan concentration and credit quality.

"Since the study shows that preparers and users are skeptical about the reliability, comparability and timeliness of fair market value accounting," says John F. Ruffle, vice-chairman of J.P. Morgan & Co. and trustee of the ARCB's Banking Research Fund, "the study should give pause to those most intent on instituting market value accounting in the banking industry."

The study was based on the results of written surveys, focus groups and interviews, including a survey distributed to the highest-ranking executives of major US banks. For more information or a copy of the study, contact Tom Ferguson, Director of Marketing, KPMG Peat Marwick, 767—5th Ave., 47th floor, New York, NY 10153.

SOURCE: *CA Magazine*, December 1992. Reprinted by permission.

Required

a. Explain why historical-cost-based net income may be a better measure of manager stewardship than net income based on fair values.

b. Give a counterargument that fair-value-based net income may better measure stewardship than the survey respondents give it credit for.

c. If both users and preparers of bank financial statements are opposed to fair value accounting, why do you think standard setters are moving in that direction?

11. One of the problems of entering into contracts, including executive compensation contracts, is incompleteness. That is, it is generally impossible to foresee all relevant events that might happen and build provisions for them into the contract. An example of contract rigidity in the face of an unforeseen event appeared in the *Wall Street Journal* (April 15, 1993) in an article entitled "Firms Get Around Big One-Time Earnings Hits to Save Executive Bonuses."

SFAS 106 requires that firms accrue employees' postretirement benefits rather than waiting until they are paid (see Section 6.4.1). The article states that because of SFAS 106 "many compensation committees want to use operating earnings—not net after the accounting change—to calculate top managers' bonuses."

For example, Chrysler Corp., which had a charge for retiree health costs of $4.7 billion in 1993, plans to ask its shareholders if it could exclude the charge to calculate bonuses. However, there is opposition by the United Shareholders Association, who believe that charges such as postretirement benefits "should be deemed a regular business cost, not an unusual expense to be ignored by board compensation committees." However, consulting firm Wyatt Co. "says it's simpler to exclude the new annual charges than to alter bonus formulas."

Required

a. If you were a shareholder, would you agree to this request? Explain why or why not.

b. If you were a senior executive affected by SFAS 106 and your request was turned down, how would you react? Explain why.

12. The incentive effects of sharing in firm payoff can also be extended down into the organization. An article entitled "IBM Will Try Big Bonus Plan to Spur Effort" appeared in the *Wall Street Journal* on February 14, 1992, and describes how IBM "has established an extensive bonus program designed to serve as a carrot," in place of a previous "stick" approach.

According to the article, for several years many IBM employees have had minimal raises, and many of them "reacted with alarm" after IBM's "senior management's base salaries rose about 35% in 1990 from 1989," excluding stock options which resulted in an even higher increase. However, IBM announced that it will be offering a "significant" bonus in 1992 to U.S. employees, "if their business unit's performance reaches its goals." The new bonus pool "is designed to step up the sort of competition IBM has been encouraging among its employees."

Furthermore, "IBM already has increased its enforcement of a ranking system that rates employees on a scale of one to four, to make sure that fewer employees get the highest rankings, and has begun to pressure many of the fours to leave." Now the new system will give those with a ranking of one or two a higher salary and bonus.

Required

a. Explain why this "carrot" approach to motivating effort may be more effective than the "stick" approach that IBM had been using. This latter approach seems to have involved minimal raises and, apparently, job security combined with close supervision.

b. What problems can you see if a large firm with many business units moves profit sharing down into the organization, as IBM appears to be doing?

13. A problem with many games is that they can have multiple Nash equilibria. This makes it difficult to predict the outcome of the game.

As an illustration of a non-cooperative game with multiple equilibria, consider the following payoff table, which is a slight adjustment of the game in question 1:

		Country 1	
		Keep	**Violate**
Country 2	**Keep**	100, 100	50, 200
	Violate	200, 50	50, 50

Required

a. Identify three Nash equilibria of this game.

b. Suppose that this game will be repeated a known, finite number of times. Suppose that the current equilibrium is in the lower left box of the table. Describe an action by country 1 which would cause a shift to a new equilibrium.

c. Suppose that the game will be repeated an infinite number of times. What equilibrium would you then predict? Explain.

Executive Compensation

10.1 Overview

In this chapter we consider **executive compensation plans**. We will see that real incentive plans follow from the agency theory developed in Chapter 9, but are more complex and detailed. They involve a delicate mix of incentive, risk, and decision horizon considerations.

> *An **executive compensation plan** is an agency contract between the firm and its manager which attempts to align the interests of owners and manager, by basing the manager's compensation on some measure of the manager's effort in operating the firm.*

Most compensation plans are based on two measures of manager effort—net income and share price. That is, the amounts of bonus, shares, options, and other components of executive pay that are awarded in a particular year depend on one or both of net income and share price performance. In conjunction with share price, the basing of compensation on net income helps control both the amount of risk these plans impose on managers and the length of their decision horizons. This role of net income is an important one, which goes beyond the role of reporting useful information to investors. An understanding of this role is important for accountants, since net income competes with other payoff measures. If net income does not have desirable hardness qualities, it will be "squeezed out" of compensation plans. If so, a major source of competitive advantage for accountants will be lost. However, to the extent that net income can maintain and increase its ability to report on manager effort, the efficiency of compensation plans will be increased. Not only will this enhance accountants' competitive advantage, it will have social benefits through the motivation of responsible executive performance.

10.2   *A Managerial Compensation Plan*

In this section we present an example of a managerial compensation plan. The following exhibit describes a plan of a U.S. firm, Rockwell International Corporation. The information appears in the firm's 1995 proxy statement, mailed to shareholders. First, notice the three components of Rockwell's managerial remuneration, namely: (1) salary; (2) an annual incentives plan, which provides for cash bonuses; and (3) a long-term incentives plan, which provides company stock to managers in a variety of ways. Observe that the total amount provided for cash bonuses depends both on dividends declared and earnings. Furthermore, note that the percentage bonus increases with earnings.

Many bonus plans require that a certain level of earnings (or other performance measure) be reached before bonuses become payable. The threshold level of earnings that must be attained is called the **bogey**. Also, such plans frequently contain an upper limit to the bonus, called the **cap**.

EXHIBIT 10.1   Rockwell International Corporation
Compensation Plans

COMPENSATION COMMITTEE REPORT ON EXECUTIVE COMPENSATION

The Compensation and Management Development Committee of the Board of Directors, which consists entirely of non-employee Directors ... has furnished the following report on executive compensation:

Compensation Philosophy and Objectives

Under the Committee's supervision, the Corporation has developed and implemented compensation policies, plans and programs intended to "pay for performance" through meeting three fundamental objectives:

- Foster the creation of shareowner value through close alignment of the financial interests of executives with those of the Corporation's shareowners
- Recognize individual and team performance through evaluation of each executive's effectiveness in meeting strategic and operating plan goals
- Pay competitively to attract, retain and motivate the high caliber of executives necessary for the Corporation's continuing leadership in the diverse markets it serves

The Committee believes this sharp focus on "pay for performance" enhances shareowner value creation as it:

- Challenges each of the Corporation's businesses to reach their full potential through achieving leadership market positions and improving long-term financial performance

- Rewards performance and motivates management to develop new products, invest in new technologies and take the management action—focused on promoting teamwork, organizational effectiveness, streamlining and empowerment—essential to assure quality, reduced product cycle times and enhanced customer responsiveness

The Committee reports to the Board of Directors following each meeting of the Committee on the substance of its discussion, data considered and action taken.

Employee Stock Ownership

The Committee believes the focus on "pay for performance" is further sharpened by aligning closely the financial interests of the Corporation's key executives with those of the shareowners. Accordingly, in July 1993 it adopted the following minimum Ownership Guidelines (multiple of base salary):

Common Stock Market Value	
Chief Executive Officer	8
Executive Vice Presidents	5
Major Business Unit Heads and Senior Vice Presidents	3
Other Business Unit Heads and Other Senior Executives	1.5

Only shares owned directly or through the Corporation's Savings Plan, but not shares subject to unexercised stock options, are considered for determining whether an executive meets the Guidelines. At November 30, 1994, the 46 executives subject to the Guidelines owned an aggregate of 1,520,643 shares of the Corporation's Common Stock, with an aggregate market value of $51.5 million. The ownership by approximately two-thirds of the executives already meets the Guidelines. Executives who do not meet the Guidelines are expected to do so within five years after the date the Guidelines are applicable to them or within eight years in case of a significant promotion.

Components of the Corporation's Compensation Plans

STRATEGY In order to carry out its "pay for performance" philosophy, the Committee sets base salaries generally somewhat below the median of other major U.S. industrial companies, and provides opportunity for above-median compensation through the Corporation's annual and long-term incentive plans which depend heavily on corporate, business unit and individual performance. The Committee considers the total compensation (earned or potentially available) of each of the Named Officers and the other senior executives in establishing each element of compensation. For the Named Officers, base compensation in a period of acceptable performance (both by the individual and the Corporation) would constitute about 20 to 30%, annual incentives about 20 to 30%, and long-term incentives about 40 to 55% of total compensation.

In its deliberations, the Committee reviews data from industry, peer group and national surveys of other major U.S. industrial companies. The surveys used by the Corporation provide reference data on large samples of industrial companies participating in national surveys that include 35 (71%) of the companies (in addition to the Corporation) included in the S&P High Technology Composite Index, a group of 12 diversified large industrial companies, four of which are included in such Index, that the Corporation believes compete with its businesses, and a group of 25 large industrial companies, six of which (in addition to the Corporation) are included in such Index, that through compensation consultants share relevant data. In addition, the Committee reviews data on a less frequent basis from a group of 15 diversified large industrial companies, eight of which are included in such Index. In determining the components of compensation based in part on survey and peer-company data, the Committee also considers the performance of other companies whose data is included in such surveys.

The Committee periodically is advised by independent compensation consultants concerning the Corporation's compensation programs in comparison to those of other companies which the consultants believe compete with the Corporation for executive talent.

Internal Revenue Code Section 162(m), enacted in 1993 and first applicable to the Corporation for its fiscal year ending September 30, 1995, provides that publicly held companies may not deduct in any taxable year compensation in excess of one million dollars paid in that year to its chief executive officer or any of its other four most highly compensated executive officers unless the compensation is "performance based" as defined in that section. Grants of stock options, on which the Corporation principally relies to provide long-term incentive compensa-

tion to the officers to whose compensation this provision might apply, are considered "performance based" compensation. Since the Committee retains discretion to fix the specific amounts of base salaries and annual incentive compensation for these officers, those elements would not qualify as "performance based" compensation for these purposes. Accordingly, to avoid loss of the tax deduction, the Committee has adopted a formal policy whereby any portion of the base, incentive or other compensation of any person whose compensation is subject to the limitation on deductibility under Section 162(m) exceeds one million dollars shall be deferred until the executive's retirement or other termination of employment.

BASE SALARY In the early part of each fiscal year, the Committee reviews with the Chief Executive Officer and the senior human resources executive and approves, with any modifications it deems appropriate, an annual salary plan for the Corporation's senior executives (other than the Chief Executive Officer). This salary plan is developed by the Corporation's human resources staff under the ultimate direction of the Chief Executive Officer based on the survey data and consultants' reports described above and performance judgments as to the past and expected future contributions of the individual senior executives.

ANNUAL INCENTIVES Near the beginning of each fiscal year, the Committee reviews with the Chief Executive Officer the Corporate Goals and Objectives for that year, including measurable financial return and shareowner value creation objectives as well as long-term leadership goals that in part require more subjective assessments. Principal 1994 financial goals included increasing earnings per share above fiscal 1993 and achieving a return on equity of not less than 19%. Shareowner value goals for 1994 included achieving a total return (stock price appreciation and dividends) exceeding a composite of the peer companies selected by the Corporation, making substantial investments in advanced technologies and product through company-sponsored research and development, and utilizing inter-business sharing of competencies, technology, product development and facilities to achieve added leverage for competitive advantage. The Corporation's long-term goals encompass its many initiatives to enhance shareowner value described above under *Compensation Philosophy and Objectives.*

After the end of the year, performance against the Corporate Goals and Objectives is evaluated and the results are considered by the Committee in awarding annual incentive compensation … to corporate executives who were not directly responsible for the management of a business unit. Individual awards to members of the senior management group, including the Named Officers other than the Chief Executive Officer, are determined by the Committee after reviewing with the Chief Executive Officer the recommended awards, taking into account the contributions made and the levels of responsibility of each of the participants. While the Committee believes achievement of the financial, shareowner value and long-term leadership goals are each important, it accords greater significance to the first two in determining the total amount available for annual incentive payments.

The incentive compensation for executives responsible for the management of business units is determined by the extent to which the respective business unit achieves goals established at the beginning of each year tailored to the particular business unit. For two of the business units, the measure is performance profit before taxes; for one of the units, it is determined by year-over-year sales growth and current-year return on sales, measured through a performance matrix; and for six of the businesses, the measure is based 65% on performance profit before taxes and 35% on the achievement of strategic goals established at the beginning of the year. Achievement of established targets is intended to provide incentive compensation at or above 100% of competitive levels; and these business unit plans include significant upward and downward leverage dependent on performance. In fiscal year 1994, executives of two of the units, which did not meet their objectives, earned only one-fourth of competitive annual incentive compensation while seven business units ranged between 99% and 200% of competitive incentive compensation levels since their performance met or exceeded established goals. Within each business unit, the amount earned by that unit under its plan is allocated among individual executives based on levels of responsibility and an assessment of their individual performance by the business unit President in consultation with the Chief Operating Officer to which the business unit reports and the senior human resources executive.

The amount available for annual incentives is determined for the Corporation's senior executives and other key management under the Corporation's Incentive Compensation Plan or, for key Allen-Bradley executives, under Allen-Bradley's Management Incentive Plan. Under the Corporation's Plan, the addition to the incentive fund for a fiscal year cannot exceed either the aggregate amount of dividends declared on the Corporation's outstanding stock during the year or an aggregate amount computed by adding 2% of the first $100 million of the applicable net earnings (defined as net income, before provision for domestic and foreign taxes based on income, of the Corporation and its consolidated subsidiaries) for the year, and 3% of the next $50 million of such earnings, and 4% of the next $25 million of such earnings, and 5% of the balance of such earnings. Generally the Committee makes awards under the Corporation's Plan in an aggregate amount well below the amount available thereunder. Under Allen-Bradley's Management Incentive Plan, the amount available for each Allen-Bradley executive's annual incentive is determined by an arithmetic formula based on Allen-Bradley's annual sales growth and return on sales; and actual awards are made upon assessment of the same factors as for other business unit plans.

LONG-TERM INCENTIVES The Corporation's 1988 Long-Term Incentives Plan (as well as the proposed 1995 Long-Term Incentives Plan described [later in this article]) provides the flexibility to grant long-term incentives in a variety of forms, including performance units, stock options, stock appreciation rights and restricted stock. Annually the Com-

mittee evaluates the type of long-term incentive it believes is most likely to achieve the Corporation's total compensation objectives.

Since fiscal 1992, the Committee has granted stock options to both the Corporation's senior and middle management groups. In fiscal 1993 and 1994, the Committee also established performance unit plans covering most of the Corporation's business units and providing long-term compensation opportunities that depend on achieving goals measured for each unit by its earnings and return on assets. The Committee also approved a new three-year performance period under Allen-Bradley's supplementary performance plan under which potential compensation is measured by achieving levels of sales growth and return on sales by the Committee for each three fiscal year performance cycle.

In determining the grants of stock options to the individual senior management group, including the Named Officers other than the Chief Executive Officer, the Committee reviewed with the Chief Executive Officer the recommended individual awards, taking into account relevant survey data and the respective scope of accountability, strategic and operational goals, and anticipated contributions of each of the members of the senior management group. In both 1992 and 1993, the long-term incentives for Mr. Davis (who then served as President of Allen-Bradley) were provided one-half through stock option grants and one-half through participation in the Allen-Bradley supplementary performance plan. The presidents of other business units for which performance unit plans have been established also were afforded one-half of their long-term incentive opportunities under those plans and one-half through stock options, with the other key executives of those units participating only in the business unit plans.

Prior to 1992, performance units were granted to senior management, generally for three-year performance cycles having cumulative earnings per share targets that determined the extent to which units were earned. Those grants produced significant long-term compensation for periods when performance objectives were fully or substantially met, including the three-year performance period covering fiscal years 1991–1993 for which performance units were granted in fiscal 1991. ... The Allen-Bradley supplementary performance plan (under which Mr. Davis received grants when he was President of Allen-Bradley) produced significant long-term compensation for the three-year performance periods ended September 30, 1993 and 1994. For the three-year performance period ended September 30, 1992, there was no payout under either the Corporation's or Allen-Bradley's plan as the minimum performance objectives were not met.

Compensation of the Chief Executive Officer

In July 1993 the Committee considered Mr. Beall's base salary which had been in effect since March 1992. Without com-mitting itself as to the timing of a future increase, it recognized Mr. Beall's expressed desire that an increase should not be authorized before March 1995 so that his total annual compensation would be more dependent on annual incentive compensation tied to the Committee's assessment of the Corporation's performance.

In November 1994, the Board of Directors adopted Corporate Governance Guidelines which provide for annual assessment by the Board, in executive session without the Chief Executive Officer's participation, of that officer's performance so that the Committee may use that evaluation in considering its action on the Chief Executive Officer's compensation.

In determining Mr. Beall's annual incentive compensation for 1994, the Committee took into account a number of factors the sum total of which it believed demonstrated unusually successful leadership. The Committee particulary considered that the Corporation exceeded each of its financial return goals for fiscal 1994, met over the last several years its share-owner value creation goal and made significant progress on each of its long-term leadership objectives. The Committee viewed these as significant achievements in a year that saw further contraction of defense spending, weak markets—some domestic, some foreign—for several of the Corporation's businesses, and successful downsizing and restructuring actions while concurrently committing necessary talent and resources to the long-term development of the Corporation's businesses. The Committee also took into account Mr. Beall's personal dedication to assuring that throughout the Corporation there is a clear commitment to customer responsiveness, quality, integrity and employment of the advanced management practices that are essential to long-term leadership of the Corporation's businesses and the enhancement of shareowner value.

In determining the number of options granted to Mr. Beall in fiscal year 1994 for future long-term incentives, the Committee took into account advice of independent compensation consultants, levels of option grants based on data from several surveys of other major U.S. industrial companies (his grant was slightly below the median of the companies surveyed according to one survey and slightly above the median according to another), data as to long-term compensation (e.g., options, restricted stock, performance plans) from selected peer companies, information on his total compensation and historical information regarding his long-term compensation opportunities together with the Committee's perception of Mr. Beall's past and expected future contributions to the Corporation's achievement of its long-term performance goals.

In December 1994, following the Committee's meeting, the Board of Executive Session received and discussed a report of the Committee that included an evaluation of the Corporation's and Mr. Beall's performance in the 1994 fiscal year and the Committee's actions as to Mr. Beall's incentive compensation for that year and long-term incentives granted to him in the form of stock options.

Compensation and Management Development Committee

William S. Sneath, *Chairman*

John D. Nichols

Richard M. Bressler

Bruce M. Rockwell

Robin Chandler Duke

Joseph F. Toot, Jr.

PROPOSAL TO APPROVE THE 1995 LONG-TERM INCENTIVES PLAN

A proposal will be presented to the meeting to approve the Corporation's 1995 Long-Term Incentive Plan (the Plan) which was adopted by the Board of Directors (with Mr. Beall, the only director eligible to participate in the Plan, not voting) on November 2, 1994, subject to approval by the shareowners of the Corporation.

The Plan would replace the Corporation's 1988 Long-Term Incentives Plan (the 1988 Plan), which has been previously adopted by the shareowners of the Corporation.

The new Plan is intended to continue to provide flexibility in adapting compensation of key employees to changes in the Corporation's business and in competitive compensation practices, as well as changes in pertinent tax and accounting provisions. The Plan would have the effect of increasing the shares available for grant of stock options or restricted stock, and for earned performance awards.

The purpose of the Plan is to foster creation of and enhance shareowner value by linking the compensation of officers and other key employees to increases in the price of the Corporation's stock or by offering the incentives of long-term monetary rewards to key employees of the Corporation or its business units directly linked to their contribution to shareowner value, thus providing means by which persons of outstanding abilities can be attracted, motivated and retained. The Plan is designed to permit the Corporation to make different types of grants to meet competitive conditions and changing circumstances.

The Plan authorizes the issuance or transfer of an aggregate of 16 million shares of Common Stock of the Corporation (Shares), provided that the total number of Shares as to which grants may be made under the Plan in any one fiscal year may not exceed 1 1/2% of the total outstanding and treasury shares. As of November 30, 1994, the closing price of the Common Stock as reported in the New York Stock Exchange—Composite Transactions was $33.875.

As of November 30, 1994, options to purchase 9,712,645 Shares were outstanding under the 1988 Plan, no performance units were outstanding under the 1988 Plan and 69,560 units were outstanding under supplementary performance plans for key employees of Allen-Bradley with respect to performance periods ending September 30, 1995 and 1996 as authorized by the 1988 Plan. In addition, payment was made on December 7, 1994 with respect to units granted under supplementary performance plans for a three-year performance period ending September 30,

1994. As of November 30, 1994, 1,150,136 Shares were available for grants under the 1988 Plan, 1,034,000 of which were granted to eligible employees on December 7, 1994. The balance of those Shares remain available for payments in respect of outstanding performance units under supplementary performance plans. In addition, as of November 30, 1994, options to purchase 587,071 Shares were outstanding under the Corporation's 1979 Stock Plan for Key Employees. No further options may be granted under those two plans. On December 7, 1994, options to purchase 706,950 Shares were granted to 597 persons (none of whom is a director or executive officer of the Corporation) under the Plan, subject to approval of the Plan by shareowners.

If the Plan is approved by shareowners, no subsequent grants of performance units, stock options or restricted stock will be made under the 1988 Plan. Outstanding performance units under supplementary performance plans with respect to performance periods not complete will remain eligible for payment in accordance with the 1988 Plan, outstanding stock options and stock appreciation rights under the 1988 Plan, the 1979 Plan and the 1981 Plan will remain exercisable in accordance with their terms, and stock appreciation rights related to outstanding stock options may be granted under any of those plans.

The Plan will be administered by the Compensation and Management Development Committee (the Committee), consisting of three or more members of the Board of Directors who are not eligible to participate in the Plan. In order to meet the requirements of Internal

Revenue Code Section 162(m), however, all grants under the Plan will be made by a Grant Committee consisting of those members of the Committee who are "outside directors" as defined for purposes of that section and regulations thereunder. In addition, the Board of Directors has authority to perform all functions of the Committee and the Grant Committee under the Plan.

The persons to whom grants are made under the Plan (Participants) will be selected from time to time by the Grant Committee in its sole discretion from among corporate officers and other key employees of the Corporation and its subsidiaries and affiliates. In selecting Participants and determining the type and amount of their grants, the Grant Committee may consider recommendations of the Chief Executive Officer of the Corporation and will take into account such factors as the Participant's level of responsibility, performance, performance potential, level and type of compensation and potential value of grants under the Plan.

The Plan permits grants to be made from time to time as performance units, nonqualified stock options, incentive stock options, stock appreciation rights and restricted stock. In addition, the Plan authorizes establishment of supplementary performance plans applicable to one or more business units of the Corporation.

Since it is within the discretion of the Grant Committee to determine which employees will receive grants under the Plan and the type and amount thereof, these matters cannot be specified at present. It is presently contemplated, however, that approximately 450 employees will be eligible to participate in performance plans established for various business units of the Corporation pursuant to the Plan, and approximately 625 employees, including Mr. Beall and the other Named Officers, will be eligible to receive grants of stock options, stock appreciation rights and restricted stock under the Plan. It is presently expected that executive officers, including Mr. Beall, would not initially participate in performance plans under the Plan unless an executive officer's principal accountability is the management of a single business unit.

It is not intended that the Plan would deprive the Board of Directors and the responsible officers of the Corporation of their authority to pay sales commission or make arrangements for other types of bonuses or incentive payments.

While the benefits that will be received by or allocated to employees eligible to receive grants under the Plan cannot be determined precisely, the following information on grants made December 7, 1994 under the 1988 Plan and the Plan may be generally indicative of annual grants under the Plan. Set forth below is information on grants made December 7, 1994 of stock options to purchase Shares pursuant to the 1988 Plan and the Plan and amounts that may be earned in respect of grants then made for the three-year performance cycle ending September 30, 1997 under business unit performance plans established pursuant to Section 4 of the Plan if the performance objectives for the respective performance plans are met, to (i) the Named Officers, (ii) the Named Officers and all other executive officers as a group, (iii) non-executive directors as a group and (iv) employees (other than executive officers) as a group.

Name and Position	Shares Underlying Options Granted	Grant Date Value[1]	Dollar Value of 100% Payout Awards for Three-Year Cycle Ending 9/30/97[2]
Donald R. Beall Chairman of the Board & Chief Executive Officer	240,000	$2,433,600	$ -0-
Kent M. Black Executive Vice President & Chief Operating Officer	105,000	1,064,700	-0-
Don H. Davis, Jr. Executive Vice President & Chief Operating Officer	105,000	1,064,700	-0-
Charles H. Harff Senior Vice President & Special Counsel	60,000	608,400	-0-
Sam F. Iacobellis Executive Vice President & Deputy Chairman for Major Programs	-0-[3]	-0-	-0-
All Executive Officers as a Group	791,300	8,023,782	392,500
All Non-Executive Directors as a Group	-0-	-0-	-0-
All Employees (Other Than Executive Officers) as a Group	949,650	9,629,451	23,606,500

(1) Valued under the Black-Scholes option pricing methodology, which produces a per option share value of $10.14 using the following assumptions and inputs: options exercised after 7 1/2 years, weighted five-year prior stock price volatility and dividend yield of 0.1835 and 3.11%, respectively, and an interest rate of 7.76% which was the zero coupon 7 1/2-year Treasury bond rate at time of grant. The actual value, if any, the employee may realize from these options will depend solely on the gain in stock price over the exercise price when the options are exercised. While the options have no value if the stock price does not increase, were the $10.14 present value of the options converted into a future stock price at the end of the 7 1/2-year period when it is assumed the options would be exercised, the shareowners of the approximately 217,790,000 shares outstanding on the grant date of those options (assuming that number of shares remains outstanding) would realize aggregate appreciation of $3,871.0 million compared to aggregate appreciation on the options of $9.1 million for the Named Officers (assuming that they held their options or the shares acquired on exercise thereof for the whole 7 1/2-year period).

(2) Amounts of potential awards (or equivalent dollar amount of awards expressed in units) that may be earned assuming all business units achieve (and do not exceed) their respective performance objectives and that there is no change in the market price of

the Corporation's Common Stock. Since the potential awards under the performance plans for some of the business units are not expressed in units and the unit values for those performance plans under which potential awards are expressed in units are not uniform, comparative information on numbers of units granted cannot usefully be presented.

(3) No options were granted to Mr. Iacobellis in view of his announced intention to retire at the end of March 1995.

Performance Plans

The Plan authorizes the establishment by the Committee of performance plans applicable to the Corporation or one or more of its business components. Each such plan must include provision for establishment of performance cycles (ending no later than September 30, 2005) of not less than three fiscal years and establishment of a performance measure and performance objectives based on criteria selected by the Committee for the Corporation or the affected business component and may provide for adjustment (up or down) of the performance objectives or modification of the performance measure, or both, if the Committee (or with its approval, the person or committee delegated to administer any plan except insofar as it relates to any executive officer) determines that conditions, involving changes in the economy, changes in law or government regulations, changes in generally accepted accounting principles or material acquisitions or divestitures, warrant. The Committee may authorize the Corporation's Chief Executive Officer to approve the definitive terms and conditions of any performance plan, including the employees or categories of employees eligible to participate in each performance plan, but the Committee's authorization is required for participation by any of the Corporation's executive officers in a performance plan. Potential awards under performance plans will be expressed as cash amounts and will be paid in cash unless the Committee decides that payment should be in Shares or a combination of Shares and cash.

Stock Options, Stock Appreciation Rights and Restricted Stock

The Plan authorizes grants to Participants of stock options, which may be either incentive stock options eligible for special tax treatment or nonqualified stock options, stock appreciation rights and restricted stock.

Under the provisions of the Plan authorizing the grant of stock options, (a) the option price may not be less than the fair market value of the Shares at the date of grant, (b) the aggregate fair market value (determined as of the date the option is granted) of the Shares for which any employee may be granted incentive stock options which are exercisable for the first time in any calendar year may not exceed $100,000, (c) stock options generally may not be exercised prior to one year nor after ten years from the date of grant and generally become exercisable in three approximately equal installments on the first, second and third anniversaries of the date of grant, and (d) at the time of exercise of a stock option the option price must be paid in full in cash or in Shares or in a combination of cash and Shares. It a participant who holds an outstanding stock option or stock appreciation right dies, the Plan permits the exercise thereof within three years of the date of death and even if it were not exercisable at such date.

The Plan permits the Committee to make determinations as to exercisability upon other termination of a Participant's employment.

The Plan permits the grant of stock appreciation rights related to a stock option (a tandem SAR), either at the time of the option grant or thereafter during the term of the option, or the grant of stock appreciation rights separate and apart from the grant of an option (a freestanding SAR). Tandem SARs permit an optionee, upon exercise of such rights and surrender of the relation option to the extent of an equivalent number of Shares, to receive a payment equal to the excess of the fair market value (on the date of exercise) of the portion of the option so surrendered over the option price of such Shares. Freestanding SAR's entitle the grantee, upon exercise of such rights to receive a payment equal to the excess of the fair market value (on the date of the exercise) of all or part of a designated number of Shares over the fair market value of such Shares on the date such rights were granted. Such payment may be made in Shares (valued on the basis of the fair market value of the Shares on the date of exercise of the stock appreciation rights), or in cash or partly in cash and partly in Shares, as the Committee may determine.

Under the Plan, the Grant Committee may also grant Shares subject to specified restrictions (restricted stock) to Participants in the Plan. Grants of restricted stock are subject to forfeiture if the grantee does not continue as an employee of the Corporation or a subsidiary or affiliate (i) for a period of three years or longer, as may be specified by the Grant Committee, from the grant date, or (ii) until performance criteria specified by the Grant Committee are met, except that in the event of a grantee's death, or retirement under a retirement plan of the Corporation after age 62 or becoming entitled to an unreduced benefit under the applicable retirement plan, before the end of the restricted period, the grantee's heirs or the grantee will be entitled to the Shares. In the case of a grantee whose employment terminates for any other reason before the end of the restricted period, the Committee, taking into account the purpose of the Plan and such other factors as in its sole discretion it deems appropriate, may waive the forfeiture of all or a portion of those Shares of restricted stock granted. During the restricted period, Shares of restricted stock have all the attributes of outstanding Shares, except that certificates for such Shares and dividends thereon are delivered to and held by the Corporation for the grantee's account. As and to the extent that Shares of restricted stock are no longer subject to forfeiture, certificates therefor and any dividends related thereto withheld by the Corporation, together with interest thereon as determined by the Board of Directors, are delivered to the grantee.

Under the Plan, stock options, freestanding SARs and restricted stock may not be granted after September 30, 2005, but tandem stock appreciation rights may be granted with respect to outstanding stock options granted before that date.

Other

During the period that stock appreciation rights are outstanding, the Corporation will accrue as an expense the amount, if any, by which the fair market value of the Shares as to which stock appreciation rights are expected to be exercised exceeds the exercise price of any related option Shares of the fair market value on the date of grant of the designated number of Shares for freestanding SARs.

Under various proposals being considered for adoption by the Financial Accounting Standards Board, publicly held issuers would be required to accrue compensation expense in respect of stock options granted to employees. The Corporation's management believes that the amounts of compensation expense it would be required to accrue if any of these proposals were adjusted would not have a material effect on the Corporation's financial statements.

In the event any change in or affecting Shares occurs, the Board of Directors may make appropriate amendments to or adjustments in the Plan or grants made thereunder, including changes in the number of Shares which may be issued or transferred under the Plan and the number of Shares and price per Share subject to outstanding options and stock appreciation rights.

In order to maintain the rights of participants in the event of a change of control of the Corporation, the Plan provides that unless prior to the occurrence of such a change the Board of Directors shall have determined otherwise by vote of at least two-thirds of its members, all performance cycles (except those under performance plans that do not provide for a change of control contingency) not then complete shall be deemed completed, the respective performance objectives shall be deemed to have been attained and all potential awards granted with respect thereto shall be deemed to have been fully earned; all outstanding stock options and stock appreciation rights then outstanding shall become fully exercisable whether or not otherwise then exercisable; and the restrictions on all Shares granted as restricted stock would lapse. A change of control is deemed to occur under the same circumstances as provided in Article III, Section 15(l)(1) of the Corporation's By-Laws, which provision was approved by the shareowners at the 1987 Annual Meeting.

The Board of Directors may at any time amend, suspend or terminate the Plan or grants made thereunder. It may not, however (except in making amendments and adjustments in the event of changes in or affecting Shares) (i) without the consent of the person affected, cancel or reduce any grant theretofore made other than as provided for or contemplated in the agreement evidencing the grant or (ii) without the approval of shareowners, change the class of persons eligible to receive incentive stock options under the Plan, increase the number of Shares that may be issued or transferred under the Plan, reduce the option exercise price of any stock option below the fair market value of the Shares covered thereby at the date of grant or decrease the forfeiture period for any restricted stock below that permitted under the Plan.

The Board of Directors recommends that you vote "FOR" the Proposal, which is presented as item (c).

SOURCE: 1995 proxy statement, Rockwell International Corporation. Reprinted by permission.

In Rockwell's case, there appears to be no formal bogey or cap with respect to the incentive compensation plan. Bonus at the rate of 2% is provided for the first $100 million of earnings (see page 318) and a bonus could theoretically increase indefinitely at the rate of 5% on earnings in excess of $175 million. However, an overall cap is provided by the provision that bonuses cannot exceed dividends declared for the year.

Furthermore, the bonus does not *automatically* go to the managers. Rather, an amount is deposited in an incentive fund which may not exceed the amounts calculated under the plan, as above. The compensation committee of the board of directors determines how much to put into the fund each year. Presumably, the compensation committee could impose a bogey and/or a cap at its discretion. More specifically, the committee will take into account the achievement of corporate goals and objectives for the year. These are based on the increase in earnings per share, return on equity, return on shares, and other specified objectives relating to R&D, divisional cooperation, and product development.

Rockwell is also proposing a new 1995 long-term incentives plan. This plan provides for the granting to executives and other senior employees of performance units, stock options, stock appreciation rights, and restricted stock. Note that performance units provide cash awards, but these are determined in relation to achievement of earnings and return on assets goals over a performance cycle of not less than three years. Stock options awarded under the plan are generally exercisable on the first, second, and third anniversaries of the award. Stock appreciation rights, payable in either shares or cash, give the awardee a payment equal to the increase in share price between the date of the award and the date of exercise. Restricted stock awards are subject to forfeiture if the grantee does not continue as an employee for at least three years after the grant.

The longer-run incentive horizon created by these awards should be clear. If incentives were based only on current earnings, as in the annual incentives portion of the plan, management might be tempted to increase earnings in the short run. This and other motivations for earnings management will be discussed in Chapter 11. While earnings management may be accomplished through accounting policy choices that do not affect cash flows, some earnings-increasing devices may be at the expense of the firm's longer-run interests. Such short-run tactics include deferral of maintenance, underinvestment in R&D, and premature disposal of facilities to realize a gain. Rockwell's long-term incentives plan will discourage dysfunctional policies such as these.

Note that for Rockwell's senior management, stock options are the primary long-term award. Options limit the downside risk to the manager, since the lowest they can be worth is zero. Also, under current accounting standards in both Canada and the United States, awarding of options does not generally result in an expense on the income statement.

The Rockwell incentive structure appears to be quite sophisticated in terms of its incentives, decision horizon, and risk properties. For our purposes, the most important point to note is that there are two main incentive components, cash bonus and stock, and these are based on both accounting- and market-based measures of performance. This gives management a vital interest in how net income is determined, both because it is a direct input into annual and long-term compensation and because, as we saw in Chapter 5, it affects share price.

We now turn to a more general consideration of executive compensation.

10.3 The Theory of Executive Compensation

In Chapter 9 we suggested that basing manager compensation on the payoff was often the only feasible way to motivate manager effort in the presence of moral hazard. From an accounting perspective, it seemed natural to regard net income as the payoff, so that the compensation contract was based on net income. Then, the properties of net income as a proxy for manager effort become important. Essentially, the higher the correlation between net income and effort the more efficient the contract, in the sense of lower agency costs. We suggested at the time that historical-cost-based net income may have desirable hardness qualities. Reasons were that historical cost net income tends to be more reliable, at least when markets do not work well, and less volatile in the sense that it is less subject than share price to economy-wide events that are out of manager control.

While this efficient contracting role for net income is on the right track, the Rockwell compensation plan suggests that real plans are more complex and detailed, involving a mix of incentive, risk, and decision horizon considerations. Consistent with Holmström's 1979 analysis (Section 9.5.1), it seems that net income must compete with other performance measures in compensation plans, just as it competes with other information sources for investors under efficient market theory. Consequently, an understanding of the role of net income in manager compensation plans is important to accountants. To the extent that accountants can improve the quality of net income for efficient contracting, this will enhance their competitive advantage as well as promote responsible manager performance.

A major problem of compensation contract design, however, is that the full impact on net income of current manager effort is usually not observable in time to form the basis of an incentive contract, despite our assumption that it was in Chapter 9. To see this, consider the payoff from manager effort exerted in the current period. Except under ideal conditions, net income lags the full payoffs from this effort. For example, profit on inventory acquired during the current period is not typically recognized if it is unsold at period-end, even though purchasing is part of current manager effort. Even for inventory sold, losses on credit sales for the period have to be estimated, despite marketing and credit policy being part of current effort.

This problem of payoff observability is even greater if we recognize that manager effort is a *set* of activities, rather than a single activity. Some of these activities have longer-run implications than others. For example, payoffs from effort devoted to advertising, capital expenditure, acquisitions, divestitures, R&D, etc. may not be known for years, yet managers must be compensated periodically. In effect, current net income captures the payoffs from some current manager activities later than others and may completely omit the payoffs from some of them.

Given these problems of using current net income as a payoff measure, we can see why share price might be a better measure. With efficient security markets, share prices will "properly reflect" all that is known about prospective payoffs from current manager actions. For example, share price will incorporate the future prospects of current R&D efforts, even though most R&D costs are written off currently under Section 3450. Furthermore, as we saw in Sections 5.3 and 5.4, share price includes the information content of net income itself.

Consequently, one might ask, why not base manager compensation only on share price? However, we should not write off accounting net income just yet. As mentioned previously, share price is affected by a host of economy-wide events such as interest rate changes, exchange rate movements, and trade agreements, which impose risks beyond those inherent in the firm's production processes themselves. Also, as discussed in Section 4.5, the presence of noise traders means that share prices do not perfectly aggregate even public information. Consequently, the use of share price as a payoff measure may impose excess risk on managers. To the extent that net income is relatively insensitive to economy-wide factors and to noise trading, the inclusion of both share price and net income in the compensation contract may be more efficient than including share price only. Indeed, this has been demonstrated by Bushman and Indjejikian (1992), Kim and Suh (1993), and Feltham and Xie (1994), whose analyses show that, in the presence of noise trading, the optimal contract includes both share price and net income as performance measures, *even though share price fully incorporates the information in net income.* These results are important, because they suggest that net income has a contracting role that goes beyond its role in informing investors.

Another reason for including net income in compensation contracts derives from recognizing manager effort as a set of activities, with both current and longer-term payoffs. The firm may wish to encourage some activities more than others. This would not be possible with share price as the only performance measure, since share price aggregates the expected payoffs from all activities. However, with both share price and net income as performance measures, the firm can adjust the relative proportions of each to exploit the fact that current net income includes the payoffs from only some manager activities in the current period. For example, suppose a firm wants to encourage the manager to undertake more R&D. Then, it can reduce the proportion of the manager's compensation on the basis of net income and increase the proportion on the basis of share price. Compensation will now rise more strongly from security market response to an increase in R&D, and there will be less compensation penalty from writing R&D costs off currently. Consequently, it will be in the manager's interest to increase R&D.

As another example, suppose that the firm has to cut costs in the short run. Net income will reflect the favourable cash flow effects of cost cutting quickly and accurately, perhaps even more so than share price, particularly if the cost-cutting measures are complex or constitute inside information, or the market is concerned about the longer-run effects of short-run cost cutting. Also, as mentioned, share price will not perfectly aggregate the cost-cutting information in the presence of noise trading. Then, the firm may wish to increase the weight of net income relative to share price in the manager's compensation.

In effect, when share price and net income differentially reflect the short- and long-run payoffs of current manager actions, the length of the manager's decision horizon can be controlled by the proportions of share-price-based and net-income-based compensation—more share-based produces a longer decision horizon and vice versa. This was demonstrated theoretically by Bushman and Indjejikian (1993), who also demonstrated that the risk-reducing role of net income remained in the presence of decision horizon considerations.

10.4   *The Role of Risk in Executive Compensation*

Regardless of the particular payoff measures included in the compensation plan, the manager typically bears risk with respect to his or her remuneration. Since managers, like other rational, risk-averse individuals, trade off risk and return, the more risk the managers bear the higher must be their *expected* compensation if reservation utility is to be attained. Thus, to motivate the manager at the lowest cost, designers of incentive compensation plans try to get the most motivation for a given amount of risk imposed or, equivalently, the least risk for a given level of motivation.

The reason why the amount of risk imposed by the incentive plan is so important is that managers cannot diversify compensation risk. Recall that investors can diversify firm-specific risk. However, managers cannot diversify their compensation risk by working for 10 different firms. Nor can they diversify by selling shares or options received under their compensation contracts, since this is usually restricted. The Rockwell plan, for example, limits managers' ability to exercise stock options, and grants of restricted stock are subject to forfeiture if the grantee does not continue as an employee for three years or longer. This implies that the grantee cannot sell these shares during this period.

Forcing managers to bear compensation risk is consistent with agency theory, which tells us that if unobservable effort is to be motivated the manager must be "under the gun" by bearing risk. Nevertheless, it may still be desirable to control risk, and there are a variety of ways whereby this can be accomplished. We have already seen, in the previous section, that inclusion of more than one performance measure in the compensation contract has risk-reduction properties.

Another factor in controlling risk is to limit the manager's **downside risk**. For example, the bogey of a bonus plan does this. That is, if the payoff is below the bogey the manager does not have to pay the firm. Also, stock options lower downside risk. While options have the potential for a considerable reward if the firm's stock price rises, the lowest they will be worth is zero. Limitation of downside risk is important, because managers do not have unlimited wealth, and fear of personal bankruptcy is probably not the best way to motivate a manager to work hard, the reason being that the manager may adopt only "safe" operating and investment strategies whereas shareholders' interests may be better served by riskier ones.

But, if downside risk is limited, it seems reasonable for upside risk to be limited too; otherwise the manager would have everything to gain and little to lose. This could lead to operating and investment strategies that are too risky for the shareholders' best interests. Thus, many compensation contracts impose caps on incentive remuneration as well as bogeys.

Another risk-reducing device is the filtering of managers' incentive pay through the compensation committee, as we saw in the Rockwell plan. The committee can take exceptional circumstances into account that a bonus formula could not. For example, suppose that a firm experiences a net loss for the year, but the loss is much less than that of other firms in the industry. The compensation committee may see fit to award a bonus even though the firm's payoff is below the bogey of the incentive plan.

More generally, **relative performance evaluation (RPE)** has the potential to reduce the manager's risk while maintaining incentives. The theory of RPE was developed by Holmström (1982). By setting bonuses or other incentive awards *relative* to the average performance of other firms in the industry, the systematic or common risk that the industry faces will be filtered out of the incentive plan, especially if the number of firms in the industry is large. Recall from agency theory that a hard performance measure is highly correlated with manager effort. Since managers cannot control economy- or industry-wide risks, basing the performance measure or measures on the difference between the firm's performance and the average performance of the industry will tighten up the correlation between effort and performance measure that is needed for an efficient contract. To see why, recall that net income is a noisy measure of firm performance (despite our argument above that it is less noisy than share price). In effect, the realization of random states of nature clouds the relationship between manager effort and firm performance (recall that, by definition, no one can control state realization), thereby imposing risk on the manager. But just as a consensus football forecast has qualities superior to those of individual forecasters (Section 4.2.2), so the average performance of firms in an industry has superior qualities as a measure of the impact of state realization on the firm. So basing the manager's compensation on firm performance relative to the industry average filters out the common industry and economy risk, leaving a performance measure that is more highly correlated with manager effort than net income itself, and hence less risky.

We can see the potential for RPE in the case of Massey-Ferguson Ltd. in Section 7.3.2. If Massey-Ferguson's management had been evaluated relative to other, similar, multinational firms, they may not have been as upset over SFAS 8 as they were, since the common exchange rate risk would have been filtered out and the resulting relative performance would have more closely reflected Massey-Ferguson's management's efforts in operating and financing the firm.

Despite the theoretical appeal of RPE, strong statistical evidence that managers are compensated this way has been hard to come by. Antle and Smith (1986) found weak evidence for RPE, and according to Pavlik, Scott, and Tiessen (1993) a survey of RPE articles shows that the ability of RPE to predict manager compensation is modest. A possible reason for the weak empirical support is given by Sloan (1993), who argues, as we have above, that net income is insensitive to economy-wide risks; therefore, inclusion of net income as a performance measure in addition to share price shields manager compensation from these economy-wide effects. As a result, RPE is not needed, since basing compensation on both share price and net income accomplishes a similar result.

The theory of executive compensation suggests, then, that the relative proportions of share-price-based and net-income-based incentives are critical in the attainment of an efficient compensation contract. This raises the question of whether real compensation plans are designed as the theory suggests. This was studied by Lambert and Larcker (1987) (LL). Using a sample of 370 U.S. firms over 1970–84 inclusive, LL investigated the relative ability of return on shares and return on equity to explain managers' cash compensation (salary plus bonus). If, for example, compensation plans and compensation committees primarily use return on shares as a payoff measure, then return on shares should be significantly related to compensation. Alternatively, if they primarily use net income as the payoff measure, return on equity (a ratio based on net income) should be significantly related to compensation.

LL found that return on equity was more highly related to cash compensation than was return on shares. Indeed, several other studies have found the same thing. This supports the risk-reduction and decision-horizon-controlling roles for net income in compensation plans that was suggested in Section 10.3.

LL also found that the relationship of these two payoff measures to cash compensation varied in systematic ways. For example, they showed that the relationship between return on equity and cash compensation strengthened when net income was less noisy relative to return on shares. They measured the relative noisiness of net income by the ratio of the variability of return on equity over 1970–84 to the variability of return on shares over the same period. The lower the noise in net income (implying a lower number of states of nature affecting net income that the manager cannot control), the higher its correlation with effort. This finding is consistent with agency theory, which suggests that a good performance measure *should* be highly correlated with effort.

LL also found that managerial compensation for growth firms' executives tended to have a lower relationship with return on equity than average. This is also consistent with the correlation argument, since, for growth firms, net income is a relatively poorer indicator of manager effort than it is for the average firm. Historical-cost-based net income tends particularly to lag behind the real economic performance of a growth firm, because this basis of accounting does not recognize value increases until they are realized. The efficient market, however, will look through to the real economic performance and value the shares accordingly. Thus, LL argue, return on equity should be less highly related to compensation than share return for such firms, which is what they found.

10.5 The Politics of Executive Compensation

The question of manager compensation has been a longstanding one in the United States and Canada. Many have argued that top managers are overpaid, especially in comparison to those in other countries, such as Japan.

In 1990, Jensen and Murphy (JM) published a controversial article about top manager compensation. They argued that CEOs were not overpaid, but that their compensation was far too unrelated to performance, where performance was measured as the change in the firm's market value (that is, the change in shareholder wealth). They examined the salary plus bonus of the CEOs of the 250 largest U.S. corporations over the 15 years from 1974 to 1988. For each year, they added the current year's and next year's salary and bonus and found that on average the CEOs received an extra 6.7 cents' compensation over the two years for every $1,000 increase in shareholder wealth. When they added in other compensation components, including stock options and direct share holdings, the CEOs still received only $2.59 per $1,000 increase in shareholder wealth.

Other aspects of JM's investigation were consistent with these findings. For example, the variability (as measured by the standard deviation) over time of CEOs' and regular workers' compensations were almost the same. JM concluded that CEOs did not bear enough risk to motivate good performance, and consequently recommended larger stock holdings by managers. With respect to the Rockwell plan, note from Exhibit 10.1 that there are guidelines which require substantial stock holdings. For example, the CEO must hold shares with a market value of eight times base salary.

Some counterarguments can be made to JM.[1] First, we would *expect* the relationship between pay and performance to be low for large firms, simply because of a size effect. Suppose that a large corporation increased in value by $2 billion last year (for example, Chrysler Corp.'s 1993 profit was approximately $2.4 billion). An increase of even 1% of this amount in the CEO's remuneration would be large enough to attract media attention.

Second, for large corporations at least, it is difficult to put much downside risk on an executive. An executive whose pay is highly related to performance would have so much to lose from even a small decline in firm value that this would probably lead to excessive avoidance of risky projects, as discussed above. If, in addition, upside risk is limited, this means a low pay-performance relationship. Despite these considerations, it does seem that the Rockwell incentive structure has considerable downside risk. From Exhibit 10.1 we see that executives of two units that failed to meet their 1994 performance objectives earned only one-quarter of competitive annual incentive compensation. Also, we are told that, with respect to the long-term incentives plan, there was no payment for the three-year performance period ending in 1994, as minimum performance objectives were not met. It seems that Rockwell has heeded JM's advice about the bearing of risk.

It should also be pointed out that the value of a given amount of compensation to a manager is lower than it might appear at first glance. Much of compensation is granted in the form of shares and options. But since the right to freely sell these is usually restricted, as we saw in the case of Rockwell, they are worth less to the manager than their current market value. The more risk-averse the manager, the greater this reduction in value.

Furthermore, restrictions on disposal also mean that the Black-Scholes option pricing formula (see Section 6.5.5) cannot be used in place of market value to estimate the value of stock options to the executive. To illustrate, Lambert, Larcker, and Verrecchia (1991) calculated the cash-equivalent value to a manager of 10,000 options with a Black-Scholes value of $351,260. If the manager is moderately risk-averse and if 50% of the manager's wealth is tied to the firm's stock price, the value of the options to the manager is only $152,300, according to their calculations.[2] If the manager is highly risk-averse this value falls to $65,900. Note from Exhibit 10.1 that Rockwell values options to executives at their Black-Scholes value. While this may represent the opportunity cost to the firm, it exceeds their value to the managers.

Finally, there are other mechanisms than incentive contracts to align manager and shareholder interests, and these reduce the need for compensation to be highly related to firm value changes. For example, the **managerial labour market** will continuously evaluate CEO performance. Managers who do not perform will not only see their reputations suffer; the salary they can expect should they change jobs or be fired will also be reduced, thereby reducing their reservation utility. Also, the **takeover market** will monitor performance. A poorly performing CEO may find his or her firm the object of a takeover bid.

SOURCE: Jim Berry. Reprinted by permission of Newspaper Enterprise Association.

Despite these counterarguments, studies such as JM's have strengthened the longstanding concern about executive salaries. The following cartoon reflects this concern.

Of course, if labour and takeover markets are to work well, they must know how much compensation the manager is receiving. It is interesting to note that in 1993 the Ontario Securities Commission adopted new regulations to require firms to give more disclosure of their executive compensation. These regulations are similar to those of the SEC (1992) in the United States, under which Rockwell Corporation (Section 10.2) reports. For example, a detailed explanation of the compensation of firms' five highest-paid executives is required, as is a report from the compensation committee justifying the pay levels. Exhibit 10.1 illustrates Rockwell's disclosure under these regulations. Presumably, the securities commissions feel that if shareholders and others have enough information to intelligently evaluate manager compensation levels and components, they will take appropriate action if these appear out of line. Whether these measures will suffice to stem the criticism or whether stronger action will be taken (for example, to limit the amount of manager compensation deductible for tax purposes) remains to be seen. Indeed, this has already happened in the Unites States—see Rockwell's discussion in Exhibit 10.1.

10.6 Summary

Executive compensation contracts involve a delicate balancing of incentives, risk, and decision horizon. To properly align the interests of managers and shareholders, an efficient contract needs to achieve a high level of motivation while avoiding the imposition of too much risk on the manager. Too much risk can have dysfunctional consequences such as shortening a manager's decision horizon, adoption of earnings-increasing tactics that are against the firm's longer-run interests, and avoidance of risky projects. Managers are particularly sensitive to risk, because they cannot diversify it away as can shareholders.

To attain proper alignment, incentive plans usually feature a combination of salary, bonus, and various types of stock plans including options. These components of compensation are usually based on two performance measures—net income and share price. We can think of these as two noisy measures of the unobservable payoff from current-period manager effort. Theory predicts that the relative proportion of each in the compensation plan depends on both their relative accuracy as performance measures and the length of manager decision horizon that the firm wants to motivate. Empirically, it appears that executive compensation is related to performance but that the strength of the relationship is low. However, for large firms at least, this low relationship is to be expected. Also, the relative proportion of net-income-based and share-price-based compensation components seems to vary as the theory predicts.

Executive compensation is surrounded by political controversy. Recently, regulators have responded by expanding the information available to shareholders and others, on the assumption that they will take action to eliminate inefficient plans, or the managers and firms that have them. Whether this is sufficient to reduce compensation concerns remains to be seen.

Notes

1. These arguments are based on R. A. Lambert and D. F. Larcker, "Firm Performance and the Compensation of Chief Executive Officers," working paper, January 1993.

2. Recall that the expected utility of a risk-averse individual declines with risk, holding expected value constant. The interpretation of the $152,300 is that the manager would be indifferent between a riskless payment of $152,300 and options with an expected value of $351,260. The options are risky because their market value will fluctuate with the value of the underlying shares and, because of restrictions laid down in the compensation contract, the manager cannot avoid this risk by selling them. A similar interpretation applies to the $65,900.

Questions and Problems

1. Below is a portion of a 1995 proxy form sent to shareholders of Miracle Corporation. It reveals that Miracle has a bonus plan for its three senior executives which allocates them 10% of before-tax profits. Also, under the Employee Stock Option Plan, share options up to 12% of capitalization may be granted to directors or employees.

MIRACLE CORP.

Executive and Management Compensation

The Corporation's five executive officers were remunerated, in total, $440,000 by way of fees, salaries and bonuses for the fiscal year ended May 31, 1995.

Included in the aforesaid sum was $280,000 paid to the three senior execu-tive officers as full-time employees of the Corporation, pursuant to individual four-year Management Agreements made between the Corporation and those senior executive officers, effective June 1, 1993. Under the terms of the Agreements, the three senior executives are entitled to receive an aggregate bonus of 10% of before-tax profits earned by the company and their base salaries are to be increased 10% per year. For the 1995 fiscal year, the three senior executive officers waived their bonus entitlements to the extent that each received dividends on shares of the Corporation held by them which dividend was declared and paid for the fiscal year ended May 31, 1995.

It is to be noted that the Directors have adopted a form of Employee Stock Option Plan under which share options of up to 12% of the capitalization of the Corporation may be granted to Directors or employees. There are presently reserved, to that end, 930,000 common shares of the Corporation; but the Corporation has not granted any option to any Director or employees as of the date of this Information Circular.

Required

a. Explain the reason for the 10% bonus plan for senior executives. Are there any dysfunctional consequences of the bonus plan? Why is it based on before-tax profits, rather than after-tax?

b. Explain why there is also an Employee Stock Option Plan.

c. To what extent would the bonus plan cause management to be concerned about accounting policies and changes in GAAP?

2. Agency theory suggests that one way to motivate managers to act in the best interests of the owners/shareholders is to link managerial compensation to firms' payoffs, such as net income or share returns. However, such a linkage imposes additional risk on the manager.

Required

a. Why is it important to control or reduce some of the risk thus imposed on managers? Explain.

b. Discuss *two* methods by which risk imposed on the managers could be reduced.

c. Many managerial compensation packages impose restrictions on *when* managers can sell off stocks granted to them as a part of their compensation. For example, some compensation packages indicate that stocks may be forfeited unless the manager continues to work for the firm for a certain number of years after the granting of the stock. Discuss the justification behind such restrictions.

d. Inclusion of shares and options in managerial compensation packages has been attributed to the desire of the owners/shareholders to provide managers an incentive to undertake policies which benefit the firm's long-term rather than short-term interests. If this is true, why not compensate the manager only on the basis of share return (for example, only by stock options)? In other words, under these circumstances, what is the justification for having a cash or a bonus element in the compensation package?

(CGA-Canada)

3. An article entitled "Study of CEOs' Compensation Finds Surprises" appeared in the *Wall Street Journal* on November 18, 1991. The article describes the findings of a study done on executive pay by Graef S. Crystal, a professor at the University of California at Berkeley, who looked at "the 1990 compensation of 1,000 chief executives." Professor Crystal "concludes that while 30% of the difference in executives' pay can be traced to company size, 'no more than 4% can be accounted for by differences in company performance.'" Thus, the article documents a very low pay-performance relationship for the companies studied. This prompted Ralph Whitworth, president of the United Shareholders Association that sponsored the study, to say: "There's just no correlation between pay and performance."

    According to the article, "Mr. Crystal takes the exercise another step, tallying up the 1,000 executives' pay and redistributing it to those whom the study showed to be more deserving." For example, the article points out that David Glass, an executive at Wal-Mart Stores Inc., received $980,000 in pay. However, according to the study Mr. Glass should have received $11 million due to the retailer's size and growth.

    On the other hand, Time Warner Inc.'s co-chiefs, Steven Ross and N. J. Nicholas, together amassed almost $100 million in compensation, which was "heavily bolstered by money made in the merger of their respective companies." However, according to the study Mr. Ross and Mr. Nicholas should have received a combined $2.5 million.

    Required

    a. What are the problems of measuring company performance in a study such as this? In your answer, include problems with both stock-based and net-income-based performance measures.

    b. What reasons are there why we would expect a low pay-performance relationship for large corporations?

4. An article entitled "Former Critic of Big Stock Plans for CEOs Now Supports Them" that appeared in the *Wall Street Journal* on December 16, 1992 describes a study of executive compensation that found firms with a higher "pay-performance sensitivity" produced higher returns for shareholders.

    According to the article, the United Shareholders Association, a Washington shareholder-rights group which once criticized the use of stock and/or stock options as a form of compensation for top executives, has now changed its tune. Now its spokespersons believe that "stock-based pay" is the best way to motivate top executives "to boost the value of a company's stock and, therefore, the payoff for shareholders."

The Association's new view comes from a study conducted by Kevin J. Murphy, an associate professor with Harvard Business School, who "suggests that companies that reward executives for stock-price increases with stock-based pay consistently perform better than those that don't."

The Murphy study, based on the 1,000 largest U.S. companies, "calculates how much the top U.S. chief executive officers earned in 1991 for each $1,000 their shareholders as a group gained in stock-price appreciation and dividends." Furthermore, the study "ranks the results" of every chief executive on a "pay-performance sensitivity" basis.

According to the article, the study found that Philip H. Knight of Nike Inc. was at the top of the "pay-performance sensitivity" because he earned $680.77 per $1,000 change in shareholder value. On the other hand, John E. Lobbia of Detroit Edison Co. was at the bottom of the "pay-performance sensitivity" for earning only two cents for each $1,000. Also, "the median sensitivity level was $5.44 per $1,000."

The study concluded that those "companies with higher sensitivity levels— whose chief executives had greater stock incentives ...—produced higher returns for shareholders over the past one, five and 10 years."

However, the article points out that there is no conclusive proof of the theory that larger "incentives" produce better "performance." Indeed, there has been some criticism of the study from companies that have low "pay-performance sensitivity" rankings. They argue that the study did not effectively take into account other "incentive plans that aren't stock based or ... tied to measures other than stock-price improvement." For example, Detroit Edison Co., the company with the lowest ranking, made a comment that it has had high shareholder returns in past years even though it lacks financial rewards for its CEO.

Required

a. Explain why basing executive compensation on a stock-price-based performance measure implicitly assumes security market efficiency.

b. According to the article, the study cautions that the finding of a positive sensitivity-return association does not prove that higher sensitivity *causes* higher returns to shareholders. Use the theory of executive compensation to explain how there might in fact be a causal link.

c. Presumably, the author of the study controlled for firm size and risk before reaching his conclusion. Explain how firm size could affect pay-performance sensitivity, other things being equal. Do the same for firm risk.

d. The United Shareholders Association seems to now support share price as a performance measure, instead of "long used" measures such as earnings per share, which provide "only a weak incentive for an executive to boost shareholder value." Do you agree? In your answer, consider the problem of controlling the executive's time horizon.

5. An article entitled "SEC to Push for Data on Pay of Executives" that appeared in the *Wall Street Journal* on January 21, 1992 describes pressures from the SEC to give more information to shareholders about the value of stock options granted to senior executives. The SEC proposals are "designed to allow investors to compare executive pay plans from company to company." "Stock options ... [are] often ... clouded by legal and financial jargon in the proxy statements sent to shareholders."

According to the article, the proposals, being brought forward by SEC Chairman Richard Breeden, "would require companies to use a specific method of valuing all stock options granted to senior officials." In this regard, "SEC economists will be studying options-pricing models to determine which one best reflects the value of options and should be made the standard for all proxy statements."

Required

Explain how better disclosure of the value of stock options awarded to executives could result in more efficient executive compensation contracts. Include the role of the managerial labour market in your answer.

6. In 1993, the OSC implemented new executive compensation disclosure rules (OSC, Form 40, Securities Act, Regulation 638/93). These require that shareholder proxy statements contain tables spelling out compensation for the five highest-paid executives, plus a report from the board's compensation committee explaining the firm's compensation practices.

Required

a. To what extent do you think that such disclosure requirements will assist the proper operation of an efficient managerial labour market? Explain.

b. If the managerial labour market is efficient (that is, analogously to an efficient securities market), would manager incentive plans based on risky performance measures such as share price and reported net income be needed? Explain why or why not.

7. An article entitled "Taking Stock—Big Firms Rely More on Options But Fail to End Pay Criticism" that appeared in the *Wall Street Journal* on March 11, 1992 describes the emphasis in many firms on issuing stock options to executives. According to the article, stock options "tend to be generous" when measured at their face value, defined as the number of shares awarded under option times the market price of the stock on the date the option is granted.

The article points out that Anthony Luiso, chairman of International Multifoods Corp., "talked its board into tripling his option grants in exchange for forgoing $1 million in pay over five years."

The article states that stock options have become very appealing, because they allow companies to decrease their large cash compensation packages for executives in exchange for stock options. Companies tell their executives that they "won't benefit unless ordinary stockholders do."

There has been some criticism about granting stock options as compensation. For instance, David Norr, an investment advisor who testified before a Senate subcommittee, states "that it is [not] necessary to provide options to retain and attract people." Furthermore, he believes that being a CEO at a major corporation should be incentive enough. Even Mr. Luiso, mentioned earlier, cannot say that stock options give him incentive to improve his performance: "I can't sit here and say if I didn't have this [stock option] program, then my decision-making process would be less good than it is now."

Furthermore, "some experts suggest tying option grants to achieving some corporate goals. The options would become available to executives only when the company, for example, improved its return on equity." Some companies such as AT&T have adopted a plan whereby stock options are granted at a higher price than the market price on the date the option is granted. Thus, the executive would only be rewarded when the stock price rises above this higher price.

Required

a. The article states that stock options are "the fastest growing segment of executive pay." Why do firms issue options, in addition to or in place of other components of executive compensation?

b. Explain why the value of options to an executive may be less than the face value of the award.

c. Do you agree that options do not cost the company anything? Explain.

d. According to the article, "most option plans reward executives for success but don't penalize them for failure." Discuss the incentive effects of this aspect of options.

8. An article entitled "FASB Moves to Make Firms Deduct Options" that appeared in the *Wall Street Journal* on April 8, 1993 states that the FASB has proposed to charge the value of stock options given to executives and employees "against a company's earnings when they are granted rather than [when] exercised." The FASB will not implement "its proposal until 1997 financial statements, at the earliest." Meanwhile, the FASB "proposed that companies disclose options' value by adding a footnote to their 1994 financial statements at the earliest." According to the article, there is a lot of opposition coming from companies, compensation consultants, and major accounting firms. The Board realizes that this new rule will cause a lot of problems especially for "start-up or small high-technology companies." These companies count on attracting top executives by giving them stock options instead of high salaries which they cannot afford.

In addition, Alan Johnson, managing director of Johnson Associates Inc., a compensation consulting firm, suggests that " 'the people who will be hurt are not the fat cats' at the top of the corporate ladder" but those who are at middle management and lower. Michael Halloran, a partner with consultants Strategic Compensation Associates, states that "most major employers would still offer stock options to top management because that's where 'there is the most impact' on individual performance."

Required

a. Are the reactions of many firms, even to the point of economic consequences to cancel existing employee stock option plans, consistent with security market efficiency? Explain. Why do you think management is so opposed to the FASB proposal?

b. The article suggests that few firms would cancel stock option plans for top management. Explain why.

c. How would you measure the cost to the firm of stock options awarded to top managers? Justify your answer.

d. The article suggests that start-up and small high-technology companies would be hardest hit. Why might executive compensation plans for such firms particularly rely on share-price-based performance measures, such as options, rather than accounting-based performance measures?

9. The article here reproduced, "American Accounting: Optional," appeared in *The Economist* (October 17, 1992). It describes some of the problems of determining the cost of executive stock options and of convincing firms to deduct this cost on their income statements.

AMERICAN ACCOUNTING: OPTIONAL

Here are three things guaranteed to irritate American businessmen: tougher rules on corporate disclosure; accounting changes that cut reported earnings per share; and anything at all that encourages talk about how much big bosses are paid. The current debate over the correct accounting treatment of stock options rolls all three into one. So expect more howls as America's Financial Accounting Standards Board (FASB) steps closer to a firm ruling that companies must treat stock options as an expense in their profit and loss accounts.

An option gives its holder the right to buy shares at a fixed price over a fixed period. It also requires its issuer to sell shares at that price, on request, even if shares in the market have climbed meanwhile to undreamed-of heights. The accounting difficulties lie in measuring the cost to the firm of issuing these options and in deciding where to put that cost in the accounts.

However those questions are resolved, tougher rules would have little effect on most firms. A typical Fortune 500 company probably grants options each year equivalent to only 1% of its total equity—though, since the average option runs for six years, outstanding options may come to equal 6% of equity. But the FASB's thinking threatens a widespread hope that options will play a bigger role in future, putting zip into the performance of middle managers as well as bosses. Many executives are piqued because they think the reform politically motivated.

They may have a point. The debate began with the recent row over bosses' pay. In February Carl Levin, a Democratic senator from Michigan, put forward a bill obliging the Securities and Exchange Commission (SEC) to require options to be valued, with a view of setting them off against revenues.

The SEC dithered. It hinted that new disclosure rules on executive pay would require stock options to be valued. But when the rules appeared in the summer, mandatory valuation had been dropped. Then up popped the FASB's chairman, Dennis Beresford, to say that, after years of handwringing over technical complexities, his board was to unveil its own proposals.

Mr. Beresford, a scholarly accountant, will have a hard time selling them. The Business Council, a powerful association of chief executives, gave him a chilly reception at Hot Springs, Virginia on October 10th. When he suggested that it might be a healthy sign if the chief executives were "sullen but not mutinous," he was bluntly told that they were both. The FASB has received more than 200 letters, even though its draft proposals have not yet been circulated.

Critics argue that the change is unnecessary, will not work and would be damaging. It is impossible, they say, to value options correctly, and wrong to reflect "opportunity cost" in actual profit and loss. For pricing the options, the obvious model seems to be the one developed by Fischer Black and Myron Scholes, two Wall Street economists. It is widely used in the options markets, but it has its critics. The FASB's current plan is to let companies themselves decide on the value of their options, taking specified factors into account. Firms would then have to treat that amount as an expense, charging it off between the date on which the option is granted and that on which it can first be exercised.

Among those grumbling loudest at such ideas are companies like PepsiCo, a soft-drinks giant, and General Mills, a food manufacturer, which have used options to top up most staff salaries. But lobbyists for small businesses and venture capitalists are also distressed. As one chief executive pointed out to Mr. Beresford at Hot Springs, Microsoft, the wonder software company, might only just be emerging into profit if it had been required to set off all its employee stock options against revenues.

A striking point—but does it weaken the case for new rules? The FASB is clearly intent on devising a standard with plenty of let-out clauses and transitional arrangements. But it has spent so much time on technical details that it is unlikely to yield ground on the basic idea. When options are given to an employee, a company has shouldered an additional cost that must be reflected somewhere. Mr. Beresford expects plenty of dire warnings about what will happen to the use of options once their cost is more openly acknowledged. But the accountants, he says, must tell it the way it is.

SOURCE: *The Economist*, October 17, 1992. © 1992 The Economist Newspaper Group, Inc. Reprinted with permission. Further reproduction prohibited.

Required

a. Explain why the Black-Scholes option pricing formula may not be suitable for determining the cost of executive stock options.

b. Use the three hypotheses of positive accounting theory to predict which firms would be most opposed to the FASB proposal for expensing stock options.

c. Given that net income does not exist as a well-defined economic construct under non-ideal conditions, explain whether you agree with FASB chairman Beresford's statement that accountants must "tell it the way it is."

10. Another common component of executive compensation plans, in addition to stock options, is the **restricted stock plan**. Under such a plan, firms award a manager shares at no cost to the manager, under the restriction that they are subject to forfeiture if the executive leaves the firm within a stipulated period of time. The Rockwell compensation plan reviewed in Section 10.2 includes such a plan, in addition to options. According to *Top Executive Compensation: 1989 Edition* (New York, N.Y.: The Conference Board, Inc., 1989)—published at about the same time as the article by Graef S. Crystal reproduced here, which appeared in *Fortune* (August 28, 1989)—a significant minority of companies has restricted stock plans for top executives, ranging from 41% of firms in the energy industry to 17% in utilities. Thus, such plans are an important component of executive compensation.

In the *Fortune* article, the author's argument is that "loser" firms still want to pay high executive compensation. To do this, they grant restricted stock instead of options, since options of loser companies have little value. The author seems to imply that restricted stock does not have sufficient incentive power to motivate executives to "turn around" the losers. As a result, the presence of a restricted stock plan is a tipoff of a loser company.

INCENTIVE PAY THAT DOESN'T WORK

Psst, Buddy, want a hot tip on the stock market? Well, whenever a company adopts a restricted-stock plan for its executives, you get out of that stock fast and invest in some other company that doesn't grant restricted stock. You may not make a killing in a single year, but over the long run you're almost sure to beat the market averages.

That advice emerges from a study I recently conducted of 161 major U.S. corporations. These were the companies I analyzed for this magazine's annual survey of CEO compensation (June 5), a group that comprised the top 100 from both the Fortune 500 and Fortune Service 500, minus companies with negative net worths, foreign corporate owners, or CEOs who served less than a year. Of these 161 companies, 61 grant restricted stock to their CEOs (and probably to other executives too). The remaining 100 do not. In general, the companies that grant restricted stock perform worse than the others, not only in return to shareholders but by a whole range of other measures as well.

What *is* restricted stock, and why should it be important to investors and not just specialists in executive compensation? To answer that question, let's go back to the 1950s and 1960s, when it was the rare company that used anything other than stock options as long-term incentive compensation. Under a classic stock option grant, the executive received the right, but not the obligation, to buy the company's stock during a ten-year period. The price he was required to pay on exercise of the option (the strike price) was the market value of a share on the day the option was granted. Obviously, if the price rose above that level, he could exercise his option and sell the shares for an immediate and risk-free gain.

Stock options offer at least some linkage between company performance and executive reward. After all, the executive doesn't make a nickel unless the stock price improves after the grant of his options. On the other hand, Warren Buffett, keen investor that he is, has observed that executives and shareholders part company when the market declines. The shareholders suffer a fall in the value of stock they bought with real money, while the executive walks away unharmed. That argument is perhaps a bit overdrawn, since the executive does sustain an opportunity loss. But then, an opportunity loss is the same as a real loss only to an economist, and not to the rest of us.

Options may sound pretty good to an executive, but what if the only place his company could compete were for best-of-breed at the local kennel club? What if his company's performance were so leaden that getting its stock price aloft would be like trying to fly the Spruce Goose? Forget about granting stock options, because they are literally not worth the paper they're printed on. But restricted stock—ah, now that looks like the ticket.

THE REAL PRICE OF RESTRICTED STOCK

Companies that award it trailed the rest over five years by these percentages:

Total return to investors	−16%
Sales growth rate	−32%
Net profit margin	−18%
Cash flow margin	−15%
Return on average equity	−28%
Return on average investment	−23%
Return on average assets	−27%
Growth in return on average investment	−15%
Growth in return on average assets	−16%

These are results from a study of 161 companies from the Fortune 500 and Service 500. An even 100 don't grant restricted stock; the rest ... do.

With restricted stock, the effective strike price is conveniently reduced all the way to zero. The company simply gives the executive the shares with the restriction that he may not sell them for a specified period, generally five years. In the meantime, he gets the dividends and can vote the shares. (Some companies use slight variations, for example offering equivalent sums of cash without issuing actual shares; I consider these the same as restricted stock.) Hence, he no longer has to lie awake nights trying to invent yet another strategy for increasing shareholder returns. To be sure, his stock may be worth more if he does. But even if he doesn't, he can still cash in. Unless he's a real worry-wart and gets insomnia over the possibility that his company will go belly up, he can't lose with restricted stock.

Not every company that adopts a restricted-stock program is a lousy performer. Witness Paramount Communications and Coca-Cola. Both grant restricted stock to their CEOs, and both have produced superior shareholder returns. But these are exceptions to an overwhelming trend.

For proof, check the table, which shows how the restricted-stock companies in this group underperformed the others. They returned less to shareholders and scored worse in several other important categories, including return on equity and return on assets. Data given are for the past five years, but the time period isn't critical. Look at sales growth or total return to investors for the past three years, or the past ten, and the same story comes through: This group is a loser.

Other facts, not reflected in the table, reinforce this conclusion:

- Not only do the losers earn considerably lower returns on their investment than the winners, but also, as each year passes, they seem to drop even further behind.
- Growth among the losers, whether in sales, in earnings, or in return on investment, is more volatile. One reason is that the losers have a higher ratio of debt to equity. If you like to ride on roller coasters, keep your money on the losers. But keep some Rolaids handy too.

- The losers are less able to find profitable ways to reinvest shareholders' earnings, so they pay out more of those earnings in dividends.
- The market truism about higher risk accompanying higher reward doesn't apply. The winners here earn their higher shareholder returns with exactly the same beta—a measure of stock price volatility, and therefore risk—as the losers.

Why should any of this be? While statistical analysis reveals the trend, it doesn't explain it. But a certain perverse explanation seems apparent. If a company's stock is rising, the board of directors can grant stock options to top executives and expect to see them well rewarded. Even if the stock is falling but directors expect it to turn around, options should pay off. But if the company is going nowhere and directors don't expect much change, then one way to make sure executives will collect on their incentive plan is to give them restricted stock. This assumes, of course, that directors for some reason want to give executives a great deal of money even when the company is performing badly.

That may not make sense. But after 23 years advising boards of hundreds of America's largest corporations, I must report that this is what a lot of directors want to do. In a way, therefore, it makes perfect sense that restricted-stock companies on the whole perform worse than others. That's why they award restricted stock in the first place.

One more thing: The losers pay their CEOs a lot more than the winners. Add together the base salary and bonus of the CEOs and it turns out that the average loser pays 12% more than the average winner. Add together base salary, bonus, and annualized long-term incentive values, and the average loser pays 41% more than the average winner. Now we know at least one reason the losers are losers. They pay their top executives too much.

So don't fall asleep next time you pick up a proxy statement. Read that remuneration section thoroughly. And look for those two little words, restricted stock. There's gold in those words.

SOURCE: Graef S. Crystal, "Incentive Pay That Doesn't Work," *Fortune,* August 28, 1989. Reprinted by permission of the author and *Fortune.* © 1989 Time Inc. All rights reserved.

Required

a. The article claims a general tendency of company directors to continue to reward executives even when the firm is performing badly. What reason is there to limit downside compensation risk for the manager of a large firm?

b. In a sense, the results seem almost "too good to be true." While the author controls for dividend payout ratio and risk of his sample firms, can you think of possible reasons why you would hesitate to avoid investing in firms simply because they have a restricted stock plan?

11. In the article here reproduced, which appeared in the *Wall Street Journal* (August 28, 1992), Gregg A. Jarrell argues against stock-price-based executive

incentive plans on the grounds that a five-year average of net income (actually, earnings per share, and other accounting performance measures) is just as highly correlated with market stock returns as is the return on the market portfolio.

TAKE THE LONG VIEW ON EXECUTIVE PAY

The furor around the Securities and Exchange Commission's current proposals on executive compensation is just the newest twist in a debate over how the management of publicly held companies should be paid.

In this debate, two schools have prevailed. The traditional school argues that incentives should be based on company performance of the kind reported in financial statements—earnings per share or return on assets. The traditionalists shy away from linking annual compensation to stock prices because stock prices are often pushed up or down by external economic factors such as interest rates.

The newer school, represented on this issue by the United Shareholder Association, says executive pay should be linked strongly to stock prices. This activist school says a tight link will lead executives to serve shareholders better—in the language of the trade, it will serve "to align" the interests of shareholder and management. The activist view is gaining ground.

But my recent research backs up the traditionalists. The research shows that longer-term accounting measures closely reflect longer-term stock performance. Yearly data produced by my colleagues had turned up a weak correlation between accounting measures and shareholder

returns. When I looked at five-year measures, however, the correlation turned out to be stronger. My results show a remarkably strong correlation between accounting performance and shareholder returns, averaged over five-year periods.

The new study covers about 600 large exchange-listed companies from the period 1963 to 1990. Six accounting measures of performance are used: earnings per share (both before and after extraordinary items), cash flow per share (defined as earnings plus depreciation), return on book equity, return on book assets and revenue growth. Stock returns include capital gains plus dividends and are adjusted for stock splits and stock dividends. For each company I measure both gross stock return and returns net of the market index, which is the value-weighted portfolio of all exchange-listed stocks. The net-of-market return is simply the difference between the gross return and any individual company and the market return over the same period.

The results are that each of the six accounting-based performance measures has a significant, positive correlation with both gross and net-of-market stock returns of individual firms. Earnings per share before extraordinary items has the tightest association with company stock returns. Remarkably, earnings per share correlates with gross stock returns for individual companies about as well as does the value-weighted market basket! In view of the central role modern finance theory gives to market returns in explaining individual stock returns, this finding—that earnings per share correlates equally well—is eye opening. Apparently, constructing the variables as five-year averages reveals the powerful longer-term connection between earnings per share and shareholder returns.

The other accounting measures are each highly correlated with stock returns, but less so than is earnings per share before extraordinary items. As a group, the several accounting variables easily dominate the market portfolio in "explaining" historical five-year average stock returns for individual firms. In essence, accounting numbers seem to be a good measure of economic factors that directly influence net-of-market stock returns of individual companies, over five-year periods.

This study also provides additional justification for using accounting-based performance measures in long-term incentive plans. The accounting measures are not greatly influenced by general market movements, in sharp contrast to the generally heavy influence of the market on individual stock returns.

This finding emphasizes the advantage that accounting-based numbers have over stock returns for setting incentive pay. Accounting-based measures are more directly linked over the longer term to things that executives are able to control, whereas stock returns are related to many things outside of their control. Holding top executives to accounting-based goals,

rather than to stock prices, should elicit better results because the true performance of executives is more directly revealed by accounting measures. Shareholders are the beneficiaries.

It is popular to urge boards of directors to link pay closely with short-term shareholder returns. Several highly publicized cases of high compensation (Time Warner, for example) have resulted from the use of this practice. This is why the SEC is singling out options for special disclosure rules. These examples of high compensation show clearly the problem with linking compensation to shareholder returns—stock prices respond to too many factors.

During 1991, for example, stock prices for most companies surged because of economy-wide declines in interest rates. This resulted in several examples of high executive compensation (from the inflated values of stock-based options) even though the companies themselves performed poorly. It was as if executives were working for Alan Greenspan and not their shareholders.

In the context of my study results—and the traditionalists' view—the SEC proposals are beside the point. The proposals focus on widening disclosure of stock-related compensation with the aim of helping shareholders monitor executives' performance. The effect of this will be to discourage the use of options; but it won't necessarily strengthen the use of the kind of accounting-based measures traditionalists favor.

From the pure activists' point of view, the SEC proposal is a bad thing, because it hurts the instrument that most clearly links stock performance to pay—the option. In reality, though, many activists have embraced populist rage at high executive pay and are focusing on the bogus issue of fairness.

The more important news here is that the choice between stock- and accounting-based incentive plans is not a choice between being for or against shareholders.

And the prospect of the SEC's costly new disclosure rules in combination with the recent spectacles of high option-based pay mean in any case that boards of directors may well move away from stock-based incentive plans.

SOURCE: Gregg A. Jarrell, "Take the Long View on Executive Pay," *Wall Street Journal*, August 28, 1992. Reprinted by permission of the *Wall Street Journal*, © 1992 Dow Jones & Company, Inc. All rights reserved worldwide.

Required

a. The market model (discussed in Section 4.3) predicts that the return on the market portfolio, in conjunction with a stock's beta, is the major determinant of that stock's realized market return. If so, explain how a five-year average of earnings per share could do equally well in explaining stocks' market returns.

b. Explain how a five-year average of earnings per share can be correlated with a firm's stock return while a single year's earnings per share exhibits "a weak correlation between accounting measures and shareholder returns."

c. Jarrell argues that his evidence works against the "newer school," which supports linking executive pay to stock prices. Explain this argument.

d. In view of the correlation evidence given by Jarrell, do you think there is any role remaining for basing executive compensation on the current year's reported net income? Explain.

Earnings Management

11.1 Overview

From Section 10.3 we see that there are strong reasons for basing management compensation on reported net income, at least in part. Net income in conjunction with share price enables a reduction in risk imposed on the manager and also enables control of the manager's decision horizon. Also, from Section 9.4.3, there are strong reasons to include financial ratio covenants in debt contracts—these can lower the cost of borrowing. In addition, we saw from Lev's study, reviewed in Section 7.6, that firms' market values can be affected by accounting policies.

For all of these reasons, managers have a strong interest in accounting policy choice. Given that managers can choose accounting policies from a set (for example, GAAP) it is natural to expect that they will choose policies so as to maximize their own utility and/or the market value of the firm. This is called **earnings management**. An understanding of earnings management is important to accountants, because it enables an improved understanding of the usefulness of net income, both for reporting to investors and for contracting.

> **Earnings management** *is the choice by a firm of accounting policies so as to achieve some specific manager objective.*

There are two complementary ways to think about earnings management. First, we can think of it as opportunistic behaviour by managers to maximize their utility in the face of compensation and debt contracts and political costs.

However, we can also think about earnings management from an efficient contracting perspective. When setting compensation contracts, firms will anticipate managers' incentives to manage earnings and will allow for this in the amount of compensation they offer. Lenders will do the same thing in deciding on the interest rates they demand. Earnings management gives managers some flexibility to protect themselves and the firm in the face of unanticipated state realizations, to the advantage of all the contracting parties.

Furthermore, managers may be able to affect the market value of their firm's shares by earnings management. For example, they may want to create the impression of smooth and growing earnings over time. Given security market efficiency, this requires them to draw on their inside information. Thus, earnings management can be a vehicle for the communication of management's inside information to investors.

These considerations lead to the interesting, and perhaps surprising, conclusion that a little bit of earnings management is a good thing. Of course, the efficiency aspects of earnings management can be pushed too far, since earnings management reduces reliability. It should not be used to rationalize misleading or fraudulent reporting. There is a fine line between earnings management and earnings mismanagement. Ultimately, the location of this line must be determined by standard setters, security commissions, and the courts.

11.2   *Evidence of Earnings Management for Bonus Purposes*

A paper by Healy (1985), entitled "The Effect of Bonus Schemes on Accounting Decisions," is perhaps the best-known empirical investigation of earnings management. Managers have inside information on the firm's net income before earnings management. Since outside parties, including the Board itself, may be unable to learn what this number is, Healy predicted that managers would opportunistically manage net income so as to maximize their bonuses under their firms' compensation plans. Here, we will review Healy's methods and findings.

Healy's paper is based on positive accounting theory (Section 8.2). It attempts to explain and predict managers' choices of accounting policies. More specifically, it is an extension of the bonus plan hypothesis, which states that managers of firms with bonus plans will maximize current earnings. By looking more closely at the structure of bonus plans, Healy comes up with specific predictions of how and under what circumstances managers will engage in this type of earnings management.

As discussed earlier, most incentive plans have more than one component. However, Healy's study was confined to firms whose compensation plans are based on current reported net income only. These will be called **bonus schemes** for the rest of this section. In Section 10.4, we saw that, for risk reduction reasons, bonus schemes may have bogies and caps. In Healy's sample, not all schemes have caps, although they all have bogeys. Figure 11.1 illustrates a typical bonus scheme.

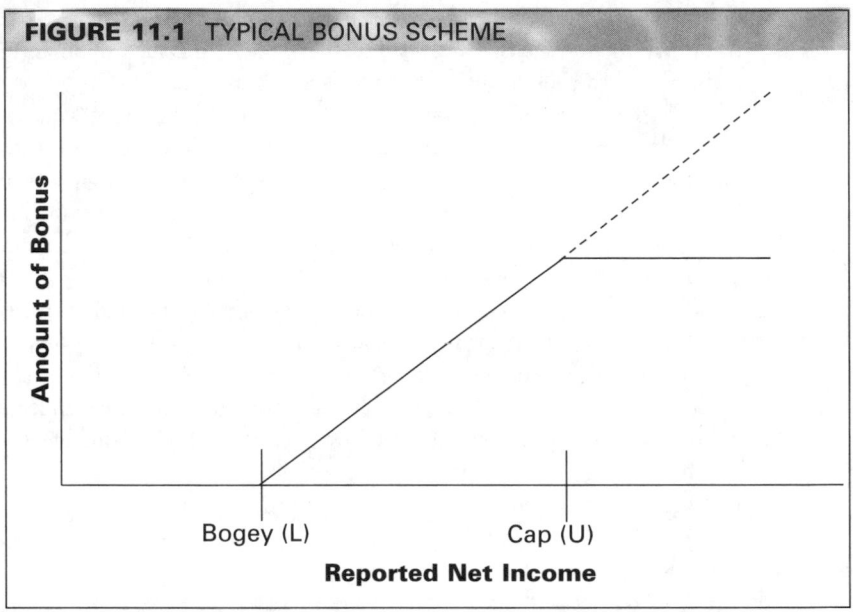

FIGURE 11.1 TYPICAL BONUS SCHEME

In the figure the bonus increases linearly (for example, 10% of net income) between the bogey and the cap. Below the bogey, bonus is zero. If there is no cap, the bonus would increase along the dotted line. Otherwise, the bonus becomes a constant for net income greater than the cap. Healy denotes the bogey and cap as L and U respectively. The bonus scheme depicted in Figure 11.1 is simpler than that of Rockwell's incentive plan, where the rate of bonus depends on both the amount of earnings and dividends. Nevertheless, the basic idea carries over. Also, the bogey of the Rockwell incentive plan is zero.

Now, consider the incentives to manage reported net income faced by a manager subject to such a scheme. If net income is low (that is, below the bogey), the manager has an incentive to lower it even further, which is called **taking a bath**. If no bonus is to be received anyway, the manager might as well adopt accounting policies to further reduce reported net income. In so doing, *the probability of receiving a bonus the following year is increased,* since current writeoffs will reduce future depreciation and amortization charges. Similarly, if net income is high (above the cap), there is motivation again to adopt accounting policies and procedures to reduce reported net income, because a bonus would be permanently lost on reported net income greater than the cap.

Only if net income is between the bogey and cap is the manager motivated to adopt accounting policies and procedures to increase reported net income. Thus, Healy refines the bonus plan hypothesis—it really only applies when net income is between the bogey and the cap.

How does a manager control net income? Healy considers two approaches. The first is by controlling various accruals, where accruals are defined broadly to include that portion of revenue and expense items on the income statement that is not represented by cash flows. The second is by changing accounting policies. Let us consider first the accruals procedure (see Table 11.1).

TABLE 11.1 DISCRETIONARY AND NON-DISCRETIONARY ACCRUALS		
Cash flow, as per cash flow statement		$1,000
Less: Amortization expense	− 50	
Add: Increase in (net) accounts receivable during the year	+ 40	
Add: Increase in inventory during the year	+100	
Add: Decrease in accounts payable and accrued liabilities during the year	+ 30	120
Net income, as per income statement		$1,120

To illustrate accruals that might be made by a manager who wanted to increase reported net income, consider the hypothetical example in Table 11.1. Note that a positive sign for an accrual means that, for given cash flow, it *increases* net income, and vice versa. For simplicity, we have assumed that there are no extraordinary income statement items and no income tax expense. Assume that explanations for the four accrual items are as follows:

- **Amortization expense** Annual amortization expense is laid down by the firm's amortization policy and its estimates of assets' useful lives. Given this policy, amortization expense is a non-discretionary accrual.

- **Increase in net accounts receivable** Assume that this derives from a decrease in the allowance for doubtful accounts, resulting from a less conservative estimate than in previous years. This accrual is discretionary, because management has some flexibility to control the amount. Other reasons for the increase could include one or more of a more generous credit policy, keeping the books open beyond the year-end, or simply an increase in volume of business. The first two of these accruals are discretionary, the third is non-discretionary.

  Thus, we see that there can be several reasons for an increase in receivables. A researcher with access only to the comparative financial statements would be unlikely to know what particular reason or reasons accounted for the increase or whether the increase was discretionary or non-discretionary or both. Nevertheless, it is clear that the manager who wishes to increase reported net income through accounts receivable accruals has several means available.

- **Increase in inventory** Assume that this derives from the firm manufacturing for stock during a period of excess manufacturing capacity. The result is to include fixed overhead costs in inventory rather than charging them off to expense as unfavourable volume variances.

  While other reasons for the increase are possible, just as in the case of accounts receivable, this illustrates that discretionary, income-increasing accruals are available for inventory as well.

- **Decrease in accounts payable and accrual liabilities** Assume that this derives from the firm being more optimistic about warranty claims on its products than it has been in previous years. Alternatively, or in addition, the decrease could be due to regarding certain borderline items as contingencies rather than accruals. Again, we see that there can be ample room for discretionary accruals in accounts payable.

The main point to note is that the manager has considerable discretion to manage reported net income within the rules of GAAP. Notice also that, for many of these discretionary accruals, it would be difficult for the firm's auditors to discover the earnings management or, if they did discover it, to object, since all of the techniques mentioned, with the exception of holding the books open past the year-end, are within GAAP. It is also clear that a similar set of discretionary accruals to *decrease* reported net income are available to the manager, simply by reversing those described above.

Healy did not have access to the books and records of his sample firms. Consequently, he was unable to determine the specific discretionary accruals made by those firms' managers. As a result, he used total accruals as a proxy for discretionary accruals. Thus, in our example, he would estimate discretionary accruals as +$120, instead of the +$170 that would be used if he had full information. The +$170 of *discretionary* accruals will raise *total* accruals by $170, regardless of what other non-discretionary accruals may be present; that is, higher total accruals contain higher discretionary accruals. Similarly, lower total accruals contain lower discretionary accruals. However, using total accruals as a proxy for discretionary accruals may get the researcher into trouble if non-discretionary accruals are large relative to discretionary. Then, finding evidence of earnings management is like finding a needle in a haystack.

Note also that total accruals can be calculated two ways. One way is to take the change in each balance sheet account that is subject to accruals and add up the changes. A short-cut approach, however, is simply to take the difference between operating cash flow and net income.

Healy obtained a sample of 94 of the largest U.S. industrial companies. He followed each company over the period 1930–80 and obtained a total of 1,527 usable observations, that is, 1,527 firm years where the bogey and (if applicable) cap for a firm's bonus scheme could be calculated. Of these, 447 observations included both a bogey and a cap.

Each observation was then classified into one of three categories, or "portfolios" as Healy calls them. Portfolio UPP consisted of observations where earnings were above the cap, portfolio LOW of observations where earnings were below the bogey, and portfolio MID where they were between the bogey and cap. The theory underlying Table 11.1 predicts that total accruals should be *greater* for the MID portfolio than for UPP and LOW—recall that income-increasing accruals have a positive sign in Table 11.1.

For the 447 observations that had both a bogey and a cap, the results are summarized in Table 11.2. We see that 46% of the 281 observations in the MID portfolio had total accruals which were positive, that is, income-increasing. This is the situation facing our firm in Table 11.1, where total accruals were +$120. The average accrual of these 281 observations was +0.0021 of total assets (accruals were deflated by total assets so that they could be compared across firms of different sizes). For the observations in the LOW and UPP portfolios, the proportions with positive total accruals was much lower—only 9% and 10% respectively. In fact, the average accruals for these observations were *negative* (income-decreasing). These results are consistent with Healy's arguments (see Figure 11.1), that firm managers whose net incomes are below the bogey and above the cap will tend to adopt income-decreasing accruals and only managers with net income between the two will tend to adopt income-increasing accruals. Thus, Healy's predictions of earnings management by managers subject to bonus schemes were supported by the empirical results.

TABLE 11.2 OBSERVATIONS WITH BOTH A BOGEY AND A CAP

	Proportion of Accruals with Given Sign		Number of Observations	Average Accruals
	Positive	**Negative**		
LOW	0.09	0.91	22	−0.0671
MID	0.46	0.54	281	+0.0021
UPP	0.10	0.90	<u>144</u>	−0.0536
			<u>447</u>	

SOURCE: P. M. Healy, "The Effect of Bonus Schemes on Accounting Decisions," *Journal of Accounting and Economics* (April 1985), p. 96, Table 2. Reprinted by permission.

Results for observations where the bonus scheme had only a bogey are summarized in Table 11.3. Here, there is no UPP portfolio. The proportions of positive and negative accruals are about the same for each portfolio. However, the average accrual is significantly greater for MID, being −0.0155 of total assets compared to −0.0367 for LOW. Thus, we can conclude that while the MID observations did not

TABLE 11.3 OBSERVATIONS WITH BOGEY ONLY

	Proportion of Accruals with Given Sign		Number of Observations	Average Accruals
	Positive	**Negative**		
LOW	0.38	0.62	74	−0.0367
MID	0.36	0.64	<u>1006</u>	−0.0155
			<u>1080</u>	

SOURCE: P. M. Healy, "The Effect of Bonus Schemes on Accounting Decisions," *Journal of Accounting and Economics* (April 1985), p. 96, Table 2. Reprinted by permission.

engage in a higher *proportion* of positive accruals, the accruals they did make were significantly *larger* (that is, less negative) on average. These results, while perhaps not as dramatic as those of Table 11.2, also are significantly consistent with Healy's arguments for earnings management by managers subject to bonus schemes.

The second approach to searching for evidence consistent with earnings management is to examine voluntary changes in accounting policies. From the firms in his sample, Healy collected 242 accounting policy changes over the 12 years 1968 to 1980 for which the effect on net income could be determined.

As Healy notes, accounting policy changes are not as desirable an earnings management vehicle as accruals. Reasons are that such changes are highly visible compared to accruals—they have to be disclosed in the annual report—and that the standard of consistency prevents a particular policy from being changed very often. Thus, accounting policy changes tend to be a blunt and inflexible weapon. Healy did not find that his sample firms used accounting policy changes the same way they used accruals. That is, policy changes were not used to increase annual reported net income in the MID range and to decrease it for LOW and HIGH incomes. Presumably, a reason is that accruals are a more effective way to accomplish this objective.

Nevertheless, it can be argued that if managers are going to change accounting policies, a good time to do it is just after introduction or amendment of a bonus plan. A manager may be motivated at that time to adopt an income-increasing accounting policy change (for example, a switch from accelerated to straight-line amortization) if a period of healthy earnings is anticipated. This policy change would increase the expected bonus in future years, particularly if there was no cap on the bonus scheme.

To test this reasoning, Healy classified his sample companies into two portfolios for each year from 1968 to 1980. One portfolio consisted of firms that adopted or modified their bonus plan in the year; the other consisted of firms that did not. If the above argument is correct, the first portfolio should have more accounting policy changes than the second.

Healy found that in 9 of the 12 years over which comparisons were made, the portfolio of firms with bonus plan changes did in fact have more accounting policy changes. This provides significant evidence that managers also use such changes as an earnings management vehicle.

However, in view of the finding that managers did not use accounting policy changes to influence individual years' net income, it seems that their use of accounting policy changes is a longer-run earnings management device. Such changes can be used to give a general upward or downward influence on net income over a period of time extending from adoption or modification of a bonus plan. Presumably, individual years in this time period can then have their reported net incomes fine-tuned by means of accruals.

It should be mentioned that earnings management studies face severe methodological problems. As mentioned earlier, a major difficulty is that discretionary accruals cannot be observed. Consequently, some proxy must be used. Using total accruals, as Healy did, introduces measurement error into the discretionary accruals variable, which makes it more difficult to detect earnings management should it exist. Another problem arises if the amount of non-discretionary accruals is correlated with net income. For example, as Kaplan (1985) has pointed out, a firm with reported net income above the cap of its bonus plan may have low non-discretionary accruals if its high income is due to an unexpected increase in demand which runs down inventory. Then, the low total accruals that are used to infer earnings management are really due to the level of the firm's real economic activity and not to low discretionary accruals. Healy was aware of these problems and conducted additional tests to control for them, which he interpreted as confirming his findings. The methodology used by Jones (1991) (see Section 8.3) provides a more refined way to estimate non-discretionary accruals. For further discussion of methodological issues in this area see McNichols and Wilson (1988), Schipper (1989), and Dechow, Sloan, and Sweeney (1994).

McNichols and Wilson (1988) also studied the behaviour of accruals in a bonus context. They confined their investigation to the provision for bad debts, on the grounds that a precise estimate of what the bad debts allowance *should* be (that is, the non-discretionary accrual) can be made. Then, discretionary accruals can be taken as the difference between this estimate and the actual bad debts provision. A precise estimate of non-discretionary accruals will reduce the problem of measurement error in the discretionary accruals variable. This approach also reduces the problem of correlation between net income and non-discretionary accruals, since the impact on the bad debts provision of the firm's level of economic activity is captured by their estimate of what the bad debts allowance should be. They found that, over the period 1969–85, discretionary bad debt accruals were significantly positive (that is, income-reducing) both for firm years that were very profitable and those that were very unprofitable (and thus likely to be below and above the bogeys and caps, respectively, of the bonus agreements). For firm years that were between these profitability extremes, discretionary accruals were much lower, and usually negative. These results are consistent with those of Healy.

More recently, Holthausen, Larcker, and Sloan (1995) (HLS) studied managers' accruals behaviour for bonus purposes. They were able to obtain data on whether managers' annual earnings-based bonuses were in fact zero, greater than zero but less than the maximum bonus, or at the maximum. These are substantially better data than Healy, who had to estimate whether earnings before discretionary accruals were below bogey, between bogey and cap, or above cap on the basis of available descriptions of bonus contracts, and *assume* that if earnings were below the bogey the manager would not receive a bonus, etc.

Using a version of the Jones (1991) model to estimate non-discretionary accruals for a sample of 443 firm-year observations over 1982–90, HLS found that managers who were at their bonus maxima managed accruals so as to lower reported earnings. This is consistent with Healy's results—see row 3 of Table 11.2 above. However, HLS did not find that managers who received zero bonus also used accruals to manage earnings downward, which differed from Healy's findings (row 1, Table 11.2). HLS concluded that methodological problems arising from Healy's procedures for estimating discretionary accruals explained why he appeared to find negative accruals for his low portfolio.

In summary, we may conclude that, despite methodological challenges, there is significant evidence that managers use accruals to manage earnings so as to maximize their bonuses, particularly when earnings are high. This evidence is consistent with the bonus plan hypothesis of positive accounting theory.

11.3   Other Motivations for Earnings Management

Managers may engage in earnings management for a variety of reasons, besides a bonus scheme. Now, we will look at these briefly.

11.3.1 OTHER CONTRACTUAL MOTIVATIONS

Healy's investigation suggests that earnings management to affect bonuses does exist. Such earnings management is an example of a **contractual** motivation, that is, the incentive for earnings management arises from the characteristics of bonus schemes, which are contracts between the firm and its managers that set forth the basis of managerial compensation.

There are other contractual motivations for earnings management. An important case arises from long-term lending contracts, which typically contain covenants to protect the lenders against actions by managers that are against the lenders' best interests, such as excessive dividends, additional borrowing, or letting working capital or shareholders' equity fall below specified levels, all of which dilute the security of existing lenders.

Earnings management for covenant purposes is predicted by the debt covenant hypothesis of positive accounting theory. Given that covenant violation can impose heavy costs, firm managers will be expected to avoid them. Indeed, they will even try to avoid being close to violation, because this will constrain their freedom of action in operating the firm. Thus, earnings management can arise as a device to reduce the probability of covenant violation in debt contracts.

Earnings management in a debt covenant context was investigated by Sweeney (1994), reviewed in Section 8.3. For a sample of firms that had defaulted on debt contracts, Sweeney found significantly greater use of income-increasing accounting changes relative to a control sample, and also found that defaulting firms tended to undertake early adoption of new accounting standards when these increased reported net income, and vice versa.

Defond and Jiambalvo (1994) also examined earnings management by firms disclosing a debt covenant violation during 1985–88. They found evidence of the use of discretionary accruals to increase reported income in the year prior to and, to a lesser extent, in the year of the covenant violation.

Somewhat different results are reported by DeAngelo, DeAngelo, and Skinner (1994), however. They studied a sample of 76 large, troubled firms. These were firms that had three or more consecutive loss years during 1980–85 and which had reduced dividends during the loss period. For 29 of these firms, the cut in dividends was forced by binding debt covenant constraints.

After controlling for the influence of declining sales and cash flows on accruals, DeAngelo et al. failed to find evidence that these 29 firms used accruals to manage earnings upward in years prior to the cut in dividends, relative to the remaining sample firms that did not face debt covenant constraints. Rather, all the sample firms exhibited large *negative* (that is, earnings-reducing) accruals extending for at least three years beyond the year of the dividend cut. DeAngelo et al. attribute this behaviour as due in part to large, discretionary non-cash write-offs. Apparently, these were to signal to lenders, shareholders, unions, and others that the firm was facing up to its troubles, and to prepare the ground for subsequent contract renegotiations which frequently took place.

It thus seems that when its troubles are profound, the firm's behaviour transcends that which is predicted by the debt covenant hypothesis and, instead, earnings management becomes part of the firm's (and its manager's) overall strategy for survival.

11.3.2 POLITICAL MOTIVATIONS

Many firms are quite politically visible. This is the case for very large firms, simply because their activities touch large numbers of people. Also, firms in strategic industries, such as oil and gas, will be visible, as will monopolistic or near-monopolistic firms such as airlines and power companies. Such firms may want to manage earnings so as to reduce their visibility. This would entail, for example, accounting practices and procedures to minimize reported net income, particularly during periods of high prosperity. Otherwise, public pressure may arise for the government to step in with increased regulation or other means to lower profitability. You will recognize that this motivation underlies the size hypothesis of positive accounting theory.

Jones (1991), reviewed in Section 8.3, found that her sample firms made significantly greater income-decreasing accruals during the year of ITC investigation than in years outside the investigation year. Also, Cahan (1992), using methodology similar to Jones, found that a sample of firms under investigation for monopolistic practices by the Department of Justice and the Federal Trade Commission during 1970–83 used more income-decreasing accruals during investigation years relative to other years in the sample period.

11.3.3 *TAXATION MOTIVATIONS*

Income taxation is perhaps the most obvious motivation for earnings management. However, taxation authorities tend to impose their own accounting rules for calculation of taxable income, thereby reducing firms' room to manoeuvre.

An exception, however, occurs with respect to the choice of the LIFO versus FIFO inventory method. In the United States, firms that use LIFO for tax purposes must also use it for financial reporting. During periods of rising prices, LIFO will usually result in lower reported profits and lower taxes, relative to FIFO. Yet, even when prices are rising, we observe that not all U.S. firms switch to LIFO. In effect, firms can either manage income down by choosing LIFO, resulting in lower taxes and increased cash flows, or manage income up by choosing FIFO, at the cost of higher taxes and lower cash flows. The question then is why.

Much positive theory research has tried to explain and predict firms' inventory policy choices. It does appear that tax savings are an important factor. For example, Dopuch and Pincus (1988) report evidence that tax savings are high for LIFO firms and that firms who remain on FIFO do not suffer large tax consequences, for reasons such as low amounts of inventory, high variability of inventory levels, high inventory turnover, and low effective tax rates. Lindahl (1989) also reports results consistent with these reasons.

From an efficient capital markets perspective, we would expect that cash savings would dominate the effects of a lower reported net income under LIFO. Then, we would expect a favourable effect on firms' share prices upon switching from FIFO to LIFO when prices are rising. Sunder (1973) was the first to document such an effect. However, subsequent research, for example Abdel-khalik and McKeown (1978), suggests the market may react negatively. This issue is still unresolved.

From a contracting perspective, one can suggest why some firms may forgo tax savings in favour of higher reported earnings under FIFO. Managerial bonuses may be favourably affected by higher reported profits, and the probability of technical violation of debt covenants will fall. However, empirical evidence that contracting variables explain LIFO/FIFO choices is not strong. For example, Abdel-khalik (1985) found that managers of LIFO firms did not suffer adverse bonus effects. Also, Hunt (1985) failed to find evidence of bonus plan effects. There is some evidence that firms with high debt-to-equity levels are more likely to use FIFO, reported by Cushing and LeClere (1992), Lindahl (1989), and Hunt (1985). However, Lee and Hsieh (1985) and Dopuch and Pincus (1988) do not find the debt-to-equity ratio to be significant.

Overall, the evidence seems to support tax savings as the most important factor in LIFO/FIFO choice. Firms that switch to LIFO have the most to gain, and vice versa. However, this raises questions about the strength of the bonus plan and debt covenant hypotheses. Perhaps other methods which do not require a cash flow sacrifice, such as accruals management and paper accounting policy changes, are sufficient for managers concerned about contract rigidities.

11.3.4 CHANGES OF CEO

A variety of income management motivations exist around the time of a change of chief executive officer (CEO). For example, the bonus plan hypothesis predicts that CEOs approaching retirement would be particularly likely to engage in a strategy of income maximization, to increase their bonuses. Similarly CEOs of poorly performing firms may income-maximize to prevent, or postpone, being fired. Alternatively, consistent with the findings of DeAngelo et al. (1994) as discussed above, such CEOs may take a bath so as to increase the probability of future earnings. This motivation also applies to new CEOs, especially if large writeoffs can be blamed on the previous CEO.

These motivations were studied by Murphy and Zimmerman (1993) (MZ). They examined the behaviour of four discretionary variables (that is, variables with earnings management potential), namely research and development (R&D), advertising, capital expenditures, and accruals. Their study included a large sample of CEO changes in U.S. companies during the period from 1971 to 1989.

Note that three of the variables examined by MZ affect the firm's *real* operations. While reducing R&D, advertising, and capital expenditures may be an effective way to increase current earnings, they are potentially quite costly to the firm, since its competitive position may be adversely affected in future. The accrual and accounting policy variables that we have considered to this point are less costly, since with the exception of LIFO inventory they are strictly paper devices with no direct effect on current or future cash flows. The possibility of using real variables such as R&D alerts us to the fact the managers have more scope to manage earnings than might be at first thought.[1] Also, it emphasizes that while GAAP may serve to constrain earnings management, it is unlikely they could ever eliminate it.

Studies such as MZ also face difficult methodological problems. For example, the probability of CEO change is affected by the firm's operating performance. But operating performance will also affect the magnitude of discretionary variables. Thus, accounts receivable may be lower if sales are down, and financially stressed firms may simply not have the cash to maintain R&D, advertising, and capital expenditures. If lower accruals, and lower expenditures on the other three discretionary variables, are observed, is this due to earnings management or to poor operating performance? Another problem is that it may be difficult to tell, in the transition year, whether any apparent earnings management is due to the new CEO or the old.

After controlling for problems such as these, MZ concluded that most of the unusual behaviour of the four discretionary variables was due to poor operating performance. For example, they found no evidence that CEOs approaching retirement income-maximized. Somewhat surprisingly, they also found little evidence that CEOs of poorly performing firms income-maximized either. Both of these findings are inconsistent with the opportunistic form of the bonus plan hypothesis. However, MZ did find evidence that incoming CEOs of poorly performing firms took baths.

It is interesting to speculate on these findings of a lack of earnings management by outgoing executives. Pourciau (1993), in a study of non-routine executive change, finds a similar result and gives extensive discussion of possible reasons. If methodological problems are ruled out, one possibility is that some poorly performing managers may have used earnings management successfully to avoid being fired. If so, they would not be included in the sample. Another possibility is that the outgoing executive engaged in income-increasing earnings management in years prior to departure, and earnings in the departure year are forced down by the inevitable reversal of these earlier discretionary accruals. Yet another possibility is that boards of directors monitor the activities of poorly performing and outgoing managers with particular care, particularly with respect to real variables such as R&D, so that opportunistic earnings management would be nipped in the bud. Furthermore, the extent of board monitoring may vary with the firm's corporate governance structure. For example, an entrenched manager who dominates the board may feel less need to manage earnings. Smith (1993) gives further discussion of issues such as these.

11.3.5 INITIAL PUBLIC OFFERINGS

By definition, firms making initial public offerings (IPOs) do not have an established market price. This raises the question of how to value the shares of such firms. Presumably, financial accounting information included in the prospectus is a useful information source. For example, Hughes (1986) shows analytically that information such as net income can be useful in helping to signal firm value to investors, and Clarkson, Dontoh, Richardson, and Sefcik (1992) find empirical evidence that the market responds positively to earnings forecasts as a signal of firm value. This raises the possibility that managers of firms going public may manage the earnings reported in their prospectuses in the hope of receiving a higher price for their shares.

Friedlan (1994) investigated this issue. For a sample of 155 U.S. IPOs during 1981–84 he examined whether the firms managed earnings upward in the latest accounting period prior to the IPO by means of discretionary accruals. Since IPO firms are usually growing rapidly, it is particularly difficult to estimate their discretionary accruals, because growth itself drives an increase in accruals, such as accounts receivable, inventories, etc. After extensive tests to control for this problem, Friedlan concluded that IPO firms did indeed make income-increasing discretionary accruals in the latest period prior to the IPO, relative to accruals in a comparable previous period. Furthermore, accruals management seemed to be concentrated in the poorer-performing sample firms as measured by operating cash flows (such firms presumably have greater motivation to increase reported income) and in the smaller sample firms (about which less may be known).

11.4   Patterns of Earnings Management

From the foregoing discussion, it is apparent that managers may engage in a variety of earnings management patterns. Here, we will collect and briefly summarize these patterns.

1. **Taking a bath** This can take place during periods of organizational stress or reorganization, including the hiring of a new CEO. If a firm must report a loss, management may feel compelled to report a large one—it has nothing to lose at this point. Consequently, it will write off assets, provide for expected future costs, and generally "clear the decks." This will enhance the probability of future reported profits. Healy also mentions that managers whose net income is below the bogey of the bonus plan may also take a bath, for similar reason—it will enhance the probability of future bonuses. In effect, the recording of large writeoffs puts future earnings "in the bank."

2. **Income minimization** This is similar to taking a bath, but less extreme. Such a pattern may be chosen by a politically visible firm during periods of high profitability. Policies which suggest income minimization include rapid writeoffs of capital assets and intangibles, expensing of advertising and R&D expenditures, successful-efforts accounting for oil and gas exploration costs, and so on. Income taxation, such as for LIFO inventory, provides another set of motivations for this pattern, as does enhancement of arguments for relief from foreign competition.

3. **Income maximization** As we saw in Healy's study, managers may engage in a pattern of maximization of reported net income for bonus purposes,

providing this does not put them above the cap. Firms that are close to debt covenant violations may also maximize income.

4. **Income smoothing** This is perhaps the most interesting earnings management pattern. We saw from Healy that managers have an incentive to smooth income sufficiently that it remains between the bogey and cap. Otherwise, earnings may be temporarily or permanently lost for bonus purposes. Furthermore, if managers are risk-averse, they will prefer a less variable bonus stream, and hence may want to smooth net income.

We considered covenants in long-term lending agreements in Section 9.4.3. Clearly, the more volatile the stream of reported net income, the higher the probability that covenant violation will occur. This provides another smoothing incentive: to reduce volatility of reported net income so as to smooth covenant ratios.

Firms may also smooth reported net income for external reporting purposes. This can convey inside information to the market and, by enabling the firm to communicate its expected longer-term earnings growth, can lower its cost of capital.

It should be apparent that these various earnings management patterns can be in conflict. Over time, the pattern chosen by a firm may vary due to changes in contracts, changes in levels of profitability, changes in CEO, and changes in political visibility. Even at a given point in time, the firm may face conflicting needs to, say, reduce reported net income for political reasons, but to smooth it for borrowing purposes. Then, the particular pattern chosen by the firm would be difficult to predict.

11.5   Is Earnings Management "Good" or "Bad"?

Probably, most people would feel that earnings management is "bad," since, as we have suggested several times in earlier chapters, it implies a reduction in the reliability of financial statement information. This raises the question of why it seems to persist. Also, why can't boards of directors, lenders, government agencies, and investors "unravel" the earnings management, so that there is no point in engaging in it?

One reason, as pointed out by Schipper (1989), is that managers have inside information and it is prohibitively costly for others to find out this information. For example, amounts of discretionary accruals would be very difficult to know, even by boards of directors. Also, other possible earnings management techniques such as accounting policy changes, timing of capital gains and losses, and provisions for restructuring can be very difficult for outsiders to interpret. For example, is a firm's sale of one of its divisions driven by necessity or by timing considerations, or is a provision for restructuring excessive? Answers to questions such as these are typically private, inside information. There must be some blockage of manager/board or manager/investor communication, or earnings management will be unravelled.

It should be emphasized that "prohibitively costly" does not mean that the unravelling of earnings management is impossible, but simply that it is not cost-effective. For example, the board of directors may be able to determine the extent of accruals manipulation by hiring an auditor to give a complete report. However, it may not feel that this is worth the cost, particularly if it had anticipated some efficient earnings management when setting the manager's compensation contract in the first place. Also, evaluating the reasonableness of gains and losses on capital assets or of the adequacy of restructuring provisions could be very costly even for analysts, large blockholders, and other sophisticated investors. Large corporations are extremely complex, often spanning several industries and conducting operations worldwide.

Also, Jones (1991) argues that individual consumers may not feel it is worth becoming informed about applications for tariff protection before the ITC, since the impact on them of price increases following a successful application would be small. Even the ITC may not bother to investigate for earnings management if it does not receive complaints from consumers.

Another reason for the persistence of earnings management is that there is a "good" side to it. We can consider the pros and cons of earnings management from both a contracting and a financial reporting perspective. From a contracting perspective the question of whether earnings management is good or bad is related to the efficient contracting versus opportunistic forms of positive accounting theory, as discussed in Chapter 8. Under efficient contracting, it is desirable to give managers some ability to manage earnings in the face of incomplete and rigid contracts. Thus we must be careful not to necessarily interpret evidence of earnings management for bonus, debt covenant, and political reasons as bad. Such an interpretation would only be valid if managers go too far and behave opportunistically with respect to existing contracts. Thus, we would expect some earnings management to persist for efficient contracting reasons.

From a capital markets perspective, earnings management can be a device to credibly convey inside information to the market, thereby affecting firms' cost of capital. To see how this could come about, consider the **blocked communication** concept of Demski and Sappington (1987). Frequently, agents obtain specialized information as part of their expertise, and this information can be prohibitively costly to communicate to the principal, that is, its communication is blocked. For example, it may be difficult for a physician to communicate to the patient exact details of an examination and diagnosis. Then, the physician's act (for example, operating on the patient) must stand in not only for the physician's surgical skills but also for the information acquired during the diagnosis. Demski and Sappington show that the presence of blocked communication can reduce the efficiency of agency contracts, since the agent may shirk on information acquisition and compensate by taking an act that, from the principal's standpoint, is sub-optional—the physician may simply sew up a badly cut hand on the basis of a cursory examination that fails to check for possible tendon or nerve damage, for example. If so, the principal has an incentive to try to eliminate or reduce the blocked communication.

In a financial reporting context, earnings management can be a device to do this. To illustrate, suppose that the board of directors (the principal) wants to encourage the manager (the agent) to communicate the firm's long-run earnings potential. This is complex inside information of the manager. If the manager simply announced this information, the announcement would not likely be credible, since the board or the market would find it prohibitively costly to verify. Suppose, however, that the firm has just realized a profit of $200 million from the sale of a division. Rather than report a net income substantially higher than what is sustainable in the long run, the manager decides to record a provision for restructuring of, say, $180 million, thereby reducing current earnings to what the manager feels is sustainable.

This way of "unblocking" the manager's inside information has some credibility, since it involves the financial statements, for which the manager has formal responsibility. If the manager reported a provision for restructuring that differed materially from internal plans, this could result in auditor objection and possible legal liability. Thus, the board may allow a reasonable amount of earnings management to persist as a way to communicate blocked, inside information to the market. Notice that the market cannot unravel this earnings management, since it is based on inside information about sustainable earning power. However, the market can use the earnings management to infer what this inside information is.

This argument that net income can convey inside information to investors while at the same time being useful for contracting purposes has been further explored by Demski and Sappington (1990). We can think, for example, of operating cash flows or some other relatively unmanaged performance measure, such as net income before extraordinary items, as reporting on manager effort. Then, they show that judicious choice and disclosure of accruals, such as the provision for restructuring mentioned above, can in addition convey value-relevant information to investors.

This "dual purpose" role for net income is encouraging and helps to meet the fundamental problem of financial accounting theory outlined in Chapter 1. However, as Demski and Sappington (1990) point out, the information conveyed by the financial statements in their model does not purport to fully convey the value of the firm. All that is claimed is that *some* value-relevant information is conveyed by net income. That is, their model does not get around our general observation that net income is only well defined under ideal conditions.

Consequently, it is still the case that the best net income for contracting need not be the same as the most useful net income for informing investors.

Dye (1988) also modelled the above capital market considerations. He envisaged two generations of shareholders—current and future. The current shareholders will sell their shares to the next generation in a future period. Given inside information, and given that it is prohibitively costly for the future shareholders to unravel the firm's earnings management, Dye showed that a manager acting on behalf of the current shareholders has an ability and incentive to manage earnings so as to maximize the selling price received by the current shareholders. In effect, in Dye's model, the firm uses earnings management to minimize its cost of capital.

Incentives to smooth can also arise from *short-term* borrowing, which typically does not impose covenants (accounts payable, for example). The more volatile its stream of cash flows, the greater the probability that the firm will be unable to pay its contractual obligations as they mature. If failure to repay means the firm goes bankrupt, the short-term lenders will suffer. Hence, the firm may engage in income smoothing to disguise its underlying cash flow volatility. As a result, lenders who look to net income as a measure of the security of their loans will be more willing to provide short-term credit. Of course, this argument only works when lenders do not see through the smoothing activity. However, as mentioned previously, accruals may provide such a smoothing vehicle, because they can be hard to detect.

11.6   Summary and Conclusions

Earnings management is motivated by contracts which depend on reported net income, by critical events such as manager retirement, takeover bids, and appeals for tariff protection, and by a desire to minimize cost of capital. There are several patterns of earnings management that firms may adopt at different times—bath, income maximization, income minimization, and income smoothing.

Earnings management is made possible by the costliness of unravelling management's inside information. There must be limits to earnings management, or investors and firm owners would quickly lose confidence in net income as a reliable measure of firm performance. However, some earnings management is desirable from the standpoint of owners and managers, both because it provides room to manoeuvre to avoid the costly consequences of contract renegotiation and because it provides a vehicle for the enhancement of firm value by communicating inside information to the market.

Our study of earnings management shows that reporting of net income goes well beyond the communication of useful information to investors as implied by single-person decision theory. Instead, choosing net income has aspects of a game, in which accounting policies are chosen for strategic reasons. Of course, reporting to investors remains as a necessary objective. The role of GAAP is to ensure socially acceptable levels of relevance and reliability.

Nevertheless, GAAP do not completely constrain a firm's choice of accounting policies and their timing. The reason, as we have seen, is that except under ideal conditions net income is not well defined, so that there are no "right answers" to many accounting questions. We can thus think of GAAP as a set of constraints. Violation of GAAP for financial reporting could result in auditor qualification, SEC investigation, and lawsuits. However, within GAAP, we can think of accounting policies as being chosen for a variety of strategic reasons to accomplish manager and firm objectives.

Note that it is information asymmetry that creates opportunities for strategic accounting policy choice. Moral hazard creates the need to compensate managers based on measures of performance, and to include covenants for the protection of lenders. Without moral hazard, managers could be paid a salary, and protection of lenders would not be of concern, in which case the management of earnings for bonus and covenant reasons would not arise. Also, managers have a lot of expert, inside information about the firm's future plans and prospects. While GAAP may help control this adverse selection problem, much inside information remains. Then, managers can use the flexibility allowed by GAAP to reveal this inside information.

Despite the reduction in reliability which accompanies earnings management, a strong case can be made that it is useful if kept within bounds. It gives managers flexibility to react to unanticipated state realizations when contracts are rigid and incomplete. It can also serve as a vehicle for the credible communication of inside information to investors. The importance to managers of being able to manage earnings can be seen with particular clarity when proposals are made to change GAAP. It is managers' reactions to changes in GAAP that create economic consequences—they would hardly react if they did not care. One reason why they may care is that changes in GAAP may constrain earnings management.

An awareness of the role of reported net income in motivating managers, and of the resulting strategic issues of earnings management, is necessary for accountants if they are to advise and evaluate accounting policy choice. Certainly, financial reporting is much more complex and challenging than simply choosing accounting and disclosure policies that best inform investors. While this role is of great importance, the legitimate interests of management also need to be taken into account. In effect, it is still the case that the best system for reporting to investors and the best system for contracting are not the same. Thus, actual financial reporting represents a compromise between the needs of these two major constituencies.

Notes

1. It should be noted that levels of expenditure on real variables may not be inside information of the manager, particularly if there is full disclosure. The reasons for changes in these variables may be inside information, however.

Questions and Problems

1. Explain why a firm's management might both believe in security market efficiency and engage in earnings management.   (CGA-Canada)

2. For an income management strategy of taking a bath, the probability of the manager receiving a bonus in a future year *rises*. Explain why.   (CGA-Canada)

3. You are a CEO operating under a bonus plan similar to the one assumed by Healy (Section 11.2). Explain whether you would react favourably or negatively to an exposure draft of a proposed change in GAAP which has the following effects on your financial statements. Treat each effect as independent of the others.

   a. The effect will be to increase liabilities. Examples of such GAAP changes include capitalization of long-term leases (*CICA Handbook*, Section 3065), recording of pension plan obligations (*CICA Handbook*, Section 3460), and recognition of postretirement benefits for employees (SFAS 106).

   b. The effect will be to increase the volatility of reported net income. An example would be the recording of foreign exchange gains (losses) on consolidation under SFAS 8.

   c. The effect will be to exert downward pressure on reported net income. An example is the PIP grant accounting controversy—see Section 7.5.

   d. The effect will be to eliminate alternative ways of accounting for the same thing. Section 3065 of *CICA Handbook* imposed uniform standards for accounting for leases, for example.   (CGA-Canada)

4. The firms in Healy's study of earnings management (Section 11.2) would have been using the historical cost basis of accounting. Suppose that firms move to greater use of valuation in their accounts, as described in Sections 6.4 and 6.5. For example, they may mark-to-market their financial assets and liabilities.

Required

Would this marking-to-market increase or decrease the potential for earnings management? Explain. (CGA-Canada)

5. The comparative balance sheet of SA Ltd. as at June 30, 1995 is as follows:

	June 30, 1995	June 30, 1994
Assets		
Current assets:		
Accounts receivable (net)	$ 76	$ 60
Inventories	35	53
Prepaid expenses	2	1
	113	114
Capital assets (net)	37	39
Long-term investments	2	2
Deferred development costs	40	39
	$192	$194
Liabilities and Shareholders' Equity		
Current liabilities:		
Bank indebtedness	$ 18	$ 4
Accounts payable	64	71
Customer advances	13	8
Current portion of long-term debt	1	2
Current portion of deferred income taxes	2	1
	98	86
Long-term debt	5	3
Deferred income taxes	0	6
Share capital	73	71
Retained earnings	16	28
	$192	$194

SA Ltd.'s 1995 income statement is as follows:

Sales	$233
Expenses:	
Cost of sales	184
Administrative and selling	35
Research and development	4
Depreciation and amortization	14
Interest	3
	240
Loss before undernoted items	(7)
Income tax recovery	7
Provision for reorganization	(12)
Net loss for the year	$ (12)

Cash flow from operations for 1995 was $7.

Required

a. Calculate the various accruals as Healy did (Section 11.2). For each accrual indicate the extent to which that accrual may contain a discretionary component and briefly explain why.

b. A manager, whose pay is related to reported net income, finds that net income for the year is below the bogey of the incentive plan. What type of earnings management might the manager then engage in? Explain why.

(CGA-Canada)

6. Following are the balance sheet and income statement of CW Ltd. for 1995 with comparative 1994 balance sheet amounts.

CW LTD.
BALANCE SHEET
As at December 31, 1995

	December 31, 1995	December 31, 1994
Assets		
Current assets:		
Cash	$ 13,598	$ 11,043
Accounts receivable (net)	6,235	5,594
Inventories	17,302	18,669
Prepaid expenses	564	562
	37,699	35,868
Fixed assets (net)	12,097	11,855
Deferred charges (net)	312	374
	$ 50,108	$ 48,097
Liabilities and Shareholders' Equity		
Current liabilities:		
Accounts payable	2,491	$ 2,578
Dividends payable	657	656
Income taxes payable	1,525	795
Current portion of long-term debt	175	175
	4,848	4,204
Long-term debt	1,770	1,862
Deferred income taxes	2,176	2,152
Minority interest in net assets of subsidiaries	220	199
Capital stock	2,070	2,070
Retained earnings	39,024	37,610
	$ 50,108	$ 48,097

The 1995 income statement is as follows:

CW LTD.
INCOME STATEMENT
For the Year Ended December 31, 1995

Sales	$56,042
Expenses:	
Manufacturing and administration	47,721
Depreciation	1,187
Interest	222
Amortization of deferred charges	80
	49,210
	6,832
Provision for income taxes	2,789
	4,043
Minority interest in net earnings	
of subsidiaries	22
Net income for the year	$ 4,021

Cash flow from operations for the year was $6,659.

Required

a. Prepare a reconciliation between net income and operating cash flow for 1995 which separately identifies the various accruals in net income.

b. Suppose that CW's managers' bonuses are tied to the firm's net income. Discuss conditions under which CW managers might have incentives to manipulate earnings downwards.

c. Discuss *two* incentives that CW managers might have to smooth earnings over time.   (CGA-Canada)

7. The article here reproduced entitled "Where's the Risk in CEOs' Rewards?" from *Fortune*, December 19, 1988 reveals some interesting insights into how many managerial bonus plans work in practice. Rather than being based on a well-defined percentage of reported net income as Healy assumed, the manager's bonus is frequently at the discretion of the board of directors. As the author documents, in such cases, the tendency is to increase bonuses in good times rather than to decrease them in bad times.

WHERE'S THE RISK IN CEOs' REWARDS?

You can't blame the troops for being suspicious. Top management wants to put us on some incentive pay plan? *Us*, out here in Division 12? They want to put more of our pay "at risk," as they say, so we can also earn greater rewards? Right. So what about Mr. Big back at headquarters? Is he going to play too? Suuurrre he is. I'll believe it when I see it.

As forms of incentive pay extend down into the ranks throughout American business experts keep stressing the importance of employees' trusting top managers. The implicit message of every board-based incentive pay plan is, "We're all in this together. When the company prospers, we all do—and when it suffers, we suffer." Trouble is, in many companies that statement is obviously false. With a few notable exceptions, the CEOs suffer little or not at all no matter what happens to the company.

[The evidence is the] profits and CEO pay for a composite of 14 of the largest companies from the Fortune 500 and Fortune Service 500. They represent a range of industries. Each had been run by the same CEO for several years, and all had experienced volatile return on equity. CEO pay was the figure reported in the aggregate remuneration section of the company's proxy statement. Generally that figure is the sum of a CEO's base salary and his bonus for annual, or short-term, performance.

[The] sample shows that CEO pay simply bears no relation to company performance. ROE may go up or down—it matters not. The CEO's pay advances with the stateliness of the *QE2* leaving New York harbor.

Is this type of analysis really fair? Suppose a company earns a magnificent return on equity of, say, 30%. Should the CEO be penalized if the next year that declines to a still extraordinary 25% (without the company's growing considerably)? The logical answer is that he should be paid munificently both years—but just a bit less in the second, since he didn't do quite as well. Or suppose a company's return on equity suffers because the CEO makes heavy investments in R&D, which may not pay off for years. Should his pay be docked? If those investments are winners, the CEO will benefit handsomely through his pay package's long-term components, such as stock options. This analysis does not consider them. Annual pay cannot reliably hope to reflect more than annual performance.

Of course these are only 14 companies, not a large sample. But this writer's experience with well over 100 major American corporations in 23 years of consulting on CEO compensation indicates that they represent a broad trend. In addition, a few of them illustrate persistent patterns in the ways CEOs are paid.

Honeywell ... exemplifies one of the commonest situations. CEO Edson W. Spencer's pay nearly mirrors return on equity when ROE is steady or rising. But when profits plummet, his pay merely dips gently. Then, when profits recover, his pay shoots up. In this case Spencer's pay was almost 50% higher in 1987 than in 1983, but Honeywell's return on equity only slightly exceeded its earlier level.

At least Honeywell demonstrates a link between pay and performance (though a far stronger link when performance is improving than when it's degenerating). At other companies, such as the transportation conglomerate CSX, there's no link at all. Returns leap and fall, but chief Hays T. Watkins's pay rises serenely above them, unaffected.

ITT looks better. When return on equity declined in 1984, the board cut chief Rand V. Araskog's pay in almost exactly the same proportion. But then, as often happens, the directors seemed to lose their nerve. ROE fell again in 1985, but this time they gave Araskog a healthy *raise*, returning his pay practically to its earlier level. After that the company turned around, and, following the usual pattern, the board awarded robust raises even though ROE barely passed its level of four years earlier.

CEO pay seems even wackier when compared with the pay of employees at the other end of the organization chart. Most factory workers, clerks, and front-line service providers face exactly the opposite pay pattern. When company performance declines, they get hit hard—put on reduced hours or laid off. But when performance improves, their pay may not respond at all, at least not for a while. So one of the principal rules of markets—greater rewards entail greater risks—has been turned on its head. Low-level workers, who receive the least rewards, end up taking the most risks. And CEOs, who

get the greatest rewards, face the least risks.

How did this odd situation develop? Mainly as a result of several factors operating together:

- Many CEOs receive huge base salaries. Remember that base salary is part of the CEO's aggregate remuneration, the part that, for practical purposes, is inert. He almost certainly gets a bonus as well, but if his base salary is $1 million, how much motivation can he have to strive for that bonus?

- Many companies' short-term incentive plans begin to generate bonus pools at levels of performance that are ridiculously puny. This writer's study of 100 major companies' bonus plans conducted a few years back showed that the typical company began to generate bonus money once it achieved a triflingly low 6% return on equity. (Last year the median ROE of the Fortune 500 was 14.4%.)

- Most executive bonus plans allow far too much discretion—and with discretion comes rationalization. It is amazing to see the clarity of vision demonstrated by CEOs and board compensation committees when it comes to spotting uncontrollable events that trigger downturns in company performance—events like rising oil prices, rising interest rates, hurricanes, and so forth. Yet it is equally amazing to see the cloudiness of vision demonstrated by the same CEOs and board compensation committees when it comes to spotting external events that spark upturns in company performance—events like falling oil prices, falling interest rates, and a booming economy. In the first case, compensation committees almost always cushion the

CEO's pay from events that he arguably cannot control. But in the second case, those committees seem to assume that great performance is always a result of CEO brilliance. Therefore pay moves sharply upward.

Such behavior could actually *increase* the volatility of company performance. If I note that every time I decrease ROE by, say, five percentage points, my pay package remains essentially the same or even goes up a bit, and that every time I increase ROE by, say, five percentage points, my package increases 60%, it won't take me long to figure that the way to maximize my income is to have a really bad year every so often and then spend the next several years being rewarded munificently for climbing out of the hole I created. Does any CEO really do this? Certainly none would admit it. But giving CEOs such a misguided incentive is asking for trouble.

There's nothing wrong with CEO pay that can't be fixed. The basis of any solution should be a return to the fundamental principle of markets, the idea that CEOs are increasingly asking employees to accept: Rewards and risks go together. Board compensation committees should make outright cuts in base salaries earned by some CEOs. After a lot of thought, not one defense comes to mind for paying a CEO $1 million a year in an inert base salary. This does not mean, however, that CEO *total* pay opportunities should decrease. Rather, the decrease in base salary could be rolled into an even larger bonus opportunity or even greater long-term incentive.

Bonus performance thresholds—the levels of profits required before bonus funds start to accumulate—ought to be increased. If a shareholder can earn a no-brainer 8% investing in 90-day T-bills, why does he want to pay an executive a bonus for earning only 6% on his investment? The CEO's bonus arrangements should also be made fully automatic, or at least mostly automatic. Such arrangements remove the temptation to rationalize.

A few major corporations pay their CEOs according to just such principles. At Bear Stearns, for example, CEO Alan "Ace" Greenberg makes do with a base salary of only $200,000. The bulk of his pay comes from an automatic bonus arrangement under which he receives a percentage of all pretax profits above a threshold figure. (The percentage changes as profits rise.) In fiscal 1987, which ended in April of that year, Bear Stearns made a lot of money, and so did Ace—$5,712,163. This fiscal year profits declined, and Greenberg's pay fell to $2,447,617. Yes, that's still a great deal, but how many CEOs anywhere took a 57% pay cut in one year for any reason?

At Walt Disney, chief Michael Eisner earns a much heftier base salary of $750,000. But he, too, has an automatic bonus arrangement, which entitles him to receive 2% of after-tax profits above a 9% return on equity. As it turns out, Eisner's threshold is much higher than Greenberg's, more than offsetting the higher base salary. Disney's performance has improved every year under Eisner, and he has quickly grown wealthy. Last year his salary and bonus came to $6,729,654.

Are these super-rich plans exemplars of how CEOs should be paid? Yes they are, because they restore risk to the chief's reward. If Bear Stearns earns less than $15 million before taxes this year *for any reason*—ineptitude or a market crash, a bad decision or an earthquake under headquarters—Ace Greenberg gets $200,000, a pittance for a CEO on Wall Street and certainly not much for the chief of a company with $32 billion in assets. But because he is willing to take that risk, the board is willing to pay him impressively when he excels.

That's the principle that smart managers are trying to spread throughout their organizations. Like all basic company values, it won't mean a thing until the man at the top embraces it.

SOURCE: Graef S. Crystal, "Where's the Risk in CEOs' Rewards?" *Fortune*, December 19, 1988. © 1988 Time Inc. All rights reserved. Reprinted by permission of the author and *Fortune*.

Required

a. A bonus plan, in theory, should align the interests of managers and shareholders by making managers want to maximize profits. Do the "riskless" bonus awards described in the article reduce this alignment? Explain.

b. The author argues that bonus performance thresholds (bogeys) be raised and that bonuses become "automatic." Would a manager who was remunerated by a high-bogey, automatic bonus plan have more or less incentive to manage income than a manager remunerated under the more flexible plans described earlier in the article? Explain.

(CGA-Canada)

8. A way to manage earnings is to manipulate the point in the operating cycle at which revenue is regarded as earned. An article entitled "Bausch & Lomb Posts 4th-Quarter Loss, Says SEC Has Begun Accounting Probe" appeared in the *Wall Street Journal* on January 26, 1995.

The article reports on questions raised by the SEC about Bausch & Lomb Inc.'s premature recording of revenue from products shipped to distributors in 1993. "Bausch & Lomb oversupplied distributors with contact lenses and sunglasses at the end of 1993 through an aggressive marketing plan, and was forced to buy back a large portion of the inventory [in 1994] when consumer demand didn't meet expectations." The oversupply amounted to around $10 million, which Bausch & Lomb claimed was not "material."

In addition, the article points out that in the fourth quarter of 1994 Bausch & Lomb had incurred $20 million in "one-time expenses" which included expenses from "previously announced staff cuts of about 2,000." Also, in the fourth quarter Bausch & Lomb took a $75 million charge in its oral-care division in order "to reduce unamortized goodwill that it recorded when Bausch & Lomb bought the business in 1988." Many analysts are saying that Bausch & Lomb are looking to sell the oral-care division, and this reduction of unamortized goodwill will make the division look better.

Required

a. What earnings management policy did Bausch & Lomb appear to be following in 1993?

b. Evaluate revenue recognition policy as an earnings management device, from management's standpoint.

c. The article refers to a $20 million writeoff in 1994 relating to staff cuts, and another $75 million writeoff in Bausch & Lomb's oral-care division. What earnings management strategy does the firm appear to have followed in 1994? Why?

9. Earnings management extends into the realm of new share offerings (IPOs), since the prospectus for a new offering includes current and recent financial statements. An article entitled "RJR Nabisco's Use of Accounting Technique Dealing with Goodwill Is Getting a Hard Look" which appeared in the *Wall Street Journal* on April 8, 1993, describes some earnings management considerations surrounding a $1.5 billion new share offering of Nabisco, a food subsidiary of RJR Nabisco Holdings.

According to the article, the parent, RJR Nabisco Holdings, has substantial goodwill on its books arising from its acquisition of Nabisco, which is being amortized at a rate of $607 million annually (generally speaking, both the *CICA Handbook*, Section 1580.58, and, in the United States, APB 17 require that goodwill from acquisitions be amortized over a period of up to 40 years). However, this goodwill amortization appears only on the books of the parent—not on those of Nabisco.

"What RJR is doing is presenting Nabisco's annual earnings without the burden of $206 million of 1992 'goodwill,' leaving this earnings-depressing item with the parent company instead." This resulted in Nabisco increasing its 1992 after-tax profit from $179 million to $345 million or from 48 cents a share to 93 cents a share.

"Nabisco executives indicated the food company could generate 1993 earnings of as much as $1.30 a share. That earnings level might justify the proposed selling price of $17 to $19 a share for the new Nabisco shares, analysts say."

The article questions whether RJR is managing the reported net income of its Nabisco subsidiary by not "pushing down" (see Section 6.3.5) goodwill to Nabisco.

Required

a. What pattern of earnings management is RJR following? Why?

b. Without considering any strategic issues surrounding the pricing of the new shares, do you think that goodwill should be pushed down to the subsidiary company?

c. Do you think the strategy of not pushing down the goodwill will be successful in raising the issue price of the new shares? Explain why or why not.

10.   The article reproduced here from *The Economist* (October 8, 1994) raises questions about earnings management around the time of initial public offerings (IPOs). We have already seen evidence of manipulation of demand and supply of new share offerings in Section 6.2.3. Perhaps earnings management is another way of manipulating the market price of newly offered shares, consistent with the evidence of Friedlan (1994) (Section 11.3.5).

INITIAL PUBLIC OFFERINGS

Sheep and Goats

Americans have a remarkable appetite for shares in initial public offerings (IPOs). Although this year's total will be well down on 1993's all-time high of $57.4 billion—companies can be reluctant to sell their shares when markets are nervous—it will still be one of the biggest on record. The puzzle is why: shares bought in IPOs are notoriously bad performers. True, prices often rise to a premium on the first day of trading, mainly thanks to demand from investors who missed out in the initial allocation. From then on, shares on average under-perform compared with the market as a whole.

Important evidence about why IPO shares often do badly is set out in two new studies by three American-based economists. Analysing the long-term performance of flotations that took place between 1980 and 1984, they found, in the first study, that firms typically went public after an unusually good set of results. After-tax profits of the firms in the sample on average rose in the financial year before the offering, then fell continuously until six years after it. Cash-flow, too, rose in the year before the IPO, and fell during the one in which it took place, but then remained stable.

Such deft timing could of course be due simply to good luck, or perhaps to demand from investors after a firm has performed well. However, there is a more sinister possibility, explored in the second study: that managers boost earnings artificially around the time of an offering in order to get the best possible price for their shares.

They have plenty of opportunity: American accounting rules allow firms going public to restate profits going back several years. These restatements must be audited, of course, but auditors allow company bosses considerable discretion in some things, such as the rate at which some assets and liabilities are depreciated, which determines "accruals," adjustments to cash-flow ostensibly made so that profits give an accurate indication of long-term performance.

The second study ranked each IPO firm according to the ratio of its accruals to a benchmark of accruals made by similar firms. It then looked at the subsequent performance of the shares. The result is striking. IPOs by firms with low accruals relative to the benchmark in the year before flotation performed much better over the following three years than those with high accruals. The fifth of IPOs with the lowest accruals-to-benchmark did significantly better than the market, while the fifth with the highest ratio badly under-performed. The finding was even stronger when firms were ranked by accruals relative to working capital.

Intriguingly, the relationship was strongest when the IPOs were ranked using accruals made in the financial year during which the floatation took place.

One possible explanation, suggest the three authors, is that managers whose firm is going public are often prevented from selling their shares for an agreed period after the IPO. If they themselves are to profit, these managers have a powerful incentive to do all they can to keep the share price high during that period, including, if need be, (legally) massaging their accounting numbers a little. Next time you are offered a sure-fire IPO, be sure to look at the firm's track record.

SOURCE: "Initial Public Offerings: Sheep and Goats," *The Economist*, October 8, 1994, p. 88. © 1994 The Economist Newspaper Group, Inc. Reprinted with permission. Further reproduction prohibited.

Required

a. The article states that "accounting rules allow firms going public to restate profits going back several years." Presumably, this is done to produce a better-looking past earnings series in the prospectus. Give an argument that this type of earnings management could be beneficial by conveying information to investors.

b. The article refers to the behaviour of accruals before and after the IPO, suggesting that firm managers may have an incentive to manipulate accruals so as to maximize the price they receive upon resale of shares they have acquired as part of the IPO.

   i. What are some of the advantages of accruals as an earnings management device from management's standpoint?

   ii. Like Healy (Section 11.2), the studies referred to in the article appear to use total accruals as a proxy for discretionary accruals. What are some of the methodological difficulties that arise because of the necessity to use total accruals as a proxy for discretionary accruals?

c. Consider the finding that low total accruals prior to an IPO are associated with better share price performance over a three-year period following the IPO. Does this reinforce or refute your argument in part **a** that earnings management conveys information to investors? Explain.

11. The article by Randall Smith, Steven Lipin, and Amal Kumar Naj, here reproduced from the *Wall Street Journal* (November 3, 1994), "Managing Profits" describes some of the earnings management devices used by General Electric to report strong, consistent earnings growth over the last decade.

MANAGING PROFITS

How General Electric Damps Fluctuations in Its Annual Earnings

The debacle at Kidder, Peabody & Co. might ruin the year for most companies.

But the roughly $750 million in losses and after-tax charges that General Electric Co. will incur this year before finally unloading Kidder will barely dent GE's smooth, consistent earnings growth. Despite those losses, some analysts believe, GE may be able to match or top last year's profit of $5.15 billion before accounting charges.

In the past decade, GE's earnings have risen every year, although net income fell in 1991 and 1993 because of accounting changes related to post-retirement benefits. The gains, ranging between 1.7% and 17%, have been fairly steady—especially for a company in a lot of cyclical businesses. As a result, GE almost seems able to override the business cycle.

How does GE do it? One undeniable explanation is the fundamental growth of its eight industrial businesses and 24 financial-services units. "We're the best company in the world," declares Dennis Dammerman, GE's chief financial officer.

But another way is "earnings management," the orchestrated timing of gains and losses to smooth out bumps and, especially, avoid a decline. Among big companies, GE is "certainly a relatively aggressive practitioner of earnings management," says Martin Sankey, a CS First Boston Inc. analyst.

To smooth out fluctuations, GE frequently offsets one-time gains from big asset sales with restructuring charges; that keeps earnings from rising so high that they can't be topped the following year. GE also times sales of some equity stakes and even acquisitions to produce profit gains when needed.

Asked several times about earnings management, Mr. Dammerman declines to discuss directly whether GE engages in the practice. Asked whether offsetting one-time gains with one-time charges could be considered earnings management, he says, "I've never looked at it in that manner." He also declines to say whether other companies use such tactics.

Most U.S. companies do try to smooth profit growth. Walt Disney Co., for example, can decide when it wants profits from a videocassette re-release of *Snow White*. Banks and insurance companies do a lot of smoothing by adjusting the level of their reserves, and many companies time write-offs carefully.

A look at GE illustrates how analysts say one giant corporation manages earnings. They add that few companies have maneuvered so successfully for so long on so large a scale. GE's size and diversity give it an unusual array of opportunities, of course. Moreover, Chairman Jack Welch relentlessly monitors GE's profit growth.

A DISMAYED MR. WELCH

Last April, when announcing that a bond-trading scheme at Kidder had generated false 1993 profits and triggered a

$210 million first-quarter charge, Mr. Welch said investors prize GE's ability "to deliver strong, consistent earnings growth in a myriad of global economic conditions. Having this reprehensible scheme ... break our more-than-decade-long string of 'no surprises' has all of us damn mad."

His dislike of surprises extends beyond what GE's operating executives tell him to what GE tells Wall Street. Russell Leavitt, a Salomon Brothers analyst, says GE executives "give you some guidance" on what other analysts' estimates are and how reasonable they are. The result, says Ben Zacks of Zacks Investment Research, is that analysts' GE estimates fall in a "very, very tight range."

GE especially prizes consistent growth because it has so many different businesses that most analysts can't track them all. For example, GE is followed by electrical-equipment analysts, most of whom have a loose grasp of financial services.

NARROWING THE DISCOUNT

GE's two major parts are an industrial conglomerate and a financial-services conglomerate, and both segments outdo their market peers. According to an analysis of data from Morgan Stanley & Co., industrial conglomerates sold at an average 20% discount to the market as of Sept. 30, based on their multiple of price to next year's anticipated earnings, while financial-services companies—banks, finance and insurance—were at a 35% discount. But partly because of its consistent earnings growth, GE sold at a discount of only 11%.

One financial calculation that helped smooth earnings at GE a few years ago was an increase in the assumed rate of future investment returns on pension funds. In 1991, a weak year at many companies, GE raised its return-rate assumption a full percentage point, to 9.5% from the 8.5% in effect for five years.

That change, by reducing GE's pension costs, helped lift what it terms the profits on its pension fund to $696 million in 1991 from $380 million in 1990, a pretax swing of $316 million. For companies like GE with overfunded pension plans, accounting rules require such changes to be reflected in corporate profits.

How much did GE's overall profit rise in 1991? Just $132 million after tax.

However, GE says the increase in its assumed return on pension assets reflected the lofty investment returns in the 1980s and wasn't any higher than rates assumed by other big companies. It says the change wasn't designed to raise reported 1991 profits.

The clearest way GE manages earnings is through restructuring charges. When GE sells a business at a profit or takes an unusual gain, it generally takes an offsetting restructuring charge of roughly equal size. In six of the years since 1983, GE has taken charges totaling $3.95 billion in this way.

Last year, when GE booked a $1.43 billion pretax gain on the sale of its aerospace business, for example, it took a $1.01 billion charge to cover costs of "closing and downsizing and streamlining of certain production, service and administrative facilities world-wide." After tax, the gain and the charge matched up exactly at $678 million.

And that 1993 charge, by anticipating some specific 1994 expenses such as "asset write-offs, lease terminations and severance benefits," is helping GE report better profit this year. Without the 1993 charge,

HOW GE OFFSETS GAINS FROM ASSET SALES

Year	Pretax Gain (millions)	Source of the Gain	Pretax Restructuring Charges (millions)
1993	$1,430	Sale of aerospace unit to Martin Marietta	$1,011
1987	858	Change in accounting for taxes and inventory	1,027
1986	50	Sale of foreign affiliate	311
1985	518	Sale of three coal properties and 37% cable stake	447
1984	617	Sales of Utal Int'l, small appliance unit, cable company	636
1983	117	Sale of radio/TV stations and Gearhart Industrial stake	147

SOURCE: General Electric Co.

some of those expenses could have reduced this year's net income. Because some of the expenses eventually would have to be paid anyway, First Boston's Mr. Sankey says, this reporting strategy allows GE to "transmute" one-time gains into future operating income.

One rationale for using this tactic: GE executives believe that many investors ignore one-time gains from asset sales in valuing companies. But clearly, taking an offsetting charge against a big gain prevents GE's earnings from getting too high in any one year; by spreading the gain into future years, the company can more easily report the steady growth that investors prefer.

Mr. Dammerman, the finance chief, says that whenever GE anticipates a gain on an asset sale or a tax or accounting change, its executives "sit down with our businesses and say, 'What are some strategic decisions that you would make to make the business better going forward?' " He says GE's use of such charges is one

way it pursues both short-term and long-term goals; without such gains, he adds, some of the spending wouldn't have been planned or would have been timed differently.

PRACTICE UNDER SCRUTINY

Richard Leftwich, an expert in financial-statement analysis at the University of Chicago business school, says analysts and regulators are questioning U.S. corporations' widespread use of restructuring charges. He wonders how companies distinguish between everyday expenses needed to remain competitive and truly extraordinary events. Such use of restructuring charges "raises real issues for how to think about what the future profits mean," he adds, "because the costs are being written off now, but the profits are being reported in the future."

Later this month, accounting rulemakers, under prodding by the Securities and Exchange Commission, are expected to sharply limit such big one-time write-offs. The new rules would force companies to spread such charges over future years or take them when the relevant expenses are actually paid rather than when planned.

While conceding the SEC "hates" such charges, Mr. Dammerman adds: "It's not like we're creating some big cookie jar" from which GE takes profits at will.

Another way GE manages its earnings is by literally buying them—by acquiring companies or assets that are immediately profitable because they throw off more income than GE's cost of financing. Much of the growth in GE Capital's earnings in the past few years has been generated by a spate of acquisitions.

"Of course we're buying earnings when we do an acquisition," says James Parke, GE Capital's chief financial officer. The financial-services subsidiary acquired assets totaling $16.9 billion in 1993 alone.

Daniel Porter, GE Capital's North American chief of retailer financial services, says he and his colleagues may hunt for acquisitions if his division might miss its annual earnings target. He says they ask: "Gee, does somebody else have some income? Is there some other deals we can make?"

RISK IN HASTY ACTION

The danger, of course, is that a headlong rush into acquisitions to book earnings could led to unwise decisions. Management's ambitious growth targets create GE Capital's biggest business risk, according to Sanjay Sharma, a Moody's Investors Service analyst.

"As growth in the commercial finance sector has become difficult to achieve because of growing bank and nonbank competition, an aggressive strategy in this sector can only be accomplished by paying higher premiums for portfolio acquisitions—in effect, by taking greater risks," Mr. Sharma says. Already, he notes, the returns on GE Capital's mushrooming trove of assets are slipping, to 1.4% in 1993 from 1.61% in 1989. To keep growing so fast without major gains from operations, GE would have to make more and more acquisitions, possibly compounding the risk.

Isn't it unsound to have earnings-report considerations drive the timing of acquisitions? Mr. Dammerman says that as long as executives keep both long-term and short-term goals in mind, "I see nothing wrong with someone saying, 'Look, I have an earnings objective for the year, and to achieve that earnings objective maybe I need to go make an acquisition.' That's fine if the individual can come up with a good acquisition."

Two former GE Capital executives say GE's financial business contains a wealth of hidden value—which they call reserves—that can be tapped to get income as needed. "Are there hidden values there? Absolutely," Mr. Parke says, though they are "impossible to measure."

One way GE stores profits for future use is, ironically, by following fairly conservative accounting practices. In fact, John W. Stanger, GE Capital's president from 1975 to 1984, says those practices would occasionally annoy managers who believed the company was "trying to bury profits" that they had racked up in a stellar year.

HANDLING USED AIRCRAFT

GE Capital also has considerable discretion over the timing of sales of warrants or equity kickers obtained in the course of lending and in deciding whether to sell or re-lease aircraft coming off lease. GE Capital has "significant ability to come up with earnings on demand," First Boston's Mr. Sankey says, because of its "diversified portfolio" and "very large amount of flexibility in how you report earnings."

Take the hypothetical example of an aircraft nearing the end of a 15-year lease. GE may have already written off most of the plane's cost, leaving its book value low. GE can potentially book a gain if it then sells the plane, Mr. Sankey says, but not if the jet is re-leased to another airline.

Mr. Parke denies that GE Capital fattens its earnings by selling aircraft. It has some discretion, he says, but this is limited because "you have to have a buyer, and you have to have the right market conditions in order to maximize the value."

The timing of sales of equity interests obtained throughout warrants—the equity operations that GE often gets for lending on especially risky buyouts—also is "very discretionary," Mr. Sankey says. But GE executives say they have only a little discretion because such sales usually depend on when a company goes public. Now holding a potentially valuable 50% stake in Montgomery Ward, however, GE Capital would have considerable say over when the retailer went public.

Such maneuvers are particularly difficult to monitor at GE Capital because the amount of information it discloses is relatively scant compared with the wealth of information about its parent company. GE Capital, for example, doesn't differentiate its income from asset sales.

"You look at their financial reports—they are pretty skinny. A lot of analysts feel frustrated because it's such a complex organization," says Richard Schmidt of Standard & Poor's Corp., the credit-rating agency. He concedes that many commercial finance companies keep their numbers close to the vest, too.

As an unregulated financial-services company, GE Capital also has more flexibility to defer write-offs than do highly regulated U.S. banks. During the 1990-91 recession, regulators required banks to take write-downs, add reserves and sell assets. But GE Capital contends that it writes off bad assets *faster* than banks do and that rating agencies and the markets are tougher than bank regulators.

THE RCA ACQUISITION

One of GE's most intriguing moves to boost its net income was in its accounting for its $6.4 billion acquisition of RCA Corp. in 1986. Anytime an acquisition is made for a price exceeding the book value of the business, the premium over book value must be recorded on the buyer's books.

In the case of RCA, one former GE executive recalls that GE allocated a disproportionate amount of this so-called goodwill to NBC, increasing the TV network's book value while reducing that of other RCA assets. GE's own annual reports appear to substantiate his recollection. In 1987, the year after the acquisition, GE raised NBC's book value to $3.8 billion from $3.4 billion. The higher book value for NBC and the resulting lower value for other RCA assets raised GE's profits on sales of some of RCA's non-NBC assets.

Among the RCA units sold, GE recorded a $110 million gain on the disposition in 1991 of NBC's interest in an

RCA-Columbia home-video joint venture. And the aerospace business was sold in 1993 at a pretax profit of $1.43 billion. That leaves NBC as the last major piece of RCA still on GE's books.

Mr. Dammerman says that boosting gains from future non-NBC asset sales didn't enter into how NBC was valued and that GE didn't know at the time which businesses would be sold. He adds that GE couldn't record profits from some RCA assets sold soon after the acquisition.

However, one consequence of assigning a higher book value to NBC eventually became apparent when GE began considering the sale of the network in the early 1990s. The higher book value raised the price GE would have had to obtain to avoid booking a loss. When GE held talks about selling NBC to Paramount Communications Inc. (now owned by Viacom Inc.), Paramount proposed to structure the sale financing in a way that would help GE avoid an immediate write-down, according to two people familiar with the negotiations. Mr. Dammerman says that although GE wanted to avoid a loss, the proposed transaction wasn't structured with that aim.

Despite some experts' doubts about earnings management, some accountants say it can be helpful as long as corporate executives try to convey a fair picture. "Some people would say maybe smoothing makes sense because it gives the best indication of the future and the long-term trend," says Peter Wilson, who specializes in financial-statement analysis at the Sloan School of Management at Massachusetts Institute of Technology.

But Howard Schilit, an accounting professor at American University in Washington, comments: "Earnings management can be very dangerous for the investor because you are creating something artificial. The numbers should reflect how the company is actually doing."

GE executives differ in how much smoothing they acknowledge. In an initial interview, GE Capital Chairman Gary Wendt said, "We do a little, not a lot." His financial chief, Mr. Parke, said, We have a lot of assets in this business. ... Obviously, there are timing issues associated with when those assets are sold."

Required

a. Evaluate the effectiveness of restructuring charges as an earnings management device. Do you agree with Professor Leftwich's reservations about such charges and with the SEC's expected limitations on such provisions? Explain.

b. Explain whether you agree with Peter Wilson, who says "maybe smoothing makes sense" or with Howard Schilit, who says "earnings management can be very dangerous."

c. One of the most interesting aspects of the article is its implications for security market efficiency. If large, complex firms such as GE have "so many different businesses that most analysts can't track them all," how can the market price of GE's shares properly reflect all that is known about the firm? To what extent do you think earnings management is a substitute for analysts in informing the market about the firm's value and prospects?

Standard Setting: Theoretical Issues

12.1 Overview

We now return to the role of standard setting that was introduced in Chapter 1. Recall that we view the standard setter as a mediator between the conflicting interests of investors and managers. The fundamental problem of financial accounting theory is how to conduct this mediation, that is, how to reconcile the financial reporting and efficient contracting roles of accounting information or, equivalently, how to determine the socially "right" amount of information.

Of course, we should not take for granted that regulation is necessary for this reconciliation. Much of the required mediation can be accomplished by market forces. Nevertheless, substantial arguments can be made that market forces alone are unable to drive the right amount of information production. Our purpose in this chapter is to review these arguments.

The extent of standard setting is a challenging one for accountants. Many aspects of firms' information production are regulated, and many of these regulations are laid down by accounting standard setting bodies themselves, in the form of GAAP. Furthermore, the amount of regulation is increasing all the time, as more and more accounting standards are promulgated.

As you are aware, many industries in recent years have been deregulated. Airlines, trucking, financial services, and telecommunications are examples of industries that have seen substantial deregulation. What would happen if the information industry was deregulated? Would this produce a flood of competition and innovation or would information production collapse into chaos? At present, the answers to these questions are not known. However, discussion of the pros and cons of standard setting helps us to see the tradeoffs that are involved and to appreciate the crucial role of information in society.

12.2   *Regulation of Economic Activity*

There are numerous instances of regulation of economic activity in our economy. Firms that have a monopoly, such as electric power companies, local telephone companies, and transportation companies are common examples. Here, regulation typically takes the form of regulation of rates, regulation of the rate of return on invested capital, or both. Public safety is an area subject to frequent regulation as, for example, in elevator inspection laws, standards for automobile tire construction, and fire protection regulations. Communications is another area that, in many countries, is deemed sufficiently sensitive to attract regulation.

Other sets of regulations affect financial institutions and securities markets. The primary reason for such regulation is to protect individuals who are at an information disadvantage. This points up the fact that information asymmetry underlies the need for regulation of information production. If there was no information asymmetry, so that managerial actions and inside information were freely observable by all, there would be no need to protect individuals from the consequences of information disadvantage.

Information asymmetry is thus frequently used to justify regulations to protect the information-disadvantaged. Insider trading rules and regulations to ensure full disclosure in prospectuses are examples. In addition to protecting ordinary investors, such regulations are also intended to improve the operation of capital markets by enhancing public confidence in their fairness.

Accounting is also strongly affected by regulations designed to protect against information asymmetry. An important role of accounting and auditing is to report relevant and reliable information, thereby reducing information asymmetry between firm insiders, the investing public, and other users. However, this role requires that accountants and auditors be credible and competent. Thus, there are laws to regulate the accounting professions which control entry and maintain high standards. Many other regulations also affect accountants. Minimum disclosure requirements for annual reports are laid down in corporations acts. Government statistical agencies and taxation authorities require financial information. Quasi-governmental bodies such as the OSC and the SEC require a variety of information disclosures for firms whose shares are publicly traded. Private bodies such as stock exchanges require periodic disclosures from firms whose securities are traded on the exchange. Finally, other private bodies, such as the CICA and the FASB, set accounting and auditing standards.

Thus, we see that accounting is a highly regulated area of economic activity. Governments are directly involved in this regulation through laws to control the creation of professional accounting bodies and their rights to public practice, and also through minimum disclosure requirements for annual reports and prospectuses, as laid down in corporations acts. Indirect government involvement comes, for example, through the creation of securities commissions. Furthermore, the professions themselves do much of their own regulating by formulating and monitoring accounting and auditing principles. Henceforth, we will use the term **central authority** to refer to any of these regulatory bodies.

In this chapter our primary concerns are the regulation of minimum disclosure requirements, generally accepted accounting and auditing standards, and the requirement that public companies have audits. We will use the term **standard setting** to denote the establishment of these various rules and regulations. Note that standard setting involves the regulation of *firms' information production decisions.* For our purposes, it does not matter whether these standards are set by direct or indirect regulation. In the case of indirect regulation, authority to set standards is clearly delegated by, or allowed by, the government. The main point to realize is that firms are not completely free to control the amount and timing of the information they produce about themselves. Rather, they must do so under a host of regulations which we shall call standards, laid down by some central authority.

Standard setting is the regulation of firms' information production decisions by some central authority.

Note that in addition to the production of information in the form of financial statements, we include an *audit* as part of a firm's information production. While an audit may not generate information directly, it adds *credibility* to the information the firm does produce. Consequently, it is an important component of the total information released by the firm.

While firms' information production decisions are highly regulated, we have witnessed several instances of *deregulation* in recent years in other industries—transportation, telecommunications, banking, and financial institutions come to mind immediately. There is little doubt that such changes, at least initially, foster substantial increases in efficiency, innovation, and price competition. Certainly, they produce dramatic changes in the structure of the industries affected.

What form would a deregulation of standard setting take? This could include cancellation of existing standards—let firms account for leases or pensions as they see fit, for example. It could also include a reduction in supervision by securities commissions and other central authorities, with greater reliance on the legal system to deter fraudulent reporting. Yet another form would be reduction or elimination of requirements for audits. Firms could be left free to determine the nature and extent of audit that they want.

Most people's reaction to suggestions such as these would be that the securities market would degenerate into chaos. Perhaps this would be the case, but, as we shall see, a surprising variety of private contractual and market forces and other mechanisms exists to produce, and credibly communicate, relevant information (by private, we mean nonregulated). A suggestion for deregulation, therefore, proposes that these private contractual and market forces be given a chance to operate more freely, just as they have in other industries where regulation was once strongly entrenched. Consequently, a large part of our analysis of standard setting is the examination of private incentives for the production of accounting information.

We shall also examine a number of characteristics of the private incentives for information production that may lead to **market failure**. By market failure we mean an inability of market forces to produce a socially "right" amount of information, that is, to produce information to the point where its marginal cost to society equals its marginal benefit.

Given the complexities of information discussed in Section 1.2, it is extremely difficult to calculate these marginal social costs and benefits. Consequently, it may seem unfair to label an inability of market forces to drive first-best production of information as a market *failure*. Nevertheless, since the purpose of regulation ideally is to restore the socially first-best solution when market forces cannot, this is the term we shall use. In effect, this socially first-best amount of information production constitutes a benchmark against which more realistic second-best production can be compared, much like the present-value accounting of Chapter 2 constitutes an ideal benchmark for asset valuation and income measurement.

In considering issues of information production, it is helpful to distinguish between two types of information that a manager may possess. One type is called **proprietary information**. This is information that, if released, would adversely affect future cash flows of the firm. Examples would be technical information about valuable patents, or plans for strategic initiatives such as takeover bids or mergers. The costs to the manager and firm of releasing proprietary information can be quite high.

The second type is called **nonproprietary information**. This is information that does not directly affect firm cash flows.[1] It includes financial statement information, earnings forecasts, details of new financing, and so on. The audit is also included in nonproprietary information. Note that nonproprietary information includes net income. Note also that it can affect the price of a firm's securities. Therefore it can affect the manager's remuneration when this depends on net income and/or share price. Thus, when we define nonproprietary information as not directly affecting future firm cash flows we mean cash flows before manager remuneration. Bear in mind that nonproprietary information can be positive or negative in its effects on firm value.

12.3   *Private Incentives for Information Production*

12.3.1 *WAYS TO CHARACTERIZE INFORMATION PRODUCTION*

While the term "production" of information may take some getting used to, we use it for two reasons. First, we want to think of information as a *commodity* that can be produced and sold. Then, it is natural to consider separately the costs and benefits of information production.

Second, we want a unified way of thinking about the various ways information production can be accomplished. Information is a complex commodity. Just what do we mean when we speak of the quantity of information produced? There are several ways to answer this question.

First, we can think of **finer information**. For example, a thermometer which tells you the temperature in degrees is a finer information system than one which only tells you if the temperature is above or below freezing—the first thermometer tells you everything that the second one does, and more. It enables a finer reading of the temperature. In an accounting context, a finer reporting system adds more detail to the existing historical-cost-based statements. Examples of finer reporting include new or expanded footnote disclosure, additional line items on the financial statements, segment reporting, and so on. In terms of our decision theory discussion of Chapter 3, finer information production means a better ability to discriminate between realizations of the states of nature. For example, in a decision problem where the relevant set of states of nature is the temperature, a thermometer which tells you degrees enables better discrimination between different temperature states than one which only tells you if the temperature is above or below freezing. We can also think of the information perspective on decision usefulness, discussed in Chapter 5, as implying finer information production.

Second, we can think of **additional information**. For example, we might add a barometer to our thermometer. In an accounting context, additional information means the introduction of new information systems to report on matters not covered by the historical cost system. Examples would include marking-to-market, which introduces the effects of changing prices into financial reporting; management discussion and analysis; and future-oriented financial information, which expands reporting responsibility to include expected future operations. In decision theory terms, additional information means an expansion of the set of relevant states of nature upon which the firm's performance depends. Thus a thermometer-barometer reports on atmospheric pressure as well as temperature. In effect, additional information can produce greater relevance in reporting. We can think of the measurement perspective on decision usefulness discussed in Chapter 6 as a move towards producing additional value-relevant information.

A third way to think about information production is in terms of its **credibility**. A thermometer which is accurate to within one degree is more credible than one which is accurate only to within five degrees. In accounting terms, more credible information is more reliable. It is often suggested that financial statements which are audited by a "Big Six" auditor are more reliable than those audited by a non–"Big Six" auditor, because the big audit firm may have more talent available or will simply have more to lose from an audit error than a small firm.[2] Similarly, an audit firm which uses a low level of materiality and high precision in its audit tests would produce a more reliable audit than a firm with higher materiality and lower precision. Also, financial statements prepared under a statutory audit would be more reliable than statements prepared under a compilation engagement, because the auditor does more work.

Fourth, we can think of a number of other mechanisms for information production, such as **signals**. We will elaborate upon these later.

In this chapter we will not need to distinguish these different ways to produce information and will refer to them all, rather loosely, as **information production**. Note that however we think of its production, more information will require higher costs.

12.3.2 *CONTRACTUAL INCENTIVES FOR INFORMATION PRODUCTION*

Incentives for private information production arise from the contracts that firms enter into. As we saw in Chapter 9, information is necessary to monitor compliance with contracts. For example, if managerial effort is unobservable, this leads to an incentive contract based on the results of the firm's operations. Then, information about net income is needed to provide a measure of results. Also, an audit adds credibility to the reported net income, so that both the owner and the manager of the firm are willing to accept reported net income as a reliable measure of managerial performance.

Similarly, when a firm issues debt, it typically includes debt covenants in the contract. Information is needed about the various ratios on which the covenants are based, so that the firm's adherence to its covenants can be monitored over the life of the debt issue. Again, an audit adds credibility to the covenant information.

Another contractual reason for private information production arises when a privately owned firm goes public. This was modelled by Jensen and Meckling (1976). The owner-manager of a firm going public, after selling all or part interest, has a motivation to increase shirking. Note that prior to the IPO the shirking problem was internalized—the owner-manager bore all the costs. The costs of shirking are the reduced profits that result. Subsequent to the new issue, the owner-manager does *not* bear all the costs—the new owners will bear their proportionate share. Thus, shirking costs the owner-manager less after going public, so he or she will engage in more of it. This is an agency cost to the new owners of the firm.

Investors will be aware of this motivation, however, and will bid down the amount they are willing to pay for the new issue by the expected amount of agency costs. In effect, the firm's cost of capital rises. Consequently, the owner-manager has an incentive to contract to limit his or her shirking and thereby raise the issue price. For example, the contract between the owner-manager and the new investors in the firm may include a *forecast*, which the owner-manager will be motivated to meet (this will be recognized as the production of *additional* information). Alternatively, the contract may provide for a lot of detail in the financial statements (*finer* information), to make it more difficult for the owner-manager to hide or bury costs of perquisites. Also, the contract may provide for an audit to increase the *credibility* of the information production. In all of these cases, the owner-manager commits to produce information that will convince investors that he or she will in fact continue to manage diligently. Investors, realizing this, will be willing to pay more for an interest in the firm than they would otherwise.

The key point here is that the firm has a *private* incentive to produce information in all of these contracting scenarios—no central authority is needed to force information production. Furthermore, since the types and amounts of information to be produced under the contract are negotiated and agreed to by all contracting parties, the right amount of information is produced, by definition. That is, the information production decision is internalized between the contracting parties. Then, the question of whether too much or too little information is produced does not arise. Failure to provide for information production in the contract will make it difficult or impossible to enforce, and thus less efficient.

In principle, the contractual motivation for information production can be extended to any group of contracting parties. Consider, for example, the relationship between the firm manager and investors. The investor's decision problem was reviewed in Chapter 3, where we concluded that investors want information about the expected return and risk of their investments. The firm manager and each investor could contract for the desired amount of information about the firm's future cash flows, financial position, and so on. The contract could provide that the investor pay for this information or, perhaps, the manager would offer it free to raise the demand for the firm's shares. Note that different investors would, in general, want different amounts of information about the firm. One investor, adept at financial analysis, might demand a very fine projection of future operations, from which to prepare an estimate of future cash flows and returns on investment. Another investor may simply want information about the firm's dividend policy. A very risk-averse investor might demand a very credible audit, at a correspondingly high cost, while another investor would prefer the least costly audit available. Other investors may not demand any information at all, particularly if their investment portfolios are well diversified. Instead, they might rely on market efficiency to price-protect them.

Unfortunately, while direct contracting for information production may be fine in principle, it will not always work in practice. The reason should be apparent from the discussion in the previous paragraph. In many cases there are simply *too many* parties for contracts to be feasible. If the firm manager was to attempt to negotiate a contract for information production with every potential investor, the negotiation costs alone would be prohibitive. In addition, to the extent that different investors want different information, the firm's costs of information production would also be prohibitive. If, as an alternative, the manager attempted to negotiate a single contract with all investors, these investors would have to agree on what information they wanted. Again, given the disparate information needs of different investors, this process would be extremely time-consuming and costly if, indeed, it was possible at all. Hence, the contracting approach only seems feasible when there are a *few* parties involved. The owner-manager incentive contracts studied in Section 9.4.2 , involved only two persons. Our long-term lending contract example in Section 9.4.3 involved a manager and a lender.

Even if contracting parties do reach an information production agreement, another problem arises. Unless the agreement can be enforced (as in a cooperative game), parties to the agreement may be tempted to violate it for their own short-run benefit. This is similar to the problem faced by cartels, where members may bolt the cartel.

It seems that while contracts are an important source of private information production, we cannot rely on them completely for the information needs of society. Accordingly, we now turn to a second set of private incentives for firms' information production. We shall call these **market-based** incentives.

12.3.3 MARKET-BASED INCENTIVES FOR INFORMATION PRODUCTION

Private incentives for managers to produce information about their firms also derive from market forces. Several markets are involved.

Consider first the market for managers. As discussed by Fama (1980), we can think of managers as being subject to a *managerial labour market*, which puts a market value on their managerial services. Rational managers will prefer a high market value, other things equal. This will raise the reservation utility they can demand in an agency employment contract. Consequently, they will be motivated to maximize the market value of the firm, since their own market value is presumably governed by their success in creating firm value.

Given that a managerial labour market motivates a manager to maximize firm value, there will be two main effects on that manager's incentive to produce information. First, there will be a reduced tendency for the manager to shirk, which means that a more efficient employment contract can be written. That is, less risk needs to be imposed on the manager in order to motivate a given level of effort. This will reduce the dysfunctional consequences of loading risk onto the manager that were discussed in Section 10.4 and, in particular, will make the manager less reluctant to release information which affects firm value.

Second, to maximize the firm's market value, the manager will want to minimize its cost of capital. This creates an incentive to release full and credible information to the market. The reason is that full and credible information increases investor confidence in the firm, with the result that the market prices of its securities will rise or, equivalently, its cost of capital will fall, other things being equal. This will show up in enhanced firm profitability and value, hence enhanced market value for the manager. The financial forecast of Mark's Work Wearhouse (Section 4.8.3) provides a good example of a full information release.

Formal models which relate information release to the firm's market value are presented by, for example, Merton (1987) and Diamond and Verrecchia (1991). In the Merton model, information asymmetry is modelled as only a subset of investors knowing about each firm. If the firm can increase the size of this subset, say by the voluntary release of information, its market value will rise, other things equal. In the Diamond and Verrecchia model, voluntary disclosure reduces information asymmetry between the firm and the market, which facilitates trading in its shares. The resulting increase in market liquidity attracts large institutional investors who, if they have to do so in future, can then sell large blocks of shares without lowering the price they receive. The firm's share price increases as a result of this greater demand.

No formal contracts or regulations are required for these effects to operate. Rather, it is the *market prices* of managers' services and firms' securities that provide the vehicle to motivate information production. It should be noted that market efficiency, whereby the markets properly interpret the firm's information, is assumed in this argument.

Another market which disciplines managers is the *takeover market*, also called the market for corporate control. If the manager does not maximize firm value, the firm may be subject to a takeover bid, which, if successful, frequently results in replacement of the manager. The more disgruntled the shareholders are, the more likely that such a takeover bid will be successful. Consequently, the takeover market also motivates managers to maximize firm value, with implications for information production similar to those of the managerial labour market.

Thus, labour markets and the market for corporate control, along with efficient securities markets, are important *noncontractual* sources of private information production. In all cases, it is *market prices* that provide the motivation—security prices and managers' market values on the labour market are affected by the quality of firms' information production decisions. The market for corporate control is beyond our scope here. The ensuing discussion will be in terms of security and labour markets only.

12.3.4 *PROPERLY WORKING MARKETS REVISITED*

The concept of a properly working securities market was discussed in Section 4.7. Such a market requires that all relevant information be in the public domain and that security market prices be efficient relative to this information. The social importance of a properly working securities market was pointed out, and we noted that capitalist economies have a variety of penalties and incentives to promote proper working.

We can define the concept of a properly working managerial labour market by analogy with a securities market. A properly working managerial labour market is one where all relevant information about managerial performance is in the public domain and the market is efficient with respect to this information. That is, the market value of a manager's services should properly reflect that manager's efforts and abilities. Note that for this definition to be fully met, managerial effort must be observable.

If both the securities market and the managerial labour market work properly, then market forces will motivate managers to produce information to the point where *the firm's* cost of capital is minimized. This will entail production of information to the point where the marginal cost to the firm of producing that information is equal to the resulting marginal benefit, where the benefit is the lower cost of capital. In other words, since we view information as a commodity, the standard economic conditions of producing information to the point where marginal cost equals marginal benefit apply. To see that production of information lowers cost of capital, think of what would happen if the firm did *not* produce information. Investors would shy away from that firm, or at least reduce the

"As an avid reader I bought their shares for the high quality of their annual reports."

SOURCE: Reproduced by kind permission of Tony Holland; first published in *Accountancy*.

amount they would be willing to pay for its securities. Thus, its cost of capital would rise. The cartoon shown here illustrates the effect of information on cost of capital. The "avid" reader has increased his demand for the firm's shares because of its high-quality financial statement information. As the demand for shares rises, their price will also rise (all other things being equal) or, equivalently, the firm's cost of capital will fall.

We can now refine our concept of *relevant information* that was included in the definition of a properly working securities market. Since the amount of information about a firm is potentially infinite, relevant information would include only that information which is *cost-effective to produce*, that is, where its marginal cost is not greater than its marginal benefits. We could hardly expect a properly working market to produce more information than this.

12.3.5 SUMMARY

There are two major sources of private incentives for firms to produce information about themselves. First, we have *contracts*, which typically require information so that compliance can be monitored and performance rewarded. The parties to a contract can agree on the type and amount of information to be produced. Therefore, the right amount is generated, by definition. Thus, there is little need for standard setting to drive information production for efficient contracting.

However, contracts break down when a large number of contracting parties are involved due to the high costs of negotiating a deal satisfactory to all parties. Contracts for information production between a firm and its shareholders fall into this category. Then, a second source of private incentives for information production is markets. Do market prices for managerial labour services and for securities operate so as to motivate managers to produce information to the point of firm value maximization? If these markets work properly, the answer is yes.

12.4 Sources of Market Failure

12.4.1 INTRODUCTION

In this section, we consider sources of market failure. First, recall from Section 12.3.4 that if markets work properly according to our definition, information will be produced to the point where the marginal costs and benefits *to the firm* are equated. However, we have defined the socially first-best amount of information as equating the marginal costs and benefits *to society*. These two criteria for information production need not yield the same result, because of **externalities** and **free-riding**.

However, even if externalities and free-riding are absent, markets will not work properly because of information asymmetry. Then, problems of moral hazard and adverse selection mean that the firm will not produce information to the point where its own cost of capital is minimized. We will discuss these various sources of market failure in turn.

12.4.2 EXTERNALITIES AND FREE-RIDING

Frequently, information released by one firm will convey information about other firms. For example, if a firm reveals a sharp increase in sales and profits, this may affect the market's expectations for other firms in the industry. Also, if a firm releases proprietary information (for example, details about a valuable patent) this could affect the market's expectations of future earnings of competing firms. Interactive effects such as these are called externalities.

The effect of externalities is to cause the private and social values of information to diverge. The Darrough and Stoughton (1990) model, reviewed in Section 9.3, of a game between a monopolist incumbent and a potential entrant to the industry also illustrates the effect of externalities. Under some conditions, the monopoly firm does not release information, so as to deter entry. While this may benefit the monopolist, it does reduce the flow of information to the market, thereby imposing a cost on society.

In Section 5.6, we noted that accounting information has characteristics of a public good. We pointed out that this makes it difficult for the firm to charge for producing this information. In effect, when the use of information by one individual does not destroy it for use by another, other investors can *free-ride* on this information. Since all investors will realize this, no one has an incentive to pay. Then, if the firm cannot recover the costs of information production it will produce less than it would otherwise.

> *An externality is an action taken by a firm or individual which imposes costs or benefits on other firms or individuals for which the entity creating the externality is not charged or does not receive revenue. Free-riding is the receipt by a firm of individual of a benefit from an externality.*

The crucial aspect of both externalities and free-riding is that the costs and benefits of information production as perceived by the firm differ from the costs and benefits to society. For example, if accounting information produced by one firm informs investors about other firms, this is a benefit to society for which the producing firm receives no benefit. Hence, the firm will underproduce relative to the first-best amount for society. A similar phenomenon operates for the free-rider problem.

Externalities and free-riding are well-known reasons used to justify regulation. The regulator steps in to try to restore the socially first-best amount of production because market forces alone fall short.

12.4.3 THE MORAL HAZARD PROBLEM

Recall that managerial effort is typically unobservable to firm owners and the market. Consequently, the effort-averse manager will shirk, other things equal (the moral hazard problem). In Section 12.3.3 we described how the managerial labour market operates to reduce this shirking. Unfortunately, while shirking may be reduced, it will not be eliminated.

To see why, note that during a manager's tenure with a firm there are likely to be periods when profits are high because of luck (more precisely, by favourable realizations of the state of nature). Then, if outsiders (such as firm owners and, in general, the managerial labour market) cannot observe the state realization, the manager (an insider) can afford to work less hard because he or she knows that the favourable state realization will lead to high profits even in the presence of shirking. In effect, unobservability of managerial effort, in conjunction with unobservability of state realization, means that outsiders cannot fully separate the effects of effort and luck in running the firm. Thus, the labour market is less able to penalize shirking, at least in periods of favourable state realizations. As another scenario, note that as the manager approaches retirement, the disciplinary effect of the labour market may become less and less. In the last period before retirement, for example, the manager may care little about market value.

Consequently, with effort unobservable and a finite number of employment periods, the managerial labour market alone cannot completely eliminate shirking—that is, the labour market does not work properly. In effect, a manager faced with a low payoff may attempt to explain it by manipulating real variables such as R&D or by biasing information release, rather than admitting the real cause was lack of effort. In fairness, however, it should be recalled that Murphy and Zimmerman (see Section 11.3) found less evidence of such manipulative behaviour than might be expected, prior to CEO turnover.

12.4.4 THE ADVERSE SELECTION PROBLEM

A second problem that arises because of information asymmetry is adverse selection. Here, one person has an information advantage and selects him/herself into a situation where this information advantage can be exploited.

In our context, there are two versions of the adverse selection problem. First, we have the problem of insider trading, which was introduced in Section 4.6.1. If opportunities exist for insiders, including managers, to generate excessive profits by trading on the basis of their insider information, persons willing to do this will be attracted to the opportunity. Then, outside investors will not perceive the securities market as a level playing field and may withdraw. This will reduce breadth and is symptomatic of the securities market not working properly. For the market to operate properly, it is necessary that there be enough traders that the buy or sell decisions of any one of them does not affect the market price of a security. Thus, the ability of insiders to earn excessive trading profits constitutes a securities market failure.

A second version of adverse selection arises when managers who are privy to bad news about the firm's future do not release that information, thereby avoiding, or at least postponing, damage to their reputation and consequent reduction in their value on the managerial labour market. This has two adverse effects. First, investors will be less able to distinguish between securities of different qualities so that managers with low-quality, bad-news securities will be encouraged to bring them to market and managers with good-news securities may not bring them to market (if the market cannot distinguish between securities of different qualities then the market price will reflect the average quality—this is called **pooling**). Second, since owners do not know that the bad news firm is doing badly, the ability of the takeover market to purge poor managers is reduced, so that the average quality of managers is lowered.

Both of these effects of failure to release bad news mean that the securities market does not work properly.

12.4.5 UNANIMITY

A characteristic of economies with markets that do not work properly is a lack of unanimity. With properly working markets, firm shareholders will be unanimously in favour of the manager maximizing the market value of the firm. When markets do not work properly, this need not be the case. Eckern and Wilson (1974) studied this problem with respect to the physical production of the firm—that is, the types and quantities of products to be produced—and showed that the manager's choice of production plan to maximize the market value of the firm would not in general be approved by all shareholders under certain market conditions.

A similar result applies to firms' production of information. Blazenko and Scott (1986) demonstrated that in an economy where the information market does not work properly, due to adverse selection, the firm manager was motivated to choose that audit quality that would maximize firm market value (recall that an audit is a form of information production). All shareholders, however, would prefer a higher-quality audit.

12.4.6 SUMMARY

Markets for information are characterized by externalities and free-riding. These problems, if sufficiently serious, can justify central authority intervention. Furthermore, because of information asymmetry, security and managerial labour markets may not operate properly. In particular, problems of moral hazard and adverse selection are symptoms of the fact that managers, and other insiders, possess private information which they can use to their advantage. Another consequence of improperly working markets is that shareholders will not necessarily be unanimous in their support of manager policies, even policies which involve firm value maximization.

We must therefore ask, are these imperfections sufficiently serious that some central authority needs to step in and regulate firms' information production decisions? Before confronting this question, we will consider some additional private forces that can potentially limit the extent of market failure.

12.5   Forces to Limit Market Failure

In this section we shall investigate additional mechanisms which limit market failure in the production of information. This is not to say that these mechanisms completely resolve market failure. However, to the extent that they reduce it, the case for regulation is diminished.

12.5.1 THE DISCLOSURE PRINCIPLE

A simple argument can be made which suggests that a manager will release all information, good or bad. This is known as the **disclosure principle**.[3] If investors know that the manager has the information, but do not know what it is, they will assume that if it was favourable the manager would release it. Thus, if investors do not observe the manager releasing it, they will assume the worst and bid down the market value of the firm's shares accordingly. For example, suppose that investors know that a manager possesses a credible forecast of next year's earnings, but they do not know what the forecast is. The manager may as well release it, as failure to do so would be interpreted by the market as the lowest possible forecast.

This argument is reinforced by the manager's incentive to keep the firm's share price from falling. A fall in share price will harm the manager through lower remuneration, if remuneration depends on share price, and/or through lower value on the labour market for managers. Since the market will assume the worst if the information is not released, any release of credible information will prevent share price and market value from falling as low as it would otherwise.

Undoubtedly, the disclosure principle operates in many situations. However, as Dye (1985) discusses, it does not always work. Note that it requires that investors *know that the manager has the information*. If they do not know this, the argument breaks down. For example, the firm may not have prepared earnings forecasts in the past and the market may not be sure whether one has been prepared this year.

A second reason for failure of the disclosure principle derives from costs of disclosure. This was examined by Verrecchia (1983), who sought to reconcile the disclosure principle with the empirical observation that managers do not always fully disclose. For example, they may delay the release of bad news. Verrecchia assumes that, if disclosure is made, it is truthful, which is consistent with the disclosure principle. However, he also assumes that there is a cost of disclosure. The cost is constant, independent of the nature of the news. For example, there may be a proprietary cost of releasing valuable patent information. Investors know that the manager has the news but do not know its nature. Nor do they know the manager's disclosure cost. Then, if information is withheld, investors do not know whether it is withheld because it is bad news or because it is good news but not sufficiently good to overcome the disclosure cost, and the disclosure principle fails.

If we rank the nature of the news on a continuum from bad to good, Verrecchia shows that for given disclosure cost there is a threshold level of disclosure. The lower the disclosure cost, the lower the threshold, and if disclosure cost is zero, the disclosure principle is reinstated.

Verrecchia (1990) extended the above model to the case where the manager's information is imperfect. That is, the manager receives a noisy signal of firm value, with the quality of the signal measured by the variance of the noise. Given risk-neutral firm valuation by the market (as would be the case if all investors were fully diversified), Verrecchia shows that the disclosure threshold is higher the lower the quality of the manager's information. The reason is that failure to disclose is perceived as less serious by the market when the manager's information is of low quality, so it exerts less pressure for disclosure. Thus, in this model, the disclosure principle is more prone to failure for poor-quality information.

Also, information released under the disclosure principle must be credible, that is, the market must know that it is truthfully revealed. Obviously, if a manager lies about next year's forecast of net income it can hardly be said that information is being disclosed. Information that is subject to verification after the event, such as a forecast, will be credible to the extent that penalties can be applied for deliberate misstatement. Another way to secure credibility is to have released information attested to by a third party, such as an auditor. However, because much inside information is not verifiable even after the fact, or subject to audit, credibility cannot always be attained.

The need for credible disclosure has been relaxed by Newman and Sansing (1993) (NS). They analyze a two-period model consisting of an incumbent firm, a representative shareholder, and a potential entrant to the industry. The firm, which is assumed to act in the shareholder's best interests, knows its value exactly. If it were not for the potential entrant, the shareholder's best interests would be served by disclosing this value, since the shareholder could then optimally plan consumption and investment over the two periods. However, this may trigger entry, in which case the incumbent firm will suffer a loss of profits and value. How should the firm report?

The answer depends on the costs to the entrant should it decide to enter the industry, and the resulting loss of profits to the incumbent. For example, if entry costs are high and there is substantial loss of profits upon entry, the incumbent firm may disclose imprecise information about its value. That is, instead of an exact disclosure, it will disclose an interval within which its value lies. If it reported its value exactly, its disclosures would not be believed, since everyone knows it has an incentive to deter entry.

Disclosure in the NS model is credible in the sense that the firm truthfully reveals an interval within which its value lies. Nevertheless, the disclosure principle fails in the sense that the firm does not report its value exactly. The NS model is consistent with range forecasts of earnings, as for Mark's Work Wearhouse (see Section 4.8.3).

Finally, as shown by Dye (1985), the disclosure principle can break down if there is a conflict between information desired by investors and information needed for contracting purposes. Suppose that the market price of a firm's shares better reflects manager effort than does net income. This could be the case if there are relatively few uncontrollable economy-wide events affecting share price, especially since share price aggregates all information held by investors. Then, share price is a more efficient variable upon which to base manager compensation than net income.

Suppose, however, that the manager has a forecast of future profitability which, if reported, would affect share price. Furthermore, assume the market knows the manager has this forecast. Reporting the forecast would reduce the ability of share price to reflect manager effort, since this ability would be swamped by the impact of the forecast on price. Thus, from a contracting perspective it may be desirable to discourage the reporting of forecasts even though a forecast provides useful information to investors. In effect, the best information for contracting may not be the best information for investor decision-making, and the investor information may not be reported for contracting reasons. Then, the disclosure principle breaks down. Dye's model provides a supplement to legal liability as a reason why reporting of forecasts is rare (Section 4.8.3).

Summary

The disclosure principle is a simple and compelling argument for release of inside information. However, it breaks down in numerous instances, and hence cannot be relied upon to solve the problem of market failure in the production of information.

12.5.2 PRIVATE INFORMATION SEARCH

To this point, our investigation of private incentives for release of inside information has centred on the manager. The argument has been that release of adequate, credible information will lower the firm's cost of capital. To the extent that the manager is motivated to maximize his or her value on the managerial labour market, lowering the firm's cost of capital will work towards this goal. Thus, the onus is on the manager to release information.

Implicit in this line of reasoning is that investors are passive. They merely react to whatever information the manager releases in deciding on their demand for the firm's securities. In effect, they are price-protected by the market. It may be, however, that many investors will be active in seeking out information. For example, they may conduct their own investigations and analyses of fundamental firm value, or hire financial analysts and other experts to assist them. They may watch closely persons that they suspect have inside information and mimic their actions.

Thus, there is a variety of ways that investors can conduct a **private information search**. Bill Cautious, in Example 3.1 did so by analysis of the annual report, using Bayes' theorem to process the resulting information. To the extent that such activities are successful, inside information is very quickly transferred to the public domain. By limiting the ability of insiders to capitalize on inside information, the severity of the adverse selection problem is reduced.

Unfortunately, private information search can be quite costly, from society's perspective, since more than one investor incurs costs to discover the same information. It would be cheaper, in terms of total resources used to generate information, if the firm produced and publicized the information only once, so that each investor would not have to rediscover it.

Hirschleifer's (1971) analysis is a classic in the area of private information search. Hirschleifer considered an exchange economy, that is, an economy without production, so that there is no scope for information search to affect the manager's effort. Then, Hirschleifer showed that the social value of information search is negative, even though individual investors may perceive it as valuable. The reason is that, without production, the amount of goods and services in the economy is fixed, so that private information search just redistributes wealth, it does not create wealth. Then, since information search has a cost, the net social effect is negative.

If we consider a production economy, private information search may improve the proper operation of markets, with resulting impacts on firms' costs of capital and manager effort. However, to the extent that a redistributive component to private information search remains, this will still constitute a cost to society.

Information search can also lead to unequal distribution of information across investors, as discussed by Beaver (1989). For example, the "big guys" may have more resources to find and analyze information, leaving the small investor at a disadvantage. This leads to suggestions, such as by Lev (1988), for regulation to require firms to release information to everyone, thereby enhancing public confidence in a fair marketplace and contributing to market depth.

12.5.3 SIGNALLING

It frequently happens that firms differ in quality. For example, a firm may have better investment opportunities than other firms. Alternatively, a firm may conduct superior R&D, leading to potentially valuable patents. Yet, disclosure of the details of high-quality projects and technology may reveal valuable proprietary information, even if it was believed by a skeptical marketplace. How can the manager credibly reveal the firm's **type**, as these underlying quality differences are called, without incurring excessive costs?

This problem of separating firms of different types has been extensively considered by means of signalling models.

A signal is an action taken by a high-type manager that would not be rational if that manager was low-type.

A crucial requirement for a signal is that it be less costly for a high-type manager than for a low-type. This is what gives a signal its credibility, since it is then irrational for a low-type to mimic a high-type.

Spence (1973) was the first to formally model signalling equilibria. He did so in the context of a job market. Given that it is less costly to a high-type job applicant to obtain a specified level of education than to a low-type, Spence showed that equilibria exist where employers can rely on the applicant's chosen level of education as a credible signal of that person's underlying competence.

A number of signals have been suggested that are relevant to accounting. One such signal is **direct disclosure**. Hughes (1986) showed how such disclosure can be a credible signal. In her model, a manager wants to reveal his or her expectation of firm value, by making a direct disclosure at the beginning of the period. Investors observe the firm's cash flows at the end of the period. They then infer the probability of the realized cash flow contingent on the manager's disclosure. For example, if the manager disclosed a high firm value but cash flow is very low, investors will assess a high probability that the disclosure was untrue, and penalties will be applied. Knowing this, the manager is motivated to report truthfully, so that in equilibrium investors can correctly infer his or her expectation of firm value.

While Hughes' model does not apply to the moral hazard problem (the manager's expectation of firm value is independent of his or her effort), it does demonstrate how direct disclosure can operate to reduce adverse selection. Firms of different types can separate themselves, so that the market value of their securities properly reflects firm value.

A variety of **indirect signals** has been studied to further understand disclosure issues. As Leland and Pyle (1977) show for an entrepreneur going public, the proportion of *equity retained* is a signal, because it would not be rational for a bad-news manager to retain a high equity position. Also, *audit quality* can be a signal of the value of a new securities issue. A rational manager would be unlikely to retain a high-quality (and high-cost) auditor when the firm is a low-type. Similar arguments relate to the choice of underwriter for a new issue. Titman and Trueman (1986) and Datar, Feltham, and Hughes (1991) developed models where audit quality is a signal.

A firm's *capital structure* also has signalling properties. There is evidence, for example, that the market value of existing common shares falls when the firm issues new shares. While dilution of existing shareholders' equity is one possibility, another explanation is the market's concern that the new shares may be issued by a low-type firm—a high-type firm would be more likely to issue bonds or finance internally, because the high value increments would then accrue to existing shareholders, or because a high-type firm would assess its probability of bankruptcy as low (thus, the probability that the bondholders would take over the firm is low).

Dividend policy can also be a signal. A high payout ratio may signal a firm as having a confident future. However, a high payout ratio could also mean that the firm sees little prospect for profitable internal financing from retained earnings. Thus, dividend policy may not be as effective a signal as others.

Accounting policy choice also has signalling properties. For example, a firm may adopt a number of conservative accounting policies. A high-type firm can do this and still report profits, while a low-type firm would report losses. Thus, conservative accounting policies can signal a manager's confident view of the firm's future. The signalling properties of accounting policy choice are related to the use of earnings management to credibly reveal inside information, as discussed in Section 11.5.

Publication of forecasts, in jurisdictions where forecasting is voluntary, is another signal. Why should a low-type firm voluntarily publish a forecast of its low quality?

Note that for signals to be applicable, the manager must have a *choice*. For example, if some central authority imposed a uniform standard of audit quality on all firms, audit quality would not be available as a signal. Indeed, Spence (1973) shows that for a viable signalling equilibrium to exist there must be a sufficient number of signals available to the manager.

This argument, that standards to enforce uniform accounting destroy managers' abilities to signal, is important for standard setting. In Section 2.5.1 we suggested that the major problem with historical cost accounting is that there is no unique way to match costs with revenues. We also suggested that standard setting bodies may then have to step in to impose uniformity. The clear implication was that diversity in reporting practices was "bad." This implication is correct, as far as it goes. Diversity in reporting practices imposes costs on investors who want to compare the performance of different entities, because it is necessary to restate the entities' financial statements to a common basis before valid comparisons can be made.

However, if we reconsider this implication in the light of signalling theory, we see that diversity may not be as bad as first suggested. To the extent that firms' choices of accounting policies signal credible information about those firms, diversity of reporting practices is desirable. This argument is reinforced by our discussion of earnings management in Chapter 11. We argued there that a little bit of earnings management is a good thing, since it gives some flexibility in the face of contract rigidities and can serve as a vehicle for the release of inside information. Obviously, earnings management is only possible if there is a sufficiently rich set of accounting policies, such as GAAP, from which to choose. Signalling theory serves as a counterargument to the continual refinement of GAAP so as to eliminate accounting policy choice.

Thus, we can see a tradeoff with respect to diversity of reporting practices. The optimal amount of diversity is not zero, despite the costs that diversity imposes, because of signalling considerations. It is important for standard setting bodies to realize the signalling potential of accounting policy choice.

12.5.4 FINANCIAL POLICY AS A SIGNAL

In this section we review a paper by Healy and Palepu (1993) (HP). HP address the question of what managers might do to signal their inside information to the efficient market. We have already discussed how market forces motivate managers to communicate information so as to maximize their firm's market value. But, since these forces are subject to various degrees of market failure, and also since noise trading can distort a firm's share price, managers of some firms may find their firms undervalued by the capital market relative to their inside information. The question then is, how can they signal the real value of the firm?

HP provide a specific illustration of the above problem. Patten Corp.[4] acquires large undeveloped tracts of land, subdivides them into lots, and sells them, with up to 90% of the financing supplied by Patten. Revenue is recognized upon sale, that is, when at least 10% of the purchase price has been received and collection of the balance is reasonably assured. This creates a potential problem of bad debt losses. However, in its 1986 financial statements Patten provided a bad debt allowance of only $10,000 on accounts receivable of $29.4 million. The firm claimed that this low amount was justified by past experience and a low current delinquency rate.

In 1987, concern appeared in the financial media that Patten's bad debt allowance was too low. Specifically, the fear was expressed that past delinquency rates may not be representative of future delinquency. Patten's share price plunged following the publication of these concerns, as investors quickly revised their beliefs about Patten's future prospects.

HP suggest several possible manager responses to convince the market of their inside information that the value of the accounts receivable is substantially as shown in the financial statements. One response is direct disclosure of credit granting and collection procedures, so as to inform the market of their integrity. Direct disclosure should be a credible signal here, since management would be foolish to overly expose itself to penalties such as loss of reputation and legal liability by disclosing incorrect information at such a critical time.

However, details of the firm's credit and collection policies are likely to be proprietary information, which could harm its competitive position—recall our discussion of the Darrough and Stoughton model in Section 9.3. Consequently, HP suggest several financial policies that could serve as indirect signals of management's information.

One such policy would be to raise private financing and/or to sell accounts receivable without recourse to a financial institution. Our discussion of contractual incentives for information production in Section 12.3.2 suggests that when there are only a few parties involved in a contract they can agree among themselves what information to provide. Here, it may be less costly for Patten to provide a private lender with information about the real value of its receivables than to provide it to the market, since, as mentioned, providing it to the market would require public release of proprietary information.

Another possibility would be for Patten to engage in a hedging strategy. Then, credit losses on accounts receivable would be offset by gains on the hedging instrument. Such a policy would be prohibitively expensive if large credit losses were anticipated. Consequently, it should be a credible signal. However, Patten would have to be careful not to get into the aggressive derivatives strategies that brought down Franklin Savings (Section 6.5.2).

Yet another signalling strategy would be for management to increase its holdings of Patten shares. This would load additional risk on to management, thereby increasing their incentive to work hard and also giving them a longer-run perspective in operating the firm.

Note the common theme in all of these signalling strategies. Management would be foolish to undertake any of them unless it really believed its inside information about asset values. This is what gives signals their credibility. The market will realize this, with the result that the fall of Patten's share price should be reversed. HP's article insightfully demonstrates the rich variety of signals available for credible communication of inside information to an efficient market.

12.6   *Is Regulation Needed?*

We are now ready to face the question that we posed at the beginning of this chapter—should the information production decisions of firms be regulated?

As the arguments presented above indicate, market failures do occur in the production of information. In addition to externalities and free-riding, additional problems derive from both moral hazard and adverse selection. With respect to moral hazard, the necessity to motivate managers that leads to the incentive contracts discussed in Section 9.4.2 leads in turn to the possibility that managers may manipulate or bias information release to disguise substandard performance. With respect to adverse selection, we have the insider trading problem and problems of manager release of bad news. All of these practices imply defects in the flow of information to the market.

These market failures do not necessarily imply that regulation of firms' information production decisions is needed, however. We have explored several mechanisms to limit the adverse consequences of these failures: auditing, the disclosure principle, and signalling, for example. Also, in Chapter 11, we argued that some earnings management was desirable to help overcome the consequences of incomplete and rigid contracts and to convey inside information to the market.

In addition, it should be emphasized that regulation carries substantial costs. These include direct costs of the bureaucracy needed to establish and administer the regulations, and compliance costs imposed on firms. Of possibly greater magnitude are *indirect costs*. One such indirect cost arises from the fact that when standards are set to enforce uniform accounting and reporting, managers' opportunity to signal is reduced. Uniform audit standards for all firms and mandatory forecasting requirements are examples of standards that would reduce signalling potential.

A second indirect cost arises because the regulator may not, and indeed probably will not, know the first-best or "socially correct" amount of information to require. This is because information is such a complex commodity, because there are conflicts between decision usefulness and contracting needs for information, and because different investors have different decision needs. Given that information regulations affect firms' financing, investment, and production decisions, the indirect costs of any "wrong" amount of information production can be large indeed.

A major theoretical reason *for* regulation derives from the problem of unanimity. In an economy in which there are market imperfections, such as those that derive from information asymmetry, it is not necessarily the case that the information production decisions of managers will be in the amounts that investors want, even if managers produce information to the point of firm value maximization. Yet, since there are a large number of investors, each with particular information demands, it seems impossible to satisfy all of them simultaneously. Consequently, investors will be in a continual state of disagreement with the amount of information produced by management. Then, investors may well react by approaching a central authority to demand standards for information production.

As we suggested in Section 1.7, in our discussion of Merino and Neimark (1982), evidence of manipulative reporting abuses leading up to the stock market crash of 1929, the Great Depression, and the creation of the SEC in 1933–34 creates a presumption that at least some regulation is socially desirable. Nonetheless, in the final analysis, the question of the extent of regulation of firms' information production decisions is unresolved. Certainly, complex cost-benefit considerations are involved. Further research in economics and related disciplines will be necessary before we have a definitive answer to the need for standard setting.

12.7 Conclusions

The question of the extent to which standards for information production should be imposed is a complex and important one for a market economy. At present, we witness substantial regulation of firms' information production decisions. These regulations include insider trading laws and laws to regulate full disclosure. They also include laws to establish accounting and auditing professions. These professions, in turn, may form bodies empowered to establish GAAP, such as the CICA and the FASB. However, it can be argued, by analogy with other industries where regulation has been eased, that deregulation of the information "industry" would result in a flood of innovation and competition, to society's advantage.

Indeed, theory suggests a number of reasons why firms would produce information in the absence of standards. These derive from the information needs of contracts and from market forces. Parties to contracts will want information to motivate effort and to reward accomplishment. Managerial labour markets and takeover markets interact with securities markets to motivate managers to release information so as to maximize the firm's market value.

Such private forces undoubtedly result in much information production. Theory also suggests, however, that even if we ignore externalities and free-riding, the amount produced by private forces alone may fall short of society's needs. The reason can be seen by means of a two-stage argument. First, contracts for information production break down when a large number of persons are involved. Consequently, we cannot rely on contracts for all of society's information needs. Second, when contracts break down, market prices (for managerial services and for securities) must take over as motivators of information production.

However, market prices are affected by two types of problems that derive from information asymmetry, namely moral hazard and adverse selection. The moral hazard problem creates the need for managerial incentive contracts based on firm performance, such as net income. Such contracts, however, may motivate managers to bias or manipulate information releases. The adverse selection problem appears as insider trading and as a disinclination by managers to report low quality and bad news. These are all symptoms of the failure of markets to drive the "right" amount of information.

A number of mechanisms, short of regulation, are available to limit market failure. These include the disclosure principle, private information search, and signalling. The question then is, do these mechanisms sufficiently eliminate market failure to the extent that regulation is not needed? The use of signals, such as voluntary issuance of future-oriented financial information, has been extensively studied by both theoreticians and empiricists in an attempt to answer this question.

It is important to realize that the preceding mechanisms need not completely eliminate market failures to preclude regulation. This is because regulation has costs. These include direct costs, such as a bureaucracy to set and enforce the standards, and compliance costs imposed on firms. More importantly, however, they include indirect costs imposed on society if the central authority mandates the "wrong" amount of information. Since information is such a complex commodity, this is quite likely to happen. Given the impact of information on firms' production, financing, and investment decisions, the costs to society here can be significant.

The question of standard setting then boils down to a cost-benefit trade-off. The costs of regulation include not only the enforcement costs, but also the costs of any wrong decisions made by the regulator. The benefits lie in reduced market failures that may persist after private market forces have done their best. At present, it is not known whether the benefits of regulation exceed the costs.

While the answer to the cost-benefit question may be unknown, it is not hard to see why investors may demand regulation. This is because of lack of unanimity. When markets are subject to imperfections, such as information asymmetry, it is no longer generally true that shareholders will agree with the amount of information privately produced by managers, even if managers produce it to the point of firm value maximization. This suggests that shareholders, frustrated by managers' information production decisions, may approach a central authority to set standards. Because of the fundamental problem of financial accounting theory, the standard setter's standards are unlikely to please everyone. As a result, the question of standard setting may need to draw on political theory as well as economics. We will explore this suggestion in Chapter 13.

Notes

1. The dividing line between proprietary and nonproprietary information is somewhat ambiguous. For example, as we saw in our review of Darrough and Stoughton (Section 9.3), the release of information that may seem nonproprietary (such as a financial forecast) could affect future cash flows if it attracts entry to the industry. Nevertheless, the distinction is a useful one. For further discussion of the interrelationships between proprietary and nonproprietary information see Dye (1986).

2. See, for example, L. DeAngelo (1981).

3. The disclosure principle is attributed to Grossman (1981) and Milgrom (1981).

4. For further discussion see Healy and Palepu (1993). Data on Patten Corp. are from Harvard Business School case #9-188-027.

Questions and Problems

1. Information has both costs and benefits to a firm. What are the costs and benefits of information production to a firm? How much information should the firm produce? (CGA-Canada)

2. Explain why a voluntary forecast can be an indirect signal but a mandated forecast cannot. (CGA-Canada)

3. "Contracting internalizes the problem of information production." Explain what this statement means. (CGA-Canada)

4. Describe the difference between a *direct* and an *indirect* signal, using a voluntary forecast as prescribed by the *CICA Handbook*, Section 4250 (see Section 4.8.3) as an example.   (CGA-Canada)

5. Discuss the extent to which (i) security market forces and (ii) managerial labour market forces operate to motivate managers to operate their firms in the best interests of the shareholders. Be sure to identify in your answer how financial accounting information enables the market forces to operate.   (CGA-Canada)

6. The notion of a market for information, unlike markets for agricultural commodities, transportation services, and so on, may be unfamiliar to most people. A main reason for this is that information is a very complex commodity.

   List four ways that we can think about the quantity of information and explain each briefly.   (CGA-Canada)

7. An "adverse selection" problem can arise from information asymmetry between issuer and buyer of securities.

   Required

   a. Explain what the adverse selection problem is in this context.

   b. How can financial accounting information reduce the adverse selection problem?

   c. Can financial accounting information eliminate the problem completely? Explain.

   d. What other ways are used to reduce the problem of inside information?
                                                                (CGA-Canada)

8. The failure of managers to release bad news is a version of the adverse selection problem. Such failure indicates that the securities market is not working properly.

   Required

   a. Why might a manager withhold bad news?

   b. To what extent does the disclosure principle operate to reduce the incentive of a manager to withhold bad news? Explain.   (CGA-Canada)

9. An article entitled "SEC Investigating Harley Stock Plunge; Angry Investors See a Leak of Results" appeared in the *Wall Street Journal* on October 25, 1991. The article describes the rapid fall in the market price of Harley-Davidson shares just prior to the release of its 1991 third-quarter earnings, which the *Journal* termed "disappointing."

   On Wednesday October 23, 1991, Harley-Davidson Inc.'s share price fell $6.625 to $52.25 before the company had a chance to report its third-quarter earnings. Over 500,000 shares were traded up until 3:32 p.m. on Wednesday, at which time the New York Stock Exchange stopped the trading of the shares. According to the article, the company was asked by the New York Stock

Exchange "to release results after the unexplained fall in the company's shares Wednesday afternoon." Furthermore, "the Securities and Exchange Commission is investigating the sudden plunge in its stock price."

The company announced that its third-quarter earnings were $8.9 million or 49 cents a share, which was higher than the previous year's third-quarter earnings of $6.5 million or 36 cents a share. However, earnings were lower than what analysts had predicted.

While several analysts said "they remain confident that the company's strong growth in the motorcycle business will continue," Lawrence Bowman, a Fidelity Investments portfolio manager, and others "expressed dismay over both the earnings and what some see as a possible early disclosure of them." Mr. Bowman believes that there was a "leak" prior to the earnings announcement.

James Ziemer, chief financial officer of Harley-Davidson Inc., "said [that] the company doesn't forecast profits and has no plans to change that policy," but indicated that the company would "fully cooperate" with any SEC investigation into what had happened.

Required

a. Explain why the market price fell so far, so quickly.

b. Does the episode constitute evidence of market failure in the production of information by Harley?

c. Given that Harley's management agrees with those analysts who feel that "the company's strong growth in the motorcycle business will continue," describe some signals that management could engage in to credibly inform the market that it is confident about a profitable future.   (CGA-Canada)

10.   XYZ Ltd. is an owner-managed retail hardware store which went public on January 1, 1995. Afterwards, Tom Harris, the fun-loving owner-manager, held 70% of the common stock and remained the chief executive of the company.

Required

a. Why is it likely that Tom Harris will shirk more as a majority shareholder relative to the time he was the owner-manager of the company prior to January 1, 1995?

b. How might potential investors protect themselves from the adverse effects of likely excessive shirking by the CEO/majority shareholder, Tom Harris, after the issuance of shares?

c. Prior to going public, does Tom Harris have an incentive to convince potential shareholders that he will not engage in excessive shirking? Discuss.

d. What steps can Tom Harris take to convince potential shareholders that he will not engage in excessive shirking?   (CGA-Canada)

11. The article here reproduced from *The Economist* (August 22, 1992) discusses some of the "creative accounting" that firms can use to make their results "look better." It argues that given full and fair disclosure the efficient market will see through these tricks and, indeed, that use of such tricks can actually harm firms by suggesting poor performance in the future.

THE PROPHET OF PROFIT

"The book they tried to ban," trumpets the cover. This time the forbidden topic is not the spooks of *Spycatcher* or the erotica of *Lady Chatterley's Lover*, but the somewhat duller subject of massaging corporate results to make them look better. *Accounting for Growth* by Terry Smith, a top analyst at UBS Phillips & Drew, a London brokerage house, is the chilling tale of "creative" accounting in the boardrooms of Britain's 200 biggest firms. Published on August 18th, the book has made national headlines and won an unrepentant Mr. Smith suspension from his job.

The 12 techniques identified by Mr. Smith are all perfectly legal but, he argues, can be used to mislead investors. They include the inconsistent use of extraordinary and exceptional items, some tricks of acquisition and disposal accounting, off-balance-sheet financing, disguising debt as equity, changing depreciation rules and capitalising costs. These practices all tend to do one of two things: increase reported profits or make a company's balance sheet look stronger. So the shares of companies using such ploys may be over-valued. As a crude rule of thumb, investors should steer clear of firms that use the criticised techniques, says Mr. Smith.

He has a point. Maxwell Communications and Polly Peck both produced a healthy-looking set of accounts months before they collapsed—and both used a full panoply of the tricks that Mr. Smith spotlights. Accounting can be as much art as science, however, and some of Mr. Smith's 12 techniques can be used in good faith, as well as bad. In any case, the most misleading will be outlawed soon by Britain's Accounting Standards Board.

Many economists have a more fundamental objection to Mr. Smith's views. In an efficient market, they argue, accounting tricks should have no effect on share prices. Provided a handful of clever analysts can find a way through the accounting jumble to the firm's true financial position and there are big investors willing to trade on that information, share prices will reflect the firm's true value because the canny investors will continue to buy or sell the shares until the right price is reached. In other words, a few informed people can set the correct price for everyone, including investors who cannot tell a profit-and-loss account from a balance sheet.

Most academic studies suggest that shareholders do indeed see through accounting tricks. As an example, take the widely held view that company analysts are obsessed with profit figures, and so if a firm can use creative accounting to beef up its earnings, its share price should rise.

Do share prices rise when actual earnings turn out higher than analysts' forecasts, and fall if profits are lower than expected? Barely. According to research by Yakov Amihud of New York University, unexpected profits and losses explain no more than 7% of a company's share price movement (relative to the market) in the two days straddling an earnings announcement. This may partly be because speculative trading dominates very short-run share-price changes. More likely, says Mr. Amihud, analysts and shareholders dislike surprising earnings statements and look at them with particular care. Share prices were more responsive to small surprises than to the bigger ones which, claims Mr. Amihud, were mostly accounting driven.

Economists have also looked at what happens when new accounting rules are introduced that alter profits. In an efficient market, these accounting changes should affect share prices only if they change the firm's underlying value (for example, by raising its tax bill). The market should see through rule changes, such as a change in depreciation rates, that are mostly presentational. And this is indeed what a long string of studies stretching back to the early 1970s has found.

Does this mean that the market sees through creative accounting? Most of these studies looked at large firms and well-publicised accounting changes. The market might take longer to spot subtler massaging of profits, especially by small and medium-sized firms.

Acccountacy regulators in Britain and America are currently working on reforms. For them the message is clear. Worry less about complaints that important information is hidden away in footnotes where only experts can find it, and rather more about making sure that the information in the accounts, however it is presented, actually gives those experts a true picture of the firm's financial position. With Maxwell Communications in mind, most effort ought to go into establishing mechanisms to stop outright fraud, which no set of accounts, however presented, can reveal.

As for Mr. Smith, his most controversial claim—that the enthusiastic use of camouflage accounting can signal poor stockmarket performance in the future—may be his most incisive. The short-term evidence is mixed. Several of the firms singled out by Mr. Smith in an earlier version of his research published in January 1991 have since performed spectacularly, though others have plunged as predicted. ... But in the longer term the shares of such companies do seem to struggle. A new study by Baruch Lev and Ramu Thiagarajan of the University of California at Berkeley examined American firms which started to use accounting ploys to boost earnings. In the first year, share prices were not affected. But over the five years after the trick was introduced, the firms' share prices underperformed the market by an average of 20-25%.

When a firm uses accounting tricks to boost earnings, it usually means that there is a lot more bad news to come, says Mr. Lev. Mr. Smith's advice to avoid firms that practise creative accounting may not be so crude after all.

Required

a. If the arguments in the article are correct, why would firm management use creative accounting to improve the appearance of their results?

b. Do you think that the ability of firms to manipulate their results within GAAP constitutes a market failure in firms' production of information? Explain why or why not.

12. An article entitled "Rash of Trading Ahead of Big Deals Raises Eyebrows" appeared in the *Wall Street Journal* on March 8, 1994. It describes the concerns about possible insider trading prior to merger announcements.

The article reports that on Monday, March 7, 1994, Martin Marietta Corp. announced that it was "launching a $55-a-share tender offer to acquire fellow defense contractor Grumman Corp." This resulted in an increase in Grumman Corp.'s share price of 36% or $14.25 to $54.125 on the New York Stock Exchange. However, on Friday, March 4, 1994, before the announcement was made, Grumman Corp.'s share price rose 8.5% and the shares were trading "nearly four times the stock's average daily volume" on the New York Stock Exchange. "A Grumman spokesman said the company had no idea why the stock had moved earlier."

Thomas Newkirk, SEC Associate Enforcement Director, believes that this kind of price increase before an announcement is made is "a source of concern." He goes on to state that "if there are people trading on inside information, they're going to be sorry." In addition, Peter Romeo, a former SEC attorney and now a partner with a law firm in Washington, D.C., finds this kind of predisclosure activity "upsetting," and believes that if share prices are influenced by insider information "it erodes the integrity of the market." He states that "the investing public can get the idea that insiders are playing games, making profits at the expense of others."

Required

a. What well-known problem of information asymmetry does this article illustrate?

b. Why is insider trading regarded as upsetting, indeed illegal?

c. Can you give an efficient-securities-markets-based argument that insider trading such as this may not be as severe a market failure as the article implies?

13. In the article reproduced here from the *Wall Street Journal* (January 29, 1992), Professor Jonathan Macey argues strongly against increasing regulation of securities markets by the SEC.

THE SEC DINOSAUR EXPANDS ITS TURF

A s in nature, adapt or die is an unavoidable fact of life in a market economy. Unfortunately, the market forces that cause private firms to adapt to new circumstances or go out of business do not operate on government bureaucracies like the Securities and Exchange Commission.

Government bureaucracies faced with the specter of obsolescence as a result of new technology or changing consumer demand are not subjected to market discipline. Nonetheless, the bureaucrats within those agencies have the same basic survival instincts as anybody else. As a result, when the traditional functions of an administrative agency are rendered obsolete, the bureaucrats will respond by expanding into previously unregulated areas.

For example, the SEC just concluded a massive investigation and enforcement proceeding against 98 banks and brokerage firms that participated in the market for debt issued by U.S. government agencies. This debt finances student loans, farm credit organizations and government-sponsored housing programs.

Nobody ever thought there was a problem in these smoothly functioning, highly efficient markets until the SEC launched its investigation. The SEC's assertion of regulatory authority over these markets was inspired by the Salomon Brothers scandal but reflects nothing but the grasping attempts of an agency without a purpose seeking to hold onto its budget.

The SEC pursued these investigations despite the fact that no public investors and no government agency that issues publicly traded debt instruments was injured in any way by the bidding practices of the brokerage firms and banks investigated. Indeed, the government agencies issuing these securities were well aware that the brokerage firms and banks bidding on their debt exaggerated the size of their orders. Nobody worried about this harmless practice until the SEC got involved.

STRONG EVIDENCE

The SEC's actions more closely resemble those of the shakedown artists portrayed in gangster films than the actions of a responsible government agency. Like the innocent merchant who pays for "protection," the brokerage firms and banks being investigated simply paid token fines totaling about $5 million to avoid having to pay bigger legal fees to defend against the lawsuits threatened by the SEC.

The SEC's fines covered virtually the entire industry and were based on the amount of business the firms did with the government. Thus, the penalties bore no relationship to any alleged wrongdoing by the firms involved. This is strong evidence that the SEC's investigation was more "shakedown" than legitimate regulatory action.

Indeed, the modern history of the SEC has been the story of a regulatory agency far more interested in inventing problems and expanding its own jurisdiction to restore its relevance than in protecting the interests of investors or issuers.

Other examples abound. Despite the fact that the Commodities Trading Act gives the Commodities Futures Trading Commission "exclusive jurisdiction" over futures contracts, since 1975 the SEC has taken the position that futures contracts involving securities are subject to the jurisdiction of the SEC. Similarly, the SEC has argued that trading in futures contracts on Ginnie Mae certificates, Treasury bills, and a variety of other, more esoteric securities (like stock index participation instruments) are subject to its approval and not that of the CFTC.

In the 1980s, the SEC attempted to wrestle from the Comptroller of the Currency regulatory authority over commercial banks that offered discount brokerage services to the public. In 1986, after much litigation, the SEC suffered the embarrassment of being told by the U.S. Court of Appeals that the statute excluding banks from regulation by the SEC was "as plain as can be."

In 1990 the SEC lost yet another lawsuit over bureaucratic turf, this time against the Business Roundtable. The Roundtable challenged an SEC rule that barred stock exchanges from listing the stock of corporations that issued certain stock with certain types of voting rights. In this litigation, the SEC took what the U.S. Court of Appeals characterized as the "surprising" position that it retained regulatory authority over virtually all of the internal affairs of U.S. corporations. These included requirements for independent directors, independent audit committees, and shareholder quorums, as well

as such other matters traditionally governed by state law as whether shareholder approval was needed for certain corporate transactions. The court declined to give the SEC authority to usurp the traditional authority of the states to regulate the internal affairs of corporations and vacated the SEC's rule.

The picture that emerges from all of this is one of the SEC as an ineffective, highly politicized agency that wastes a tremendous amount of resources in turf-grabbing.

The complex disclosure and anti-fraud rules that burden those who wish to issue securities, launch tender offers or proxy contests, or even simply to communicate with their fellow shareholders all spring from the same basic—and outmoded—regulatory philosophy: that issuers and investors benefit from a regulatory system of mandatory disclosure. Historically, the justification for the SEC's rules has been that market forces do not generate the information investors and other market participants need to make informed decisions about how to allocate capital.

Whatever the merits of this pro-disclosure philosophy 60 years ago, times have changed. In particular, three closely related economic developments have greatly diminished society's need for the SEC.

First, as financial markets have developed, they have become more efficient. An efficient capital market is one in which the current price of a security fully reflects all available information about the future cash flows to investors in that security.

Securities markets have become steadily more efficient as market professionals who compete to find mis-priced securities have emerged in massive numbers. These market professionals—arbitragers, portfolio managers, investment analysts, brokers and industry specialists employed by investment banks, among others—engage in basic research to locate mis-priced securities in order to gain trading profits. Their trading ensures that stock prices reflect the fundamental values of issuing corporations. As markets have become more efficient, society's need to devote resources to support a statutory regime of mandatory disclosure designed and enforced by the SEC has disappeared. Any information that was supplied by the force of law is now supplied by the marketplace.

Second, the development of superior mechanisms for coping with risk also deprives the SEC of a justification for existing. Not only has the rise of institutional investors enabled small investors to hire sophisticated intermediaries, but these investors have acquired important tools for dealing with risk. Portfolio insurance, as well as the emergence of markets for options, futures and other derivative financial products, enables investors to eliminate the very sorts of investment risks that the SEC is charged with regulating.

Put simply, investors' opportunities to hedge are greater than ever before. And while these hedging opportunities are not costless, the markets are sending a pretty clear signal that they are less costly and more effective than the dubious regulatory alternative provided by the SEC.

MODERN FINANCIAL THEORY

Finally, in the years since the Roosevelt administration gave birth to the SEC, financial economists have invented portfolio theory and the capital asset pricing model, which give investors additional tools for reducing risk that are far superior to the bureaucratic alternative offered by the SEC. The lessons provided by these cornerstones of financial theory are now well understood and are put into practice every day by investment firms.

Portfolio theory provides a precise model for how diversification works—not just to reduce risk, but to eliminate certain types of risk from the investment process. Among the lessons of modern financial theory is that the risks associated with owning a portfolio of securities are not related to the particular risk characteristics of individual securities in the portfolio, because these risks can be eliminated through diversification. Thus, there is considerably less demand for the firm-specific disclosure rules promulgated and enforced by the SEC than once was believed.

It is true, of course, that fraud continues to exist as a possibility even in the most efficient markets. But the opportunities for manipulation and fraud are probably less now than at any time in history. Moreover, rules against fraud existed long before there was an SEC, and such rules are all that are needed now.

SOURCE: Jonathan Macey, "The SEC Dinosaur Expands Its Turf," the *Wall Street Journal,* January 29, 1992. Reprinted by permission of the *Wall Street Journal,* © 1992 Dow Jones & Company, Inc. All rights reserved worldwide.

Required

a. Professor Macey argues that private information search by market professionals is sufficient to ensure proper operation of securities markets. Do you agree? Explain why or why not.

b. Professor Macey argues that better understanding of risk reduction through diversification, and increased availability of financial instruments for risk reduction and control, eliminate much of the need for the SEC to reduce investors' risks by means of regulation. Do you agree? Explain why or why not.

c. If Professor Macey's recommendation that the role of the SEC be reduced to one of enforcing rules against fraud were adopted, do you think this would increase or decrease the proper operation of markets? Be sure to consider the cost of regulation in your answer.

Standard Setting: Political Issues

13.1 Overview

In Chapter 12 we saw that, from the perspective of economic theory, the question of regulation of accounting and reporting standards is unsettled. While we can suggest a number of contractual and market-based incentives for private information production, we simply do not know whether market failures that would follow from deregulation of firms' information production decisions would be more or less costly to society than the various costs of the standard setting process. It does appear, however, that the problem of market failure is quite fundamental. Information asymmetry (and the resulting problems of moral hazard and adverse selection), which creates the demand for information production by firms, also creates a demand for regulation of that information production. This is because of the problem of unanimity—the amount of information that firms would privately produce need not, and in general will not, equal the amount that investors want. As a result, investors may push for regulation to remedy the perceived deficiency.

This suggests that standard setting is fundamentally as much a political process as an economic one. Such a viewpoint is consistent with the concept of constituencies of accounting, with the size hypothesis of positive accounting theory in Section 8.2, and with the game theoretic and agency theoretic views of constituency conflict in Chapter 9. It seems natural to expect that the various accounting constituencies would appeal to the political process when their conflicting interests cannot be resolved by contractual or market forces.

Our first objective in this chapter is to review two theories of regulation. The first, the **public interest theory**, takes the view that regulation should maximize social welfare. This was the viewpoint of Chapter 12. The second, the **interest**

group theory of regulation, suggests that individuals form coalitions, or constituencies, to protect and promote their interests by lobbying the government. These coalitions are viewed as in conflict with each other, to obtain their share of benefits from regulation.

Our second objective is to examine the *processes* of standard setting. Besides being of interest in their own right, we will learn that these processes are largely consistent with the interest group theory of regulation.

Our third objective is to consider the criteria that standard setters need to consider if their standards are to be acceptable. While decision usefulness and reduction of information asymmetry are necessary for any standard, we shall see that much more is needed. Specifically, the standard must be acceptable to its various constituencies. This requires a careful attention to due process by the standard setter.

13.2   *Two Theories of Regulation*

13.2.1 *THE PUBLIC INTEREST THEORY*

The public interest theory of regulation was implicit in our examination of standard setting in Chapter 12. This theory suggests that regulation is the result of a public demand for correction of market failures. In this theory, the central authority, also called the regulatory body or the regulator, is assumed to have the best interests of society at heart. It does its best to regulate so as to maximize social welfare. Consequently, regulation is thought of as a tradeoff between the costs of regulation and its social benefits in the form of improved operation of markets. Chapter 12 addressed these various costs and benefits.

While this view represents an ideal of how regulation should be carried out, there are problems with its implementation. It can be argued, from the standpoint of how regulation works in practice, that the theory is superficial and perhaps naive. Our discussion here is based on Stigler (1971), Posner (1974), and Peltzman (1976).

One problem with the public interest theory is the very complex task of deciding on the right amount of regulation. This is particularly true for a complex commodity like information where, as Chapter 12 makes clear, it is effectively impossible to please everyone. Then, the door is left open for other theories of how the amount of regulation is determined.

An even more serious problem, however, lies in the motivation of the regulatory body. Given the complex nature of its task, it is difficult for a legislature to monitor the operations of the regulator. In effect, the ability of the legislature to force the regulatory body to act in the public interest is weak, because of the complex nature of regulation and the fact that costly and lengthy hearings would be needed for the legislature to know whether the regulator is doing a good job. This opens up the possibility that the regulatory agency will operate on its own behalf rather than on behalf of the public. The situation here is reminiscent of the manager in our agency theory discussion of Example 9.2, who was motivated to shirk because his or her action was unobservable to the owner. Thus, the public interest theory represents a sort of first-best approach to regulation. In practice, the first-best solution may not be attainable, because of problems of implementation. This leads directly to another theory.

13.2.2 THE INTEREST GROUP THEORY

The interest group theory of regulation takes the view that an industry operates in the presence of a number of interest groups (or constituencies, as we have used the term in earlier chapters). Consider any manufacturing industry as an example. The firms in the industry compose an obvious interest group, as do its customers. Another interest group would be environmentalists, who would be concerned about the industry's social responsibility. These various interest groups will lobby the legislature for various amounts and types of regulation. For example, the industry itself may demand regulation to protect it against foreign price competition or against encroachments on its operations by related industries. Customers may form groups to lobby for quality standards or price controls. Environmentalists may lobby for emission control regulations from factories, and so on. These various constituencies can be thought of as *demanders* of regulation. Note that the nature and extent of the regulation they demand will differ across constituencies.

The political authority, or legislature, can also be thought of as an interest group, which has the power to *supply* regulation. The interests of the political authority lie in retaining power. Consequently, they will supply regulation to those constituencies that they believe will be most effective and useful in helping them retain power. The regulatory body is then in the middle. It is the *vehicle* whereby regulation is supplied. It attempts to maximize its own welfare while at the same time *balancing the demands* of the various constituencies.

In effect, the interest group theory of regulation takes the view that regulation is a commodity for which there is a demand and a supply. The commodity will be allocated to those constituencies which are most politically effective in convincing the legislature to grant them regulatory favours.

While it may seem rather cynical, the interest group theory may well be a better predictor of how regulation really works than the public interest theory. Before considering the extent to which the theory fits the regulation of the information industry, we will examine the standard setting process.

13.3   *Standard Setting in Canada and the United States*

13.3.1 *THE CANADIAN INSTITUTE OF CHARTERED ACCOUNTANTS (CICA)*

Accounting Standards Committee

The *CICA Handbook* contains standards for financial accounting and for auditing, as laid down by the Accounting Standards Board and the Auditing Standards Board (AuSB) respectively of the Canadian Institute of Chartered Accountants. The *CICA Handbook* is the major source of accounting and auditing standards in Canada. Its authority is enhanced because it has a special legal status. For example, the Canada Business Corporations Act, Regulation 44, states:

> The financial statements referred to in paragraph 155(1)(a) of the Act shall, except as otherwise provided by this Part, be prepared in accordance with the standards, as they exist from time to time, of the Canadian Institute of Chartered Accountants set out in the *CICA Handbook*.

The Accounting Standards Board is authorized by the Board of Governors of the Canadian Institute of Chartered Accountants to publish reports on its own responsibility. The CICA Board of Governors has also authorized the AuSB to publish reports on its own responsibility. There is also a third CICA standard setting body, the **Public Sector Accounting and Auditing Committee (PSAAC)**.

PROCESS OF STANDARD SETTING   The following points should be noted about the process of setting standards for the *CICA Handbook*:

- The Accounting Standards Board publishes accounting standards "on its own authority." Presumably, this is to give it a measure of independence from the CICA itself and reduce the possibility of interference in its deliberations.

- New standards require the approval of at least two-thirds of the members of the Board. This is substantially more than a simple majority, thereby decreasing the possibility of approval of a standard that is only marginally acceptable to the Board. This will also tend to produce a process of compromise in the creation of a new standard. Dissenting members will be in a stronger position than they would be if only a simple majority was required and thus would be less likely to feel that their views and concerns had been ignored.

- Two-thirds or more of the Board's members must be members of the CICA. This may water down the two-thirds voting requirement—to the extent that CICA members who "think alike" may gang up on non-CICA members. However, Board members will be selected to represent both official languages and also major geographical regions. In addition, they should comprise a broad range of occupational backgrounds and experience. It is noteworthy that provision is made for the appointment of five members from organizations representing financial analysts, business executives, academics, and other professional accounting organizations. Thus, while the CICA retains majority representation on the Board, some attempt has been made to broaden representation, both from different areas of the CICA and from other accounting constituencies.

- While not mentioned explicitly in the terms of reference, it should be noted that exposure drafts enable interested parties to react to a proposed standard before it is finalized. It is possible that significant change will be made in a new standard before it is finalized, depending on constituent reaction.

- Membership on the Accounting Standards Board is voluntary, that is, these are not full-time, salaried positions. In effect, the organizations that employ the Board members bear the costs. Whether this is a desirable state of affairs is difficult to say. An alternative scenario might be one in which Board members were full-time, paid employees (like FASB members in the United States). Of course, this would require that considerably more money be raised to support the Board's activities. To the extent that this was raised from a variety of different constituencies, this would broaden the base of financial support for the standard setting process. However, we saw in Chapter 12 that the direct costs of setting and administering standards were only a part, and probably a small part, of the overall costs of standard setting. Nevertheless, such an alternative scenario might reduce any possible concerns arising from the fact that, at present, the organizations that employ the Board members, mainly professional accounting firms, may "call the tune." Yet another possibility would be to discontinue the Accounting Standards Board, and adopt GAAP as laid down by the FASB (Section 13.3.3) and/or the International Accounting Standards Committee (Section 13.4).

- The *CICA Handbook* says little about how a particular topic is placed on the agenda of the Accounting Standards Board. Presumably, Board members and full-time Institute staff are close enough to public practice to know what topics require attention. Also, the Accounting Standards Board is advised by the **Standards Advisory Board**. This is a body with widely based membership set up to provide an outside perspective on priorities for possible new standards.

- It should be apparent that the issuance of a new standard will require considerable time. First, background research is needed. Then, a project proposal must be prepared and approved, followed by a statement of principles. The exposure draft stage will also take considerable time. It seems that the procedures for due process in establishing a new standard carry a time penalty. This reduces the ability of the Board to respond to new issues as they arise. In effect, the Board may be able to react to problems only after they have arisen.

  However, the Board can also issue **Guidelines**. These are interpretations of existing *CICA Handbook* recommendations or opinions on other matters for which a *CICA Handbook* provision does not exist. While Guidelines do not have the authority of *CICA Handbook* recommendations, they do have the potential to enable a relatively quick reaction when a need arises.

- Also, the **Emerging Issues Committee (EIC)** was established in 1988 by the Accounting Standards Board to provide a forum for timely review of emerging accounting issues that are likely to receive divergent or unsatisfactory treatment in practice in the absence of some guidance. The EIC has 14 voting members, including 10 from public practice and 4 from industry, 2 of which are nominated by the Financial Executives Institute. Its pronouncements require a consensus, defined as the existence of no more than two dissenting members of those present at the meeting. The EIC represents a major step towards improving the timeliness of the standard setting process.

Our main observation from this discussion is that the various steps to create a new standard suggest that the process is quite "political." In other words, many of the various constituencies of accounting are invited to take part, either as part of the process leading to insertion of an item into the Board agenda, as members of the Board itself, or as respondents to exposure drafts. If the process was strictly economic, as was implicit in our discussion in Chapter 12, such broad-based representation would not be necessary.

13.3.2 THE ONTARIO SECURITIES COMMISSION (OSC)

Here, we select for analysis the securities commission of Ontario. The Ontario Securities Commission (OSC) regulates the largest stock exchange in the country (Toronto Stock Exchange) and is one of the most active securities commissions. Hence, it is a logical candidate for analysis.

Role of the OSC

According to the *Securities Act* of Ontario, the OSC may, where it appears to be in the public interest, make any decision:

i) with respect to the manner in which any Ontario Stock Exchange carries on business;

ii) with respect to any bylaw, ruling, instruction or regulation of any such exchange;

iii) with respect to trading on or through any such exchange or with respect to any security listed or posted for trading on such an exchange; and

iv) to ensure that issuers of securities from (iii) above comply with the regulations of the *Securities Act*.

In summary, the role of the OSC is to regulate all securities trading in Ontario, including both the securities themselves and the exchanges on which they are traded.

Authority and Power of the OSC

The authority of the OSC is endowed by the *Securities Act*. The Act allows that an order made by the OSC may be enforced in the same manner as any order or judgement of the Ontario Court and may be varied or discharged upon an application made by notice. Orders made by the OSC may include:

i) an order to cease trading of a specific security or of all securities on a given Ontario Stock Exchange;

ii) an order of investigation with respect to a specific security or trading practice, including summoning witnesses and requiring production of evidence;

iii) an order of property seizure;

iv) an order to freeze property; and

v) suspension or cancellation of a firm or intermediary's registration for trading.

Structure of the OSC

The upper portion of the OSC structure consists of eight commissioners, including a chairman (chief executive officer) and a vice chairman. All commissioners are appointed by the Lieutenant-Governor in Council for Ontario; they are usually appointed for a three-year term, but may be removed at any time by the Lieutenant-Governor in Council. During their term, the chairman and vice chairman are full-time public servants; the remaining six commissioners are required to give such time as may be necessary for the due performance of their duties, which consist mainly of weekly hearings and any other meetings/hearings which may be required from time to time.

The chairman and vice chairman are usually selected for appointment by the Premier of Ontario; the remaining six commissioners are selected by decision of the chairman and vice chairman. The objective of the OSC in selecting commissioners is to appoint members with diversity of experience, covering all specialized areas of securities trading. For this reason, the appointed commissioners usually include an expert financial analyst and a geological consultant.

The appointed commissioners are assisted in their duties by an administrative staff of approximately 100 civil servants, including accountants, lawyers, and investigators. The administrative staff are under the supervision of the director (chief administrative officer), who reports directly to the chairman. Reporting to the director, in turn, are the chief legal investigation officer, the deputy director of registration, the deputy director of administration, and the deputy director of filings, each of whom supervises his or her own administrative staff. It should be stressed that the final decisions of the OSC are made by the commissioners, and that the reports and actions of the administrative staff occur solely to assist the commissioners in decision-making and to carry out any actions required as a result of their decisions.

For specialized legal decisions, the OSC consults the Chief Counsel, an experienced lawyer appointed by the Lieutenant-Governor in Council to render legal opinions and represent the OSC in court as needed. The Chief Counsel, who is also paid on a per diem basis, has no day-to-day functions.

The OSC may also appoint experts from any field, as required, for investigations.

OSC's Relation to the CICA Handbook

Prior to 1978 the *Securities Act* provided a detailed prescription for the annual financial statement contents of companies whose securities were publicly traded. However, in 1978, the Act recognized the *CICA Handbook*'s Accounting and Auditing Recommendations as the appropriate authority for standards of financial reporting. Currently, OSC National Policy Statement 27 (1992) states that GAAP "has the meaning ascribed to this term by the *CICA Handbook.*"

However, certain exceptions from GAAP are permitted. If the issuer of financial statements is a foreign-based company whose stock is publicly traded in Ontario, the issuer may use applicable foreign accounting principles. Exceptions from GAAP may be allowed for Canadian companies when one of the following is true:

- The OSC is satisfied that GAAP statements are not reasonably practicable
- The OSC previously accepted non-GAAP statements and is certain that the circumstances of the previous decision have not changed

Also, the OSC issues standards where these do not directly affect the financial statements. For example, MD&A (Section 4.8.2) and requirements for disclosure of executive compensation (Section 10.5) are OSC standards.

13.3.3 THE FINANCIAL ACCOUNTING STANDARDS BOARD (FASB)

Establishment and Purpose of the FASB

The **Financial Accounting Standards Board (FASB)** was established in 1973. Its purpose is to establish and improve standards of financial accounting and reporting for the guidance and education of the public in the United States. To accomplish this, the FASB attempts to improve the usefulness of financial reporting by focusing on consistency and comparability, by updating standards (if necessary) for changes in the business and economic environment, and by improving the public understanding of the nature and purpose of information contained in financial reports.

In conducting its activities, the FASB is guided by certain perceptions. These include: objectivity in decision-making, consideration of the views of its constituents, promulgation of standards only when the expected benefits exceed the expected costs, implementation of changes in a manner which minimizes disruption to existing practice, and review and (if necessary) amendment of past decisions. It should be noted that the FASB is a body distinct from the **American Institute of Certified Public Accountants (AICPA)**. While the AICPA is one of the sponsoring bodies and endorses FASB standards, it will be clear from the following that many other bodies are also involved in sponsoring the FASB.

Structure of the FASB

The FASB is the operational arm of a three-part organizational structure for financial accounting standard setting; the other two parts are the Financial Accounting Foundation and the Financial Accounting Standards Advisory Council. We will now discuss the structure of each of these entities.

FINANCIAL ACCOUNTING FOUNDATION (FAF)   The Financial Accounting Foundation (FAF) consists of 16 trustees, each of whom can serve no more than two consecutive three-year terms. Of these trustees, 13 are elected from sponsoring organizations as follows:

Organization	Number of Trustees
American Accounting Association (an association of academic accountants)	1
AICPA	4
Financial Analysts Federation	1
Financial Executives Institute	2
National Association of Accountants	1
Securities Industry Association	1
Various government accounting groups	3
	13

Of the remaining trustees, two are elected by the above trustees; of these two, one must be from the commercial banking industry and one from the business community in general. The sixteenth trustee is the senior elected AICPA official.

The FAF raises funds for all three groups in the structure, appoints FASB board members and reviews FASB performance, and appoints Financial Accounting Standards Advisory Council members.

FINANCIAL ACCOUNTING STANDARDS ADVISORY COUNCIL (FASAC)   The Financial Accounting Standards Advisory Council (FASAC) consists of a minimum of 20 (and usually 35 to 40) members appointed by the FAF. Although the breakdown of membership by profession is not specified as it is for the FAF, the membership should consist of individuals from diversified interests.

The FASAC acts as the liaison between FASB and the business and economic communities: it advises on priorities of projects and potential projects, and on the suitability of FASB's preliminary positions on issues (as perceived by those communities).

FINANCIAL ACCOUNTING STANDARDS BOARD (FASB)   The FASB consists of seven board members, appointed by the FASAC for a maximum of two five-year terms. Although background is taken into account when selecting board members, it is considered secondary to such qualifications as accounting knowledge, integrity, discipline, and judicial temperament. A majority of five of the seven members in favour is required to pass a new standard.

FASB board members are expected to be independent, both in fact and in appearance. To accomplish this, they must sever all ties with previous employers, declare conflict of interest if necessary, and not accept fees or honoraria from any institution other than the FASB.

Standard Setting Process of the FASB

In setting and updating accounting and reporting standards, the FASB places heavy emphasis on *due process*. The process usually encompasses the following stages:

- **Preliminary evaluation of problems related to accounting and reporting standards**   This evaluation of problems may be done by FASAC, the Emerging Issues Task Force (discussed below), FASB research staff, professional groups, or the SEC. Regardless of who identifies the problem, it is then brought to the attention of FASAC, which advises FASB on its importance and urgency.

- **Admission to the agenda of FASB**   To be admitted to the FASB agenda, an issue must be evaluated by FASAC and FASB to determine whether it meets criteria for admission. Specifically, the issue must be sufficiently significant, alternative solutions must be sufficiently different to be controversial, and there must be a high likelihood that the FASB can resolve the issue to the satisfaction of the business and economic communities. If the problem is not immediately admitted to the agenda, it may still be assigned to FASB research staff for further study.

- **Early deliberations** This stage consists of more careful examination of the issue by the FASB. In addition to discussions by the FASB board members, early deliberations may involve creation of a special task force or advisory council to formalize contact with constituencies, or even (for major issues) conducting public hearings.

- **Tentative resolution** This involves a more formal description of the board members' views and of any consensus which may have developed. Once this consensus has been achieved, FASB publishes documentation of its proposed solution (an exposure draft, for example) to focus public interest on the issue.

- **Further deliberations** Once responses to an exposure draft are received, FASB deliberates further to analyze these responses. If the responses are sufficiently contradictory and controversial, this stage may also involve public hearings. Depending on the amount of response and the agreement between responses, there are three possibilities for this stage:

    - The project is terminated (if it is determined to be insignificant or unresolvable)
    - Another exposure draft is issued
    - A final pronouncement is issued

- **Final resolution** This stage consists of the issuance of a Final Pronouncement. The Final Pronouncement may be a Statement of Financial Accounting Standards, an Interpretation Statement, or a Technical Bulletin, depending on how significant the problem has finally been determined to be.

- **Subsequent review** After a Final Pronouncement has been issued, FASB periodically reviews its decision to determine whether further supplementation is needed.

13.3.4 THE SECURITIES AND EXCHANGE COMMISSION (SEC)

In the United States, the SEC was founded in 1933 to regulate trading in the securities of firms whose securities are traded in more than one state and which meet certain size tests. As part of its mandate, the SEC has the responsibility to ensure that investors are supplied with adequate information. Consequently, it has the authority to issue accounting standards for firms under its jurisdiction. However, in ASR 150, the SEC delegated this responsibility to the FASB.

This is not to say that the SEC does not intervene in standard setting from time to time. For example, the SEC overrode SFAS 19, which required oil and gas companies to use successful-efforts accounting for exploration costs (recall our discussion in Section 7.6). This was done by means of ASR 253 (1978), which allowed use of either full-cost or successful-efforts accounting, and also proposed RRA, initially as supplementary information. As a result of this intervention, the FASB issued SFAS 25 in 1978, which amended SFAS 19 to allow both cost methods.

Nevertheless, it can be argued that instances such as these are "the exceptions that prove the rule," and that it is correct to say the SEC effectively delegates standard setting authority to the FASB.

13.4 The International Accounting Standards Committee (IASC)

13.4.1 ESTABLISHMENT AND OBJECTIVES OF THE IASC

The **International Accounting Standards Committee**[1] was established in 1973 by agreement between accountancy bodies in Australia, Canada, France, Germany, Japan, Mexico, the Netherlands, the United Kingdom and Ireland, and the United States.

The objectives of the IASC are:

- To formulate and publish in the public interest accounting standards to be observed in the presentation of financial statements and to promote their worldwide acceptance and observance

- To work generally for the improvement and harmonization of regulations, accounting standards, and procedures relating to the presentation of financial statements

The establishment of the IASC is part of the increased globalization and integration of economic activity which has taken place in recent years. In particular, this globalization includes securities markets, with many corporations listed on stock exchanges in two or more countries. Consequently, preparers of annual reports of large, multinational corporations are finding it necessary to prepare these reports to satisfy the securities legislation of more than one jurisdiction. For example, foreign firms that wish to trade their securities in the United States must satisfy SEC requirements. These include filing annual financial statements either in accordance with U.S. GAAP or, if the statements are prepared under GAAP of some other jurisdiction, with a reconciliation of net income and balance sheet line items with U.S. GAAP.

To the extent that international accounting standards become acceptable to securities commissions as a substitute for local GAAP, costs of multiple exchange listings will fall. This should lower firms' costs of capital as they are better able to tap broader sources of financing.

13.4.2 STRUCTURE OF THE IASC

The membership of the IASC consists of the professional accountancy bodies which belong to the International Federation of Accountants (IFAC). As at January 1994, there were 109 member bodies in 80 countries. The business of the IASC is conducted by a board of representatives of accountancy bodies in 13 countries, including Canada, and up to four other organizations with an interest in financial reporting. Currently the Board includes representation of one such organization, the International Coordinating Committee of Financial Analysts' Associations.

The Board is advised by an international Consultative Group that includes representatives of users and preparers of financial statements and standard setting bodies, as well as observers from intergovernmental organizations. Current membership of the Consultative Group includes, among others, the FASB and the International Organization of Securities Commissions (IOSCO). This latter organization, established in 1984, promotes international harmonization of the regulation and trading of securities.

The IASC is funded by the professional accountancy bodies and other organizations on its Board, by IFAC, and by contributions from multinational companies, financial institutions, accounting firms, and other organizations.

13.4.3 THE DEVELOPMENT OF INTERNATIONAL ACCOUNTING STANDARDS

One of the objectives of the IASC is to harmonize as far as possible the diverse accounting standards and accounting policies of different countries, by means of a due process whereby Board representatives, member bodies, members of the Consultative Group, other organizations and individuals, and the IASC staff are encouraged to submit suggestions for new topics which might be dealt with in International Accounting Standards. Once a topic is admitted to the agenda, a Steering Committee develops a Statement of Principles. Each Steering Committee is chaired by a Board representative and usually includes representatives of the accountancy bodies in at least three other countries. Steering Committees may also include representatives of other organizations that are represented on the Board or the Consultative Group or that are expert in the particular topic.

The Steering Committee prepares an "Exposure Draft" based on the Statement of Principles. Publication of an exposure draft requires approval of at least two-thirds of the IASC Board. Comments are invited from all interested parties during the exposure period. The Steering Committee reviews the comments and prepares a draft International Accounting Standard. A final Standard requires the approval of at least three-quarters of the Board.

During the development process, the Board may decide that the needs of the topic under discussion would be better served by issuing a Discussion Paper for comment. Issuance of a Discussion Paper requires approval of a simple majority of the Board.

13.4.4 *AUTHORITY OF THE IASC*

The IASC does not have the power to require compliance with International Accounting Standards, hence their adoption is voluntary. Nevertheless, a 1993 IASC survey[2] revealed that 11 countries had adopted some or all IASC standards as their own and a further 9 countries use IASC standards as a basis for developing their own national standards. Furthermore, a growing number of companies disclose that their financial statements conform to international accounting standards. Indeed, the *CICA Handbook* (paragraph 1501.05) states the desirability for Canadian firms that report in an international environment of disclosing conformity with international standards.

13.5   *Relationship to Theories of Regulation*

Our description of the standard setting process shows that it is characterized by due process. For example, in Canada, the United States, and internationally, major constituencies of financial statement preparers are represented. Also, there are provisions for public hearings, exposure drafts, and, generally, for openness, as well as requirements for majority or super-majority votes in favour before new standards are issued.

This due process characteristic is consistent with conflict-based theories of constituency interaction. The sources of market failure in the production of information discussed in Chapter 12 imply that market forces cannot always be relied upon to generate the "right" accounting standards and procedures. Yet, the complexities arising from the diverse information needs and interests of investors and managers make it effectively impossible for standard setters to calculate the "right" accounting standards either. We simply do not know how to calculate the best tradeoff between the conflicting uses of information by investors and managers which is required by the public interest theory of regulation. This is why the choice of accounting standards is better regarded as a conflict between constituencies than as a process of calculation. The Accounting Standards Board, the FASB, and the IASC are players in a complex game where affected constituencies choose strategies of lobbying for or against a proposed new standard.

If the players of the game are to accept the outcome (that is, the issuance or non-issuance of a new standard and, if it is issued, its specific reporting requirements) they must feel that the process was fair, and that their strategy at least had a chance of working. The willingness of players to accept a new standard is enhanced if they feel that their views were heard. This explains the attention to due process as a way of moderating the inherent constituency conflict in standard setting.

These considerations suggest that the interest group theory of regulation may be a better predictor of new standards than the public interest theory, since the interest group theory formally recognizes the existence of conflicting constituencies. To pursue this question further, we next consider some of the conflict leading up to a specific new FASB standard.

13.6   An Example of Constituency Conflict

In the absence of a comparable Canadian standard, we described SFAS 115, "Accounting for Certain Investments in Debt and Equity Securities," in Section 6.5.4. However, we did not consider the process that led up to SFAS 115. Here, we consider aspects of this process, which provide an interesting and important example of the problems of developing a new standard. Exhibit 13.1 reproduces an article by Robin Goldwyn Blumenthal which appeared in the *Wall Street Journal*, September 11, 1992, following the release of an exposure draft by the FASB. The exposure draft specified that at least some securities held by firms be valued at fair value. Recall that this implies market value if reliably available. Otherwise, fair value can be determined by present value, use of models, or other appropriate techniques. The problems of gains trading, and of volatility of reported net income under the new proposed standard, were considered in Section 6.5.4. Here, our main interest is in the constituency conflicts leading up to SFAS 115.

EXHIBIT 13.1 FASB Moves Closer to Forcing Banks to Value Securities Near Market Prices

NEW YORK—The Financial Accounting Standards Board moved a step closer to implementing controversial rules that would require banks to value many of their securities closer to market prices.

In issuing its exposure draft, the FASB formally proposed rules on accounting for securities held as investments; the proposal is similar to a compromise approach outlined in July. Although there appears to be solid support for the proposal by six of the seven members on FASB's board, there is likely to be continuing strong opposition to the proposal during the comment period by banks, which in the past year have bought record amounts of securities.

"It's a huge change in accounting," said Donna Fisher, manager of accounting policy at the American Bankers Association. In effect, the proposal would make it more difficult for banks to classify securities as long-term investments, and thus account for them at original cost rather than market value. Although the proposal would affect any company that invests in marketable equity securities and debt securities, it would have the greatest effect on financial institutions such as banks, whose investments in those securities represent about 30% of their total assets, Ms. Fisher said.

GAINS TRADING

The proposal, which is intended to standardize accounting methods on investments in securities for various industries, also attempts to address a practice by banks called gains trading, in which securities that have appreciated in value are sold to recognize gains while those that have fallen in value are held as long-term investments and thus recorded at original cost.

Under existing accounting rules, "there was a perception that people were inappropriately reporting something at cost when in fact they were not holding on to [the securities] for the long term," said Robert C. Wilkins, an FASB project manager.

The FASB, the chief rule-making body for accountants that is based in Norwalk, Conn., has been under pressure for several years from the Securities and Exchange Commission to hold investment securities at more up-to-date values, known as marking to market. SEC Chairman Richard Breeden began voicing his support for marking to market all investment securities two years ago.

Although the FASB had at one point considered eliminating the current three categories of investment securities and forcing companies to mark all of them to market, it abandoned that approach because it couldn't figure out how to mark related liabilities to market, Mr. Wilkins said. In July, the FASB also eased its approach to declines in value of debt securities held as "available for sale." These would be booked to shareholders' equity on the balance sheet, rather than reducing profits on the income statement.

PLUSES AND MINUSES

Walter Schuetze, the SEC's chief accountant, said the proposal had pluses and minuses. "The plus is that more marketable securities will be accounted for at market in the balance sheet," Mr. Schuetze said. However, he pointed out that under this proposal, there is room for "so-called psychoanalytic accounting," which allows management to classify three different ways the same securities at the time they are purchased.

Mr. Schuetze also said the proposal didn't adequately address gains trading, and that it failed to give enough guidance on when to write down stocks and bonds when the decline in market price is deemed to be "other than temporary."

Banking representatives, however, had other views on the proposal. "They don't come out and say you must mark securities to market but the net effect we think will be very close," said Ms. Fisher of the American Bankers Association. She said that if the proposal is adopted, banks would need to try to reduce volatility in their capital accounts, possibly by investing in shorter-term securities.

Bankers say that for the most part they purchase intermediate-term securities with a maturity of two to five years. "Most of our securities are short term," said William J. Rossman, chief executive officer of Mid-State Bank in Altoona, Pa., and president of Robert Morris Associates, a trade group of commercial lenders. "You're not going to find too many banks taking short-term funds and investing in 30-year bonds."

The proposed rules must now go through a public comment period, in which the FASB undoubtedly will be hearing from opponents. The exposure draft could take effect as early as 1994 if it is approved.

Treasury Undersecretary Jerome Powell, in remarks to a mortgage bankers group, warned that market value accounting would make bank earnings very volatile and add to the credit crunch.

Diane Casey of the Independent Bankers Association of America, a group of 6,000 community banks, said the fight to soften the proposed rule is "far from over." The association contends that the proposal will hurt community banks and discourage many of them from purchasing local school district and sewer authority bonds, many of which aren't actively traded.

Before considering constituency conflicts, consider the effects of full marking-to-market, which Exhibit 13.1 mentions the FASB had considered at one point. Full marking-to-market would not only involve fair valuation of all of a firm's securities, both assets and liabilities, but also involve including the unrealized gains and losses in reported net income, with consequent volatility. (This volatility would be reduced to the extent that a firm's holdings of financial liabilities hedged its holdings of financial assets.) Note also that full marking-to-market would eliminate the ability of firms to engage in gains trading. If securities were valued at market, with gains and losses included in income as they occurred, management would not control the timing of these gains and losses. Also, there would be no effect on the bottom line upon sale, so that gains trading would be eliminated.

As might be expected, full marking-to-market would be objected to by banks, since they hold large amounts of financial assets and liabilities. Banks would see both the volatility of their earnings increase (to the extent this was not hedged) and their ability to engage in earnings management severely reduced. Exhibit 13.1 describes the objections of the American Bankers Association, Robert Morris Associates, and the Independent Bankers Association of America, all representing management.

In addition, the U.S. Treasury was concerned about economic consequences. It felt that marking-to-market would affect banks' operating and financial strategies, to the point where they would be unwilling to lend long-term, which would affect the availability of credit in the economy. This concern arises because as interest rates vary so does the market value of fixed-term securities. Since the longer the term the greater the market value variation in response to a given change in interest rates, banks would cut down on long-term lending in order to reduce volatility of earnings. Consequently, the Treasury strongly opposed the proposed standard.

In addition, the original proposal for full marking-to-market accounting faced technical difficulties. Certain financial liabilities, such as banks' deposit liabilities, were difficult to value, because of core deposit intangibles. It appears that models to provide values in the face of these difficulties were not available.

Obviously, if a standard has technical difficulties, it can be even more strongly attacked by its opponents. To make matters worse, if financial liabilities were excused from the standard, then they could not hedge gains or losses on financial assets, thereby making concerns about volatility even greater.

However, Exhibit 13.1 also describes the support of another powerful constituency, the SEC, for full marking-to-market. This support is not hard to understand. As an agency whose role is to protect investors and encourage the proper operation of securities markets, the SEC would be expected to favour the conveying of fair values to investors. Also, the SEC favoured the recording of these fair values in the accounts (as opposed to footnote presentation), since, with such recording, gains trading would be eliminated.

Obviously, the FASB was in a difficult position as it tried to produce a standard which would be generally acceptable. Nevertheless, SFAS 115 passed in 1993, along the lines discussed in Section 6.5.4. The standard takes effect for fiscal years beginning after December 15, 1993.

It is interesting to note some of the compromises that were made in the standard, relative to the original goal of full mark-to-market accounting. First, liabilities are excluded, due to measurement difficulties. Second, to reduce volatility, some debt securities continue to be valued at cost (strictly speaking, at lower-of-cost-or-market) under SFAS 115. Recall that these are securities for which the firm "has the positive intent and ability" to hold them to maturity. Marking-to-market is required for trading securities and for available-for-sale-securities. Third, to further reduce volatility, unrealized gains and losses on available-for-sale securities are excluded from reported net income and reported in a separate category of shareholders' equity.

Presumably, the above compromises were made to reduce the objections of management. However, as a result, gains trading is not eliminated, and may even be encouraged since firms could realize gains merely by transferring securities from held-to-maturity to trading. However, by placing severe constraints on the ability both to classify securities as held-to-maturity in the first place and to reclassify, the FASB hopes to minimize the incidence of gains trading. Furthermore, expanded disclosure requirements under SFAS 115 would be more likely to reveal gains trading profits than before. In addition, if a firm were to sell *part* of its held-to-maturity securities before maturity, this would be inconsistent with intent to hold and would likely result in the remaining securities being reclassified to trading or available-for-sale.

These constraints on gains trading were apparently made to satisfy the SEC. Had the SEC decided not to go along, this would have put the FASB in a very difficult position.

13.6.1 CONCLUSION

There seems little doubt that a standard such as SFAS 115 is decision useful to investors—for example, recall our discussion of Barth (1994) in Section 6.6. Furthermore, the reduction in information asymmetry between management and investors that results from investors' enhanced knowledge of security values, and from reductions in gains trading, will improve the working of securities markets, with consequent social benefits. However, while these are valuable improvements, it should be clear that much more is required if a standard is to succeed. An acceptable compromise between the interests of affected constituencies is also essential. We will now consider the criteria for a successful standard in greater generality.

13.7 Criteria for Standard Setting

We have seen that there are a number of factors which affect the process of standard setting. Standards should be decision useful, but they should also be acceptable to other constituencies—in particular, management. This puts the standard setter in a conflict situation and it is difficult to predict what an acceptable resolution of this conflict will be. Nevertheless, we now suggest some criteria which should be kept in mind when trying to understand standard setting.

13.7.1 DECISION USEFULNESS

The criterion of decision usefulness underlies the information and measurement perspectives on financial reporting, and the empirical capital market studies. Recall that the more informative, that is, the less noisy, is an information system the stronger will be investor reaction to information produced by the system, other things equal. Thus, empirical evidence that security prices respond to accounting information suggests that investors find that information useful.

This suggests that a necessary condition for the success of a new standard is that it be decision useful. Of course, this can be hard to assess beforehand, since the market has not yet had a chance to respond to the standard. Nevertheless, the theory of rational investor decision-making can be used to *predict* decision usefulness. For example, in their study reviewed in Section 7.4, Collins and Salatka predicted that SFAS 52 earnings were more informative than those of SFAS 8, and provided some evidence to this effect. Also, as argued in Chapter 6, the incorporation of valuations into financial reporting will increase decision usefulness to the extent that this tightens up the linkage between current and future performance.

However, while decision usefulness may be a necessary criterion for a successful standard, it is not sufficient to ensure success. We saw in Section 5.6 that, because of certain public good characteristics of accounting information, we cannot be sure that the standard which has the greatest decision usefulness is best for society. Since investors do not directly pay for accounting information, they may "overuse" it. Thus, a standard could appear to be decision useful, yet society would be worse off because the costs of producing the information were not taken into account. Furthermore, changes in standards can impose contracting costs on firms and their managers. This is another source of cost that needs to be taken into account. In effect, as implied by the fundamental problem of financial accounting theory, standard setters must consider other criteria than decision usefulness.

13.7.2 REDUCTION OF INFORMATION ASYMMETRY

We saw in Section 12.3.3 that market forces operate to motivate management and investors to generate information. Standard setters should be aware of these forces and take advantage of them to the extent possible, to reduce the need for standards. Unfortunately, market forces alone cannot ensure that the right amount of information is produced. As we saw in Section 12.4, one of the reasons for this is information asymmetry. Consequently, as suggested by Lev (1988), standard setters should use reduction of information asymmetry in capital and managerial labour markets as a criterion for new standards. Beyond any decision usefulness that such new standards possess, reduction of information asymmetry improves the operation of markets, since investors will perceive investing as more of a "level playing field." This will expand market breadth, reduce the "lemons" phenomenon and generally produce social benefits from properly working markets.

Standard setters should also be aware of the informativeness of market price itself as a conveyor of information. As discussed in Section 4.5, the efficient market price of a firm's shares reflects, with noise, what is publicly known about that firm. Furthermore, more is publicly known about large firms than small firms to the extent they are in the public eye and have analyst and media following. Consequently, we would expect the extent of information asymmetry between managers and investors to be greater for small firms, suggesting that standard setters should require at least as high disclosure standards for small firms as for large firms. In this regard, it is interesting that while the *CICA Handbook* applies to all profit-oriented enterprises, certain disclosure exemptions for small firms are allowed with respect to segment disclosure (paragraph 1700.07) and earnings per share (paragraph 3500.06)

However, it should be noted that reduction of information asymmetry as a criterion is again a necessary condition for a successful standard but not a sufficient one. Just as decision useful information has a cost, so does reduction of information asymmetry. Consequently, it is hard to know when standards to reduce information asymmetry cease to be cost-effective.

13.7.3 *ECONOMIC CONSEQUENCES OF NEW STANDARDS*

As mentioned above, one of the costs of a new standard is the cost imposed on firms and managers to meet that standard. This goes beyond the out-of-pocket costs of producing the newly mandated information. Costs are also created by contract rigidities, as in an increased probability of violating debt covenants and effects on the level and volatility of managers' future bonus streams. These costs can affect operating and financial policies. Furthermore, to the extent that new standards require the release of proprietary information, firms' future profitability can be unfavourably or favourably affected by the reduction of competitive advantage.

The reduction in managers' freedom to choose from different accounting policies that frequently results when a new standard is implemented is also a source of economic consequences. We argued in Section 12.5.3 that firms can signal inside information by accounting policy choice. Also, earnings management can reveal inside information, as discussed in Section 11.3. Obviously, if accounting policy choice is constrained, there is a reduction in the extent to which these private forces for information production can operate.

Finally, the Darrough and Stoughton model in Section 9.3 suggests that the greater the degree of competition in an industry the better the disclosure, other things equal. As a result, there may be less need for accounting standards in some industries than others.

These considerations suggest that standard setters should weigh the possible economic consequences of new standards as an important source of cost which will affect both the need for the standard and the willingness of constituencies to accept it. Of course, it may be that the economic consequences of a new standard will be overstated during the debate leading to the standard. For example, would banks really stop long-term lending if their long-term investments have to be fully marked-to-market? Probably not, but the costs to banks of long-term lending would increase and, as a result, the charges to borrowers would likely rise.

13.7.4 THE POLITICAL ASPECTS OF STANDARD SETTING

Economic consequences leads directly to our last criterion, namely the political aspects of standard setting. Standard setters, in effect, must engineer a consensus sufficiently strong that even a constituency that does not like a new standard will nevertheless go along with it. This is the "delicate balancing" act that Zeff referred to (see Section 7.2). As should be apparent from Sections 13.3 and 13.4, the structure of standard setting bodies, both nationally and internationally, is designed to encourage such a consensus.

We conclude that the standard setting process seems most consistent with the interest group theory of regulation. Certainly, technical, and even theoretical, correctness is not sufficient to ensure the success of a standard. As we argued in Section 7.3.5, SFAS 8 was more consistent with the economic theory of exchange rate determination than its successor standard SFAS 52. Yet SFAS 8 met with such resistance that it was replaced. While careful attention to due process may be time-consuming, such attention seems essential if costly and embarrassing retractions are to be minimized. Too many of these will threaten the existence of the standard setting body itself.

13.7.5 SUMMARY

Accounting standard setters can be guided by decision usefulness and reduction of information asymmetry. However, these criteria are not sufficient to ensure successful standard setting. The legitimate interests of management and other constituencies also need to be considered, as does careful attention to due process. Because of the fundamental problem of financial accounting theory, it seems that the actual process of standard setting is better described by the interest group theory of regulation than by the public interest theory.

13.8   Conclusions

In a sense, this whole book comes to a focus on standard setting. We saw, in Chapter 2, that under ideal conditions accounting and reporting standards are not needed, since there is only one way to account, on the basis of the present values of firms' future cash flows. Indeed, under ideal conditions one can question whether financial accounting is needed at all.

Fortunately, in view of our conclusion in Section 2.6 that accountants would not be needed under ideal conditions, such conditions do not exist. As a result, financial accounting becomes much more challenging. Information asymmetry is a major source of this challenge.

We have seen two major types of information asymmetry. The first is adverse selection. That is, managers and other insiders typically know more than outside investors about the state and prospects of the firm. Here, the accounting challenge is to convey information from inside to outside the firm, thereby improving investor decision-making, limiting the ability of insiders to exploit their information advantage, and enhancing the operation of capital markets.

The second type of information asymmetry is moral hazard. That is, the effort exerted by a manager is unobservable to shareholders and lenders in all but the smallest firms. Here, the accounting challenge is to provide a hard measure of managerial performance, that is, one that is highly correlated with manager effort. This enables incentive contracts to control manager performance, protect lenders, and inform the managerial labour market.

It is important to realize that the accounting system that best meets the first challenge is unlikely to best meet the second. Specifically, investors need decision-relevant information to help them predict future firm performance. This implies not only a lot of information release, including extensive footnotes, MD&A, and even financial forecasts, but also market- and present-value-based information. However, problems of volatility and possible subjectivity of market and present values reduces the correlation of net income with manager performance. To the extent that historical cost accounting is less subject to these problems, it can be argued that it better meets the challenge of enabling efficient contracts.

It is this need for financial reporting to fulfill a dual role of meeting investors' information needs and the needs of efficient contracting that creates the fundamental problem of financial accounting theory. Investors, including securities commissions acting on their behalf, push for additional information, including valuation information. Management pushes the other way when they perceive that proposed standards will affect their flexibility under the contracts they have entered into and inhibit their ability to communicate with the market through accounting policy choice. The standard setter must then seek a compromise between these conflicting interests. The structure of standard setting bodies is designed to facilitate such a compromise.

With the increasing globalization of commerce, including securities markets, the need for international accounting standards will expand. However, the difficulties of standard setting will also increase. In addition to investor-manager conflict, new constituencies will arise representing different levels of economic development, different business practices, and different cultures. Standard setting bodies will have to adapt to take these additional challenges into account.

Notes

1. Much of the material in this section is taken from International Accounting Standards Committee, *International Accounting Standards 1994* (Basingstoke, Hants: Burgess Science Press, 1994).

2. Reported in *IASC Insight*, June 1993.

Questions and Problems

1. Contrast the public interest and interest group theories of regulation with respect to:

    a. The role of the regulatory body

    b. Their implications for the amount of the regulated commodity or service to be supplied   (CGA-Canada)

2. A debate concerning the public interest theory and the interest group theory of regulation took place at a 1989 conference entitled "Accounting Standard Setting Towards the Year 2000." Refer to the article by Chris Robinson reproduced here from *The Bottom Line* (April 1989).

DOES POLITICS TRIUMPH OVER CONTENT IN STANDARD SETTING?

MONTREAL—The hottest issue in standard setting is the philosophical question of how they should be set.

One side argues that standard setting is a process of trading off the economic and social interests of different parties who are affected by accounting, regardless of the technical quality of the standards.

The other side counters that better standards can come closer to reflecting economic reality, and standard setters should try to resist pressures to compromise.

The two schools of thought came face to face in Montreal on March 10 at Concordia University's research conference, "Accounting Standard Setting Towards the Year 2000: Meeting the Challenges."

Stephen Zeff of Rice University, past president of the American Accounting Association, chronicled the rise of economic consequences arguments that have plagued standard setters in the U.S.

For example, in the 1960s, intervention by government prevented the Accounting Principles Board from requiring the cost reduction method of accounting for investment tax credits, because the government wanted businesses to show higher income to bolster confidence.

In Canada, the oil and gas industry also lobbied against the cost reduction method of accounting for government grants, but here the standard setters won the battle. Zeff commented that Canada seems to be less adversarial than the U.S., and that the existence of provincial securities commissions to offset federal power seems to help Canadian standard setters resist corporate lobbying.

George Gorelik of the University of British Columbia characterized a standard-setting agency as an open system, vulnerable to outside influences. Accounting standards are man-made for a social purpose, and the agency which sets them must respond to society's demands.

Dhia AlHashim, director of the Centre for International Business at California State University at Northridge, proposed a policy-making body with representatives elected from the affected groups. The standards would still be administered by the technical experts, but wider participation in the process should lead to more acceptable standards.

Rashad Abdel-khalik, of the University of Florida, argues that substituting market values for historic cost would provide better information that management would be less able to manipulate.

Abdel-khalik noted that, under historic cost rules, management can choose to recognize income by selling or holding assets, reorganizing its debt and deferring or recognizing losses. If market values are used, the opportunities to time income recognition are greatly reduced, and the resultant financial statements are much more relevant to users.

Alex Milburn, a partner with Clarkson Gordon and past president of the Canadian Academic Accounting association, lamented that the profession had given in to political lobbying too easily. Accepting the process view will erode the credibility of the accounting profession and the financial statements it produces and audits.

He argued that techniques such as present value accounting still offer much promise in developing a rigorous accounting measurement system.

Gorelik and Arthur Wyatt, former member of the Financial Accounting Standards Board, suggested that the adoption of a specific conceptual framework by a standard-setting body is an important means of fending off lobbying by affected economic interests. It provides the basis for all subsequent standards.

Canada does not have such a conceptual framework, and opinion in the profession on its usefulness remains divided.

In a final panel discussion, the speakers seemed to agree that both points of view are important. Better standards are possible, but the economic interests of those affected by accounting standards will continue to influence the rules that can be set.

Kelly Gheyara, conference chairman,

and Farhad Simyar, chairman of Concordia's Department of Accountancy, organized the conference, which attracted about 120 participants from across Canada and the U.S. CGA-Quebec and CGA-Canada provided financial support.

SOURCE: Reprinted with permission from *The Bottom Line*, April 1989.

Required

For each of the following speakers mentioned in the article, indicate which theory their views are closest to, and why:

- Zeff
- Gorelik
- AlHashim
- Abdel-khalik
- Milburn   (CGA-Canada)

3. An interesting example of the constituency conflict that underlies the interest group theory of regulation appears in the article reproduced here from *The Bottom Line* (April 1990), which describes pressures from industry to change the voting procedure for new accounting standards by the FASB. Specifically, industry wants a five-out-of-seven majority required to pass a new standard, rather than a simple majority as was the case when the article was written.

FASB UNDER FIRE ON VOTE REQUIREMENT

NEW YORK—The U.S. Financial Accounting Standards Board is hunkered down in its bomb shelter, trying to fend off the slings and arrows of outraged corporations fighting to discourage new accounting regulations.

According to pressure from such influential lobbying organizations as the Business Roundtable, the Financial Accounting Foundation (the FASB's oversight body) has called for a new voting procedure. It would require five board members out of seven to vote for a new accounting standard, rather than the current simple majority of four out of seven.

The FASB, the Security and Exchange Commission staff and the powerful Congressional Oversight and Investigations Subcommittee of the House Energy and Commerce Committee, among others, have helped throw up defensive barricades.

The board of directors of the American Institute of CPAs, however, has aligned itself with the raiders—business executives, led by Roundtable task force Chairman and Citicorp CEO John Reed. They hope that a "supermajority" requirement would give FASB directors pause before creating new regulations.

They're particularly upset about some recent FASB regulations, such as the one tightening the method of accounting for post-retirement benefits.

The FASB points out, however, that since its inception in 1973, only 15 of the 104 accounting standards it adopted were passed by one vote. But the AICPA, which sets auditing standards, requires 12 out of its 17 Auditing Standards Board members to vote for passage.

In a "letter of advice" to the FAF, the AICPA said the majority of its directors "favoured the supermajority" requirement for the FASB.

The foundation, which is scheduled to vote on this issue on April 26, has studied the matter almost every two years since 1977 without coming to a decision.

One of the reasons might be that a change in the voting requirement actually would eliminate dissent rather than encourage it, according to Dr. Douglas Carmichael, Professor of Accounting at New York City University's Baruch College of Business.

"As long as a FASB Board member knows his negative vote won't prevent a proposal, which he doesn't completely agree with, from passing, he feels he has the luxury to vote against it under the present system," says Dr. Carmichael, who was formerly AICPA's vice president for Auditing. "But, if it requires five votes, that member will be more reluctant to express his doubt."

According to another highly respected technician who has been involved in much of the profession's activities for at least 15 years, this current supermajority proposal is "just silly." He told *The Bottom Line*, "I personally see no reason for this change. Somehow we manage to operate in this country with a simple majority voting in Congress and the Supreme Court. I should think the accounting profession can live with it."

That's the opinion of the Congressional subcommittee that serves as a watchdog over the SEC and the accounting and investment communities.

In a letter to SEC Chairman Richard Breeden, House Committee Chairman John Dingell (Dem., Michigan) expressed his pleasure that "the establishment of accounting standards has been handled well" in recent years by the FASB under SEC supervision. It has "evolved into an independent and principled standard-setting body, staffed by dedicated professionals, and operated under fair and open procedures."

He noted, however, that his subcommittee "is concerned about a series of events indicating that the FASB is the target of an external political-pressure campaign by certain elements in the business community ... to actually change the FASB's voting requirements and slacken the pace of its work."

"Undue interference in the FASB's activities cannot be tolerated if the public is expected to retain confidence in accounting standards issued for its protection. Majority voting," he noted, "works at the SEC, which has the authority to establish accounting standards directly."

He also pointed out that a simple majority is used by other government bodies "that make important national decisions every day. Due process assures that majority decisions in the federal government will ultimately be fair and responsive, just as it does at FASB."

Chairman Dingell then called upon the SEC to supply the subcommittee with information on what communications it has had with outside groups regarding FASB procedures, as well as the SEC's opinion on the need for any changes at the board, and what steps the commission is taking "to protect" the board's "independence."

At press time, a subcommittee spokesperson told *The Bottom Line*, "There has been no response as yet" from the SEC, although a commission source told *The Bottom Line* that "the staff is inclined to keep the status quo. The commissioners may not even vote on the matter, but just let it stand as is."

SOURCE: Reprinted with permission from *The Bottom Line*, April 1990.

Required

a.   Identify four constituencies from the article who have an interest in the proposed new voting requirement.

b.   Explain why the industry favours the five-out-of-seven voting rule.

(CGA-Canada)

4.   Refer to the article "FASB Moves Closer to Forcing Banks to Value Securities Near Market Prices" (*Wall Street Journal*, September 11, 1992), reproduced in Section 13.6.

Required

a.   Describe how the structure of standard setting in the United States is designed to facilitate the resolution of constituency conflicts such as those described in the article.

b.   Explain why a more-than-majority vote by FASB members is required to pass a new standard.

5.   An article entitled "Few Support Any New Rules on Derivatives" appeared in the *Wall Street Journal* on January 6, 1995. It describes some of the considerations surrounding possible increased regulation of the market for derivative financial instruments.

The article states that the chiefs of the Federal Reserve, the SEC, the Commodity Futures Trading Commission, and the Treasury Department are against trying "to contain the risks" in derivatives. "Derivatives are contracts with values linked to underlying assets that are … used … to defray the risks of interest-rate changes." However, instead of lessening risk, "certain derivative strategies can magnify the risks," contributing "to huge losses in professionally managed portfolios." For example, Orange County, California, went bankrupt when it incurred huge losses from its derivative portfolio. Many feel that it is not always the risk associated with the derivatives that causes the problems but "the misdeeds and misjudgments of individual investors and dealers," which is believed to be the case in Orange County. "Rep. Jim Leach (R., Iowa), chairman of the House Banking and Financial Services

Committee, … introduced a bill calling for greater disclosure, and tighter oversight of derivatives markets." Leach wants to have "a Federal Derivatives Commission to establish principles and guidelines that existing financial regulators would follow in overseeing and requiring disclosure by financial institutions that trade derivatives."

Required

a. Use the public interest theory of regulation to evaluate the pros and cons of increased regulation of derivatives.

b. To what extent will Section 3860 of the *CICA Handbook* and/or SFAS 105 and 107 reduce the need for increased government regulation? Explain your answer.

6. An article entitled "Bank Regulators Expected to Drop Plan Pegged to Market Value of Securities" appeared in the *Wall Street Journal* on November 9, 1994. It indicates that federal bank and thrift regulators will not require capital calculations for regulatory purposes to be made in accordance with SFAS 115. Rather, unrealized gains and losses arising from changes in the market value of "available for sale" securities under SFAS 115 can be excluded in the calculation of regulatory capital. "Financial institutions are required to keep a minimum level of capital, based on a percentage of assets." According to the article, banks believe that unrealized gains and losses would have had a major impact on their reported capital if there were shifts in the market value of "available for sale" securities.

Kenneth Guenther, executive vice president of the Independent Bankers Association, is happy about the change in the rule. He states that "as interest rates rose this year, many banks witnessed big declines in the value of their 'available for sale' bonds." He believes that SFAS 115 would have made " 'perfectly healthy banks … [face] serious and unwarranted regulatory restrictions.' "

Required

a. Explain why excluding unrealized gains and losses from regulatory capital will reduce the concerns by bankers about SFAS 115.

b. According to Mr. Guenther of the Independent Bankers Association, SFAS 115 would have made "perfectly healthy banks" face "serious and unwarranted regulatory restrictions." Can a bank with a securities portfolio worth less than cost be perfectly healthy? Explain.

c. To what extent will this move by bank regulators compromise the objectives of SFAS 115? Explain.

7. The article by Ford S. Worthy reproduced here from *Fortune* (June 1, 1992) describes some of the controversies surrounding a movement to greater use of valuations in GAAP.

THE BATTLE OF THE BEAN COUNTERS

In this battle of regulatory titans, Richard Breeden, head of the Securities and Exchange Commission, weighs in at seven pounds, zero ounces. Alan Greenspan, chairman of the Federal Reserve Board and Breeden's opponent in a fierce debate that could lead to sweeping changes in the way companies measure financial performance, tips the scales at a few pounds more—or less. Ludicrous? Not according to generally accepted accounting principles, or GAAP (pronounced *gap*). GAAP calls for recording and maintaining most corporate assets and liabilities based on their original cost a practice akin to measuring a person's size by his birth weight (as we just have).

Should anything be done about this kind of gross distortion of financial reality? Yes, says Breeden. He is campaigning vigorously for a new approach that could ultimately shelve the use of historical costs in favor of current, or market, values. In his camp are Comptroller General Charles Bowsher, who heads the General Accounting Office; Edmund Jenkins, a partner at Arthur Andersen & Co., who chairs a high-level accounting industry group that is studying financial reporting standards; and a number of influential economists. Squared off against them is a powerful crowd that includes Greenspan, Treasury Secretary Nicholas Brady, Federal Deposit Insurance Corp. Chairman William Taylor, and, it seems, virtually every banker and bank regulator in the country.

The stakes in this seemingly esoteric argument over the bean counter's art are potentially large and wide-ranging. Greenspan and other defenders of the status quo argue that jettisoning established accounting conventions for new, untested rules depending upon highly subjective estimates of market values would undermine investors' and depositors' confidence in banks. Such a change could also encourage bankers to abandon their traditional role as providers of long-term credit and holders of long-term securities.

Those risks must be taken seriously. But the risks of inaction may be even greater. Exhibit A in the case for change: the collapse and bailout of the savings and loan industry, now expected to cost taxpayers at least $150 billion before it's over. Though different accounting rules might not have averted this disaster, greater reliance on market values would have signaled impending doom far earlier and could have forced regulators to shut down thrifts while their losses were still manageable. Says Edward J. Kane, a finance professor at Boston College and an authority on the S&L fiasco: "Misleading accounting practices allow zombie institutions to conceal the depth of their insolvency."

Even now, traditional accounting may be allowing banks, which finally seem on the mend, to delude themselves, regulators, and investors about their true health. On average, banks' financial statements show them holding capital equal to about 7% of the historical value of their assets. But Emory University economist George J. Benston, an expert on bank capitalization, maintains that if their balance sheets, which are still burdened with bad real estate loans, were marked to their current market value, many banks and thrifts would appear insolvent or close to it.

The task of deciding how best to reform GAAP falls to an unusual organization, the Financial Accounting Standards Board. Its rulings effectively have the force of law. That power is bestowed upon it by the SEC, which has statutory authority over the accounting practices that companies must follow. Yet FASB's seven members are chosen by a private foundation and its bills are paid in part by its main constituents, which are large corporations and accounting firms. Its stated aim is to devise "neutral" accounting standards that provide information without regard for any particular policy result. In fact, FASB's dry, academic-minded deliberations, conducted in public in a classroom-like space at its offices in Norwalk, Connecticut, sometimes lead to pronouncements that profoundly affect society (see box).

WHAT ELSE FASB WILL HIT YOU WITH

Retirement Benefits

Talk about big numbers. Between now and the first quarter of 1993, corporate America's reported net income—and, in turn, its stockholders' equity—will shrink by an estimated $225 billion thanks to a new FASB rule now being phased in. The product of nearly 11 years' work, Statement 106 requires large public companies to begin taking charges for the cash they expect to pay out one day for medical and other nonpension benefits promised to retired employees and their families.

Up to now, such costs have been recognized as expenses as they were paid each year. In shifting from pay-as-you-go to accrual accounting, companies must acknowledge a huge "catch-up" liability—the total present value of future commitments already made to present retirees and employees. They may account for this burden by taking a single big bath—as IBM ($2.3 billion) and General Electric ($1.8 billion) did last year—or they may spread the cost over 20 years, as General Motors (estimated catch-up obligation: $16 billion to $24 billion) is likely to do. Nonpublic companies whose pension plans cover fewer than 500 people have until 1995 to comply.

The new rule is a prime example of FASB's influence on the real world. By forcing managers to take account of the huge costs of retirement programs, costs that in many cases were poorly understood, "FASB has done companies a real service," says Harold Dankner, a partner at Coopers & Lybrand. Already the new rule is prompting some stunned employers to begin exploring ways to reduce the benefits of future retirees.

Income Taxes

With its recent adoption of Statement 109, FASB will make the byzantine realm of income tax accounting slightly less incomprehensible. The new rule, which all companies must begin following by the end of the first quarter of next year, is the result of years of intense lobbying by companies seeking to overturn a highly complex and restrictive income tax standard that FASB issued in 1987 but never enforced. Companies henceforth will be able to recognize in current financial statements tax benefits such as loss carry-forwards, as long as they expect eventually to be able to realize a benefit in the tax returns they file with Uncle Sam. Previously they were not permitted to recognize a tax benefit from a loss carry-forward in financial statements until they actually produced income against which the carry-forward could be offset.

Stock Options

Despite unremitting opposition, FASB recently renewed its effort to find a way to recognize the cost of the incentive stock options that so many companies use to compensate key executives. Right now most options to buy shares in the future are not deemed by generally accepted accounting principles to be an expense for the companies that hand them out, even though they unquestionably have value—oodles of it—to the managers on the receiving end. Trouble is, reasonable people cannot agree on a method to determine the value. If FASB's rulemakers don't come up with an answer soon, says Paula Todd, a principal and compensation consultant at Towers Perrin, "there's a risk that Congress may enact something worse than the current rules."

So far FASB appears inclined to side with market value proponents, though just how far it will go remains uncertain. Late last year it finalized a rule, Statement 107, that will require companies with more than $150 million in assets to disclose the "fair value" of securities, loans, and a wide range of other financial instruments that they hold, beginning with reports issued for fiscal years that close after December 15, 1992. Smaller companies will have three extra years to comply. Fair value as defined by FASB is the amount at which an asset or a liability can be exchanged in a current transaction between a willing buyer and a seller who is not under duress. Because the forthcoming disclosures are to appear as footnotes to financial statements, they won't alter earnings or the values reported on balance sheets, which will continue to be produced on the basis of GAAP.

Even so, the new disclosure rule was strenuously opposed by banks and many nonfinancial companies. They fear it is merely the first step in a radical overhaul of the GAAP system, which already contains some projections about the future alongside its historical-cost foundation. At Breeden's urging, FASB is hashing through a proposal that would go beyond Statement 107 and require companies to recognize—either on their income statements or on their balance sheets—fluctuations in the market values of certain securities and related liabilities.

Also on its agenda: possible changes in when and how loans are written down once they are deemed impaired and new rules for the accounting treatment of plants, equipment, and real property whose value seems to have permanently fallen. GAAP now gives companies considerable leeway in each of these situations—leeway they often use to manage the earnings they report. Says Donald Nicolaisen, Price Waterhouse's national director of accounting: "These proposals are all related. They reflect the same gnawing concern that historical cost accounting doesn't work anymore."

Bankers, the group most directly affected by these new notions, concede that a few current practices need reform. The most notable of these is known as "gains trading," the practice of selling your winners (bonds on which you have paper gains) while holding your losers (bonds with unrealized losses) in order to boost reported earnings. Such cherry picking is made possible by rules that allow bonds to be accounted for at cost rather than market value as long as the company claims it intended to hold them until they matured.

But the moneymen argue vehemently that trying to mark assets and liabilities to market is a cure far worse than the original disease. Their first line of defense: It is virtually impossible to come up with verifiable estimates of what many financial instruments are worth. The assumptions and guesstimates required, banks contend, make the end result meaningless.

Take commercial loans, which account for about a third of the assets on many banks' balance sheets. "Our portfolio has tens of thousands of highly customized loans, mostly to small and midsize companies," says Susan Bies, chief financial officer for First Tennessee National, a Memphis bank holding company with $7.9 billion in assets. If such loans traded on a well-developed secondary market, determining their value would be a snap. But most trade infrequently or not at all.

So calculating each loan's present value depends on how you answer a battery of tough questions. Will a borrower pay off the loan early if interest rates go up by two (or three or four) percentage points? Under what conditions might he convert from an adjustable-rate loan to a fixed-rate one? How vulnerable is his collateral to an economic downturn? Says Bies: "In good conscience, different banks can come up with different forecasts and arrive at vastly different estimates of value for similar loans."

Valuing other crucial items on a bank's balance sheet is even slipperier. Banks profit by lending money held in low-interest checking and savings accounts to other customers at far higher rates of interest. The stability and long-term nature of these so-called core deposits endow them with considerable worth beyond their face value. But they don't trade; nor is there any good way to forecast future cash flows, because they can always be withdrawn at any time. Economist Benston, who is a market value enthusiast, admits no one has come up with a satisfactory way to value core deposits.

Others raise an even more basic objection to market value accounting. They argue that showing the price a 20-year loan could fetch were it sold today is simply not an appropriate way to measure the performance of a bank that fully expects to be around 20 years hence when that money is due to be repaid. Weighing in last year against what became FASB's Statement 107, Lester Stephens Jr., Chase Manhattan's corporate controller, wrote: "These values represent a 'fire sale' valuation that will gyrate up and down as interest rates and credit factors change. This doomsday portrayal can be very damaging to the uneducated user."

Or perhaps even to educated users. For Stephens and other bankers, the doomsday scenario is built upon a belief that Wall Street—and maybe regulators as well—will severely penalize them if the more volatile earnings that market value accounting would bring show up on their income statements. "A 1% change in interest rates would cause a 3% flip-flop in the value of our bond portfolio. That would have a significant impact on our earnings," says P. Michael Brumm, chief financial officer for Cincinnati's Fifth Third Bancorp. In that case he predicts banks will try to dodge such swings by stuffing their investment portfolios with far more short-term bonds, whose market values are less susceptible than long-term securities to big up and down movements.

Banks might also be far less apt to hold bonds issued by small municipalities, speculates Gary Anderson, CFO at Zion Bancorp. in Salt Lake City. This debt is often relatively risky, not actively traded, and thus more prone to wide swings in value. Since banks are major buyers of municipal bonds, such a shift would make it harder and costlier for cities to raise capital for urgent needs such as rebuilding bridges and upgrading schools.

Treasury Secretary Nick Brady contends that market value accounting "could even result in more intense and frequent credit crunches." In an insistent letter to the chairman of FASB, Brady maintained that temporary declines in the market value of assets, if recognized on the balance sheet, "would result in immediate reductions in bank capital and an inevitable retrenching in bank lending capacity."

Now here's the case for making a change, despite these worries. It is undeniable that interest rate shifts send the value of a bank's loans, say, spiraling up and down, though current accounting practice allows such changes to remain undisclosed to the outside world. While no one can be certain how investors and creditors might respond to a clearer picture, it seems doubtful that the reality hidden by GAAP would come as a complete surprise to Wall Street analysts, who supposedly earn their big salaries by parsing balance sheets in search of the truth—and who presumably find, if not the whole truth, at least a good deal of it.

True, some banks with unexpectedly spikier earnings probably would get punished. But a former Fed economist, who asks not to be identified because he remains part of the banking industry, maintains that on the whole, Wall Street will accept with equanimity financial statements that look more volatile. Another close market value enthusiast, a respected economist at a major bank, agrees and adds, "If you're not sufficiently capitalized to withstand the true volatility inherent in your balance sheet, taxpayers are better off knowing that unsettling fact sooner rather than later."

Consider again the lessons of the S&L mess. In 1981 the S&L industry's collective balance sheet showed $28 billion in capital, according to retrospective figures gathered by Richard Pratt, former chairman of the Federal Home Loan Bank Board, the main overseer of thrifts in the 1980s. Yet, on a market value basis, the industry's liabilities exceeded assets in 1981 by a staggering $178 billion. If financial statements had given off even a whiff of such gross insolvency, regulators—and legislators too—would have had little choice but to force sick institutions to find additional capital or, failing that, to close them before their difficulties multiplied.

Three years ago the Office of Thrift Supervision, the successor to the Home Loan Bank Board, began requiring the thrifts it supervises to submit detailed cash flow and interest rate information about their loan portfolios and other balance sheet items. OTS feeds the data through an elaborate model that estimates how sudden changes in interest rates might affect the market values of assets and liabilities.

The model was designed primarily to help thrifts better understand and manage their interest rate exposure. As a byproduct it also produces approximations of the market value of an institution's capital, the crucial margin of safety for uninsured creditors and the federal deposit insurance fund. Though OTS officials remain harshly critical of shifting to market value accounting, some grudgingly admit this new information could prove useful. Says one: "It's potentially an important red flag."

While FASB ponders how far to push market value accounting, a few companies are moving ahead on their own. Two years ago Roosevelt Financial Group, a St. Louis-based thrift holding company with $2 billion in assets, began including in its financial statements what it calls net market value, in essence the difference between the market value of its assets and the market value of its liabilities. Interestingly, Roosevelt's most recent net market value is 9% *lower* than the company's book value according to GAAP.

Despite such negative tidings, CEO Stanley Bradshaw praises market value accounting with the fervor of a preacher delivering the gospel. He gives the back of his hand to the argument that such calculations are impractical, acknowledging that might have been true when interest rate swaps, mortgage-backed securities, financial futures, and other innovations didn't exist or were not widely traded. But the proliferation of such products over the past decade, he says, along with the development of complex mathematical pricing models, now makes it feasible to estimate market values for most financial instruments. Though this depends on a lot of assumptions, Bradshaw argues that the judgment required is no more extensive or imprecise than what GAAP currently expects of bankers in estimating, say, loan loss reserves.

Some investors also see big benefits from publishing market value estimates. Says Thomas Jones, chief financial officer at Teachers Insurance and Annuity Association, which provides retirement and insurance plans for college and universities: "Policy holders and regulators will have more insight into whether liquidity and safety concerns are warranted, and investors will get a clearer fix on possible hidden values." One such financial Spindletop burbles on the books of SunTrust Banks, a $35 billion bank holding company headquartered in Atlanta. SunTrust has long disclosed market value information for its investment securities, though not its loans. The annual eye popper: the revelation that its vaults contain shares of Coca-Cola Co. that a subsidiary received as an underwriting fee when Coke went public in 1919. That stock, which remains on SunTrust's balance sheet at its original value of $110,000, is now worth almost $1 *billion*.

Among companies committed to market value accounting, none is more sold on the idea than the Federal Home Loan Mortgage Corp., a New York Stock Exchange-listed company created by Congress to buy home mortgage loans from banks and other lenders. Freddie Mac first began experimenting with market value management concepts in the mid-1980s and since 1989 has issued a full-fledged market value balance sheet as a supplement to its regular quarterly financial statements. It is probably the only company whose present disclosures satisfy the requirements of FASB's Statement 107, which all big companies will have to start complying with eight months from now.

Freddie Mac Chairman Leland Brendsel believes the real appeal of market value accounting lies in the managerial insight it provides. He insists, for example, his complete computerized market-value

model gives managers more realistic guidance about how to limit exposure to interest rate changes than could ever be gleaned from historical numbers.

How is FASB likely to proceed? Slowly, if the past is a guide, and that's probably not a bad speed. While the value of the insight offered by market value accounting is compelling, the nitty-gritty of adopting such a new approach on a comprehensive scale will require a lot more hard work and thought.

John Spiegel, chief financial officer of Atlanta's SunTrust, strikes what seems the right balance on this contentious issue. He recognizes the power of analyzing balance sheets through a market value lens, an exercise that he and his colleagues perform regularly for the better "feel" it gives them in hedging interest rate risks. And unlike most bankers, he doesn't object to FASB's Statement 107, which limits market value information to footnotes. But before going further, Spiegel argues, it's important to find out whether such information will really help users of financial statements make better decisions. In other words, let the disclosures FASB has already decreed serve as a laboratory to test the feasibility, and ultimate value, of market values.

Required

Suppose that you are a member of the FASB. Evaluate the desirability of new valuation-oriented standards, such as marking-to-market and others described in the article, from the standpoints of:

- Decision usefulness for investors
- Reduction of information asymmetry (that is, impact on the proper operation of securities markets)
- Economic consequences
- Political fallout

8. In the article here reproduced, "The SEC Says: Mark to Market!" from *Accounting Horizons* (March 1991), Arthur Wyatt discusses the background of the SEC's call in 1990 for mark-to-market accounting of securities held by financial institutions. It seems that the 1974 intervention of Arthur Burns, the then Federal Reserve chairman, was instrumental in persuading the AICPA Accounting Standards Executive Committee to vote down a proposal to value bank portfolios at market. According to Wyatt, the retention of historical cost accounting led to the savings and loan debacle and the SEC's subsequent endorsement of mark-to-market accounting.

THE SEC SAYS: MARK TO MARKET!

No, this title is not intended for the lead article in an April Fool's Day publication. Neither is it designed to attract attention but have little relationship to the thrust of this commentary. Rather, it reports a fact, possibly the most significant initiative in accounting principles development in over 50 years. That great bastion of historical cost accounting, the Securities and Exchange Commission, has encouraged, some might say dictated, the use of market-based measures to value certain debt securities, a new level of relevance in financial reporting.

The dramatic change in SEC thinking culminated in testimony of SEC Chairman Richard C. Breeden before the Committee on Banking, Housing and Urban Affairs of the United States Senate on September 10, 1990. That testimony was presented in connection with hearings concerning issues involving financial institutions and accounting principles that arose out of the savings and loan industry deterioration in the United States. While the specifics of that testimony will be dealt with more thoroughly in subsequent paragraphs, in substance Chairman Breeden called for use of market-based measures of valuation for debt securities held as assets by financial institutions.

MARK TO MARKET CONSIDERED—AND REJECTED—BY OTHERS

Before considering some of the ramifications—and opportunities—of the Breeden initiative, some background is helpful to develop the setting in which the initiative was introduced. The issue of mark-to-market[1] accounting is certainly not new.

---

(1) Throughout this commentary the terms "mark to market" and "fair value" are used somewhat interchangeably. As attention is focused more on specific applications, the distinctions in these terms will become more significant. At the general level of the current discussion, however, the imprecision should be of little consequence.

The Accounting Principles Board considered moving to a mark-to-market valuation approach for investments in certain financial instruments in the early 1970s, but no agreement was reached. The FASB undertook a limited project involving the same issues in the mid-1970s and eventually issued SFAS 12 dealing with marketable equity securities in late 1975.

The principal concerns with historical cost accounting for investment securities are that gains can be recognized as income is needed to meet earnings projections by selectively selling appreciated securities (so-called "gains trading"), and that recognition of losses can be delayed almost indefinitely by holding depreciated securities and representing that the decline in value is only temporary. Some have argued that the historical cost model promotes an unsound investment management policy —sell the winners and hold the losers. Others have noted that the model permits an overstatement of shareholders' equity because of delays in the recognition of losses.

The principal concerns expressed about the mark-to-market approach are that market values are often not reliable and are sometimes costly to obtain, that inappropriate volatility is reported in the income statement, and that the approach is often suggested for use on a piecemeal basis, i.e., only certain assets are proposed to be so accounted for or only certain types of entities would be affected. Until Chairman Breeden's testimony these concerns, among others, have been sufficient to forestall recognition of mark-to-market for investment securities except for limited circumstances or in certain specialized industries.

CERTAIN INDUSTRIES USE MARK-TO-MARKET IN SOME SITUATIONS

Specific accounting guidance on investment securities is limited, and even that which exists is inconsistent among industries. Thus, banks divide their investment securities into two categories, trading and investing. Trading securities are marked to market with gains and losses reported in income. Investing securities are reported at historical cost, with a provision required for permanent impairment. Permanent impairment is deemed to exist when market value is lower than carrying amount and the bank no longer "has the ability and intent to hold these securities on a long-term basis." Savings and loans have a similar classification system, and permanent impairment is recognizable when a market decline has occurred and the savings and loan no longer has "both the ability and intent to hold the debt instrument to maturity." Credit unions have similar guidance, but such guidance uses "hold to maturity," "long-term basis," and "foreseeable future" as the intended holding period. The insurance industry guidance uses "ability and intent to hold the bonds until maturity." The result of these differences in the various existing AICPA audit guides and FASB standards is that an unlevel playing field is perceived to exist among entities that are competitors for at least certain kinds of business.

THE SAVINGS AND LOAN INDUSTRY ACCOUNTING SHORTCOMING

Of particular concern recently has been the experience of savings and loans even before the massive failures occurred. In earlier times savings and loans' regular operating activities generated mortgage loan receivables, generally on single family residences or up to four unit apartment buildings. The mortgages were serviced monthly and often held to maturity. When interest rates began to rise in the late 1960s, savings and loans began to package mortgages to sell them, a process that accelerated during the late 1970s and 1980s. Even during the package-and-sell process, however, some low rate mortgage receivables continued to be held. Sale of them would have generated losses and thereby reduced capital, with the consequent limitation under Federal regulations on the ability to write new mortgages.

Thus, the notion of "selling winners" and "holding losers" was applied not only to investments in stocks and bonds, but also to mortgage receivables in the savings and loan industry. Some have argued that on a real economic basis, i.e., if the losses on underwater mortgages had been recognized at an earlier date, many savings and loans would have been recognized as insolvent years prior to the time they eventually failed. Some speculate that had such accounting been required the magnitude of the current savings and loan bailout would be markedly lower.

The issue of valuing investment securities at historical cost or on a fair value basis has generally been approached as a conceptual issue, wherein the arguments have focused on the objectives of financial accounting, or on practical grounds, wherein assertions have been made regarding lack of reliability and the cost to arrive at market values. Little attention has been directed to the economic consequences flowing from each alternative.

With the savings and loan debacle projected to cost taxpayers $500 billion or more, new focus is directed at this accounting issue and the role it may have played in contributing to the savings and loan losses. One assertion that merits study is that the accounting information produced for savings and loan managers under the historical cost model, combined with the banking regulatory restrictions on capital adequacy, helped generate bad management decisions, decisions to sell securities on which gains has arisen but to hold securities with inherent losses. In any event, the issue of marking investments to market has clearly emerged from a principally academic environment to become an issue of pressing practical significance.

BREEDEN TESTIMONY IS UNEQUIVOCAL

The focus on this accounting issue was highlighted by the testimony of SEC Chairman Richard C. Breeden before the Committee on Banking, Housing and Urban Affairs of the U.S. Senate in September 1990. That testimony dealt with a number of matters involving the savings and loan industry and its accounting requirements. A final section dealt with "The Proper Role of Financial Reporting: Market Based Accounting." A few quotations from this testimony, while admittedly out of context, convey the principal thrust of the Breeden testimony.

"Financial institutions are in the business of buying and selling financial instruments, all of which have a value measured in terms of current market conditions. Determining the current value of an institution's assets, not recording their original cost, should increasingly be the goal toward which we must work."

"The Commission recognizes that transforming the accounting standards of banks and thrifts from a cost to a market-based standard is a complex undertaking, and we realize that studies are currently under way concerning these issues. The objective of these efforts should be to achieve financial reporting that uses appropriate market-based measures of valuation at the earliest possible date."

"… [Historical cost accounting] … was developed in a vastly different economic environment than the one in which most institutions function today. Today financial institutions actively manager their interest earning asset and interest bearing liability portfolios to maximize net income and to manage interest rate risk. This 'asset/liability' management often requires frequent buying and selling of investment securities to restructure asset and liability maturities. The continued use of the historical cost model in this environment is inappropriate because of the diminished relevance of the resulting financial information."

Chairman Breeden also recognized that any move to increase the use of market-based measures in the accounts requires "careful and deliberate planning." Concerns exist over the reliability of market-based measures and the costs of implementation and ongoing compliance. Even so, recognition is increasing that historical cost amounts for many monetary items can be misleading to financial statement users and lead to economically unsound decisions by business managers. Clearly it is the obligation of accountants to seek improvements in the reporting process.

FEDERAL RESERVE BOARD INTERVENTION DERAILED EARLIER MARK-TO-MARKET MOVE

In early October 1990 *The Wall Street Journal*, reporting on these developments, noted: "The SEC has been down this road before. John C. Burton, a Columbia professor and former SEC chief accountant, recalls that in 1974, when bank portfolios 'were very much underwater,' the [AICPA] Accounting Standards Executive Committee was ready to shift those holdings to current prices. Mr. Burton says he lined up the five commissioners to vote for the plan.

"Arthur Burns, then the Federal Reserve Chairman, called Mr. Burton to a special meeting to discuss the plan—on Christmas Eve. The Federal chief praised Mr. Burton, his former student, as an accounting theorist. Then he informed Mr. Burton that he 'should advise the commissioners that they were taking a grave risk with the economic future of the U.S. in the interest of a somewhat dubious accounting principle.'

"The next day, the commissioners withdrew their support for the plan."

In retrospect, many now believe that it is clear that the grave risk undertaken was to continue a measurement system for certain financial instruments that lacked both relevance and correspondence to underlying economics. The lesson has been a costly one.

FOLLOW-UP ACTIVITY TO BREEDEN INITIATIVE

The immediate result of the Breeden testimony was a meeting involving representatives of the AICPA, the FASB, and the SEC. At this meeting, it was decided that the AICPA Accounting Standards Executive Committee (AcSEC) would undertake the responsibility to develop an appropriate accounting standard to meet the concerns of Chairman Breeden. AcSEC already had a project under way involving these issues and was more likely than the FASB to meet the time deadline of the end of 1991.

The top accounting policy makers of the six largest public accounting firms expressed concern, however, about whether AcSEC was the most appropriate body to deal with these issues. They noted, for example, that it was likely a final standard would conflict with various FASB pronouncements dealing with marketable securities, insurance accounting, and possibly other areas as well. In late October agreement was reached that the FASB should undertake a limited project dealing with debt instruments and attempt to accelerate its procedures to meet the SEC time constraints. Such a project could conceivably involve an amendment to SFAS 12. The FASB would also continue to develop its pending exposure draft calling for increased disclosure of fair values for financial instruments.

MARK-TO-MARKET ACCOUNTING—AN EVOLUTIONARY DEVELOPMENT

Any move to mark-to-market (or fair value) basis for a significant part of the variety of investment securities held by business enterprises will be a dramatic development in the evolution of accounting. For over 50 years many have asserted that the relevance of the information reported in financial statements has been suspect because of the suffocating influence on current practice of accounting inadequacies prior to the 1929 stock market crash and ensuing depression. Under the historical cost model accounting has become increasingly divorced from economics. Too many came to rely on accounting numbers as if they reflected economic reality when only those trained in accounting (and a few others) understood well the actual basis for the reported numbers, and thus any defects they may have contained. The savings and loan crisis simply provided new evidence of existing accounting inadequacies that some had been pointing to for a number of years.

The focus on mark-to-market accounting for investment securities reflects the emerging conceptual focus on the balance sheet, on the critical nature of asset and liability measurements if balance sheets are to reflect faithfully the resources and obligations of the reporting entity. While this focus is of equal concern for unregulated entities and for nonfinancial entities, it is vital for the partially regulated financial institutions. Such regulation historically has been based in part on the magnitude of capital, or shareholders' equity. Any accounting which artificially enhances capital is subverting the intent of the regulation. Up to now, regulators have used (and misused) accounting in order to make it appear that capital adequacy standards had been met. Mark-to-market accounting will force regulators to focus more attention on their own capital adequacy guidelines and reduce the artificiality of the regulatory process.

Of course, one of the by-products of a focus on the balance sheet is that the income statement results will demonstrate increased volatility. That might be a concern if such volatility were artificial, but it is the relatively smooth patterns of reported income by business enterprises over the past 50 years or so that many believe are artificial. While managers tend to desire smoothness rather than volatility, the role of accounting is to approximate the real world as closely as possible. Too many existing accounting standards artificially smooth real world volatility.

It is possible, of course, that the FASB may try to achieve the appropriate balance sheet improvement while at the same time minimizing volatility by reporting market value fluctuations directly in equity. While that approach has some conceptual shortcomings, it may have some merit in the short run, particularly if the FASB deals only with certain investment securities and not with any liabilities. That approach would also be more palatable to those who desire to achieve the appearance of smoothness in reported earnings for those who use income statements. In the past (e.g., SFAS 12, 15, 52, 87) the Board has faced the same pressures and decided to reflect the market variations in equity. Clearly, the principal focus in the current concern on remeasurement of financial instruments is on the balance sheet and not on the income statement.

OPPORTUNITIES FOR NEW RESEARCH INITIATIVES

The new initiative by the SEC to embrace mark-to-market valuation for investment securities of financial institutions provides new incentives for academic research and involvement. Many practical issues will arise for which research assistance can be significant. The conceptual ramifications need additional exploration as well.

Should the immediate project be limited to investment assets and omit liabilities? If so, what are the ramifications for highly leveraged entities with significant investment assets? Should investment assets include mortgage (and loan) receivables? What surrogates are reliable (and reasonable from a cost perspective) for investment assets that have no ready markets? What basis, if any, exists to limit any new standards only to financial institutions? If such a limitation is desirable, how does a complex entity report, if it is partly a financial institution? What levels of capital adequacy will meet regulatory needs if mark-to-market measures are adopted? What are the benefits, and shortcomings, of limiting mark-to-market to investment securities? What are the ramifications of the artificial smoothing created under the historical cost model? What are the ramifications of reporting value fluctuations directly in equity?

These, and many other, issues will require careful thought as the change to a market valuation model is considered. It has taken more than 50 years to see a major crack in the armor of historical cost accounting. The research avenues to explore as we move toward a more relevant measurement system in accounting are varied and exciting. For this, Chairman Breeden and the SEC merit great credit in their call to "mark to market."

SOURCE: Arthur Wyatt, "Commentary," *Accounting Horizons*, March 1991. Reprinted by permission.

Required

a. Why was the Federal Reserve opposed to mark-to-market accounting in 1974?

b. This 1974 episode illustrates a tradeoff between decision usefulness and economic consequences. It was the avoidance of economic consequences by retaining historical cost accounting that, according to Wyatt, "helped generate bad management decisions ... to sell securities on which gains had arisen but to hold securities with inherent losses." Presumably there was not enough information disclosed about security values to enable investors to realize what was going on.

In view of this episode, do you think that SFAS 115 represents a better tradeoff between usefulness and economic consequences? In your answer, consider the compromises that SFAS 115 made short of full mark-to-market accounting and evaluate the extent to which the resulting standard will prevent recurrence of a debacle such as that which befell the savings and loan industry.

9. The announcement reproduced here appeared in *Financial Accounting Series* (December 27, 1994). It reports that the FASB agreed not to require recognition of an expense for options granted to employees, including managers. This represents a backing off from a 1993 exposure draft which proposed that compensation expense be recorded equal to the fair value of options granted.

FASB AGREES NOT TO REQUIRE EXPENSE RECOGNITION FOR STOCK OPTIONS

The FASB has agreed to work toward improving disclosures about employee stock options and related arrangements in the notes to financial statements rather than requiring an expense charge for all options. The Board expects to encourage, rather than require, companies to adopt a new method that accounts for stock compensation awards based on their estimated fair value at the date they are granted.

Companies would be permitted, however, to continue accounting under the present requirements, which do not require an expense charge for most options.

In June 1991, the FASB issued an Exposure Draft on accounting for employee stock options, which would have required expense recognition for virtually all employee stock option plans. The Board has been redeliberating the issues for several months based on comment letters received, public hearing testimony, and much other information. The Board has been concentrating on ways to improve the method of estimating the value of options.

"The Board remains convinced that employee options have value and are compensation," said FASB Chairman Dennis R. Beresford. "However, in the final analysis, the Board decided that there simply isn't enough support for the basic notion of requiring expense recognition. Different constituents had different reasons for disagreeing with our conclusions on expense recognition, but most favored expanded note disclosures rather than changes to the current accounting requirements."

The approach that the FASB will now pursue would allow companies to continue following existing accounting rules, which result in zero compensation expense for most existing plans. However, those companies that do not recognize expense would have to disclose in a note to the financial statements the effect on net income had the company recognized expense for them based on FASB-specified guidelines.

According to Project Manager Diane W. Willis, "one of the important objectives of this project was to eliminate the bias against variable plans, such as option plans with terms that vary on company performance. Current rules require expense charges for many variable plans, while no expense is recognized for otherwise similar fixed plans. The new accounting method would eliminate this bias, so the Board decided to encourage companies to adopt it. The proposed disclosures for those who continue to follow existing accounting standards will permit users to compare companies that elect the new accounting with companies that do not."

Having reached this conclusion, the FASB needs to complete reconsideration of its 1993 Exposure Draft because its provisions will form the basis for the disclosures and elective accounting described above. The Board hasn't decided yet whether it will issue a final standard based on this conclusion or whether it will issue another Exposure Draft for public comment. That decision will be made when redeliberations are completed, probably in the second quarter of 1995. At this time, no decision has been made on an effective date for a new standard.

Required

a. With which theory of regulation is the 1993 exposure draft and subsequent change of policy most consistent? Explain.

b. To what extent will the new policy, which encourages expense recognition but allows an alternative footnote disclosure of the option cost, serve as a satisfactory substitute for mandatory expense recognition as originally proposed? Explain.

   Note: The distinction in the announcement between fixed and variable plans may need some explanation.

   Chapter 13B of ARB 43 provides that when options are granted to a manager with the exercise price equal to or greater than the current market value of the optioned shares, no compensation expense shall be recognized. This was modified by APB 25 (1972) for variable plans, that is, plans in which the number of shares which the manager may acquire and/or the price to be paid are not determinable until some time after the grant date. For such plans, compensation expense shall be recognized to the extent that the current market value of the optioned share exceeds the current market value of an option on that share. Thus, an expense may need to be accrued under a variable plan, while no expense will be recorded under a fixed plan when option exercise price is at least equal to current share market value.

10. In *Financial Accounting Series* (October 18, 1993), Mr. Dennis R. Beresford, the FASB chairman, vigorously and eloquently defends the FASB's proposed new rules on accounting for stock-based compensation (see article reproduced here). The FASB proposals require a measure of the cost of such plans to be deducted in arriving at reported net income. The proposals have drawn wide criticism from industry and some legislators.

FASB TO HOLD PUBLIC HEARINGS ON STOCK COMPENSATION

The FASB has announced that it will hold public hearings on its Exposure Draft, "Accounting for Stock-Based Compensation," in March at both East Coast and West Coast locations. The East Coast hearings will probably be held in the Norwalk, Connecticut area, and the West Coast hearings will most likely be in the San Francisco area. More details on the date, time, and place of each hearing will be announced in a future edition of *Status Report*.

NOTES FROM THE CHAIRMAN

Our regular readers know that the Board has proposed new rules that would significantly change the accounting for stock-based compensation. This project

was originally undertaken in 1984 at the request of many groups including the AICPA and major accounting firms. At the time we added this project to our agenda, issues surrounding executive pay did not exist and, thus, had nothing (and still have nothing) to do with our undertaking this project.

In some respects, the stock compensation project is no different from any other project the Board undertakes. Inevitably there are certain characteristics of all projects that we must accept and address. First, the proposed answers are likely to be controversial. After all, the difficult questions that need FASB action often produce strongly held views and disagreement. Second, an FASB pronouncement may have consequences that some consider undesirable.

Our proposal has drawn strong opposition and today is the most controversial project we have on our agenda. The issue has even escalated to Washington where Congress has stepped into the act. Certain members of Congress have decided to fight our proposal through the legislative process and have introduced legislation that would countermand the FASB's position. On the other hand, other members of Congress have introduced legislation that would *require* a charge to earnings for stock options if the FASB does not act.

I know there are some who believe that Congressional intervention into the standard-setting process is a good thing if it can stop our stock compensation project. After all, when U.S. citizens are unhappy with the way things are in this country, we always have the option to "write to our Congressman." In this instance, some in Congress have listened to their constituents and are taking what they consider appropriate measures. To quote one Congressman, "From a public-policy, job creation, and competitiveness perspective [the proposed accounting] simply is unnecessary and unusually disruptive."

As indicated by that quote, a major objection to our proposal centers on perceived economic consequences of requiring the recognition of compensation cost in the income statement. We have been told that our proposal could cause lasting damage to U.S. companies and their employees. Many of our critics argue that the Board should take a broader view of standard setting and be more mindful of the economic impact of all of our proposals, starting with this one.

In my view those arguments are inconsistent with the primary objective of financial reporting, which is to provide useful information to decision makers. If the Board were to adopt as an objective avoiding economic consequences perceived to be undesirable, it would be abandoning neutrality as a fundamental precept. Consequences unfavorable to one interest are invariably favorable to others. Seeking to select and favor any specific interest, no matter how virtuous or powerful, is inconsistent with credible, useful financial reports.

If financial information is to be useful, it must report economic activity without coloring the message it conveys in a manner that would influence behavior in a particular direction. Thus, it must not, for example, intentionally favor one party or type of transaction over another. Instead, it must provide a neutral scorecard on the economic effects of decisions.

Neutrality in standard setting does not mean that accounting should not influence human behavior. Changes in behavior naturally follow from more complete and representationally faithful financial statements. We expect that changes in financial reporting will have economic consequences, just as economic consequences are inherent in *existing* financial reporting practices. For example, as a result of the new accounting for retiree health care benefits, many employers understood the magnitude of their obligations for the first time and took steps to better manager their exposure to future costs.

To abandon neutrality could result in the establishment of accounting and reporting standards that conceal the economic impact of certain transactions from those who use financial statements rather than reporting it to them. One need only look to the collapse of the thrift industry to demonstrate the consequences of abandoning neutrality in the standard-setting process. During the 1970s and 1980s, regulatory accounting principles were altered to obscure problems in troubled institutions because preserving the industry was considered a "greater good." Today, however, many observers believe that the effect of that action was to delay corrective action and hide the true dimensions of the problem.

Should those who measure and report on economic events somehow screen the information before reporting it to achieve some objective like job creation or competitiveness? In FASB Concepts Statement No. 2, "Qualitative Characteristics of Accounting Information" (paragraph 102), the Board observed:

> Indeed, most people are repelled by the notion that some "big brother," whether government or private, would tamper with scales or speedometers surreptitiously to induce people to lose weight or obey speed limits or would slant the scoring of athletic events or examinations to enhance or decrease someone's chances of winning or graduating. There is no more reason to abandon neutrality in accounting measurement.

The Board continues to hold that view. We do not set out to achieve or avoid particular economic results through accounting pronouncements. We could not if we tried. As a private entity, the FASB has neither the authority nor the competence to weigh various, and often conflicting, national goals. Nor do we seek that

authority or that competence. Our sole mission is to improve, through accounting standards, the usefulness of financial statements so that public and private decision makers can make better decisions.

Costs of transactions exist whether or not the FASB mandates their recognition in financial statements. For example, not requiring the recognition of the cost of stock options or ignoring the liabilities for retiree health care benefits does not alter the economics of the transactions. It only withholds information from investors, creditors, policy makers, and others who need evenhanded information to make informed decisions and, eventually, impairs the credibility of financial reports.

Some have argued that improved disclosures about stock options should be adequate for users of financial statements. But the Board believes that disclosure is not an adequate substitute for recognition. If disclosure and recognition were equal alternatives, why not just disclose information about depreciation, pensions, and retiree health benefits, or, for that matter, cash salaries? But even with improved disclosures, only the most sophisticated users could reasonably estimate the financial statement impact of recognizing all compensation costs. Many individual investors and others could not. For them, accurate comparisons between entities of profit margins, rates of return, income from operations, and the like would be impossible. Therefore, the Board decided that compensation cost for employee stock options should be recognized in the income statement, just like any other cost of operations.

In summary, the FASB must continue to strive for accounting that is evenhanded and, therefore, a faithful representation of the economic facts of a situation. To abandon neutrality would be unfair to those who use and depend on financial statements and would thrust the Board into a public policy making role, a role for which we are not chartered or equipped to perform. Our one and only public policy making role is to maintain the integrity of generally accepted accounting principles so that decision makers, including public policy decision makers like Congress, are all on an equal footing.

Financial statements are one of the basic tools used in capital markets for communicating information about economic events. The U.S. capital market system is well developed and efficient because of users' confidence that the financial information they receive is reliable. Corporations, accounting firms, users of financial statements, and most other interested parties have long sup-

ported the process of establishing accounting standards in the private sector without intervention by Congress or other branches of government. Despite numerous individual issues on which the FASB and many of its constituents have disagreed, that support has continued. The resulting system of accounting standards and financial reporting, while not perfect, is the best in the world.

I hope you agree that a legislative solution to accounting for stock-based compensation or other financial reporting issues being considered by the FASB would be wrong. If you would like a copy of my letter to Senator Lieberman, who is sponsoring legislation that would affect the accounting for stock compensation, please call the FASB at (203) 847-0700, ext. 270.

Dennis R. Beresford, Chairman
Financial Accounting Standards Board

Required

a. Given that the FASB is a standard setting body, are the views of its chairman more in accordance with the public interest or the interest group theory of regulation? Explain.

b. Given that net income, unlike speed or weight, does not exist as a well-defined economic construct, is complete neutrality attainable? Explain why or why not.

c. Mr. Beresford equates neutrality in measurement with decision usefulness. Do you agree? Explain why or why not.

d. In the same issue of *Financial Accounting Series*, the FASB announced public hearings on stock compensation. With which theory of regulation are public hearings most consistent? Explain. If standard setting was completely neutral, would public hearings be necessary? Explain why or why not.

11. In the "Notes from the Chairman" reproduced here, which appeared in *Financial Accounting Series* (December 27, 1994), Mr. Beresford describes certain revisions to the FASB's strategic plan for international activities.

NOTES FROM THE CHAIRMAN

Strategic Plan for International Activities: Evaluation and Revision

We recently undertook an evaluation of our strategic plan for international activities. The evaluation consisted of a review of the plan's objectives, underlying postulates, and implementation strategy as well as the outcomes of various international activities initiated under the plan. As a result of that evaluation, the plan was essentially reaffirmed although some revisions were made in light of our experiences and of changes in the standard-setting environment. A revised plan has been developed that will be published next month.

In 1991, the FASB recognized the need for a strategy that provides flexibility to evolve with the changing international environment while also providing a structure to direct future initiatives. What emerged was the FASB's strategic plan for international activities. It set forth objectives and initiatives to pursue while actively participating in developing an acceptable level of international comparability. In the original plan, we had the following as one of our focal points for standard-setting efforts:

- To encourage the equality of financial statement requirements for foreign and domestic companies in their utilization of U.S. capital markets.

We have presented this as a specific objective in the revised plan, rather than a broad area of interest. Presenting as an objective the equality of financial reporting requirements acknowledges that the move toward international comparability must be comprehensive, and the FASB should, where possible, contribute to the process at all levels. This helps to reinforce our commitment to maintaining comparability and understandability in the internationalization process.

We also have revised one of the underlying premises of the original plan. That was that domestic financial reporting needs would continue to be the FASB's first priority and that other national standard setters would likewise look first to their domestic needs. The FASB would bring international considerations to bear on the domestic projects as much as possible and, in addition, would give them high priority and increased attention in their own right.

However, as originally stated, this premise suggested that we could choose the level of international involvement that we felt appropriate. We have concluded that the line between domestic and international issues is not that clear. Almost every FASB project now is a matter of current interest and activity in at least one other country or the International Accounting Standards Committee. The FASB's obligation to its domestic constituents demands that it attempt to narrow the range of difference between U.S. and foreign standards. To do that we must work with other standard setters around the world to the extent necessary to achieve greater comparability. Accordingly, we have revised that premise in our new plan in response to our experiences.

An evaluation of our international efforts revealed that due consideration had been given to and action had been taken on almost all the initiatives set forth in the original plan. Some of those initiatives are still under way, and many have been carried over into the revised plan.

The revised plan also contains a number of new initiatives, and we look forward to increasing our contribution to the international accounting environment.

Overall, the original plan served us well. The main thrust of that plan continues to provide a solid foundation for the FASB's efforts to improve international comparability. We believe that the FASB has an important role to play in the international accounting environment. We plan to continue with our current international contributions, and we recognize that our role is evolving, as is that of other national and international accounting organizations. Evaluating where we have been and setting our course for the future through our strategic plan for international activities helps us to keep pace with the dynamic accounting environment.

Dennis R. Beresford
Financial Accounting Standards Board

Required

a. Mr. Beresford states that the "FASB's obligation to its domestic constituents demands that it attempt to narrow the range of difference between U.S. and foreign standards." To what extent is international comparability of financial accounting practices desirable according to efficient security market theory?

b. Of particular interest is Mr. Beresford's statement that "The FASB would bring international considerations to bear on the domestic projects as much as possible. ... " Use the interest group theory of regulation to evaluate the extent to which this component of the FASB plan would make it more difficult to set new accounting standards.

12. An article entitled "Big Board, SEC Fight over Foreign Stocks" which appeared in the *Wall Street Journal* on May 13, 1992 describes the reservations of the SEC concerning a proposal by the New York Stock Exchange to list foreign stocks for trading.

William H. Donaldson, the New York Stock Exchange's chief, wants "to soften strict U.S. rules so that foreign companies with looser financial disclosures can be traded on the Big Board." However, SEC Chairman Richard Breeden says no.

Mr. Breeden does agree that more foreign shares should be listed; however, he does not want U.S. investors exposed to "undue risk by allowing foreign companies to follow looser accounting and disclosure standards." For example, he points out that "the German accounting system, unlike that of the U.S., doesn't require companies to disclose cash reserves, which can be used to offset losses in a bad quarter."

According to the article, Mr. Breeden believes that "American companies would be disadvantaged." For instance, if General Motors has to report a liability for postretirement benefits and a German company like Daimler-Benz does not, then which company will look better to investors? he asks.

On the other hand, Mr. Donaldson feels that investors pay too much in overseas commissions to buy foreign stocks. The New York Stock Exchange will make sure that "only the biggest and best foreign companies" be allowed on the stock exchange. Also, the New York Stock Exchange will further protect investors by having them "sign special disclosure forms acknowledging the potentially greater risks of foreign stocks."

Required

a. According to the SEC, one of the problems of listing the stocks of foreign countries is the different accounting standards in the various countries involved. Specifically, German companies need not disclose cash reserves. What type of earnings management would such companies be likely to engage in, and why?

b. It is claimed that American companies would be disadvantaged, due to stricter U.S. accounting standards. Do you agree? Explain, using efficient securities markets theory.

c. How might large multinational firms benefit if they prepared financial statements according to international accounting standards, and these financial statements were accepted by the SEC? (CGA-Canada)

13. The article by William C. Freund reproduced here appeared in the *Wall Street Journal* (August 27, 1993). Mr. Freund argues for freer access by foreign firms to U.S. capital markets.

THAT TRADE OBSTACLE, THE SEC

When the German auto giant Daimler-Benz recently agreed to adhere to nearly all U.S. accounting practices, thus allowing it to become the first German company listed on the New York Stock Exchange, the changes were hailed as a sign that foreign firms will begin operating in accordance with Securities and Exchange Commission requirements. But Daimler-Benz, greatly in need of capital, was a special case; few other foreign firms are expected to follow its lead. Indeed, if the SEC continues to insist that foreign firms abide by America's anachronistic accounting standards, it will strangle U.S. markets and do irreversible harm to the U.S. as the world's dominant financial center.

At issue are SEC rules that drive the trading of world-class companies into more costly, less liquid foreign markets. What makes the issue urgent is that capital markets can be as important as physical exports and imports in helping reduce the U.S. trade deficit. Moreover, new research shows that the obstructionist SEC rules serve no useful purpose.

INTELLECTUAL ARROGANCE

The greatest roadblock to transnational listings on the New York Stock Exchange is the SEC requirement that companies reconcile their financial statements to U.S. Generally Accepted Accounting Principles (GAAP) standards. There is an intellectual arrogance in maintaining that GAAP rules, as enforced by the SEC, are the best in the world and must be followed in U.S. markets.

For example, the SEC finds unacceptable German rules that allow companies to plow back earnings into so-called blind reserves. German companies argue that their investors have benefited from accounting practices that average out earnings over years, moderating earnings volatility and focusing management attention on longer-run earnings performance.

The SEC's contention that it must safeguard U.S. investors from inadequate disclosures by foreign firms is a mirage in the modern world of low-cost, high-speed communications. Former SEC Commissioner Philip R. Lochner Jr. noted on this page last November that "many SEC rules are arbitrary and were written in an era when U.S. securities markets could exist in splendid isolation." He continues, "The fact is that U.S. citizens buy foreign stocks anyway, they just do so on foreign exchanges and at greater cost than if those foreign securities could be bought here."

Even more fundamental is the question whether SEC disclosure rules make for a more efficient market in the U.S. than exists in leading foreign stock exchanges not governed by these rules.

A number of scholars have examined this issue in a variety of ways. Most recently, Profs. William Baumol of New York University and Burton Malkiel of Princeton evaluated the efficiency of European and Pacific Rim stock exchanges by testing whether professional investors had any advantage over broad stock market averages. If stock prices reflected most everything shown about a company—that is, if foreign disclosure of accounting and other information was adequate—the uninformed investors would do as well as the experts. Between 1982 and 1991, professionally managed portfolios did not outperform broad stock market averages on a persistent basis. There are now about a dozen studies confirming that the risk-adjusted performance of professionals matches the market averages, attesting to the efficiency of European and Pacific Rim markets.

Messrs. Baumol and Malkiel conclude that "taken as a whole, the evidence supports the view that markets for the shares of non-U.S. companies appear to be as efficient as those for U.S. firms. ... Thus, informed investors can expect that the shares of non-U.S. companies are reasonably priced in relation to those of other firms. If this is the case, there is good reason to doubt that investors would benefit at all from any additional disclosure."

SEC rules requiring foreign firms to reconcile their domestic financial reports with U.S. GAAP standards may actually be counterproductive. They many reduce investor mastery of the pertinent facts and lull investors into a false sense of confidence. Indeed, studies have found that home country accounting standards practiced in other countries have, in many instances, provided more rather than less information. Mechanically reconciling foreign accounting data to U.S. GAAP standards will often suggest a comparability that does not exist.

Under the guidance of the International Accounting Standards Committee, efforts are under way to develop greater international accounting uniformity. But even more important toward this end is the pressure coming from the increasingly powerful institutional investors. These investors have been more effective than the SEC in prying loose meaningful financial data from global companies.

The final argument against SEC intransigence in recognizing foreign financial reporting is that the purported protection of American investors is a victory of theory over practice. Since the SEC's regulatory arm does not reach beyond national borders, U.S. investors trading abroad are denied all SEC regulatory safeguards. They are also denied the lower transactions costs and greater liquidity generally available in U.S. markets. Overall, the U.S. market is prevented from competing in a service where U.S. comparative advantage is undisputed.

The SEC has shown little give on the issue of foreign listings so far. Indeed, when Daimler-Benz agreed to adhere to U.S. accounting standards, the SEC's chief economist declared that "the brave move by Daimler-Benz ... makes it more likely that fair play will be the rule of this growing world game." But other giant international firms are unlikely to use Daimler as a model. Only where their need to raise capital in the U.S. is very intense are they likely to submit to the SEC's regulatory jurisdiction.

The Big Board has proposed a number of safeguards to alert the investing public to any differences in accounting procedures. Under its proposals, the sole exception to the GAAP reporting rules would be about 200 world-class foreign issuers, companies with revenues of at least $5 billion for the most recent fiscal year, a market capitalization in excess of $2 billion, and an average weekly trading volume outside the U.S. of at least $1 million or 200,000 shares. For these large, highly visible companies, the SEC would accept independently audited home-country financial statements as long as these include a written explanation of the material differences between home-country accounting practices and U.S. GAAP.

A SEPARATE TABLE

To protect U.S. investors further, the Big Board has suggested that transactions in world-class foreign-company shares be listed in a separate table, or at least identified with an asterisk or other appropriate symbol to alert investors to different disclosure standards. All of these are good suggestions.

SEC rules need regular review to determine their impact on the efficiency and competitiveness of U.S. securities markets. Such a review is currently under way in the SEC's so-called Market 2000 study. The issue of foreign listings needs to be resolved—the sooner the better.

Required

a. Mr. Freund quotes evidence that European and Pacific Rim security markets are efficient. Explain how an inability of market professionals to outperform the market index constitutes evidence of security market efficiency.

b. In view of the ability of firms to manage earnings (see Section 11.5 and, in particular, question 11 of chapter 5), do you feel that U.S. firms are at a disadvantage by being unable to "plow back earnings into so-called blind reserve"? In your answer, evaluate the argument made by German companies that "investors have benefited from accounting practices that average out earnings over years."

c. What are the advantages to both domestic investors and foreign firms of easier access to U.S. capital markets by foreign firms? To what extent would the safeguards proposed by the Big Board (that is, the NYSE) protect investors while retaining the advantages of easier access?

Bibliography

ABDEL-KHALIK, A. R., "The Effect of LIFO-Switching and Firm Ownership on Executive Pay," *Journal of Accounting Research* (Autumn 1985), pp. 427-447.

ABDEL-KHALIK, A. R. AND J. C. MCKEOWN, "Understanding Accounting Changes in an Efficient Market: Evidence of Differential Reaction," *The Accounting Review* (October 1978), pp. 851-868.

AKERLOF, G. A., "The Market for 'Lemons': Quality Uncertainty and the Market Mechanism," *Quarterly Journal of Economics* (August 1970), pp. 488-500.

ALCHIAN, A., "Uncertainty, Evolution and Economic Theory," *Journal of Political Economy* (June 1950), pp. 211-221.

ANTLE, R. AND A. SMITH, "An Empirical Examination of the Relative Performance Evaluation of Corporate Executives," *Journal of Accounting Research* (Spring 1986), pp. 1-39.

BALL, RAY, "The Earnings-Price Anomaly," *Journal of Accounting and Economics* (June-September 1992), pp. 319-345.

BALL, RAY AND P. BROWN, "An Empirical Evaluation of Accounting Income Numbers," *Journal of Accounting Research* (Autumn 1968), pp. 159-178.

BANZ, R. W., "The Relationship Between Return and Market Value of Common Stocks," *Journal of Financial Economics* (March 1981), pp. 3-18.

BARNEA, A., J. RONEN, AND S. SADAN, "Classificatory Smoothing of Income with Extraordinary Items," *The Accounting Review* (January 1976), pp. 110-122.

BARTH, M. E., "Fair Value Accounting: Evidence from Investment Securities and the Market Value of Banks," *The Accounting Review* (January 1994), pp. 1-25.

BEAVER, W. H., "The Information Content of Annual Earnings Announcements," *Journal of Accounting Research*, (Supplement, 1968), pp. 67-92.

BEAVER, W. H., *Financial Reporting: An Accounting Revolution*, Second Edition (Englewood Cliffs, N.J.: Prentice Hall, 1989).

BEAVER, W. H., "What Should Be the FASB's Objectives?" *The Journal of Accountancy* (August 1973), pp. 49-56.

BEAVER, W. H., R. CLARKE, AND W.F. WRIGHT, "The Association Between Unsystematic Security Returns and the Magnitude of Earnings Forecast Errors," *Journal of Accounting Research* (Autumn 1979), pp. 316-340.

BEAVER, W. H. AND J. DEMSKI, "The Nature of Income Measurement," *The Accounting Review* (January 1979), pp. 38-46.

BEAVER, W. H., P. KETTLER, AND M. SCHOLES, "The Association Between Market-Determined and Accounting-Determined Risk Measures," *The Accounting Review* (October 1970), pp. 654-682.

BEAVER, W. H. AND W. R. LANDSMAN, *The Incremental Information Content of FAS 33 Disclosures* (Stamford, Conn.: FASB, 1983).

BENSTON, G. J., "Required Disclosure and the Stock Market: An Evaluation of the

Securities Exchange Act of 1934," *American Economic Review* (March 1973), pp. 132-155.

BERNARD, V. L., "Cross-Sectional Dependance and Problems in Inference in Market-Based Accounting Research," *Journal of Accounting Research* (Spring 1987), pp. 1-48.

BERNARD, V. L., "Capital Markets Research in Accounting During the 1980s: A Critical Review," working paper, University of Michigan, 1989.

BERNARD, V. L. AND R. G. RULAND, "The Incremental Information Content of Historical Cost and Current Cost Income Numbers: Time Series Analysis for 1962-1980," *The Accounting Review* (October 1987), pp. 707-722.

BERNARD, V. L. AND T. L. STOBER, "The Nature and Amount of Information in Cash Flows and Accruals," *The Accounting Review* (October 1989), pp. 624-652.

BERNARD, V. L. AND J. THOMAS, "Post-Earnings Announcement Drift: Delayed Price Reaction or Risk Premium?" *Journal of Accounting Research* (Supplement, 1989), pp. 1-36.

BETTS, N. M. AND G. D. RICHARD-SON, "The Income Statement Classification Debate Revisited: Were Recent Revisions to CICA Handbook Section 3450 Justified?" working paper, University of Waterloo, April 15, 1993.

BLACK, F. AND M. SCHOLES, "The Pricing of Options and Corporate Liabilities," *Journal of Political Economy* (May/June 1973), pp. 637-654.

BLAZENKO, G. AND W. R. SCOTT, "A Model of Standard Setting in Auditing," *Contemporary Accounting Research* (Fall 1986), pp. 68-92.

BOLAND, L. A. AND I. M. GORDON, "Criticizing Positive Accounting Theory," *Contemporary Accounting Research* (Fall 1992), pp. 147-170.

BROWN, L. D., P. A. GRIFFIN, R. L. HAGERMAN, AND M. ZMIJEWSKI, "Security Analyst Superiority Relative to Univariate Time-Series Models in Forecasting Quarterly Earnings," *Journal of Accounting and Economics* (April 1987), pp. 61-87.

BROWN, S. J. AND J. B. WARNER, "Measuring Security Price Performance," *Journal of Financial Economics* (September 1980), pp. 205-258.

BUSHMAN, R. M. AND R. J. INDJEJI-KIAN, "Accounting Income, Stock Price and Managerial Compensation," *Journal of Accounting and Economics* (January/April/July 1993), pp. 3-23.

CAHAN, S. F., "The Effect of Antitrust Investigations on Discretionary Accruals: A Refined Test of the Political-Cost Hypothesis," *The Accounting Review* (January 1992), pp. 77-95.

CANADIAN INSTITUTE OF CHAR-TERED ACCOUNTANTS, *CICA Handbook*, (Toronto, Ontario: CICA, 1995).

CHRISTIE, A. A. AND J. ZIMMER-MAN, "Efficient and Opportunistic Choices of Accounting Procedures: Corporate Control Contests," *The Accounting Review* (October 1994), pp. 539-566.

CLARKSON, P., A. DONTOH, G. RICHARDSON, AND S. SEFCIK, "The Voluntary Inclusion of Earnings Forecasts in IPO Prospectuses," *Contemporary Accounting Research* (Spring 1992), pp. 601-626.

COLLINS, D. W. AND S. P. KOTHARI, "An Analysis of the Intertemporal and Cross-Sectional Determinants of Earnings Response Coefficients," *Journal of Accounting and Economics* (July 1989), pp. 143-181.

COLLINS, D. W., S. P. KOTHARI, J. SHANKEN, AND R.G. SLOAN, "Lack of Timeliness and Noise as Explanations for the Low Contemporaneous Return-Earnings Association," working paper, University of Iowa, 1994.

COLLINS, D. W. AND W. K. SALATKA, "Noisy Accounting Earnings Signals and Earnings Response Coefficients: The Case of Foreign Currency Accounting," *Contemporary Accounting Research* (Fall 1993), pp. 119-159.

CRANDALL, R. H., "Government Intervention—the PIP Grant Accounting Controversy," *Cost and Management* (September/October, 1983), pp. 57-59.

CUSHING, B. E. AND M. J. LECLERE, "Evidence on the Determinants of Inventory Accounting Policy Choice," *The Accounting Review* (April 1992), pp. 355-366.

DARROUGH, M. N., "Disclosure Policy and Competition: Cournot vs. Bertrand," *The Accounting Review* (July 1993), pp. 534-561.

DARROUGH, M. N. AND N. M. STOUGHTON, "Financial Disclosure Policy in an Entry Game," *Journal of Accounting and Economics* (January 1990), pp. 219-243.

DATAR, S. M., G. A. FELTHAM, AND J. S. HUGHES, "The Role of Audits and Audit Quality in Valuing New Issues," *Journal of Accounting and Economics* (March 1991), pp. 3-49.

DE ANGELO, L. E., "Auditor Size and Auditor Quality," *Journal of Accounting and Economics* (December 1981), pp. 183-199.

DEANGELO, H., L. DEANGELO, AND D. J. SKINNER, "Accounting Choice in Troubled Companies," *Journal of Accounting and Economics* (January 1994), pp. 113-143.

DECHOW, P. M., "Accounting Earnings and Cash Flows as Measures of Firm Performance: The Role of Accounting Accruals," *Journal of Accounting and Economics* (July 1994), pp. 3-42.

DECHOW, P. M., R. G. SLOAN, AND A. P. SWEENEY, "Detecting Earnings Management," working paper, University of Pennsylvania, February 1994.

DEFOND, M. L. AND J. JIAMBALVO, "Debt Covenant Violation and Manipulation of Accruals," *Journal of Accounting and Economics* (January 1994), pp. 145-176.

DEMSKI, J., *Information Analyis* (Reading, Mass.: Addison-Wesley, 1972).

DEMSKI, J., "Positive Accounting Theory: A Review," *Accounting, Organizations and Society* (October 1988), pp. 623-629.

DEMSKI, J. AND D.E.M. SAPPINGTON, "Delegated Expertise," *Journal of Accounting Research* (Spring 1987), pp. 68-89.

DEMSKI, J. AND D.E.M. SAPPINGTON, "Fully Revealing Income Measurement," *The Accounting Review* (April 1990), pp. 363-383.

DHALIWAL, D. S., K. J. LEE, AND N. L. FARGHER, "The Association Between Unexpected Earnings and Abnormal Security Returns in the Presence of Financial Leverage," *Contemporary Accounting Research* (Fall 1991), pp. 20-41.

DIAMOND, D. W. AND R. E. VERRECCHIA, "Disclosure, Liquidity, and the Cost of Capital," *The Journal of Finance* (September 1991), pp. 1325-1359.

DOPUCH, N. AND M. PINCUS, "Evidence on the Choice of Inventory Accounting Methods: LIFO vs. FIFO," *Journal of Accounting Research* (Spring 1988), pp. 28-59.

DORAN, B. M., D. W. COLLINS, AND D. S. DHALIWAL, "The Information Content of Historical Cost Earnings Relative to Supplemental Reserve-Based Accounting Data in the Extractive Petroleum Industry," *The Accounting Review* (July 1988), pp. 389-413.

DYCKMAN, T. R. AND A. J. SMITH, "Financial Accounting and Reporting by Oil and Gas Producing Companies: A Study of Information Effects," *Journal of Accounting and Economics* (March 1979), pp. 45-76.

DYE, R. A., "Disclosure of Nonproprietary Information," *Journal of Accounting Research* (Spring 1985), pp. 123-145.

DYE, R. A., "Proprietary and Nonproprietary Disclosures," *Journal of Business* (April 1986), pp. 331-366.

DYE, R. A., "Earnings Management in an Overlapping Generations Model," *Journal of Accounting Research* (Autumn 1988), pp. 195-235.

EASTON, P. D. AND T. S. HARRIS, "Earnings as an Explanatory Variable for Returns," *Journal of Accounting Research* (Spring 1991), pp. 19-36.

EASTON, P. D. AND M. E. ZMIJEWSKI, "Cross-Sectional Variation in the Stock-Market Response to Accounting Earnings Announcements," *Journal of Accounting and Economics* (July 1989), pp. 117-141.

EASTON, P. D., T. S. HARRIS, AND J. A. OHLSON, "Aggregate Accounting Earnings Can Explain Most of Security Returns," *Journal of Accounting and Economics* (June-September 1992), pp. 119-142.

ECKERN, S. AND R. WILSON, "On the Theory of the Firm in an Economy With Incomplete Markets," *The Bell Journal of Economics and Management Science* (Spring 1974), pp. 171-180.

Exxon 1993 Annual Report (Irving, Tex.: Exxon Corp., 1994).

FAIRFIELD, P. M., "P/E, P/B and the Present Value of Future Dividends," *Financial Analysts Journal* (July/August 1994), pp. 23-31.

FAMA, E. F., "Agency Problems and the Theory of the Firm," *Journal of Political Economy* (April 1980), pp. 288-307.

FELTHAM, G. A. AND J. A. OHLSON, "Valuation and Clean Surplus Accounting for Operating and Financial Activities," *Contemporary Accounting Research* (Spring 1995), pp. 661-687.

FELTHAM, G. A. AND J. XIE, "Performance Measure Congruity and Diversity in Multi-task Principal/Agent Relations," *The Accounting Review* (July 1994), pp. 429-453.

FINANCIAL ACCOUNTING STANDARDS BOARD, *Statement of Financial Accounting Concepts No. 1: Objectives of Financial Reporting by Business Enterprises* (Norwalk, Conn.: FASB, 1978).

FINANCIAL ACCOUNTING STANDARDS BOARD, *Statement of Financial Accounting Concepts No. 2: Qualitative Characteristics of Accounting Information* (Norwalk, Conn.: FASB, 1980).

FINANCIAL ACCOUNTING STAN-
DARDS BOARD, *Statement of Financial
Accounting Standards No. 8: Accounting for the
Translation of Foreign Currency Transactions
and Foreign Currency Financial Statements*
(Norwalk, Conn.: FASB, 1975).

FINANCIAL ACCOUNTING STAN-
DARDS BOARD, *Statement of Financial
Accounting Standards No. 19: Financial
Accounting and Reporting by Oil and Gas
Producing Companies* (Norwalk, Conn.:
FASB, 1977).

FINANCIAL ACCOUNTING STAN-
DARDS BOARD, *Statement of Financial
Accounting Standards No. 25: Suspension of
Certain Accounting Requirements for Oil and
Gas Producing Companies* (Norwalk, Conn.:
FASB, 1979).

FINANCIAL ACCOUNTING STAN-
DARDS BOARD, *Statement of Financial
Accounting Standards No. 33: Financial
Reporting and Changing Prices* (Norwalk,
Conn.: FASB, 1979).

FINANCIAL ACCOUNTING STAN-
DARDS BOARD, *Statement of Financial
Accounting Standards No. 52: Foreign
Currency Translation* (Norwalk, Conn.:
FASB, 1981).

FINANCIAL ACCOUNTING STAN-
DARDS BOARD, *Statement of Financial
Accounting Standards No. 69: Disclosures about
Oil and Gas Producing Activities* (Norwalk,
Conn.: FASB, 1982).

FINANCIAL ACCOUNTING STAN-
DARDS BOARD, *Statement of Financial
Accounting Standards No. 80: Accounting for
Futures Contracts* (Norwalk, Conn.: FASB,
1984).

FINANCIAL ACCOUNTING STAN-
DARDS BOARD, *Statement of Financial

Accounting Standards No. 87: Employers'
Accounting for Pensions* (Norwalk, Conn.:
FASB, 1985).

FINANCIAL ACCOUNTING STAN-
DARDS BOARD, *Statement of Financial
Accounting Standards No. 105: Disclosure of
Information about Financial Instruments with
Off-Balance-Sheet Risk and Financial
Instruments with Concentrations of Credit
Risk* (Norwalk, Conn.: FASB, 1990).

FINANCIAL ACCOUNTING STAN-
DARDS BOARD, *Statement of Financial
Accounting Standards No. 106: Employers' Ac-
counting for Postretirement Benefits Other Than
Pensions* (Norwalk, Conn.: FASB, 1990).

FINANCIAL ACCOUNTING STAN-
DARDS BOARD, *Statement of Financial
Accounting Standards No. 107: Disclosures
about Fair Value of Financial Instruments*
(Norwalk, Conn.: FASB, 1991).

FINANCIAL ACCOUNTING STAN-
DARDS BOARD, *Statement of Financial
Accounting Standards No. 115: Accounting for
Certain Investments in Debt and Equity
Securities* (Norwalk, Conn.: FASB, 1993).

FOSTER, G., "Briloff and the Capital
Market," *Journal of Accounting Research*
(Spring 1979), pp. 262-274.

FOSTER, G., C. OLSEN, AND T.
SHEVLIN, "Earnings Releases, Anomalies,
and the Behavior of Security Returns," *The
Accounting Review* (January 1977), pp. 574-
603.

FRIEDLAN, J. M., "Accounting Choices of
Issuers of Initial Public Offerings,"
Contemporary Accounting Research (Summer
1994), pp. 1-31.

GHICAS, D. AND V. PASTENA, "The
Acquisition Value of Oil and Gas Firms:

The Role of Historical Costs, Reserve Recognition Accounting, and Analysts' Appraisals," *Contemporary Accounting Research* (Fall 1989), pp. 125-142.

GJESDAL, F., "Accounting for Stewardship," *Journal of Accounting Research* (Spring 1981), pp. 208-231.

GONEDES, N. AND N. DOPUCH, "Capital Market Equilibrium, Information Production, and Selected Accounting Techniques: Theoretical Framework and Review of Empirical Work," *Journal of Accounting Research* (Supplement, 1974), pp. 48-129.

GREIG, A. C., "Fundamental Analysis and Subsequent Stock Returns," *Journal of Accounting and Economics* (June-September 1992), pp. 373-411.

Grossman, S., "On the Efficiency of Competitive Stock Markets Where Traders Have Diverse Information," *The Journal of Finance* (May 1976), pp. 573-585.

Grossman, S., "The Informational Role of Warranties and Private Disclosure about Product Quality," *Journal of Law and Economics* (December 1981), pp. 461-484.

HANLEY, K. W., C.M.C. LEE AND P. J. SEGUIN, "The Marketing of Closed-End Fund IPOs: Evidence from Transactions Data," *Journal of Financial Intermediation* (forthcoming).

HANNA, J. R., D. B. KENNEDY, AND G.D. RICHARDSON, *Reporting the Effects of Changing Prices: A Review of the Experience with Section 4510* (Toronto, Ontario: CICA, 1990).

HARRIS, T. S. AND J. A. OHLSON, "Accounting Disclosures and the Market's Evaluation of Oil and Gas Properties," *The*

Accounting Review (October 1987), pp. 651-670.

HARRIS, T. S. AND J. A. OHLSON, "Accounting Disclosures and the Market's Valuation of Oil and Gas Properties: Evaluation of Market Efficiency and Functional Fixation," *The Accounting Review* (October 1990), pp. 764-780.

HEALY, P. M. "The Effect of Bonus Schemes on Accounting Decisions," *Journal of Accounting and Economics* (April 1985), pp. 85-107.

HEALY, P. M. AND K. G. PALEPU, "The Effect of Firms' Financial Disclosure Strategies on Stock Prices," *Accounting Horizons* (March 1993), pp. 1-11.

HIRSCHLEIFER, J., "The Private and Social Value of Information and the Reward to Inventive Activity," *American Economic Review* (September 1971), pp. 561-573.

HOLMSTRÖM, B., "Moral Hazard and Observability," *The Bell Journal of Economics* (Spring 1979), pp. 74-91.

HOLMSTRÖM, B., "Moral Hazard in Teams," *The Bell Journal of Economics* (Autumn 1982), pp. 324-340.

HOLTHAUSEN, R. W. AND D. F. LARCKER, "The Prediction of Stock Returns Using Financial Statement Information," *Journal of Accounting and Economics* (June-September, 1992), pp.373-411.

HOLTHAUSEN, R. W., D. F. LARCKER, AND R. G. SLOAN, "Annual Bonus Schemes and the Manipulation of Earnings," *Journal of Accounting and Economics* (February 1995), pp. 29-74.

HUGHES, P. J., "Signalling by Direct Disclosure Under Asymmetric Information,"

Journal of Accounting and Economics (June 1986), pp. 119-142.

HUNT, H. G., "Potential Determinants of Corporate Inventory Accounting Decisions," *Journal of Accounting Research* (Autumn 1985), pp. 448-467.

IJIRI, Y., *Theory of Accounting Measurement*, Studies in Accounting Research, No. 10 (Sarasota, Fla.: American Accounting Association, 1975).

INTERNATIONAL ACCOUNTING STANDARDS COMMITTEE, "1993 Survey of the Use and Application of International Accounting Standards," IASC Insight (June 1993), pp. 17-19.

International Accounting Standards Committee, *International Accounting Standards 1994* (Basingstoke, Hants: Burgess Science Press, 1994).

JENSEN, M. C., "The Modern Industrial Revolution, Exit, and the Failure of Internal Control Systems," *The Journal of Finance* (July 1993), pp. 831-880.

JENSEN, M. C. AND W. H. MECKLING, "Theory of the Firm: Managerial Behavior, Agency Costs and Ownership Structure," *Journal of Financial Economics* (October 1976), pp. 305-360.

JENSEN, M. C. AND K. J. MURPHY, "CEO Incentives—It's Not How Much You Pay, But How," *Harvard Business Review* (May/June, 1990), pp. 138-149.

JONES, J., "Earnings Management During Import Relief Investigations," *Journal of Accounting Research* (Autumn 1991), pp. 193-228.

KAPLAN, R. S., "Comments on Paul Healy," *Journal of Accounting and Economics* (April 1985), pp. 109-113.

KIM, O. AND Y. SUH, "Incentive Efficiency of Compensation Based on Accounting and Market Performance," *Journal of Accounting and Economics* (January/April/July 1993), pp. 25-53.

KORMENDI, R. C. AND R. LIPE," Earnings Innovations, Earnings Persistence, and Stock Returns," *Journal of Business* (July 1987), pp. 323-346.

KROSS, W., "Stock Returns and Oil and Gas Pronouncements: Replications and Extensions," *Journal of Accounting Research* (Autumn 1982), pp. 459-471.

LAFFONT, J. J., *The Economics of Uncertainty and Information* (Cambridge, Mass.: MIT Press, 1984).

LAMBERT, R. A. AND D. F. LARCKER, "An Analysis of the Use of Accounting and Market Measures of Performance in Executive Compensation Contracts," *Journal of Accounting Research* (Supplement, 1987), pp. 85-125.

LAMBERT, R. A. AND D. F. LARCKER, "Firm Performance and the Compensation of Chief Executive Officers," working paper, (January 1993).

LAMBERT, R. A., D. F. LARCKER, AND R.E. VERRECCHIA, "Portfolio Considerations in Valuing Executive Compensation," *Journal of Accounting Research* (Spring 1991), pp. 129-149.

LEE, J. C.-W. AND D. A. HSIEH, "Choice of Inventory Accounting Methods: Comparative Analysis of Alternative Hypotheses," *Journal of Accounting Research* (Autumn 1985), pp. 468-485.

LELAND, H. E. AND D. H. PYLE, "Information Asymmetries, Financial

Structure, and Financial Intermediation," *The Journal of Finance* (May 1977), pp. 371-387.

LEV, B., "The Impact of Accounting Regulation on the Stock Market: The Case of Oil and Gas Companies," *The Accounting Review* (July 1979), pp. 485-503.

LEV, B., "Toward a Theory of Equitable and Efficient Accounting Policy," *The Accounting Review* (January 1988), pp. 1-22.

LEV, B., "On the Usefulness of Earnings: Lessons and Directions from Two Decades of Empirical Research," *Journal of Accounting Research* (Supplement, 1989), pp. 153-192.

LEV, B. AND S. R. THIAGARAJAN, "Fundamental Information Analysis," *Journal of Accounting Research* (Autumn 1993), pp. 190-215.

LINDAHL, F. W., "Dynamic Analysis of Inventory Accounting Choice," *Journal of Accounting Research* (Autumn 1989), pp. 201-226.

LINTNER, J., "The Valuation of Risky Assets and the Selection of Risky Investments in Stock Portfolios and Capital Budgets," *Review of Economics and Statistics* (February 1965), pp. 13-37.

LYS, T., "Mandated Accounting Changes and Debt Covenants: The Case of Oil and Gas Companies," *Journal of Accounting and Economics* (April 1984), pp. 39-65.

MAGLIOLO, J., "Capital Market Analyis of Reserve Recognition Accounting," *Journal of Accounting Research* (Supplement, 1986), pp. 69-108.

MARK'S WORK WEARHOUSE LTD., *Annual Report, January 30, 1993* (Calgary, Alta.: Mark's Work Wearhouse Ltd., 1993).

MCNICHOLS, M. AND G. P. WILSON, "Evidence of Earnings Management from the Provision for Bad Debts," *Journal of Accounting Research* (Supplement, 1988), pp. 1-31.

MERINO, D. B. AND M. D. NEIMARK, "Disclosure Regulation and Public Policy: A Sociohistorical Reappraisal," *Journal of Accounting and Public Policy* (Fall 1982), pp. 33-57.

MERTON, R. C., "A Simple Model of Capital Market Equilibrium with Incomplete Markets," *The Journal of Finance* (July 1987), pp. 483-510.

MIAN, S. L. AND C. W. SMITH, JR., "Incentives for Unconsolidated Financial Reporting," *Journal of Accounting and Economics* (January 1990), pp. 141-171.

MILGROM, P., "Good News and Bad News: Representation Theorems and Applications," *Bell Journal of Economics* (Autumn 1981), pp. 380-391.

MILLIGAN, J. W., "How the Government Railroaded Franklin Savings," *Institutional Investor* (January 1991), pp. 50-60.

MURPHY, K. J. AND J. L. ZIMMERMAN, "Financial Performance Surrounding CEO Turnover," *Journal of Accounting and Economics* (January/April/July 1993), pp. 273-316.

NEWMAN, P. AND R. SANSING, "Disclosure Policies with Multiple Users," *Journal of Accounting Research* (Spring 1993), pp. 92-112.

OHLSON, J. A., "On the Nature of Income Measurement: The Basic Results," *Contemporary Accounting Research* (Fall 1987), pp. 1-15.

OHLSON, J. A., "The Theory of Value and Earnings, and an Introduction to the Ball-Brown Analysis," *Contemporary Accounting Research* (Fall 1991), pp. 1-19.

ONTARIO SECURITIES COMMISSION, "Annual Information Form and

Management's Discussion and Analysis of Financial Condition and Results of Operations-Policies," OSC Policy Statement No. 5.10, OSC *Bulletin* (November 10, 1989), pp. 4275-4299.

ONTARIO SECURITIES COMMISSION, "Statement of Executive Compensation," Form 40, Securities Act, Regulation 638/93, *The Ontario Gazette*, Vol. 126-39 (September 25, 1993), pp. 1203-1216.

ONTARIO SECURITIES COMMISSION, "OSC National Policy Statement No. 27," OSC *Bulletin* (December 18, 1992), pp. 6055-6144.

OU, J. A. AND S. H. PENMAN, "Financial Statement Analysis and the Prediction of Stock Returns," *Journal of Accounting and Economics* (November 1989), pp. 295-329.

PAVLIK, E. L., T. W. SCOTT, AND P. TIESSEN, "Executive Compensation: Issues and Research," Journal of Accounting Literature (1993), pp. 131-189.

PELTZMAN, SAM, "Toward a More General Theory of Regulation," *The Journal of Law and Economics* (August 1976), pp. 21-240.

POSNER, R. A., "Theories of Economic Regulation," *Bell Journal of Economics and Management Science* (Autumn 1974), pp. 335-358.

POURCIAU, S., "Earnings Management and Nonroutine Executive Changes," *Journal of Accounting and Economics* (January/ April/July 1993), pp. 317-336.

PRATT, J. W., "Risk Aversion in the Small and in the Large," *Econometrica* (January-April, 1964), pp. 122-136.

RAIFFA, H., *Decision Analysis: Introductory Lectures on Choices Under Uncertainty* (Reading, Mass.: Addison-Wesley, 1968).

RAMAKRISHNAN, R.T.S. AND J. K. THOMAS, "Valuation of Permanent, Transitory and Price-Irrelevant Components of Reported Earnings," working paper, Columbia University Business School (July 1991).

SCHIPPER, K., "Commentary on Earnings Management," *Accounting Horizons* (December 1989), pp. 91-102.

SECURITIES ACT, *Revised Statutes of Ontario, 1990*, Vol. 11, Chapter 5.5 (Toronto, Ont.: Queen's Printer for Ontario, 1991).

SECURITIES AND EXCHANGE COMMISSION, *Accounting Series Release No. 150* (Washington, D.C.: SEC, 1973).

SECURITIES AND EXCHANGE COMMISSION, *Accounting Series Release No. 253* (Washington, D.C.: SEC, 1978).

SHARPE, W. F., "Capital Asset Prices: A Theory of Market Equilibrium Under Conditions of Risk," *The Journal of Finance* (September 1964), pp. 425-442.

SLOAN, R. G., "Accounting Earnings and Top Executive Compensation," *Journal of Accounting and Economics* (January/April/July 1993), pp. 55-100.

STOBER, T. L., "Summary Financial Statement Measures and Analysts' Forecasts of Earnings," *Journal of Accounting and Economics* (June-September, 1992), pp. 347-372.

SMITH, A., "Earnings and Management Incentives: Comments," *Journal of Accounting and Economics* (January/April/July 1993), pp. 337-347.

SPENCE, M., "Job Market Signalling," *Quarterly Journal of Economics* (August 1973), pp. 355-374.

STIGLER, G. J., "The Theory of Economic Regulation," *The Bell Journal of Economics and Management Science* (Spring 1971), pp. 3-21.

SUNDER, S., "Relationship Between Accounting Changes and Stock Prices:

Problems of Measurement and Some Empirical Evidence," *Journal of Accounting Research* (Supplement, 1973), pp. 1-45.

SWEENEY, A. P., "Debt-Covenant Violations and Managers' Accounting Responses," *Journal of Accounting and Economics* (May 1994), pp. 281-308.

THORNTON, T. AND M. BRYANT, *GAAP vs. TAP in Lending Agreements: Canadian Evidence* (Toronto, Ont.: The Canadian Academic Accounting Association, 1986).

TINIC, S., "A Perspective on the Stock Market's Fixation on Accounting Numbers," *The Accounting Review* (October 1990), pp. 781-796.

TITMAN, S. AND B. TRUEMAN, "Information Quality and the Valuation of New Issues," *Journal of Accounting and Economics* (June 1986), pp. 159-172.

VERRECCHIA, R. E., "Discretionary Disclosure," *Journal of Accounting and Economics* (December 1983), pp. 179-194.

VERRECCHIA, R. E., "Information Quality and Discretionary Disclosure," *Journal of Accounting and Economics* (March 1990), pp. 365-380.

WARFIELD, T. D. AND J. J. WILD, "Accounting Recognition and the Relevance of Earnings as an Explanatory Variable for Returns," *The Accounting Review* (October 1992) pp. 821-842.

WATTS, R. L. AND J. L. ZIMMERMAN, *Positive Accounting Theory* (Englewood Cliffs, N.J.: Prentice-Hall, 1986).

WATTS, R. L. AND J. L. ZIMMERMAN, "Positive Accounting Theory: A Ten Year Perspective," *The Accounting Review* (January 1990), pp. 131-156.

WEIL, R. L., "Role of the Time Value of Money in Financial Reporting," *Accounting Horizons* (December 1990), pp. 47-67.

WILSON, G. P., "The Incremental Information Content of the Accrual and Funds Components of Earnings After Controlling for Earnings," *The Accounting Review* (April 1987), pp. 293-322.

ZEFF, S. A., "The Rise of Economic Consequences," *The Journal of Accountancy* (December 1978), pp. 56-63.

Internet Resources

The following finance and accounting information sources can be accessed at these Internet addresses:

The Certified General Accountants' Association of Canada
http://www.cga-canada.org

The Canadian Institute of Chartered Accountants   **http://www.cica.ca/**

The American Institute of Certified Public Accountants   **http://www.rutgers.edu/ Accounting/raw/aicpa/home.htm**

The Globe & Mail Report on Business
http://www.globeandmail.ca/

The Economist   **http://www.economist.com/**

The Wall Street Journal   **http://info.wsj.com/**

Rockwell International Corporation (U.S.)
http://www.rockwell.com/

The Securities and Exchange Commission (U.S.)   **http://www.sec.gov/**

Index